# SOCRATES

The Garland Reference Library
of the Humanities
Volume 844

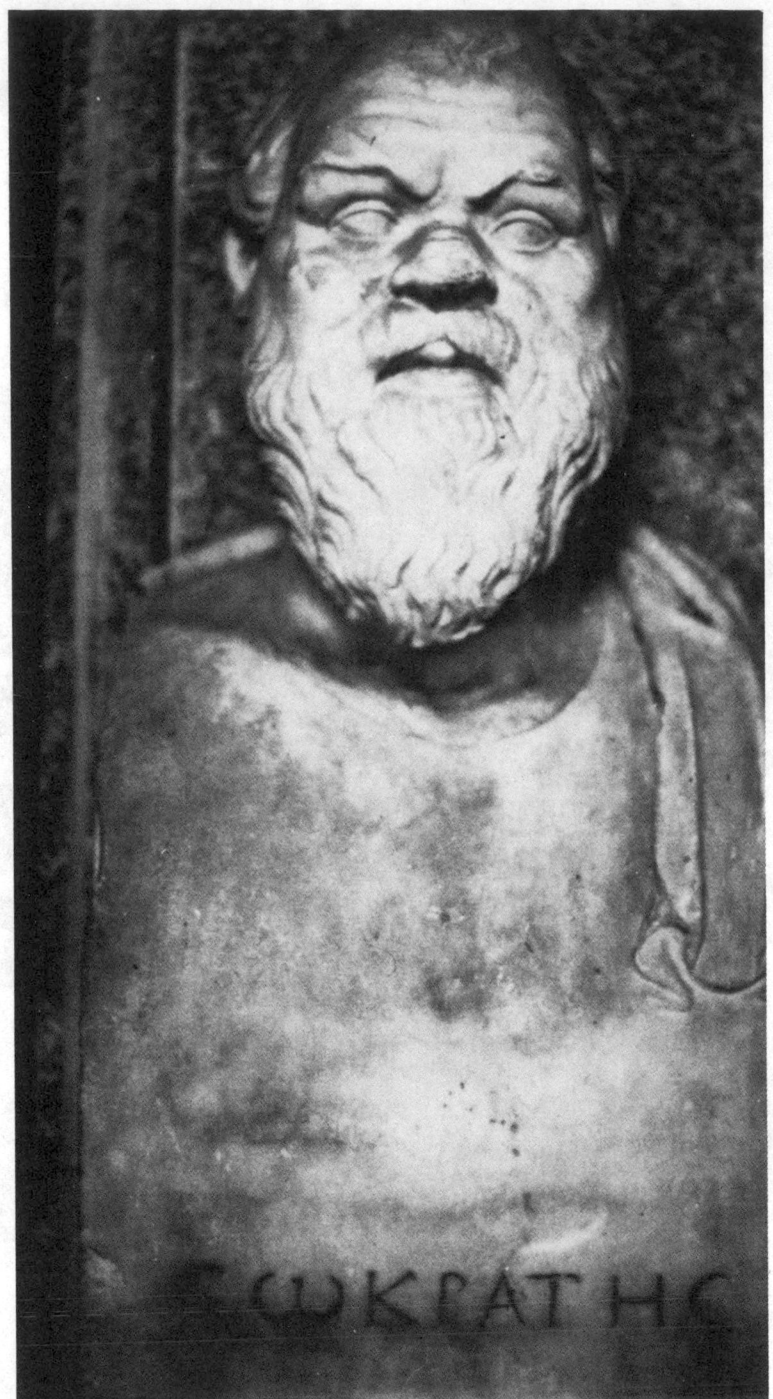
ϹωΚΡΑΤΗϹ

# SOCRATES

*An Annotated Bibliography*

Luis E. Navia
Ellen L. Katz

GARLAND PUBLISHING, INC.
NEW YORK & LONDON
1988

**Library of Congress Cataloging-in-Publication Data**

Navia, Luis E.
Socrates: an annotated bibliography / Luis E. Navia, Ellen L. Katz
p. cm — (Garland reference library of the humanities; v. 844)
Includes index.
ISBN 0–8240–5740–6 (alk. paper)
1. Socrates—Bibliography. I. Katz, Ellen L. II. Title.
III. Series: Garland reference library of the humanities; vol. 844.
Z8824.34.N38 1988
[B317]
016.183'2—dc19 88–10264
CIP

Printed on acid-free, 250-year-life paper
Manufactured in the United States of America

# CONTENTS

# FOREWORD

As far as we have been able to ascertain, this annotated bibliography on Socrates is the first work of its kind to be published. There are exhaustive annotated bibliographies on Aristophanes and Plato, and other major philosophical and literary figures have been the object of similar scholarly research. But up to the present no such project has been undertaken exclusively around the person and influence of Socrates. The only available bibliographical work on Socrates is Andreas Patzer's *Bibliographia Socratica* which contains over two thousand entries. These are, however, unannotated, and can only give us an idea of the extent of the literature that has grown around Socrates. There are also unannotated bibliographies appended to major Socratic studies. V. de Magalhães-Vilhena's *Le problème de Socrate* contains close to one hundred pages of entries, and other works, such as Coleman Phillipson's *The Trial of Socrates* and W.K.C. Guthrie's *Socrates* include several pages of meaningful and well-researched bibliographical information. There are, moreover, a few works that include annotated bibliographies, but in these cases, the number of entries is exceedingly limited and always built around some specific aspect of Socratic scholarship. The present work hopes to serve the useful purpose of offering a compilation of over nineteen hundred annotated entries of works about Socrates, satisfying thereby a need that has been felt for quite some time in the scholarly world.

In the preparation of this work, we faced and made certain decisions concerning its orientation, character, and scope. Concerning the latter, we decided to embrace the Socratic literature without any restrictions as to time, content, or style, concentrating our attention on works written in or translated into English, French, German, ancient Greek, Italian, Latin, Portuguese, and Spanish. But instead of choosing a limited period (for instance, the Socratic literature of the seventeenth century), or a circumscribed theme (such as the trial of Socrates), or a given style (for example, only monographs and articles), we opted for including items from all periods (since the time of Socrates himself to our own), covering all possible aspects of the Socratic problem generally understood (from biographical and philosophical works to specific studies), written in all sorts of genres and contexts (from monographs to audio-visual materials)—in sum, items from the entire spectrum of Socratic scholarship and literature.

But, of course, our decision to be as comprehensive as possible means that this bibliography can only offer a representative selection of annotated works. The literature that has been created around the memory, philosophy, and influence of Socrates is so immense and complex, that the expectation of compiling a truly exhaustive bibliography is probably bound to remain an unrealizable project. Still, we are convinced that we have taken into account very many of the most significant works on Socrates, not only in philosophy, but in other fields such as history and literature.

The second decision that we faced was whether to include in the annotations critical comments besides those of a purely descriptive nature. Critical annotations, while possibly useful and even enlightening, necessarily reveal the author's points of view, interpretations, and prejudices, and may often do little justice to the annotated works. Like condensed reviews, they pass judgment in a few lines on works of great complexity, and thus they may be ultimately misleading. And in the context of Socratic scholarship, where there is so great a number of mutually exclusive interpretations and divergent points of view, and where our own philosophical conceptions determine so decisively our final assessment of Socrates and of what has been said and written about him, the injection of critical comments or evaluation statements about the annotated works might prove to be a bibliographical hindrance. Accordingly, we have chosen to remain strictly on a descriptive level, giving simply a general account of the annotated works, without becoming entangled in the often tempting practice of passing judgment on them.

The third decision involved the complex issue of distinguishing Socrates and the works about him from the primary sources and the literature about them. When we speak of primary sources, we have in mind the writings of Aristophanes, Xenophon, and Plato. In the instance of the first two, it is relatively easy to establish a line of demarcation between them and the image of Socrates created by them. Of the eleven extant comedies of Aristophanes, only one deals primarily with Socrates, and the strictly Socratic works of Xenophon are only a part of his entire literary creation. Thus, it is relatively easy to make a selection of works by and about Aristophanes and Xenophon in which the major emphasis is the Socratic image. The case of Plato, on the other hand, is very different. The personalities and philosophies of Socrates and Plato appear so intimately fused throughout the Platonic writings, that there have been some scholars, such as John Burnet and A.E. Taylor, who have concluded that everything attributed by Plato to Socrates can be unquestionably associated with the historical Socrates, and this includes even those metaphysical and cosmological ideas of the middle and late dialogues which in the eyes of other scholars belong exclusively to the mature mind of Plato. There have been other interpreters of Plato's works who view the Platonic Socrates as nothing but a literary construction on Plato's part. In either case, however, it would be practically impossible to separate Plato, whether as a reporter of Socrates' views or as the creator of the Socratic myth, from Socrates himself. Accordingly, a bibliography of works on Socrates would turn out to be a bibliography of the Platonic literature.

The resolution of this issue entails some tentative stance vis-à-vis the Socratic problem, that is, the problem concerning the historical character of Socrates in the context of the many and seemingly discordant testimonies about him. We have opted for an eclectic stance which avoids a position of skepticism (as exemplified by O. Gigon and A.H. Chroust), as well as the hypothesis of one true Socrates (that is, the thesis that resolves the Socratic problem by relying exclusively on one of the primary sources). We maintain that no single Socratic witness can be accorded complete credibility, and that all the sources of testimony contain elements that are biographically and ideologically significant. Thus, it is our conviction that while a perfectly authentic portrait of the historical Socrates will probably always remain a chimerical representation, there are sufficient bits of information about him which, if treated critically and sympathetically, may yield a reasonably clear and complete image. It is on the basis of this assumption that we have approached the mountains of literature that deal with Socrates.

We have divided the book into twenty-three sections. Obviously, in the classification of the entries an element of subjective judgment has been present. Many of the annotated items could belong to two or three sections, and in those cases we have given a full annotation of the work in one of the sections and a reference to it in other sections. The sections on the primary sources (Aristophanes, Xenophon, and Plato) contain entries on a small representative selection of works, and the section on the secondary sources include annotations of a few significant Socratic testimonies from post-Socratic classical times. In most cases we have transliterated ordinary Greek words such as ἀκρασία, λόγος, ἀρετή, ἔρως, ἔλεγχος, and ψυχή, but less common words and phrases, as well as Greek titles, have been written in Greek. Cross-references (Ref.) are generally given at the end of the entries, and the *Index of Authors* is based on the entry numbers.

We would like to express our gratitude to Alicia S. Navia and Kenneth Katz for their affectionate and unfailing assistance in the preparation of the manuscript. We also wish to thank Ms. Phyllis Korper, the editor at Garland Publishing, for her guidance and support.

## JOURNALS AND PERIODICALS

*Abhandlung der philosophischen Klasse der königlich Preussischen Akademie.* Berlin.

*Acta ad archaeologiam et artium historiam pertinentia.* Institutum Romanum Norvegaie et Oslo.

*Acta Antiqua Academiae Scientiarum Hungaricae.* Budapest.

*Acta Classica Universitatis Scientiarum Debreceniensis.* University of Kossuth. Debrecen (Hungary).

*Aitia.* Philosophy-Humanities Magazine. SUNY at Farmingdale. Farmingdale, N.Y.

*Alma Mater.* Revue Universitaire de la Suisse Romande. Geneva (Switzerland).

*Altertum.* Deutche Akademie der Wissenschaft. Berlin.

*America.* National Catholic Weekly Review. New York.

*The American Bar Association Journal.* Chicago.

*The American Journal of Archeology.* Princeton, N.J.

*The American Journal of Philology.* The John Hopkins Press. Baltimore, Md.

*The American Philosophical Quarterly.* Bowling Green State University. Bowling Green, Oh.

*Anales de Historia antigua y medieval.* Instituto de Estudios Clásicos. Buenos Aires.

*Analysis.* Oxford (England).

*Ancient Philosophy.* Duquesne University. Pittsburgh.

*Ancient Society.* Catholic University. Louvain (Belgium).

*Ancient World.* Chicago.

*Annales de la Faculté des Lettres et Sciences Humaines d'Aix.* Aix (France).

*Annali del Liceo Clasico G. Garibaldi di Palermo.* Palermo (Italy).

*Annali della Scuola Normale Superiore di Pisa.* Pisa (Italy).

*Annuaire de la Societé Suisse de Philosophie.* Basel (Switzerland).

*Annuaire de l'Institut de Philologie et d'Histoire Orientales et Slaves.* Université Libre de Bruxelles. Brussels.

*Antaios.* Zeitschrift für eine freie Welt. Stuttgart (West Germany).

*Antichthon.* The Journal of the Australian Society for Classical

Studies. Sydney University Press. Sydney (Australia).

*Antike.* Zeitschrift für Kunst und Kultur der Altertumswissenschaft. Berlin.

*Antike Kunst.* Basel (Switzerland).

*Antike und Abendland.* Berlin.

*Anuario Filosófico.* Universidad de Navarra. Pamplona (Spain).

*Apeiron.* Department of Classical Studies. Monash University. Clayton, Victoria (Australia).

*Appunti di Filologia greco-latina.* Chivazzo (Italy).

*Aquinas.* Ephemerides Thomisticae. Pontificia Universita Lateranense. Vatican City.

*Archaiognosia.* Athens.

*Archeion.* Revue Internationale d'Historie des Sciences. Paris.

*Archiv für Geschichte der Philosophie.* Berlin.

*Archiv für Philosophie.* Stuttgart (West Germany).

*Archives de Philosophie.* Recherches et Documentation. Paris.

'Αρχαιολογικὰ 'Ανάλεκτα ἐξ 'Αθηνῶν. Athens.

*Atena e Roma.* Rassegna trimestrale dell' Associazone Italiana di Cultura classica. Florence (Italy).

*Athena.* Athens.

*Atlantic Monthly.* Boston.

*Atti del Istituto Veneto di Scienze, Lettere ed Arti.* Venice (Italy).

*Atti dell' Accademia Pontaniana.* Naples (Italy).

*Atti della reale Accademia di Torino. Turin (Italy).*

*Atti di Scienze morali e politici della Società nazionale di Scienze, Lettere ed Arti in Napoli.* Naples (Italy).

*Bibliotheca Sacra.* Oberlin, Ohio.

*Boletín del Instituto de Estudios Helénicos.* Facultad de Filosofía. Barcelona (Spain).

*Breslauer Philologische Abhandlundgen.* Wroclaw [Breslau] (Poland).

*Bulletin de l'Association Guillaume Budé.* Paris.

*Bulletin de la Societé Française de Philosophie.* Paris.

*Bulletin des Lettres de l'Académie Royale de Belgique.* Brussels.

*Bulletin of the American Society of Papyrologists.* Columbia University. New York.

## *JOURNALS AND PERIODICALS*

*Bulletin of the Institute of Classical Studies of the University of London. London.*

*California Studies in Classical Antiquity.* Berkeley, Ca.

*The Canadian Journal of Philosophy.* University of Calgary Press. Calgary (Canada).

*The Catholic World.* A Monthly Magazine of General Literature and Science. New York.

*The Christian Century.* An Ecumenical Weekly. Chicago.

*The Christian Review.* Boston.

*Classica et Mediaevalia.* Danish Journal of History and Philology. Copenhagen.

*The Classical Bulletin.* Department of Classical Languages. Saint Louis University. St. Louis, Mo.

*Classical Folia.* Studies in the Christian Perpetuation of the Classics. Catholic Classical Association of Greater New York. New York.

*The Classical Journal.* Classical Association of the Middle West and South. University of Georgia. Athens, Ga.

*Classical Philology.* The University of Chicago Press. Chicago.

*The Classical Quarterly.* Classical Association. Oxford University Press. Oxford.

*The Classical Review.* Classical Association. Oxford University Press. Oxford.

*The Classical Weekly.* Fordham University. New York.

*The Classical World.* Classical Association of Atlantic States. Duquesne University. Pittsburgh, Pa.

*Commentary.* The American Jewish Committee. New York.

*Convivium.* Milan (Italy).

*Der altsprachliche Unterricht.* Arbeitshefte zu seiner wissenschaftlichen Begründung und praktischen Gestalt. Stuttgart (West Germany).

*Deutsches Museum.* Abhamdlungen und Berichte. Munich (West Germany).

*Diálogos.* University of Puerto Rico. Río Piedras (Puerto Rico).

*Dialogue.* Marquette University. Milwaukee, Wi.

*Diogenes.* International Council of Philosophy and Humanities Studies. Paris.

*Dioniso.* Bolletino dell' Istituto nazionale del Dramma antico. Syracuse (Italy).

*Dionysius.* Dalhousie University. Halifax, Nova Scotia (Canada).

*Diotima*. Athens.

*Doitsu Bangaku*. Tokyo.

*The Dublin University Magazine*. Dublin.

*The Durham University Journal*. University of Durham. Durham (England).

*Educational Theory*. University of Illinois. Champaign, Il.

*Emerita*. Boletín de Lingüística y Filología Clásica. Instituto Antonio de Nebrija. Madrid.

*The Emory University Quarterly*. Emory University. Atlanta, Ga.

*Eos*. Commentarii Societatis Philologae Polonorum. Wroclow [Breslau] (Poland).

Ἐπιστημονικὴ Ἐπετηρὶς τῆς φιλοσοφικῆς Σχολῆς τοῦ Πανεπιστημίου Ἀθηνῶν. Athens.

*Eranos*. Acta Philologica Suecana. Uppsala (Sweden).

*Eranos-Jahrbuch*. Leiden (Holland).

*Estudios Filósoficos*. Instituto Superior de Filosofía. Valladolid (Spain).

*Ethics*. An International Journal of Social, Political and Legal Philosophy. The University of Chicago Press. Chicago.

*Etudes Théologiques et Religieuses*. Montpellier (France).

*Giornale Critico della Filosofia Italiana*. Florence (Italy).

*Giornale di Metafisica*. Genoa (Italy).

*Gnomon*. Kritische Zeitschrift für die gesamte klassische Altertumswissenschaft. Munich.

*Greece and Rome*. The Clarendon Press. Oxford.

*Greek, Roman and Byzantine Studies*. Duke University. Durham, N.C.

*Gymnasium*. Vierteljahrsschrift für Kultur der Antique und humanistische Bildung. Heidelberg (West Germany).

*Habis*. Arqueología. Filología Clásica. Universidad de Sevilla. Seville (Spain).

*Harvard Studies in Classical Philology*. Harvard University. Cambridge, Mass.

*The Harvard Theological Review*. The Faculty of Divinity. Harvard University. Cambridge, Mass.

*Helikon*. Rivista di Tradizione e Cultura classica. Messina (Italy).

*Hermathena*. A Series of Papers on Literature, Science and Philosophy. London.

## JOURNALS AND PERIODICALS

*Hermeneus.* Maanblad voor de antieke Cultuur. Zwolle (Holland).

*Hermes.* Zeitschrift für klassische Philologie. Wiesbaden (West Germany).

*The Hibbert Journal.* London.

*Historia.* Wiesbaden (West Germany).

*Historische Zeitschrift.* Munich (West Germany).

*The History of Philosophy Quarterly.* Bowling Green State University. Philosophy Documentation Center. Bowling Green, Ohio

*History of Political Thought.* Exeter (England).

*History Today.* London.

*Hudson Review.* New York.

*Human Studies.* University of Western Ontario. London, Ontario (Canada).

*Humanistisches Gymnasium.* Leipzig.

*Idealistic Studies.* Worcester, Mass.

*Illustrated London News.* London.

*L'Information Littéraire.* Paris.

*The International Journal for Philosophy and Religion.* Dordrecht (Holland).

*The International Journal of Ethics.* Chicago.

*The International Philosophical Quarterly.* Fordham University. New York.

*International Studies in Philosophy.* An International Journal of General Philosophic Inquiry. State University of New York at Binghamton. Binghamton, N.Y.

*Interpretation.* A Journal of Political Philosophy. Queens College (CUNY). New York.

*Iura.* Rivista internazionale di Diritto romano e antico. Naples (Italy).

*Iyunn.* A Hebrew Philosophical Quarterly. Hebrew University of Jerusalem. Jerusalem.

[*Jahrbücher für klassischen Philologie*] *Neue Jahrbücher für Philologie und Paedagogik.* Leipzig.

*The Journal of Aesthetics and Art Criticism.* American Society for Aesthetics. Temple University. Philadelphia, Pa.

*The Journal of Chinese Philosophy.* Boston, Mass.

*The Journal of Classical and Sacred Philology.* Cambridge (England).

*The Journal of Classical Studies.* Classical Society of Japan. Kyoto University. Kyoto (Japan).

*The Journal of Critical Analysis.* Port Jefferson, N.Y.

*The Journal of Hellenic Studies.* London.

*The Journal of the History of Ideas.* Temple University. Philadelphia.

*The Journal of the History of Philosophy.* University of California Press. Berkeley, Ca.

*The Journal of Philosophy.* Columbia University. New York.

*The Journal of Thought.* University of Oklahoma. Norman, Ok.

*The Journal of Value Inquiry.* Dordrecht (Holland).

*Kant-Studien.* Philosophische Zeitschrift. Berlin.

*The Kenyon Review.* Kenyon College. Gambier, Ohio.

*Kinesis.* Southern Illinois University. Carbondale, Il.

*Koinonia.* Organo dell' Associazone di Studi tardoantichi. Naples (Italy).

*Korrespondenzblatt für die höheren Schulen Württembergs.* Stuttgart (West Germany).

*Lampas.* Tijdschrift voor Nederlandse classici. Middelburg (Holland).

*L'Année Philosophique.* Paris.

*La Nouvelle Revue.* Paris.

*La Parola del Passato.* Rivista di Studi Classici. Naples (Italy).

*Laval Théologique et Philosophique.* Université Laval. Québec (Canada).

*Le Temps de la Réflection.* Gallimard. Paris.

*Les Etudes Classiques.* Namur (Belgium).

*Liberal Education.* Association of American Colleges. Washington, D.C.

*L'Information Historique.* Paris.

*L'Information Littéraire.* Paris.

*Logos.* Mexico.

*Logos.* Rivista di Filosofia. Naples (Italy).

*Lustrum.* Internationale Forschungsberichte aus dem Bereich des klassischen Altertum. Göttingen (West Germany).

*Maia.* Rivista di Letterature classiche. Rome.

*Man and World.* An International Philosophical Review. Dordrecht (Holland).

*Materiali e Discussioni per l'Analisi dei Testi classici.* Pisa (Italy).

*Mémoires de l'Académie Royale des Inscriptions et Belles Lettres.* Paris.

*Mind.* A Quarterly Review of Psychology and Philosophy. Oxford.

*Mnemosyne.* Bibliotheca Classica Batava. Leiden (Holland).

*The Modern Language Quarterly.* University of Washington. Seattle, Washington.

*The Modern Schoolman.* A Quarterly Journal of Philosophy. Saint Louis University. St. Louis, Mo.

*Monatschrift für die Geschichte und Wissenschaft des Judentum.* Wroclaw [Breslau] (Poland).

*The Monist.* Hegeler Institute. La Salle, Il.

*Museum Helveticum.* Revue suisse pour l'Etude de l'Antiquité classique. Basel (Switzerland).

*The National Quarterly.* New York.

*Neue Jahrbücher für das klassische Altertum.* Leipzig/Berlin.

*Neue Jahrbücher für Philologie und Paedagogik.* Leipzig.

*New England Magazine.* Boston.

*The New Scholasticism.* The American Catholic Philosophical Association. The Catholic University of America. Washington, D.C.

*The New York Daily News.* New York.

*The New York Times.* New York.

*The North American Review.* University of Northern Iowa. Cedar Falls, Ia.

*Nosotros.* Buenos Aires.

*Nous.* Indiana University. Bloomington, Ind.

*The Open Court.* Chicago.

*Orpheus.* Rivista di Umanità classica e cristiana. Catania (Italy).

*Paideia.* Brescia (Italy).

*The Partisan Review.* New York.

*Pedagogia e Vita.* Brescia (Italy).

*Pensamiento.* Revista de Investigación e Información Filosófica. Madrid.

## *JOURNALS AND PERIODICALS*

[*The Personalist*]. *Pacific Philosophical Quarterly*. University of Southern California. Los Angeles, Ca.

*Phi Beta Kappa*. Washington, D.C.

*The Philological Quarterly*. London.

*Philologische Wochenschrift*. Leipzig.

*Philologus*. Zeitschrift für klassische Philologie. Berlin.

*Philosophia*. Athens.

*The Philosophical Forum*. Boston University. Boston, Mass.

*Philosophical Inquiry*. Adelphi University. Garden City, N.Y.

*Philosophical Investigations*. University College of Swansea. Wales (England).

*The Philosophical Quarterly*. Oxford.

*Philosophical Review*. New York.

*Philosophy*. The Journal of the Royal Institute of Philosophy. Cambridge (England).

*Philosophy and Literature*. John Hopkins University Press. Baltimore, Md.

*Philosophy and Phenomenological Research*. Brown University. Providence, R.I.

*Philosophy and Rhetoric*. Pennsylvania State University. University Park, Pa.

*Philosophy East and West*. A Quarterly Journal of Asian and Comparative Thought. University of Hawaii. Honolulu, Hawaii.

*Phoenix*. The Journal of the Classical Association of Canada. University of Toronto. Toronto.

*Phronesis*. A Journal for Ancient Philosophy. Assen (Holland).

*Phrontisterion*. University of Ibadan. Ibadan (Nigeria).

*Platon*. Δελτίον τῆς ῾Εταιρείας ῾Ελλήνων Φιλολόγων . Athens.

*Political Theory*. An International Journal of Political Philosophy. Beverly Hills, Ca.

Πρακτικὰ τῆς ᾿Ακαδημίας ᾿Αθηνῶν. Athens.

*Proceedings of the American Philosophical Society*. Philadelphia, Pa.

*Proceedings of the Aristotelian Society*. London.

*Proceedings of the Boston Area Colloquium in Ancient Philosophy*. Boston College. Chesnust Hill, Mass.

*Proceedings of the British Academy*. London.

## *JOURNALS AND PERIODICALS*

*Proceedings of the Cambridge Philological Society*. Cambridge University. Cambridge (England).

*Proceedings of the Classical Association*. London.

*Proceedings of the Society for Psychical Research*. London.

*Proteus*. Rivista di Filosofia. Rome.

*Prudentia*. A Journal Devoted to the Intellectual History of the Hellenistic and Roman Periods. University of Auckland. Auckland (New Zealand).

*Quaderni di Storia*. Pisa (Italy).

*Quaderni Urbinati di Cultura classica*. Rome.

*The Queen's Quarterly*. Kingston, Ontario.

*Rassegna di Filosofia*. Istituto di Filosofia dell' Università di Roma. Rome.

*Rendiconti della Pontificia Accademia di Archeologia*. Rome.

*Rediconti della Realle Accademia del Lincei*. Rome.

*Réseau*. Revue Interdisciplinaire de Philosophie Morale et Politique. Mons (Belgium).

*Revista de Estudios Clàsicos*. Instituto de Lenguas y Literature Clásicas. Mendoza (Mexico).

*Revista de Filosofía*. Madrid.

*Revista de Filosofía de la Universidad de Costa Rica*. San José (Costa Rica).

*Revista Latinoamericana de Filosofía*. Buenos Aires.

*Revista Portuguesa de Filosofía*. Braga (Portugal).

*Revista Venezolana de Filosofía*. Caracas (Venezuela).

*The Review of Metaphysics*. A Philosophical Quarterly. Catholic University of America. Washington, D.C.

*Revue Belge de Philologie et d'Histoire*. Mechelen (Belgium).

*Revue de l'Enseignement Philosophique*. Aurillac (France).

*Revue de l'Histoire des Religions*. Paris.

*Revue de Philologie*. Paris.

*Revue de Théologie et Philosophie*. Lausanne (Switzerland).

*Revue de l'Université de Bruxelles*. Brussels.

*Revue de l'Université d' Ottawa*. Ottawa.

*Revue de Metaphysique et de Morale*. Paris.

*Revue des Deux Mondes*. Litterature, Histoire, Arts et Sciences.

Paris.

*Revue des Etudes Anciennes.* Paris.

*Revue des Etudes Grecques.* Paris.

*Revue des Sciences Humaines.* Lille (France).

*Revue des Sciences Philosophiques et Théologiques.* Paris.

*Revue de Théologie et de Philosophie.* Ancienne Académie. Lausanne (Switzerland).

*Revue Internationale de Philosophie.* Wetteren (Belgium).

*Revue Philosophique.* Paris.

*Revue Philosophique de France et de l'Etranger.* Paris.

*Revue Universitaire.* Litterature, Histoire, Arts et Sciences. Paris.

*Rheinisches Museum für Philologie.* Frankfurt.

*Rivista Critica di Storia della Filosofia.* Milan (Italy).

*Rivista di Cultura Classica e Medioevale.* Rome.

*Rivista di Filosofia.* Turin (Italy).

*Rivista di Filosofia Classica.* Turin (Italy).

*Rivista di Filosofia e Scienze.* Rome.

*Rivista di Filosofia Neoscholastica.* Universita Cattolica del Sacro Cuore. Milan (Italy).

*Rivista d'Italia.* Lettere, Scienza ed Arte. Rome.

*Rivista di Studi Classici.* Turin (Italy).

*Rivista Filosofica.* Pavia (Italy).

*Rivista Internazionale di Filosofia del Diritto.* Milan (Italy).

*Romanistische Versuche und Vorarbeiten.* Bonn.

*Sandalion.* Quaderni di Cultura classica, cristiana e medievale. Sassari (Italy).

*Sapienza.* Rivista Internazionale di Filosofia e di Teologia. Naples (Italy).

*Séances et Travaux de l'Académie des Sciences Morales et Politiques.* Paris.

*Siculorum Gymnasium.* Rassegna semestrale della Facoltà di Lettere e Filosofia dell' Università di Catania. Catania (Italy).

*Sitzungsberichte der Wiener Akademie.* Vienna.

*Social Research.* New School for Social Research. New York.

*Sociologia Internationalis.* Berlin.

*Sophia.* Rassegna critica di Filosofia e Storia della Filosofia. Padua (Italy).

*The Southern Journal of Philosophy.* Memphis State University. Memphis, Tn.

*The Southern Literary Messenger.* Washington, D.C.

*The Southern Review.* A Literary and Critical Quarterly Magazine. Louisiana State University. Baton Rouge, La.

[*The Southwestern Journal of Philosophy*]. *Philosophical Topics.* University of Arkansas. Fayetteville, Ark.

*The Spectator.* London.

*Studii Classice.* Bucharest.

*Studi Urbinati di Storia, Filosofia e Letteratura.* Urbino (Italy).

*Studies in the History of Philosophy.* Columbia University. New York.

*Studium Generale.* Berlin.

*Symbolae Osloenses,* aupiciis Societatis Graeco-Latinae. Oslo.

*Talanta.* Proceedings of the Dutch Archeological and Historical Society. Amsterdam.

*Teaching Philosophy.* Bowling Green State University. Bowling Green, Ohio.

*Theologische Studien und Kritiken.* Gotha (East Germany).

*Theology Today.* Princeton, N.J.

*Theoria.* A Journal of Studies in the Arts, Humanities and Social Sciences. University of Natal Press. Pietermaritzburg (South Africa).

*The Thomist.* A Speculative Quarterly Review. Washington, D.C.

*Thought.* A Review of Culture and Ideas. Fordham University Press. New York.

*Tijdschrift voor Filosofie.* Louvain (Belgium).

*The Times Literary Supplement.* London.

*Traditio.* Studies in Ancient and Medieval History, Thought and Religion. Fordham University Press. New York.

*Transactions and Proceedings of the American Philological Association.* Chico, Ca.

*Transactions of the Peirce Society.* A Quarterly Journal in American Philosophy. State University of New York at Buffalo. Buffalo, N.Y.

*Transactions of the Royal Society of Canada.* Ottawa.

## *JOURNALS AND PERIODICALS*

*Tulane Studies in Philosophy*. Tulane University. New Orleans, La.

*University: A Princeton Magazine*. Princeton University. Princeton, N.J.

*Wiener Studien*. Zeitschrift für klassische Philologie und Patristik. Vienna.

*Würzburger Jahrbücher für die Altertumswissenschaft*. Würzburg (West Germany).

*Zeitschrift für die Neutestamentliche Wissenschaft*. Berlin.

*Ziva Antika*. Skoplje (Yugoslavia).

# Socrates

# BIBLIOGRAPHIES AND INDEXES

1 "A Bibliography of Philosophy for 1933." *The Journal of Philosophy*, 31 (1934), pp. 456-492.

Presents scholarly philosophical literature published in English, French, German, and Italian, in 1933. Includes a section on Greek philosophy, and on Socrates and Plato (pp. 457-458).

2 "A Bibliography of Philosophy for 1934." *The Journal of Philosophy*, 32 (1935), pp. 450-495.

Contains bibliographical information on philosophical literature published during 1934 in English, French, German, Italian, and other languages. Includes a section on Socrates and Plato (pp. 456-457).

3 "A Bibliography of Philosophy for 1935." *The Journal of Philosophy*, 33 (1936), pp. 450-495.

Covers scholarly literature published in 1935. Contains a section on Socrates and Plato (pp. 456-457).

4 Ast, D. Frederick. *Lexicon platonicum sive vocum platonicarum*. New York: Burt Franklin, 1969 (3 vols.).

Originally published in 1835 (2 vols.). Greek index of the Platonic *corpus* by reference to the Stephanus edition (Paris, 1578). Gives Latin equivalences of the important Greek terms. Standard Platonic lexicon.

5 Baldwin, James M., ed. "Socrates." *Dictionary of Philosophy and Psychology*. Gloucester, Mass.: Peter Smith, 1960 (3 vols.), Vol. 3, Part 1, pp. 479-482.

Unannotated bibliography of modern Socratic literature.

6 Bonitz, H. *Index aristotelicus*. Berlin, 1870.

General *index nominum* and *rerum* of the Aritotelian *corpus*.

Distinguishes the references to the historical Socrates from those which appear to involve the Socrates who acts as Plato's mouthpiece.

7 Brisson, L. "Platon: 1958-1975." *Lustrum* 20 (1977), pp. 5-304.

Includes bibliographical entries of works on Plato and Platonic scholarship published between 1958 and 1977. Provides brief summaries and comments.

8 Cherniss, Harold. "Plato: 1950-1957." *Lustrum* 4 (1959), pp. 5-308; 5 (1960), pp. 321-648.

Includes bibliographical entries of works on Plato and Platonic scholarship published between 1950 and 1957. Provides brief summaries and comments.

9 Des Places, Eduard. *Lexique de la langue philosophique et religieuse de Platon. Platon. Oeuvres complètes.* Paris: Les Belles Lettres, 1920.

Constitutes the last two volumes (14 and 15) of the Greek-French edition of Plato's works. Furnishes lexicographical information on the major philosophical and theological terms used by Plato. Contains also a bibliography which is divided into two sections: general works of Plato, and works which discuss specific terms used throughout the dialogues.

10 Dover, Kenneth J. "Aristophanes: 1938-1955." *Lustrum* 2 (1957), pp. 52-112.

Includes bibliographical entries of works on Aristophanes and Aristophanic scholarship published between 1938 and 1955. Provides brief summaries and comments.

11 Dubois, J. "Bulletin d'histoire de la philosophie grecque." *Revue des Sciences Philosophiques et Théologiques*, 33 (1949), pp. 267-303.

Reviews (pp. 296-303) recent books on Socrates, specifically works by T. Déman, O. Gigon, R. Guardini, A. J.

Festugière, and W. Jaeger.

12 Gelzer, T. "Hinweise auf einige neuere Bucher zu Aristophanes." *Museum Helveticum*, 21 (1964), pp. 103ff.

Contains summaries of and comments on several works on Aristophanes published in 1962 and 1963. Among the authors included are E. Fraenkel, C. F. Russo, W. Kassies, W. Kraus, R. Hosek, P. Haendel, and C. M. J. Sicking.

13 Magalhães-Vilhena, V. de. "Bibliographie." *Le problème de Socrate. Le Socrate historique et le Socrate de Platon.* Paris: Presses Universitaires de France, 1952, pp. 471-566.

Contains sections on bibliographies, dictionaries, and lexicons; on primary and secondary sources; and on modern philological, philosophical, and historical Socratic scholarship. Constitutes the most extensive unannotated Socratic bibliography aside from that of Andreas Patzer. Ref. 391.

14 McKirahan, Richard D. *Plato and Socrates: A Comprehensive Bibliography, 1958 to 1973.* New York: Garland Publishing, 1978.

Includes 4620 unannotated entries on Plato and Socrates. Divides the entries on Plato into the following categories: general studies, Plato's life and his relations to others, the Platonic *corpus*, Plato as a writer, Plato's thought, and Plato's terminology. Includes close to 400 entries on Socrates (pp. 501-548), divided into various categories: general studies, the sources of our information about Socrates, Socrates' life and relations to others, Socrates' thought, and Socrates and Plato in ancient art. Provides an index of authors, as well as abundant cross-references.

15 Montuori, Mario. "Bibliography of 18th Century Writings on Socrates." *De Socrate iuste damnato.* Amsterdam: J. C. Gieben, 1981, pp. 147-153.

Contains 132 unannotated entries of works on Socrates published in the seventeenth, eighteenth, and early nineteenth centuries. Ref. 398.

16 Murphy, C. T. "A Survey of Recent Works on Aristophanes and Old Comedy." *Classical World* 65 (1972), pp. 261-273.

Includes bibliographical entries with brief annotations and comments.

16a Navia, Luis E. "Bibliography." *Socrates: The Man and His Philosophy*. Lanham, Md.: University Press of America, 1985, pp. 335-356.

Contains over 360 unannotated entries of works on Socrates. Ref. 304.

17 Organ, Troy Wilson. *An Index to Aristotle in English Translation*. Princeton, N.J.: Princeton University Press, 1949.

Distinguishes between the references to Socrates as a historical person or as a Platonic dramatic character, and 'Socrates' as a common name (*i.e.*, 'anybody').

18 Patzer, Andreas. *Bibliographia Socratica*. Freiburg: Verlag Karl Alber, 1985.

Contains 2301 unannotated entries of works on Socrates and Socratic scholarship. Provides an index of names and subjects.

19 Sturz, Friedrich W. *Lexicum xenophonteum*. Hildesheim: G. Olms, 1964 (4 vols.).

Reprint of the 1801-1804 edition (Leipzig: J. A. Barth). General Greek index of major terms and names contained in Xenophon's works, with Latin equivalencies.

20 Todd, O. J. *Index aristophaneus*. Cambridge, Mass.: Harvard University Press, 1932.

General Greek index of major terms and names contained in Aristophanes' comedies, with Latin equivalencies.

# PRIMARY SOURCES - ARISTOPHANES

The major primary sources include Aristophanes' *Clouds*, the dialogues of Plato, and writings of Xenophon which deal specifically with Socrates (the *Apology*, the *Memorabilia*, and the *Symposium*). In this section, an effort has been made to give a varied and selective sample of bibliographical entries of the primary sources. Surely, the actual number of editions and translations of these sources is far greater than what could be gathered from the following pages.

The *Clouds* is one of Aristophanes' eleven extant comedies. Written and performed in 423 B.C., it underwent a revision by its author, which, although probably never performed in ancient times, constitutes the basis of the Mss. which have come down to us. The *editio princeps* (which includes all the Aristophanic comedies with the exception of *Lysistrata* and *Thesmophoriazusae*) was published in Venice by Marcus Musurus in 1508. Various Greek and Latin editions have been published since that time, and a vast number of translations into many languages have been made.

The comedy calls for a cast of twelve characters (probably played by only three actors) and the usual chorus of twenty-four voices (which is a personified group of clouds). Five among the characters occupy the dramatic foreground: Strepsiades, Phidippides, Socrates, and two personifications of the Just Discourse and the Unjust Discourse. In the comedy, we witness the plight of an old peasant (Strepsiades) whose troubles stem from a deteriorating economic condition which has been caused by the ill behavior of his lazy son (Phidippides). In desperation, the old man seeks the assistance of Socrates who is the head of an institution (the Thinking Establishment), where the curriculum promises to make the students experts in the art of deception through language. Socrates spends his time suspended in a basket from which he prays to his beloved Clouds who have come to take for him the place of the gods. After a short course of instruction, Strepsiades loses his sense of reality and degenerates into a confused old man. At a later point, Phidippides also joins the Socratic institution, and he, too, becomes perverted under the Sophistical influence of Socrates. The old man, however, eventually comes to his senses upon seeing the unhappy transformation of Phidippides who has changed himself into an irreligious, disrespectful, and boastful man who does not hesitate to abuse his aged father. The comedy ends with the burning of the Socratic school and with the disbanding of the disciples, while Socrates himself barely succeeds in escaping alive. Amid countless jokes and nonsensical scenes, the portrait of Socrates which emerges from the *Clouds* is that of a socially dangerous man whose influence cannot but be a great source of concern to law-abiding and honest citizens. Ultimately he proves to be the embodiment of Sophistical tendencies and practices, as well as of the spirit of scientific curiosity which characterized the earlier philosophers, and it is precisely on this account that he is presented to the audience as a detrimental presence among the Athenians.

Undoubtedly, Socrates was ridiculed on the stage by other poets of the Old Comedy, as can be seen from the fragments of Ameipsias (*Connus* 9e), Cratinus (*Cheirons* 231e), Eupolis (352e), and others (collected in *Comicorum Graecorum Fragmenta* by A. Meineke, Berlin, 1839-1857, and by T. Kock, Leipzig, 1880-1888). But the *Clouds* seems to be the only comedy exclusively devoted to Socrates. There are scattered references to him in some of the other Aristophanic comedies, as when in *Birds* 1280-1281, for instance, we encounter the following lines in reference to the new Athenian intellectuals:

> They were all crazy.... They wore their hair long, they went hungry and crazy, they socratized, they carried sticks!

Other references include *Wasps* 1037ff., *Birds* 1553ff., and *Frogs* 1491-1499. These brief references, however, do not add anything new to the Socratic portrait created in the *Clouds*.

The following entries include selective examples of the numerous editions and translations of the *Clouds*.

21 "Aenaoi Nefelai." *Musique de la Grèce antique*. Compact phonodisc. Saint-Michel de Provence: Harmonia Mundi, 1979, 1 min, 25 sec.

Musical performance by the Atrium Musicae de Madrid of the chorus from the *Clouds* (275-277) Ἀέναοι Νεφέλαι.... Based on a fifteenth century Munich manuscript. Recreates the authentic sound of Aristophanic music, specifically the chorus hymn sung immediately after Socrates' fervent invocation to the Clouds. Directed by Gregorio Paniagua, with authentic instrumentation.

22 *Aristophane*. Translated by Alphonse Willems. Paris:

Hachette et Cie., 1919 (2 vols.).

French translation with notes and commentary of Aristophanes' comedies. Includes the *Clouds* (*Les nuées*) in Vol. 1, pp. 269-415.

23 *Aristophanes' Clouds: Purpose and Technique*. Edited by Raymond K. Fisher. Amsterdam: Adolph M. Hakkert, 1984.

Presents a detailed textual analysis with extensive Greek passages.

24 *Aristophanis Comoedia*. Edited by F. H. Hall and W. M. Geldart. Oxford: The Clarendon Press, 1970 (2 vols.).

First edition published in 1900. Contains the Greek text of all the extant works of Aristophanes. The *Clouds* is included in Vol. 1.

25 *Clouds. Aristophanes: The Eleven Comedies*. New York: Liveright Publishing Corp., 1943 (2 vols.), Vol. 1, pp. 295-377.

Anonymous prose translation originally published by the Athenian Society (London, 1912). Contains a brief introduction in which Aristophanes' purpose in writing the *Clouds* is interpreted in terms of his desire to expose and ridicule the Sophists. Regards the Aristophanic Socrates as a comic stereotype of Sophism, and alleges that neither the comic poet nor his audience was able (or willing) to understand the immense gap that actually separated Socrates from the Sophists.

26 *Clouds. Aristophanes*. Translated by Benjamin B. Rogers. Cambridge, Mass.: Harvard University Press (The Loeb Classical Library), 1959 (3 vols.), Vol. 1, pp. 262-401.

Greek text with an accompanying English translation. Contains a brief introduction by Benjamin B. Rogers in which it is maintained that the aim of the comedy was to mount an attack on the Sophistical system of education which dominated Athenian intellectual circles during the last decades of the fifth century B.C. Argues that in choosing Socrates as the embodiment of the Sophistical movement, Aristophanes was notoriously unjust, and that there is no reason to believe that the audience took seriously his attack on Socrates. Interprets Socrates' references in the *Apology* to Aristophanes as an ironical device designed to expose the worthlessness of the official indictment.

27 *Clouds. The Complete Greek Drama*. Edited by Whitney J. Oates and Eugene O'Neill, Jr. New York: Random House, 1938 (2 vols.), Vol. 2, pp. 536-601.

Translator anonymous. Same prose translation as in *Aristophanes: The Eleven Comedies*. Ref. 25.

28 *Clouds*. Edited by Kenneth J. Dover. Oxford: The Clarendon Press, 1968.

Greek text with philological and historical annotations.

29 *Clouds*. Edited by W. J. M. Starkie. Amsterdam: Hakkert, 1966.

Greek text with philological annotations. Reprint of the edition of 1911.

30 *Clouds. Five Comedies of Aristophanes*. Translated by Benjamin B. Rogers. Garden City, N.Y.: Doubleday & Company, 1955, pp. 149-214.

Annotated English verse translation with a brief introduction. Other comedies in the volume are the *Birds*, the *Frogs*, the *Wasps*, and *Lysistrata*.

31 *Clouds*. Translated by Benjamin B. Rogers. *Fifteen Greek Plays*. New York: Oxford University Press, 1943, pp. 545-601.

English verse translation prefaced by a summary of the comedy's argument.

32 *Clouds*. Translated by Moses Hadas. *The Complete Plays of Aristophanes*. Edited by Moses Hadas. New York: Bantam Books, 1962, pp. 101-141.

Unannotated English prose translation.

33 *Clouds*. Translated by Richard Cumberland. *Greek Literature in Translation*. Edited by George Howe and Gustave A. Harrer. New York: Harper & Brothers, 1924, pp. 324-370.

English translation with an introduction.

34 *Clouds*. Translated by William Arrowsmith. Ann Arbor: The University of Michigan Press, 1962.

English verse translation. Sketches by Thomas McClure. Includes notes and a glossary, as well as a short introduction which discusses the relationship between Aristophanes and Socrates.

35 *Comédies d' Aristophane*. Translated by M. Artaud. Paris: Librairie Firmin Didot Frères, Fils et Cie., 1859 (2 vols.).

Annotated French translation of Aristophanes' eleven comedies. Includes a general introduction. Presents the *Clouds* (*Les nuées*) in Vol. 1, pp. 135-202.

36 *Comedies of Aristophanes*. Edited by Alan H. Sommerstein. Warminster, England: Aris & Phillips, 1982 (4 vols.).

Greek text accompanied by a prose translation and explanatory notes. The *Clouds* is contained in Vol. 3.

37 *Four Plays of Aristophanes*. Translated by James H. Mantinband. Lanham, Md.: University Press of America, 1983.

English poetic translation with a few annotations. Includes the *Clouds* (pp. 1-74). Contains an introduction in which the translator argues that the Aristophanic Socrates is only a caricature of the historical man.

38 *Les nuées. Aristophane*. Translated by C. Poyard. Paris: Librairie de L. Hachette et Cie., 1860, pp. 95-143.

French translation with annotations and an introduction.

39 *Nubes*. Edited by J. van Leeuwen. Leiden: A. W. Sijthoff, 1968.

Greek text with extensive annotations in Latin and a detailed index. Includes a prolegomena.

40 *Nuvole*. Translated by B. Marzuelo. *Socrate: Tutte le testimonianze da Aristophane e Senofonte ai padri Cristiani*. Edited by Gabriele Giannantoni. Bari: Editori Laterza, 1971, pp. 1-73.

Annotated Italian translation. Ref. 143.

41 *Oeuvres*. Paris: Collection Budé, 1923-1930 (5 vols.).

Greek text edited by V. Coulon and French translation by H. van Daele.

42 *The Plays of Aristophanes*. Translated by Frere, Hickie, Mitchell and Cumberland. London: J. M. Pen & Sons, 1911 (2 vols.).

Contains a general introduction by John Hookman Frere, originally written in 1820. The *Clouds* (translated by T. Mitchell) is found in Vol. 2, pp. 111-174. The text is edited by Ernest Rhys.

## PRIMARY SOURCES - XENOPHON

The works of Xenophon which are particularly important as Socratic testimonies are the *Symposium*, the *Memorabilia*, and the *Apology*. It is generally believed that writings such as the *Oeconomicus* do not shed much light on the life and ideas of the historical Socrates, even though his presence in them has literary significance. There is only one passage in the *Anabasis* (III,i,5-7) in which he is mentioned, and such is also the case with the *Hellenica* (I,7,15). The most varied opinions concerning the value of Xenophon as a genuine Socratic witness have been advanced, and these opinions range from the most negative or skeptical attitude to the most enthusiastic assessment of his reports on Socrates' life and philosophy.

As in the instance of the Platonic dialogues, many attempts have been made to establish a chronology of Xenophon's writings, but here, too, there remains much ground of scholarly disagreement. All that can be said to the satisfaction of everybody is that such writings were written sometime after Xenophon's participation in the Greek expeditionary force that accompanied Cyrus the Younger in 401 B.C. Likewise, as in the case of Plato, there is no agreement as to the authenticity of some of the works attributed to him; the *Apology*, for instance, has been regarded as authentic by some scholars and as a patently spurious work by others.

The *Apology* is avowedly Xenophon's attempt to exonerate Socrates from the charge of having behaved arrogantly towards the jurors of the court of the King Archon, and it is in the context of that apologetic endeavor that Xenophon reveals various interesting details concerning Socrates' trial and attitudes on that occasion. The *Symposium*, on the other hand, recounts for us the details of an informal gathering in which Socrates and several among his friends participated. The dramatic scene and some of its themes are reminiscent of Plato's *Symposium*, but the precise literary relationship between both works remains a matter of controversy among scholars. The *Memorabilia* appears to be divided into two unequal parts, namely, a strictly apologetic section (I,i,1 - I,ii,64), in which Xenophon endeavors to answer the specific charges contained in the official indictment levelled against Socrates, and a lengthy collection of reminiscences of Socrates' conversations, many of which were allegedly heard by Xenophon himself. The *Oeconomicus*, generally viewed as a non-Socratic work, portrays Socrates as engaged in conversations on subjects such as household maintenance and farming. It has often been maintained that the presence of Socrates in the *Oeconomicus* does not transcend the level of a mere literary device for the expression of Xenophon's own ideas.

The *editio princeps* of Xenophon's works was published by Junta (Venice, 1516). Later more complete editions appeared under the direction of Aldus (Venice, 1525), H. Stephanus (Geneva, 1561 and 1581), and J. Lenklau (Frankfurt, 1594). More recent editions of the Greek text include those of J. C. Zeune (Leipzig, 1778-), J. C. Schneider (Leipzig, 1790-), B. Weiske (Leipzig, 1798-), G. F. Schaefer (Leipzig, 1811-), L. Dindorf (Leipzig, 1824-), Schneider and Dindorf (Oxford, 1810-), and G. Sauppe (Leipzig, 1863-). E. C. Marchant's edition (annotated below in the Loeb Classical Library edition) was published originally by the Clarendon Press at Oxford (1900-).

The following entries include a small selection of recent editions and translations.

43 *Anabasis*. Translated by Carleton L. Brownson. *Xenophon in Seven Volumes*. Cambridge, Mass.: Harvard University Press (The Loeb Classical Library), 1980 (Vol. 3).

Greek text with an accompanying English translation. Mentions Socrates (III,i,5-7) in the context of Xenophon's request for advice concerning his joining the expedition to Persia. Reports that Socrates advised him to consult the Delphic oracle and to follow precisely its directive. Indicates Socrates' response to Xenophon's intention to participate in the expedition, and raises the issue of the possible charge of Laconism to which such participation might give rise (Cf. *Memorabilia* I,i,4).

44 *Apologia de Sócrates*. Edited and translated by J. S. Stavrou. Panamá: Facultad de Filosofía y Letras, 1954.

Spanish translation of Xenophon's *Apology*. Includes an introductory essay and annotations.

45 *Apologia de Sócrates*. Edited by S. Rodriguez Brasa. Salamanca: Colegio de San Estanislao, 1957 (2 vols.).

Presents in Vol. 1 the Greek text of the *Apology*, and in Vol. 2 the Greek text and an accompanying Spanish translation.

46 *Apologie de Socrate*. Edited and translated by M. Beleze. Paris: Auguste Dehalain, 1829.

Greek text of the *Apology* with a French translation. Includes also an interlinear translation in which the order of the Greek text has been altered in order to render it more accessible to French readers. Prefaces each chapter with a short summary of its contents.

47 *Apology. Xenophon's Minor Works.* Translated by J. S. Watson. London: George Bell & Sons, 1888, pp. 192-201.

Annotated English translation of Xenophon's *Apology*. Contains an introduction in which it is maintained that this work is a fragmentary, dry, and spiritless piece which, judging from the excellence of Xenophon's authentic writings, cannot be rightly attributed to him. Suggests that the inferior writer of the *Apology* is the same who forged the last chapter of the *Cyropaedia*.

48 *Apology* (*Socrates' Defence to the Jury*). Translated by O. J. Todd. *Xenophon in Seven Volumes.* Cambridge, Mass.: Harvard University Press (The Loeb Classical Library), 1979 (7 vols.), Vol. 4, pp. 637-663.

Greek text with an accompanying English translation. Contains an introduction in which it is argued that it is impossible to determine the literary relationship between the *Apology* and the *Memorabilia* (*i.e.*, whether the former was meant to be the conclusion of the latter). Maintains, moreover, that the date of composition of the *Apology* (the authenticity of which is taken for granted) cannot be determined. Notes that there is not enough evidence to speak confidently concerning the literary relationship between Xenophon's work and the Platonic *Apology*.

49 *Banquet - Apologie de Socrate.* Edited and translated by François Ollier. Paris: Societé d'Editions Les Belles Lettres, 1961.

Includes the Greek text and a French translation of the *Symposium* and the *Apology*. Provides a synopsis of each work.

50 *Cyropaedia and the Hellenica*. Translated by J. S. Watson and Henry Dale. London: George Bell & Sons, 1891.

English translation. Includes a biographical notice of Xenophon. Discusses his meeting with Socrates at an early age, and endorses the opinion that from that time on, he was firmly attached to the philosopher. Discusses briefly the *Memorabilia* and the *Symposium*, and comments on the alleged rivalry between Xenophon and Plato. Adds a chronological table to the *Hellenica*.

51 *De philosophia morali in Xenophontis de Socrate commentariis tradita*. Edited by L. Dissen. Göttingen, 1812.

Contains Latin translations of excerpts from the *Memorabilia*. Aims at the reconstruction of Socrates' moral philosophy as this reveals itself in Xenophon's testimony.

52 *Die sokratischen Schriften*. Translated by E. von Bux. Stuttgart: Kröner, 1956.

Presents an annotated German translation of Xenophon's Socratic writings: *Apology*, *Memorabilia*, *Symposium*, and *Oeconomicus*.

53 *Erinnerungen an Sokrates*. Edited and translated by R. von Preiswerk. Zürich: Rascher, 1953.

Contains an annotated German translation of the *Memorabilia*.

54 *Hellenica*. Translated by Carlton L. Brownson. *Xenophon in Seven Volumes*. Cambridge, Mass.: Harvard University Press (The Loeb Classical Library), 1968, Vols. 1 and 2.

Greek text with an accompanying English translation. Mentions Socrates (I,vii,15) in the context of the account of the trial of the generals of Arginusae in 406 B.C. Describes Socrates as one of the prytanes, and as the only one who refused to put the question (whether the generals should be tried for treason in a group) to the Assembly's vote. Explains Socrates' defiance of the popular will as a manifestation of his unwillingness to act contrary to the laws.

55 *History of My Time.* Translated by Rex Warner. Baltimore: Penguin Books, 1966.

English translation of the *Hellenica.* Emphasizes (in the introduction) Xenophon's Spartan sympathies.

56 *Jenofonte, Sócrates. Toda la obra del gran historiador a propósito de su maestro. Apología de Sócrates. El Banquete. Recuerdos socráticos. De lo económico. Cartas.* Edited and translated by J. B. Bergua. Madrid: Bergua, 1954.

Contains a Spanish translation of the Socratic writings of Xenophon: *Apology*, *Symposium*, and *Memorabilia.* Includes a translation of the *Oeconomicus* and his letters. Provides an introduction and annotations.

57 *La Morale de Socrate.* Edited by J. Fravre. Paris, 1888.

Contains French translations of selected passages from the *Memorabilia.*

58 *Les choses memorables de Socrate. Ouvrage de Xénophon.* Translated by François Charpentier. Amsterdam: Etienne Roger, 1699.

French translation of the *Memorabilia.* Appended to Charpentier's *La vie de Socrate* (Amsterdam: Etienne Roger, 1699). Ref. 206.

59 *The March of the Ten Thousand.* Translated by H. G. Dakyns. London: Macmillan, 1901.

English translation of the *Anabasis.* Contains Dakyns' "A Sketch of Xenophon's Life" (pp.i-lxxx). Provides abundant annotations to the text, and includes a detailed chronology and a map of the expedition. Ref. 514.

60 *The March Up Country.* Translated by W. H. D. Rouse. Ann Arbor: The University of Michigan Press, 1964.

English translation of the *Anabasis*. Includes a map of the route taken by the Greek army. Presents in the preface a discussion of Xenophon's Spartan sympathies, and a description of the intellectual life of his time. Notes the importance for him of the spirit of open debate as embodied in the person of Socrates.

61 *The Memoirs of Socrates.* London, 1871.

Contains an English translation of excerpts from the *Memorabilia*, prefaced by a short introduction.

62 *Memoirs of Socrates and the Symposium.* Translated by Hugh Tredennick. Baltimore: Penguin Books, 1970.

English translation of the *Memorabilia* and the *Symposium*. Includes a glossary of proper names.

63 *Memoirs of Socrates with the Defense Before His Judges.* Translated by Sarah Fielding. London: C. Pope, 1762.

English translation of the *Memorabilia* and the *Apology*.

64 *Memorabili.* Translated by R. Laurenti. *Socrate. Tutte le testimonianze da Aristofane e Senofonte ai padri Cristiani*, edited by Gabriele Giannantoni. Bari: Editori Laterza, 1971, pp. 74-263.

Annotated Italian translation of the *Memorabilia*. Ref. 143.

65 *Memorabilia.* Edited by Charles Anthon. New York: Harper & Brothers, 1879.

Includes the Greek text as well as critical and explanatory notes, and an introduction. Contains (in the introduction) sections which discuss the design and plan of Xenophon's work, the arrangement of the subjects, the precepts of Socrates reduced to a system, the historical value of Xenophon's testimony, and the divine voice of Socrates.

66 *Memorabilia.* Translated by E. C. Marchant. *Xenophon in Seven Volumes.* Cambridge, Mass.: Harvard University Press (The Loeb Classical Library), 1979 (7 vols.), Vol. 4, pp. 1-359.

Greek text with an accompanying English translation. Provides a brief analysis of the *Memorabilia.* Considers this work to be the result of several decades of literary activity on Xenophon's part, and to be actually the outcome of the compilation of separate writings. Recognizes the influence of Antisthenes on the ideological tone of the *Memorabilia.* Emphasizes the impossibility of making definite assertions concerning the actual historical relationship between Xenophon's work and Plato's dialogues.

67 *The Memorable Thoughts of Socrates.* Translated by Edward Bysshe. London: Cassell & Co., 1901.

English translation of the *Memorabilia.* Originally published in 1712. Contains a reprint of the revised edition of 1722. Provides an introduction in which Xenophon is referred to as a philosophical man of action. Considers his writing to be clear and precise. Endeavors to explain the manner in which Xenophon was able to bring together, in a direct and simple way, the views on life imparted to him by his friend Socrates. Observes that although Xenophon had strong feelings towards Socrates, he did not want to idealize him.

68 *Memorables (Recuerdos socráticos).* Edited and translated by Juan David García. Mexico: Secretaría de Educación Pública, 1945.

Contains a Spanish translation of selections from the *Memorabilia.*

69 *Oeconomicus (On the Management of a Farm and Household). Xenophon's Minor Works.* Translated by J. S. Watson. London: George Bell & Sons, 1888, pp. 71-147.

Annotated text. Prefaces each chapter with a brief synoptical statement. Regards the *Oeconomicus* as a well-organized dialogue concerning Socrates' philosophy of domestic management, and as a complement to the

*Memorabilia* (which is viewed as the expression of Socrates' moral philosophy).

70 *Oeconomicus*. Translated by E. C. Marchant. *Xenophon in Seven Volumes*. Cambridge, Mass.: Harvard University Press (The Loeb Classical Library), 1979 (7 vols.), Vol. 4, pp. 361-525.

Greek text with an accompanying English translation. Introduction: Argues that even though certain indications point to an early date of composition, the tone of the *Oeconomicus* should convince us that at least in its final form it belongs to a late stage in Xenophon's life. Views the Socrates of the *Oeconomicus* as a literary figure mostly unrelated to the historical Socrates. Interprets Ischomachus as a genuine mouthpiece for Xenophon's own ideas.

71 *Recollections of Socrates and Socrates' Defense Before the Jury*. Translated by Anna Benjamin. Indianapolis: The Bobbs-Merrill Company, 1965.

English translations of the *Memorabilia* and the *Apology*, based on E. G. Marchant's edition (Oxford Classical Texts Series). Discusses in the introduction the relationship between Xenophon and the Socratic literature, and suggests that Xenophon's works present three types of Socratic literature: (1) the Socratic discourses or dialogues, (2) the Socratic apologetics, and (3) the recollections.

72 *Records de Sòcrates*. Edited and translated by Carles Riba. Barcelona: Editorial Catalana, 1923.

Contains the annotated Greek text of the *Memorabilia* with an accompanying Catalonian translation. Includes a preface in which comments are made about the structure and contents of the work. Gives a brief bibliographical notice about the manuscripts and the major Greek editions.

73 *Symposium*. Edited by Samuel Ross Winans. Boston: John Allyn, 1888.

Provides the Greek text with extensive annotations. Includes a preface in which Xenophon is described as a man who possessed little poetic imagination, and whose life exemplified not the dialectical but the practical side of Socrates' philosophy. Notes that Xenophon was one of the first to employ the philosophical dialogue, and argues that there is an immense difference in style between his writings and those of Plato. Considers Xenophon's account less pretentious and more trustworthy than that of Plato.

74 *Symposium (The Banquet)*. Translated by O. J. Todd. *Xenophon in Seven Volumes*. Cambridge, Mass.: Harvard University Press (The Loeb Classical Library), 1979 (7 vols.), Vol. 4, pp. 527-635.

Greek text with an accompanying English translation. Introduction: Maintains that the *Symposium* must be viewed not as a historical conversation but as a literary attempt to portray Socrates in a moment of social relaxation and enjoyment, and as an endeavor to develop a corrective to the more exalted representation of him presented in Plato's *Symposium*. Emphasizes the realism and vividness of Xenophon's work, and assigns the year 421 B.C. as its literary date.

75 *Symposium (The Banquet)*. *Xenophon's Minor Works*. Translated by J. S. Watson. London: George Bell & Sons, 1888, pp. 148-191.

Annotated text. Contains brief summary statements for each chapter. Introduction: Includes short biographical notices on all the participants. Assumes the veracity of Xenophon's assertion concerning his presence at the conversation, and assigns the year 424 B.C. as its literary date.

76 *Xénophon. Morceaux choisis*. Edited and translated by G. Daubresse and P. Courtin. Wetteren: Scaldis, 1954 (2 vols.).

Contains French translations of passages from the *Anabasis*, the *Cyropaedia*, and the *Memorabilia*.

77 *Xenophon's Socratic Discourse: An Interpretation of the Oeconomicus*. Ithaca, N.Y.: Cornell University Press, 1970.

Includes a translation of the *Oeconomicus* by C. Lord.

Interpretation and annotations by Leo Strauss.

78 *Xenophontis Opera Omnia.* Edited by E. C. Marchant. Oxford: The Clarendon Press, 1900 (5 vols.).

Provides the Greek text of the entire extant Xenophontean *corpus.* Volume 2 contains the *Memorabilia*, the *Oeconomicus*, the *Symposium*, and the *Apology*.

# PRIMARY SOURCES - PLATO

Many attempts have been made to determine the dates of composition and chronological sequence of Plato's dialogues, but such endeavors have only yielded certain general historical parameters of tentative value. We cannot be certain, for instance, whether Plato began the composition of his dialogues only after Socrates' death, or whether, as Diogenes Laertius reports (iii, 35), some of the early dialogues were actually written during the last years of Socrates' life. In general the tendency among scholars is to distinguish three major groups of dialogues, different from one another not only with respect to their composition time, but also in regard to their style, content, and philosophical orientation. The groups are (1) the early dialogues, which include dialogues such as the *Euthyphro*, the *Apology*, the *Lysis*, and the *Charmides*; (2) the middle dialogues, among which we can place dialogues like the *Symposium*, the *Phaedrus*, and the *Republic*; and (3) the late dialogues such as the *Laws* and the *Critias*. The early dialogues are said to be those written before the year 385 B.C., while the late dialogues belong to the last twenty years of Plato's life (367-347 B.C.). It is also generally believed that, as we construct the chronology of the dialogues in terms of early, middle, and late dialogues, we can notice a change in the presence of the historical Socrates. Thus, whereas his presence is unmistakable in the early dialogues, it tends to recede more and more into the background as we move towards the late dialogues, until, as in the case of the *Laws*, it disappears altogether from the dramatic scene. It is obviously for this reason that the early dialogues are often regarded as genuine examples of Socratic discourses, and as an abundant source of information concerning the historical Socrates. It is important to bear in mind, however, that there have been scholars for whom such an interpretation of the Socratic problem as this confronts us in Plato's writings is inadequate or plainly mistaken, as has been stressed by John Burnet, A. E. Taylor, and Eric A. Havelock. According to Burnet and Taylor, we would not be unjustified in asserting that everything attributed by Plato to Socrates, either in terms of biographical information or in the form of philosophical ideas, reflects reasonably accurate historical information.

The oldest classification of the Platonic dialogues belongs to Aristophanes of Byzantium, a scholar of the third century B.C., and it seems that it was on the basis of such classification that Thrasyllus, a bibliographer of the time of Tiberius, arranged the dialogues and the letters into nine tetralogies. Included in these thirty-nine Platonic works, however, there are dialogues that later scholarship has chosen to regard as spurious or inauthentic, although there is by no means a universally accepted list of authentic dialogues. The following list of dialogues (arranged by their order of appearance in the Stephanus edition) includes those whose authenticity is generally taken for granted:

| | |
|---|---|
| *Euthyphro* | *Charmides* |
| *Apology* | *Laches* |
| *Crito* | *Lysis* |
| *Phaedo* | *Menexenus* |
| *Theaetetus* | *Statesman* |
| *Sophist* | *Republic* |
| *Euthydemus* | *Laws* |
| *Protagoras* | *Epinomis* |
| *Hippias Minor* | *Timaeus* |
| *Cratylus* | *Critias* |
| *Gorgias* | *Parmenides* |
| *Ion* | *Symposium* |
| *Philebus* | *Phaedrus* |
| *Meno* | *Hippias Major* |

The oldest printed edition of Plato's writings was published by A. P. Manutius and Marcus Musurus (Venice, 1513). An edition (which included Proclus' commentary) was published by Valder and Simon Grynaeus a few years later (Basel, 1534), and in 1556 the Stephanus edition appeared in Paris. This was published again in 1578 with a Latin translation of all the Platonic writings. Later Greek editions include those of I. Bekker (with a Latin translation; Berlin, 1816-1823, 10 vols.); G. Stallbaum (with commentary; Leipzig, 1821-1825, 12 vols.); J. G. Baiter, J. C. Orelli, and A. G. Winckelmann (Zurich, 1839-1841, 21 vols.); R. B. Hirzschig and C. E. C. Schneider (Paris, 1856-1873, 3 vols.); and M. Schanz (Leipzig, 1875-1879). More recently, there are editions by John Burnet, W. R. M. Lamb *et al*, and Maurice Croiset (which are annotated below).

79 Ἅπαντα Πλάτωνος. Athens: Hetaireia Hellenikon Ekdoseon, 1956-1966 (18 vols.).

Contains (vols. 1 to 14) a modern Greek translation of Plato's works, and (vols. 15 to 18) the ancient Greek text (based on C. F. Hermann's edition). The translation, the general introduction, and the annotations are by G. Kouchtsoglou.

80 *Apologia de Sócrates, Critón, Laques, Fedón.* Edited and translated by María Juanas Ribas and Agustín Gonzalez Gallego. Barcelona: Editorial Bruguera, 1974.

Contains a Spanish translation of the *Apology*, the *Crito*, the *Laches*, and the *Phaedo*. Includes an introduction and a bibliography.

81 *The Apology*. Edited by G. Stock. Oxford: The Clarendon Press, 1961.

Reprint of the 1887 edition. Contains the Greek text, with an introduction and detailed notes. Provides indexes to the notes in English and Greek, and a Greek-English glossary.

82 *Apology*. Edited by James J. Helm. Chicago: Bolchazy-Carducci Publishers, 1981.

Greek text of the Burnet edition of Plato's works. Includes grammatical annotations.

83 *Apology and Crito. Man and Man: The Social Philosophers.* Edited by Saxe Commins and Robert N. Linscott. New York: Random House. 1947, pp. 184-226.

English translations. Presents each dialogue as an expression of a distinct moral problem. Views the *Apology* as a defense of what constitutes the good life, and the *Crito* as Socrates' definitive statement of his commitment to social responsibility.

84 *Apology of Socrates.* Edited by Harold Williamson. London: Macmillan, 1963.

Contains the Greek text of the *Apology* with abundant annotations. Presents in the introduction a summary of the dialogue, and comments on the different representations of Socrates created by Aristophanes, Xenophon, and Plato.

85 *The Apology, Read by Ralph Richardson.* Phonodisc. New York: Caedmon Records, No. 2050, 1971 (2 discs).

Reading of Plato's *Apology* by Ralph Richardson. Uses B. Jowett's translation. Notes by Marianne Mantell.

86 *The Collected Dialogues of Plato, Including the Letters.* Edited by Edith Hamilton and Huntington Cairns. Princeton: Princeton University Press (Bollington Series), 1961.

Contains twenty-eight dialogues and the Platonic letters. The English translations are by various translators (including Jowett). Contains a general introduction by Huntington Cairns, and individual prefaces to the dialogues and the letters by Edith Hamilton. In the introduction, Cairns argues against a mystical interpretation of Plato and his works, and sees Plato's explorations as a manifestation of his firm grasp of logical principles. Contains an index of names and subjects.

87 *Critón.* Edited and translated by M. Rico Gomez. Madrid: Instituto de Estudios Politicos, 1957.

Spanish translation of the *Crito.* Includes an introductory essay and critical annotations.

88 *Der Tod des Sokrates. Eine Interpretation der platonischen Schriften Euthyphron, Apologie, Kriton und Phaidon.* By Romano Guardini. Berlin: H. Küpper, 1943.

Contains a German translation of the dialogues indicated in the title. Includes Guardini's analysis and commentaries on their significance. Examines Socrates at the moment of his trial and death, and attempts to clarify his views concerning his mission and death. Provides a lengthy discussion on Plato's theory of Ideal Forms as this emerges in the *Phaedo.* English translation by Basil Wrighton as *The Death of Socrates: An Interpretation of the Platonic Dialogues Euthyphro, Apology, Crito, and Phaedo* (New York: Sheed and Ward, 1948). English translation of the dialogues by F. J. Church.

89 *The Dialogues of Plato and the Seventh Letter.* Translated by Benjamin Jowett and J. Harward. Chicago: Encyclopaedia Britannica, 1984.

Volume 7 of Great Books of the Western World (edited by Maynard Hutchins). Includes Jowett's translation of the dialogues and a translation of the Seventh Letter by J. Harward (from *The Platonic Epistles*, translated by J. Harward, Cambridge: Cambridge University Press).

90 *The Dialogues of Plato.* Translated by Benjamin Jowett. Oxford: The Clarendon Press, 1964 (4 vols.).

Originally published in 1872 (5 vols.). English translation with analyses and introductions to the individual dialogues. Reprinted by Macmillan (1892).

91 *The Dialogues of Plato.* Translated by Benjamin Jowett. New York: Random House, 1937 (2 vols.).

Reprint of the 1892 edition (London: Macmillan). General introduction by Raphael Demos. Contains twenty-eight dialogues of Plato. Does not include the *Letters*, the *Hippias Major*, and several dialogues of doubtful authenticity. Provides marginal summary statements and a comprehensive general index. Volume 1 contains the early or Socratic dialogues. Ref. 679.

92 *Die platonischen Schriften.* Edited and translated by Paul Friedländer. Berlin: Walter de Gruyter & Co., 1930.

Contains a German annotated translation of the Platonic *corpus*.

93 *Early Socratic Dialogues.* Edited by Trevor L. Saunders. New York: Penguin Books, 1987.

Contains a general introduction by T. J. Saunders. Includes English translations of the following dialogues: *Ion* (trans. T. J. Saunders), *Laches* (trans. I. Lane), *Lysis* and *Charmides* (trans. D. Watt), *Hippias Major* and *Hippias Minor* (trans. R. Waterfield), and *Euthydemus* (trans. T. L. Saunders). Includes fragments of Aeschines of Sphettus (trans. T. L. Saunders) and a bibliography.

94 *Euthyphro, Apology, Crito, Phaedo, Phaedrus.* Translated by Harold N. Fowler. *Plato in Twelve Volumes.* Cambridge,

Mass.: Harvard University Press (The Loeb Classical Library), 1971 (12 vols.), Vol. 1.

Greek text with an accompanying English translation. Contains a general introduction by W. R. M. Lamb which presents a brief outline of the biography and writings of Plato. The individual dialogues are prefaced by short introductions.

95 *Euthyphro, Apology, Crito.* Translated by F. J. Church. Indianapolis: The Bobbs-Merrill Company, 1948.

Includes the death scene from the *Phaedo*. English translation revised and prefaced by Robert D. Cummings. The preface discusses the social components of the dialectic as represented in the three translated dialogues. Suggests that while each dialogue advances different approaches and points of view, they all present complementary perspectives for the examination of related problems.

96 *Euthyphro, Apology of Socrates, and Crito.* Edited by John Burnet. Oxford: The Clarendon Press, 1924.

Greek text accompanied by extensive annotations of philosophical, philological, and historical interest.

97 *Five Dialogues: Euthyphro, Apology, Crito, Meno, Phaedo.* Translated by G. M. A. Grube. Indianapolis: Hackett Publishing Company, 1984.

Contains English translations of the complete text of the five dialogues.

98 *Five Great Dialogues.* Translated by Benjamin Jowett and edited by Louise R. Loomis. New York: Walter J. Black, 1942.

Contains the *Apology*, the *Crito*, the *Phaedo*, the *Symposium*, and the *Republic*. The introduction (by the editor) presents the development of Socratic and Platonic thought from a historical perspective.

99 *Four Dialogues of Plato, Including the Apology of Socrates.*

Edited and translated by John Stuart Mill. London: Watts & Co., 1946.

Contains three individual chapters on the *Protagoras*, the *Phaedrus*, and the *Gorgias*, with passages translated by Mill and with explanatory comments and paraphrases. Devotes a separate chapter to the *Apology*, which includes the entire translated text. Prefaces the translations and commentaries with an introductory essay ("On Genius") in which Mill speaks of the decadence of education in the modern world, and of the absence of genius: "Ten centuries of England and France cannot produce as many illustrious names as the hundred and fifty years of little Greece."

100 *Frühdialoge. Laches, Charmides, Lysis, Der grössere Hippias, Der kleinere Hippias, Protagoras, Euthydemus, Ion, Menexenus.* Translated by R. von Rufener. Zurich: Artemis-Verlag, 1960.

German translation of some of the early dialogues. Introduction by O. Gigon.

101 *Gorgias.* Translated by Terence Irwin. Oxford: The Clarendon Press, 1979.

Contains a detailed introduction and abundant annotations, including an analysis of the main divisions and some of the interlocking themes of the dialogue. Provides extensive etymological observations.

102 *Great Dialogues.* Edited by H. Warmington and Philip G. Rouse. Translated by W. H. D. Rouse. New York: The New American Library, 1968.

Contains English translations of the following dialogues: *Ion*, *Meno*, *Euthydemus*, *Symposium*, *Republic*, *Apology*, *Crito*, and *Phaedo*. Provides a summary of the *Republic* (by J. C. G. Rouse), and a pronunciation index of Greek names and words.

103 *Laches, Protagoras, Meno, Euthydemus.* Translated by W. R. M. Lamb. *Plato in Twelve Volumes.* Cambridge, Mass.: Harvard University Press (The Loeb Classical Library), 1957 (12 vols.), Vol. 2.

Greek text with an accompanying English translation. Provides brief introductions to the individual dialogues.

104 *The Last Days of Socrates: Euthyphro, the Apology, Crito, Phaedo.* Translated by Hugh Tredennick. New York: Penguin Books, 1982.

Provides the translated text of the four dialogues which are annotated and prefaced by short introductions. Includes a general introduction which outlines the intellectual and political background of Socrates' trial and death. Contains also brief comments about Socrates' biography, intellectual development, and the relationship between him and Plato.

105 *Le philosophe retrouvé, précédé de Criton.* Edited and translated by Jacques Rolland de Renéville. Lausanne: Editions L'Age d'Homme, 1978.

Contains a French translation of the *Crito* and the *Philosopher*, with some annotations.

106 *Les pages immortelles de Platon.* Edited by J. Guitton. Paris: Buchet-Chastel, 1960.

Contains French translations of selected passages from the *Gorgias*, the *Republic*, the *Phaedo*, the *Symposium*, the *Apology*, the *Phaedrus*, the *Theaetetus*, the *Laws*, the *Meno*, and the *Seventh Letter*. Provides brief explanatory comments on the selections. Spanish edition: *El pensamiento vivo de Platón* (Buenos Aires: Editorial Losada, 1967).

107 *Meno.* Edited and translated by R. W. Sharples. Chicago: Bolchazy-Carducci Publishers, 1985.

Greek text with an accompanying English translation. Includes a commentary (67 pp.) with grammatical notes and a select bibliography. Uses for the Greek text that of R. S. Bluck (Cambridge University Press, 1961).

108 *Obras Completas.* Madrid: Aguilar, S.A. de Ediciones, 1966.

Translations into Spanish by María Araujo, Francisco García, Luis Gil, José A. Miguez, María Rico, Antonio Rodriguez, and Francisco de P. Samaranch. Contains all the Platonic *corpus*, including the Letters, the dialogues of questionable authenticity, and the *Definitions*. Introduces each dialogue with a short preface, and provides numerous annotations. Offers an introductory chapter by José A. Miguez. Ref. 645.

109 *Oeuvres Complètes*. Translated by Maurice Croiset. Paris: Societé d'Editions Les Belles Lettres, 1925 (13 vols.).

Contains a biographical essay on Plato, and includes all the works of the Platonic *corpus*, including those of doubtful authenticity. Introduces each dialogue with a brief explanatory preface.

110 *Oeuvres de Platon*. Translated by Victor Cousin. Paris: Bassage Frères, Libraires, 1826 (13 vols).

Annotated French translation of the Platonic *corpus*.

111 *Opera Platonis*. Edited by Henricus Stephanus. Paris, 1578 (3 vols.).

Originally published in Paris, 1556. Greek text, edited with the assistance of Joannes Serranus. Dedicated to Queen Elizabeth of England, King James VI of Scotland, and the Consuls of the Republic of Bern. Contains all of Plato's works included in the tetralogies of Thrasyllus. The pages of each volume are subdivided into five parts designated by letters ([a], b, c, d, e). The page numbers and the subdivisions are used as standard reference pagination in all subsequent major editions of Plato's works. References are given by Stephanus' volume, page, and letter, because in his edition page numbers and letters are sometimes repeated in more than one volume. An appendix contains the spurious Platonic texts: *On Virtue*, *Demodocus*, *Sisyphus*, *Eryxias*, and *Axiochus*.

112 *The Phaedrus, Lysis and Protagoras of Plato*. Translated by J. Wright. London: Macmillan, 1925.

Presents a literal English translation, with brief introductions to each one of the dialogues.

113 *Plato. Phaedo.* Translated by David Gallop. Oxford: The Clarendon Press, 1975.

Presents an English translation based on Burnet's Oxford translation. Contains detailed notes and exegetic comments.

114 *Plato: Portrait of Socrates.* Edited by R. W. Livingstone. Oxford: Oxford University Press, 1938.

Contains the *Apology*, the *Crito*, and the *Phaedo*, in an English translation largely based on the Jowett translation. Provides a general introduction, as well as a separate introduction to the Platonic works included. Gives a general account of Plato's representation of Socrates by appealing to a variety to modern parallels.

115 *Plato's Apology: An Interpretation, With a New Translation.* Edited and translated by Thomas G. West. Ithaca, N.Y.: Cornell University Press, 1979.

English translation. Includes an extensive section of accompanying notes which provide information on historical details, as well as etymological and semantic discussions of critical terms. Focuses on Plato's portrayal of the trial rather than on his historical accuracy. Approaches Plato's work as a finely crafted poem -- each part being analyzed both independently and in its relationship to the entire work. Stresses the tension between philosophy and politics, and sees the dialogue as an introduction to the other major themes of Plato's writings.

116 *Plato's Phaedo.* Edited and translated by G. M. A. Grube. Indianapolis: Hackett Publishing Co., 1977.

Includes an English translation with an introduction. Disagrees with Hackforth's interpretation that the theory of Ideal Forms was known and familiar to Socrates' audience.

117 *Plato's Phaedo, Edited with an Introduction and Notes.*

Edited by John Burnet. Oxford: The Clarendon Press, 1911.

Includes the Greek text of the *Phaedo* and an English translation. Provides extensive annotations, and Greek and English indexes to the notes. Contains an introduction which advances Burnet's thesis concerning the Platonic Socrates, specifically the contention that everything attributed by Plato to Socrates can be regarded as historically accurate. Maintains that there is no early or late Platonic Theory of Ideas, because such theory belongs both to Socrates and to Plato. Regards the views on the immortality of the soul expressed by Socrates in the *Phaedo* as having belonged to the historical Socrates. Ref. 678.

118 *Plato's Phaedo*. Translated by R. Hackforth. Cambridge: Cambridge University Press, 1972.

English translation with an introduction by R. Hackforth. Considers the *Phaedo* perhaps the greatest achievement in Greek literature. Argues that the fundamental purpose of the dialogue is to deepen, through the agency of the Platonic Socrates, the basic Socratic teaching, namely, that a person's supreme concern should always be the care of the soul and the furthering of moral and spiritual values, as well as the application of that insight to conduct.

119 *Plato's Protagoras: A Socratic Commentary*. Translated by B. A. F. Hubbard and E. S. Karnofsky. Chicago: The University of Chicago Press, 1984.

Contains an English translation of the *Protagoras*, as well as a foreword by M. F. Burnyeat and a 'Socratic' commentary by the translators.

120 *Plato: The Trial and Death of Socrates*. Translated by Lane Cooper. Ithaca, N.Y: Cornell University Press, 1941.

Contains the *Apology*, the *Crito*, and selected passages from the *Phaedo*, in an annotated English translation. Includes a chronological table of Socrates' life.

121 *Platon. Oeuvres Complètes*. Translated and edited by Léon

Robin. Paris, 1940-1942 (2 vols.).

Annotated French translation of Plato's works. The *Parmenides* and the *Timaeus* are translated and annotated by J. Moreau.

122 *Platone. Eutifrone.* Translated by B. Mazzantini. Turin, 1945.

Italian translation of the *Euthyphro.* Annotations and introduction by C. Mazzantini. Attempts to show in the introduction that the critical attitude developed by Socrates in the *Euthyphro* with respect to religious claims is basically in accord with the fundamental guidelines of Catholic theology.

123 *Platone. I Dialoghi, l'Apologia e le Epistole.* Edited and translated by E. Turolla. Milan: Rizzoli, 1964 (3 vols.).

Annotated Italian translation. Originally published in Milan in 1953. Presents in the annotations and introduction (by Turolla) an interpretation of Plato along distinctive neo-Platonic lines.

124 *Platonis Opera.* Edited by John Burnet. Oxford: The Clarendon Press, 1900 (5 vols.).

Published as part of the Scriptorum Classicorum Bibliotheca Oxoniensis. Greek text (with a brief introduction in Latin) of all the Platonic *corpus.* Includes all the dialogues (and the Letters) of Stephanus' three main volumes, as well as those found in Stephanus' Appendix. Provides numerous philological notes concerning Ms. variations.

125 *Sämtliche Werke.* Edited by W. F. von Otto *et al.* Hamburg: Rowohlt, 1958-1960 (6 vols.).

Reprint of Schleiermacher's German translation of Plato's works (1836). Contains Schleiermacher's original introductions to the individual dialogues.

126 *Select Dialogues of Plato.* Translated by Henry Cary. New

York: Harper & Brothers, 1891.

Contains the following dialogues: *Apology*, *Crito*, *Phaedo*, *Gorgias*, *Protagoras*, *Phaedrus*, *Theaetetus*, *Euthyphro*, and *Lysis*. Prefaces each dialogue with a brief introduction.

127 *Socrate selon Platon. Textes choisis et présentés.* Edited by André Bonnard. Lausanne, 1945.

Contains French translations of selections from the Platonic dialogues. Argues in its commentary that the 'real' Socrates has tended to disappear as a result of the endeavors of scholars, especially philologists, who have sought to recreate the image of the historical Socrates. Maintains that the Socrates who deserves to be called truly historical is the figure who emerges from the dialogues of Plato, for it is precisely this Socrates who has exercised an immense influence on the history of ideas.

128 *The Trial and Death of Socrates*. Audio-cassette. Pasadena, Ca.: Audio Book Company, n.d., 1 hour, 22 min. (2 cassettes).

Audio-cassette set. Narrated by Thomas Mitchell. Contains dramatically arranged sections from the *Apology*, the *Crito*, and the *Phaedo* (Jowett's translation). Concludes with the description of Socrates' death from the *Phaedo*.

129 *Trial and Death of Socrates*. Translated by G. M. A. Grube. Indianapolis: Hackett, 1984.

Contains an English translation of the *Apology*, the *Crito*, and the death scene from the *Phaedo*.

130 *The Works of Plato*. London: George Bell & Sons, 1915 (7 vols.).

Vol. 1: *Apology, Crito, Phaedo, Gorgias, Protagoras, Phaedrus, Theaetetus, Euthyphro, Lysis*. Translated by H. Cary. Vol. 2: *Republic, Timaeus, Critias*. Translated by Henry Davis. Vol. 3: *Euthydemus, Sophist, Meno, Statesman, Cratylus, Parmenides, Symposium*. Translated by G. Burges. Vol. 4: *Philebus, Charmides, Laches, Menexenus,*

*Hippias, Ion, Alcibiades (I and II), Theages, Rivals, Hipparchus, Minos, Clitophon, Epistles.* Translated by G. Burges. Vol. 5: *Laws.* Translated by G. Burges. Vol. 6: *The Doubtful Works.* Translated by G. Burges. Includes an additional volume which provides a summary and an analysis of the dialogues, as well as an analytical index. The individual dialogues are prefaced by short introductions.

131 *The Works of Plato.* Selected and Edited by Irwin Edman. New York: The Modern Library, 1956.

Originally published by Simon & Schuster (New York, 1928). Contains an introductory chapter which deals extensively with Socrates (pp. xvi-xxii). Includes the following dialogues (translated by Jowett): *Lysis*, *Euthyphro*, *Apology*, *Crito*, *Phaedo*, *Protagoras*, *Phaedrus*, *Symposium*, *Republic*, and *Theaetetus*.

132 *The Works of Plato.* Translated by Floyer Sydenham and Thomas Taylor. New York: AMS Press, 1972 (5 vols.).

Reprint of the edition of 1804 which carried the following subtitle: *His Fifty-five Dialogues and Twelve Epistles, Translated from the Greek; Nine of the Dialogues by Floyer Sydenham, and the Remainder by Thomas Taylor.*

## COLLECTIONS

133 *The Ethics of Socrates.* Edited by Miles M. Dawson. New York: Haskill House Publishers, 1974.

Presents extensive quotations from the writings of Plato and Xenophon which reveal Socrates' thoughts on human conduct. Includes relevant passages from the testimonies of Aristotle, Cicero, Epictetus, Lucretius, Longinus, Marcus Aurelius, Plutarch, Plotinus, and Seneca, which reflect important connections that can be traced to the ethics of Socrates. Supplies a running commentary which connects the quotations. Contains a detailed analytical table of contents.

134 *Four Texts on Socrates.* Edited and translated by Thomas G. West and Grace S. West. Ithaca, N.Y.: Cornell University Press, 1984.

Contains English translations of the *Euthyphro*, the *Apology*, and the *Crito*, as well as selections from the *Clouds*. Provides an introduction by Thomas G. West in which Socrates' political philosophy is presented as an alternative to modern liberalism and to Marxism. Furnishes brief summary statements of the four texts offered.

135 *The Greek Commentaries on Plato's Phaedo.* Edited by L. G. Westerink. Amsterdam: North Holland, 1976 (2 vols.).

Contains the Greek text and an English translation of the commentaries of Damascius and Olympiodorus on the *Phaedo*. Includes extensive annotations.

136 *The Life and Death of Socrates.* London: J. M. Dent & Sons, 1923.

Introduction by George Grote. Contains passages from the *Memorabilia* and from Plato's dialogues (*Symposium*, *Apology*, *Crito*, and *Phaedo*).

137 *The Life of Socrates, by Plato, Xenophon, and His Disciples; With Many Curious and Interesting Anecdotes of the Same and*

*Other Celebrated Greek Philosophers.* Augusta, Ga.: Chronicle Office, 1807.

Includes excerpts from Plato's early dialogues, from the *Memorabilia*, and from several secondary sources.

138 *Plato: Apology of Socrates and Crito; with Extracts from the Phaedo and Symposium, and from Xenophon's Memorabilia.* Edited by Louis Dyer. Waltham, Mass.: Blaisdell Publishing Company, 1908.

Edition revised by Thomas D. Seymour. Greek text of the works indicated in the title. Provides summary statements of the textual material and numerous annotations about the meanings and usages of major words and phrases. Furnishes a comprehensive Greek-English vocabulary. Introduction: Discusses various historical, philosophical, and cultural themes that are relevant to the understanding of Socrates' life and doctrine. Reviews in detail the structure and functioning of the Athenian juridical system.

139 *The Question of Socrates.* Edited by Richard Levin. New York: Harcourt, Brace & World, 1961.

Collects a number of English translations of primary and secondary testimonies: Aristophanes' *Clouds* (complete) and excerpts from the *Wasps*, the *Birds*, and the *Frogs*; the complete text of the *Euthyphro*, the *Apology*, and the *Crito*, and excerpts from the *Gorgias*, the *Symposium*, *Theaetetus*, the *Phaedo*, the *Republic*, and the letters; and Xenophon's *Apology* (complete) and excerpts from his *Hellenica*, *Anabasis*, *Memorabilia*, and *Epistles*. Includes also passages from the Attic orators (Andocides, Isocrates, and Aeschines), Aristotle, Diogenes Laertius, and Athenaeus. Contains a chronological table.

140 *Socrate. Antologia di Testi.* Edited by Antonio Capizzi. Florence: La Nuova Italia, 1974.

Collects a great variety of testimonies (in Italian translation) from primary and secondary sources, and divides the material into four sections: the life of Socrates, the accusations and the trial, his thought and method, and the Socratic legend. Includes statements from recent philosophers and scholars.

141 *Socrate nella letteratura socratica antica.* Edited by Giuseppe Cambiano. Milan: Principato Editore, 1970.

Contains a brief introductory chapter on Socrates and his historical and cultural context. Includes Italian excerpts from the *Clouds*, Diogenes Laertius' *Life of Socrates*, the *Memorabilia*, and Aristotle's *Metaphysics*. Gives the complete translated texts of Plato's *Apology* and *Crito*, and Xenophon's *Apology*.

142 *Socrate. Portraits et enseignements.* Paris: Presses Universitaires de France, 1972.

Contains French translations of sections of Plato's dialogues, Xenophon's works (*Memorabilia*, *Apology*, *Symposium*), Aristophanes' *Clouds*, and Diogenes Laertius (Books ii and iii). Translated by Anne Marie Fraisse and Jean-Claude Fraisse. Notes in the preface (p. 5) the paradoxical character of compiling an anthology of writings on Socrates -- "*une anthologie consacrée au seul philosophe peut-être qui n'ait jamais écrit.*" Includes an appendix which contains statements about Socrates from Plato to Alain.

143 *Socrate. Tutte le testimonianze da Aristofane e Senofonte ai padri Cristiani.* Edited by Gabriele Giannantoni. Bari: Editori Laterza, 1971.

Contains Italian translations of Aristophanes' *The Clouds*; the fragments of the comic poets which mention Socrates; Xenophon's *Memorabilia*, *Oeconomicus*, *Symposium*, *Apology*, and passages from the *Anabasis* and the *Hellenica*; the Aristotelian references to Socrates; and a vast collection of texts from Aristoxenus to the Fathers of the Church. Includes an introduction by Giannantoni, as well as abundant annotations.

144 *Socrates: A Source Book.* Edited by John Ferguson. London: Macmillan, 1970.

Contains a wide variety of primary and secondary source materials in English translation: Plato's *Apology*, *Crito*, and *Alcibiades I*, and Diogenes Laertius' *The Life of Socrates* are reproduced in full. Selections from the following authors are included: Plato, Xenophon, Aristophanes (and other comic poets), Diogenes Laertius, the Athenian orators (Andocides, Isocrates, and Aeschines), Aristotle, Cicero, Seneca, Apuleius, Julian, Plutarch, Stobaeus, the Christian Fathers (from Saint Justin to Cyril of Alexandria), the lexicographers, and the commentators on classical texts. Includes also the testimony of Libanius (*On the Silence of Socrates* and *The Defense of Socrates*). Introduction: Discusses the following issues: The nature and scope of the sources, the educational mission of Socrates, the historical and intellectual background of Socrates' life, the details of his life, his relationship to the Sophists, and his contribution to philosophy. Ref. 414.

145 "Socrates." *Greek Philosophy: A Collection of Texts.* Edited by Cornelia J. de Vogel. Leiden: E. J. Brill, 1957 (3 vols.), Vol. 1, pp. 113-156.

Presents a collection of selected ancient texts which are supplied with notes and explanations. Includes translated passages from Plato's *Apology*, the speech of Alcibiades in Plato's *Symposium*, and excerpts from the *Theaetetus*, the *Gorgias*, the *Meno*, and the *Crito*. Contains passages from the *Memorabilia*.

146 "Socrates." *Plato and His Dialogues.* Edited by G. L. Dickinson. New York: W. W. Norton & Co., 1932, pp. 32-54.

Strings together various passages from the *Clouds* (translated by B. B. Rogers) and the Platonic dialogues (from several translations) in order to form a comprehensive portrait of Socrates.

147 "Socrates." *Source Book in Ancient Philosophy.* Edited by Charles M. Bakewell. New York: Charles Scribner's Sons, 1907, pp. 86-141. New York: Gordian Press, 1973, pp. 104-141.

Contains one passage from Aristotle's *Metaphysics* (1078b) and selections from the *Memorabilia* (Watson's translation) and from the *Phaedo* and the *Meno* (Jowett's translation). Includes Plato's *Apology* (Jowett's translation).

148 *Socrates: The Wisest and the Most Just?.* Edited by Meg

Parker. New York: Cambridge University Press, 1980.

Contains English translations of selected passages from the writings of Plato, Xenophon, and Aristophanes, with brief commentaries.

149 *The Socratic Enigma.* Edited by Herbert Spiegelberg. New York: The Library of Liberal Arts, 1964.

Collects quotations and brief statements on Socrates (translated into English) from 306 writers who are classified into five groups: antiquity, early Christianity, the Middle Ages, the Renaissance, and modern times. Structures the latter group into nine sections: British, American, French, German, Italian, Oriental, Russian, Scandinavian, and Spanish. Includes eulogistic testimonies, as well as some which the editor classifies as belonging to the anti-Socratic literature (*e.g.*, from Tertullian and Bentham). Contains brief biographical notices on all the represented authors.

150 *Socratic Testimonies.* Edited by Luis E. Navia. Lanham, Md.: University Press of America, 1987.

Contains English translations (by various translators) of Aristophanes' *The Clouds*; Xenophon's *Symposium*, *Memorabilia* (selections), and *Apology*; Plato's *Theages*, *Euthyphro*, *Apology*, *Crito*, and *Phaedo* (selections); and Diogenes Laertius' *The Life of Socrates.* Includes Alcibiades' speech in Plato's *Symposium.* Provides a general introduction which discusses various aspects of the Socratic problem, and separate introductions to the chapters. Furnishes abundant annotations for the testimonies, and contains an extensive bibliography. Ref. 401.

151 *Socraticorum Reliquiae.* Edited by Gabriele Giannantoni. Naples: Edizioni Dell' Ateneo, 1983 (3 vols.).

Includes Greek and Roman testimonies about the Socratics. Volumes 1 and 2 give the Greek and Latin texts, and Volume 3 furnishes annotations and discussions (in Italian). Volume 2 (pp. 409-692) contains texts dealing with Diogenes of Sinope.

## SECONDARY SOURCES

The annotations included in this section contain references and comments on works of classical writers which deal primarily with Socrates (or in which he is given a prominent place), on Aristotle's allusions to Socrates, and on the so-called Socratic letters. The testimony of Diogenes Laertius clearly shows that during the six centuries following Socrates' death, there was great interest in his life and ideas, and that he was the object of much biographical, anecdotal, and even scholarly study among a great variety of authors. Most of the sources quoted or mentioned by Diogenes, however, are not extant, and of others, only fragments remain. The works of the minor Socratics, for instance, are no longer available except for brief passages, although, judging from Diogenes' reports, such writings, mostly in the form of dialogues, must have been quite numerous. Some of their fragments have been collected, as is the case with those of Antisthenes which are gathered in texts such as F. Dümmler's *Antisthenica* (Bonn, 1882), A. G. Winkelman's *Antisthenis Fragmenta* (Zurich, 1842) and J. Humble's *Antisthenis Fragmenta* (Gand, 1931-1932).

It would be inappropriate in the present context to make specific reference to even a small number of the works and *loci* where Socrates is mentioned in the secondary literature, for statements about his life, character, and philosophy, are found in the writings of practically all major classical authors. Among them, however, there are some who go beyond merely mentioning or making a passing reference to Socrates. Such is the case, for instance, with Aristoxenus, a pupil of Aristotle, who wrote a non-extant *Life of Socrates*, and in whose fragments there are repeated (and unfavorable) comments about him and his ideas (F. Wehrli, *Die Schule des Aristoteles, Texte und Kommentar*, Basel, 1945). In the writings of Cicero, Seneca, Epictetus, Dio Chrysostom, Plutarch, Maximus of Tyre, Aulus Gellius, Aelian, Aelius Aristides, John Stobaeus, and Suidas (or *The Suda*), there are extended or at least numerous comments on Socrates' life, character, and philosophy. In general, we may affirm that all these mountains of references do not add anything entirely new to what can be gathered either from the primary sources or from the major secondary sources (annotated below).

There are several collections of classical Socratic references, the most useful among which are John Ferguson's *Socrates: A Source Book* (Ref. 144), Gabriele Giannantoni's *Socrate: Tutte le testimonianze da Aristofane e Senofonte ai padri cristiani* (Ref. 143) and *Socraticorum reliquiae* (Ref. 151), and H. Spiegelberg's

*The Socratic Enigma* (pp. 21-49, Ref. 149). The Aristotelian references have been collected in various texts, two of which are Thomas Déman's *Le Témoignage d' Aristote sur Socrate* (Ref. 702) and Luis E. Navia's *Socrates: The Man and His Philosophy* (pp. 211-251, Ref. 304). Selected Aristotelian passages on Socrates are translated in Italian in Antonio Banfi's *Socrate* (Ref. 184).

152 *Aeschinis Socratici reliquiae.* Edited by Heinrich Krauss. Leipzig: B. G. Teubner, 1911.

Doctoral dissertation. (K. Ludwigs Universität, Giessen). Contains the Greek text of the fragments of Aeschines' works, specifically from his *Alcibiades*, *Axiochus*, *Aspasia*, *Callias*, *Miltiades*, *Rinon*, *Telauges*, and various dialogues of doubtful authenticity. Provides a short Latin preface which deals with the sources for the texts, and includes abundant Latin commentaries and a bibliography.

153 Apuleius. *On the God of Socrates. The Works of Apuleius.* Translated by Thomas Taylor. London: George Bell & Sons, 1914, pp. 350-373.

English translation of *De deo Socratis*. Composition date: second century A.D. *Editio princeps* by Andreas in 1469. Discusses the Socratic experience of the divine voice or sign which is interpreted as being intimately related to the Platonic concept of God or the divine. Expands on various themes relevant to polytheistic myths and beliefs about gods, demons, and lemures. Argues that "the power of beholding a divine form" (that is, the Socratic experience) may be possessed by any person, and that, accordingly, there should not be anything surprising in Socrates' ability to hear and sense his own δαιμόνιον. Explains the Socratic experience in terms of a manifestation of the divine, and as a manifestation of the moral conscience developed by Socrates. Argues for a polytheistic interpretation of Socrates' concept of the divine.

154 Aristotle. *The Complete Works of Aristotle.* Edited by Jonathan Barnes. Princeton, N.J.: Princeton University Press (Bollingen Series), 1984 (2 vols.).

Revised English Oxford translation (various translators). Contains the entire extant Aristotelian *corpus*, with numerical references based on I. Bekker's edition of the Greek text (Berlin, 1831). Provides a general index and an index of proper names.

There are many editions of the Greek text of the Aristotelian corpus. Among them, the following can be cited: I. Bekker (Berlin, 1831; Oxford, 1837, 5 vols.), A. Schwegler (Tübingen, 1848, with a German translation), and H. Bonitz (Bonn, 1849). A Greek edition with an accompanying Latin translation was prepared by A. F. Didot (Paris, 1846, 5 vols.); it includes an exhaustive index of names and subjects. The standard pagination presently in use in scholarly editions is based on that of Bekker. As might be expected, there are innumerable English translations and editions of Aristotle's works, the most useful of which appears to be the edition by J. Barnes annotated above (Ref. 154).

There are no writings by Aristotle specifically about Socrates. His name, however, appears in a wide variety of contexts in slightly over fifty places. These Aristotelian references can be divided into five categories: (1) those in which 'Socrates' functions as an instance of a proper name and is used as a grammatical or logical example; (2) those in which the sense is conveyed that the allusion is to Socrates as a literary character of Plato's dialogues; (3) those in which it is clear that what Aristotle had in mind was the historical Socrates; (4) those which comment on the λόγοι σωκρατικοί in general; and (5) those which mention Socratic sources other than Plato. Obviously, our understanding of the line of demarcation between the second and third categories varies widely depending on our interpretation of the Socratic problem in general and the relationship between Plato's Socrates and Socrates as a historical person in particular.

The first of these categories is not particularly important, since in them the name of Socrates functions merely as a proper noun, and any other name could have been used in its place, as can be seen in *Topics* 103a, *Sophistical Arguments* 160b and 166b, *Metaphysics* 981a, and *Rhetoric* 1356b.

The second category, on the other hand, appears to shed light on Aristotle's understanding and assessment of the Socrates who speaks in the Platonic dialogues, and it seems reasonable to assume that in those references Aristotle has in mind the character created by Plato rather than the historical Socrates. The following are the principal among such references: *On Generation and Corruption* 335b; *Politics* 1260a, 1261a, 1261b, 1262b, 1263b, 1264a, 1264b, 1265a (in which Aristotle speaks of the Socrates of Plato's *Laws*, a dialogue in which in fact Socrates does not appear), 1291a, 1316a, 1316b, 1342a, 1342b; *Rhetoric* 1367b. The reference in *On Generation and Corruption* (335b) mentions the introduction of the theory of Ideal Forms by the Socrates of the *Phaedo*, while the reference in *Rhetoric* 1367b alludes to Socrates' advice concerning the importance of keeping in mind the nature of one's audience as one delivers a speech (Cf. *Menexenus* 225d). Most of the references in the *Politics*, on the other hand, involve specific Aristotelian criticisms of the political views advanced by Plato in the *Republic* and in the *Laws*.

The third category includes references which may be assumed to deal with the historical Socrates, and the most indicative among them are the following: *Sophistical Arguments* 183b (a comment about Socrates' confession of ignorance); *Parts of Animals* 642a (an observation about Socrates' attempts to deal with the problem of definition); *Problems* 953a (a statement about Socrates' atrabilous character or μελαγχολία ); *Metaphysics* 987c and 1078b (concerning Socrates' preoccupation with ethical issues and ethical definitions, and concerning the difference between Socrates' and Plato's stance vis-à-vis the theory of Ideal Forms); *Metaphysics* 1086b (a reference to Socrates' role in the *genesis* of the theory of Ideal Forms, and to his unwillingness to regard universals as existing apart from particulars); *Nicomachean Ethics* 1127b (about Socrates' irony); *Nicomachean Ethics* 1116b, 1144b, 1145b, and 1147b (specifically concerning Socrates' understanding of the relationship between knowledge and virtue, and concerning his denial of the possibility of *akrasia*, a doctrine rejected by Aristotle); *Magna Moralia* 1182a, 1183b, 1187a, 1190b, 1198a, and 1200b (comments which reiterate those made in the *Nicomachean Ethics*); *Eudemian Ethics* 1216b, 1229a, and 1230a (comments on Socrates' concept of virtue in general and courage in particular); *Eudemian Ethics* 1235a (an allusion to Socrates' view that what is not useful should be thrown away, as in the case of one's corpse); *Eudemian Ethics* 1247b (a reference to Socrates' reported comment that wisdom sometimes comes to us by sheer luck; cf. *Euthydemus* 279d); *Rhetoric* 1390b (a statement about the vulgarity and stupidity of Socrates' children); *Rhetoric* 1393b (comments on Socrates' objections to the system of sortition used by the Athenians for choosing most public officials); *Rhetoric* 1398a (an allusion to Socrates' refusal to accept an invitation from Archelaus of Macedon); *Rhetoric* 1398b (on Socrates' reported lack of dogmatism in his conversations); *Rhetoric* 1419a (observations about Socrates' mode of questioning).

In the fourth category there are three indicative references: *Politics* 1265a (where the λόγοι σωκρατικοί are said to be graceful, original, and profound); *Rhetoric* 1415b (a comment about their ethical import); and *Poetics* 1447a.

The only reference in the fifth category is found in *Rhetoric* 1399a: here, Aristotle speaks of the Socrates of Theodectes (c. 375-334 B.C.), a tragic poet and orator, from whom only fragments remain, in none of which Socrates' name appears.

155 Athanaeus of Naucratis. *Deipnosophistae.* Translated by Charles B. Gulick. Cambridge, Mass.: Harvard University Press (The Loeb Classical Library), 1941 (7 vols.).

Greek text with an accompanying English translation. Composition date: late second century A.D. *Editio princeps* by Aldine in 1524. Makes abundant references to Socrates and the Socratics in the context of a three-day long conversation among twenty-four guests whose main nominal subject of discussion is food and cookery. Sets the conversation in Rome during the author's time. Belongs to the sort of literary genre known as 'symposium literature,' and is wealthy in anecdotal and gossipy information (typical of the literature exemplified by Diogenes Laertius). Attributes to various characters views and comments about Socrates and his associates: *e.g.*, Masurius challenges the evidence for Socrates' participation in military campaigns, and questions various points of chronology in Plato's reports; Pontianus of Nicomedia disputes the historical and biographical value of Plato's references to places, events, and persons. Assumes often a clearly anti-Socratic stance.

156 Diogenes Laertius. *Socrates. Lives of Eminent Philosophers.* Translated by R. D. Hicks. Cambridge, Mass.: Harvard University Press (The Loeb Classical Library), 1966 (2 vols), Vol. 1, pp. 148-176.

Greek text with an accompanying English translation. Book ii (18-47) of Diogenes' biographical and doxographical work. Date of composition: early third century A.D. *Editio princeps* by M. Meibomius (Amsterdam, 1692-1693, 2 vols.), with an accompanying Latin translation. Recounts in anecdotal style hosts of reports about Socrates' life and ideas. The sources quoted or mentioned are Plato, Mnesimachus, Aristophanes, Alexander, Aristoxenus, Duris, Timon, Idomeneus, Xenophon, Favorinus, Demetrius of Byzantium, Aristippus, Ion of Chios, Aristotle, Pamphilia, Satyrus, Hieronymus of Rhodes, Ameipsias, Hermippus, Antisthenes, Justus of Tiberias, Dionysodorus, and Apollodorus. Its treatment of Socrates can be divided into various non-sequential parts: biographical comments on Socrates (dates, activities, marriages, children, military service, acquaintances, trial, and death); doxographical observations concerning his ideas and opinions; doxographical notes about opinions and views on the part of his contemporaries and successors; descriptions of his character and habits; a seemingly *verbatim* statement of the official indictment; and Diogenes' own assessment of the character and philosophical views of Socrates. All the references to Plato's dialogues can be corroborated directly by an appeal to the dialogues themselves, and most of the references to Xenophon can be supported by Xenophon's own writings. The first reference to the *Clouds* ii, 18) is unverifiable and is probably a mistake. The references to Aristotle's reports concerning Socrates' alleged trip to Delphi and his marriage to Myrto are not found in Aristotle's extant writings. The comments and references to Xanthippe are partly sustained by passages in Xenophon.

157 Isocrates. *Busiris*. *Isocrates in Three Volumes*. Translated by Larue van Hook. Cambridge, Mass.: Harvard University Press (The Loeb Classical Library), 1968, Vol. 3, pp. 100-131.

Greek text with an accompanying English translation. Date of composition: c. 390 B.C. Eulogizes Busiris (a mythological Egyptian king), and appears to be a reply or a correction to a composition of Polycrates on the same subject (*Defense of Busiris*). Mentions Socrates (222) in the context of its assessment of Polycrates' *Indictment of Socrates*, and maintains that Polycrates' work fails in its intention to denigrate Socrates: by alleging that Alcibiades was Socrates' disciple, argues Isocrates, Polycrates unintentionally praised the philosopher, for Alcibiades was a man who "far excelled all his contemporaries." Insists, however, that Alcibiades was never a genuine disciple of Socrates.

158 Libanius. *Apologia Socratis. Libanii Opera.* Edited by R. Foerster (Teubner edition). Leipzig, 1903-1927 (12 vols.), Vol 5.

Greek text with annotations. Date of composition: fourth century A.D. Libanius' *Declamation 1* (*Apologia Socratis*) is cast in the form of a forensic speech, the main object of which is the vindication of Socrates and his exoneration from the accusations posthumously levelled against him by Polycrates in his *Indictment of Socrates*. Some have argued, however, that Libanius' *real* purpose was the defense of the Emperor Julian (see Markowski, Ref. 1084). Libanius' *Apologia Socratis* remains our most important source of information about Polycrates' non-extant work, and serves as the basis for the reconstruction of the latter. Libanius' efforts are directed at the refutation of accusations such as (1) that Socrates was a perverse Sophist whose influence was detrimental to the Athenian youth; (2) that he encouraged the Athenians to despise their city and its laws; (3) that he undermined the principles of the democracy; (4) that he neglected and even rejected the gods of the city; (5) that he expressed contempt for the great poets; (6) that he condoned criminal acts; (7) that his private vices were even greater than his public ones; (8) that he practiced and taught idleness and political indifference; and (9) that he corrupted Critias and Alcibiades. Libanius' defense is ostensively directed at Anytus (the accuser in Polycrates' work) who is ironically charged with hypocrisy and dereliction of duty for not having prosecuted Socrates before 399 B.C. The Socrates who emerges from Libanius' work is a blameless philosophical victim who was entrapped by cunning and unscrupulous political enemies.

159 Libanius. *Apologie des Sokrates.* Edited and translated by Otto Apelt. Leipzig: Verlag von Felix Meiner, 1922.

German translation of *Apologia Socratis*, with an introduction and critical annotations. Ref. 158.

160 Libanius. *Apology of Socrates.* Translated by G. Salway.

*Socrates: A Source Book*. Edited by John Ferguson. London: Macmillan, 1970, pp. 257-289.

English translation of *Apologia Socratis.* Ref. 158.

161 Libanius. *On the Silence of Socrates.* Translated by M. Crosby and W. H. Calder. *Socrates: A Source Book.* Edited by John Ferguson. London: Macmillan, 1970, pp. 251-257.

English translation of one of Libanius' declamations. The translation originally appeared in *Greek and Byzantine Studies* 3 (1960), pp. 185-202. Composition date: fourth century A.D. Speaks of the accusations against Socrates and of his absolute blamelessness, and of the wickedness of those who sentenced him. Condemns his accusers for having imposed upon him, besides the death sentence, the additional penalty of silence in prison, an illegal penalty with which Socrates did not comply. Describes his serene and joyful behavior in prison, and emphasizes the fact that his enemies were eventually compelled to repent. [Structured as a forensic oration, Libanius' piece has been interpreted as a defense of paganism at a time when the Christian Roman authorities were bent on banning and persecuting the last representatives of the old Greco-Roman world.]

162 Lucian. *Dialogues of the Dead. Lucian's Dialogues.* Translated by Howard Williams. London: G. Bell & Sons, 1913, pp. 88-167.

English translation of Lucian's *Dialogi mortuorum.* Composition date: second century B.C. Creates fictional and satirical conversations in the underworld among various philosophers and famous men of ancient Greece, among whom Diogenes of Sinope and Crates of Maroneia are given a prominent place. Introduces the ghost of Socrates (Dialogue xx) in the context of a conversation between Menippus the Cynic and Aecus. Portrays Socrates as being still engaged in questioning and as being interested in the affairs of the Athenians, and in the company of friends such as Charmides and Phaedrus.

163 Lucian. *The Fisherman. Selected Satires of Lucian.* Edited and translated by Lionel Casson. Garden City, N.Y.: Doubleday & Co., 1962, pp. 334-363.

Annotated English translation of Lucian's *Piscator*. Composition date: second century A.D. Sequel to *Philosophies for Sale*. Creates an imaginary dialogue in the Athenian Potters' Quarter and in the temple of Athena on the Acropolis. Involves various philosophers and personified characters (Lucian, Socrates, Empedocles, Plato, Chrysippus, Diogenes of Sinope, Aristotle, Philosophy, Truth, Good Sense, Virtue, and others). Depicts the philosophers who, on a short leave from Hades, have returned to torture and kill Lucian for having ridiculed them. Describes how Socrates, after having begun by urging his fellow-philosophers to stone Lucian to death, changes his mind and advises them to have him tried in the court of philosophy. Concludes with a scene in which Lucian joins Philosophy and descends with Socrates and the philosophers from the Acropolis.

164 Lucian. *Lucian in Eight Volumes.* Translated by A. M. Harmon, K. Kilburn, and M. D. Macleod. Cambridge, Mass.: Harvard University Press (The Loeb Classical Library), 1972 (8 vols.).

Greek text with an accompanying English translation of Lucian's extant works.

165 Lucian. *Philosophies for Sale. Selected Satires of Lucian.* Edited and translated by Lionel Casson. Garden City, N.Y.: Doubleday & Co., 1962, pp. 314-333.

Annotated English translation of Lucian's *Vitarum auctio*. Composition date: second century A.D. Describes an imaginary slave market in which Zeus and Hermes auction various philosophers such as Pythagoras, Diogenes of Sinope, Epicurus, Chrysippus, and Socrates. Depicts Socrates as a pederast who swears by strange divinities (*e.g.*, the Dog), who has set up his own republic with outlandish laws, and who believes in the existence of non-physical entities (*i.e.* the Platonic Ideal Forms) that exist in the realm of nothingness.

166 Phaedrus. *Socrates ad amicos. Phaedri Augusti liberti fabularum Aesopiarum*, III, ix. *Corpus poetarum latinorum.* Edited W. S. Walker. London: Henry G. Bohn, 1849, p. 592.

Date of composition: first century A.D. Short fable written in the style of the traditional fables of Aesop.

Describes a scene in which passers-by ridicule Socrates for having built for himself a humble house: "Fancy a man like you building such a poky house," they remark; to which Socrates replies: "I only hope that I can find enough true friends to fill it."

167 Phaedrus. *Friends Indeed. Fables of Aesop.* Translated by S. A. Handford. Baltimore: Penguin Books, 1954, p. 202.

English translation of Phaedrus' *Socrates ad amicos.* Ref. 166.

168 Plutarch. *Le démon de Socrate de Plutarque.* Translated by E. Des Places. *Le Sage et son démon, précédé de 'Le démon de Socrate de Plutarque'.* Edited by Henri Pourrat. Paris: A. Michel, 1950.

French translation of Plutarch's *De genio Socratis.* Ref. 169.

169 Plutarch. *On the Sign of Socrates.* Translated by Phillip H. De Lacey and Benedict Einarson. *Plutarch's Moralia in Fifteen Volumes.* Cambridge, Mass.: Harvard University Press (The Loeb Classical Library), 1968 (15 vols.), Vol. 7, pp. 372-509.

Greek text of *De genio Socratis*, with an accompanying English translation and a brief introduction. Forms part of Plutarch's *Moralia* (575b-598f). Composition date: c.95 B.C. Dramatic setting: early fourth century B.C. A dialogue on Socrates' spiritual voice or sign, narrated by Caphisias. Reviews at length various interpretations of the Socratic experience, and describes several characteristics associated with it. Attributes to various participants in the dialogue interpretations such as these: that the Socratic 'sign' was the mere act of sneezing on Socrates' part; that it was only a gross superstition of his; and that it was an actual communication from the divine realm [this interpretation being probably that of Plutarch himself]. Recounts a multitude of political and social circumstances of the early fourth century B.C., and gives an overview of the various meanings attached at that time to concepts such as τὸ δαιμόνιον and ὁ δαίμων.

170 Plutarch. *Three Selections from Plutarch's Genius of Socrates.* Translated by Kenneth S. Guthrie. Melford, Mass.:

The Prophet Publishing House, 1904.

English translation of selected passages from Plutarch's *De genio Socratis*. Ref. 169.

171 Themistius. Περὶ τοῦ λέγειν. *Plaidoyer d'un socratique contre le Phèdre de Platon. XXVI Discours de Thémistius.* Edited and translated by Hubert Kesters. Louvain: Editions E. Nauwelaerts, 1959.

Contains the Greek text of Themistius' work with an accompanying French translation. Provides an exhaustive analysis of the text and abundant philological annotations. Date of composition: fourth century A.D. Constitutes a rhetorical oration in which the author, while wishing to remain an authentic disciple of Socrates, condemns the Socratic-Platonic attack on rhetoric typified by the *Phaedrus*. Argues that the adversaries of rhetoric have robbed philosophy of its principal tool for communicating truth and intellectual enlightenment to the masses, namely, public speaking. Maintains that the true goal of the Socratic search for the truth is to bring the Socratic message to all human beings, not merely to the members of a confined philosophical circle. Reminds Socrates of the fact that Apollo did not only speak to the few, but that his words were intended to reach the mass of humankind.

## *Socrates' Epistles*

Seven letters attributed to Socrates have come down to us from antiquity. It is reasonably certain, however, that they are late forgeries of Alexandrian origin. Both philosophically and biographically they appear to be of little value, as they simply reiterate details found in the genuine sources, particularly in Xenophon. In the first letter, for instance, Socrates, writing possibly to Archelaus of Macedon, reminds him that he is not a Sophist or retailer of educational merchandise (I,i), and later on (I,viii), he speaks of how his divine sign came to him during the battle of Delium. In the sixth letter, he writes of his frugality (VI,ii) and poverty (VI,viii), and of the relationship between clear thinking and happiness (VI,v), and in the seventh, he comments on his unwillingness to cooperate with the Thirty (VII,i).

172 *Die Briefe des Sokrates und der Sokratiker.* Edited by

Johannes Sykutris. Paderborn: Verlag Ferdinand Schöningh, 1933.

Gives a detailed analysis of the seven letters attributed to Socrates and the twenty-eight letters attributed to the minor Socratics. Contains the Greek text of the letters.

173 "Die Briefe des Sokrates und der Sokratiker." Edited by Liselothe Köhler. *Philologus*, 20 (Supplement No. 2), (1928), pp. 1-141.

Editor's inaugural professorial dissertation, University of Zurich, 1925. Contains the Greek text of the Socratic letters with a German translation and a commentary.

174 "Socrates and His Circle." *Socrates: A Source Book.* Edited by John Ferguson. London: Macmillan, 1970, pp. 333-335.

Presents brief passages from the Socratic letters, translated into English. Ref. 144.

175 "Sokrates und Archelaos. Zum I. Sokratesbrief." *Museum Helveticum*, 49 (1982), pp. 71-81.

Presents the text of the first Socratic letter, with a commentary by M. Imhof.

176 *Socratis, Antisthenis et aliorum socraticorum epistolae.* Paris: S. Cramoisy, 1637.

Contains the Greek text of the letters of Socrates and the minor Socratics, and a Latin translation by Leo Allotius.

177 *Socratis et Socraticorum Epistolae. Epistolographi Graeci.* Edited by Rudolf Hersher. Paris, 1873, pp. 609ff.

Contains the annotated Greek text of the Socratic letters.

178 *Socratis et Socraticorum, Pythagorae et Pythagoreorum quae feruntur epistolae.* Edited by Johannes Conrad Orellius. Leipzig: Libreria Weidmannia, 1815.

Includes (pp. 3-64) the Greek text of the letters attributed to Socrates, Xenophon, Aristippus, Aeschines, Simon, Plato, and Phaedrus. Adds a Latin translation (pp. 67-112), abundant annotations in Latin, and a variety of short Latin dissertations by several scholars on the meaning and authenticity of the letters.

## GENERAL STUDIES

The works annotated in this section include books, monographs, articles, and notices which deal with Socrates' biography and philosophy in a general way, or in which various aspects of his philosophical doctrines or of his influence in the development of ideas are discussed.

179 Adorno, Francesco. *Introduzione a Socrate.* Bari: Editori Laterza, 1970.

Deals extensively with various issues related to the Socratic problem, and contains a lengthy section on the history of modern Socratic scholarship. Includes a detailed bibliographical section which provides notices about the primary and secondary sources, and about recent studies on them.

180 Alberti, E. *Sokrates. Ein Versuch über ihn nach den Quellen.* Göttingen: Dieterische Buchhandlung, 1869.

Conducts a general examination of the life and philosophy of Socrates, with particular emphasis on the examination of the relative value of the primary sources. Accepts the criterion developed by Schleiermacher which calls for a critical integration of the testimonies of Plato and Xenophon. Comments in detail on the controversy surrounding Socrates' alleged early interest in natural philosophy in general and Anaxagoras in particular. Ref. 331.

181 Anderson, Maxwell. "Socrates and His Gospel." *Barefoot in Athens.* New York: William Sloane Associates, 1951, pp. vii-xvi.

Serves as a preface to Anderson's play *Barefoot in Athens.* Discusses the political, historical, and judicial circumstances of Socrates' trial and execution. Speaks of the three Socratic 'gospels': (1) the gospel according to the young Plato (*i.e.*, the Platonic writings in which Socrates' allegiance to the democratic ideals of Pericles is accurately depicted); (2) the gospel according to the older

Plato (*i.e.*, after Plato had become Socrates' Judas and had turned against him and Athens); and (3) the gospel according to Xenophon. Views the second gospel as a collection of fabrications and lies motivated by Plato's political and ideological considerations and interests. Ref. 1777.

182 Baker, Albert E. "Socrates." *Prophets for an Age of Doubt.* London: The Centenary Press, 1934, pp. 37-84.

Recounts the major biographical aspects of Socrates, with special attention given to his experience of the divine voice (which is compared with the experience reported by Saint Joan of Arc). Gives an account of Socrates' principal philosophical doctrines, and emphasizes his conviction concerning the unity of the virtues, and the identity of virtue and true knowledge. Other 'prophets' discussed in the book include Job, Pascal, and Newman.

183 Bakewell, Charles M. "The Unique Case of Socrates." *The International Journal of Ethics*, 20 (1909-1910), pp. 10-28.

Suggests that the difficulty in understanding Socrates stems from the fact that he was a man of genius. Concludes that he can be regarded as a "philosophical prophet and priest, an Isaiah come to meet a religious crisis that had taken the form of a philosophical dispute."

184 Banfi, Antonio. *Socrate.* Milan: Garzanti, 1944.

Reviews the major aspects of the life and philosophy of Socrates. Contains a chapter entitled "La fama di Socrate" which provides Italian translations (with brief commentaries) of passages which deal with Socrates from the writings of Aristotle, Hamann, Hegel, Kierkegaard, Schleiermacher, and Nietzsche. Speaks of Socrates' philosophy as a living experience in which there is nothing abstract and nothing doctrinaire.

185 Bastide, Georges. *Le moment historique de Socrate.* Paris: Librairie Felix Alçan, 1939.

Reviews the main themes associated with the philosophy of Socrates. Calls attention to the parallels that can be drawn between Socrates and Kant: the Socratic idea of moral commitment can be viewed as an anticipation of the Kantian categorical imperative. Regards the Socratic call for self-knowledge as a prelude to the Cartesian *cogito*. Observes that Socrates' appeal to self-knowledge is the essence of his philosophy, and is the foundation of a profound spirituality.

186 Bedell, Gary. *Philosophizing with Socrates: An Introduction to the Study of Philosophy*. Lanham, Md.: University Press of America, 1980.

Discusses the historical problem of Socrates, and develops a general study of philosophy, using the Socratic presence and ideas as a point of reference for its explorations. Studies the following themes: Socrates' commitment to the philosophical life, the nature and scope of the Socratic method, the problem of knowledge and learning, the meaning of dialectic and definition, the relationship between the citizen and the state, the nature and significance of ethical questions, and the meaning of philosophy.

187 Belmont, Paul. *Le testament de Socrate*. Paris: Hermann et Cie., 1938.

Reviews the major themes associated with the philosophy of Socrates, and outlines the principal ways in which he has been a source of intellectual and moral influence in the development of culture and philosophy.

188 Benson, Arthur Christopher. "Socrates the Athenian." *Men of Might: Studies of Great Characters*. London: E. Arnold, 1921.

Devotes the first chapter to a general discussion of the personality and philosophy of Socrates, and to the analysis of the relationship between theory and practice in him. Other figures studied in subsequent chapters include Mahomet, Saint Bernard, Savanarola, Michelangelo, Carlo Borromeo, Fénelon, John Wesley, George Washington, Henry Martyn, David Livingstone, and Father Damien.

189 Birmbaum, Walter. *Sokrates. Urbild abendländischen Denkens*. Göttingen: Müsterschmidt, 1973.

Gives an overview of Socrates' life, political and social context, and last days. Begins and concludes its account of Socrates' philosophy by emphasizing its relevance and actuality in our own time: "*Sokrates ist und bleibt aktuell.*" Views Socrates as the prototype of the philosopher in the Western world.

190 Blackie, John S. *Four Phases of Morals: Socrates, Aristotle, Christianity, Utilitarianism*. New York: Charles Scribner's Sons, 1892, pp. 1-135.

Gives a general account of the life and philosophy of Socrates, and directs its attention initially to two questions: (1) As an ethical philosopher, what did Socrates wish to reform?, and (2) In the work of his reform, who were his antagonists? Regards Xenophon as "the only safe authority" with respect to Socrates' philosophy, and identifies two main propositions as being the basis of this philosophy: (1) that man is naturally a sympathetic and social animal, and (2) that man is naturally a reasoning animal whose passions can be tempered, and whose conduct can be regulated by reason.

191 Blum, Alan F. *Socrates: The Original and Its Images*. London: Routledge & Kegan Paul, 1978.

Focuses on the Socratic pursuit which epitomizes the relationship between the activity of an individual and the theories or principles he espouses. Interprets the Socratic ethical position in an Aristotelian manner: life is a course of action which aims at some good. Discusses the Socratic dialectic as an attempt to identify that which is good. Contains a concluding chapter which examines in detail the role and significance of the Delphic oracle in the formation and development of Socrates' philosophical mission.

192 Boas, George. *Rationalism in Greek Philosophy*. Baltimore: The John Hopkins Press, 1961.

Contains references and allusions to Socrates in the context of a comprehensive study of the role of rationalism in the development of ancient Greek thought. Maintains that the doctrine of innate ideas can be attributed to Socrates, and concludes that his educational method is understandable on the assumption that according to him, the pupil already possesses in himself the desired answers. Comments on the diverse portraits of Socrates that come from Aristophanes, Xenophon, and Plato.

193 Böhringer, A. *Der philosophische Standpunkt des Sokrates.* Karlsruhe, 1860.

Pamphlet (42 pp.) in which the major themes of Socratic philosophy are outlined and integrated into a system of ideas.

194 Boutroux, Emile. "The Search for a Science of Morality." *The State Versus Socrates: A Case Study in Civic Freedom.* Edited by John D. Montgomery. Boston: The Beacon Press, 1954, pp. 197-202.

Excerpted from Boutroux' *Historical Studies in Philosophy* (translated by Fred Rothwell, London: Macmillan, 1912, pp. 68-73). Attributes to Socrates the establishment of morality on a scientific foundation. Maintains that in appreciating this endeavor on his part, we should be able to reconcile the apparently contradictory and paradoxical aspects of his character and philosophy. Traces the influence and development of the Socratic method from Plato to Hegel, specifically with respect to ethical inquiries. Ref. 195.

195 Boutroux, Emile. "Socrate, fondateur de la science morale." *Etudes d'histoire de la philosophie.* Paris, 1897, pp. 8-73.

Originally published in 1883. Reviews the major aspects of Socrates' life and philosophy. Regards Xenophon's *Memorabilia* as the most important source of information concerning Socrates' ideas. Views Plato's *Apology* as an essentially historical document, and argues against its interpretation as a rhetorical piece born out of Plato's imagination. Supports its position by referring to Socrates' prophecy (*Apology* 39c-d) concerning the advent of many youthful accusers of the Athenians, a prophecy that appears not to have been fulfilled. Notes that if the *Apology* were a fictional composition, Plato would not have included such prophecy. Attaches great historical weight to the testimony of Xenophon. Regards Socrates as the founder of ethics as a scientific and systematic discipline. Calls attention to the great affinity between Socrates and Pascal. Other philosophers discussed in the volume are Aristotle, Jacob Boehme, Descartes, and Kant.

196 Brandis, C. A. "Grundlinien der Lehre des Sokrates." *Rheinisches Museum für Philologie*, 1 (1827), pp. 118-150.

Gives a general account of the fundamental principles on which Socrates' philosophy is based, and stresses the primacy of self-knowledge and subjectivity. Endeavors to arrive at those ideas that can be regarded as genuinely Socratic. Emphasizes the role played by Socrates as a counterbalancing force against the ideas of the Sophists. Comments favorably on the value of Diogenes Laertius' Socratic testimony.

197 Brochard, Victor. *Estudios sobre Sócrates y Platón*. Translated by León Ostrov. Buenos Aires: Editorial Losada, 1940.

Spanish translation of seven articles by Victor Brochard, including "L'Oeuvre de Socrate" and "Le Devenir dans la philosophie de Platon." Ref. 198, 577.

198 Brochard, Victor. "L'Oeuvre de Socrate." *L'Année Philosophique*, 12 (1902), pp. 1-11.

Stresses the enigmatic and paradoxical character of Socrates' life and thought -- a circumstance which has attracted scholars and historians, and has constantly called for a solution. Notes that with respect to Socrates no one has or will have ever spoken the final word. Regards Socrates' work as ultimately incomplete, and adds that he himself must have been perfectly aware of the unfinished nature of his mission. Interprets Socratic ethical philosophy as a type of utilitarianism.

199 Brun, Jean. *Socrate*. Paris: Presses Universitaires de France, 1960.

Contains an introduction on the Socratic problem, as well as chapters on the life of Socrates, the formula 'Know thyself' and self-knowledge, the Socratic 'demon' or divine experience, and Socratic irony. Devotes three concluding chapters to Socrates' physiognomy (with references to

Nietzsche's comments), to his trial and death, and to his philosophical legacy. Regards the life, death, and thought of Socrates as a mystery. Notes, however, that there is enough information about him which allows us to shed some light on the significance of his presence in the history of ideas.

200 Brun, Jean. *Socrates.* Translated by Douglas Scott. New York: Walker & Co., 1962.

English translation of Brun's *Socrate.* Ref. 199.

201 Buron, Pièrre-Emile. *La vie de Socrate l'admirable.* Combourg: Atimco, 1983.

Presents an illustrated biography of Socrates, with various fictional dialogues included in the narration. Speaks of Socrates as a man whose long and intense existence was devoted to the teaching of love and wisdom.

202 Busse, Adolf. *Sokrates. Die grossen Erzieher.* Berlin: Reuther & Reichard, 1914.

Develops a general description of Socrates on the basis provided by Plato's Socratic or early dialogues. Maintains that even though there is nothing in Aristotle's testimony which cannot be found in that of Plato, the Aristotelian comments on Socrates are significant because they clearly separate his philosophical stance from that assumed by Plato, particularly with respect to the theory of Ideal Forms.

203 Cabral Pinto, F. *Sócrates, um filósofo bastardo.* Lisbon: Livros Horizonte, 1985.

Discusses the meaning and influence of the Sophistical movement on Socrates, and stresses the anti-dogmatic tendencies of the Sophists. Devotes one chapter to the examination of the Socratism that can be associated with the historical Socrates, and emphasizes in a separate chapter the anti-Socratic themes that can be linked to Plato and Platonism. Speaks of Socrates as an example of the 'bastard philosopher' who is mentioned by Plato in the *Republic* and who is there condemned to exile. Explores in a concluding chapter the political causes and circumstances of Socrates' trial. Concludes with comments on the significance of Socrates' prophetic words in *Apology* 39d, and notes that even though he died in a physical way, he remains alive in each consciousness that strives for freedom and understanding.

204 Callot, Emile. *La doctrine de Socrate*. Paris: Marcel Rivière, 1970.

Gives a comprehensive outline of the major philosophical ideas associated with Socrates, and devotes particular attention to the Socratic search for knowledge in self-consciousness, the primacy of ethical considerations, the identity between knowledge and virtue, and the importance of critical thinking. Argues that the kernel of the Socratic doctrine is found in Socrates' concept of moral knowledge (*la science morale*), to which a vision of God is intimately united.

205 Chaignet, A. E. *La vie de Socrate*. Paris, 1868.

Provides a general account of the principal aspects and circumstances of Socrates' life, and contains a brief survey of his philosophical doctrines.

206 Charpentier, François. *La vie de Socrate*. Amsterdam: Etienne Roger, 1699.

Originally published in Paris in 1650. Gives a biographical sketch of the life and philosophy of Socrates, drawn chiefly from the testimonies of Xenophon, Plato, and Diogenes Laertius. Constitutes the earliest extensive account of Socrates in modern times. Includes a French translation of Xenophon's *Memorabilia* (*Les Choses mémorables de Xénophon*). Ref. 58.

207 Cooper, John Gilbert. *The Life of Socrates*. London: R. Dodsley, 1749.

Recounts the major aspects and moments of Socrates' life, and gives a summary of some of his philosophical contributions. Makes a special effort to discredit the accusations created by Aristophanes in the *Clouds*, and argues against the anti-Socratic tradition that goes back to the writings of Aristoxenus and Lucian.

208 Cordova Iturburu, Cayetano. *Vida y doctrina de Sócrates. El hombre, el maestro, el ciudadano.* Buenos Aires: Editorial Atlántida, 1940.

Provides a general account of the life and doctrine of Socrates, basing its narrative on Xenophontean and Platonic testimonies. Endeavors to reconstruct a portrait of Socrates in which various elements are well integrated: Socrates as a man, as the propounder of a set of philosophical ideas, and as a living participant in the Athenian polity.

209 Cornford, Francis MacDonald. *Before and After Socrates.* Cambridge: Cambridge University Press, 1932.

Presents the contributions of ancient Greek thought to modern times through the seminal figure of Socrates. Endeavors to elucidate the process by which Greek Milesian rationalism failed to satisfy Socrates' aspirations, and discusses the ways in which Plato and Aristotle integrated Socratic ideas into their philosophies. Stresses the role played by Socrates in the reorientation of philosophical thought from the study of nature to the study of human conduct.

210 Cornford, Francis MacDonald. *Principium Sapientiae: The Origins of Greek Philosophical Thought.* New York: Harper Torchbooks, 1965.

Discusses various themes related to Socrates in the context of a general exposition of the origins of Greek philosophy: Socrates' early cosmological interests and speculations (p. 40); the differences between Socratic and Platonic philosophies (pp. 45ff, 66ff, 84ff); Socrates' relationship to the Apollonian cult (pp. 68 and 125); his attitude to life after death (pp. 69ff); his trances (pp. 86ff) and personality (pp. 124ff); his position vis-à-vis religion (pp. 138ff); and the nature of the indictment against him (pp. 133ff).

211 Cortés, Eugenio S. "La palabra socrática." *Revista de*

*Filosofia de la Universidad de Costa Rica*, 22 (1984), pp. 151-156.

Observes that it is common to present the person of Socrates as a paradigm of the philosophical teacher, and his ideas as an example of a great philosophical contribution. Notes, however, that he expressed disdain for philosophy and for the teaching of philosophy, and that this is evident, not only by the fact that he refused to write down his ideas, but by the very basis of his thought, which calls for the recognition of one's ignorance.

212 Cotton, Gerard. *Socrate*. Brussels: Office de Publicité, 1944.

Deals in an introductory section with the details of Socrates' life, especially the circumstances of his trial and death. Contains translated excerpts from the *Memorabilia* and the *Phaedo*.

213 Cresson, André. *Socrate. Sa vie, son oeuvre, avec un exposé de sa philosophie*. Paris: Presses Universitaires de France, 1947.

Gives a general account of the life of Socrates, and outlines the principal themes associated with his philosophy.

214 Cross, Robert N. *Socrates: The Man and His Mission*. London: Methuen & Co., 1914.

Studies the major aspects of Socrates' life and personality: boyhood, education, and youth; his appearance and character; his domestic and family life; his public and political life; and his teaching activities. Examines the relationship between him and his 'enemies' and the State at large, and devotes individual chapters to his ethics, his religion, the impact of Aristophanes' *Clouds*, and the trial and execution. Relies chiefly on the testimonies of Plato and Xenophon, and makes passing references to the secondary sources.

215 Cushman, Robert E. "The Socratic Perspective." *Therapeia: Plato's Conception of Philosophy*. Westport, Conn.: Greenwood

Press, n.d., pp. 3-29.

Chapter 1. Contains three sections: (1) Socrates, the integral man; (2) a revolution in perspective; and (3) the prophetic soul and teleology. Stresses the idea that Socrates did not attempt to instil knowledge but only to awaken thought. Argues that any systematic attempt to construct a deliberate and systematic exposition of Socratic thought involves a gross insensitivity to Socrates' spirit. Notes that for Plato Socrates was the integral man -- that is, the man of perfect moral and intellectual integrity.

216 Davidson, Robert F. "The Role of the Philosopher: The Sophists and Socrates." *Philosophies Men Live By*. New York: Holt, Rinehart & Winston, 1974, pp. 1-24.

Originally published in 1947. Serves as an introductory chapter for a work which discusses various philosophical and intellectual views from Socrates to contemporary times. Begins with an examination of the meaning and function of philosophy and its development among the Sophists. Comments on their moral relativism and skepticism, and introduces Socrates as the major counterbalancing force against Sophistical thought. Explores briefly the Socratic problem, and notes that the Socrates of the Platonic early dialogues may be regarded as a reasonably historical figure. Emphasizes Socrates' conviction that knowledge leads to virtue, and stresses the social function of his mission and the paradigmatic nature of his quest for truth.

217 Dijk, I. van. *Socrates*. Haarlem, 1923.

Develops a general overview of the major philosophical ideas associated with Socrates, and argues against all interpretations that see in him a moralist or a philosopher primarily concerned with moral or ethical issues.

218 Drakakes, Stellos P. Ἡ ζωὴ καὶ ὁ θάνατος τοῦ Σωκράτους. Iraklion, Greece: Ephemerides Ide, 1932.

In modern Greek. Gives a general presentation of the life and death of Socrates by stringing together various passages from the Platonic dialogues. Includes an introductory section on Aristophanes' *Clouds*.

219 Durant, Will. "The Present Significance of the Socratic Ethic." *Philosophy and the Social Problem.* New York: Macmillan, 1917, pp. 5-35.

Comments on the major themes of Socrates' philosophical contributions. Acknowledges that the great discovery of the Sophists was the importance of the individual, but stresses the fact that it was Socrates who made that discovery valuable by identifying the individual's commitment to philosophy with the quest for the good. Emphasizes Socrates' recognition of the identity between the interest of the community and the interest of the individual.

220 Duvall, T. G. "Greece, the Cradle of Western Civilization - Socrates." *Great Thinkers. The Quest of Life for Its Meaning.* New York: Oxford Univesity Press, 1937, pp. 41-52.

Presents the historical background of Athens at the time of Socrates, and comments on his significance in the development of culture and philosophy. Observes that the Socratic endeavor was rooted in "the tacit assumption of a moral and spiritual nature in man, something divine and self-revealing which gives life all its dignity and worth."

221 Eastman, Max. "Socrates: The Herald of Logic." *Seven Kinds of Goodness.* New York: Horizon Press. 1967, pp. 67-75.

Gives a general biographical account of Socrates, with specific comments on his physiognomy and daily activities. Views as his most important contribution his insistence on arriving at the precise definitions of moral states and virtues, and regards him as the herald of logical thinking. Emphasizes the signficance of the Socratic concept of the soul -- a concept on which "his zeal for verifiable definition seems to have broken down," and which appears to be an emotional idea. Concludes with comments on Socrates' trial and execution.

222 Eitrem, Samson. *Sokrates.* Oslo: H. Aschehoug & Co., 1952.

Discusses the major biographical and ideological themes associated with Socrates. Begins with a study of the Athenian world of Socrates' time, and introduces the Socratic philosophy by examining the significance of the idea of *logos* in Socrates' mind. Devotes individual chapters to his relationship with Aspasia, Xanthippe, Alcibiades, and the Delphic Oracle.

223 Eliot, Alexander. *Socrates: A Fresh Appraisal of the Most Celebrated Case in History*. New York: Crown Publishers, 1967.

Part 1 ("The Evidence") gives an account of the principal aspects of Socrates' life and character: his emergence during the Athenian Golden Age, his frugality, his curiosity, his erudition and modesty, his 'peculiar' piety, his relationship with women, his associates, his trial and execution, and his 'immortalization' through the agency of Plato. Draws attention to Socrates' silence about the conduct of the Athenians during the Peloponnesian War. Discusses the presence of Socrates in Aristotle's writings and in the works of art of Hellenistic times. Comments on Nietzsche's reaction to him, and on the influence of Socratic philosophy on Zen Buddhism, existentialism, and religious people in general. Part 2 recreates in a dialogical form the last days of Socrates: his trial and refusal to escape, and his death.

224 Emerson, Ralph Waldo. *Two Unpublished Essays: The Character of Socrates and The Present State of Ethical philosophy*. Boston: Lamson, Wolffe & Co., 1895.

"The Character of Socrates" is the Bowdain Prize Dissertation of 1820 at Harvard University. Speaks of Socrates' character as uncommon and admirable. Gives a survey of the political and cultural world of Socrates' Athens, and a brief summary of his biography, as well as a eulogistic account of the virtues that accompanied his personality.

225 Festugière, A. J. *Socrate*. Paris: Flammarion, 1934.

Reviews the major biographical and philosophical aspects and themes associated with Socrates. Maintains that his confession of ignorance was a sincere and genuine expression of intellectual perplexity and of a desire to become enlightened. Explores the significance and implications of this confession of ignorance. Notes that the true greatness of Socrates consists in his having led Greece to the age of reason, as if from a stage of adolescence to a stage of mature humanity. Concludes with a series of remarks on

Socrates' late devotion to music, which is understood as a devotion to the spiritual harmony of the universe.

226 Forbes, John Thomas. *Socrates*. New York: C. Scribner's Sons, 1905.

Contains an introductory chapter on the political conditions, the civic ideals, and the religion of Socrates' time. Includes also a chapter on the pre-Socratics. Discusses various interpretations of Socrates' teaching, and gives an elaborate presentation of its method and content. Devotes a separate chapter to the 'personal issues' of Socrates' life: the Athenians' attitude towards him, and the details of his trial and execution. Concludes that the Socratic ideal is limited inasmuch as it emphasizes the intellectual, not the moral aspects of the human experience. Suggests that the Socratic ideal can only be completed through the commitment made possible by the Christian faith.

227 Fouillée, Alfred. *La Philosophie de Socrate*. Paris: Ladrange, 1874 (2 vols.).

Reconstructs the biography of Socrates, and maintains that the testimonies of Xenophon, Plato, and Aristotle are in basic agreement, not only with respect to the details of his life, but also in what concerns his philosophical conceptions. Interprets his fits of abstraction as deep moments of spiritual self-absortion in which he manifested a profound sense of disdain for material things and events. Views his trial and execution as the unfolding of a divine and providential design which revealed the incompleteness of his vision of the Good: an unjust sentence, therefore, had to have ultimately a just purpose. Considers Socrates' chief contributions to ethics his effort to disassociate moral values from egoistic and utilitarian purposes, and his endeavor to establish an independent foundation for ethics. Praises him for having insisted on the primacy of ethics over metaphysics, science, and politics. Maintains that his originality consists in his discovery of the psychological and ethical significance of the concept of *psyche*. Argues that the Socratic method has ultimately a metaphysical goal. Emphasizes the systematic theological doctrines of Socrates.

228 Galli, Gallo. "Socrate." *Platone.* Milan: Edizione Pergamena, 1974, pp. 35-99.

Reviews the general biographical and philosophical aspects of Socrates. Sees him as the natural offspring of the same movement that brought about the rise of Sophistical philosophy, but also as the force which came to oppose that philosophy. Places special emphasis on the positive aspects of Socrates' maieutics.

229 Genta, Jordán B. *El filósofo y los sofistas. Curso de introducción a la filosofía. Diálogos socráticos de Platón.* Buenos Aires: Lumen, 1949.

Presents a series of twenty-nine university lectures which deal mostly with the presence and influence of Socrates. Discusses, among others, the following themes: the teaching of Socrates and the problem of Alcibiades; self-knowledge and the confession of ignorance; the relationship between virtue and knowledge; and the apparent failure of Socrates and his real success; and the concept of the soul as this is elaborated in the *Phaedo.*

230 Gomes, A. Sousa. *A filosofia de Sócrates.* Lisbon: Gazeta do Sul, 1970.

Pamphlet (3 pp.) which states briefly various biographical and ideological points associated with Socrates. Emphasizes his commitment to rationalism.

231 Gomez Robledo, Antonio. *Sócrates y el socratismo.* Mexico: Fondo de Cultura Económica, 1966.

Begins with a discussion of the Socratic problem, towards which it adopts an eclectic stance. Discusses the social and political context of Socrates' time, and recounts the major moments of his life. Reviews the circumstances of his trial and execution, and concludes with comments on the parallelism betweem Socrates and Jesus.

232 Griggs, Edward H. *Socrates, Teacher and Martyr.* Croton-on-Hudson, N.Y.: Orchard Hill Press, 1932.

Gives a brief biographical sketch of Socrates, and brings

to the foreground his contributions (both his doctrines and his example) as a great moral leader. Views as his major achievement the revelation that through a moral and noble life, it is possible to give eternal meaning to our transient lives.

233 Grote, George. *Life, Teachings, and Death of Socrates.* New York: Stanford & Delisser, 1859.

Extracted from Grote's *History of Greece* (Vol. 6, pp. 7-219). Reviews the major biographical and ideological aspects associated with Socrates. Calls attention to the remarkable agreement between the testimonies of Xenophon and Plato.

234 Gulley, Norman. *The Philosophy of Socrates.* London: MacMillan, 1968.

Deals with the philosophy of Socrates in four sections: (1) the Socratic method of *elenchus*, and the gap that separates Socrates' dialectics from Sophistical eristics; (2) the Socratic paradoxes, specifically the idea that knowledge is virtue and ignorance is evil; (3) Socrates' political and religious views; and (4) the Socratic concept of the soul. Argues against the tendency of emphasizing the skeptical and agnostic elements in Socrates' thought. Ref. 306.

235 Guthrie, W. K. C. *The Greek Philosophers: From Thales to Aristotle.* New York: Harper Torchbooks, 1960.

Carries out a general review of the history of Greek philosophy from the Milesian rationalists to Aristotle. Deals with Socrates and the Sophists (Chapter 4, pp. 63-80) who are viewed as representatives of a shift towards humanism and as a reaction to the strictly cosmological and metaphysical tendencies of their predecessors. Understands the Socratic presence as an opposing force to the skeptical attitudes of the Sophistical movement, and develops its analysis of the Socratic philosophy on the basis of the examination of Socrates' central doctrine that virtue is knowledge.

236 Guthrie, W. K. C. *Socrates.* London: Cambridge University Press, 1971.

Originally published as Part 2 of Guthrie's *A History of Greek Philosophy* (Vol. 3, Cambridge University Press, 1969). Discusses all the major themes and issues concerning Socrates, such as the Socratic problem, the sources of information, the life and character of Socrates, and his philosophical significance. Contains an abundance of annotations and references to primary and secondary sources, as well as an extensive (unannotated) bibliography and an *index locorum*. Deals with Socrates both biographically and philosophically from a comprehensive point of view and without seeking to defend any one given interpretation of his ideas. Attempts thereby to reconstruct a general and embracing representation of his life and philosophy. Ref. 1031, 1913.

237 Guthrie, W. K. C. *Socrates and Plato*. Brisbane: University of Queensland Press, 1958.

Pamphlet (27 pp.) which reprints two popular lectures given by Guthrie as part of the Macrossan Lectures at the University of Queensland in Brisbane. Deals separately with Socrates and Plato. Emphasizes the intellectual and linguistic aspects of Socrates' teaching. Views the following as the most important among Socrates' ideas: his confession of ignorance as a preamble for the acquisition of true knowledge, his conviction that virtue and knowledge are fundamentally identical, and his belief that all evil is ultimately the result of ignorance.

238 Gutierrez, Alberto. *Sócrates, el padre de la moral*. Buenos Aires: Editorial L.E.Y.C.A., Nocito & Raño, 1943.

Pamphlet (46 pp.) which recounts the major biographical information about Socrates. Concludes with comments on the comparison between his death and that of Jesus, and notes that in both instances we come upon individuals who died for the sake of truth, justice, goodness, and love.

239 Hadas, Moses and Smith, Morton. "The Image of Socrates." *Heroes and Gods: Spiritual Biographies in Antiquity*. New York: Harper & Row, 1965, pp. 49-59.

Discusses the process through which Socrates became the paradigm of aretalogy in ancient times, and concludes that it was in and through the dialogues of Plato that such a process was possible, and that it was through the Platonic idealization that Socrates succeeded in reaching the highest position of spirituality in the history of culture. Comments on the testimonies of Aristophanes and Xenophon, and notes that, while the former is simply a grossly unfair characterization, the latter remains a superficial and prosaic rendition of the Socratic phenomenon. Recounts the generally accepted details of Socrates' life, and summarizes passages from some of the early dialogues.

240 Hadot, P. "La figure de Socrate." *Eranos-Jahrbuch*, 43 (1974), pp. 51-90.

Studies the representation of Socrates as this is embodied in the testimonies of Plato and Xenophon, and notes that this representation turns out to be an idealization of the Wise Man who has become the human standard of the absolute Good, and who reveals himself to us as a bridge between divine wisdom and the human condition.

241 Holberg, Ludvig. *Socrates og Epaminondas. Samlede Skrifter.* Copenhagen, 1931.

Contains a Danish biography of Socrates, originally published in 1739. Portrays Socrates as a philosophical and moral paradigm worthy of imitation.

242 Hopkinson, Leslie White. "Socrates." *Greek Leaders.* Freeport, N.Y.: Books for Libraries Press, 1969, pp. 79-101.

Originally published in 1918 (Houghton Mifflin Company). Presents a general biographical sketch of Socrates, and provides lengthy quotations from the *Clouds* and from Plato's *Apology* and *Symposium.* Notes that "Socrates is a man impossible to describe without contradictions." Observes that the confusion of Socrates with the Sophists is similar to the confusion of socialists with anarchists in the early twentieth century.

243 Hübscher, Arthur. *Sokrates.* Frankfurt am Main: Verlag August Lutzeyer, 1950.

Reviews the main aspects of Socrates' life and philosophy, and provides numerous excerpts from primary and secondary sources, as well as from recent works. Includes poems on Socrates by Hördelin and Meyer.

244 Irmscher, Johannes. *Sokrates. Versuch einer Biographie.* Leipzig: Verlag Philipp Reclam, 1982.

Constructs a general biographical account of Socrates. Devotes a concluding chapter to a brief examination of the sources. Contains a detailed chronological table from 624 B.C. to 399 B.C.

245 Jacques-Trève [Ducat, Louise]. *L'Evangile de Socrate.* Paris: Societé d'Editions Litteraires et Techniques, 1935.

Discusses in Part 1 the cultural, political, and social milieu which made possible Socrates' advent. Devotes Part 2 to an exposition of his philosophical ideas. Develops a mixture of narrative (reminiscent of the Christian gospels) and philosophical commentary in order to put forth the main contentions of Socrates' message. Speaks of him as the true incarnation of a god, and quotes from a fictitious letter attributed to Xenophon.

246 Jaeger, Werner. "The Memory of Socrates." *The State Versus Socrates: A Case Study in Civic Freedom.* Edited by John D. Montgomery. Boston: The Beacon Press, 1954, pp. 19-34.

Reprinted from Jaeger's *Paideia: The Ideals of Greek Culture* (translated by Gilbert Highet, New York: Oxford University Press, 1939, Vol. 2, pp. 13-27). Reviews various interpretations of the significance of Socrates, from ancient times to the twentieth century, and comments on the sources of information about him. Discusses at length Nietzsche's reaction to Socrates, and outlines the two major schools of Socratic scholarship: the one exemplified by Maier and the other by Burnet and Taylor. Notes that even though these two schools stand apparently in vast opposition to each other, there is a sense in which they can be reconciled, specifically by an appeal to the paradoxical and multi-dimensional mind and personality of Socrates.

247 Jaspers, Karl. "Socrates." *The Great Philosophers: The Foundations.* Translated by Ralph Manheim. New York:

Harcourt, Brace & World, 1962, pp. 15-31.

English translation of Jaspers' "Sokrates" (in Part 1 of *Die grossen Philosophen I*, Munich: R. Piper & Co. Verlag, 1957). Deals with Socrates as an example of a paradigmatic individual (like Buddha, Confucius, and Jesus), and as a man whose presence has decisively determined the course of human history. Recounts Socrates' biography and intellectual development, and outlines the details of his trial and execution. Speaks of the 'Platonic transfiguration of Socrates', and argues against the tendency of attributing Plato's metaphysical ideas to Socrates. Reviews the development of his influence, and mentions several interpretations of his philosophy among ancient, medieval, and modern scholars. Supports Jaeger's eclectic approach to the Socratic problem, and emphasizes the spirit of openness and freedom that emanates from the Socratic experience.

248 Kelly, Eugene, editor. *New Essays on Socrates*. Lanham, Md.: University Press of America, 1984.

Contains the papers and commentaries presented at a conference on Socrates held at the New York Institute of Technology and sponsored by the Long Island Philosophical Society on October 23, 1983. Includes contributions on a wide spectrum of Socratic scholarship by John P. Peterman (Ref. 1214), James Haden (Ref. 931), Thomas C. Brickhouse and Nicholas D. Smith (Ref. 1124), Luis E. Navia (Ref. 543), Eric A. Havelock (Ref. 623), Michael Henry (Ref. 934), James Kostman (Ref. 1427), Elinor J. West (Ref. 1231a), Michael Soupios (Ref. 1009), Richard E. Hart (Ref. 1077), Victorino Tejera (Ref. 561), Christopher P. Mooney (Ref. 960), and Walter Watson (Ref. 1297).

249 Kelly, Eugene. "Socrates Today." *New Essays on Socrates*. Lanham, Md.: University Press of America, 1984, pp. xi-xx.

Serves as an introduction to *New Essays on Socrates*. Explains the process which made the Socrates conference possible, and comments briefly on the content of the papers presented. Emphasizes the relevance of Socrates' philosophical contributions for our contemporary world. Ref. 248.

250 Kendrick, A. C. "The Life and Philosophy of Socrates." *The*

*Christian Review*, 10 (1845), pp. 155-181.

Gives a general account of Socrates' life and character, and summarizes the main themes associated with his philosophical teachings.

251 Kessidi, F. C. [*Socrates*]. Moscow: Mysl, 1976.

In Russian. Provides a general and comprehensive analysis of Socrates and his philosophy. Sees him as an advocate of the moderate democratic party in Athens, and as a law-abiding citizen who taught and practiced the greatest respect for the government of the polity. Observes that according to Socrates, philosophy is not limited to theory and speculation alone, but is a highly practical endeavor. Emphasizes the importance of self-knowledge for Socrates, and notes that in his view, true freedom can only be attained in self-knowledge. Concludes with the statement that the issues raised by Socrates remain even today the very core of all philosophical inquiries.

252 Kessler, Herbert. *Warum Sokrates modern ist*. Mannheim: Verlag Sokrates, 1976.

Discusses the overall significance of the term 'Sokratismus,' and outlines the meaning and implications of the Socratic quest for the truth in the process of self-understanding. Attaches special importance to Socrates' work and mission as an educator and as a creator of moral values.

253 Kesters, H. *Kérygmes de Socrate. Essai sur la formation du message socratique*. Louvain: Editions Nauwelaerts, 1965.

Deals with a vast number of themes and issues, such as the authenticity of the *Clitophon*, the Socratic method in the *Euthydemus* and in the *Apology*, and the Socratic thesis concerning the identity of virtue and knowledge.

254 King, Thomas Starr. *Socrates: An Oration*. San Francisco: Harr Wagner Publishing Co., 1924.

Introduction and notes by Ernest Carroll Moore. Gives a general biographical account of Socrates. Praises him for his moral earnestness and intellectual integrity.

255 Köchly, Herman. "Sokrates und sein Volk." *Akademische Vorträge*. Zurich, 1859, pp. 219-386.

Attempts to delineate the character of Socrates against the background of his historical and political circumstances. Provides a summary statement of the history of his times. Maintains that Plato's *Apology* preserves far more faithfully than any other Platonic work the character and philosophy of the historical Socrates.

256 Kraus, René. *The Private and Public Life of Socrates*. Translated by Barrows Mussey. New York: Doubleday, 1940.

Originally published in French. Recreates Socrates' biography in a fictional and highly imaginative manner. Remains generally faithful to the information provided by Plato and Aristotle, but often goes far beyond it. Constitutes an attempt to construct a quasi-historical narrative which serves as a political and social allegory for the purpose of shedding light on certain contemporary political issues.

257 Krokiewicz, Adam. *Sokrates*. Warsaw: Pax, 1958.

In Polish. Develops a general psychological analysis of Socrates' personality, with special emphasis on the ethical aspects of his life and thought. Contains chapters on Aristophanes' accusations against Socrates, on Socrates' spirit of contradiction, on the meaning and use of dialectics, on Plato and the minor Socratics, and on Socrates' trial and execution.

258 Kronska, Irena. *Sokrates*. Warsaw: Wiedza Powszechna, 1964.

In Polish. Develops a general exposition of the life, personality, and philosophy of Socrates, with comments on the Socratic problem and the influence of Socratic thought. Includes in the second part a number of translated passages from Aristophanes, Xenophon, Plato, Diogenes Laertius, and Plutarch.

259 Kuhn, Helmut. *Sokrates. Ein Versuch über den Ursprung der Metaphysik*. Berlin: Verlag Die Runde, 1934.

Examines the rise of metaphysical issues from the matrix furnished by Socrates' questioning, specifically from his confession of ignorance. Concludes with comments on the relationship between his questioning stance and Plato's endeavor to transcend it. Portrays a philosophical figure of Socrates which displays distinct traces of Kierkegaard's interpretation of him.

260 Kühnemann, Eugen. *Grundlehren der Philosophie: Studien über Vorsokratiker, Sokrates und Plato*. Stuttgart: W. Spemann, 1899.

Devotes Part 2 (pp. 165-478) to the study of the philosophical contributions of Socrates and Plato. Reviews (pp. 165-238) several major issues associated with Socrates, *e.g.*, the background of Sophistical thought, Socrates' endeavor to transcend the impasse created by the skepticism of the Sophists, and the Socratic thesis that virtue and knowledge are identical.

261 Labriola, Antonio. *Socrate*. Edited by Benedetto Croce. Bari, 1909.

Originally published as *La dottrina di Socrate secondo Senofonte, Platone ed Aristotele*, in *Atti della Reale Accademia di Scienze Morali et Politiche di Napoli*, 6 (1871); reprinted in Milan in 1961, edited by Luigi Dal Pane (Feltrinelli Editore). Includes chapters on the historical character of Socrates, his philosophical value, the Socratic method, Socrates' ethics, and his idea of the Good, the knowledge of God and the soul. Approaches the Socratic problem by excluding all the Platonic passages in which the theory of Ideal Forms and Plato's psychological views play a significant role, or in which there is any deviation from the Xenophontean testimony. Regards Aristotle's testimony as useful but not crucial, since it is derived entirely from Xenophon and Plato. Views the testimony of Xenophon as the true source of our information concerning Socrates' personality and thought. Rejects the idea that Xenophon was incapable of understanding and appreciating Socrates' philosophy. Contrasts sharply Socratic philosophy and Platonic philosophy, and insists that Xenophon's testimony can give us the criterion to distinguish the one from the other. Rejects all efforts to invest Socrates with any mystical ideas or tendencies, although emphasizes his compliance with religious rituals and practices. Notes that Socrates was successful in establishing a metaphysical conception of nature.

262 Labriola, Antonio. *Socrates.* Translated by Rangel de Andrade. Rio de Janeiro: Companhia Brasil Editora, 1939.

Portuguese translation of Labriola's *Socrate.* Ref. 261.

263 Lamartine, Alphonse de. "Socrates." *Memoirs of Celebrated Characters.* New York: Harper & Brothers, 1854 (3 vols.), Vol. 2, pp. 5-16.

English translation of part of Lamartine's *Mémoires.* Explores the significance of the two best known moments of Socrates' death: his trial and his execution. Concludes that he was "neither wiser, more virtuous, neither more religious than all the other philosophers of antiquity, but the most witty and the most amiable of Athenian citizens."

264 Lasaulx, E. von. *Des Sokrates Leben, Lehre und Tod.* Stuttgart: Verlag Freies Geistesleben, 1958.

Originally published in 1857. Presents a brief exposition of Socrates' main philosophical contributions, and gives a sketch of his life, with emphasis on the circumstances surrounding his trial and execution.

265 Leider, Kurt. *Sokrates.* Hamburg: Verlag Friedrich Matthies, 1970.

Pamphlet (28 pp.). Gives a general exposition of the main themes of Socrates' philosophy.

266 Leonard, William Ellery. "The Personality and Influence of Socrates." *The Open Court*, 29 (1915), pp. 313-318.

Comments that "Socrates is more than the facts of his life and more than the Socratic teaching; for both are but derivative verbs of action from a concrete substantive being." Gives a general sketch of the main doctrines associated with Socrates, and emphasizes his importance as a source of moral values.

267 Leonard, William Ellery. "Socrates." *The Open Court*, 29 (1915), pp. 19-31, 110-112, and 151-162.

Gives a general biographical sketch of Socrates, and provides a summary statement of his philosophical doctrines. Includes photographs and illustrations.

268 Leonard, William Ellery. *Socrates, Master of Life.* Chicago: Open Court, 1915.

Develops an imaginative yet critical interpretation of the personality of Socrates, and stresses the value of the practical teachings that ensue from his example and virtues.

269 MacIlwaine, W. "The Mission of Socrates." *The Dublin University Magazine*, 82 (1873), pp. 300-313.

Outlines the major philosophical ideas associated with Socrates, and discusses his contributions as an educator, especially with respect to the understanding and development of ethical values.

270 Manetti, Giannozzo. *Vita Socratis.* Florence: Bibliotheca di De Homine, 1974.

Edited and annotated by M. Montuori. First modern edition of Manetti's Latin biography of Socrates, which was originally published in 1440. Portrays Socrates as a wise and worthy philosopher who fulfilled with perfection his civic and religious obligations. Written in the style of a eulogy. Recounts the generally accepted facts of Socrates' life.

271 Manetti, Giannozzo. *Vita Socratis et Seneca.* Florence: Leo S. Olschki Editore, 1979.

Originally published in 1440. Introduction and annotations by Alfonso de Petris (in the 1979 edition).

272 Martin, Alfred W. "Socrates -- Wisest of Men." *Great Moral Leaders.* New York: The International Press, 1933, pp. 25-44.

Provides a biographical and philosophical sketch of Socrates. Views him as a paradigm of intellectual integrity. Other figures discussed in the volume are Jeremiah, Saint Francis of Assisi, Erasmus, Carlyle, and Emerson.

273 Martin, Gottfried. *Sokrates in Selbstzeugnissen und Bilddokumenten.* Hamburg: Rowohlt, 1967.

Provides a general exposition of the biography and philosophy of Socrates, and furnishes numerous illustrations of art works which depict Socrates and other Greek philosophers. Includes chapters on themes such as the problem of the sources, Socrates and the Delphic oracle, the Socratic spiritual voice or sign, Socratic irony, the value of Aristotle's testimony, and the interpretations of Hegel and Nietzsche.

274 Martinetti, Piero. "Socrate." *Rivista di Filosofia*, 1 (1939), pp. 1-38.

Maintains that the presence of Socrates in the history of civilization is so absolutely decisive and central that it would make little sense to opt for a position of complete agnosticism with respect to our knowledge of his life and thought. Draws special attention to the importance of religious and mystical themes in the development of his philosophy.

275 Mason, Cora C. *Socrates: The Man Who Dared to Ask.* Boston: The Beacon Press, 1954.

Presents various generally accepted biographical details about Socrates. Aims at an audience of young readers (from fifteen to twenty years old). Emphasizes the integrity, honesty, and earnestness of Socrates, and calls attention to his unwillingness to remain satisfied with ideas and assumptions based on authority or tradition. Stresses his independence and boldness.

276 Mason, R. J. and Wakefield, H. *Socrates, the Man and His*

*Teaching*. London: Oxford University Press, 1955.

Intended for readers whose first language is other than English. Presents a general introduction (pp. 1-14) which outlines the major aspects of Socrates' life and the main characteristics of his historical and political context. Provides abbreviated renditions of the *Apology*, the *Crito*, and the *Phaedo* (translated by F. J. Church), and contains maps and diagrams.

277 Mayer, Frederick. "Socrates." *The Great Teachers*. New York: The Citadel Press, 1967, pp. 45-54.

Gives a general account of Socrates' historical and political context, and comments on the major primary sources, as well as on various interpretations of the significance of Socrates' philosophy (*e.g.*, the assessments of the humanists of the Renaissance, Hegel, Kierkegaard, Nietzsche, Bertrand Russell, and John Burnet). Recounts the main events of Socrates' life, and concludes with remarks about his role as an ideal teacher: "The function of the teacher, according to Socrates, is to awaken the average man."

278 McCormick, John F. "Philosophy Looks at Life." *The Catholic World*, 143 (1936), pp. 709-715.

Comments on the fundamental task of philosophy, which is conceived as the examination of human existence, and on its overall goal, which is defined as the attainment of happiness. Examines how different philosophies approach the issue of the meaning of happiness, and concludes that it is Socrates' philosophy that provides the most meaningful approach, suggesting that he would rebuke us for attempting to relate happiness to material possessions.

279 McCrindle, J. W. *Socrates the Reformer and Martyr of Philosophy*. Calcutta: The Baptist Mission Press, 1863.

Pamphlet (27 pp.). Lecture delivered at the Doventon College. Recounts the generally accepted facts of Socrates' life, and develops a eulogistic statement about his personality and thought. Speaks of Socrates as "by far the greatest and best character of all heathen antiquity."

280 McKeon, Richard. "The Choice of Socrates." *Great Moral Dilemmas in Literature, Past and Present*. Edited by R. M. MacIver. New York: Cooper Square Publishers, 1964, pp. 113-133.

Discusses various interpretations to which Socrates' paradoxical philosophy and life have given rise, and reviews several solutions given to the Socratic problem. Devotes particular attention to the paradox of Socrates' death -- the death of a just man who was found guilty and sentenced by a legally constituted jury. Comments at length on his refusal to escape from prison and on the paradoxical issue raised by the *Crito*. Argues that "the final choice of Socrates, which brought his life to its close, was the consequence, logical as well as historical, of the choices and decisions which made up his life."

281 Mendelssohn, Moses. *Leben und Charakter des Sokrates als Einleitung zu seinem Phaedo.* Hamburg: F. Meiner, 1979.

Originally published in Berlin in 1764. Contains a lengthy introductory monograph on the life and personality of Socrates, which constitutes a eulogistic summary of the biographical information about him known and accepted in the late eighteenth century. Recreates Plato's *Phaedo*, using the Platonic characters and dramatic setting, but injects into the dialogue certain philosophical ideas and expressions typical of the rationalism associated with Mendelssohn. Rejects the Platonic arguments for the immortality of the soul (which the author calls 'chimerical'), and substitutes in their place arguments based on what is designated as "proofs from the harmony of moral truths." Presents a portrait of Socrates in the garb of a philosopher of the eighteenth century.

282 Mendelssohn, Moses. *Phaedon: Or the Death of Socrates.* London: J. Cooper, 1789.

Anonymous English translation of Mendelssohn's *Leben und Charakter des Sokrates als Einleitung zu seinem Phaedo.* Reprinted in 1973 by Arno Press, Chicago. Ref. 281.

283 Merleau-Ponty, Maurice. "Socrate." *Eloge de la philosophie.* Paris: Librairie Gallimard, 1953.

Lecture delivered on January 15, 1953, at the Collège de France. Refers to Socrates as the patron of philosophy, and emphasizes the element of challenge and openness of his philosophical outlook (which is contrasted with the closed and structured outlook typical of the professional philosophers of the present time). Stresses the paradoxical nature of Socrates' life and death, and sees in him a paradigm of philosophical commitment in which conflict and struggle are essential. Draws attention to his conviction that absolute knowledge is an illusion.

284 Merleau-Ponty, Maurice. "Socrates." *In Praise of Philosophy*. Translated by John Wild and James M. Edie. Evanston, Ill.: Northwestern University Press, 1963, pp. 33-41.

English translation of Merleau-Ponty's "Socrate." Ref. 283.

285 Meunier, Mario. *La lègende de Socrate*. Paris: L'Edition D'Art, H. Piazza, 1926.

Gives a biographical exposition of Socrates' philosophy. Includes discussions of themes such as the birth and education of Socrates, the influence of the Sophists, Socrates' relationship with Prodicus, the presence of Alcibiades, Socrates' military service, the Socratic circle, Socrates' practical wisdom, and his trial and execution.

286 Millet, René. *Socrate et la pensée moderne*. Paris: Plon-Nourrit, 1920.

Presents a biographical and thematic exposition of Socrates, and assumes an eclectic stance towards the sources. Regards Socrates' commitment to the freedom of thought as one of his most important and most lasting contributions. Attempts to discover in the contemporary ideological world clear vestiges of the influence of Socratic thought.

287 Mills, Dorothy. "Socrates." *The Book of the Ancient Greeks*. New York: G. P. Putnam's Sons, 1925, pp. 361-378.

Reviews briefly the generally accepted biographical

information about Socrates, and quotes extensively from the *Apology* and the *Phaedo*. Speaks of Socrates as one of the "gifts of Greece to the world." Integrates bits of information from Plato and Xenophon into one continuous narrative.

288 Mirgeler, Albert. *Sokrates*. Hellerau: Verlag Jakob Hegner, 1926.

Gives a general exposition of Socrates' biography and philosophy, and devotes considerable effort to the clarification of the relationship between Socrates and Plato. Observes that even though Socrates and Plato are two distinct and different philosophers, the latter was able to capture clearly and eloquently the essence of the former's thought.

289 Mitchison, N. M. and Crossman, R. H. S. *Socrates*. London: Hogarth Press, 1937.

Provides a short biography of Socrates, and sheds light on the political and social conditions of Athens in the late fifth century B.C. Deals mostly with the externalities of Socrates and his world, and discusses in a minimal way the philosophical components of his presence. Uses various modern instances and analogies in order to clarify some of the conditions of Socrates' world: *e.g.*, the crowded cicumstances of contemporary Madrid can give us some idea of the circumstances of Athens in the late fifth century B.C.

290 Mondolfo, Rodolfo. *Sócrates*. Buenos Aires: Ediciones Losange, 1955.

Discusses the historical and cultural context of Socrates' life, and gives a brief account of the present state of the Socratic problem. Reviews several themes associated with Socrates' philosophy: *e.g.*, the role of the *elenchus* as an intellectual and spiritual purification, and the identity of virtue and knowledge. Concludes with a chapter on the influence and present relevance of Socrates' philosophy.

291 Mondolfo, Rodolfo. *Sócrates*. Buenos Aires: Eudeba, 1959.

Originally published in 1941 as part of Mondolfo's *Moralistas griegos. La conciencia moral de Homero a Epicuro* (pp. 61ff.). Rejects the conclusion of those scholars who argue that all efforts to reconstruct the historical Socrates are useless, but accepts the reality of his enigmatic and paradoxical character as this has been revealed to us by the various sources. Argues that the Socratic problem should not be faced initially from a skeptical viewpoint, but from a perspective from which we can refine and improve the efforts of historians to delineate Socrates' character and philosophy. Emphasizes the significance of the Socratic concept of *psyche* understood in a metaphysical sense. Rejects the attempt to attribute hedonistic or utilitarian foundations to Socrates' ethics. Calls attention to the unity of theory and practice, thought and action, in Socrates' concept of philosophy.

292 Montée, Pierre. *La philosophie de Socrate.* Paris: A. Durand, 1869.

Gives a brief account of the life of Socrates, and reviews the major sources of information about him. Presents a general outline of the main philosophical ideas of Socratic thought, and emphasizes the development of its method, the search for wisdom in the self, and the identity of knowledge and virtue.

293 Montgomery, John D., editor. *The State Versus Socrates: A Case Study in Civic Freedom.* Boston: The Beacon Press, 1954.

Includes nineteen selections and articles by authors from Plato to twentieth century writers. Structures its contents around the theme of Socrates' trial and execution, but some of its components address other themes. Presents two selections which give an estimate of Socrates as a defendant, while seven of them argue the case for the prosecution, and six take the case for the defense. Includes four selections which outline the general contributions of Socrates. Contains a concluding selection which examines the justification for establishing a comparison between Socrates and Jesus. Includes the following authors: Werner Jaeger (Ref. 246), Paul E. More (Ref. 297), Alfred E. Taylor (Ref. 1109), René Kraus (Ref. 467), Alban D. Winspear (Ref. 1171), Eduard Zeller (Ref. 361), George Grote (Ref. 1260), Friedrich Nietzsche (Ref.

1724), Vilfredo Pareto (Ref. 806), Plato, Gustav F. Wiggers (Ref. 353), Karl R. Popper (Ref. 1282), Coleman Phillipson (Ref. 1093), Emile Boutroux (Ref. 194), and John S. Mill (Ref. 1599). Contains an introduction by the editor ("The Unfinished Trial"). Ref. 1089.

294 Montuori, Mario. *Socrate. Fisiologia di un mito.* Florence: G. C. Sansoni, 1974.

Reconstructs the historical portrait of Socrates within the context of the Athens of his time, and emphasizes the unity of humanity and philosophy in him. Examines the various legends that have flourished under his name, and pays close attention to the background, circumstances, and processes associated with his indictment and execution. Reviews in particular the content of the accusations of impiety and corruption. Discusses the possible political and philosophical motives which may have led Plato to alter the human and philosophical figure of Socrates. Observes that the Delphic pronouncement about Socrates' wisdom is a Platonic invention, as is the whole delineation of Socrates' philosophy in the *Apology*. Discusses the transformation of the Socratic myth and of the Socratic problem since the eighteenth century.

295 Montuori, Mario. *Socrates: Physiology of a Myth.* Chicago: Bolchazy-Carducci Publishers, 1981.

Published in *London Studies of Classical Philology*, 6 (1981). English edition of Montuori's *Socrate*. Ref. 294.

296 More, Paul E. "Socrates." *Shelburne Essays. Sixth Series. Studies of Religious Dualism*. New York: Phaeton Press, 1967, pp. 242-273.

Originally published in 1898 (New York: Houghton, Mifflin & Co.). Views the testimonies of Xenophon and Plato as being in basic agreement concerning the externalities of Socrates' character and biography, and as thoroughly reliable. Regards Plato's account, however, as the true source of information concerning Socrates' philosophical stance, and maintains that the philosophy of Plato is a faithful extension of Socratic ideas. Recounts the details of Socrates' biography, and comments on his relationship with women such as Xanthippe, Myrto, Aspasia, and Diotima (who is assumed to have been a historical character).

297 More, Paul E. "Socrates the Man." *The State Versus Socrates: A Case Study in Civic Freedom*. Edited by John D. Montgomery. Boston: The Beacon Press, 1954, pp. 35-52.

Excerpted from More's "Socrates." Ref. 296.

298 Moreau, J. "Socrate, son milieu, son actualité." *Bulletin de l'Association Guillaume Budé*, 1 (1951), pp. 19-38.

Argues that the real originality of Socrates consists in the fact that he understood well the moral sources of the social and political decadence of his time. Comments on his conviction that all moral disorder is itself a product of the absence of true self-knowledge. Concludes with observations concerning the everlasting aspects of Socrates' legacy: his contempt for opinions based merely on tradition and authority, his inflexible sense of justice, and his willingness to sacrifice his own life for the sake of his convictions.

299 Moszkowski, Alexander. *Sokrates der Idiot; eine respektlose Studie*. Berlin: Eysler & Co., 1917.

Collects a variety of pieces which portray aspects of Socrates who is presented in a less than complimentary fashion. Deals in the first section with the Pythia's pronouncement about Socrates' wisdom, and in the other sections, creates various dialogues in which he speaks with characters such as Polus, Crito, and Cebes.

300 Murray, Gilbert. "The Message of Socrates." *Classics in Sociology*. Edited by Donald MacRae. Port Washington, N.Y.: Kennikat Press, 1971, pp. 105-110.

Originally published in 1960. Raises questions about the meaning of 'progress' (as this is conceived in modern times), in the context of the presence and contributions of Socrates. Notes that for him, the true idea of progress is unrelated to material, scientific, or technological changes, but can only be actualized in the improvement of human existence in its spiritual, intellectual, and ethical dimensions. Emphasizes Socrates' attempt to teach people the art of clarifying their ideas and their language, and comments on the intentional misuse of words by the political system. Stresses the urgency of applying the Socratic method to counterbalance the abuse of language.

301 Muzzey, David Saville. "Socrates, the Champion of Intellectual Piety." *Spiritual Heroes: A Study of Some of the World's Prophets.* New York: Doubleday, Page & Co., 1902, pp. 65-97.

Constitutes a general biographical essay in which an account is given of Socrates' major philosophical contributions, with special attention paid to what is called his rationalistic religiosity.

302 Navia, Luis E. "A Certain Man Named Socrates." *An Invitation to Philosophy* by Nicholas Capaldi, Eugene Kelly, and Luis E. Navia. Buffalo: Prometheus Books, 1981, pp. 35-56.

Discusses the transformation of Greek thought towards subjectivism brought about by Socrates and the Sophists. Explains the emergence and significance of the Sophists, and emphasizes their skepticism. Recounts the generally accepted facts of Socrates' life, and deals with the major ideas associated with his philosophy: subjectivity, intellectual optimism and moral confidence, the Socratic method, the confession of ignorance, and individualism.

303 Navia, Luis E. "The Philosophical Impulse: The Case of Socrates." *The Fundamental Questions.* Edited by Eugene Kelly and Luis E. Navia. Dubuque, Iowa: Kendall/Hunt, 1985, pp. 1-51.

Uses Socrates and his thought as a starting point for the study of philosophy. Reproduces the *Apology* and Book 1 of the *Republic*, as well as excerpts from the *Phaedrus*, the *Theaetetus*, the *Phaedo*, and the *Memorabilia*. Regards Socrates as a paradigm of the philosophical impulse. Reviews the outlines of his biography. Discusses the Socratic problem and the sources of information. Examines Socrates' choice of the spoken word, and gives an account of his intellectual midwifery. Reviews the historical circumstances of his trial, and discusses his concept of philosophy as a systematic search for self-enlightenment.

304 Navia, Luis E. *Socrates: The Man and His Philosophy*. Lanham, Md.: University Press of America, 1985.

Undertakes a general and comprehensive study of the life, character, and philosophy of Socrates. Reviews in separate chapters the testimonies of Aristophanes, Xenophon, and Plato. Outlines in an introductory chapter the social and political condition of Athens in Socrates' time, and devotes the two concluding chapters to the examination of his philosophical contributions. Argues that the various representations of Socrates which emerge from the primary sources do disclose a portrait that is basically consistent and unified, in spite of their divergent orientations. Examines the testimony of Aristotle, and quotes all the Aristotelian references to Socrates. Contains a bibliography of over 360 unannotated entries.

305 Nebel, Gerhard. *Sokrates*. Stuttgart: Ernst Klett Verlag, 1969.

Provides a general exposition of the life and philosophy of Socrates. Includes chapters on Hegel's interpretation of Socrates' thought, on Nietzsche's assessment of the value of the Socratic presence, and on Socrates' irony. Speaks of Socrates as a man of extraordinary spiritual strength, for whom death was ultimately an act of pride. Regards his God as a manifestation of the *deus philosophorum* who communicated with him through the medium of a spiritual voice or sign.

306 Neumann, Harry. "Review of *The Philosophy of Socrates* by Norman Gulley." *The Journal of the History of Philosophy*, 8 (1970), pp. 335-338.

Raises questions about the relationship between the Platonic Socrates and Gulley's understanding of Socrates, specifically with respect to the nature of the soul and its moral freedom. Disagrees with Gulley's premise that the Socratic *elenchus* is primarily a link in the history of philosophical methods. Argues that the *elenchus* implies the real conversion of the soul, and, as such, it remains the "heart and soul" of philosophy. Ref. 234.

307 Nohl, H. *Sokrates und die Ethik*. Leipzig, 1904.

Discusses the general tenets and implications of the ethical ideas associated with Socrates, in particular his contention that knowledge and virtue are essentially the same, and that ignorance is the necessary condition of evil. Comments on the relationship of Socrates' ethical ideas and the medical views and practices of the late fifth century B.C.

308 O'Brien, Michael J. *The Socratic Paradoxes and the Greek Mind.* Chapel Hill, N.C.: The University of North Carolina Press, 1967.

Examines the import and significance of the paradoxes apparently entailed in the Socratic-Platonic convictions that no one chooses evil willingly and knowingly, and that evil is always the result of ignorance. Sets those convictions within the cultural world of ancient Greece, specifically against the background of Greek intellectualism. Raises the question, "To what, apart from the private genius of Socrates and Plato, can we attribute the ethical paradoxes?" Devotes the greater part of its effort to the analysis of the dialogues, mainly the early dialogues. Argues in its final assessment that Plato's ethical philosophy ultimately embodies a unified set of doctrines composed of two seemingly discordant elements: the Socratic paradoxes (directly inherited from Socrates' intellectualism) and the doctrine of the partition of the soul. Concludes that those elements are not logically incompatible, but constitute a developmental structure in which the Platonic concept of *eros* forms a connecting bridge. Notes that with respect to the Socratic problem, we must recognize the biographical aspects of many of Plato's dialogues, but insists that the Burnet-Taylor hypothesis should be rejected, since it is clear that Plato did not bind himself to biographical or doctrinal accuracy in his portrayal of Socrates.

309 Ortega, Teófilo. *Sócrates.* Barcelona: Araluce, Editor, 1935.

Creates a variety of scenes and dramatic sequences for the purpose of illustrating the character and philosophy of Socrates.

310 Osborn, E. B. *Socrates and His Friends.* London: Hodder & Sloughton, n.d.

Describes the historical background of Socrates' time, and gives an account of Athens in the fifth century B.C. Comments on Socrates' reaction, if he were able to return to his birthplace in the twentieth century. Devotes one chapter to the three images of Socrates created by Aristophanes, Xenophon, and Plato, and one chapter to his philosophical contributions (which are referred to as his 'spiritual discoveries'). Contains two chapters on Socrates' trial and execution, and an epilogue which discusses his relevance to our own contemporary political world.

311 Ozmon, Howard. "Socrates." *Twelve Great Philosophers*. Mankato, Minn.: Oddo Publishing, 1968, pp. 5-7.

Presents a brief biographical sketch of Socrates, intended primarily for children and young readers. Describes the main events of his life and his major ideas. Contains a glossary for the entire volume. Illustrations by Rodney Furan.

312 Palmer, L. M. "Review of *Socratic Humanism* by Laszlo Versényi." *The Journal of the History of Philosophy*, 7 (1969), pp. 79-81.

Identifies the aim of *Socratic Humanism* as an attempt to recapture with purity the Socratic doctrine, and as an endeavor to discover what exactly Socrates was and why so many thinkers have called themselves Socratic. Discusses the author's injunction that all hypotheses about Socrates must conform to the Aristotelian testimony. Considers the work to be fresh and novel, while still presenting a traditional Socratic portrait. Ref. 346.

313 Petander, Karl. *Sokrates, personlighetstankens fr*ö*kunnare* [*Socrates, a Prophet of the Idea of Personality*]. Stockholm: Natur och Kultur, 1950.

In Swedish. Develops a general exposition of the life and philosophy of Socrates. Regards him primarily as a practical moral philosopher. Rejects the idea that the Platonic representation of Socrates can be viewed as historically accurate.

314 Phelps, William F. *Socrates.* New York: Phillips & Hunt, 1879.

School textbook, part of the Chautauqua Textbook Series. Gives a general account of Socrates' life and philosophy. Contains brief English translations of excerpts from the *Meno* and the *Alcibiades I.*

315 Phillipson, Coleman. *The Trial of Socrates.* London: Stevens & Sons, 1928.

Ref. 1094.

316 Phillipson, R. "Sokrates. Eine Gedenkfeier." *Humanistisches Gymnasium*, 1932, pp. 2-14.

Commemorates the 24th centenary of Socrates' birth. Reviews the major themes of his philosophy, and stresses the lasting influence of his method and his place of importance as a thinker of innovative ideas in ethics and scientific thought.

317 Piat, C. *Socrate.* Paris: Collection Les grandes Philosophes, 1900.

Attempts to create a comprehensive representation of Socrates' life and thought by integrating in an eclectic fashion the testimonies of Plato, Xenophon, and Aristotle.

318 Pöhlmann, Robert von. *Sokrates und sein Volk.* Leipzig: R. Oldenbourg, 1899.

Examines the biography and ideology of Socrates within the social and political background of the Athenian world of the late fifth century B.C.

319 Pratt, James Bisset. "On the Philosophy of Socrates." *The Open Court*, 21 (1907), pp. 513-522.

Provides a brief discussion on the parameters of the Socratic problem. Presents a schematic analysis of the major philosophical ideas that can be attributed to Socrates according to (1) Aristotle, (2) Plato, and (3)

Xenophon. Includes photographs of a bust of Socrates, of his prison, and of the Acropolis.

320 Reinaga, Fausto. *Sócrates* y *yo*. La Paz: Ediciones Communidad Amaútica Mundial, 1983.

Presents a series of reflections in which the author establishes a sharp contrast between Socrates' truth and his own: the former constitutes the origin of the intellectual and political oppression with which European culture has enslaved the rest of the world, whereas the latter represents a call to freedom for the enslaved and oppressed all over the world. Describes 'the Socratic Imperative' which has dominated the affairs of the white race in these terms: *Miente* y *mata* ("Lie and kill").

321 Riezu, Jorge. "Vigencia y actualidad de Sócrates." *Estudios Filósoficos*, 20 (1971), pp. 113-130.

Reviews the significance and relevance of Socrates in the contemporary philosophical world, and stresses the quasi-mystical character of his life and death, and the non-temporal and universal texture of his doctrines. Interprets the Socratic dialogue as a rigorous method for the quest for truth. Views the Socratic questioning as the genuine kernel of Socrates' philosophy.

322 Ritter, Constantin. *Sokrates*. Tübingen: H. Laupp, 1931.

Brief analysis (87 pp.) of all the major aspects and themes associated with Socrates. Contains several appendices which deal with the sources.

323 Robin, Léon. "Socrate." *La pensée grecque et les origines de l'esprit scientifique*. Paris: La Renaissance du Livre, 1923, pp. 178-193.

Regards Socrates as the most important figure in the history of Greek philosophy, but notes that our information about him is exceedingly deficient, and that the sources of testimony are greatly in disagreement. Views Aristotle's testimony as most significant. Compares the philosophical revolution brought about by Socrates with that associated with Descartes.

324 Robin, Léon. "Socrates." *Greek Thought and the Origins of the Scientific Spirit*. Translated by M. R. Dobie. New York: Russell & Russell, 1967, pp. 148-160.

English translation of Robin's "Socrate." Ref. 323.

325 Romundt, Heinrich. *Die Vollendung des Sokrates*. Berlin, 1885.

Examines the life and philosophy of Socrates, and stresses the high degree of integration between his habits and character on the one hand, and his ideological convictions on the other.

326 Rotta, Paolo. *Socrate*. Brescia: Editrice La Scuola, 1943.

Discusses the life of Socrates under three headings: the sources, his times and culture, and the details of his life. Gives a general account of his philosophy, and examines the relationship between him and the Sophists.

327 Santas, Gerasimos X. *Socrates: Philosophy in Plato's Early Dialogues*. Boston: Routledge & Kegan Paul, 1982.

Discusses three major aspects of the Socrates of Plato's early dialogues: the philosopher and the citizen, the Socratic method, and Socrates' ethical convictions. Makes references to the testimonies of Aristophanes and Xenophon (in Chapter 1), but devotes most of its attention to the testimony of Plato. Offers the view that it is only this latter testimony that should be regarded as historically and philosophically significant. Maintains that the alleged contradiction between Socrates' stance in the *Apology* and the views he expresses in the *Crito* is more apparent than real, although agrees with Grote's assessment that these two Platonic works are ultimately very one-sided. Examines the nature and scope of the Socratic method (Socrates' questions and assumptions, and his various definitions and arguments). Reviews in detail the meaning and implications of Socrates' doctrine about the relationship between knowledge and virtue. Ref. 1318.

328 Sauvage, Micheline. *Socrate et la conscience de l'homme*. Paris: Editions du Seuil, 1957.

Contains a great number of photographs and illustrations of interest for Socratic scholarship. Deals with three aspects of Socrates: his life and the Athenian world of the late fifth century B.C.; the pedagogical activities of Socrates; and the development of the Socratic myth. Illustrates various pictorial representations of Socrates throughout the ages. Provides a collection of texts from the primary and secondary sources, and from modern times. Includes excerpts from the writings of Aristophanes, Plato, Xenophon, Saint Augustine, Clement of Alexandria, Montaigne, Descartes, Kierkegaard, Valéry, Merleau-Ponty, F. M. Cornford, and others.

329 Sauvage, Micheline. *Socrates and the Conscience of Man.* Translated by Patrick Herpburne-Scott. New York: Harper & Brothers, 1960.

English translation of Sauvage's *Socrate.* Ref. 328.

330 Sauvage, Micheline. *Sócrates y la conciencia del hombre.* Translated by I. G. de Ramales. Madrid: Editorial Aguilar, 1958.

Spanish translation of Sauvage's *Socrate.* Ref. 328.

331 Schleiermacher, F. D. E. "Uber den Werth des Sokrates als Philosophen." *Abhandlung der philosophischen Klasse der Königlich Preussichen Akademie der Wissenschaft aus den Jahren 1814-1815*, 1818, pp. 51-68.

Reprinted in Schleiermacher's *Sämtliche Werke* (Berlin, 1834-1864, Vol. 2, pp. 287-300). Examines the issue of the precise meaning of Socrates' confession of ignorance, against the background furnished by his commitment to act as a servant of the Delphic god. Argues that in his confession of ignorance, Socrates could not have expressed a genuine lack of knowledge, and that beneath his irony there must have lurked an absolute and positive state of knowledge. Regards Socrates as the true founder of dialectic philosophy. Comments on the relationship between Socrates and Diogenes of Sinope, and views the latter as a caricature of the former, although recognizes a genuine common element between them, specifically, their independence from sensual pleasure. Attaches historical significance to Plato's *Apology*. Insists that for an adequate understanding of Plato's philosophy, it is essential to begin with an examination of Socrates. Introduces a criterion for assessing the relative historical value of Xenophon's and Plato's testimonies: we must ask what Socrates may have been *besides* what Xenophon reports of him without contradicting the traits of character and principles of life which he definitely sets up as Socratic, and what Socrates must have been to have given Plato the occasion and the right to represent him as he does in his dialogues. Speaks of Socrates' philosophy as the true awakening of the idea of knowledge.

332 Schremf, C. *Sokrates, seine Persönlichkeit und seine Glaube.* Stuttgart: F. Frommann, 1927.

Regards the philosophy of Socrates, not as a completed and perfected system of ideas, but as a collection of seminal thoughts and intuitions, and as a starting point, expressed in terms of fragmented utterances. Notes that Socrates' thought rests on the strength of his extraordinary and complex personality.

333 Sears, E. I. "Socrates and His Philosophy." *The National Quarterly*, 13 (1866), pp. 1-33.

Gives a general account of Socrates' life and character. Provides a summary statement of his philosophical ideas.

334 Silverberg, Robert. *Sócrates.* México: Editorial Diana, 1967.

Spanish translation of Silverberg's *Socrates.* Ref. 335.

335 Silverberg, Robert. *Socrates.* New York: G. P. Putnam's Sons, 1965.

Offers a general exposition of Socrates' life and philosophy. Attaches special significance to his devotion and commitment to open and honest conversation.

336 Spitzer, Doreen C. *"Know Thyself": A Leader's Guide to the Study of Socrates.* Boston: The Beacon Press, 1954.

Pamphlet (46 pp.). Contains a section entitled "Foreground

and Background" which discusses the historical context of Socrates and the sources of information. Gives a schematic presentation of the major biographical and ideological aspects of Socrates.

337 Strong, Leonard A. *The Man Who Asked Questions: The Story of Socrates.* London: Thomas Nelson & Sons, 1934.

Gives a general exposition of Socrates' life and philosophy. Emphasizes the openness of his philosophical method and stance, and stresses the absence of dogmatism in his approach to the search for truth.

338 Thomas, Norman. "Socrates." *Great Dissenters.* New York: W. W. Norton & Co., 1961, pp. 19-48.

Devotes Chapter 2 to a study of Socrates. Views him as a paradigm of dissent and individualism, especially in the final moments of his life. Gives a general account of the political and social conditions in which he lived, and summarizes the main aspects of his life and philosophy. Quotes at length from the *Apology*, the *Crito*, and the *Phaedo.* Other figures discussed in the book are Galileo, Thomas Payne, Wendell Phillips, and Gandhi.

339 Tofallis, Kypros. *Socrates: Man and Philosopher.* London: The Greek Institute, 1978.

Originally published in 1967. Gives a brief exposition (53 pp.) of Socrates' biography and philosophy.

340 Toman, Josef. *Sokrates.* Prague: Ceskoslovensky Spisovatel, 1975.

In Czech. Presents a general biographical and philosophical exposition of Socrates. Includes a glossary of names and places.

341 Tovar, Antonio. *Socrate. Sa vie et son temps.* Translated by H. E. de Medico. Paris: Payot, 1954.

French translation of Tovar's *Vida de Sócrates.* Ref. 342.

342 Tovar, Antonio. *Vida de Sócrates.* Madrid: Revista de Occidente, 1947.

Gives a detailed account of the sources of information concerning the life and philosophy of Socrates, and assumes an eclectic position towards the Socratic problem. Reconstructs the biography of Socrates from a variety of sources, and provides a summary of the principal philosophical themes associated with him.

343 Tsanoff, Radoslav. *The Great Philosophers.* New York: Harper & Row, 1964.

Deals with Socrates in Chapter 1 ("The Philosophers of Antiquity," pp. 28-48). Introduces the subject with an exploration of the Sophistical movement, and identifies the denial of the possibility of real knowledge as the main element of this movement. Recounts the major aspects of the life and character of Socrates, and outlines the Socratic problem as this has been treated by various historians and philosophers. Concludes with a discussion of the method and teachings of Socrates, and draws attention to the ways in which he was able to transcend the epistemological and ethical impasse created by skepticism of the Sophists. Adds a brief account of the minor Socratics.

344 Turlington, Bayly. *Socrates: The Father of Western Philosophy.* New York: Franklin Watts, 1969.

Gives a general account of Socrates' life and philosophy. Speaks of him as a major benefactor to the Western world. Contains a complete English translation of the *Apology*. Provides a chronological table.

345 van Buskirk, William R. "Socrates." *The Saviors of Mankind.* Freeport, N.Y.: Books for Libraries Press, 1971, pp. 291-338.

Originally published in 1929. Criticizes those studies of Socrates which fail to provide enough background information about him and which do not allow us to come to know him as a man. Considers him a practised 'soldier' whose mature life coincided with the death struggle of his city. Presents some historical background, including the central role of Aspasia in Athenian politics.

346 Versényi, Laszo. *Socratic Humanism*. Westport, Conn.: Greenwood Press, 1963.

Distinguishes the Socrates of the early dialogues (*e.g.*, the *Apology*) from the Socrates of the later dialogues (*e.g.*, the *Symposium*), and affirms that it is the former who represents Socratic humanism. Identifies as elements of this humanism the focusing of thought on questions which directly concern humankind, and the endeavor to resolve such questions without transcending that which is human. Attempts to present Socrates' philosophy independently of the interpretations of the Socratics. Begins with a discussion of the Sophistical movement, and shows how it was influential in directing philosophy away from natural philosophy towards human issues. Regards the Sophistical movement as a preparation for Socrates' thought. Considers the knowledge of oneself, more than the knowledge of Socrates' own ideas, to be the ultimate end of the Socratic maieutics. Ref. 312.

347 Versfeld, Marthinus. *The Socratic Spirit*. Cape Town: University of Cape Town Press, 1971.

Inaugural professorial lecture delivered on May 12, 1971, at the University of Cape Town. Identifies the Socratic spirit as a commitment to dialogue, liberty, and perfect intellectual honesty.

348 Vircillo, Domenico. *Socrate e la filosofia*. Soveria Mannelli: Rubbettino Editore, 1883 (2 vols.).

Presents a general discussion of the philosophy of Socrates, and includes chapters on themes such as the meaning of Socrates' trial, the roots of his ideas, and his concepts of love and dialectics. Includes an appendix and a bibliography specifically relevant to the Socratic problem.

349 Vlastos, Gregory. "The Paradox of Socrates." *The Philosophy of Socrates: A Collection of Critical Essays*. Edited by Gregory Vlastos. Notre Dame, Ind.: University of Notre Dame Press, 1980, pp. 1-21.

Published in *Queen's Quarterly*, 64 (1958), pp. 496-516. Serves as the introduction to Vlastos' anthology. Brings to light the paradoxical character of Socrates' life and philosophy, and emphasizes the intensive and dynamic nature of his presence. Views the figure of Socrates revealed by Plato as the truly historical and philosophically significant representation of him, and downgrades the value of Xenophon's testimony as a simplistic characterization of limited philosophical import. Regards the testimonies of Plato and Xenophon as standing in irreconcilable disagreement. Subjects to critical analysis several ideas associated with the Platonic Socrates in an attempt to develop a solution to the Socratic paradox. Speaks of the Socratic method as one of the great achievements of humanity, and reiterates the significance of Socrates' conviction that an unexamined life is not worth living.

350 Vlastos, Gregory, editor. *The Philosophy of Socrates: A Collection of Critical Essays*. Notre Dame, Ind.: University of Notre Dame Press, 1980.

Originally published in 1971 (Doubleday). Includes essays by Gregory Vlastos (Ref. 349), A. R. Lacey (Ref. 388), Kenneth J. Dover (Ref. 444a), Richard Robinson (Ref. 986), George Nakhnikian (Ref. 966), S. Marc Cohen (Ref. 1348), Gerasimos X. Santas (Ref. 1488), M. F. Burnyeat (Ref. 1337), James J. Walsh (Ref. 1035), A. D. Woozley (Ref. 1303a), and Reginald E. Allen (Ref. 862). Includes a bibliography and an *index locorum*.

351 Warner, Rex. "Socrates." *The Greek Philosophers*. New York: New American Library, 1958, pp. 49-71.

Reviews the major philosophical contributions of Socrates, as these played an important role within the development of Greek philosophy in general. Regards his philosophical stance as a clear example of intellectualism. Concludes with extended quotations from the *Gorgias*.

352 Wiggers, Gustav F. *A Life of Socrates*. London: Taylor & Walton, 1840.

Recounts the major biographical and ideological aspects of Socrates, and stresses his predicament vis-à-vis the Athenian world: an exceptional and excellent individual who was compelled to live amid a climate of mediocrity, frivolity, and incompetence. Views Socrates' trial as the result of his anti-democratic convictions and tendencies, but interprets his position not as a manifestation of a devotion towards the oligarchical party of his time, but as a commitment to a system of aristocratic government in which only the best among the citizens will hold political power.

353 Wiggers, Gustav F. "The Critic of Incompetence." *The State Versus Socrates: A Case Study in Civic Freedom.* Edited by John D. Montgomery. Boston: The Beacon Press, 1954, pp. 154-159.

Excerpted from Wiggers' *A Life of Socrates* (pp. lxxi-lxxxix). Ref. 352.

354 Wilson, H. "Socrates and His Philosophy." *The Southern Literary Messenger*, 29 (1859), pp. 14-29.

Gives a general account of the life and philosophy of Socrates.

355 Wilson, Pearl C. *The Living Socrates.* Owings Mills, Md.: Stemmer House, 1975.

Presented as a contribution to the literature of teaching. Quotes liberally from the dialogues of Plato in order to shed light on the character and personality of Socrates. Notes that the Socratic method of teaching undermined the Greek system of education which relied heavily on the memorization of poetic works.

356 Winspear, Alban D. and Silverberg, Thomas. *Who Was Socrates?* New York: The Cordon Company, 1939.

Endeavors to explain the personality and philosophy of Socrates from the point of view of historical materialism. Views Socrates as the product of economic, political, and social circumstances. Speaks of the young Socrates as a democratic, radical, skeptic, and materialistic free artisan, who in time and as the result of material prosperity, became an ally of the oligarchical conservatives. Interprets the ultimate mission of Socrates as the unfolding of an oligarchical conspiracy of an elitist ideology against the ordinary Athenian masses, and deems his freedom of opinion as a disguised absence of moral principles. Attempts to resolve the apparent contradiction between the judgments of those who praise Socrates and those who condemn him.

357 Wolff, Francis. *Socrate*. Paris: Presses Universitaires de France, 1985.

Gives a general account of the life and philosophy of Socrates, and examines the various sources of information about him. Distinguishes the historical Socrates from the Socratism developed by the different schools and philosophical movements that trace back their origins to him.

358 Woody, Thomas. "In Utopia." *Life and Education in Early Societies*. New York: Macmillan, 1949, pp. 429-432.

Discusses the life, philosophy, and impact of Socrates in the Athens of the late fifth century B.C. Emphasizes his conviction that knowledge leads necessarily to virtue, and his stress on the importance of physical education, including his belief in the urgency of maintaining an adequate diet.

359 Zeller, Eduard. *Socrates and the Socratic Schools*. Translated by Oswald J. Reichel. New York: Russell & Russell, 1962.

Originally published in London in 1877 (Longmans, Green & Company). English translation of Zeller's *Sokrates und die Sokratiker*. Ref. 360.

360 Zeller, Eduard. *Sokrates und die Sokratiker*. Leipzig, 1889.

Contains three general divisions: (1) the state of culture of Greece in the fifth century B.C.; (2) Socrates; and (3) the minor Socratics. Deals in Part 1 with two interrelated themes, namely, the intellectual development of Greece and the progress of Greek philosophy during Socrates' time. Discusses in Part 3 the contributions of Xenophon, Aeschines, the Megarian and the Elean-Eretrian schools, the Cynics, and the Cyrenaics. Devotes Part 2 to an exhaustive examination of Socrates, and addresses itself to the following main subjects: the life and character of Socrates; the sources and characteristics of his philosophy; his philosophical method; the substance of his teaching (which is seen as being exclusively concerned with ethics); his ideas of God, nature, and man; his relationship with Plato and the Sophists; and the details of his trial and execution. Views Socrates' philosophy as being intimately related to his life and character, and regards his life as a paradigm of human excellence. Argues that we must assume *a priori* that there must have been more in Socrates than we can gather from the testimony of Xenophon, and that we must appeal to Plato for an adequate appreciation of Socratic thought. Accepts the canon proposed by Schleiermacher, that is, a view that regards the testimonies of Plato and Xenophon as being fundamentally different, yet complementary.

361 Zeller, Eduard. "The Victim of His Times." *The State Versus Socrates: A Case Study in Civic Freedom.* Edited by John D. Montgomery. Boston: The Beacon Press, 1954, pp. 191-193.

Excerpted from Zeller's *Socrates and the Socratic Schools.* Regards Socrates' trial as a political anachronism in which his accusers sought to restore certain principles and ideas which they had lost the right to defend. Views the utter state of moral and political decadence of Socrates' time as a permeating atmosphere which he endeavored to dissipate, but for which the accusers condemned him: in condemning him, therefore, they were condemning themselves. Ref. 360.

362 Zuccante, Guiseppe. *Socrate. Fonti. Ambiente. Vita. Dottrina.* Milan, 1909.

Discusses the sources of information about Socrates, his social and political background, the details of his life, and the major elements of his philosophy. Maintains that the fundamental aim of Socrates' mission was to bring about a profound transformation into the realm of ethics. Argues that the testimony of Aristotle is especially significant for the task of constructing a reliable portrait of Socrates' philosophy on the basis of the testimonies of Plato and Xenophon.

## THE SOCRATIC PROBLEM - GENERAL WORKS

Annotated in this section are works in which the Socratic problem is discussed in a general and comprehensive way, and in which there is an attempt to explore the significance and value of several among the primary sources. Included, too, are unannotated references to works in which emphasis is made on one of the primary sources, but in which there are substantive comments on the Socratic problem in general; the full annotations of these specific studies will be found in subsequent sections.

363 Amory, F. "Socrates: The Legend." *Classica et Mediaevalia*, 35 (1984), pp. 19-56.

Notes that Socrates is often regarded as a mediating influence in the context of many philosophical and religious disputes, and that this role assigned to him is a consequence of his ironical stance vis-à-vis a great variety of intellectual issues. Observes, however, that as soon as the Socratic ironical element is set aside, Socrates becomes either an impostor (as in the *Clouds*) or an extraordinary and earnest philosopher (as in the Platonic dialogues). Suggests that there may be a third way of interpreting him, namely, the way proposed by Aristoxenus: Socrates becomes therein an irascible and passionate man. Concludes that this third way may be closer to the actual historical Socrates. Points out the fact that since medieval times, Socrates has been viewed mostly as a martyr of philosophical truth, and that his philosophical message has been reduced to the Apollonian "Know thyself" or simply to a call to self-knowledge.

364 Boeck, A. "De Socratis rerum physicarum studio." *Kleine Schriften*. Berlin, 1874 (4 vols.), Vol. 4, pp. 430-436.

Ref. 727.

365 Capizzi, Antonio. "Il problema socratico." *Sophia*, 25 (1957), pp. 199-207.

Outlines the major issues related to the Socratic problem. Comments on V. de Magalhães-Vilhena's two main works on

Socrates and the Socratic problem. Provides a bibliography of related contributions, specifically of books and articles on Socrates from 1940 to 1957. Ref. 391, 641.

366 Caprariis, V. de. "Per una interpretazione di Socrate." *La Parola del Passato*, 2 (1947), pp. 168-188.

Argues that an adequate reconstruction of the character and personality of Socrates is possible only through a critical appeal to all the primary and secondary sources, and through the contextual study of the circumstances in which his ideas and life were unfolded.

367 Chroust, Anton-Hermann. "Socrates: A Source Problem." *The New Scholasticism*, 19 (1945), pp. 52ff.

Ref. 586.

368 Chroust, Anton-Hermann. *Socrates: Man and Myth. The Two Socratic Apologies of Xenophon.* Notre Dame, Ind.: University of Notre Dame Press, 1957.

Ref. 511.

369 Diès, Auguste. "Socrate." *Autour de Platon.* Paris: Gabriel Beauchesne, 1927 (2 vols.), Vol. 1, pp. 127-243.

Ref. 594.

370 Dubbs, Homer H. "The Socratic Problem." *The Philosophical Review*, 36 (1927), pp. 287-306.

Ref. 595.

371 Dupréel, Eugène. *La légende socratique et les sources de Platon.* Brussels: Robert Sand, 1922.

Assumes a radically skeptical position towards the solution of the Socratic problem and the reconstruction of the historical Socrates. Maintains that the entire *corpus* of Socratic literature (primary and secondary) ultimately embodies a monumental romantic fiction, from which it is no longer possible to disentangle any definite biographical or ideological facts. Claims, too, that even the common allegation that Socrates left no writings is also nothing but another piece of the Socratic legend. Speaks of the character of Socrates as a *prête-nom* of a romantic legend.

372 Dupréel, Eugène. "Socrate et l'histoire de la philosophie grecque." *Revue de l'Université de Bruxelles*, 26 (1920), pp. 42-63.

Advances clearly and emphatically the theme developed in Dupréel's *La légende socratique et les sources de Platon*. Reiterates the contention that Socrates is so inextricably intertwined with a collection of legends, that it is impossible to separate the historical man from the romantic figure created in literature and philosophy.

373 Fischer, Josef L. *Sokrates nelegendární* [*Socrates the Non-legendary*]. Prague: Státní Pedagogicke Nakladatelsví, 1965.

Attempts to reconstruct the real 'historical' Socrates. Argues that the disagreements found among the major sources (primary and secondary) are often exaggerated by scholars, and that if we take into account the idiosyncratic peculiarities of the various Socratic witnesses, an accurate picture of the historical Socrates can be developed. Attaches importance to the testimony of Aristoxenus which has stood the proof of its veracity. Contains an English summary of the principal ideas advanced in the original Czech text.

374 Fite, Warner. "Socrates the Martyr." *The Platonic Legend*. New York: Charles Scribner's Sons, 1934, pp. 97-112.

Examines the sources of information about Socrates (mainly Plato and Xenophon), and delves into the question of whether Socrates can be truly viewed as a martyr of free speech. Concludes that only the portrayal of Socrates which emerges from the Platonic *Apology* can give us any justification for such a conception of him. Notes that historically the figure of Socrates is as blurry as that of Jesus.

375 Fresco, M. F. *Socrates. Zijn Wijsgerige betekenis* [*Socrates.*

*His Philosophical Meaning*]. Assen, Holland: Van Gorcum, 1983.

Discusses Socrates from the wider perspective of the issue of the interpretation of major historical figures. Approaches the case of Socrates by raising questions concerning the significance of *Verstehen* and hermeneutical understanding. Examines the main sources of information concerning Socrates: Aristophanes, Euripides, Phaedo, Euclides, Plato, Aristotle, and others. Devotes its final section to an examination of the meaning of Socrates' philosophy.

376 Friere, Antonio. "Socrates no pensamento Grego." *Revista Portuguesa de Filosofia*, 37 (1981), pp. 133-177.

Examines the portraits of Socrates which emerge from the testimonies of Plato, Xenophon, Aristophanes, and Aristotle, and concludes that it is in Plato that we can surely find the most reliable representation. Regards Xenophon's testimony as only complementary, and that of Aristophanes as definitely misguiding. Comments at length on the phenomenon of the Socratic voice or sign, and discusses the major philosophical currents that preceded and succeeded Socrates among the Greeks.

377 Garnier, Jean-Jacques. "Premier mémoire sur Platon. Caractère de la philosophie socratique." *Mémoires de l'Académie Royale des Inscriptions et Belles Lettres*, 23 (1768), pp. 137-163.

Establishes a comparison between Plato and Xenophon as Socratic witnesses, and reaches the general conclusion that it is Plato who gives us a real and human portrait of Socrates. Speaks of Xenophon's testimony as simplistic and monotonous. Appears to anticipate Schleiermacher's ideas with respect to a possible solution to the Socratic problem.

378 Gigon, Olof. "Review of Magalhães-Vilhena, *Le problème de Socrate*." *Gnomon*, 27 (1955), pp. 259-266.

Argues that in spite of the efforts of scholars for over two thousand years, the Socratic problem has not yet been given a proper and strict methodological treatment. Outlines the approach for the development of the proper method, and observes that this involves a critical separation of those sources and texts that are decidedly historical from those whose aim is apologetic, eulogistic, accusatory, or anecdotal. Ref. 391.

379 Gigon, Olof. *Sokrates. Sein Bild in Dichtung und Geschichte.* Bern: A. Francke, 1947.

Generally rejects the historical value of Xenophon and Aristotle as genuine Socratic witnesses, and favors with reservations the Platonic testimony. Insists, however, that most of the Socratic literature is really only a complex of myths and legends from which it has not been possible to derive a body of definite historical material. Maintains that the paucity and scarcity of the extant fragments of the works of the Socratics (other than Plato and Xenophon) should not lead us directly to question their reliability.

380 Gomperz, Heinrich. "Die Sokratische Frage als geschichtliche Problem." *Historische Zeitschrift*, 129 (1924), pp. 395-418.

Reviews the nature and scope of the Socratic problem, and explores various possibilities of finding a solution for it. Assumes an eclectic stance towards the issue of the historical Socrates. Defends the authenticity of Xenophon's *Apology*. Maintains that of all the Socratics, it was Antisthenes who was probably closest to Socrates, and who most faithfully inherited the Socratic message.

381 Hackforth, Reginald. "Great Thinkers: Socrates." *Philosophy*, 8 (1933), pp. 259-272.

Dicusses various aspects of the Socratic problem, and notes that Xenophon has often been judged too severely. Attaches great historical value to the Xenophontean testimony, and observes that Plato's devotion to philosophy may have been a hindrance for him as a reliable Socratic witness. Devotes considerable efforts to the elucidation of the main philosophical tenets that can be attributed to Socrates. Notes that the greatness of Socrates consists in his clarity of conceptual understanding of the basic problems of human nature, and in his commitment to communicate to others all his insights.

382 Hackforth, Reginald. "Review of *The Socratic Problem* by A. K. Rogers." *Mind*, 8 (1933), pp. 502-503.

Considers Rogers' work to be a careful, valuable, and temperate investigation. Questions its argument for a mystical interpretation of some of the elements of Socrates' philosophy. Ref. 408.

383 Hadas, Moses and Smith, Morton. "Socrates: A Modern Perspective." *Makers of the Western Tradition: Portraits from History*. Edited by J. Kelley Sowards. New York: St. Martin's Press, 1972 (2 vols.), Vol. 1, pp. 59-69.

Reprinted from Hadas' and Smith's "The Image of Socrates," in *Heroes and Gods*, edited by Ruth Nanda Anshen (1965, Vol. 13). Regards Socrates as the Greek paradigm for aretalogy (*i.e.*, the worship of and reverence for nobility and virtue) -- a paradigm created by Plato as an image that transcends its historical origin, that is, the historical Socrates. Notes that there are no actual historical records on the basis of which we can make definitive statements about Socrates (except perhaps about the year of his death). Views the Socratic legend that ensues mostly from Plato's testimony, as a kind of 'hagiology' whose main purpose is moral edification. Speaks of the Aristophanic caricature of Socrates as a significant corrective to the Platonic idealization.

384 Havelock, Eric A. "The Evidence for the Teaching of Socrates." *Transactions of the American Philological Association*, 65 (1934), pp. 282-295.

Notes that the Socratic dialogues or discourses were not inspired by a desire to portray accurately a historical character, but by a need to express a given moral philosophy. Observes that for this purpose the dialogical literary genre was standard in the early fourth century B.C.

385 Havelock, Eric A. "The Socratic Problem: Some Second Thoughts." *Essays in Ancient Greek Philosophy*, 2 (1983), pp. 147-173.

Explores the Socratic problem, first by presenting various views and arguments, and then by examining the writing styles of ancient writers other than Plato (*e.g.*, apologetic literature, such as the *Apology of Palamedes* by Gorgias). Investigates the change from an oral tradition to a written form of expression, and comments on the effect of this change on the Greek cultural consciousness.

386 Joël, Karl. *Der echte und der xenophontische Sokrates*. Berlin, 1893-1901 (2 vols.).

Regards Socrates as the representative *par excellence* of the rationalistic ideal of his time, and views as his major contribution his commitment to establish ethics on the basis of reason. Devotes considerable attention to the Socratic doctrine concerning the identity of knowledge and virtue. Explains the apparent paradox entailed in this doctrine in terms of the extraordinary strength of Socrates' character. Views the Socratic ethical position as essentially deterministic ("primitively deterministic"), for in it, the will is entirely unfree and thoroughly under the bondage of reason. Accounts for the one-sidedness of the Socratic doctrine by viewing it as a starting moment in the history of the philosophy of mind: "Every beginning is one-sided, and Socrates constitutes the beginning of the *Geistesphilosophie*." Regards the doctrine of the identity of knowledge and virtue as genuinely Socratic, but the doctrine of self-control imputed by Xenophon to Socrates as a reflection of the influence of Antisthenes on Xenophon. Considers most of Xenophon's testimony as a manifestation of Cynic influences (especially in the *Symposium*), not as a biographical or historical source of information about the historical Socrates. Expresses general skepticism concerning the possibility of reconstructing the historical Socrates from the extant sources: both Socratic and anti-Socratic writings were often born out of a desire on the part of their authors to imitate, correct, or refute one another. Argues that the correct understanding of the Socratic discourses compels us to reconsider many of the accepted claims about Socrates. Views the Platonic Socrates as a sublime ideal for Plato, the Xenophontean Socrates as Xenophon's own pedagogical paradigm, and the Socrates of Antisthenes as the Cynic's model for imitation and emulation. Ref. 568.

387 Labriola, Antonio. *Socrate*. Edited by Benedetto Croce. Bari, 1909.

Ref. 261.

388 Lacey, A. R. "Our Knowledge of Socrates." *Socrates: A Collection of Critical Essays.* Edited by Gregory Vlastos. Notre Dame, Ind.: University of Notre Dame Press, 1980, pp. 22-49.

Provides a detailed and documented short review of the sources of historical and philosophical information about Socrates, specifically Xenophon, Plato, Aristophanes, and Aristotle. Reaches the conclusion that just as there may not be a definite and clear road that may lead us directly to the historical Socrates, there is no justification for "throwing up our hands and treating him as a myth." Views the early dialogues of Plato as our most important source, but is unwilling to regard any one specific testimony as absolutely reliable.

389 Levi, Adolfo. "Sul pensiero di Socrate." *Studi di filosofia greca.* Edited by L. Alfieri and M. Untersteiner. Bari, 1950, pp. 217-220.

Accounts for the multiplicity of divergent and often contradictory interpretations of Socrates' personality and philosophy as the result of the diversity and discordant nature of the extant original testimonies.

390 Lundgren, Lars O. *Sokratesbilden. Fran Aristofanes till Nietzsche.* Stockholm: Almquist & Wiksell International, 1978.

Text in Swedish with a brief summary in English. Examines the different ways in which Socrates has been seen in Western literature, from classical times to the end of the nineteenth century. Raises questions such as, How does this author describe Socrates, and what does he think is important about him? Is his attitude positive or negative? Contains chapters on the Socrates of Aristophanes, Plato, and Xenophon; the early Socratic literature; Aristotle and the Fathers of the Church; the Middle Ages and the Renaissance; the seventeenth and the eighteenth centuries; and the nineteenth century, with special emphasis on Schleiermacher and Nietzsche. Provides an annotated bibliography.

391 Magalhães-Vilhena, V. de. *Le problème de Socrate. Le Socrate historique et le Socrate de Platon.* Paris: Presses Universitaires de France, 1952.

Provides a detailed account of the present state of the Socratic problem, and reviews the history of that problem and the very many solutions given to it fron the time of Aristotle to the twentieth century. Devotes individual chapters to the examination of the Platonic, Xenophontean, and Aristotelian portraits of Socrates, and three separate chapters to (1) the discussion of the value of the Aristotelian testimony, (2) the analysis of the Aristotelian references to Socrates, and (3) the review of the sources on which such references could have been based. Devotes one third of the book to the analysis of Socratism and Platonism. Concludes by rejecting the skepticism and despair of those who deny the possibility of reconstructing a reliable image of Socrates, but warns against the temptation of using only one source to the exclusion of all others. Maintains, nevertheless, the primary importance of the Platonic testimony. Observes that each generation evolves its own interpretation of Socrates through a dialectical interaction with preceding interpretations. Contains an appendix on the minor Socratics and an extensive unannotated bibliography of primary, secondary, and modern sources and references to Socrates. Ref. 378.

392 Magalhães-Vilhena, V. de. *Socrate et la lègende platonicienne.* Paris: Presses Universitaires de France, 1952.

Ref. 641.

393 Maier, Heinrich. *Socrate, la sua opera e il suo posto nella storia.* Translated by G. Sanna. Florence: La Nuova Italia, 1943-1944.

Italian translation of Maier's *Sokrates, sein Werk und seine geschichtliche Stellung.* Ref. 394.

394 Maier, Heinrich. *Sokrates, sein Werk und seine geschichtliche Stellung.* Tübingen: J. C. B. Mohr, 1913.

Subjects the Socratic problem and the traditional reconstructions of Socratic philosophy to an exhaustive analysis. Notes that, on the whole, it is impossible to reconstruct with any degree of certainty Socrates' thought: "The historians who have tried to turn Socrates into a 'philosopher' and who have attempted to discover his philosophical doctrine have ignored too easily the fact that he wrote nothing at all" (pp. 294-295). Regards the Platonic dialogues *qua* Socratic testimonies as fictitious specimens of λόγοι σωκρατικοί, but does accord some historical value to some of Plato's writings (*e.g.* the *Apology*, the *Crito*, and Alcibiades' speech in the *Symposium*). Argues that Xenophon's Socratic writings are mostly panegyrical, although it does not reject the historical basis of his association with Socrates. Insists that the Xenophontean testimony makes use of the most diversified fruits of the literature of its day, and is generally (as much as that of Aristotle) valueless from a historical point of view. Concludes that the greatness of Socrates cannot be measured by judging him as a speculative thinker, but as the creator of a new attitude towards life. Calls attention to the parallels between Socrates and Kant.

395 Martin, Gottfried. *Sokrates in Selbstzeugnissen und Bilddokumenten*. Hamburg: Rowohlt, 1967.

Ref. 273.

396 Martin, Victor. "Le problème du Socrate historique." *Revue de Théologie et de Philosophie*, 23 (1933), pp. 217-242.

Reviews various interpretations and solutions of the Socratic problem, and examines the possible common denominators found among the primary sources. Argues that the areas of agreement among them are wider than their disagreements.

397 Montuori, Mario. *De Socrate iuste damnato*. Amsterdam: J. C. Gieben, 1981.

Ref. 398.

398 Montuori, Mario. "The Rise of the Socratic Problem in the Eighteenth Century." *De Socrate iuste damnato*. Amsterdam: J. C. Gieben, 1981, pp. 9-25.

Serves as an introductory essay to Montuori's *De Socrate*

*iuste damnato.* Acknowledges the fact that the Socratic problem became a significant historical issue only after the investigations of Schleiermacher, "because the studies of the age of Illuminism ignored and knew nothing about the world of history." Notes, however, that there was an abundance of important Socratic studies in the seventeenth and eighteenth centuries. Comments at length on Hegel's interpretation of Socrates' presence in the history of ideas, and reviews the development of the understanding of Socrates among eighteenth century scholars.

399 Montuori, Mario. *Socrate. Dal mito alla storia.* Athens, 1967.

Ref. 1090.

400 Mueller, Gustav E. "Another Approach to Socrates." *The International Journal of Ethics*, 43 (1933), pp. 429-439.

Examines the Socratic portrait as it emerges through his relationships with Xenophon, Aristophanes, Plato, Antisthenes, and Aristippus. Concludes that Socrates appeared at a fatal time in the history of Greek culture, a time in which the Athenians were unwilling to accept the truth, and in which Plato's idealism was born.

401 Navia, Luis E. "Outlines of the Socratic Problem." *Socratic Testimonies.* Edited by Luis E. Navia. Lanham, Md.: University Press of America, 1987, pp. 3-41.

Serves as the introduction to *Socratic Testimonies.* Discusses the major roots and causes of the Socratic problem, specifically Socrates' unwillingness to set his ideas into writing, his paradoxical personality, his apparent ideological elusiveness, and the seemingly contradictory and divergent character of the testimonies about him. Rejects the attitude of complete skepticism taken by some scholars, as well as the hypothesis of 'one true Socrates' (*i.e.*, the exaggerated reliance on only one of the primary sources). Maintains that in spite of the differences among the sources, it is possible to construct a reasonably cohesive and comprehensive biographical and ideological image of the historical Socrates, although admits that there are many important aspects of his personality and thought that will probably never be fully clarified. Comments on the bibliographical history of the principal sources. Ref. 150.

402 Pater, Walter. "Plato and Socrates." *Plato and Platonism*. New York: Macmillan, 1908, pp. 66-87.

Highlights the distinctions between the Socrates of Xenophon and the Socrates of Plato, and concludes that the historical Socrates constitutes a paradoxical embodiment of both representations. Speaks of him as the anticipator of the Christian way of life. Notes that his moral and religious reflections had a profound influence on Plato, and that whenever we speak of Plato we are really speaking of the Platonic Socrates.

403 Pfleiderer, E. *Sokrates, Plato und ihre Schüler*. Tübingen: H. Laupp, 1896.

Lengthy monograph (921 pp.) Supports the thesis that it is mostly in Xenophon, not in Plato, that the image of the historical Socrates can be found. Regards the testimony of Plato as an expression of his own ideas and not as an account of Socrates' thought. Interprets the Socratic phenomenon of the divine voice or sign in terms that confine it to a strictly rational and social dimension.

404 Pöhlmann, Robert von. "Das Sokratesproblem." *Aus Altertum und Gegenwart*. Munich, 1911, pp. 1-117.

Assumes a thoroughly skeptical stance towards any attempt to reconstruct the personality and philosophy of the historical Socrates. Views the primary and secondary testimonies as mixtures of historical and fictional elements, from which a body of solid facts cannot be retrieved. Regards the association of Alcibiades with Socrates mostly as a fictional creation of Plato, and is skeptical about the historical value of the *Apology*. Draws attention to the religious and mystical traits attributed to Socrates and to his reported attachment to the civic aspects of religion.

405 Randall, John Herman. "The Historical and the Platonic Socrates." *Plato: Dramatist of the Life of Reason*. New York: Columbia University Press, 1970, pp. 93-102.

Ref. 659.

406 Ricci, Marcello. *Socrate, padre del nichilismo. Struttura logica e significato teoretico del discorso socratico.* L'Aquila, Italy: L. U. Japadre Editore, 1971.

Ref. 1475.

407 Rogers, Arthur Kenyon. "The Ethics of Socrates." *The Philosophical Review*, 34 (1925), pp. 117-143.

Considers the Socrates of Plato and the Socrates of Xenophon to be very far apart from each other, and the Socrates of Aristophanes to be irreconcilable with Xenophon's portrait, and as having significant points of contact with the Platonic representation. Suggests that Socrates was the first great expert in the art of debunking, whose search for definitions was an attempt to expose ignorance rather than to establish a scientific terminology.

408 Rogers, Arthur Kenyon. *The Socratic Problem*. New Haven, Conn.: Yale University Press, 1933.

Develops a comprehensive examination of the Socratic problem on the basis provided by three assumptions: (1) that regardless of Plato's own extensions and additions to the portrait of the historical Socrates, he meant to give us the general *sort* of man Socrates really was; (2) that in some of his dialogues, Plato combined genuine Socratic doctrines with intellectual interests of his own; and (3) that we must recognize the existence of a limit in the first two assumptions, namely, that Plato neither functioned as a mere biographer, nor used Socrates' name simply to present his own views. Regards Xenophon's testimony as useful but strictly secondary. Argues against the Burnet-Taylor hypothesis (the thesis that whatever Plato reports about Socrates must be treated as genuinely Socratic). Rejects the authenticity of the Platonic second letter. Constructs a chronology of the early dialogues as follows: *Apology*, *Crito*, *Euthyphro*, *Laches*, *Ion*, *Charmides*, *Lysis*, *Cratylus*, *Gorgias*, *Meno*, *Euthydemus*, *Protagoras*, *Symposium*, *Phaedo*, *Republic*, and *Phaedrus*. Ref. 382.

409 Romero, Francisco. "La cuestión socrática." *Nosotros* (Buenos Aires), No. 227 (1928), pp. 111ff.

Compares the Socratic problem with the issue which surrounds the historical Jesus, and notes that in both cases we come upon an enormously influential presence which determines the course followed by culture, and that in both cases we find ourselves facing the impossibility of delineating the precise image and doctrine of the historical person.

410 Rossetti, Livio. "La questione socratica. Un problema mal posto." *Rivista Critica di Storia della Filosofia*, 38 (1983), pp. 3-24.

Argues that the frame of reference within which the Socratic problem has been posed is ill-founded, and that by simply establishing comparisons among the diverse Socratic testimonies, little progress can be expected towards the resolution of the problem. Insists that the issue should not merely be to delineate the historical from the legendary Socrates, but to construct a reasonable picture of the popular ethical and political ideas of Socrates' time in order to gain a clear understanding of the extent to which he departed from those ideas.

411 Rossetti, Livio. "Recenti sviluppi della questione socratica." *Proteus*, 6 (1971), pp. 161-187.

Argues that the investigation of the Socratic problem has been generally limited to the examination of the major sources and testimonies. Comments that for a more adequate approach to the issue it is necessary to take into account a host of minor sources and testimonies.

412 Rossi, P. "Per una storia della storiografia socratica." *Problemi di storiografia filosofica.* Edited by A. Banfi. Milan, 1951, pp. 85-140.

Provides a detailed discussion of the history of the Socratic problem, with special attention given to the ways in which its implications were treated by Hegel, Kierkegaard, and Nietzsche. Comments on the postulation of and reactions to the Burnet-Taylor hypothesis concerning the historical value of Plato's portrayal of Socrates.

413 Schleiermacher, F. D. E. "Uber den Werth des Sokrates als Philosophen." *Abhandlung der philosophischen Klasse der Königlich Preussichen Akademie der Wissenschaft aus den Jahren 1814-1815*, 1818, pp. 51-68.

Ref. 331.

414 Schroeder, F. M. "Review of *Socrates: A Source Book* by John Ferguson." *Phoenix*, 26 (1972), pp. 411-412.

Sees Ferguson's work as addressed primarily more to the Socratic problem than to the examination of Socrates. Suggests that more material should have been included from Socratics like Antisthenes, Aristippus, and Aeschines. Praises the inclusion of the first English translation of Libanius' *Apology*. Ref. 144.

415 Shorey, Paul. "The Question of the Socratic Element in Plato." *Selected Papers*. New York: Garland Publishing, 1980 (2 vols.), Vol. 1, pp. 316-323.

Ref. 676.

416 Stern, V. "Socrates." *Altertum*, 3 (1957), pp. 195-205.

Argues against a pessimistic view concerning the possibility of reconstructing an adequate biographical and ideological portrait of Socrates. Notes that in spite of the limitations inherent in all the sources, such a portrait can indeed be satisfactorily developed.

417 Strycker, Emile de. "Les témoignages historiques sur Socrate." *Mélanges Henri Grégoire. Annuaire de l'Institut de Philologie et d'Histoire Orientales et Slaves*, 10 (1950), pp. 199-230.

Argues that Xenophon's testimony should not be viewed as being based on that of Plato, but concedes that the former may have made occasional use of the latter. Emphasizes the priority of Plato's testimony over that of Xenophon with respect to ideological and biographical information about Socrates. Maintains that in spite of the inadequacy and scarcity of absolutely reliable sources, there is no justification for a stance of complete skepticism concerning the historical Socrates.

418 Vogel, Cornelia J. de. "Il Socrate di Olof Gigon." *Antologia della critica filosofica, I: L'età antica.* Edited by P. Rossi. Bari: Laterza, 1961.

Italian version of Vogel's "Une nouvelle interprétation du problème socratique." Ref. 420.

419 Vogel, Cornelia J. de. "The Present State of the Socratic Problem." *Phronesis*, 1 (1955), pp. 26-35.

Reviews the current views and interpretations of the Socratic problem, with special reference to Magalhães-Vilhena's contribution towards its solution.

420 Vogel, Cornelia J. de. "Une nouvelle interprétation du problème socratique." *Mnemosyne*, 1951, pp. 30-39.

Criticizes the solution of the Socratic problem which concludes (as in Gigon's analysis) that the Socrates revealed by the sources is mostly a romantic creation that may bear little resemblance to the historical phenomenon. Ref. 379.

421 Vogel, Cornelia J. de. "Who Was Socrates?" *The Journal of the History of Philosophy*, 1 (1963), pp. 143-161.

Ref. 564.

422 Wright, Jonathan. "The Legend of Socrates." *The Open Court*, 38 (1924), pp. 513-522.

Criticizes E. Dupréel's *La légende socratique et les sources de Platon*, and rejects the suggestion that the real source of Xenophon's *Memorabilia* was the testimony of Plato. Ref. 371.

## ARISTOPHANES AND THE ARISTOPHANIC SOCRATES

This section includes a selection of general works on Aristophanes, as well as of studies specifically concerned with the description and significance of his representation of Socrates in the *Clouds*.

423 Adkins, A. W. H. "Clouds, Mysteries, Socrates, and Plato." *Antichthon*, 4 (1970), pp. 13-24.

Examines Socrates' comments in the *Clouds* about the rites of religious initiation. Observes that by imputing to him a clearly abusive language about the rites, Aristophanes' intention was to elicit from the audience a reaction of anger towards the philosopher. Analyzes various passages from the Platonic dialogues which contain references to the mysteries and rites of initiation. Ref. 624.

424 Ambrose, Philip. "Socrates and Prodicus in the *Clouds*." *Essays in Ancient Greek Philosophy*, 2 (1983), pp. 129-144.

Attempts to clarify the relationship between the historical Socrates and the Aristophanic character. Calls attention to the contribution of Prodicus of Ceos towards the formation of Aristophanes's portrayal of Socrates. Views this portrayal as a composite of various contemporary thinkers, and Prodicus as a prominent ingredient in that composite.

425 Ambrosino, D. "Nuages et sens. Autour des *Nuées* d'Aristophane." *Quaderni di Storia*, 9 (1983), pp. 3-60.

Studies the possible origin of Aristophanes' symbol of the clouds, and observes that this origin is linked to certain pre-Socratic concepts related to the relationship between language and thought. Views the symbolic clouds as a mediating element between man and reality. Emphasizes their important symbolic function: they can easily deceive human beings, strengthen weak language, and even destroy the very foundations of society.

426 Anselmet, Raymond A. "Socrates and the *Clouds*: Shaftesbury and a Socratic Tradition." *The Journal of the History of*

*Ideas*, 39 (1978), pp. 171-182.

Reviews Shaftesbury's interpretation of Aristophanes' *Clouds*. Notes Shaftesbury's awareness of the controversy concerning the effect of the comedy on the eventual fate of Socrates, and emphasizes the effort on Shaftesbury's part to challenge his readers to appreciate the ethical stand entailed by the conduct of the historical Socrates.

427 Arnott, Peter D. *Greek Scenic Conventions in the Fifth Century B.C.*. Oxford: The Clarendon Press, 1962.

Reviews the pertinent evidence on the basis of which we can make definitive statements concerning the physical staging of Greek dramas, tragedies as well as comedies. Discusses, among other details, the use of a permanent stage-altar.

428 Barzin, M. "Sur les *Nuées* d' Aristophane." *Bulletin de la Classe des Lettres de l'Académie Royale de Belgique*, 54 (1968), pp. 378-388.

Argues that the testimony of Aristophanes concerning the allegation that Socrates was once the head of an educational institution should merit attention, even if it stands in direct opposition to what Plato reports in the *Apology*. Notes that the fact the *Clouds* was performed for the sake of an audience who knew Socrates and his activities makes it unlikely that the poet would have indulged in gross distortion of the actual image of the philosopher.

429 Böhringer, A. *Uber die Wolken des Aristophanes*. Karlsruhe, 1863.

Developes as its central thesis the idea that Aristophanes' *Clouds* should not be interpreted as an attack either against philosophy, science, or even the Sophistical movement, or against Socrates as a person, but as a denunciation of the Athenians' urge to rely on superficial notions for the explanation of things. Views Strepsiades, not Socrates, as the real protagonist and therefore the central focus of ridicule of the comedy.

430 Boruchwitsch, H. "Aristophanes als Herausgeber seiner

Komödien." *Acta Antiqua Academiae Scientiarum Hungaricae*, 21 (1973), pp. 89-95.

Maintains that the extant version of the *Clouds* is a revised version of the comedy. Notes that in its revised version it contains contradictions and sequences that lack continuity and cohesiveness.

431 Borukhovic, V. C. ["Aristophanes and Alcibiades."] *Acta Antiqua Academiae Scientiarum Hungaricae*, 7 (1959), pp. 329-336.

In Russian. Argues that the failure of Aristophanes' *Clouds* can be related to the great political influence of Alcibiades who had been ridiculed by the poet in the character of Phidippides, the young man who, like Alcibiades, had become Socrates' disciple.

432 Bowder, Diana, editor. "Aristophanes." *Who Was Who in the Greek World*. Ithaca, N.Y.: Cornell University Press, 1982, pp. 58-59.

Gives a brief biographical notice of Aristophanes. Interprets his presence in Plato's *Symposium* as a suggestion that although he portrays Socrates as a dangerous Sophist in the *Clouds*, his stage mockery was accepted in good humor.

433 Brelich, A. "Aristofane come fonte per la storia dell' educazione ateniese." *Dioniso*, 43 (1969), pp. 385-398.

Argues that the major point of the *Clouds* is to oppose the traditional and archaic system of Athenian education to the ideological and educational reforms introduced by Socrates and the Sophists.

434 Camon, F. "Datazione delle seconde Nube di Aristofane e delle ieromnemonia di Iperbolo." *Giornale Italiano di Filologia*, 14 (1961), pp. 54-62.

Reviews the evidence concerning the two versions of the *Clouds*, and concludes that the revised version must have been written after the year 421 B.C.

435 Cantarella, R. "Das Werk des Aristophanes." *Altertum*, 3 (1957), pp. 205-211.

Provides a general study of the significance of Aristophanes' works. Emphasizes his commitment to come to grips with those critical and important issues which affected the Athens of his time, and stresses his attempt to address them through the medium of his comic art. Comments on the political and social context of his work.

436 Cavaignac, E. "Pythagore et Socrate." *Revue de Philologie*, 33 (1959), pp. 246-248.

Analyses Aristophanes' *Birds* 1553-1564, and concludes that on the evidence provided by these lines, it is clear that Socrates was influenced by the Pythagorean belief in reincarnation before the year 414 B.C.

437 Chiapelli, Alessandro. "Il naturalismo di Socrate et le prime *Nubi* di Aristophane." *Rendiconti della Reale Accademia del Lincei*, 1886, pp. 284-302.

Reviews the issue of Socrates' early interest in natural philosophy, and places this issue against the background provided by his characterization as a philosopher in the style of the Milesian philosophers in the *Clouds*. Argues that the Aristophanic description may be well grounded on historical circumstances, and that it is possible that in his youth Socrates may have been genuinely interested in scientific speculations.

438 Cousin, Victor. "Socrate. De la part que peut avoir eue dans son procès la comédie des *Nuées*." *Fragments Philosophiques*. Geneva: Slatkine Reprints, 1970, pp. 82-87.

Originally written in 1815 and published in Paris in 1865. Rejects the interpretation that sees in the *Clouds* a harmless and merely playful characterization of Socrates, and maintains that the seeds of the indictment of 399 B.C. can be clearly detected in the comic performance of 423 B.C. Examines the testimonies of the *Apology*, the *Phaedo*, and the *Symposium*, and concludes that the relationship between Aristophanes' comedy and Socrates' execution can be compared to that between the first and last acts of a tragedy. Notes that although the *Clouds* did not give rise to the accusations, it nevertheless paved the way for them.

439 Croiset, Maurice. *Aristophane et les partis à Athènes.* Paris, 1906.

Examines the career of Aristophanes as a comic poet, and reviews his relationship with the various political tendencies and clubs of post-Periclean Athens. Accepts as historical his aristocratic and oligarchical leanings, but views him as basically independent from any specific political party. Regards him as belonging in "heart and soul" to the moderate democracy which was attached to the soil and its traditions. Discusses his eleven extant comedies. Notes that his basic intention in the *Clouds* was "to show how the Athenian character, simple and honest under the influence of tradition, might be changed and even depraved by philosophy and rhetoric." Argues that Aristophanes' use of Socrates was the result of the poet's inadequate understanding of the philosopher: "If Aristophanes had known him well, and if he had been devoted to the interests of the aristocracy, instead of combating him, he ought to have considered him his strongest ally."

439a Croiset, Maurice. *Aristophanes and the Political Parties at Athens.* Translated by James Loeb. London: Macmillan, 1909.

English translation of Croiset's *Aristophanes.* Ref. 439.

440 Dearden, C. W. *The Stage of Aristophanes.* London: The Athlone Press, 1976.

Discusses various aspects relevant to the theatrical production of Aristophanes' comedies, and to the physical structure and organization of the classical theater in general. Includes discussions on the following topics: the theatrical background (the festivals), the archeology and architecture of the theater, the stage, the theatrical mechanisms, the actors, the chorus, the costumes, the masks, and the actual production and performance of the comedies. Comments on Socrates as an Aristophanic character (pp. 24, 28, 66, 82, 97, and 125ff.), and on his costume (p. 115) and mask (p. 123).

441 Demand, N. "Plato, Aristophanes, and the Speeches of

Pythagoras." *Greek, Roman and Byzantine Studies*, 23 (1982), pp. 179-184.

Maintains that the doctrines of the Pythagoreans, as well as of Socrates and his disciples, are the target of ridicule by Aristophanes in various parts of his *Ecclesiazusae*, and notes that the influence of Pythagoras on Socrates can be clearly detected in the Platonic *Republic*.

442 Des Places, Eduard. "Socrate, directeur de conscience." *Revue des Etudes Grecques*, 51 (1938), pp. 395-402.

Maintains that the portrait of Socrates created by Aristophanes is a reasonably accurate representation of the historical Socrates. Comments in detail on *Clouds* 476-490, as well as on passages from Plato and Xenophon which appear to allude to traits found in the Aristophanic Socrates. Discusses the relationship between the reputation enjoyed by Socrates and the reputation promised by the chorus of clouds to Strepsiades if he succeeds in learning well Socrates' lessons.

443 Dover, Kenneth J. "Aristophanes' Speech in Plato's *Symposium*." *The Journal of Hellenic Studies*, 86 (1966), pp. 41-50.

Observes that a satisfactory explanation of Plato's feelings and attitude towards Aristophanes remains an unresolved issue because Plato's views on popular values are not free of complications. Suggests that Plato meant Aristophanes' story (that once human beings were double creatures with two heads and two bodies, and were cut in two by order of Zeus) not as comedy, but as unsophisticated folklore. Points out the elements of paradoy and irony in Alcibiades' speech.

444 Dover, Kenneth J. *Aristophanic Comedy*. Berkeley, Ca.: University of California Press, 1972.

Examines all the major themes and issues related to Aristophanes' comedies: the nature of the evidence (the texts, the identification of speakers, stage directions, and chronology); the theatrical conditions in the fifth centur, B.C.; the function of comedy as illusion, instruction, and entertainment; and the structure and style of comic poetry. Provides a synopsis and an analysis of all the extant Aristophanic comedies, and discusses their main political, social, and philosophical implications and ramifications. Includes two chapters on Aristophanes' comic predecessors and contemporaries, and on later comic developments. Devotes one chapter to the *Clouds* (pp. 101-120). Provides an extensive synopsis of this comedy, and comments on its revision in 417 B.C. and on the details of its production in 423 B.C. Discusses the three major themes of the comedy, namely, science, rhetoric, and morality. Concludes with comments on the relationship between the Aristophanic Socrates and the historical Socrates. Emphasizes the contrast between the former and the Socrates of Plato, Xenophon, and Aristotle. Argues that Aristophanes foisted upon Socrates practices and beliefs which could have belonged to any other intellectual. Expresses skepticism over the attempt to reconcile the Aristophanic Socrates with the traditional Socrates by an appeal to the idea that the latter passed through a scientific and/or Sophistical stage of development. Suggests that Aristophanes simply failed to recognize the true differences between Socrates and other intellectual figures of his time.

444a Dover, Kenneth J. "Socrates in the *Clouds*." *The Philosophy of Socrates: A Collection of Critical Essays.* Edited by Gregory Vlastos. Notre Dame, Ind.: University of Notre Dame Press, 1980, pp. 50-77.

Part of the Introduction to the *Clouds*, edited with commentary by Dover (Oxford: The Clarendon Press, 1968). Examines the portrait of Socrates created by Aristophanes, summarizes the comedy's plot, and gives a brief description of its characters. Reviews various explanations offered to resolve the conflict between Aristophanes' Socratic testimony on the one hand, and on the other those of Plato and Xenophon. Concludes with comments on the effect of the *Clouds* on Athenian public opinion in general and on Socrates' fate in particular.

445 Edmunds, Lowell. "Aristophanes' Socrates." *Proceedings of the Boston Area Colloquium in Ancient Philosophy*, 1 (1985), pp. 209-230.

Regards the *Clouds* as a comic endeavor to ridicule two

major aspects of Socrates, namely, his playful and deceitful irony and his spiritual voice or sign. Establishes a relationship between Strepsiades' anticipation of a 'voice' from the Clouds and Socrates' own experience of his spiritual voice.

446 Ehrenberg, Victor. *The People of Aristophanes: A Sociology of Old Attic Comedy*. New York: Schocken, 1962.

Originally published in 1943. Develops an analysis of a variety of Aristophanic characters, as well as of the nature and composition of the typical Athenian audiences who attended the performances of the comedies. Devotes Chapter 10 to the examination of issues related to Athenian education and religion, and comments on the place and role of Socrates in that context.

447 Erbse, H. "Sokrates im Schatten der aristophanischen *Wolken*." *Hermes*, 82 (1954), pp. 385-420.

Interprets the *Clouds* as implying that Aristophanes recognized an immense gap between the moral danger inherent in the teachings of the Sophists and the moral teachings of Socrates. Argues that there is no accusation of atheism against Socrates in the *Clouds*, and that he is not even charged with extravagant scientific endeavors. Insists that the difficulty with Socrates' teachings (in the comedy) is the immediate effect on Strepsiades who obviously only misunderstood him. Concludes that the *Clouds* is not an attack against philosophy, but a veiled vindication of the righteousness of Socrates.

448 Everett, E. "Socrates and Aristophanes." *The North American Review*, 14 (1822), pp. 273-296.

Examines the portrayal of Socrates in Aristophanes' *Clouds*, and explores the various possible reasons that might have led the comic poet to use Socrates as the object of his representation in the comedy.

449 Fabrini, P. "Sulla rappresentabilità delle *Nuvole* di Aristofane." *Annali della Scuola Normale Superiore di Pisa*, 5 (1975-1976), pp. 1-16.

Observes that there is nothing in the extant version of the *Clouds* that might suggest its inability to be performed according to the means and requirements of ancient Greek dramatic practices. Adds that there are no indications that imply that the extant version is incomplete.

450 Frese, R. "Die 'aristophanische Anklage' in Platons *Apologie*." *Philologus*, 18 (1926), pp. 376-390.

Reviews the references to Aristophanes in Plato's *Apology*, and comments on the significance of what Socrates refers to as the old accusations against him levelled by the comic poet. Emphasizes the historical importance of the Aristophanic portrayal of Socrates. Argues that Plato did not impute to Aristophanes the responsibility for the indictment against Socrates, and that the effect of the *Clouds* was negligible in the context of the trial. Maintains that the reference to Aristophanes in the *Apology* can be interpreted as a way in which Plato sought to show the worthlessness of the legal accusations: these were as senseless as Aristophanes's charges.

451 Gelzer, T. "Aristophanes und sein Sokrates." *Museum Helveticum*, 13 (1956), pp. 65-93.

Concludes that the worst accusation against Socrates in the *Clouds* is idleness and garrulity. Notes, however, that Aristophanes' accusation is not directed personally against Socrates, but against him as a symbol of the dangers inherent in the new educational ideas introduced by the Sophists. Attempts to discover various characteristics in the Aristophanic Socrates that are also found in the testimonies of Xenophon and Plato. Examines Aristophanes' characterizations of Cleon and Euripides, and compares them with his portrayal of Socrates.

452 Gerlach, F. D. *Aristophanes und Sokrates*. Basel, 1876.

Pamphlet (30 pp.) which discusses the Aristophanic portrait of Socrates in the *Clouds*, and the effect of the comedy on his eventual fate.

453 Goguel, E. *Aristophane et Socrate*. Strasbourg, 1859.

Studies the Aristophanic portrayal of Socrates in the *Clouds*, and speculates that Aristophanes' main reason for having chosen him as the object of ridicule was the philosopher's ability to serve as the stereotype of the decadent educational influence of the Sophists.

454 Goosens, R. "Le vrai sens d'un vers des *Nuées* (414)." *Les Etudes Classiques*, 16 (1949), pp. 22-28.

Examines *Clouds* 414ff, where the chorus promises to Strepsiades various blessings that would result from Socrates' teaching ("And thy soul wilt inure all wants to endure," etc.). Observes that these lines were often taken to be a genuine description of Socrates' own characteristics, and notes that the Aristophanic passage gives an idea of the attributes which young Athenians expected to find in their Sophistical teachers.

455 Greene, P. "Strepsiades, Socrates, and the Abuse of Intellectualism." *Greek, Roman and Byzantine Studies*, 20 (1979), pp. 15-20.

Establishes a comparison between Aristophanes' introduction of Strepsiades as a man who is not initiated into the world of 'higher' learning, and Socrates' comments in the *Theaetetus* concerning a person who is not yet acquainted with philosophy. Reviews Aristophanes' portrayals of anti-intellectualism (Strepsiades) and of intellectualism (Socrates).

456 Grene, D. "The Comic Technique of Aristophanes." *Hermathena*, 50 (1937), pp. 87-125.

Analyzes the comic art of Aristophanes as it reveals itself in the representation and use of three characters: Cleon, Socrates, and Euripides.

457 Grube, G. M. A. "Comedy: Aristophanes." *The Greek and Roman Critics*. London: Methuen & Co., 1965, pp. 22-32.

Discusses the role and importance of the Aristophanic comedy in the development of literary and social criticism. Views Aristophanes' ridicule of Socrates as an attack against the rhetorical education promoted by the Sophists, and notes that Socrates' activities were truly unrelated to that kind of education. Detects clearly Euripidean themes in the debate between the Just and the Unjust Discourses.

458 Harvey, F. D. "*Nubes* 1493ff. Was Socrates Murdered?" *Greek, Roman and Byzantine Studies*, 22 (1981), pp. 339-343.

Comments on E. C. Kopff's interpretation of the concluding scene of the *Clouds*, and argues, contrary to Kopff's view, that it clearly conveys the sense that Socrates and his disciples were able to escape from the burning of their school. Ref. 466.

459 Havelock, Eric A. "The Socratic Self as It is Parodied in Aristophanes' *Clouds*." *Yale Classical Studies (22): Studies in Fifth Century Thought and Literature*. Edited by Adam Parry. Cambridge: Cambridge University Press, 1972, pp. 1-18.

Argues, on the basis of specific observations on the common vocabulary of the *Clouds* and the Platonic dialogues, that there is indeed an intimate relationship between the portrayal of Socrates created by Aristophanes and that developed by Plato.

460 Hommel, H. "Aristophanes über die Nilschwelle." *Rheinesches Museum für Philologie*, 94 (1951), pp. 315-317.

Discusses *Clouds* 268-274, that is, Socrates' invocation to the Clouds. Notes that this invocation makes allusion to the four cardinal points (north, east, west, and south). Comments in particular on Socrates' reference to "the mystical waves of the Nile."

461 Hulley, Karl K. "A Note on Aristophanes' *Clouds* 804-813." *The Classical Journal*, 69 (1974), pp. 223-225.

Examines the choral passage of the *Clouds* (804-813), and concludes that it is addressed to Strepsiades rather than to Socrates.

462 Jaeger, Werner. "The Comic Poetry of Aristophanes." *Paideia: The Ideals of Greek Culture*. Translated by Gilbert Highet. New York: Oxford University Press, 1965 (2 vols.), Vol. 1, pp.

358-381.

Reviews the cultural and philosophical significance of Aristophanic comedy, and stresses the ideological transformation of the Old Comedy brought about by Aristophanes. Emphasizes the fact that with him, the comic stage became "the censorship of Athens." Recognizes in the Aristophanic Socrates a caricature that serves as a focal point in order to subsume various educational and cultural tendencies which the poet deemed to be socially detrimental: the Sophistical movement, the passion for rhetoric and eristics, and the preoccupation with scientific questions. Views in Aristophanes' hatred for rationalism the principal theme of the *Clouds*.

463 Karavites, P. "Socrates in the *Clouds*." *The Classical Bulletin*, 50 (1973), pp. 65-69.

Maintains that the vast gap that separates the Aristophanic Socrates from the Socrates of Plato and Aristotle is ultimately explainable by reference to the fact that Aristophanes' main concern was to depict on the stage only the outward or external characteristics of Socrates. Comments on Socrates' physical ugliness and carelessness about his external appearance.

464 Kleve, K. "Anti-Dover or Socrates in the *Clouds*." *Symbolae Osloenses*, 58 (1983), pp. 23-27.

Argues against the interpretation of the Aristophanic Socrates developed by K. J. Dover in his *Aristophanic Comedy*. Observes that Kierkegaard's interpretation of Socrates' irony, and our present understanding of the Socrates, lead us to the conclusion that the gap that separates the Aristophanic Socrates from the historical man is less wide than is often believed. Ref. 444.

465 Kock, T. "Aristophanes als Dichter und Politiker." *Rheinisches Museum für Philologie*, 39 (1884), pp. 118ff.

Stresses the ideological and political intentions which motivated Aristophanes in his exposure of Socrates: beneath the comic scenes, there was an absolutely serious purpose.

466 Kopff, E. C. "*Nubes* 1493ff. Was Socrates Murdered?" *Greek, Roman and Byzantine Studies*, 18 (1977), pp. 113-122.

Argues for the interpretation of the concluding lines of the *Clouds*, according to which, with the burning of the Thinking Establishment, Socrates and his disciples were killed. Concludes that as early as 418 B.C. (the probable year of the revision of the *Clouds*), Aristophanes had already announced his solution to the 'problem' posed by Socrates' presence in Athens. Ref. 458.

467 Kraus, René. "The Godless Scientist: Indictment by Ridicule." *The State Versus Socrates: A Case Study in Civic Freedom*. Edited by John D. Montgomery. Boston: The Beacon Press, 1954, pp. 62-79.

Extracted from Kraus' *The Private and Public Life of Socrates* (pp. 251-267). Recreates in a fictionalized fashion the circumstances which surrounded Aristophanes' production of the *Clouds*. Describes the reaction of the audience to the various scenes, and suggests that Aristophanes' ridicule was directed specifically at the person of Socrates, and that the ultimate result of the comedy was the social undoing of the philosopher. Ref. 256.

468 Lever, Katharine. *The Art of Greek Comedy*. London: Methuen, 1956.

Discusses in the first two chapters the origins and early developments associated with Greek comic poetry, and devotes the third chapter to the examination of Old Comedy in Athens. Concentrates its attention in three subsequent chapters on Aristophanic comedy. Regards Aristophanes as a moralistic teacher and as a conservative patriot who sought to counterbalance the effects of educational and moral decandence (as exemplified by Socrates and the Sophists).

469 Lord, Louis E. *Aristophanes: His Plays and His Influence*. New York: Cooper Square Publishers, 1963.

Contains chapters on the origins of Greek comedy, on the Athens of Aristophanes, and on his comedies. Discusses in other chapters the influence of Aristophanes on the literature of Greece and Rome, and the Renaissance, and on

German, French, and English writers. Deals briefly with the Aristophanic portrayal of Socrates (pp. 40-45), and regards such a portrayal as an obvious travesty of the historical reality.

470 Marzullo, B. "Strepsiade." *Maia*, 6 (1953), pp. 99-124.

Analyzes the word στρέφειν ('to twist or bend') and its cognates, as they are used throughout the *Clouds*. Calls attention to the clear relationship between Strepsiades' character and conduct, and the meaning implied by his name. Comments on the custom of Athenian parents to give their children high-sounding names, as in the case of Strepsiades' own name.

471 Meautis, G. "La scène de l'initiation dans les *Nuées* d'Aristophane." *Revue de l'Histoire des Religions*, 108 (1938), pp. 92-97.

Comments on the characteristics given by Aristophanes to Socrates and the Thinking Establishment, and in particular to the scene of Strepsiades' initiation into the Socratic school. Argues that there are clear parallels between the Aristophanic scene and certain passages from Euripides' *Bacchantes*.

472 Melero Bellido, Antonio. *Atenas y el pitagorismo. Investigación en las fuentes de la comedia.* Salamanca: Universidad de Salamanca, 1972.

Examines the advent and development of Pythagoreanism in Athens and the role of Pythagorean sects in Athenian life in the fifth century B.C. Studies in Chapter 5 ("Sócrates y *Las Nubes* de Aristófanes") the differences between the two versions of the *Clouds*, and concludes that the Pythagorean references in the comedy belong almost exclusively to the first original version, and that the attack against Socrates is on a more personal level in the second version.

473 Montuori, Mario. "Socrate tra *Nuvole* prime e *Nuvole* seconde." *Atti di Scienze morali e politici della Società nazionale di Scienze, Lettere ed Arti in Napoli*, 77 (1966).

Argues that the two versions of the *Clouds* do not differ with respect to the characterization and condemnation of Socrates, and that in both he appears as a corrupting Sophistical influence among the Athenian youth.

474 Müller, K. O. "Aristophanes." *A History of the Literature of Ancient Greece*. Translated by George C. Lewis and John W. Donaldson. London: Longmans, Green & Co., 1884 (3 vols.), Vol. 2, pp. 19-48.

Outlines the biographical information of Aristophanes, and reviews chronologically the content, significance, and mode of production of all his extant comedies. Interprets the *Clouds*, not as an attack on Socrates, but as an indictment of the new education made popular by the Sophists. Views this comedy as an oblique and superficial representation of the historical Socrates.

475 Murray, Gilbert. "The New Learning: Socrates." *Aristophanes: A Study*. New York: Russell & Russell, 1964, pp. 85-105.

Analyzes the plot of the *Clouds*. Rejects the ordinary interpretation of the comedy which sees in it an attack against the Sophistical movement and a travesty of the truth with respect to Socrates and the Sophists. Recognizes as unmistakable the direct imitation of various characteristics of Socrates on Aristophanes' part. Concludes that the comedy is not a passionate attack on some subject that roused the poet's indignation, but a study of the new and strange phenomenon which attracted and amused the poet, namely, the teachings of Socrates.

476 Naumann, H. "Die Gestalt des Sokrates und ihre Wirkungen auf die Weltliteratur." *Der altsprachliche Unterricht*, 12 (1969), 2, pp. 64-103.

Examines the role and significance of the presence of Socrates in Aristophanes and Plato, and argues that he stood in their minds as a paradigm of the unity of life and doctrine. Comments on the replacement of the Socratic presence by the character of Cato in the writings of Plutarch, Sallust, Seneca, and Dante.

477 Neumann, Harry. "Socrates in Plato and Aristophanes." *The American Journal of Philology*, 90 (1969), pp. 201-214.

Examines and compares the portrayals of Socrates in the *Clouds* and in the opening sections of the *Republic*. Calls attention to the contrast between the Socrates who challenges Strepsiades' religious beliefs and the Socrates who does not question the conventional ideas of the aged Cephalus. Stresses the great gap that separates the Platonic Socrates from the Aristophanic Socrates. Notes that in the *Republic* philosophy manifests itself as a worthy undertaking that can guide human beings to the love of a common good, whereas in the *Clouds* it appears in the garb of Sophistical moral opportunism.

478 Nussbaum, Martha. "Aristophanes and Socrates on Learning Practical Wisdom." *Yale Classical Studies (26): Aristophanes: Essays in Interpretation*. Edited by Jeffrey Henderson. Cambridge: Cambridge University Press, 1980, pp. 43-97.

Examines the action and speeches in the *Clouds*, and endeavors to reconstruct from them Aristophanes' ideas about ethical values and education. Attempts to show that the *Clouds* delivers a clear political message, namely, that democracy engenders violence and disregard of human rights. Comments on the possible relationship between this message and Plato's own contempt for democracy.

479 Petrie, R. "Aristophanes and Socrates." *Mind*, 20 (1911), pp. 507-520.

Explores the significance of Socrates' references to Aristophanes in the *Apology*. Argues against the Burnet-Taylor thesis concerning the relationship between the historical Socrates and the Platonic Socrates, and against Taylor's view of Socrates as an adherent of an Orphic-Pythagorean cult. Specifically rejects Taylor's contention that the real accusation against Socrates was related to his alleged Orphic and Pythagorean tendencies. Supports its position by an examination of the Aristophanic Socrates. Ref. 496.

480 Petruzzellis, N. "Aristofane e la sofistica." *Dioniso*, 20 (1957), pp. 38-62.

Discusses various theories about the significance and nature of Old Comedy. Comments on Aristophanes' interpretation and representation of the Sophists and Socrates, and argues that it is not possible to reach a final determination as to whether his portrayal of Socrates is the result of an intentional distortion or of a mistaken understanding of his activities and ideas. Argues that Aristophanes was able to capture well the kernel and practice of Sophistical teaching, even though his characterization of Socrates may have been ill-founded.

481 Philippson, R. "Sokrates' Dialektik in Aristophanes' *Wolken*." *Rheinisches Museum für Philologie*, 81 (1932), pp. 30-38.

Studies the reasoning employed by Socrates in the *Clouds*. Maintains that there is more agreement than divergence among the primary sources concerning the actual ideas of Socrates, and that this applies even to Aristophanes' testimony. Argues that Aristophanes was well acquainted with the personality and ideas of Socrates, and that his rendition of Socratic dialectics is more faithful and accurate than what may appear at first sight. Notes that Aristotle's testimony is valuable, as it reveals a true description of Socrates' philosophy.

482 Pippidi, D. M. "Aristote et Aristophane. En marge de la théorie aristotelique de la comédie." *Studii Classice*, 1 (1959), pp. 197-206.

In Rumanian, with an abstract in French. Discusses Aristotle's interpretation of the origin and meaning of comic poetry. Notes the fundamental incompatibility between his interpretation and the evidence provided by the extant texts of Old Comedy.

483 Pucci, P. "Saggio sulle Nuvole." *Maia*, 12 (1960), pp. 3-42 and 106-129.

Maintains that in using Socrates as an object of ridicule, Aristophanes sought to dramatize various popular misconceptions and prejudices about Socrates and the Socratic circles. Notes that even though Socrates' philosophy was not properly portrayed in the *Clouds*, there are in the comedy adequate characterizations of certain aspects of the historical Socrates, specifically his external appearance, his ordinary behavior, and his dialectical method.

484 Reckford, K. J. "Aristophanes' Ever-flowing Clouds." *The Emory University Quarterly*, 22 (1967), pp. 222-235.

Examines the philosophical and dramatic functions of the cloud-imagery in the *Clouds*.

485 Röck, Hubert. "Aristophanischer und geschichtlicher Sokrates." *Archiv für Geschichte der Philosophie*, 18, (1912), pp. 175-195.

Maintains that the atheism attributed by Aristophanes to Socrates can also be attributed to the historical Socrates. Stresses the importance of Aristophanes' general characterization of Socrates as a source of genuine historical information about him.

486 Rosenstrauch, H. "Quomodo Aristophanes lusu verborum sophistas ludibrio habuerit." *Eos*, 51 (1961), pp. 45-54.

Examines various issues related to Aristophanes' portrayal of Socrates in the *Clouds*, and concludes that the poet's real intention was to expose to ridicule the ideas and practices of the Sophists, especially Prodicus and Protagoras. Written in Polish, with a summary in Latin.

487 Rossetti, Livio. "Le *Nuvole* di Aristofane. Perchè furono una commedia e non una farsa." *Rivista di Cultura Classica e Medioevale*, 16 (1974), pp. 131-136.

Maintains that Aristophanes' *Clouds* was conceived by its author not as a farce but as a comedy, and that it is for this reason that he endeavored to create a dramatic scene reasonably close to the actual facts. Notes that there are no traces among the Sophists which may suggest anything comparable to Socrates' Thinking Establishment as this is depicted by Aristophanes.

488 Rötscher, Heinrich T. *Aristophanes und sein Zeitalter*. Berlin, 1827.

Discusses the cultural and political background of

Aristophanes, and draws attention to his opposition to the educational and rationalistic ideas of the Sophists in general and of Socrates in particular. Stresses the negative and detrimental consequences of Socrates' ideas as these were interpreted by Aristophanes. Gives an account of the Hegelian interpretation of Socrates as the first major representative of the principle of subjectivity. Regards Xenophon's testimony as the most impartial and accurate source of our knowledge about the historical Socrates.

489 Sarri, Francesco. "Rilettura delle *Nuvole* di Aristophane come fonte per la conoscenza di Socrate." *Rivista di Filosofia Neoscholastica*, 65 (1973), pp. 532-550.

Endeavors to account for the comic representation of Socrates in the *Clouds* by reference to Aristophanes' need to present his characters in the light of the understanding of common and ordinary Athenian audiences. Argues that such a theatrical requirement necessitates the transformation of Socrates into a composite character who is an Orphic priest, a natural philosopher, and a Sophist -- all at the same time. Suggests that the ordinary Athenian audiences would have been unable to appreciate the differences between Socrates and the Sophists or the natural philosophers.

490 Schmid, Wolfgang. "Das Sokratesbild der *Wolken*." *Philologus*, 97 (1948), pp. 209-228.

Examines the Aristophanic characterization of Socrates in the *Clouds* with special emphasis on the traits that make him appear as a Sophist. Concludes that the actual resemblance between Socrates and the Sophists is not merely accidental or superficial.

491 Segal, Charles. "Aristophanes' Cloud-Chorus." *Arethusa*, 2 (1969), pp. 143-161.

Analyzes the function of the chorus of clouds in Aristophanes' *Clouds*, and attempts to explain the apparent change in the message of the chorus at the conclusion of the comedy. Argues that any interpretation of the *Clouds* must address these problems: (1) the role of the chorus; (2) the function of the debate between the Just and the

Unjust Discourses; and (3) the very abrupt change of the chorus of clouds at the end of the comedy. Notes that the final speech of the chorus is presented in an Aeschylean framework.

492 Solomos, Alexis. Ὁ ζωντανὸς Ἀριστοφάνης [*The Living Aristophanes*]. Athens: 1961.

In modern Greek. Provides a full discussion of Aristophanes' life, works, and socio-political context, and analyzes each one of his extant comedies. Includes comments on the ancient staging and production of the comedies, against the background of modern theatrical practice. Identifies the author as being responsible for the direction and production of several ancient comedies for the Greek National Theater.

493 Strauss, Leo. *Socrates and Aristophanes*. New York: Basic Books, 1966.

Endeavors to shed light on the relationship among the portrayals of Socrates created by Plato, Xenophon, and Aristophanes, and reaches the conclusion that they are not incompatible. Maintains that the Aristophanic Socrates is a reflection of an early stage in Socrates' life. Analyses closely all the extant Aristophanic comedies. Adds some critical notes on Nietzsche's interpretation of Socrates.

494 Süvern, W. *Uber Aristophanes' Wolken*. Berlin, 1826.

Examines the Aristophanic characterization of Socrates in the *Clouds* against the background provided by the testimonies of Plato and Xenophon. Concludes that Aristophanes' error consisted in his gross confusion of Socrates with the Sophists.

495 Symonds, John A. "Aristophanes." *Studies of the Greek Poets*. New York: Harper & Brothers, 1917 (2 vols.), Vol. 2, pp. 171-215.

Reviews all the major aspects related to Aristophanic comedy. Begins with an analysis of Heine's critique of Aristophanes, and discusses the fanciful and grotesque ingredients of his comic poetry. Pays close attention to his conservative tendencies and to his political and social intentions, and, in that context, examines the role played by the historical Socrates in the formation of the Aristophanic Socrates. Concludes with a comparison of the testimonies of Plato and Aristophanes which are conceived as two radically opposed yet complementary sources of information about Socrates and his time: "By Plato we are taught how dignified and humane the Greeks could be, by Aristophanes how versatile and human they were."

496 Taylor, Alfred E. "The φροντιστήριον." *Varia Socratica: First Series*. Oxford: James Parker & Co., 1911, pp. 129-177.

Examines in detail the Aristophanic description of the Socratic φροντιστήριον, and endeavors to establish parallels between such a description and what can be affirmed about the Socratic circle. Emphasizes the mystic and religious elements of both, and concludes that we find in both all the characteristics of some sort of Orphic and Pythagorean community. Ref. 1071.

497 Tejera, V. "The *Symposium*: Socrates, Eros, and Aristophanes." *Plato's Dialogues One by One: A Structural Interpretation*. New York: Irvington Publishers, 1984, pp. 339-358.

Argues that the common belief that Aristophanes was anti-Socratic stems from a misunderstanding of the *Clouds*. Suggests that Aristophanes does not present an individual as the protagonist, but a composite representation of several traits. Explores in detail Diotima's conversation with Socrates in the *Symposium*, as well as Aristophanes' ideas about love.

498 Thompson, W. H. "On the *Nubes* of Aristophanes." *The Journal of Philosophy* (London), 12 (1883), pp. 171-173.

Interprets Aristophanes' *Clouds* as a manifestation of the bitter antagonism between the comic poets on the one hand and, on the other, the intellectuals who were suspected of exercising a pernicious influence on the youth. Classifies among the intellectuals persons such as the Sophists, dialecticians, rhetoricians, speculative philosophers, scientists, free-thinkers -- all of whom are merged into the character of Socrates. Suggests that in constructing his Socratic portrait, Aristophanes was merely giving expression to public opinion, and that he was not specifically attempting to falsify the character of the historical Socrates.

499 Vlastos, Gregory. "On 'The Socrates' Story'." *Political Theory*, 7 (1979), pp. 533-536.

Ref. 1112.

500 Walcot, P. "Aristophanic and Other Audiences." *Greece and Rome*, 43 (1971), pp. 35-50.

Discusses the relationship between the audience and the performers in Greek comedy, and discusses specifically the parabasis in which the chorus directly addresses the audience. Comments on the appearance of living Athenians in Aristophanes' comedies (*e.g.*, Socrates in the *Clouds*). Mentions the story by Aelian that Socrates, while witnessing the performance of the *Clouds*, would stand up so that the audience could compare him with the character on the stage. Argues that the revised parabasis was the result of Aristophanes' unhappiness with the audience's reaction. Reminds us that the comedies were meant to be performed not simply read.

501 Weber, Hermann. *Aristophanes and His Sense of the Comic: A Comparative Study of the Meaning of Old Comedy*. Doctoral dissertation. The University of Texas at Austin, 1968.

Shows that the comic element in Aristophanes's works is expressed in concrete contents that are drawn from Greek life in the fifth century B.C. Stresses the importance of understanding adequately the tragic and comic elements of Greek theater as a means for appreciating fully classical Greek culture which is epitomized in Socrates and in Aristophanes. Notes that their realizations about life are similar: they refrain from criticizing the world as they find it, and accept it in a spirit of joy. Maintains that the ultimate purpose of Aristophanic art is to expose the futility and emptiness of all human pretentiousness.

502 Webster, Thomas B. L. *Greek Theater Production*. London: Methuen, 1956.

Discusses in great detail the production and performance of Greek tragedies and comedies. Deals with the construction and arrangement of the stage, the organization of the sequences of scenes, the use of masks and costumes, and other physical and practical aspects related to ancient drama. Contains useful material which can help a twentieth century person understand more fully the mechanics involved in Aristophanes' *Clouds*. Recounts (p. 60) the anecdote in which Socrates is said to have been present during the performance of the *Clouds* in 423 B.C. -- as strangers and foreigners would ask, "Who is this man Socrates?," the philosopher would silently stand before the audience as if wishing to reply, "Here is the man himself."

503 Whitman, Cedric H. *Aristophanes and the Comic Hero*. Cambridge, Mass.: Harvard University Press, 1964.

Contains one chapter on the *Clouds* in which the portrait of Socrates as a comic hero is analysed. Views the genesis of Aristophanes' creation as a reaction to the new educational system introduced in Athens by the Sophists, and regards the *Clouds* as a less than satisfactory account of the "war between the generations" in Athens. Emphasizes the role and significance of Aristophanes as a *poet* more than as a moralistic teacher. Notes that in his comedies, the comic hero attains to "supreme selfmanship" through which he develops "the ability to get the advantage of somebody or some situation by virtue of an unscrupulous, but thoroughly enjoyable exercise of craft."

## XENOPHON AND THE XENOPHONTEAN SOCRATES

This section includes a selection of general biographical and critical works and notices on Xenophon, and works which discuss his Socratic testimony.

504 Anderson, J. K. *Xenophon*. New York: Charles Scribner's Sons, 1974.

Provides a biography of Xenophon, and sketches various aspects of his life: as a historian, as a literary man, as a soldier, and as a moralist. Accepts as authentic the tradition that views him as a direct disciple of Socrates, and argues that in writing about Socrates, he must have recognized his own inferiority to Plato. Regards the Xenophontean testimony as historically valuable.

505 Armin, Hans von. *Xenophons Memorabilien und die Apologie des Sokrates*. Copenhagen: A. F. Host & Son, 1923.

Also published by the Royal Danish Academy of Science (Philosophy-History Section), No. 8, 1923. Studies the structure and content of Xenophon's *Apology*, and attempts to elucidate its relationship to the *Memorabilia* in general and with the defense part of the *Memorabilia* in particular. Accepts the authenticity of the *Apology*, and argues for the thesis that it must have been written before the Platonic *Apology*. Reaches this conclusion particularly on the basis of Xenophon's comment that Socrates' μεγαληγορία had remained unaccounted for by earlier writers. Claims that, as compared with Xenophon's *Apology*, the Platonic *Apology* offers a more adequate explanation of Socrates' behavior in court. Views certain sections of the *Memorabilia* as furnishing summary statements of the *Apology*. Attaches historical value to Xenophon's testimony.

506 Baker, W. W. "An Apologetic for Xenophon's *Memorabilia*." *The Classical Journal*, 12 (1916-1917), pp. 293-309.

Examines the question of the authenticity and biographical value of Xenophon's writings. Maintains that even though he might not have been an intimate member of the Socratic circle, many of his 'recollections' (as those left for us in his *Memorabilia*) are probably the result of his direct acquaintance with Socrates. Attempts to refute the suggestion that Xenophon made ample use of Plato's writings in order to compose his own. Argues that the multiplicity of representations of Socrates that have come down to us is explainable by the fact that Socrates himself was a many-sided man: thus, the pictures drawn of him may all be partially true in spite of their profound differences.

507 Berns, Laurence. "Socratic and Non-Socratic Philosophy: A Note on Xenophon's *Memorabilia* 1:1:13 and 14." *The Review of Metaphysics*, 28 (1974), pp. 85-88.

Examines Xenophon's classification of madness into six types and his enumeration of six pre-Socratic positions. Reviews Socrates' treatment of these categories and his appeal to moderation both as a theoretical stance and as a practical principle. Interprets the Socratic appeal to moderation as an effort to do justice to the cognitive meaning of ordinary experience and speech. Shows how Socrates' approach is a mean between the ways of the many and the ways of the speculative despisers of the many.

508 Bowder, Diana, editor. "Xenophon." *Who Was Who in the Greek World*. Ithaca: N.Y.: Cornell University Press, 1982, pp. 209-210.

Provides a brief biographical notice on Xenophon, together with short abstracts of some of his works. Suggests that the Xenophontean Socrates may be truer to life than the Platonic Socrates.

509 Breitenbach, L. "Wer ist der κατήγορος in Xenophons Commentarien?" *Neue Jahrbücher für Philologie und Paedagogik*, 39 (1869), pp. 801-815.

Reviews the textual evidence for the identity of the accuser mentioned in Xenophon's *Memorabilia*, and identifies him as Meletus.

510 Busse, Adolf. "Xenophons Schutzschrift und *Apologie*." *Rheinisches Museum für Philologie*, 89 (1930), pp. 215-229.

Discusses the possible ideological influence of Diogenes of Apollonia in the composition of Xenophon's *Memorabilia*, specifically, I,i and IV,iii. Finds in Xenophon's *Apology* a mosaic of expressions and ideas found in his other works. Reviews the testimonies of Xenophon and Aristotle, which are judged to be of great historical value, in spite of their secondary importance in comparison to that of Plato. Maintains that it is possible to distinguish three levels in the composition of the first book of the *Memorabilia*: (1) a series of actual recollections, (2) a direct answer to the charges of Polycrates, and (3) specific comments on the Socratic literature.

511 Chroust, Anton-Hermann. *Socrates: Man and Myth. The Two Socratic Apologies of Xenophon.* Notre Dame, Ind.: University of Notre Dame Press, 1957.

Provides a textual and exhaustive analysis of Xenophon's *Apology* and *Memorabilia* (I,i,1-I,ii,64), and an examination of the content and significance of his Socratic testimony. Interprets the literature of the early fourth century B.C. about Socrates as having been occasioned by a political and ideological controversy between two groups: the Socratics who sought to vindicate the memory of Socrates, and who were generally opposed to the restored democracy, and the new Sophists who, like Polycrates, saw in the Socratic movement a source of social and political danger. Reaches the following conclusions: (1) the Xenophontean apologetic writings were occasioned by the Sophistical anti-Socratic literature exemplified by the pamphlet of Polycrates; (2) Xenophon's apologies are only incidentally concerned with the historical Socrates and his trial; (3) our sources of information about Socrates furnish us with unsatisfactory and often contradictory reports which are the basis of the Socratic 'legend' from which it is impossible to recreate a reliable portrait of Socrates; (4) at the basis of Xenophon's testimony it is possible to discern the presence of Antisthenes, although it is impossible to determine precisely the relationship between the Antisthenean Socrates and the historical Socrates; (5) in general, the entire ancient literary tradition about Socrates can be viewed as a collection of efforts to create a legend which is far removed from historiography and biography; and (6) the only assertion that can be made about the historical Socrates is that we know practically nothing about him. Adds that it is not possible to clarify the reasons that led Plato to create his version of the Socratic legend.

Includes a partial reconstruction of Polycrates' pamphlet (pp. 99-100).

512 Chroust, Anton-Hermann. "Xenophon, Polycrates, and the Indictment of Socrates." *Classica et Mediaevalia*, 16 (1955), pp. 1-77.

Endeavors to reconstruct Polycrates' Κατηγορία Σωκράτους mostly on the basis of Libanius' *Apologia Socratis*, and seeks to clarify the relationship between Polycrates' work and the defense part of Xenophon's *Memorabilia*. Argues that Polycrates' work appears to be based on historical facts, and notes that, on that assumption, we can conclude that Socrates must have been a man more immersed in political activities than is generally believed.

513 Croiset, Alfred. *Xénophon, son caractère et son talent*. Paris, 1873.

Reviews the biography of Xenophon, gives an account of his personality, and assesses the merits of his literary production. Accepts as highly probable a return of Xenophon to Athens before the year 395 B.C., and places the date of composition of the *Memorabilia* between 399 and 395 B.C. Maintains that in his testimony of Socrates, Xenophon made use of those aspects and ideas of the philosopher which were in accord with his own temperament and idiosyncrasy.

514 Dakyns, H. G. "A Sketch of Xenophon's Life." *The March of the Ten Thousand*. Translated by H. G. Dakyns. London: Macmillan, 1901, pp. i-lxxx.

Serves as the introduction to Dakyns' translation of the *Anabasis*. Gives a detailed biographical account of Xenophon. Discusses his relationship with Socrates, and views the presence of the latter as a decisive influence on the spiritual and intellectual development of the former. Assumes that the Xenophontean testimony is mostly based on actual recollections, and suggests that the relationship between Xenophon and Socrates was a truly intimate one. Ref. 59.

515 Delatte, Armand. *Le troisième livre de souvenirs socratiques*

*de Xénophon.* Liége-Paris, 1933.

Maintains that certain parts of the *Memorabilia* were written shortly after the year 355 B.C., and that Book III belongs certainly to a date later than those of Xenophon's minor works. Regards the first half of Book III as a statement of Xenophon's political ideas. Speaks of the "*heureuse adaptation*" made by Xenophon of Socrates' ideas -- a happy adaptation to the political, social, economic, and military circumstances of the fourth century B.C.

516 Dissen, Ludolph. *De philosophia morali in Xenophontis de Socrate commentariis tradita.* Göttingen, 1812.

Provides a systematic presentation of Socrates' philosophical principles and opinions as these are reported by Xenophon. Suggests that the Xenophontean account may be partly inaccurate, since it appears to contain elements that belong mostly to Xenophon, not to the historical Socrates, as in the instance of the utilitarian ethical ideas advanced in the *Memorabilia.*

517 Durbach, L. "L'Apologie de Xénophon dans l'*Anabase.*" *Revue des Etudes Grecques*, 5 (1893), pp. 374ff.

Maintains that Xenophon's acquaintance with Socrates is mostly fictional, and claims that the use of Socrates' name in Xenophon's writings is ultimately a device through which he sought to lend credibility to the exposition of his own views.

518 Edelstein, Emma. *Das xenophontischen und platonischen Bild des Socrates.* Heidelberg, 1935.

Examines the portrayals of Socrates given by Xenophon and Plato. Reviews in particular the defense part of the *Memorabilia*, and establishes a comparison between it and the Platonic *Apology*.

519 Erbse, H. "Aristipp und Sokrates bei Xenophon (Bemerkungen zu *Mem.* 2,1)." *Würzburger Jahrbücher für die Altertumswissenschaft*, 6b (1980), pp. 7-19.

Notes that the way in which Xenophon uses Aristippus'

arguments in *Memorabilia* II,ii shows that this chapter is not merely the result of excerpting or compiling from other sources. Observes that his primary aim is to vindicate Socrates from the accusation of corrupting others through the simple distortion of his teachings. Concludes that the chapter of the *Memorabilia* under analysis corresponds well to the overall objective of the entire work.

520 Erbse, H. "Die Architektonik im Aufbau von Xenophons *Memorabilien*." *Hermes*, 89 (1961), pp. 257-287.

Argues in favor of the view which sees in the *Memorabilia* a unified work whose different parts are tied together by a unifying principle, which was Xenophon's conviction that Socrates' character and actions were absolutely contrary to what the accusations suggested about him. Rejects as unsound the notion that parts of the *Memorabilia* should be regarded as a separate pamphlet which was artificially used by later editors as a preface to the main body of the work. Gives hints which are useful for the reconstruction of Polycrates' pamphlet.

521 Flacelière, Robert. "A propos du *Banquet* de Xénophon." *Revue des Etudes Grecques*, 74 (1961), pp. 93-118.

Recognizes the centrality of the idea of love in Xenophon's *Symposium*, and argues against the interpretation of this work which places other ideas (such as 'the noble' or 'the good') at the center of its discussions. Views the *Symposium*, not as a collection of unrelated anecdotal conversations, but as a unified and well-structured composition. Maintains that in writing the *Symposium*, Xenophon had as his main purpose to enhance and rectify the Platonic portrait of Socrates.

522 Fritz, Kurt von. "Antisthenes und Sokrates in Xenophons *Symposion*." *Rheinisches Museum für Philologie*, 84 (1935), pp. 19-45.

Analyzes and comments on the personalities and ideas of Antisthenes and Socrates as these are portrayed by Xenophon in the *Symposium*, and stresses the dramatic mastery with which Xenophon deals with them. Maintains that Xenophon's characterization of Socrates could have been influenced by Aeschines, and could have also been a manifestation of his desire to correct Antisthenes' narrow appreciation of Socrates' personality.

523 Fritz, Kurt von. "Das erste Kapitel des zweiten Buches von Xenophons *Memorabilien* und die Philosophie des Aristipp von Kyrene." *Hermes*, 93 (1965), pp. 257-279.

Maintains that the first chapter of the second book of the *Memorabilia* is a late addition to the work, an addition inserted by Xenophon himself in order to refute the doctrines of Aristippus. Notes that the arguments attributed to Socrates in that chapter are weak and unconvincing, and probably belong to Xenophon.

524 Fritz, Kurt von. "Zur Frage der Echtheit der xenophontischen *Apologie des Sokrates*." *Rheinisches Museum für Philologie*, 80 (1931), pp. 36-68.

Rejects the authenticity of Xenophon's *Apology*. Argues that this work contains clearly un-Socratic elements, and that some of its themes may have been borrowed from a non-extant non-Socratic work. Downgrades the historical and biographical value of the *Apology*.

525 Gebhardt, Ernst. *Polykrates' Anklage gegen Sokrates und Xenophons Erwiderung*. Doctoral dissertation. Johann Wolfgang Goethe Universität, Frankfurt, 1957.

Reconstructs Polycrates' indictment against Socrates, and endeavors to shed light on its 'proofs', specifically, its references to Homer, Pindar, and Theognis, and the arguments involving Socrates' harmful influence on Alcibiades and Critias. Reviews Xenophon's response to Polycrates in the *Memorabilia*. Includes an extended bibliography.

526 Gemoll, W. "Ἄρρενες ἔρωτες." *Philologische Wochenschrift*, 1933, pp. 1356-1357

Argues that the interpretation of Socrates's concept of love given by Xenophon in the *Symposium* is probably more historically accurate than that given by Plato in his *Symposium*.

527 Gemoll, W. "Der Eros in den *Symposien* Xenophons und Platons." *Philologische Wochenschrift*, 1934, pp. 30-32.

Maintains that both Xenophon and Plato attribute to Socrates a complete rejection of pederasty. Notes that according to Xenophon's testimony, Socrates urges us to love, not the physical body, but virtue and nobility, while Plato in his *Symposium* emphasizes Socrates' idea of a spiritual love in which the soul should be the sole object of desire.

528 Gigon, Olof. *Kommentar zum ersten Buch von Xenophons Memorabilien.* Basel: Reinhardt, 1953.

Originally published in 1947. Examines Book I of the *Memorabilia*, and argues in favor of the thesis that the defense part of Xenophon's work (*i.e.*, I,i,1-I,ii,64) is an integral component thereof, and that it should not be viewed as an independent apologetic pamphlet. Interprets the *Memorabilia* as a carefully planned and well organized work, not as a mere collection of unrelated literary pieces originally not intended for publication. Stresses the virtual impossibility of drawing a separating line between the actual historical Socrates and the Socrates of the literary (mostly fictional) traditions (to which Xenophon's testimony belongs). Maintains that the Platonic and Xenophontean *Apologies* must be interpreted on the assumption of the existence of earlier apologetic writings which are not extant. Disputes some of Maier's conclusions concerning the Socratic problem. Ref. 394.

529 Gigon, Olof. *Kommentar zum zweiten Buch von Xenophons Memorabilien.* Basel: Reinhardt, 1953.

Examines the content and structure of Book II of the *Memorabilia*, and develops further arguments in support of the conclusions reached in *Kommentar zum ersten Buch von Xenophons Memorabilien.* Ref. 528, 544.

530 Gigon, Olof. "Xenophons *Apologie des Sokrates.*" *Museum Helveticum*, 3 (1946), pp. 210ff.

Examines the structure and content of Xenophon's *Apology*, and concludes that its historical and biographical value is minimal.

531 Higgins, W. E. *Xenophon the Athenian: The Problem of the Individual and the Society of the Polis*. Albany, N.Y.: State University of New York Press, 1977.

Examines various biographical, historical, and literary aspects of Xenophon. Argues in favor of a more positive reassessment of Xenophon from a literary point of view and as an important Socratic witness. Discusses the relationship between Xenophon and the Athenian polity, and his views concerning the relationship between the State and the individual. Devotes one chapter (pp. 21-43) to an analysis of the relationship between Xenophon and Socrates. Recognizes as the unifying principle of his testimony his efforts to define precisely the concept of Socratic justice within the structure of political existence. Argues against those who minimize the philosophical and historical significance of Xenophon's portrait of Socrates, and rejects Kierkegaard's low estimate of the worth of such a portrait. Discovers throughout Xenophon's Socratic writings a concerted effort to answer Socrates' questions about justice.

532 Hornstein, F. "Komposition und Herausgabe der xenophontischen *Memorabilien*." *Wiener Studien*, 36 (1914), pp. 122-139; 37 (1915), pp. 63-87.

Argues that the *Memorabilia* contains basically three independently written sections: I,i-ii (written as a direct response to Polycrates); IV (written after I,i-ii); and the rest of the work (written later on).

533 Joël, Karl. *Der echte und der xenophontische Sokrates*. Berlin, 1893-1901 (2 vols.).

Ref. 386.

534 Krohn, A. *Sokrates und Xenophon*. Halle, 1874.

Reviews the Xenophontean testimony in general and Xenophon's claim to have been a direct and intimate witness of the Socratic presence in particular. Concludes that his account and 'recollections' of Socrates are largely the result of the influence of the Cynics, specifically Antisthenes. Argues that the Xenophontean Socrates is really only an expression of various ideas developed by the early Cynics. Calls attention to the parallels that can be drawn between the Xenophontean Socrates and Kant.

535 Lincke, K. *De Xenophontis libris socraticis.* Jena, 1890.

Examines in detail Xenophon's Socratic writings, mainly the *Memorabilia* and the *Apology*. Concludes that their historical and ideological value as Socratic testimonies is very limited, and that they reveal, not the direct presence of Socrates, but the influence of Cynic ideas (mainly those of Antisthenes) on Xenophon himself.

536 Lincke, K. "Xenophon und die Stoa." *Neue Jahrbücher für das Klassische Altertum*, 17 (1906), pp. 673-691.

Discovers in the extant text of Xenophon's Socratic writings interpolations of a Stoic origin which bear nevertheless the literary and ideological character of the actual Xenophontean writings.

537 Luccioni, Jean. *Les idées politiques et sociales de Xénophon.* Paris, 1948.

Argues that Xenophon was able to capture from Socrates only those ideas that were in agreement with his own inclinations, and that only in his mature age was he able to develop an adequate understanding of some of the teachings of his master. Observes that it was through the assimilation of these teachings that Xenophon succeeded in clarifying and organizing his political and social ideas.

538 Luccioni, Jean. *Xénophon et le socratisme.* Paris: Presses Universitaires de France, 1953.

Deals with the following major topics: (1) the relationship between Xenophon and Socrates; (2) the apologetic works of Xenophon (the *Apology* and the *Memorabilia*); the relationship between Xenophon's writings and the λόγοι σωκρατικοί; (4) the historical and political contributions of Xenophon. Regards him as a true Socratic, but notes that his Socratism is characteristic of a man who was endowed with a somewhat mediocre spirit ("*un esprit moyen*").

539 Mesk, J. "Die Anklagerede des Polykrates gegen Sokrates." *Wiener Studien*, 32 (1911), pp. 56-84.

Argues that there is some harmony between Xenophon's vindication of Socrates in the introductory sections of the *Memorabilia* and Libanius' *Apologia Socratis*, and that this applies especially to the issue involving the charge concerning Socrates' use and abuse of quotations from the poets (*Memorabilia* I,i,56; Libanius, lxi,14ff). Attributes to Libanius' work a greater sense of structure and organization than what can be attributed to that of Xenophon.

540 Morrison, J. S. "Socrates and Antiphon." *The Classical Review*, 5 (1955), pp. 8-11.

Discusses the meeting between Socrates and Antiphon in the *Memorabilia* (I,vi,1-15). Argues against those who insist on identifying Antiphon with a non-Athenian Sophist of the same name.

541 Morrison, J. S. "Xenophon, *Memorabilia* 1:6: The Encounter of Socrates and Antiphon." *The Classical Journal*, N.S. 3 (1953), pp. 3-6.

Identifies the Antiphon of the examined passage from the *Memorabilia* with Antiphon of Rhamus, the anti-democratic ideologist who was executed after the collapse of the oligarchical government of 411 B.C. in Athens. Suggests that that passage of the *Memorabilia* is intended as a defense of Socrates against the attack of Antiphon, specifically with respect to Socrates' asceticism, his refusal to accept fees for instruction, and his claim to be able to teach politics without being engaged in political activities.

542 Müller, K. O. "Xenophon and Ctesias." *A History of the Literature of Ancient Greece*. Translated by George C. Lewis and John W. Donaldson. London: Longmans, Green & Co., 1884 (3 vols.), Vol. 2, pp. 183-201.

Reviews the biography, style, literary intentions, and individual works of Xenophon. Maintains that even though it is not possible for us to form an adequate idea of the philosophical depth of Socrates from the writings of Xenophon, it is in them, not in Plato's dialogues, that we can find a genuine representation of the teachings and character of Socrates. Supports Athenaeus' contention that Plato's *Symposium* was written as a rebuttal to Xenophon's own *Symposium*.

543 Navia, Luis E. "A Reappraisal of Xenophon's *Apology*." *New Essays on Socrates*. Edited by Eugene Kelly. Lanham, Md.: University Press of America, 1984, pp. 47-65.

Examines in detail the content and structure of Xenophon's *Apology*, and reaches the conclusion that this brief Xenophontean work deserves to be evaluated in a more favorable light than has been customary among modern scholars. Pays particular attention to the context and intentions related to the writings of the *Apology*, and emphasizes its restricted and clearly defined scope, which can be characterized as an attempt to give an account of Socrates' μεγαληγορία during his trial. Regards Xenophon's testimony as valuable, and notes that it may well reveal a historically genuine aspect of Socrates which is missing from Plato's testimony. Ref. 561.

544 Neitzel, H. "Zur Interpretation von Xenophon, *Mem.* 2,6,13ff." *Würzburger Jahrbücher für die Altertumswissenschaft*, 7 (1981), pp. 51-61.

Maintains that a careful examination of *Memorabilia* II,vi,10-14 does not support Gigon's conclusion concerning the composition of the passages. Ref. 529.

545 Neumann, Harry. "Review of *Xenophon's Socratic Discourse: An Interpretation of the Oeconomicus* by Leo Strauss." *The Journal of the History of Philosophy*, 11 (1971), pp. 239-243.

Notes that Strauss' Xenophon reflects an attitude whereby philosophy is inseparable from irony, and that this attitude reveals and conceals at the same time the Socratic enterprise. Acknowledges that Strauss' Xenophon counter-balances in an effective way some of the contemporary prejudices which have attempted to downgrade the value of Xenophon's Socratic testimony. Ref. 559.

546 Oost, S. I. "Xenophon's Attitude Toward Women." *The Classical World*, 71 (1977), pp. 225-236.

Notes that Xenophon's ideas about women vary depending on the influence of Socrates on him: in his Socratic writings, he is more inclined to speak favorably about women, while in his non-Socratic works, he appears to share the ordinary views of the Greeks of his time.

547 Rapaport, A. "Ad Xenophontis *Convivium*." *Eos*, 13 (1925), p. 134.

Maintains that the dramatic date of Xenophon's *Symposium* coincides with the Peace of Nicias (421 B.C.), and that, accordingly, Xenophon (contrary to his assertion) could not have been present at the conversation. Notes that neither in antiquity nor in modern times has his literary presence in the *Symposium* been taken in a historical sense.

548 Richter, Ernst. "Xenophon-Studien." *Jahrbücher für klassischen Philologie*, 19 (1893), pp. 59-154.

Maintains that both in style and in content there is hardly any difference between Xenophon's Socratic writings and his non-Socratic writings. Supports this contention by examining and comparing the characterizations of Socrates and Kind Agesilaus, the accounts of Socrates' greatness and the excellence attributed to the Spartans, and the portrayals of Socrates and Cyrus. Insists that Xenophon's characterization of Socrates bears a closer relation to a generalized and idealized human type than to a specific historical person, and that, accordingly, the historical and biographical value of his Socratic testimony is quite minimal. Suggests that there are four different Xenophontean *Apologies*: three contained in the *Memorabilia*, and the actual *Apology*. Questions the historical character of Xenophon's direct acquaintance with Socrates.

549 Robin, Léon. *Les mémorables de Xénophon et notre connaissance de Socrate."* *L'Année Philosophique*, 21 (1910), pp. 1-47.

Reviews the *Memorabilia* and concludes that the value of Xenophon's testimony is most limited as a historical and biographical account of Socrates, and even more limited as a source of information concerning his philosophy. Refers to Socrates as a hero whose true history has never been written.

550 Roquette, Adalbert. *De Xenophontis vita dissertatio.* Königsberg, 1884.

Gives a general biographical account of Xenophon. Places composition of the *Memorabilia* between the years 384 and 380 B.C.

551 Rossetti, Livio. "Alla ricerca dei λόγοι σωκρατικοί perdutti, II-III." *Rivista di Studi Classici*, 23 (1975), pp. 87-99 and 361-381.

Ref. 820.

552 Schaerer, René. "Xénophon et la sagesse socratique." *L'Homme antique et la structure du monde intérieur d'Homère à Socrate.* Paris: Payot, 1958, pp. 343-353.

Discusses the nature and scope of Xenophon's representation of Socrates, and comments on his interpretation of Socratic wisdom as a practical philosophical stance.

553 Sheeks, Wayne. "Isocrates, Plato, and Xenophon Against the Sophists." *The Personalist*, 56 (1975), pp. 250-259.

Reviews the testimonies of Isocrates and Xenophon in order to determine the extent to which they are in agreement with Plato's negative and uncomplimentary assessment of the Sophistical movement. Examines Xenophon's representation of Socrates against the background of the ideas of the Sophists.

554 Shero, L. R. "Plato's *Apology* and Xenophon's *Apology*." *The Classical Weekly*, 20 (1926), pp. 107-111.

Ref. 1166.

555 Simeterre, M. R. *La théorie socratique de la vertue-science selon les Mémorables de Xénophon.* Paris, 1938.

Studies the problem of the relationship between virtue and knowledge as this is formulated and solved by the Xenophontean Socrates. Attaches great value to Aristotle's Socratic testimony. Regards the endeavor to reconstruct the image of the historical Socrates from the sources as *un jeu de patience* in which every bit of information, no matter how small or marginal, should be taken into account. Collects and comments on the passages of Xenophon which deal specifically with Socrates' concept of virtue.

556 Strauss, Leo. "The Spirit of Sparta or the Taste of Xenophon." *Social Research*, 6 (1939), pp. 502-536.

Discusses the influence of Spartan institutions and ideals on the formation and development of Xenophon's thought. Deals with the Xenophontean portrait of Socrates, to which it attaches historical importance.

557 Strauss, Leo. *On Tyranny: An Interpretation of Xenophon's Hiero*. New York, 1948.

Attempts to vindicate the veracity of Xenophon's Socratic testimony in general and the historical value of the *Memorabilia* in particular. States its basic criterion concerning the analysis of the Xenophontean Socrates in these terms: "What the attitude of the citizen-philosopher Socrates was can be ascertained only by a comprehensive and detailed analysis of Xenophon's Socratic writings" (p. 94).

558 Strauss, Leo. *Xenophon's Socrates*. Ithaca, N.Y.: Cornell University Press, 1972.

Reviews Xenophon's Socratic writings, and examines the origins and scope of his political ideas, and the significance of the Socratic presence in his life and thought. Endeavors to restore to a place of importance the value of Xenophon's testimony about Socrates, both as a biographical account and as a clear statement of Socratic ideas.

559 Strauss, Leo. *Xenophon's Socratic Discourse: An Interpretation of the Oeconomicus*. Ithaca, N.Y.: Cornell University Press, 1970.

Reviews the content of Xenophon's *Oeconomicus* against the background of the question as to the historical value of his reports on Socrates. Observes that of the four major Socratic witnesses (Xenophon, Plato, Aristophanes, and

Aristotle), it was Xenophon alone who "showed by deed that he was willing to be a historian." Concludes that the major source of our knowledge of Socrates is by necessity the Socratic writings of Xenophon. Ref. 545.

560 Taylor, Alfred E. "Socrates and the Myths." *The Classical Quarterly*, 27 (1933), pp. 158-159.

Notes that in the testimony of Xenophon the basis for the accusations against Socrates is based on his alleged lack of respect towards the poets, not on his refusal to accept the ordinary mythological tales about the gods.

561 Tejera, Victorino. "Ideology and Literature: Xenophon's *Defense of Socrates* and Plato's *Apology*." *New Essays on Socrates*. Edited by Eugene Kelly. Lanham, Md.: University Press of America, 1984, pp. 151-159.

Serves as a commentary on Navia's "A Reappraisal of Xenophon' *Apology*." Regards Xenophon's work as a brief and cunningly constructed piece of political ideology, more than as a historical account of Socrates' trial. Views Plato's *Apology* also as an ideologically oriented document, and as a creation far more artistic than that of Xenophon: while the latter addresses itself to limited and temporary issues, the former aims at shedding light on the entire human condition. Ref. 543.

562 Thesleff, H. "The Interpretation and Date of the Symposia of Plato and Xenophon." *Bulletin of the Institute of Classical Studies of the University of London*, 25 (1978), pp. 157-170.

Argues for the existence of two layers in the composition of Xenophon's *Symposium*: (1) an initial version which could have influenced the composition of Plato's *Symposium*, and (2) a final version which could have been affected by Plato's work.

563 Toole, H. J. "Xenophon's *Apologia* and Its Relations to the Platonic *Apologia* and to the Accusatory Pamphlet of Polycrates." *Platon*, 28 (1976), pp. 3-8.

In modern Greek, with an English abstract. Defends the authenticity of Xenophon's *Apology*, and argues that it is basically dependent on Plato's *Apology*.

564 Vogel, Cornelia J. de. "Who Was Socrates?" *The Journal of the History of Philosophy*, 1 (1963), pp. 141-161.

Argues for the idea that there is a basic agreement between the testimonies of Xenophon and Plato: "Our most important sources do not contradict but confirm one another." Notes, however, the absence of irony and philosophical depth in the Xenophontean Socrates. Argues that it is possible to develop a historically accurate portrait of Socrates as a philosopher, and that the most prominent feature of that portrait is his attachment to reason and to ethical convictions founded on metaphysical ideas.

565 Vrijlandt, P. *De Apologia Xenophontea cum Platonica comparata*. Leyden, 1920.

Develops a detailed textual analysis of Plato's and Xenophon's *Apologies*. Regards them as basically independent works.

566 Walton, Craig. "Xenophon and the Socratic Paradoxes." *The Southern Journal of Philosophy*, 16 (1978), pp. 687-700.

Endeavors to interpret the Socratic paradoxes (*i.e.*, the theses that virtue and wisdom are ultimately identical, and that the possession of wisdom precludes the commission of evil deeds) by an appeal to five themes in the testimonies of Xenophon and Plato, such as the ideas of practice and craftmanship, the reality of human ignorance, the principle of utility, and the use of dialectics. Observes in its conclusion that the two Socratic paradoxical ideas express the principles of self-knowledge and active wisdom, and that these two principles are basically independent of each other.

567 Wegehaupt, J. *De Dione Chrysostomo Xenophontis sectatore*. Gotha, 1896.

Reviews various passages in Dio Chrysostom's *Orationes* which may be viewed as echoes of certain passages in Xenophon's Socratic writings. Argues that the alleged summary of Socratic teachings found in *Oratio* xiii was taken in all probability from the pseudo-Platonic *Clitophon*.

568 Weissenborn, H. *De Xenophontis in commentariis scribendis fide historica*. Jena, 1910.

Short dissertation on Xenophon's Socratic writings. Rejects the judgment of K. Joël concerning the value of Xenophon's testimony. Reaches the following general conclusions: (1) that such testimony is not borrowed from Cynic sources; (2) that, unlike Plato, Xenophon did not use Socrates as a vehicle for his own ideas; (3) that the contradictions allegedly found in Xenophon vanish under the light of a better understanding of the texts; and (4) that the doctrines attributed to Socrates by Xenophon are genuinely Socratic. Ref. 386.

569 Wellman, Robert R. "Socratic Method in Xenophon." *The Journal of the History of Ideas*, 37 (1976), pp. 307-318.

Studies the common criticism levelled at Xenophon which alleges that his Socrates does not become engaged in the sort of eristical *elenchus* associated with the Platonic Socrates. Maintains that an examination of the *Memorabilia* and the *Oeconomicus* reveals the presence of the idea of Socratic maieutic. Concludes that this idea rather than the practice of eristics is the fundamental component of the Socratic method, and that this can be appreciated even in Xenophon's testimony.

570 Wilamowitz-Möllendorf, U. von. "Die xenophontische *Apologie*." *Hermes*, 32 (1897), pp. 99ff.

Rejects the authenticity of Xenophon's *Apology*. Maintains that the essential parts of this work were written under the direct influence of the Platonic *Apology*.

571 Wimmel, W. "Zum Verhältnis eineger Stellen des Xenophontischen und des platonischen Symposions." *Gymnasium*, 64 (1957), pp. 230-250.

Establishes a comparison between the *Symposium* of Xenophon and that of Plato, and concludes that it is not possible to determine whether they owe their origin to a common source, their similarities notwithstanding. Places their respective dates of composition after 386 B.C. and between 385 and 372 B.C.

## PLATO AND THE PLATONIC SOCRATES

The entries of this section include a representative sample of general works on Plato and his philosophy, and works in which emphasis is made on the significance of the Socratic problem as this is directly related to the Platonic Socrates.

572 Adam, A. M. "Socrates *quam mutatis ab illo.*" *The Classical Quarterly*, 12 (1918), pp. 121-139.

Reviews and criticizes the thesis advanced by Burnet and Taylor concerning the Socratic problem. Raises various objections to their contention that the Platonic Socrates should be viewed as an accurate and faithful representation of the historical Socrates.

573 Alsina, J. "Sócrates, Platón y la verdad." *Boletín del Instituto de Estudios Helénicos*, 1 (1967), pp. 39-43.

Notes that in spite of the fact that Plato acted as the apologist and supporter of Socrates and his ideas, the gap that separates them is immense, especially with respect to the approach to the quest for the truth: Socrates searched without restrictions and in an atmosphere of complete openness, but Plato wished to impose certain doctrines as if they were unquestionable dogmas (as can be gathered from passages from the *Laws*).

574 Baur, F. C. "Das Christliche des Platonismus, oder Sokrates und Christus." *Drei Abhandlungen zur Geschichte der Alten Philosophie und ihres Verhältnisses zum Christentum*. Edited by Eduard Zeller. Leipzig, 1876, pp. 228ff.

Ref. 1561.

575 Beamer, Elbert Monroe. *The Socratic Image in Plato*. Doctoral dissertation. Syracuse University, 1972.

Distinguishes an 'image' from a 'protrait': the latter imitates faithfully the original, while the former is open to distortion and may provide information by means of artistic transformation. Notes that the quest for a historical portrait of Socrates has blinded us to the possibility of finding a genuine Socratic image. Speaks of the futility of searching for a historical Socratic portrait. Develops an image of Socrates as this is found in Plato's writings, and attributes to this image three characteristics: (1) a 'likeness' to the original, (2) a dianoetic function, and (3) a poetic function. Observes that Plato, as a poet and an artist, created an image of Socrates in order to give us a paradigm of the true philosopher, and that to do this, he had to transform and even distort the original data of his recollections. Concludes that the Platonic Socrates is more meaningful as an image than as a mere portrait.

576 Berger, H. "Plato's Flying Philosopher." *The Philosophical Forum*, 13 (1982), pp. 385-407.

Contrasts the way in which Plato characterizes Socrates with the ways in which other philosophers (*e.g.*, Parmenides and Anaxagoras) are depicted in the dialogues. Notes that the latter are invariably portrayed negatively and in an anti-Socratic light, whereas Socrates is always presented positively and as an ideal philosopher.

577 Brochard, Victor. "Le devenir dans la philosophie de Platon." *Etudes de philosophie ancienne et de philosophie moderne.* Paris: Vrin, 1926.

Maintains that the skepticism expressed by the Platonic Socrates in the *Apology* with respect to the problem of the immortality of the soul, can be confidently attributed to the historical Socrates. Argues that the views expressed by Socrates in the *Phaedo* concerning immortality should be regarded as expressions of Plato's own ideas and not as authentic Socratic thoughts.

578 Brumbaugh, Robert S. "Plato and Socrates." *Plato for the Modern Age.* Westport, Conn.: Greenwood Press, 1979, pp. 29-50.

Originally published by Cromwell-Collier Publishing Company in 1962. Examines the background and details of Socrates' trial as this is recounted in the *Apology*. Views this Platonic work as an accurate, yet polished and edited account of the actual trial. Reviews the arguments of Socrates in the *Crito*, and suggests that these stand in no contradiction with his arguments in the *Apology*. Summarizes and comments on various Platonic dialogues with special emphasis on the Platonic representation of Socrates (*Phaedo*, *Euthyphro*, *Lysis*, and *Charmides*). Regards these dialogues as Plato's literary efforts to leave for us an outline of authentic Socratic themes. Concludes with comments on Plato's choice of the dialogue as a vehicle for expression, and on his use of Socrates as the protagonist for his dialogues.

579 Burnet, John. *Platonism*. Berkeley: University of California Press, 1928.

Expresses the author's last supporting statements concerning his fundamental thesis with respect to the Socratic problem: that is, that Plato can be viewed as the biographer and doxographer of Socrates. Observes that the Platonic dialogues "do not give us Plato's own philosophy" (pp. 12-13), but a literary formulation of Socrates' philosophical stance. Reiterates the contention that the theory of Ideal Forms has an origin that precedes Plato and can already be found in Socrates' thought. Regards the Platonic dialogues as documents in which we come face to face with the "really and truly" historical Socrates, and as a "marvelously accurate and truthful representation of him." Views the philosophy of Socrates as a development of Pythagoreanism.

580 Burnyeat, M. F. "Socratic Midwifery, Platonic Inspiration." *Bulletin of the Institute of Classical Studies of the University of London*, 24 (1977), pp. 7-16.

Argues that the Platonic comparison of Socrates with a midwife has to be understood in the context of certain dialogues (*e.g.*, the *Theaetetus* and the *Symposium*), and that it should not be associated with the historical Socrates.

581 Cairns, Huntington. *Legal Philosophy from Plato to Hegel*. Baltimore: The Johns Hopkins Press, 1949, pp. 29-76.

Attempts to bring together the various references to the concept of 'law' which appear throughout the Platonic dialogues. Begins with a reference to the *Minos*, where Plato states that it is the discovery of reality which law seeks: Socrates endeavors to arrive at a definition of 'law' and leads to the conclusion that law is different from that which is recognized as legal. Emphasizes the distinction between nature and convention, as this distinction appears in several Platonic contexts. Comments on the role played by the Laws in the *Crito*.

582 Campbell, Lewis, editor. *Select Passages from the Introductions to Plato by Benjamin Jowett*. New York: John Murray, 1895.

Reproduces passages from the introductions to the Platonic dialogues in Jowett's translation. Ref. 90.

583 Capizzi, Antonio. "La testimonianza platonica. Contributo alla ricerca di una determinazione dell' elemento socratico nei dialoghi." *Rassegna di Filosofia*, 6 (1957), pp. 205-221 and 309-337.

Maintains that by analyzing the views attributed by Plato to Parmenides and Zeno, it is possible to develop a criterion in order to distinguish those elements in the dialogues which belong to Socrates from those which are Platonic additions. Notes that the genuinely Socratic elements appear with equal regularity from the *Apology* to the *Theaetetus*.

584 Capizzi, Antonio. *Socrate e i personaggi filosofi di Platone*. Rome: Edizioni dell' Ateneo, 1970.

Reviews and analyzes the ideological portrait of Socrates which emerges from Plato's dialogues, and discusses various other Platonic characters. Ref. 647.

585 Capuzzi, Frank A. *Socrates Manikos: An Essay on the Death of a Hero-Seer*. Doctoral dissertation. Duquesne University, 1972.

Represents an attempt to give an account of the artistic unity of Plato's works. Speaks of this unity as having been realized through a tragic myth, which is itself the artistic imitation of Socrates' life. Observes that philosophy begins with the sense of wonder, and that this sense is the *locus* of Plato's thought. Notes that this thought is centered in Socrates, who constitutes for Plato "philosophy in act." Reappraises the traditional grounds for developing a chronology of the dialogues. Emphasizes the supreme artistry of Plato's work and of his effort to achieve artistically the ultimate philosophical destiny, namely, self-knowledge. Notes that for the Platonic Socrates, "philosophy is the name of the rebirth [he] promises for the right kind of soul -- the steadiest kind of soul."

586 Chroust, Anton-Hermann. "Socrates: A Source Problem." *The New Scholasticism*, 19 (1945), pp. 52ff.

Expresses skepticism concerning the possibility of recreating a genuinely historical representation of Socrates from the available sources. Insists that it was not Plato's intention to construct such a representation for posterity, and that the Platonic Socrates may not be even a remote facsimile of the historical Socrates.

587 Cornford, Francis MacDonald. "Plato's Commonwealth." *The Unwritten Philosophy and Other Essays*. Edited by W. K. C. Guthrie. Cambridge: Cambridge University Press, 1967, pp. 47-67.

Establishes a comparison between the Athenian political world of the early fourth century B.C. and that of Europe after World War I. Describes Plato's disappointment with politics in general and democracy in particular, and discusses the significance of Socrates' execution for the development of Plato's political views. Outlines the Platonic ideal State, and establishes a parallelism between it and communist regimes and the Catholic Church. Concludes with a dramatic scene (drawn in the style of Dostoevski's "The Grand Inquisitor") in which Socrates is tried and sentenced before the Platonic nocturnal council (proposed in Plato's *Laws*).

588 Crombie, I. M. *The Midwife's Apprentice*. London: Routledge & Kegan Paul, 1965.

Presents the conclusions of the author's *An Examination of Plato's Doctrines* (London: Routledge & Kegan Paul, 1962) without all the supporting arguments. Does not attempt to offer an account of what Plato says but, through its interpretation, a demonstration of the significance of his philosophical contributions. Argues that during Plato's generation it was undoubtedly Socrates who represented the greatest influence on intelligent Athenians, and of whom Plato wished to leave a permanent record for posterity. Suggests that the major assumption that can be made regarding Socratic thought is that when in a dialogue Socrates advances strongly a particular idea, it is most likely that Plato considered such an idea a faithful representation and development of Socrates' thought.

589 Crossman, R. H. S. *Plato Today*. London: George Allen & Unwin, 1939.

Brings Plato into the contemporary world of politics in order to elicit from him comments on issues such as British democracy, American education, the New Deal, the modern family, communism, and Nazism. Attempts to explain the reasons and causes for the ultimate failure of Plato's political philosophy. Contains one chapter on Socrates in which his ideological relationship is discussed. Implies that even though Plato's political thoughts may have originated from genuine Socratic ideas, their general political outlooks should not be viewed as identical.

590 Demos, Raphael. *The Philosophy of Plato*. New York: Charles Scribner's Sons, 1939.

Aims at reconstructing the philosophy of Plato from his works without appealing to any secondary sources of criticism and interpretation. Maintains that the Socratic influence on Plato was so profound and decisive that it became an integral component of his own mind. Does not attempt to distinguish the Socratic from the Platonic elements in the dialogues.

591 Deschoux, M. "La singularité de Platon." *Métaphysique. Histoire de la Philosophie. Recueil d'Etudes offert à Fernand Brunner*. Neuchâtel: La Baconnière, 1981, pp. 25-32.

Regards Plato's dialogues as a great testimony about Socrates as a man and as a philosopher, but notes that Plato's work goes far beyond being a mere historical record, as it deals with the problems of philosophy at large, and is therefore both historical and dogmatic. Adds, however, that Plato's dogmatism does not preclude him from remaining open to developing ideas.

592 Dewey, John. "The 'Socratic Dialogues' of Plato." *Studies in the History of Philosophy*, 2 (1935), pp. 3-23.

Views the Socratic or early dialogues as "critical preparatory try-outs" in which the questions answered and solved in the later dialogues are raised and formulated. Maintains that the positions advanced in the Socratic dialogues are consistent with the teachings of the *Republic*, and can be construed as dialectical refutations of certain philosophers who claimed to be Socratic.

593 Diès, Auguste. "La transposition platonicienne." *Autour de Platon*. Paris: Gabriel Beauchesne, 1927 (2 vols.), Vol. 1, pp. 400-449.

Discusses the transformations undergone by the philosophy of Socrates in the Platonic dialogues. Distinguishes two interrelated kinds of transformations (*transpositions*): (1) a literary transformation which constitutes a change in style, and (2) a doctrinal transformation which entails the actual development of Platonism out of Socrates' thought.

594 Diès, Auguste. "Socrate." *Autour de Platon*. Paris: Gabriel Beauchesne, 1927 (2 vols.), Vol. 1, pp. 127-243.

Contains three major sections: The Socratic Question, the Platonic Socrates, and the Socratic Legend. Includes also separate sections on Taylor's interpretation of the Socratic problem, on the views advanced by Burnet, von Armin, H. Gomperz, and Duprél, and on W. D. Ross' assessment of Aristotle's Socratic testimony. Speaks of Socrates as a "*predicateur de l'action droite*", whose entire life was controlled by a unifying mission, namely, the moral and intellectual reformation of humanity.

595 Dubbs, Homer H. "The Socratic Problem." *Philosophical Review*, 36 (1927), pp. 287-306.

Examines Plato's representation of Socrates, and concludes

that it should be regarded as a faithful portrayal of the historical Socrates at least with respect to its essential features. Argues against the view (advanced by Hegel and Schleiermacher) which maintains that Xenophon's lack of philosophical originality renders him a more reliable Socratic witness than Plato.

596 Duncan, Patrick. "Socrates and Plato." *Philosophy*, 15 (1940), pp. 339-362.

Endeavors to trace the genesis and development of the theory of Ideal Forms as this is advanced in the *Republic*, the *Phaedo*, and the *Phaedrus*. Does not make a specific distinction between the contribution of Socrates to that theory and Plato's own contribution.

597 Dupréel, Eugene. *La légende socratique et les sources de Platon*. Brussels: Robert Sand, 1922.

Ref. 371.

598 Dupréel, Eugene. "Socratisme et platonisme." *Congrès des Societés Philosophiques Americaine, Anglaise, Belge, Italienne, et de la Societé Française de Philosophie. Communications et Discussions*. Paris, 1921, pp. 266ff.

Questions the historical value of Plato's representation of a philosophy that can be associated with the actual Socrates. Speaks of Plato's dialogues (inasmuch as they appear to portray Socrates) as imaginary creations born out of a desire to resolve philosophical issues. Rejects the idea of a genuinely Socratic period in the development of Plato's thought. Concludes that the historical thought of Socrates is truly indiscernible. Maintains that if we insist on reconstructing the authentic philosophy of Socrates, we must appeal to the testimony of Euripides, "*puisqu'il nous est fortement attesté qu'Euripide se fit l'echo de Socrate*" (p. 271).

599 Edelstein, Emma. *Das xenophotisches und platonisches Bild des Sokrates*. Heidelberg, 1935.

Ref. 518.

600 Edelstein, L. "Platonic Anonymity." *The American Journal of Philology*, 83 (1962), pp. 1-22.

Interprets Plato's choice not to include himself in his dialogues as a clear manifestation of his great debt to Socrates. Adds, however, that his choice may have been influenced by Pythagorean ideas, according to which the pursuit of philosophy should always be an impersonal and collective undertaking.

601 Eisner, Robert. "Socrates as Hero." *Philosophy and Literature*, 6 (1982), pp. 106-118.

Argues that in his creation of the portrait of Socrates, Plato endeavored to superimpose a new type of myth (the myth of the philosopher as hero) on the myths of earlier times. Views the Platonic Socrates as a focal point for the convergence of the traditional features of the Homeric warrior, although such features are modified in Socrates for the purpose of supporting a distinct philosophical content. Discovers a number of specific analogies between the Platonic Socrates and the Homeric Odysseus.

602 Field, Guy C. *Plato and His Contemporaries*. London: Methuen & Co., 1930.

Contains chapters on Plato's life and work (early years, personal characteristics, the Academy, and the dialogues), on the moral and political background, and on the literary and philosophical background. Rejects the view that sees the dialogues as an accurate representation of the historical Socrates, and finds a logical weakness in the arguments of those who, in order to strengthen the historical reliability of Plato, attempt to discredit Xenophon's *Memorabilia* as an intentional fiction.

603 Field, Guy C. *Socrates and Plato*. Oxford: Parker & Co., 1913.

Pamphlet (40 pp.). Examines the contentions of A. E. Taylor and John Burnet concerning Plato's testimony about Socrates, specifically "that the portrait drawn in the Platonic dialogues of the personal and philosophical individuality of Socrates is in all its main points strictly historical," and "that, consequently, the views put in the mouth of Socrates by Plato were really held by him." Argues that the evidence available from the testimonies of Xenophon and Aristotle, and even from that of Plato himself, points decisively away from such a view of the Socratic problem. Insists on recognizing a clear ideological difference between Socrates and Plato. Ref. 579.

604 Field, Guy C. "Socrates and Plato in Post-Aristotelian Tradition." *The Classical Quarterly*, 18 (1924), pp. 127-136; 19 (1925), pp. 1-14.

Examines the Peripatetic and Academic traditions, and the biographical and doxographical traditions, and concludes that there is unanimity among the later writers that the dialogues represent Plato's own thought, but that there is no agreement as to the extent to which the dialogues present a historical picture of Socrates. Adds that there is no evidence in the literature consulted to connect Socrates with the Pythagoreans: "In fact, most of the evidence, such as it is, is rather the other way." Ref. 496.

605 Fox, Adam. *Plato for Pleasure.* London: John Westhouse, 1945.

Contains chapters on Plato's dialogues, on his life and character, on the main themes of his philosophy (dialectics, mathematics, myths, and theology), on various problems related to the interpretation of Platonic philosophy, and on his political views. Includes a translation of the *Euthyphro*, preceded by a summary of the dialogue. Concludes with an extended bibliography and with two appendices which give the pagination of the Stephanus edition and a schematic list of the dialogues (indicating authenticity as accepted by A. E. Taylor), together with comments on their literary structure, probable date of composition and literary date, and major themes.

606 Fraisse, J. C. "Ascétisme et valeur de la vie chez Platon." *Revue Philosophique*, 149 (1959), pp. 104-108.

Argues that the philosophical portraits of Socrates given by Plato in the *Phaedrus*, the *Symposium*, and the *Phaedo* stand in mutual agreement, specifically with respect to the two basic Socratic principles which they convey, namely, a reliance on spontaneity and an adherence to a rigorous asceticism. Notes that these two principles do not contradict each other.

607 Friedländer, Paul. *Plato: An Introduction.* Translated by Hans Meyerhoff. Princeton, N.J.: Princeton University Press, 1969.

English translation of Friedländer's *Platon. Sein Wahrheit und Lebenswirklichkeit.* Ref. 608.

608 Friedländer, Paul. *Platon. Sein Wahrheit und Lebenswirklichkeit.* Berlin: W. de Gruyter & Co., 1954.

Collection of essays on a variety of themes and topics related to Plato: the concepts of εἶδος, δαίμων, and ἔρως; the theory of Ideal Forms; the Platonic Academy; the presence of Socrates in Plato; the use of irony, dialogue, and myth by Plato; Platonic intuition and construction, and their relationship to the philosophies of Bergson and Schopenhauer; the concept of ἀλήθεια as viewed by Heidegger, and the use of dialogue as understood by Jaspers; the authenticity of the Platonic letters; and Plato as a physicist, geographer, jurist, and city planner. Concludes with a chapter entitled "Socrates Enters Rome." Ref. 1661.

609 Friedländer, Paul. "Socrates in Plato." *Plato: An Introduction.* Translated by Hans Meyerhoff. Princeton, N.J.: Princeton University Press, 1969, pp. 126-136.

English translation of Chapter 6 of Part 1 of Friedländer's *Platon.* Examines Plato's choice to place Socrates at the center of his philosophical dramas, and concludes that what is truly encountered in this circumstance is something that goes far beyond a mere testimony of gratitude of the pupil towards his teacher. Views the literary presence of Socrates in Plato as a clear manifestation of the immense influence of the Socratic spirit in the entire development of Platonic thought, and as a direct effort on Plato's part to answer the questions originally raised by Socrates. Rejects as artificial the distinction between 'Socratic' dialogues and 'Platonic' dialogues, and regards as false the idea that the influence of Socrates grew fainter as Plato became older.

610 Gerke, Alfred. "Eine Niederlage des Sokrates." *Neue Jahrbücher für das Klassische Altertum*, 41 (1918), pp. 145-191.

Emphasizes the opposition between Socrates and Plato, and suggests that in some of the Platonic texts we can clearly detect an effort on Plato's part to struggle against the constraints placed upon him by Socrates' teachings. Indicates that in some respects Plato's philosophical accomplishment constitutes something like the overthrow of Socrates' thought.

611 Giannantoni, Gabriele. "Il primo libro della *Repubblica* di Platone." *Rivista Critica di Storia della Filosofia*, 12 (1957), pp. 123-145.

Argues that the views and arguments attributed to Socrates in the first book of the *Republic* are specifically designed to convey a sense about the limitations inherent in the Socratic method. Notes that it is possible to detect a change on Plato's part with respect to his attitude towards Socrates, as one compares the beginning of the *Republic* with earlier dialogues. Views the first book of the *Republic* as an introduction to the more constructive (and more Platonic) arguments of the rest of the work.

612 Goergemanns, H. "Sokrates in den platonischen Frühdialogen." *Gymnasium*, 91 (1984), pp. 135-148.

Comments on the Platonic portrait in the early dialogues, with special emphasis on their fictional character and the traditional picture of Socrates which has emerged from them. Includes a bibliography.

613 Greene, William C. "The Spoken and the Written Word." *Harvard Studies in Classical Philology*, 60 (1951), pp. 23-59.

Proposes to resolve various aspects of the Socratic problem (as this emerges especially in the context of Plato's testimony) by distinguishing those early dialogues which are mostly biographical from those in which Plato came to expound his own philosophy, there being a gradual transition between the former and the latter. Suggests that his early dialogues may have been based on actual notes of Socrates' conversations taken by Plato himself.

614 Grote, George. *Plato and the Other Companions of Socrates.* London: John Murray, 1875 (3 vols.).

Furnishes a comprehensive examination of the biography, writings, and philosophy of Plato and the Socratics. Deals in Chapter 1 with the rise and development of philosophy in Greece before Socrates' time and during his time. Devotes most of Chapter 2 to the study of Zeno and Gorgias, and the growth of dialectics. Discusses the biography of Plato in Chapter 3, and the structure, composition, and chronology of his writings in Chapters 4, 5, and 6. Examines (beginning in Chapter 7) all the Platonic dialogues listed in Thrasyllus' arrangement. Reviews in subsequent chapters a great amount of biographical and ideological information pertaining to the minor Socratics, including Xenophon. Views Socrates as the pivotal point at which philosophy became concerned with human issues, and as the originator of the elenchical method. Constructs its historical and philosophical portrait of Socrates by appealing to the testimony of Plato (who is viewed neither as in opposition to Socrates, nor yet as identical with him), and to the testimonies of Xenophon and the other Socratics.

615 Grube, G. M. A. "Burnet and the *Phaedo*." *Plato's Thought.* London: Methuen & Co., 1935, pp. 291-294.

Appendix 1 of Grube's work. Maintains that Burnet's position with respect to the Socratic problem, namely, that the Platonic portrayal of Socrates is historically and ideologically accurate, is based to a great extent on a mistaken interpretation of the *Phaedo*. Observes that this interpretation gives a Pythagorean origin to the theory of Ideal Forms (viewing Cebes and Simmias as familiar with this theory). Argues against Burnet on the basis of an analysis of the text of the *Phaedo*. Ref. 117, 579.

616 Gulley, Norman. "Ethical Analysis in Plato's Earlier Dialogues." *The Classical Quarterly*, N.S. 2 (1952), pp. 74-82.

Maintains that the uncertainties and hesitations (*i.e.*, lack of a definite commitment on Socrates' part to a given idea) which abound in the early dialogues, are explainable as a consequence of Plato's own early searching and wavering mind, not as a representation of the uncertainties of the historical Socrates.

617 Gustarelli, A. *Socrate et Platone*. Milan, 1953.

Contains synoptical statements which survey and summarize the *Apology*, the *Crito*, the *Euthyphro*, the *Phaedrus*, the *Phaedo*, and *Republic* I.

618 Guthrie, W. K. C. *Plato. A History of Greek Philosophy*. Cambridge: Cambridge University Press, 1976, Vol. 4.

Deals with the biography of Plato and with his dialogues up to the *Republic*. Presents the dialogues by reference to the aim and philosophical lesson of each one of them, rather than by reference to general philosophical themes.

619 Guthrie, W. K. C. "Plato's Views on the Nature of the Soul." *Plato (II): Ethics, Politics, and Philosophy. A Collection of Critical Essays*. Edited by Gregory Vlastos. Garden City, N.Y.: Doubleday, 1971, pp. 230-243.

Originally published in *Recherches sur la tradition platonicienne, Entretiens* (Vol. 3), Fondation Hardt pour l'Etude de l'Antiquité Classique (Geneva: Vandoeuvres, 1957, pp. 2-19). Addresses itself to the following questions: What were Plato's beliefs about the nature of the human soul? In what sense did he predicate immortality to it? Do the dialogues speak with internal consistency about the soul? Maintains that the seeds of Plato's concept of the soul can be traced back to Socrates, and that even when the former went beyond the latter, no state of contradiction can be found among them: Plato held firmly to the Socratic thesis that the chief purpose of human life is the care of the soul, and that the ultimate aim of philosophy is the looking after the welfare of the soul. Agrees with E. Ehnmark with respect to the idea that for Socrates the soul is immortal and is destined to an everlasting and blessed existence. Concedes, however, that the specific doctrines and myths of the *Phaedo* go beyond the stance adopted by Socrates. Observes that it may be impossible to state with precision Socrates' views on the nature of the soul. For further comments, see p. 260 (Ref. 929). Ref. 1192.

620 Hager, F. P. "Vom sokratischen Zweifel zur platonischen Gewissenheit. Ein beispielhafter Weg des Philosophierens." *Museum Helveticum*, 34 (1977), pp. 99-121.

Comments on the relationship between Socrates and Plato, and notes how Plato's intellectual journey led him away from the initial stage of Socratic doubtfulness, towards the recognition of the Ideal Forms and the Divine as the true sources of knowledge.

621 Hamilton, Edith. "Plato." *The Ever-Present Past*. New York: W. W. Norton & Company, 1964. pp. 38-47.

An address given before the Classical Association of the Atlantic States. Discusses several biographical aspects of Plato, and focuses on his role as a writer. Comments at length on the influence of Socrates on him, by making remarks on the *Gorgias*, the *Apology*, and the *Phaedo*. Makes some passing references to Christian themes that are evoked as one reads Plato's works.

622 Hare, R. M. *Plato*. New York: Oxford University Press, 1982.

Gives a general account of Plato's philosophical contributions. Contains chapters on the life and times of Plato and his predecessors, and on a variety of themes related to his thought. Discusses the influence of Socrates on Plato (pp. 4-6, 13-22, 26ff, 37-41, 47-54, 72-74). Notes that such influence was so decisive that Plato "resolved to devote his life to the exposition and development of [Socrates'] ideas" (p. 6). Observes also that Socrates' philosophy is "so continuous with that of Plato that scholars have found it hard to decide which views belonged to which" (p. 14). Maintains, however, that while certain ideas can be safely attributed to Socrates (*e.g.*, his overwhelming concern with the difference between opinion and knowledge), other ideas belong more properly to Plato (*e.g.*, the doctrine of the soul, with its three parts and its communion with a world of Ideal Forms). Refers to its own approach to the Socratic problem as "fairly orthodox."

623 Havelock, Eric A. "The Orality of Socrates and the Literacy of Plato: With Some Reflections on the Historical Origins of Moral Philosophy in Europe." *New Essays on Socrates*. Edited by Eugene Kelly. Lanham, Md.: University Press of America, 1984, pp. 67-93.

Discusses the roles played by Socrates and Plato in the introduction of literacy and the development of moral philosophy in the late fifth and early fourth centuries B.C. in Greece. Views Socrates as an oralist and Plato as a textualist, and shows, by examining a variety of terms such as *psyche* and *arete*, the change undergone by language from a spoken and heard form to a written and seen form, which was essential for the genesis of moral ideas among the Greeks. Regards Plato's theory of Ideal Forms as the ultimate expression of the process of alphabetization. Rejects categorically the ideological distinction introduced by scholars between 'early' and 'late' dialogues, and does not share the belief that in certain 'Socratic' or 'early' dialogues (unlike in the 'Platonic' or 'late' dialogues) it is possible to discover the presence of the historical Socrates.

624 Hawtrey, R. S. "Plato, Socrates, and the Mysteries." *Antichthon*, 10 (1976), pp. 22-24.

Argues against A. W. H. Adkins' allegation that Plato did not attribute to Socrates any language of religious initiation in the early dialogues in order to avoid shocking Athenian readers. Ref. 423.

625 Horneffer, Ernst. *Platon gegen Sokrates.* Leipzig, 1904.

Reviews several Platonic dialogues (such as the *Protagoras*, the *Laches*, and the *Hippias Major*), and concludes that in some of their arguments and passages a clear opposition between Socrates and Plato can be discerned, and that the presence of this opposition makes it impossible to accept the thesis that Socrates acted in the dialogues as the mouthpiece for Plato's ideas. Views the major thrust of the *Laches*, for instance, as an attack against the ethical intellectualism of Socrates, and suggests that the ultimate purpose of the *Hippias Major* is to undermine the Socratic conviction that virtue and knowledge are identical, and that no one chooses evil willingly and knowingly. Regards the *Apology* as an essentially historical document. Draws attention to the mystic and prophetic aspects of the Socratic presence.

626 Huit, C. *La vie et l'oeuvre de Platon.* Paris: Shorin & Fils, 1893 (2 vols).

Devotes Vol. 1 to a reconstruction of the biography of

Plato. Presents Socrates as the crucial influence on Plato's life and philosophy. Discusses in Vol. 2 the order and content of Plato's dialogues.

627 Hyland, Drew A. "Why Plato Wrote Dialogues." *Philosophy and Rhetoric*, 1 (1968), pp. 38-50.

Takes seriously the theoretical principle of Platonic interpretation which focuses on the central place of those aspects of Plato's writings peculiar to the dialogue form: dramatic setting, personalities involved and relationships among them, and others. Includes a brief interpretation of the dramatic situation of the *Crito*.

628 Irwin, Terence. *Plato's Moral Theory: The Early and Middle Dialogues.* Oxford: Oxford University Press, 1978.

Maintains that the ethical positions of Socrates and Plato stand in opposition towards each other within the thesis defended by both, namely, that the only final good for human beings is happiness. Argues that for Socrates virtue is external to happiness, and is a mere means that leads to happiness; while for Plato, virtue is a part of happiness, and is, therefore, a good in itself. Develops its main theme by analyzing two major points of the early dialogues: the Socratic *elenchus* and Socrates' model of ethics as a craft. Finds these two points in irreconcilable conflict, and insists that Plato resolved the conflict by eliminating the idea of ethics as a craft, and by introducing his theory of Ideal Forms as the basis for ethics. Develops a portrait of Socrates as a reductionist utilitarian. Ref. 690, 1350, 1404, 1425.

629 Jordan, Nehemiah. *The Wisdom of Plato: An Attempt at an Outline*. Lanham, Md.: University Press of America, 1981 (2 vols.).

Challenges the traditional interpretation of Plato's dialogues which sees in them three distinct groups of writings: early, middle, and late. Challenges also the idea that the Socrates of the 'early' dialogues can be viewed as the truly historical Platonic Socrates. Maintains that such a categorization of the Platonic *corpus* is mostly arbitrary and unjustified, and develops the idea that *all* the dialogues of Plato constitute an organic whole in which the fundamental theme is the development of the exploration of the problem of meaning. Constructs a tentative chronology, and introduces a number of novel interpretational ideas about some of the individual dialogues.

630 Kafka, Gustav. *Sokrates, Platon und der sokratische Kreis.* Munich: E. Reinhardt, 1921.

Reviews the major biographical information about Socrates, Plato, and some of the minor Socratics. Endeavors to shed light on the ideological relationship between Socrates and Plato.

631 Kahn, Charles H. "Did Plato Write Socratic Dialogues?" *The Classical Quarterly*, 31 (1981), pp. 305-320.

English version of Kahn's "Platon a-t-il écrit des dialogues socratiques?" Ref. 632.

632 Kahn, Charles H. "Platon a-t-il écrit des dialogues socratiques?" *Bulletin de la Societé Française de Philosophie*, 74 (1980), pp. 45-77.

Argues that it is reasonable to assume that Plato wrote little or nothing before the year 390 B.C., that is, before the time when he abandoned his political ambitions. Notes that the so-called Socratic dialogues belong to a period after 390 B.C., and that their true purpose is not merely to present Socratic themes and issues, but to pave the way for the exposition of Plato's own ideas, specifically the doctrines of recollection and of the Ideal Forms.

633 Laguna, Théodore de. "Burnet's Socrates." *Mind*, 43 (1934), pp. 50-62.

Reviews and criticizes Burnet's assertions (specifically in his edition of the *Phaedo*) concerning the historical and biographical value of Plato's portrayal of Socrates. Expresses reservations about the contention that everything attributed by Plato to Socrates can be construed as being historically accurate. Ref. 117, 579.

634 Levi, Adolfo. "Socrate o Platone." *Rivista di Filosofia Classica*, 46 (1918), pp. 256-271.

Examines and criticizes the thesis advanced by Burnet and Taylor concerning the historical authenticity of the Platonic Socrates. Insists on distinguishing a genuine Socratic philosophy from the extensions and amplifications created by Plato around the figure of Socrates. Ref. 117, 579, 686, 687, 688, 689.

635 Levinson, Ronald B. *In Defense of Plato.* Cambridge, Mass.: Harvard University Press, 1954.

Deals with the alleged misrepresentations of Plato on the part of his detractors. Discusses the ideas of R. H. S. Crossman, W. Fite, O. Neurath, and K. Popper, among others. Proposes to mount a defense of Plato and his philosophy by (1) stating the nature of the criticisms and attacks; (2) classifying and cataloguing them; and (3) demonstrating by textual analyses and cultural references the frequency of erroneous and occasionally malicious misinterpretations of Plato. Argues that his detractors base their conclusions on vicious mistranslations, severe historical inaccuracies, and fanciful speculations. Questions the correctness of Popper's allegations concerning Plato's 'betrayal' of Socrates' philosophy in general and of his political ideas in particular. Ref. 589, 1283.

636 Lodge, Rupert C. "On a Recent Hypothesis Concerning the Platonic Socrates." *Proceedings of the Sixth International Congress of Philosophy*. New York, 1927, pp. 559ff.

Reviews and criticizes the Burnet-Taylor interpretation of the Platonic Socrates. Questions its major contention, and suggests that the gap that separates the historical Socrates from the Platonic portrayal of him may be more real than Burnet and Taylor were willing to admit. Ref. 117, 579, 686, 687, 688, 689.

637 Lodge, Rupert C. "What Plato Knows." *Transactions of the Royal Society of Canada*, 45 (1951), pp. 19-34.

Argues that Plato, Socrates' chief disciple, must have understood well the kernel of Socratic philosophy, and that it is through the study of the Platonic dialogues that one may succeed in discovering the direction of Socrates' message.

638 Louis, Savine. "Ein Versuch zur Losung Sokratischen Problems." *Philosophia*, 7 (1977), pp. 241-265.

Argues that Plato attributed to Socrates two basically different doctrines, and that Plato endeavored laboriously to hide their differences by means of "a dialectic of deceit." Concludes that such doctrines surface in a variety of pairs of themes: Socratic and Platonic ignorance, Socratic and Platonic divine voice, and Socratic and Platonic irony. Notes, with respect to the Socratic problem, that the most adequate approach should involve a search for a common denominator among the various testimonies.

639 MacKenzie, Mary M. *Plato on Punishment*. Berkeley: University of California Press, 1982.

Presents a discussion of Plato's views on punishment as these emerge primarily in the *Protagoras*, the *Gorgias*, the *Republic*, and the *Laws*. Examines these views in the context of Plato's time and culture, and deals with the relationship between his penology and his ideas in general. Comments on classical and current perspectives on punishment. Maintains that Plato's views are basically reformist and humanitarian, although some element of the deterence idea may be detected in them. Argues that the Platonic position is a corollary of the Socratic thesis that no one does wrong willingly and knowingly.

640 Magalhães-Vilhena, V. de. *Le problème de Socrate. Le Socrate historique et le Socrate de Platon*. Paris: Presses Universitaires de France, 1952.

Ref. 391.

641 Magalhães-Vilhena, V. de. *Socrate et la lègende platonicienne*. Paris: Presses Universitaires de France, 1952.

Presents a general discussion of the Socratic Problem, but concentrates its attention on the Platonic portrayal of Socrates. Establishes a sharp distinction between the historical Socrates and the legendary Socrates created by Plato. Expresses a radically skeptical attitude towards the possibility of reconstructing a reliable and accurate representation of the historical Socrates. Includes an appendix on the Socratic doxography and an extensive bibliography.

642 Masaracchia, A. "Il *Charmide* di Platone." *Maia*, 3 (1950), pp. 161-180.

Presents an interpretation of the *Charmides* in which this dialogue is seen as the critical point at which Plato began to develop his own philosophy away from the ideas associated with Socrates.

643 McKim, Richard C. *Diotima's Doubt and the Platonic Critique of Socrates: The Early and Middle Dialogues as Studies in the Failure of Socratic Method*. Doctoral dissertation. Princeton University, 1982.

Argues that Plato chose the dramatic form in order to maintain a clear distance between himself as an author and his characters, specifically Socrates. Challenges the interpretation which sees Socrates as the mouthpiece for Plato's ideas. Notes that Plato presents the Socratic *elenchus* as an ineffective method of transforming moral belief into moral knowledge. Supports this idea by an examination of passages from the *Symposium*, the *Phaedrus*, the *Theaetetus*, the *Sophist*, the *Republic*, the *Meno*, and the *Phaedo*.

644 Merlon, Philip. "Form and Content in Plato's Philosophy." *The Journal of the History of Ideas*, 8 (1947), pp. 406-430.

Examines Plato's Socratic and non-Socratic dialogues, as well as his letters, in an effort to determine to what extent he revealed his ideas. Suggests that Plato did not attempt to impart his philosophy, but that he kept himself 'alive' during sixty years of philosophizing, the dialogue form providing for him the possibility and freedom to do so. Concludes that he consistently refused to identify himself with any particular or specific ideological position.

645 Miguez, José A. "Introducción a Platón." *Platón. Obras Completas*. Madrid: Aguilar, 1966, pp. 11-97.

Serves as an introduction to the Spanish edition of Plato's works. Contains sections on the development of pre-Socratic philosophy and the sources and intepretations of the pre-Socratics, a synopsis of the Platonic system, and an extensive bibliography. Views the emergence of Socratic philosophy as a reaction against the ideas of the Sophists. Assumes an eclectic position vis-à-vis the Socratic problem, but stresses the primacy of Plato's testimony both biographically and philosophically. Ref. 108.

646 Miller, J. W. "The Development of the Philosophy of Socrates." *The Review of Metaphysics*, 6 (1952-1953), pp. 551-561.

Supports the Burnet-Taylor approach to the Socratic problem (*i.e.*, the essentially historical accuracy of the Platonic Socrates). Examines the dramatic dates of some of the dialogues, and attempts to construct a tentative chronology by reference to which the development of Socrates' thought can be traced.

647 Montuori, Mario. "I presocratici e Socrate nella testimonianza platonica." *Giornale Critico della Filosofia Italiana*, 50 (1971), pp. 452-467.

Examines critically A. Capizzi's *Socrate e i personaggi filosofi di Platone*. Ref. 584.

648 Moore, Jared S. "A Suggestion Regarding Plato and Socrates." *Mind*, 44 (1935), pp. 68-69.

Reviews and criticizes Burnet's interpretation of Plato's testimony. Concludes that the theory of Ideal Forms in its earlier form was neither purely Socratic nor purely Platonic, but a development created by Plato of what he had learned from Socrates. Distinguishes three stages in the development of the dialogues: (1) the early dialogues, in which the only purpose is to present Socrates' ideas; (2) the middle dialogues, in which Plato formulates his own philosophy which he recognizes as a logical development of Socrates' thought; and (3) the late dialogues, in which Plato is influenced more by Pythagorean ideas than by

Socrates' views. Ref. 579.

649 Mueller, Gustav E. *What Plato Thinks.* Chicago: Open Court, 1937.

Develops a scene in which Plato is present at a seminar in which he is asked questions about the meaning of Platonic love, his relationship with Socrates, his ideas concerning the soul, the ethical ideal of the golden mean, the meanings of art and beauty, the basis and significance of idealism, and the nature of the gods. Makes abundant use of various Platonic dialogues such as the *Charmides* and the *Hippias Major*.

650 Naumann, H. "Die Gestalt des Sokrates und ihre Wirkungen auf die Weltliteratur." *Der altsprachliche Unterricht*, 12 (1969), pp. 64-103.

Ref. 476.

651 Navia, Luis E. "Plato: The Man Who Saw Beyond." *An Invitation to Philosophy* by Nicholas Capaldi, Eugene Kelly, and Luis E. Navia. Buffalo: Prometheus Books, 1981, pp. 57-78.

Reviews the major aspects of Plato's biography and philosophy. Stresses the following themes as fundamental to Plato's thought: the immortality of the soul, the theory of two worlds, knowledge as recollection, the ideal State, and the perfection of the soul. Examines the relationship between Socrates and Plato, and concludes that the Platonic dialogues should be interpreted as preparatory exercises which may predispose the mind for a translinguistic understanding of reality. Stresses the importance of the historical Socrates in the early dialogues, and supports the view that the middle and late dialogues give expression to Platonic extensions and amplifications of Socratic themes which, although not necessarily contradicting Socrates' ideas, transcend by far the ideological and methodological parameters of the historical Socrates.

652 Neumann, Harry. "Socrates in Plato and Aristophanes." *The American Journal of Philology*, 90 (1969), pp. 201-214.

Ref. 477.

653 Okada, S. "What Encouraged Plato to Write the Dialogues?" *The Journal of Classical Studies*, 13 (1965), pp. 1-14.

In Japanese with a summary in English. Maintains that Plato's abandonment of poetry and commitment to philosophy were entirely the consequence of the influence of Socrates, and that in writing his dialogues, he simply wanted to report faithfully the very words of his philosophical master.

654 Parker, P. "The Historical Socrates in the Light of Professor Burnet's Hypothesis." *Harvard Studies in Classical Philology*, 27 (1916), pp. 67-75.

Clarifies the precise meaning of Burnet's position vis-à-vis the Socratic problem. Questions the conclusions to which Burnet arrives in his analysis of the *Phaedo*, and criticizes the idea that the historical and the Platonic Socrates should be viewed as basically one and the same. Ref. 117, 579.

655 Pater, Walter. "Plato and Socrates." *Plato and Platonism*. New York: Macmillan, 1908, pp. 66-87.

Ref. 402.

656 Patzer, H. "Die philosophische Bedeutung der Sokratesgestalt in den platonischen Dialogen." *Parusia. Studien zur Philosophie Platons und zur Problemgeschichte des Platonismus. Festgabe für J. Hirschberger.* Edited by K. von Flasch. Frankfurt: Minerva Verlag, 1965, pp. 21-43.

Maintains that the early dialogues (*e.g.*, the *Euthyphro* and the *Apology*) reveal primarily the presence of Socrates as a man, that is, as a philosopher on a human level, whereas the later dialogues (*e.g.*, the *Phaedo* and the *Symposium*) give expression to themes and concerns that transcend the historical Socrates (*e.g.*, the development of the doctrine of Ideal Forms).

657 Pfleiderer, E. *Sokrates, Plato und ihre Schüler.* Tübingen: H. Laupp, 1896.

Ref. 403.

658 Preiswerk, R. *Neue philologische Untersuchungen zum 1. Buch des platonischen Staates.* Freiburg, Switzerland, 1939.

Maintains that the first book of the *Republic* represents an effort on Plato's part to draw a faithful portrait of Socrates. Observes, however, that it is possible to identify certain passages which appear to be later additions, introduced by Plato in order to use the dialogue (originally conceived as an independent work) as the introductory book of the *Republic.* Argues that an authentic Socratic portrait can be reconstructed by deleting the added passages.

659 Randall, John Herman. "The Historical and the Platonic Socrates." *Plato: Dramatist of the Life of Reason.* New York: Columbia University Press, 1970, pp. 93-102.

Stresses the incompatibility of the testimonies of Xenophon and Plato, and maintains that in both there must be elements of *Dichtung* and *Wahrheit.* Reviews (by reference to Ueberweg-Praechter's *Das Sokratesproblem*) the various hypotheses advanced with respect to the issue of the historical Socrates. Recognizes in the Platonic *Apology* a reliable source of information concerning Socrates' personality, but insists that this document is not an accurate historical account but a summary statement of what Socrates meant to Plato. Concedes that our lack of reliable historical information about Socrates' philosophy does not allow us to make definite statements concerning the precise relationship between that philosophy and the ideas developed by Plato.

660 Rindone, Elio. "L'Ideale del filosofo in Platone." *Aquinas,* 27 (1984), pp. 75-104.

Reviews the representation of the ideal philosopher which Plato constructed around the person and thought of Socrates. Maintains that such a representation discloses for us a man in love with truth and in search for the meaning of Being, who confronted the moral crisis of his time by proposing a universal and rational morality, and who avoided the sort of nostalgic stagnation which might be the natural solution for a great mind living in the midst of decadent circumstances.

661 Robin, Léon. "La philosophie grecque de M. John Burnet." *Revue de Metaphysique et de Morale*, 2 (1917), pp. 210-224.

Reviews and criticizes Burnet's contention that the Platonic Socrates should be construed as an accurate representation of the historical Socrates. Rejects this approach to the Socratic problem. Ref. 117, 579.

662 Robin, Léon. "Sur une hypothèse récente relative à Socrate." *Revue des Etudes Grecques*, 29 (1916), pp. 129-165.

Provides a thorough critique of the Burnet-Taylor thesis. Argues that such a thesis is supported by a series of seemingly historical and objective assumptions which are ultimately only ingenious conjectures. Questions the rejection of the Aristotelian testimony by Burnet and Taylor in view of their acceptance of a testimony that is of later origin than that of Aristotle (*i.e.*, that of Proclus). Ref. 117, 579, 686, 687, 688, 689.

663 Robinson, Richard. *Plato's Earlier Dialectic*. Ithaca, N.Y.: Cornell University Press, 1942.

Assumes that the Platonic dialogues can be arranged in three groups, and that the earlier group (the Socratic dialogues) can be subdivided into two groups: (1) the dialogues dominated by an emphasis on the Socratic *elenchus*, and (2) those which exhibit the development of a method of dialectics. Examines in detail the structure and development of the Socratic *elenchus* and the search for definitions. Devotes the second half of the book to the elucidation of Plato's dialectics which is viewed as a development of the Socratic approach. Ref. 1401.

664 Rogers, Arthur Kenyon. *The Socratic Problem*. New Haven, Conn.: Yale University Press, 1939.

Ref. 408.

665 Ross, W. D. "The Problem of Socrates." *Proceedings of the Classical Association*, 1933, pp. 7-24.

Questions the adequacy of the Burnet-Taylor interpretation of the relationship between the Platonic Socrates and the historical Socrates. Accepts as reliable Aristotle's testimony concerning the origin of the Platonic theory of Ideal Forms, according to which, it was Plato, not Socrates, who separated the Forms from individual things. Notes that the Socratic discourses should be read on the assumption that they may give us a *vraisemblance*, not a biographically accurate portrait of Socrates, and that this must have been Aristotle's own view. Observes that the effectiveness of Aristophanes' portrayal of Socrates would have been minimal, had it been devoid of some historical basis. Ref. 117, 579, 686, 687, 688, 689.

666 Ross, W. D. "Socrates, Plato, and the Platonists." *Aristotle's Metaphysics*. Oxford: The Clarendon Press, 1924 (2 vols.), Vol. 1, pp. xxxiii-lxxvi.

Ref. 708.

667 Rudberg, G. "Der platonische Sokrates." *Symbolae Osloenses*, 7 (1928), pp. 1-24.

Argues that the most authentic historical portrait of Socrates given by Plato is to be found in the early dialogues. Maintains that as one moves into the later dialogues, one finds Platonic ideas and concerns being mixed with genuine Socratic thoughts, and that the mysticism of certain late Platonic passages is altogether foreign to Socrates' actual stance. Notes that in the late dialogues Socrates recedes more and more into the background, until he becomes a mere dramatic name.

668 Rudberg, G. "*Protagoras*, *Gorgias*, *Menon*. Eine platonische Ueberganszeit." *Symbolae Osloenses*, 30 (1953), pp. 30-41.

Attempts to determine the precise point in the *Protagoras*, the *Gorgias*, and the *Meno*, where the ideas of the historical Socrates are replaced by those of Plato.

669 Ryle, Gilbert. *Plato's Progress*. Cambridge: Cambridge University Press, 1966.

Rejects the idea that Aristotle was a strict disciple of Plato. Argues that Plato's dialogues were composed mainly for oral delivery, and that many of them were presented at the games festivals. Suggests that Plato put into writings some of the words and doctrines which can be generally attributed to Socrates. Develops an original chronology for the composition of the dialogues, and offers a novel interpretation of the *Apology* (which is viewed, along with the *Crito*, not as an example of Plato's early writing). Rejects the authenticity of the Platonic letters. Ref. 683.

670 Sarf, Harold. *Establishing a Framework for Conceptualizing Socrates as Plato's Theoretical Teacher.* Doctoral dissertation. University of California, Berkeley, 1979.

Observes that it is impossible to study Plato's philosophical contribution without assessing the doctrines, moral sentiments, and methods of inquiry of the historical Socrates. Studies in Part 1 the question of the historical identity and impact of Socrates on Athens from perspectives that are independent of Plato. Discusses in Part 2 the evidence for the classification and chronology of Plato's dialogues, and seeks to clarify the issue of whether it is possible to discern a development in them by reference to the presence of Socrates. Concludes that the early dialogues reveal basic historical traits of Socrates, whereas the middle dialogues exhibit theoretical modifications of an unquestionable Platonic origin.

671 Schaerer, René. *La question platonicienne. Etude sur le rapport de la pensée et de l'expression dans les Dialogues.* Neuchâtel, 1938.

Insists on recognizing the presence of an 'inspired' Socrates (*le Socrate inspiré*) between the Socrates of the early dialogues (who confesses his ignorance) and the Socrates of the later dialogues (who appears to have attained to clear philosophical knowledge). Finds the presence of the inspired Socrates in *Meno* 81a-d, *Symposium* 201d, *Menexenus* 236a, *Phaedrus* 235c and 244a, and *Phaedo* 70c, 97b-c, and 107d. Accepts with reservations the idea that the primary sources are in basic agreement, and notes that it was Socrates' nature to appear differently to different witnesses and to accommodate himself to the diverse kinds of people with whom he was related.

672 Schleiermacher, Friedrich. *Introductions to the Dialogues of*

*Plato*. Translated by William Dobson. New York: Arno Press, 1973.

Originally published in 1836 (Cambridge: Deighton). Contains Schleiermacher's introductions to Plato's dialogues, prefaced by a general introduction. Concludes that the dialogue form was essential to Plato's philosophy, embodying as it does the Socratic method. Notes that through an analysis of the style as well as of the doctrine, one can determine the proper sequence of the dialogues.

673 Schuré, Edouard. *Hermes and Plato*. Translated by F. Rothwell. London: William Rider & Son, 1919.

Examines the development, scope, and nature of ancient occult Egyptian traditions, particularly those related to the mystery cult of Isis and Osiris, and discusses the role played by Hermes in this context. Deals with the nature of the mysteries of Eleusis, and with Plato's relationship to those mysteries. Discusses in Part 2, Chapter 1, the presence of Socrates in the formation of Plato's thought. Argues that while Plato received from Socrates a decisive impulse towards philosophy, the actual development of Plato's metaphysical ideas was greatly determined by his initiation into the mysteries.

674 Schwartz, E. "Sokrates und Plato." *Charakterköpfe aus der antiken Literatur*. Leipzig, 1943, pp. 54-73.

Examines the ideological relationship between Socrates and Plato. Speaks of Socrates as the greatest rationalist of his time, and dicusses the kind of rationalism which Plato inherited from him. Emphasizes the role played by Socrates in the emergence of the individual conscience as the ultimate source of ethical values.

675 Sesonske, Alexander. "Plato's Apology, *Republic I*." *Phronesis*, 6 (1961), pp. 29-36.

Maintains that it is in the first book of the *Republic* that Plato first begins to move away from Socrates, and notes that the opening sections of the *Republic* can be rightfully called 'the Apology' of Plato. Adds, however, that in spite of the distance that eventually came to separate

Plato from Socrates, Plato remained invariably attached to the basic principles of Socrates' thought.

676 Shorey, Paul. "The Question of the Socratic Element in Plato." *Selected Papers.* New York: Garland Publishing, 1980 (2 vols.), Vol. 1, pp. 316-323.

Originally published in *Proceedings of the Sixth International Congress of Philosophy* (Harvard University), London: Longmans, Green & Co., 1927, pp. 576-583. Examines various solutions to the Socratic problem, and concludes that even though the problem may never have a final solution, it is justifiable to assume that Plato would have allowed himself to put into Socrates' mouth ideas which were really his very own. Argues that the testimonies of Xenophon and Aristotle are mainly dependent on that of Plato, and that Aristophanes' testimony is nothing but an irresponsible caricature. Notes that the Socrates of Plato is an idealized mouthpiece for the expression of Plato's own ideas, and that the Platonic Socrates is mostly the protagonist of dramatic creations. Affirms that our knowledge of Socrates is confined to the recognition of the greatness of his personality, and to the acceptance of those traits that are common to the testimonies of Plato, Xenophon, and Aristotle. Gives an account of the genesis and meaning of the Platonic theory of Ideal Forms.

677 Shorey, Paul. "Review of *Platon, Phédon, texte établi et traduit par Léon Robin.*" *Selected Papers.* New York: Garland Publishing, 1980 (2 vols.), Vol. 1, pp. 464-467.

Originally published in *Classical Philology*, 21 (1926), pp. 264-267. Considers Robin's translation "always interesting and often instructive." Questions several of Robin's interpretations, but agrees with his rejection of Burnet's idea concerning the Pythagorean roots of Socrates' thought.

678 Shorey, Paul. "Review of *Plato's Phaedo.* Edited with an introduction by John Burnet." *Selected Papers.* New York: Garland Publishing, 1980 (2 vols.), Vol. 1, pp. 460-462.

Originally published in *Classical Philology*, 8 (1913), pp. 232-234. Considers Burnet's translation the "soundest, most accurate, and least misleading" of all translations. Praises Burnet as a master of practical annotations.

Questions as not clearly demonstrated the allegation concerning the Pythagorean elements in Socrates' thought. Ref. 117.

679 Shorey, Paul. "Review of *The Dialogues of Plato*, translated by Benjamin Jowett." *Selected Papers*. New York: Garland Publishing, 1980 (2 vols.), Vol. 1, pp. 364-387.

Originally published in *The American Journal of Philology*, 13 (1892), pp. 349-372. Evaluates Jowett's work as much more than a translation, although expresses reservations about his theory of translation. Acknowledges Jowett's faithfulness and success in adhering to his prescribed method. Considers his introductory essays to the dialogues as exquisite and "filled with modernity, breadth of view, gentle wisdom, and playful urbanity." Suggests, however, that there is an occasional lack of precision in the formulation of philosophical questions, which leads to "errors, misleading statements, and fantastic analogies." Provides a partial list of translation errors. Ref. 91.

680 Shorey, Paul. *What Plato Said*. Chicago: The University of Chicago Press, 1933.

Provides a summary of the entire Platonic *corpus*, including the dialogues of questionable authenticity. Gives a general account of Plato's biography, and discusses his relationship with Socrates. Devotes one chapter to the overall structure of the Platonic dialogues, and examines the various hypotheses concerning their chronology. Deals briefly with the classification of the dialogues given by Diogenes Laertius and the tabulation made by G. Grote.

681 Sichirollo, L. *Antropologia e dialettica nella filosofia di Platone*. Milan, 1957.

Contains two essays by Sichorollo and the Italian translation of two contributions by J. Stenzel and A. Kojève on Hegel's interpretation of Greek philosophy. Discusses in the first essay the meaning of Socrates' thought as this was understood by Plato. Argues that the development of Plato's philosophy can be interpreted as an attempt to solve some of the issues raised by Socrates and by the fact of his execution. Concludes, however, that the developed form of Plato's philosophy involves the rejection of

Socraticism. Bases its conclusions on the examination of the *Meno*, the *Republic*, and passages from the seventh letter.

682 Sider, David. "Did Plato Write Diaologues Before the Death of Socrates?" *Apeiron*, 14 (1980), pp. 15-18.

Examines five reports from the fourth century B.C. which indicate the possibility that some of Plato's early dialogues were written before 399 B.C.

683 Sparshott, F. E. "Review of *Plato's Progress* by Gilbert Ryle." *Phoenix*, 22 (1968), pp. 73-79.

Considers the work to be boldly speculative, closely reasoned, and adequately documented, as well as brilliantly written. Regards some of the evidence to be somewhat illusory, and objects to Ryle's assumption that history is generally free from anomalies. Ref. 669.

684 Sweeney, Leo. "A. E. Taylor on Socrates and Plato." *The Southwestern Journal of Philosophy*, 8 (1977), pp. 79-99.

Examines Taylor's thesis that the theory of Ideal Forms expressed by Socrates in dialogues such as the *Phaedo*, the *Republic*, the *Philebus*, and others, can be rightfully attributed to the historical Socrates. Argues that an analysis of the *Philebus* shows the inadequacy and artificiality of Taylor's interpretation. Notes that in some of Taylor's works (*e.g.*, *Plato: The Man and His Work*) one can recognize the exegetical bind in which he is compelled to involve himself. Ref. 686, 687, 688, 689.

685 Tarrant, Dorothy. "Plato as Dramatist." *The Journal of Hellenic Studies*, 75 (1955), pp. 82-89.

Acknowledges that the dialogue form is an excellent medium for the presentation of Socratic inquiry and philosophy, but notes that much more than this goes into the construction of a Platonic dialogue. Makes a dramatic study of various passages of Plato's dialogues, and concludes that he was a dramatist at heart.

686 Taylor, Alfred E. *Plato.* London: Butler & Tanner, 1926.

Presents an analysis of Plato's dialogues by emphasizing the social, economic, and political context of his times, rather than by assuming a predetermined perspective -- that is, exegesis rather than criticism or praise. Argues that Plato would not have deliberately misrepresented Socrates' thought, and that his main program was to preserve for posterity a faithful and loving portrait of Socrates. Develops an analysis of individual dialogues. Contains a chronological table. Ref. 684.

687 Taylor, Alfred E. "Plato's Biography of Socrates." *Proceedings of the British Academy*, 1918, pp. 93-132.

Reiterates the thesis advanced by the author in other works, namely, that the Socrates of the Platonic dialogues is by no means a fictional vehicle for the expression of Plato's ideas, but a historical and real person, whose views are faithfully recorded in the dialogues.

688 Taylor, Alfred E. *Socrates.* Westport, Conn.: Greenwood Press, 1951.

Approaches Socratic thought with the assumption that Plato's portrait of Socrates is substantially accurate, acknowledging, however, that this does not mean that the Platonic Socrates is presented by Plato with all his historical and biographical traits. Questions the dominant trend of the nineteenth century which refused to accept the historical Socratic value of the writings of Plato, Xenophon, and Aristotle.

689 Taylor, Alfred E. *Varia Socratica: First Series.* Oxford: James Parker & Co., 1911.

Collects in one volume five essays on Socrates: "The Impiety of Socrates" (Ref. 1108), "On the Alleged Distinction in Aristotle Between Σωκράτης and ὁ Σωκράτης" (Ref. 711), "Socrates and the Δισσοὶ λόγοι," "The φροντιστήριον" (Ref. 496), and "The Words εἶδος and ἰδέα in Pre-Socratic Literature." Stresses in the first two essays the thesis that the portrait drawn in the Platonic dialogues of the personal and philosophical individuality of Socrates is strictly historical. Argues that in using

Socrates' name, Plato did not transfigure him but simply showed his adequate understanding of him.

690 Tejera, Victorino. "Methodology of a Misreading: A Critical Note on T. Irwin's *Plato's Moral Philosophy*." *International Studies in Philosophy*, 10 (1978), pp. 131-136.

Discusses the method of reading and interpreting Plato's works which is found among dogmatic scholars, specifically among the 'Neopythagorean' and 'Platonist' scholars. Regards this method as one that involves mistranslations and inauthentic dialogues, and as one that ignores the various uses of 'Socrates' by Plato. Argues that this method (as exemplified by T. Irwin's work) takes no account of the tone of the conversational exchanges in the dialogues, and violates the dialogical integrity of Plato's works by seeing in them philosophical treatises. Ref. 628.

691 Tejera, Victorino. *Plato's Dialogues One by One: A Structural Interpretation*. New York: Irvington Publishers, 1984.

Attempts to develop an interpretation of the Platonic dialogues without making any assumptions concerning their chronology, and without seeking to impose an external doctrine on them. Endeavors to uncover the observable design of each one of the dialogues explored. Presents twenty papers which are divided into various sections, some of which focus on the Socratic element in Plato. Contains an extensive bibliography and abundant references. Ref. 497, 1522, 1523, 1524, 1525, 1526, 1527, 1528, 1529, 1530.

692 Thesleff, H. "The Interpretation and Date of the Symposia of Plato and Xenophon." *Bulletin of the Institute of Classical Studies of the University of London*, 25 (1978), pp. 157-170.

Ref. 562.

693 Valgimigli, Manara. *Platone. Apologia di Socrate*. Bari, 1929.

Published as part of *Poeti e filosofi de Grecia* (Bari, 1941). Discusses and emphasizes the Platonic idealization of Socrates as a paradigm of philosophical existence.

694 Vives, J. "De la intransigencia socrática a la intolerancia platónica." *Doro syn oligo. Homenatje a Josep Alsina*. Edited by C. Millares. Barcelona: Editorial Ariel, 1969, pp. 121-133.

Argues that Plato's firm commitment to certain absolute and immutable ethical values has its roots in Socrates' total dedication to the search for the truth.

695 Vogel, Cornelia J. de. "Who Was Socrates?" *The Journal of the History of Philosophy*, 1 (1963), pp. 143-161.

Ref. 564.

696 Winspear, Alban D. *The Genesis of Plato's Thought*. New York: S. A. Russell, 1940.

Discusses the relationship between Socrates and the Pythagoreans, and concludes that he was closely bound in friendship to leading Pythagoreans who criticized democracy, and who had a cosmopolitan rather than a local political perspective, on account of which they alarmed the conservative Athenians. Recognizes, however, major differences between Socrates and the Pythagoreans.

697 Woodruff, Paul. "The Skeptical Side of Plato's Method." *Revue Internationale de Philosophie*, 40 (1986), pp. 22-37.

Examines the nature and scope of the skepticism that can be attributed to Socrates and Plato, and notes that even though Socrates makes the claim that he knows nothing, he still knows how terms ought to be defined and also what kind of answers are philosophically satisfactory. Observes that the skepticism of Socrates is a temporary state of suspension, which (one may assume) is superseded by Platonic dialectics.

# THE ARISTOTELIAN TESTIMONY

This section contains annotations of works which deal specifically with Aristotle's testimony on Socrates. It also includes several references to more general works which present brief discussions of the Socratic problem as this is related to Aristotle's comments on Socrates.

698 Bokownew, P. "Sokrates Philosophie in der Darstellung des Aristoteles." *Archiv für Geschichte der Philosophie*, 27 (Neue Folge 20, 1914), pp. 295-304.

Examines Aristotle's testimony on Socrates, and concludes that such testimony furnishes us with the most reliable source of information concerning Socratic philosophy. Maintains that Aristotle's comments on Socrates should not be construed as being dependent on Plato's writings, and that Aristotle was successful in capturing those original Socratic themes which have exercised a decisive influence on the history of ideas.

699 Brown, Sarah H. "Socratic Method and Aristotle's Definition of the Good." *The International Journal of Ethics*, 43 (1933), pp. 329-338.

Comments on Burnet's suggestion that Socrates' doctrine of reminiscence resembles Aristotle's theory of induction, specifically in the recognition of the universal in the particular case. Examines Aristotle's view concerning the necessity of overcoming the paradox between what we already know (*i.e.*, right opinion, which makes it possible to us to search for the truth), and what we do not know.

700 Chroust, Anton-Hermann. "A Comment on Aristotle's *On Noble Birth*." *Wiener Studien*, 6 (1972), pp. 19-32.

Ref. 735.

701 Chroust, Anton-Hermann. "Socrates in the Light of Aristotle's Testimony." *The New Scholasticism*, 26 (1952), pp. 327-365.

Reviews the Aristotelian testimony about Socrates, and reaches the conclusion that, on the whole, it is essentially useless, since it reveals nothing of value that cannot be found in older sources. Expresses a general attitude of skepticism towards the possibility of shedding definitive light on the historical Socrates. Interprets the Apollonian (Delphic) statement ("Know thyself") as an expression of Socrates' desire to attain to a clear understanding of the limitations of the human powers of reasoning and action.

702 Déman, Thomas. *Le témoignage d'Aristote sur Socrate.* Paris: Societé d'Edition Les Belles Lettres, 1942.

Collects the Aristotelian references to Socrates, and provides critical comments about them. Argues that there is no reason to accuse Aristotle of inaccurate reporting, and that the correct approach to his testimony is to discover his methodology in a way which agrees with our historical demands. Emphasizes the importance of Socrates' devotion to ethical inquiries (which assume with him a strictly scientific texture), and regards Aristotle's testimony in this regard as quite valuable. Supports the idea that Aristotle's comments on Socrates should be used as a criterion in order to distinguish in the Platonic writings those elements which belong to Socrates from those which belong to Plato. Rejects the suggestion of Burnet and Taylor which alleges that the 'separation' of the Ideal Forms from particular objects was proposed originally by Socrates. Ref. 579, 686, 687, 688, 689.

703 Gigon, Olof. "Die Sokratesdoxographie bei Aristoteles." *Museum Helveticum*, 16 (1959), pp. 174-212.

Reviews the references to Socrates in Aristotle's works, and concludes that such references are neither particularly revealing nor especially reliable. Maintains that there is no justification for attaching significant historical value to Aristotle's Socratic testimony. Comments in particular on the Aristotelian attribution of a double role to Socrates in the development of Greek philosophy, namely, the creation of a method for the investigation of natural phenomena, and the emphasis on strictly ethical issues.

704 Magalhães-Vilhena, V. de. *Le problème de Socrate. Le Socrate*

*historique et le Socrate de Platon.* Paris: Presses Universitaires de France, 1952.

Ref. 391.

705 Mulhern, J. J. "Aristotle and the Socratic Paradoxes." *The Journal of the History of Ideas*, 35 (1954), pp. 293-299.

Ref. 963.

706 Rogers, G. K. "A Note on Socrates and Aristotle." *Mind*, 34 (1925), pp. 471-475.

Advances a reinterpretation of Aristotle's evidence that Socrates was concerned only with definitions and inductive investigations. Argues that to the Greek mind, the problem of the 'universal' was realistically, not psychologically approached. Notes that the editorial insertion of phrases into the Aristotelian texts may have added more confusion than clarification.

707 Ross, W. D. "The Problem of Socrates." *Proceedings of the Classical Association*, 1933, pp. 7-24.

Ref. 665.

708 Ross, W. D. "Socrates, Plato, and the Platonists." *Aristotle's Metaphysics.* Oxford: The Clarendon Press, 1924 (2 vols.), Vol. 1, pp. xxxii-lxxvi.

Discusses besides several general themes the Aristotelian Socratic testimony, to which it attaches special importance as a means to shed light on the ideological differences between Socrates and Plato. Opposes Taylor's unfavorable assessment of the Aristotelian testimony. Ref. 711.

709 Santas, Gerasimos X. "Aristotle on Practical Inference, the Explanation of Action, and *akrasia.*" *Phronesis*, 14 (1969), pp. 162-189.

Studies various themes and issues related to Aristotle's *Nicomachean Ethics* (Book 7), and deals specifically with his understanding of and response to Socrates' denial of the possibility of *akrasia*.

710 Seddon, Frederick A. "Megalopsychia: A Suggestion." *The Personalist*, 53 (1975), pp. 31-37.

Comments on various (mostly negative) assessments of *Nicomachean Ethics* IV, iii, where Aristotle describes the character and behavior of the man of great soul (or the man of proper pride). Argues that this Aristotelian image can be interpreted as "a kind of Galtonian composite image of Socrates and Aristotle himself," and that the features of Socrates' excellence of character, especially as these are outlined in Plato's *Apology*, can be clearly discerned in the Aristotelian description in the *Nicomachean Ethics*.

711 Taylor, Alfred E. "On the Alleged Distinction Between Σωκράτης and ὁ Σωκράτης." *Varia Socratica: First Series*. Oxford: James Parker & Co., 1911, pp. 40-90.

Argues against the view of Aristotle as an independent and critically important Socratic witness, and defends the idea that all significant Aristotelian remarks about Socrates can be traced back to the Platonic writings. Regards Aristotle's testimony as lacking in higher criticism, and claims that it adds little or nothing to the knowledge of Socrates that is derived from Plato. Dismisses as inconsequential the use or lack of use of the definite article in the context of Aristotle's references to Socrates. Rejects the usefulness of the canon proposed by W. Fitzgerald (*Selections from the Nicomachean Ethics*, 1850, p. 163), which appeals to Aristotle's grammatical usage in order to distinguish the historical from the Platonic Socrates in the Aristotelian *corpus*.

712 Walsh, James J. "The Socratic Denial of *Akrasia*. *The Philosophy of Socrates: A Collection of Critical Essays*. Edited by Gregory Vlastos. Notre Dame, Ind.: University of Notre Dame Press, 1980, pp. 235-263.

Ref. 1035.

713 Waterfall, Donald Ernest. *Plato and Aristotle on 'akrasia'*. Doctoral dissertation. Princeton University, 1969.

Ref. 1038.

714 Wiggins, D. "Weakness of Will, Commensurability, and the Objects of Deliberation and Desire." *Essays on Aristotle's Ethics*. Edited by A. O. Rorty. Berkeley: University of California Press, 1981, pp. 241-265.

Discusses Aristotle's understanding and critique of Socrates' denial of *akrasia*.

## SPECIFIC BIOGRAPHICAL LITERATURE

The annotations included in this section are of works and notices which deal with some specific biographical aspect of Socrates, as well as of works which discuss his relationship with some of his contemporaries and predecessors (for instance, the Sophists, Anaxagoras, Euripides, Antisthenes, Isocrates, Archelaus, and others), and of works which deal with writings attributed to Socrates.

715 Afnan, Ruhi M. *Zoroaster's Influence on Anaxagoras, the Greek Tragedians, and Socrates*. New York: The Philosophical Library, 1969.

Reviews the ideological influence of Persian philosophy in general and Zoroaster's ideas in particular on the Greek world of the second half of the fifth century B.C. Makes specific references to Pericles, Aspasia, Anaxagoras, Aeschylus, Euripides, and Socrates. Deals in Chapter 5 (pp. 129-154) with various principles of Socrates' philosophy in which Zoroaster's indirect influence can be detected, and these principles include the transcendence of the creative mind, the doctrine of perfection, the doctrine of Ideal Forms, and the Socratic conception of love (as outlined in the *Symposium*).

716 Alatzoglou-Themelis, G. "Protagoras und Sokrates." *Philosophia*, 8-9 (1978-1979), pp. 117-143.

In modern Greek, with an abstract in German. Analyzes and compares the philosophical outlooks associated with Protagoras and Socrates, and deals specifically with their approaches to religion and polytheism, education, and relativism. Establishes a contrast between Socrates' profession of ignorance and Protagoras' claim to wisdom. Attempts to show that, far from being ideological adversaries, Socrates and Protagoras shared many ideas and convictions, including their methods and general philosophical interest. Notes their agreement on several issues: the abandonment of natural philosophy, the rejection of popular polytheism, their interest in political education, the conviction that virtue can be taught, and their adherence to a utilitarian view of values.

717 Amelung, W. "Notes on Representations of Socrates and of Diogenes and Other Cynics." *The American Journal of Archeology*, 31 (1927), pp. 281-296.

Comments on a marble statue of Socrates (second century B.C.) which appears to represent him at age fifty. Notes that two bas-relief works from Pompeii and Orvieto are of a similar nature.

718 Babut, D. "Anaxagore jugé par Socrate et Platon." *Revue des Etudes Grecques*, 91 (1978), pp. 44-76.

Comments on the autobiographical statements made by Socrates in *Phaedo* 96a-99d, and concludes that his alleged relationship with Anaxagoras' philosophy, although probably not altogether historical, cannot be viewed as merely fictional. Notes that by allowing Socrates to make such statements, Plato was in fact revealing a great deal concerning the ideological gap that eventually separated him from his master.

719 Baily, D. M. "A Caricature of Socrates." *The American Journal of Archeology*, 78 (1974), p. 427.

Comments on a small clay lamp of the first or second century A.D., which depicts a seated figure. Identifies this figure as a caricature of Socrates.

720 Baker, Howard. "A Portrait of Aesop." *Persephone's Cave: Cultural Accumulations of the Early Greeks*. Athens, Ga.: The University of Georgia Press, 1979, pp. 79-111.

Discusses the relationship between Aesop and Socrates (pp. 105-107). Notes that it was not accidental that Socrates should have chosen to versify at the end of his life some of Aesop's fables. Stresses the physical similarities between Aesop and Socrates (especially their ugliness), their 'peculiar' kind of wisdom, and their constant jesting and irony. Quotes from an adage by Erasmus (*Sileni Alcibiadis*), in which a vivid description of Socrates' physical appearance is given.

721 Barns, J. "A New Gnomologium: With Some Remarks on Gnomic Anthologies." *The Classical Quarterly*, 44 (1950), pp. 126-137.

Discusses the issue of the antiquity of the collections of aphorisms (*i.e.*, the gnomologia), some of which have been traditionally attributed to Socrates (especially on the authority of Stobaeus). Argues that parts of these collections have their origins, not directly in the actual Socratic circle, but in the early fourth century B.C., at which time they were promoted in the literary groups related to Isocrates.

722 Bentley, Richard. "Dissertation upon the Epistles of Socrates." *Dissertations upon the Epistles of Phalaris, Themistocles, Socrates, Euripides, and the Fables of Aesop*. London: George Bell & Sons, 1883.

Originally published in London (Henry Mortlock, 1699). Examines the letters attributed to Socrates (*e.g.*, to King Archelaus), as well as those attributed to Xenophon. Attempts to show their spurious character and their late date of composition.

723 Bicknell, P. J. "Sokrates' Mistress Xanthippe." *Apeiron*, 8 (1974), pp. 1-5.

Argues for the view that Myrto was Socrates' actual wife, whereas Xanthippe was only his mistress. Suggests that Xanthippe had Lesbian inclinations.

724 Blackwood, Russell *et al.* "*Gorgias* 482b." *The Classical Journal*, 57 (1962), pp. 318-319.

Brief notice which discusses Socrates' oath in *Gorgias* 482b. Notes that this oath by "the Dog" is a reference to Anubis, the dog-headed Egyptian god, which was connected to the judgment of souls after death, and with their degree of truthfulness. Mentions several other instances of Socrates' custom of swearing by "the Dog" (*Apology* 22a, *Phaedo* 98e, etc.), and finds in them a confirmation of the view that, in playfully swearing in such a way, he was in fact invoking the name of a divinity which symbolized truth and sincerity. Points out that in *Republic* 367a, the dog is said to be "your only true philosopher" because it is able to see the true characters of people. Ref. 777.

725 Blank, David L. "Socrates vs. Sophists on Payment for Teaching." *Classical Antiquity*, 4 (1985), pp. 1-49.

Summarizes the popular complaints concerning the Sophists' accumulation of wealth through their teaching, and examines the reasons given by Plato and Xenophon as to why Socrates did not charge any fees for his services. Emphasizes the interpretation of Socrates' decision as a result of his desire to teach people regardless of their ability to pay.

726 Bock Cano, L. de. "Estudio sobre el léxico de las cartas de Sócrates." *Habis*, 8 (1977), pp. 23-55.

Develops a lexicographical analysis of the first, sixth, and seventh Socratic letters. Concludes that more than seventy-five percent of the language of the letters can be identified as belonging to late Hellenistic Greek. Notes, however, that although the author of the letters lived probably in the second century A.D., his inspiration can be traced back to genuine Platonic traditions.

727 Boeck, A. "De Socratis rerum physicarum studio." *Kleine Schriften*. Berlin, 1874 (4 vols.), Vol. 4, pp. 430-436.

Reviews various issues related to Socrates' alleged early interest in natural philosophy in general and in the ideas of Anaxagoras in particular, and comments on the areas of agreement and disagreement in this regard among the testimonies of Aristophanes, Plato, and Xenophon.

728 Breckenridge, J. D. "Multiple Portrait Types." *Acta ad archaeologiam et artium historiam pertinentia*, 2 (1965), pp. 9-22.

Comments on several issues related to the multiple artistic representations of famous ancient personages. Studies specifically the instances of art works which represent Socrates, Sophocles, and Euripides.

729 Brickhouse, Thomas C. and Smith, Nicholas D. "The Origin of Socrates' Mission." *The Journal of the History of Ideas*, 44

(1983), pp. 657-666.

Discusses Socrates' conviction that his philosophical mission was intimately related to the Delphic pronouncement concerning his exceptional wisdom. Observes that many commentators have seen only confusion in this regard on Socrates' part, and attempts to show how the Delphic oracle was actually the seminal source which can best account for the direction of Socrates' life and for his philosophical activities.

730 Bruyne, L. de. "Aristote ou Socrate? A propos d'une peinture de la Via Latina." *Rendiconti della Pontificia Accademia di Archeologia*, 42 (1969-1970), pp. 173-193.

Argues that the principal figure in the so-called 'Lesson in Medicine' (or 'The Philosophers' Discussion), a painting found in the Via Latina, is Socrates and not, as is often believed, Aristotle. Maintains that what the painting actually represents is not a lesson in medicine, but a discussion led by Socrates on the question of the immortality of the soul.

731 Calder, W. M. "Socrates at Amphipolis (*Apology* 28e)." *Phronesis*, 6 (1961), pp. 83-85.

Argues that on the basis of *Apology* 28e it is reasonable to affirm that Socrates did participate in the Athenian campaign in Amphipolis in 422 B.C.

732 Carrau, Ludovic. "La sophistique et Socrate." *Revue de Deux Mondes*, 1886, pp. 136-159.

Explores the relationship between Socrates and the Sophists, and points out the common elements between them, as well as the moral gap that separates Socratic philosophy from the relativism of the Sophists.

733 Chiapelli, Alessandro. "Il naturalismo di Socrate e le prime *Nubi* d'Aristofane." *Rediconti della Realle Accademia del Lincei*, 1886, pp. 284-302.

Ref. 437.

734 Chiapelli, Alessandro. "Nuove ricerche sul naturalismo di Socrate." *Archiv für Geschichte der Philosophie*, 4 (1891), pp. 369-413.

Strengthens the thesis advanced in Chiapelli's "Il naturalismo di Socrate et le prime *Nubi* d'Aristofane." Regards as historical the relationship between Socrates and Archelaus. Ref. 437.

735 Chroust, Anton-Hermann. "A Comment on Aristotle's *On Noble Birth*." *Wiener Studien*, 6 (1972), pp. 19-32.

Examines Aristotle's reference to Socrates' marriage or marriages, and concludes that the available evidence leads us to believe that Socrates first lived with Xanthippe, a woman of humble origin, whom he never married, and that later on he actually married Myrto, who became the mother of Sophroniscus and Menexenus. Notes also that the evidence suggests that Socrates kept Xanthippe in his house even after his marriage with Myrto, and that Myrto died shortly before Socrates' own death.

736 Chroust, Anton-Hermann. "Socrates and Pre-Socratic Philosophy." *The Modern Schoolman*, 29 (1952), pp. 119-135.

Discusses the evidence for associating Socrates with the natural philosophers, and comments on his denial of any interest on his part in their speculations, specifically as affirmed in the *Apology* (19c-d) and in the *Memorabilia* (I,i,11-15).

737 Chroust, Anton-Hermann. *Socrates: Man and Myth. The Two Socratic Apologies of Xenophon.* Notre Dame, Ind.: University of Notre Dame Press, 1957.

Ref. 511.

738 Clark, Pamela M. "A Cock to Asclepius." *The Classical Review*, 2 (1952), pp. 146-147.

Examines the possible meaning of Socrates' statement about his owing a cock to Asclepius. Notes that cocks were offered to Asclepius as a token of gratefulness after the recovery from some illness. Suggests that Socrates' offering was in payment for the recovery of Plato from the illness which kept him from being present at Socrates' death. Argues against the usual interpretation which sees in Socrates' offering a sacrificial payment for his being liberated from the illness of being alive in the physical world.

739 Cocke, Zitella. "In Praise of Xanthippe." *New England Magazine*, 37 (1907-1908), pp. 241-246.

Mounts a defense of Xanthippe who has been slandered and maligned throughout time. Presents examples of the vilification to which she has been subjected: "Xanthippe was a shrewish wife," "To scold was her delight in life," etc. Discredits Xenophon's portrayal of Xanthippe, and criticizes Socrates himself for his style of living, suggesting that in New England he "would have been in the divorce court before he had taken his second dancing lesson."

740 Cope, E. M. "The Sophists." *The Journal of Classical and Sacred Philology*, 1 (1854), pp. 145-188.

Argues against the endeavors of scholars like G. Grote who attempt to clear the Sophists of the unfavorable imputations made by Plato and Aristotle. Maintains that the weight of the evidence is sufficient to compel us to see in the Sophists the champions of rhetorical deceptiveness and philosophical superficiality, and that on this assumption, the opposition between Socrates and the Sophistical movement must be regarded as historically genuine.

741 Daniel, J. and Polansky, R. "The Tale of the Delphic Oracle in Plato's *Apology*." *Ancient World*, 2 (1972), pp. 83-85.

Ref. 1130.

742 Davies, C. "Socrates." *History Today*, 20 (1970), pp. 799-805.

Examines Socrates' efforts to heal what were seen as wounds on Athenian society inflicted by the Sophists. Acknowledges that, while he was unsuccessful in his efforts, he had a profound effect on the development of philosophical thought.

743 Delatte, Armand. "La figure de Socrate dans l'*Apologie* de Platon." *Bulletin des Lettres de l'Academie Belgique*, 36 (1950), pp. 213-226.

Ref. 1131.

744 Demos, Raphael. "What Is It That I Want?" *Ethics*, 55 (1945), pp. 182-195.

Considers the question raised in the title to be the root of the controversy between Socrates and the Sophists, specifically with respect to the meaning of virtue. Argues that Socrates agreed that one ought to fulfill one's nature, as the Sophists urged, but that one's nature is more than merely one's physical concerns. Examines the Socratic distinction between 'real' and 'apparent' desire.

745 Dhondt, U. "Filosofie en He Geweld van het Woord." *Tijdschrift voor Filosofie*, 47 (1985), pp. 195-213.

Discusses the responses of Socrates, Plato, and Aristotle to the position held by the Sophists, namely, that human values are caught in a process of constant change, and that all moral ideas are relative. Explains how Socrates and Plato sought to defend the possibility of philosophy, and endeavored to transcend Sophistical relativism. Observes that for Socrates, virtue is ultimately the true expression of human reason.

746 Dienelt, K. "Das Porträt des Sokrates." *Gymnasium*, 62 (1955), pp. 206-210.

Comments on the Napolitan bust of Socrates, and notes that it reveals to us the natural features of his physiognomy. Contrasts this representation with those in which an idealized Socrates appears as if he had fully conquered the unbecoming and primitive characteristics of his natural self.

747 Dihle, A. "Die Bedeutung der Gestalt des Sokrates für die Entstehung der Biographie." *Studien zur griechschen*

*Biographie.* Göttingen, 1956, pp. 13-34.

Ref. 1132.

748 Dodds, E. R. "Euripides the Irrationalist." *The Ancient Concept of Progress.* Oxford: The Clarendon Press, 1973, pp. 78-91.

Acknowledges the friendship between Socrates and Euripides, and looks for some trace in the latter's works of his reaction to the teachings of Socrates. Examines the *Medea*, the *Hecuba*, and other tragedies, and concludes that while in many passages there appears to be some reaction to Socrates' thought, Euripides' ideas were in fact developed independently from the Socratic influence, and were derived in part from the works of the last natural philosophers (*e.g.*, Diogenes of Apollonia) and from some of the Sophists (*e.g.*, Protagoras).

749 Dontas, S. A. "Διατὶ ὁ μέγιστος τῶν φιλοσόφων Σωκράτης δὲν ἔγραφε τίποτε." Πρακτικὰ τῆς 'Ακαδημίας 'Αθηνῶν, 31 (1956), pp. 379-388.

Maintains that Socrates abandoned his trade as a sculptor when he was about forty years of age, and that he did so because of medical reasons, specifially hypermetropia and presbyopia. [Presbyopia is an eye condition characterized by a loss of elasticity in the ocular lens.] Claims that it was at that time that he became attached to philosophy, but that his medical condition did not allow him to set his ideas in writing. [There is a reply by B. Eginetos to Donta's claim. Ref. 753.]

750 Dunshirn, A. *Der Humor des Sokrates.* Doctoral dissertation. University of Vienna, 1982.

Bases its analysis of Socrates' humor on Erich Heintel's concept of humor. Avoids discussing the Socratic problem, and concentrates its attention on the Platonic Socrates. Criticizes Kierkegaard's interpretation of Socrates and Socratic irony, and develops an analysis of Socrates' humor by a study of the *Crito*, the *Apology*, the *Euthyphro*, the *Protagoras*, and the *Charmides.* Interprets Socrates' humor as an expression of his efforts to expose in a cheerful way the inadequate narrowness of all human intellectual endeavors, and as a manifestation of his profound love of all those human values which are grounded on a firm faith in the benevolent presence of the gods. Speaks of Hegel's interpretation of Socrates as a perceptive and penetrating one. Concludes by recognizing in Socrates' humor, not an enrichment of philosophy itself, but a reflection of the inevitable futility of all human philosophical efforts.

751 Dupré, R. "Socrate." *Bulletin de l'Association Guillaume Budé*, 5 (1948), pp. 77-90.

Outlines the activities of Socrates as an Athenian citizen and against the background of Athenian everyday life.

752 Duruy, Victor. "Lutte entre la religion et la philosophie au temps de Socrate." *Revue des Deux Mondes*, 1887, pp. 44-77.

Discusses the conflict between philosophical thought (as exemplified by Socrates and the Sophists) and the religious polytheism of ordinary Athenians in the late fifth century B.C. Interprets Socrates' indictment and trial as clear manifestations of that conflict.

753 Eginetos, B. "Περὶ τοῦ φιλοσόφου Σωκράτους." *Platon*, 9 (1957), pp. 47-52.

Argues that all available evidence points to the conclusion that Socrates enjoyed good sight throughout his life. Rejects the claims made by M. Dontas concerning Socrates' condition of presbyopia. Ref. 749.

754 Eibl, Hans. *Delphi und Sokrates. Eine Deutung für unsere Zeit*. Salzburg: Akademischer Gemeinschaftsverlag, 1949.

Reviews in Part 1 the basic available information concerning the Delphic oracle: its history, its significance for Greek polytheism, its political and cultural role, and its influence on Athenian statesmen. Explores in Part 2 the biography and doctrine of Socrates, and in particular his relationship to the Apollonian oracle. Views the development of his life and thought as being intimately related to the oracle.

755 Eldridge, Michael. *Philosophy as Religion: A Study in Critical Devotion.* Doctoral dissertation. The University of Florida, 1985.

Ref. 903.

756 Elmore, J. "A Note on the Episode of the Delphic Oracle in Plato's *Apology.*" *Transactions and Proceedings of the American Philological Association*, 38 (1907).

Comments briefly on the meaning and historicity of Plato's report in the *Apology* about the Delphic pronouncement concerning Socrates' wisdom.

757 Erbse, H. "Sokrates und die Frauen." *Gymnasium*, 73 (1966), pp. 201-220.

Argues that the views attributed by Plato to Socrates concerning love and women must be balanced by an appeal to the testimony of Xenophon. Emphasizes the historical value of Xenophon's testimony with respect to Socrates' ideas about love and women.

758 Ferguson, John. "On the Date of Socrates' Conversion." *Eranos*, 1964, pp. 70-73.

Associates Socrates' 'conversion' with the Delphic pronouncement about his wisdom, and places the pronouncement around the year 421 B.C. Argues that Socrates' marriage to Xanthippe must have taken place shortly after 421 B.C.

759 Fiore, Benjamin. *The Function of Personal Example in the Socratic and Pastoral Epistles.* Doctoral dissertation. Yale University, 1982.

Discusses the rhetorical device of personal example used in the Pastoral letters, and compares them to the Socratic letters. Finds both kinds of letters to belong to the same literary genre, and to exhibit similar methods, aims, and even content. Notes their common time of composition. Devotes one chapter to the detailed examination of the Socratic letters.

760 Fitton, J. W. "That was no Lady, that was..." *The Classical Quarterly*, 20 (1970), pp. 56-66.

Argues that what is usually considered malicious gossip, that is, that Socrates lived with Xanthippe and Myrto at the same time, should not be discounted. Concludes that he probably lived with Xanthippe and had a child with her, before marrying and having children with Myrto.

761 Franz, Marie-Louise von. "The Dream of Socrates." Translated by Elizabeth Welsh. *The Analytical Psychology Club of New York*, 1954, pp. 16-35.

Analyses Socrates' dreams in the *Crito* and in the *Phaedo* according to Jungian psychoanalytic techniques, and claims to reveal interesting aspects of his personality, specifically the presence of clearly outlined archetypal images.

762 Fritz, Kurt von. "Antisthenes und Sokrates in Xenophons *Symposion*." *Rheinisches Museum für Philologie*, 84 (1935), pp. 19-45.

Ref. 522.

763 Gabaldón Marquez, Joaquín and Anzola Carrillo, Antonio. *La risa de Sócrates y otras risas*. Buenos Aires: Imprenta Losada, 1962.

Contains two letters (in Parts 1 and 2), one from Gabaldón to Anzola, and one from Anzola to Gabaldón, and in both, the theme of Socrates' constant joviality and good temper is brought to the surface. Develops the idea that it was through the medium of laughter and joviality that Socrates was able to communicate his most serious thoughts.

764 Gautier, R. "Les dernières paroles de Socrate." *Revue Universitaire*, 64 (1955), pp. 274-275.

Comments on Socrates' words to Crito (*Phaedo* 118a) concerning his owing a cock to Asclepius. Argues that these words were probably uttered in a state of mental aberration or derangement caused by the effect of the hemlock poison which he had just drunk.

765 Giannantoni, Gabriele. "La pritania di Socrate nel 406 a.C." *Rivista Critica di Storia della Filosofia*, 17 (1962), pp. 3-25.

Argues that the foundation of Socrates' political thought consists in his absolute commitment to obey and respect the laws. Attempts to reconstruct the historical details of Socrates' position and behavior at the trial of the generals of Arginusae in 406 B.C., in order to delineate precisely Socrates' political stance towards the laws.

766 Gildersleeve, B. L. "Socrates and Xanthippe." *The Southern Review*, 2 (1867), pp. 172-200.

Reviews the references to Xanthippe found in the primary and secondary sources, and comments on the transformation undergone by her character in later literature.

767 Godel, Roger. "Socrate et Diotime." *Bulletin de l'Association Guillaume Budé*, 4 (1954), pp. 3-30.

Studies the evidence for and the significance of Socrates' alleged encounter with Diotima, the Mantinean woman, as reported by Plato in *Symposium* 201d-212b.

768 Godel, Roger. *Socrate et Diotime*. Paris: Les Belles Lettres, 1955.

Presents an extended version (64 pp.) of Godel's article on Socrates and Diotima. Argues that the Socratic teaching allegedly derived from Diotima is strikingly similar to certain ideas found in Indian philosophy, specifically those ideas related to the concept of love. Ref. 767.

769 Godley, A. L. *Socrates and the Athenian Society of His Day*. London: Seeley & Co., 1896.

Analyzes the position of Socrates within the social and political context of Athens in the late fifth century B.C., and emphasizes the double character of his stance: as a faithful and law-abiding citizen, and as a relentless and perceptive critic.

770 Gomperz, Heinrich. "Isokrates und die Sokratik." *Wiener Studien*, 27 (1905), pp. 163-207.

Studies the relationship between Isocrates and the 'Socratic discourses', and between the eristics of Isocrates and his school, and the dialectics of the Socratics. Comments on the influence of Socrates on Isocrates.

771 Gooch, Paul W. "Socrates: Devious or Divine?" *Greece and Rome*, 32 (1985), pp. 32-41.

Discusses various issues concerning Socrates' reputation both during his lifetime and after his death. Mentions the ancient custom of celebrating his traditional birthday, a custom reserved in antiquity for saints or great statesmen, rarely for philosophers. Notes that after the Middle Ages, the custom of celebrating Socrates' birthday was reinstituted by the Florentine Platonist Marsilio Ficino in 1474. Maintains that if Socrates is 'divine,' it is not in the Judeo-Christian sense, but on account of his intellectual and moral accomplishments.

772 Grosvenor, Gilbert, editor. *Everyday Life in Ancient Times.* Washington, D.C.: The National Geographical Society, 1961.

Contains general descriptive essays by Edith Hamilton and Richard Stillwell on life in ancient Greece. Includes a color plate of a painting by H. M. Herget, which portrays a symposium with Socrates in a central position, and an accompanying introduction entitled "Socrates Enjoys a Banquet" (pp. 242-243).

773 Grube, G. M. A. "Thucydides, Socrates, Isocrates." *The Greek and Roman Critics.* London: Methuen & Co., 1965.

Comments on various ideas on literary criticism which can be gathered from the writings of Thucydides and Isocrates. Discusses the influence of Socrates and the Socratic circle in the development of literature and rhetoric, but notes that, aside from the contribution of Plato, we know hardly anything concerning the writings of the Socratics. Maintains that *Memorabilia* III,x contains a passage which is probably based on the views of the historical Socrates with respect to the meaning and function of art: the artist can combine different elements of the real world, and can represent the spiritual dimension (*i.e.*, the soul) by imitating purely physical features.

774 Hamilton, Edith. "The Greek Way." *Everyday Life in Ancient Times.* Edited by Gilbert Grosvenor. Washington, D.C.: The National Geographic Society, 1961, pp. 169-184.

Speaks of Socrates as the exception in Athenian history, inasmuch as he was the only man in Athens who was actually killed for his ideas and opinions. Contrasts the liberty of speech and thought enjoyed by the Athenians with the spirit of oppression of later times in Europe, during which innumerable tortures and deaths were the ordinary fate of intellectual and religious dissidents.

775 Hatzfeld, Jean. "Socrate au procès des Arginuses." *Revue des Etudes Anciennes*, 13 (1940), pp. 165-171.

Reviews the Platonic and Xenophontean testimonies concerning Socrates' role in the trial of the generals tried in Athens in 406 B.C. in the aftermath of a naval battle off the Arginusae Islands. Comments on the legal and political meaning of Socrates' refusal to side with the majority of Athenians who sought to prosecute the generals. Argues that the account given in the *Memorabilia* is less reliable that those contained in Plato's *Apology* and in the *Hellenica*, and that Socrates was only one of the prytanes during the trial of the generals. Suspects that the version of the *Memorabilia* involves another occasion during which Socrates was the head of the Assembly.

776 Heinsius, Theodor. *Sokrates nach dem Grade seiner Schuld zum Schutz gegen neuere Verunglimpfung.* Leipzig, 1839.

Draws attention to Socrates' struggle against the teachings of the Sophists, and emphasizes the unity of life and thought in him. Criticizes the Hegelian interpretation of the Socratic philosophy and the Sophistical movement for its distortions and misrepresentations, specifically with respect to its understanding of the primary sources.

777 Hoerber, Robert G. "The Socratic Oath 'By the Dog'." *The Classical Journal*, 58 (1963), pp. 268-269.

Refers to the notice by R. Blackwood *et al.* on Socrates' oath by 'the Dog' in *Gorgias* 482b. Supports the interpretation which links Socrates' swearing habit with the Egyptian conception of Anubis, the dog-headed god, as the judge of veracity. Adduces other instances (besides those mentioned by Blackwood) in which the Socratic oath could be viewed as an invocation to Truth (*Cratylus* 411b, etc.). Ref. 724.

778 Hoffmann, E. "Der pädagogische Gedanke bei den Sophisten und Sokrates." *Neue Jahrbücher für Wissenschaft und Jugendbildung*, 1930, pp. 59-68.

Discusses the educational premises, assumptions, goals, and methodologies of the Sophists, and contrasts their philosophical stance and ideals with those of the Platonic Socrates.

779 Humbert, J. *Socrate et les petits socratiques.* Paris: Presses Universitaires de France, 1967.

Examines the relationship between Socrates and the minor Socratics (Antisthenes, Aristippus, Aeschines, and others), and comments on the transformation undergone by the Socratic message among them. Argues that correct solution of the Socratic problem requires our taking into account all the Socratic witnesses. Concludes that Socrates can be best understood as a philosopher who did not wish to impart a dogmatic doctrine, and who made possible a variety of philosophical alternatives.

780 Imbert-Gourbeyre, A. *De la mort de Socrate par la ciguë.* Paris, 1875.

Studies the available evidence concerning the precise manner of Socrates' execution, namely, death by hemlock poisoning. Comments on the Athenian customs and laws with respect to capital punishment, and notes that the testimonies that attribute Socrates' death to hemlock poisoning are in full agreement with the general historical information of the Athenian practice in the late fifth century B.C.

781 Irwin, Terence. "Euripides and Socrates." *Classical*

*Philology*, 78 (1983), pp. 183-197.

Comments on Euripides' description of incontinence or moral weakness in the *Hippolytus* and the *Medea*, and maintains that he attempted therein to resolve the Socratic paradox concerning the relationship between knowledge and virtue. Adds that the attempt to demonstrate that the tragedian dismissed the Socratic paradox has not been successful.

782 Jackson, B. Darrell. "The Prayers of Socrates." *Phronesis*, 16 (1971), pp. 14-37.

Examines the twenty-one prayers found in Plato's dialogues (twelve of them said by Socrates). Classifies them as biographical, literary, or philosophical, and argues that two of their functions include the dramatic exemplification of Plato's religious ideas, and the strengthening of his vindication of Socrates against the charge of irreligiosity.

783 Joël, Karl. "Der λόγος Σωκρατικός." *Archiv für Geschichte der Philosophie*, 8 (1895), pp. 466-483; 9 (1896), pp. 50-65.

Discusses the issue concerning Socrates' refusal to confine his ideas to the written medium, and concludes that his choice can be understood as a consequence of the fact that his philosophical views were never dogmatic or final. Maintains that a correct understanding of the nature and purpose of the λόγος Σωκρατικός should compel us to reassess many of the apparently historical and biographical claims made about Socrates.

784 Katsimanis, Kyriakos S. "Messages delphiques et socratisme." *Philosophia*, 4 (1974), pp. 155-167.

Explores the import of the Delphic command ("Know thyself") and its relationship to Socrates' philosophical mission. Argues that the Delphic command is not really an exhortation to find knowledge introspectively, but a call for philosophical resignation. Concludes that Socrates' response was ultimately ambivalent, and that the Delphic command ultimately led him to philosophical reflection.

785 Kekule von Stradonitz, Reinhard. *Die Bildnisse des Sokrates*.

Berlin: Verlag der kӧngl. Akademie der Wissenschaften, 1908.

Provides an annotated commentary on forty-one ancient busts of Socrates.

786 Kerferd, G. B. *The Sophistic Movement*. London: Cambridge University Press, 1981.

Provides a general examination of the historical development and conceptual contributions of the Sophistical movement from 450 to 400 B.C. Gives an account of the history of the interpretations of that movement, and discusses its structure as a social phenomenon. Deals in detail with individual Sophists (Protagoras, Gorgias, Prodicus, Hippias, Antiphon, Thrasymachus, and others), and examines the relationship between Socrates and them. Recognizes in Socrates certain clearly Sophistical tendencies and themes, but emphasizes the existence of a philosophical gap (both in method and content) between him and the Sophists in general.

787 Kӧhler, Liselothe. "Die Briefe des Sokrates und der Sokratiker." *Philologus*, 20 (Supplement Band, No. 2), (1928), pp. 1-141.

Ref. 173.

788 Krell, David F. "Socrates' Body." *The Southern Journal of Philosophy*, 10 (1972), pp. 443-451.

Discusses the apparent paradox of Plato's portrayal of Socrates as a lover of souls, and the physical depiction of Socrates throughout the dialogues. Concludes that in the Platonic Socrates there is a "long-hidden resource for interpreting man's embodied existence as flesh," and for transcending "ascetic Platonism." Calls attention to the anomaly of Socrates' body -- how it looked and what it did, and suggests that as the Socratic dialectic threatened and challenged the conservative spirit of the Athenian polity, so, too, Socrates' physical appearance called into question the traditional ideals of beauty and virtue.

789 Lasson, A. *Sokrates und die Sophisten*. Berlin, 1909.

Discusses the characterization of the Sophists primarily given by Plato, and examines the ideological relationship between the Platonic Socrates and the Sophists.

790 Lönborg, S. "Socrates and Xanthippe." *Theoria*, 15. *A Philosophical Miscellany Presented to A. Nyman.* Lund: Greerup, 1949, pp. 198-204.

Argues that Socrates' comments to Xanthippe, as reported in the *Phaedo*, do not reveal an attitude of disdain or indifference towards her.

791 Luzac, J. *Lectiones atticae. De digamia Socratis.* Leyden, 1809.

Collects a number of unfavorable and derogatory statements, reports, anecdotes, and references about Socrates among classical authors. Comments on the rift between the Aristotelians and the Platonists, and accounts for the antipathy towards Socrates on the part of some of the Aristotelians (*e.g.*, Aristoxenus) in terms of that rift.

792 Martinazzoli, F. "Alcesti e Socrate." *Dioniso*, 1949, pp. 56-62.

Compares Euripides' description of the death of Alcestis with Plato's rendition of Socrates' death. Notes that the relationship that could have existed between Euripides and Socrates was founded, not so much on a ground of intellectual affinity, but on a common orientation and on similar emotional attitudes.

793 Mazon, P. "Méletos accusateur de Socrate." *Revue des Etudes Anciennes*, 15 (1942), pp. 177-190.

Examines the evidence concerning Meletus, and concludes that he was the son of a tragic poet also named Meletus, who had successfully participated in a competition shortly after the year 468 B.C. Notes also that the younger Meletus had himself composed tragic pieces by the time of Socrates' trial, when he must have been around thirty years of age.

794 Mieli, A. "L'epoca dei sofisti e la personalità di Socrate." *Archeion*, 11 (1929), pp. 178-189.

Argues that the real personality of Socrates can be best appreciated by an appeal to the testimony of Aristophanes, not by relying on the writings of Plato or Xenophon. Comments on the role of the Sophists in the continuation of the speculations of their predecessors.

795 Minadeo, R. "Socrates' Debt to Asclepius." *The Classical Journal*, 66 (1971), pp. 294-297.

Argues that Socrates' debt to Asclepius (as this is mentioned at the end of the *Phaedo*) is to be interpreted as an expression of gratitude towards the god for having protected him while in this life.

796 Mingazzini, P. "Su alcuni ritratti di Socrate." *Rendiconti della Pontificia Accademia di Archeologia*, 43 (1970-1971), pp. 47-53.

Notes that the headless statue of a seated thinker in the Ludovisi collection is probably not a representation of Socrates. Argues that the bust of Socrates in the Musée des Thermes may be the work of Lysippus, and comments on Diogenes Laertius' reference to a bronze statue made by that sculptor.

797 Montuori, Mario. "Nota sull' oracolo a Cherefonte." *Quaderni Urbinati di Cultura classica*, 39 (1982), pp. 113-118.

Rejects the historical character of the Delphic pronouncement concerning Socrates, and suggests that the oracular incident may have been invented by Plato in order to counterbalance the accusation of corruption levelled against Socrates, and also in order to secure for himself and for other Socratics a safe return to Athens after their exodus in 399 B.C.

798 Nemes, Z. "On Socrates' Public and Political Attitude." *Acta Classica Universitatis Scientiarum Debreceniencis*, 14 (1978), pp. 19-22.

Examines the admiration and respect on Socrates' part

towards Aristides the Just, and argues that this attitude had its roots in Socrates' childhood because of the ties between his family and Aristides' family.

799 Nestle, Wilhelm. "Die Entwicklung der griech. Aufklärung bis auf Sokrates." *Neue Jahrbücher für das Klassische Altertum*, 4 (1899), pp. 177-203.

Examines the position and role of Socrates within the Athenian enlightenment of the late fifth century B.C., and discusses in particular the ideological relationship between him and Euripides. Shows how the typical themes which emerge in the tragic poetry of Euripides can be found, albeit in a very different form, in the philosophy of Socrates, especially as he is portrayed by Plato.

800 Nestle, Wilhelm. "Sokrates und Delphi." *Korrespondenzblatt für die höheren Schulen Würtenbergs*, 17 (1910), pp. 81-91.

Reviews the various testimonies concerning the Delphic pronouncement that impelled Socrates towards his philosophical pilgrimage.

801 Neumann, Harry. "Socrates and the Tragedy of Athens." *Social Research*, 35 (1968), pp. 426-444.

Maintains that Socrates did not partake in the Laconic predilections and inclinations which can be detected in Athenian writers such as Thucydides, and that the courage and honesty which are generally associated with the Athenian character are genuinely philosophical in a Socratic sense.

802 Notopoulos, James A. "Socrates and the Sun." *The Classical Journal*, 37 (1942), pp. 260-274.

Examines the significance of the use of the sun as the offspring of the Good in the *Republic*, and against the background provided by various references to the sun in the *Apology* and other Platonic dialogues. Views such references as attempts to create an organic intellectual symbol close to the heart of Socrates, and as a testimony of how he conceived the sun -- that is, as a god *in excelsis*. Argues that Plato's use of the sun in its scientific and religious character as the symbol of the Good is partly explainable by reference to Socrates' own life. Reviews the mentions of the sun in the *Apology*, and comments on the worship of the sun among the Athenians of Socrates' time. Regards the statements of the Athenian stranger in the *Laws* as significant for the reconstruction of the historical Socrates' views about the sun. Concludes with the observation that the historical Socrates typifies both the religious and scientific traditions and beliefs of the Athenians about the sun.

803 Ober, W. B. "Did Socrates Die of Hemlock Poisoning?" *Ancient Philosophy*, 2 (1982), pp. 115-121.

Examines the Platonic description of Socrates' death (in the *Phaedo*), and comments on our modern toxicological knowledge of the effects of hemlock poisoning. Suggests that on the basis of that knowledge, we can attach to Plato's account only a literary value.

804 Ojoade, J. O. "Socrates. Was He Really a Sophist?" *Phrontisterion*, 5 (1967), pp. 48-61.

Argues that the primary testimonies lead us to a double conclusion, namely, that Socrates was and was not a Sophist. Notes, however, that what this really entails is that he shared many important characteristics with the Sophists, while differing in certain critical ways from them.

805 Oświecimski, S. "Socrates fueritne sophistes?" *Eos*, 56 (1969), pp. 242-255.

In Polish, with an abstract in Latin. Reviews the evidence concerning the relationship between Socrates and the Sophists, and observes that he was close to them in what concerns their ideas on natural philosophy, but far removed from them with respect to their understanding of knowledge.

806 Pareto, Vilfredo. "The Menace to Society: The Issue of Social Utility." *The State Versus Socrates: A Case Study in Civic Freedom*. Edited by John D. Montgomery. Boston: The Beacon Press, 1954, pp. 111-117.

Excerpted from Pareto's *The Mind and Society* (translated by Andrew Bongiorno and Arthur Livingstone, New York: Harcourt, Brace & Co., 1935, Vol. 4, pp. 1694-1701). Uses the special terminology developed by the author in his sociological analysis of human behavior: Class A individuals are those who aim at undermining group persistences, at substituting logical for non-logical conduct, and at deifying reason, while Class B individuals are those who defend group persistences, stand for tradition, and are favorable to non-logical conduct. Maintains that from a sociological point of view, there was no real gap between the Sophists and Socrates, or between Socrates and Plato, as they all belonged to Class A. Argues that their doctrines had no immediate effect on their socio-political context, as such doctrines were in themselves effects of the social disintegration of their times. Regards Socrates' condemnation and execution as understandable social phenomena, but as clearly stupid and useless acts.

807 Parke, H. W. "Chaerephon's Inquiry about Socrates." *Classical Philology*, 56 (1961), pp. 249-250.

Comments on the Platonic and Xenophontean reports about Chaerephon's visit to the Delphic oracle. Argues that Xenophon's allusion to the circumstance that the oracular pronouncement was given to Chaerephon in the presence of many people gives his report some historical value. Places Chaerephon's visit around the year 431 B.C.

808 Petrakos, V. C. "Ψηφιδωτὰ ἐκ Μυτιλήνης." Ἀρχαιολογικὰ Ἀνάλεκτα ἐξ Ἀθηνῶν, 2 (1969), pp. 239-243.

Comments on the discovery of a floor mosaic in front of the church of Saint Therapon in Mytilene. Observes that one of the figures of the mosaic appears to represent Socrates.

809 Pingler, Andreas. "Sokrates in der Kunst der Neuzeit." *Antike*, 14 (1938), pp. 281-294.

Reviews pictorial representations of Socrates from classical times to the middle of the eighteenth century.

810 Plumb, Robert K. "Socrates Linked to Find in Athens." *The*

*New York Times*, December 25, 1953, p. 25.

Reports the archeological discovery of the floor of the court building where Socrates was tried and sentenced. Recounts the descriptive reconstruction of the building by Professor Homer A. Thompson of the American School of Classical Studies. Notes also the discovery of a small business structure near the court building, at the southwest corner of the ancient agora, in which hobnails were found, together with a drinking cup with the name 'Simon' inscribed on it. Observes that according to Professor Thompson this cup might have belonged to Simon the shoemaker, who was a friend of Socrates and an author of Socratic dialogues.

811 "Portrait of Socrates Found." *The New York Times*, October 27, 1963, p. 87.

Unsigned news report which announces the discovery of a fresco portrait of Socrates in excavations at the ruins of Ephesus. Notes that the portrait measures seven by eleven inches.

812 Pottelbergh, R. "De sokratische zoekmethode volgens Platoons *Phaidoon* 101d." *Revue Belge de Philologie et d'Histoire*, 1944, pp. 236-245.

Discusses the relationship between Anaxagoras' natural philosophy and Socrates' thought. Observes that the latter can be understood as an attempt to transcend the former. Affirms that this attempt entails the postulation of an 'ultimate hypothesis' in which we can clearly discern the genesis of the Platonic theory of Ideal Forms.

813 Ramage, E. S. "An Early Trace of Socratic Dialogue." *The American Journal of Philology*, 82 (1961), pp. 418-424.

Comments on a passage of the Δισσοὶ Λόγοι (i,12-14), and notes that we find in it perhaps the oldest example of a genuine Socratic dialogue (the clearly Sophistical texture of the source notwithstanding). Observes that it is quite possible that its author could have actually heard some of Socrates' actual conversations.

814 Raskin, H. D. *Sophists, Socrates, and Cynics.* London: Croom Helm, 1983.

Examines the aspect of Greek intellectual history which is characterized by the spoken word, and explores the interconnectedness among the Sophists, Socrates, and the Cynics. Observes that Antisthenes can be classified more as a Socratic than as a Cynic.

815 Re, M. C. de. "L'estremo voto di Socrate." *Sophia*, 25 (1957), pp. 290-294.

Interprets Socrates' offering of a cock to Asclepius as a gesture on his part to express his gratefulness towards the god for his removing from him through death the stain of the condemnation by the Athenians.

816 Reilly, Joseph J. "Women One Would Like to Have Known." *The Catholic World*, 156 (1942), pp. 53-55.

States that Socrates is "the most unchallengeable contribution of Greece to the world's Hall of Immortals," and that Xanthippe's weakness was her failure to understand and appreciate the genius and depth of her husband. Creates an account given by Xenophon concerning Xanthippe's frustrations with Socrates' character and activities.

817 Richter, G. M. A. "A New Portrait of Socrates." *Essays in Memory of K. Lehmann.* Edited by L. F. Sandler. New York: New York Institute of Fine Arts, New York University, 1964, pp. 267-268.

Examines a bust of Socrates found in the collection of G. M. Fiamingo in Rome.

818 Roberts, Steven V. "Athens Ruin May Be Jail of Socrates." *The New York Times*, March 21, 1976, pp. 17.

Describes the archeological work of Professor Eugene Vanderpool of the American School of Classical Studies at Athens, through which the unearthing of what could have been Socrates' prison has taken place. Reports on the archeological find on the south-west corner of the ancient agora. Summarizes Vanderpools's statements concerning the find, and recounts some of the details of the *Phaedo*. Emphasizes the tentative nature of the conclusions about the find, but stresses the probability of its actually being directly related to Socrates' prison. Ref. 849.

819 Rossetti, Livio. "Alla ricerca dei λόγοι Σωκρατικοί perduti." *Rivista di Studi Classici*, 22 (1974), pp. 424-438.

Comments on various testimonies concerning Socrates' ἐγκράτεια, and notes that their sources may be traced to a lost writing of Antisthenes which was itself probably based on Plato's *Symposium* 175a-b and 220c-d. Comments also on Diodorus' report concerning Socrates' attempt to save Theramenes in 404 B.C, and argues for the historicity of this report (Xenophon's silence on the matter notwithstanding). Maintains that Diodorus' information may have been based on a non-extant Socratic discourse.

820 Rossetti, Livio. "Alla ricerca dei λόγοι Σωκρατικοί perduti, II-III." *Rivista di Studi Classici*, 23 (1975), pp. 87-99 and 361-381.

Observes that Lysias' *Apology of Socrates* may have been a pamphlet written around 393 B.C. in response to that of Polycrates. Argues that Lysias' work appears to have stressed the political implications of Socrates' teachings. Discusses *Memorabilia* I,iii,3-13, and notes that this passage could have been based on a lost dialogue by Antisthenes. Claims that the Xenophon of this dialogue is not the same as the author of the *Memorabilia*, but an older man who was the author of *The Constitution of the Athenians*.

821 Rossetti, Livio. *Aspetti della letteratura socratica antica*. Chieti: Libera Università degli Studi G. D'Annunzio, 1977.

Discusses the political context of the end of the fifth century B.C., specifically with respect to the circumstances which led to the writing of Socratic dialogues during the first decades of the fourth century B.C. Comments on Polycrates' pamphlet and on the Socratics' reaction to it. Reviews the literary productions of Plato and the Socratics, and deals in particular with the issue of whether Socratic dialogues were written before Socrates' death. Comments in detail on dialogues attributed to Aeschines and Phaedo.

822 Rossetti, Livio. "Il momento conviviale dell' eteria socratica e il suo significato pedagogico." *Ancient Society*, 7 (1976), pp. 29-77.

Discusses the pedagogical methods developed by Socrates, and emphasizes the fact that his young disciples remained attached to him even in their later years, and that their attachment was strengthened through their social gatherings (the 'symposia') in which Socrates participated. Observes the contrast in this respect between Socrates and the Sophists. Notes the pedagogical importance and fruitfulness of *il momento conviviale* in educational practice.

823 Rossetti, Livio. "Spuren eineger ἐρωτικοὶ λόγοι aus der Zeit Platons." *Eranos*, 72 (1974), pp. 185-192.

Discusses a reference by Plutarch to various Socratic discourses (writings) which are not extant, specifically one of which Cebes was the author (or in which he plays the major part), and several dialogues on Alcibiades. Comments on Libanius' reference (in *De Socratis silentio*) to a 'symposium' dramatically set in Damon's house.

824 Rossetti, Livio. "Tracce di un λόγος Σωκρατικός alternativo al *Critone* e al *Fedone*. *Atena e Roma*, 20 (1975), pp. 34-43.

Maintains that various references in Xenophon's *Apology*, as well as in Diogenes Laertius, point to the existence of a non-extant account of Socrates' last days, and suggests that such an account could have been a more accurate and historical description of the actual facts surrounding the end of Socrates' life.

825 Rowe, C. J. "Plato and the Sophists as Teachers of Virtue." *History of Political Thought*, 4 (1983), pp. 409-427.

Examines the meaning and scope of Socrates' favorite question to the Sophists, namely, whether they were able to fulfill their claim to be able to teach virtue. Finds such a question to be apparently puzzling, since what Socrates and the Sophists understood by virtue entails two different things. Attributes the differences between their understandings of virtue to their divergent views concerning the meaning of success, and to the Socratic conviction that all questions about virtue can be resolved rationally in favor of virtue.

826 Sarri, Francesco. "Isocrate come testimone del messaggio socratico." *Rivista di Filosofia Neoscholastica*, 66 (1974), pp. 40-58.

Examines the scope and content of Isocrates' testimony on Socrates. States that even though Isocrates did not develop a full understanding of philosophy, his intellectual curiosity was keen and wide. Argues that Isocrates' acquaintance with Socrates renders his testimony valuable, although it has often been ignored by scholars. Maintains that his grasp of Socrates' personality and ideas can be an important source of insight in our endeavor to establish a criterion in order to distinguish the historical Socrates from the Platonic Socrates.

827 Schanz, M. "Sokrates als Dichter." *Hermes*, 29 (1894), pp. 597-603.

Reviews and comments on the traditions according to which Socrates composed poetical works during his last years.

828 Schefold, K. "Sokratische Wolkenverehrer." *Antike Kunst*, 2 (1959), pp. 21-26.

Comments on ancient representations of Sileni which appear to depict the figure of Socrates in the act of contemplating or worshipping clouds.

829 Schuhl, Pierre Maxime. "Socrate et le travail rétribué." *Revue Philosophique*, 151 (1961), pp. 91-92.

Provides a brief statement on Socrates' views concerning the justification of being remunerated for one's work, and contrasts his critical and negative stance towards the Sophists' practice of demanding fees for their teaching, and his approval of pay given to simple artisans.

830 Shero, L. R. "*Apology* 26d-e and the Writings of Anaxagoras." *The Classical Weekly*, 35 (1941-1942), pp. 219-220.

Discusses the references made in the *Apology* to Anaxagoras and his scientific speculations, and to Socrates' statement that Meletus must have confused him with Anaxagoras.

831 Sichère, B. "Socrate musicien." *Revue de Metaphysique et de Morale*, 77 (1972), pp. 183-196.

Comments on the role and significance of music for Socrates, and notes that for him, music constituted an applied form of philosophy, and that he conceived of it as the most ordered expression of language.

832 "Site of Trial of Socrates Is Unearthed." *The New York Times*, June 22, 1970, p. 2.

Unsigned news report. Describes the archeological discovery of the Stoa of the Basileus (the Porch of the King), the court building in which the trial of Socrates is believed to have been held. Gives an account of the work of the American School of Classical Studies under Professor Leslie Shear in the unearthing of the building which is presently located twenty feet below street level at the southern end of the ancient agora. Describes the discovery of the stone benches used by the jurors, and identifies the site as the court building associated with Socrates' trial.

833 Snell, Bruno. "Das früheste Zeugniss über Sokrates." *Philologus*, 97 (1948), pp. 125-134.

Examines the presence of Socratic ideas in the tragedies of Euripides, specifically in *Medea*.

834 *Socrates in the Agora*. The American School of Classical Studies. Princeton: Princeton University Press, 1978.

Prepared by Mabel Lang. Presents the Athenian agora as the setting for Socrates' practice of philosophy. Provides photographs of archeological sites and artifacts, as well as diagrams and a comprehensive historical narrative.

835 "Socrates Not So Bald." *The New York Times*, January 24, 1926, Section 2, p. 1.

Unsigned news report. Describes a fourth century B.C.

Parian marble statuette of Socrates exhibited at the British Museum. Notes the prominent feature of Socrates -- a snub nose. Observes that on the evidence provided by the statuette Socrates appears not to have been completely bald. Notes that the statuette is the most perfect specimen of its kind in existence made within a measurable time after Socrates' death.

836 "Socrates Statuette in British Museum." *The New York Times*, August 10, 1926, p. 3.

Unsigned news report. Describes the discovery in Alexandria of an eleven-inch statuette of Socrates made of Parian marble. Notes the special interest of the find, since it coincides with the discovery of a head of Jesus in Jerash.

837 Stewart, Douglas J. "Socrates' Last Bath." *The Journal of the History of Philosophy*, 10 (1972), pp. 253-260.

Discusses Plato's inclusion of what appears to be a trivial incident in the *Phaedo* (116a) -- Socrates' last bath. Notes that the bath may have some meaning as part of an Orphic ritual. Suggests that the fact that Plato indicates his absence from the scene of Socrates' death clearly implies that the *Phaedo* in general should be construed as a dramatic account, not as a journalistic report of Socrates' hours.

838 Stillwell, Richard. "Greece: The Birthplace of Science and Free Speech." *Everyday Life in Ancient Times*. Edited by Gilbert Grosvenor. Washington, D.C.: The National Geographic Society, 1961, pp. 185-266.

Places Socrates and Protagoras at the center of the rise of philosophical thinking.

839 Stone, I. F. "I. F. Stone Breaks the Socrates Story." *The New York Times*, April 8, 1979, Section 6, pp. 22ff.

Ref. 1106.

840 Strycker, Emile de. "The Oracle Given to Chaerephon about

Socrates." *Kephalaion: Studies in Greek Philosophy and Its Continuation*. Holland: Van Gorcum & Co., 1975, pp. 39-49.

Raises the question, "What role did the oracle really play in Socrates' life?" Argues that, historically speaking, the oracle does not represent the catalyst which initiated Socrates' philosophical activity, and emphasizes the fact that in the Platonic dialogues (aside from the *Apology*) the oracle given to Chaerephon is not even mentioned.

841 Tarrant, Dorothy. "The Touch of Socrates." *The Classical Quarterly*, 32 (1938), pp. 167-173.

Examines the concluding section of the *Theages* in which the claim is made that Socrates' physical proximity and touch had spiritually efficacious effects. Maintains that even though this claim may have had its roots in *Theaetetus* 150c and in *Memorabilia* I,i,4, it really goes far beyond the traditions associated with Plato and Xenophon, and that its presence constitutes an argument against the authenticity of the *Theages*. Reviews other references to the efficaciousness of touch in Greek literature and in the Bible.

842 Taylor, Alfred E. "Parmenides, Zeno, and Socrates." *Proceedings of the Aristotelian Society*, 14 (1915-1916), pp. 234-289.

Deals with the historical basis for the encounter between Socrates and Parmenides and Zeno, as this is reported by Plato. Maintains that we can assume the overall historical character of this encounter.

843 Thompson, H. "Sokrates in the Agora." Πρακτικὰ τῆς Ἀκαδημίας Ἀθηνῶν , 55 (1980), pp. 252-282.

Furnishes an archeological description of the ancient Athenian Agora: the open spaces, the porches and buildings, the shops and money-tables, and the courts and the prison. Notes that such a description is of great value in the endeavor to understand the philosophical and daily activities of Socrates, for it sheds light on his style of life and on the dramatic settings in which he is presented in the testimonies.

844 Toole, H. "Αἱ ἱστορικαὶ χρονολογίαι ἐν τῷ βίῳ τοῦ Σωκράτους." Ἐπιστημονικὴ Ἐπετηρὶς τῆς φιλοσοφικῆς Σχολῆς τοῦ Πανεπιστημιου Ἀθηνῶν, 24 (1973-1974), pp. 372-382.

Reviews the various accepted and assumed dates of Socrates' life. Maintains that his death happened during his sixtieth year, and that little authentic biographical information about his dates can be obtained by a mere reading of Plato's dialogues.

845 Toole, H. "A quel socratique doit-on attribuer la laideur de Socrate?" *Athena*, 75 (1974-1975), pp. 303-317.

Raises the issue concerning the origin of the idea that Socrates was an exceedingly ugly man. Observes that while there are no references to Socrates' ugliness in Plato's early dialogues, comments about his unpleasant physical appearance are made in the *Symposium* and in the *Theaetetus*. Maintains that the original comments about Socrates' ugliness must have been made by Phaedo in his *Zopyrus*, a dialogue written before 370 B.C.

846 Toole, H. "The Social Status of Socrates as Inferred from His Military Service and Other Information." *Platon*, 27 (1975), pp. 147-152.

In modern Greek, with an English abstract. Argues that the attribution of poverty to Socrates is really the result of a legend or myth created by his followers. Notes that from the fact that he served as a hoplite in the Athenian army, we can conclude that he was a man of modest yet sufficient means. Observes that there is no historical basis for speaking of his father as a mason, or of his mother as a midwife. Maintains that Socrates must have owned a house and sufficient money to lend it on interest.

847 Toole, H. "Socrate était-il une personne mystique et superstitieuse?" *Athena*, 75 (1974-1975), pp. 318-334.

Observes the difference between Plato's and Xenophon's representations of Socrates: in the former, he is presented as a mystic, whereas in the latter, superstition, not mysticism, occupies the foreground. Notes, however, that in spite of this difference, both sources depict Socrates as a man firmly convinced of the divine nature of his mission. Argues against a 'realistic' (or positivistic) interpretation of Socrates, and suggests that if he had been a 'realistic' philosopher, he would not have appeared before the jury as readily as he did.

848 Trainor, Paul. "Immortality, Transcendence, and the Autobiography of Socrates in the *Phaedo*." *The Southern Journal of Philosophy*, 21 (1983), pp. 595-610.

Views Socrates' autobiographical statements in the *Phaedo* as a philosophical 'argument' through which Simmias and Cebes are 'converted' to his belief in immortality. Concludes that Socrates' narration discloses the nature of his own immortality, and constitutes a fundamental manifestation of his existence.

849 Vanderpool, Eugene. "The Prison of Socrates." *Illustrated London News*, 264, No. 6 (1976), pp. 87-88.

Argues that the so-called Poros Building, adjacent to the ancient Athenian agora, appears to be the location of the Desmoterion or state prison, where Socrates was imprisoned and executed. Comments on the finding of a statuette of Socrates found in the ruins of the the building, and notes that this piece may date back to the destruction of the building in Hellestic times. Ref. 818.

850 Vermeule, C. C. "Socrates and Aspasia." *The Classical Journal*, 54 (1958), pp. 49-55.

Discusses (among other things) various portraits of Socrates and Aspasia which belong to late classical times, and notes that these artistic pieces often exaggerate the satyrical features of the philosopher.

851 Vincent, J. "Le type historique de Socrate dans l'art grec." *L'Information Historique*, 37 (1975), pp. 107-112.

Divides the iconography of Socrates into three different types which correspond to the general periods of development of Greek art. Notes that each iconographic type reflects the aesthetic requirements of the individual periods.

852 Vlastos, Gregory. "On 'The Socrates Story'." *Political Theory*, 7 (1979), pp. 533-536.

Ref. 1112.

853 Walters, H. B. "A Portrait-Statuette of Socrates." *The Journal of Hellenic Studies*, 45 (1925), pp. 255ff.

Comments on the realism of a statue of Socrates at the British Museum, and notes that its origin is Alexandrian (fourth century B.C.).

854 Woodbury, Leonard. "Socrates and Archelaus." *Phoenix*, 25 (1971), pp. 299-309.

Examines the report from Diogenes Laertius (ii,23) concerning Socrates' trip to Samos in the company of Archelaus, and attempts to reconcile this report with Socrates' own statements about his unwillingness to step beyond the boundaries of Attica (*Crito* 52b, *Phaedrus* 230c-d). Interprets Diogenes' report (which apparently comes from Ion of Chios) as linking Socrates' trip to the Athenian campaign in Samos in 440 B.C. Discusses Aristoxenus' statement concerning Socrates' relationship with Archelaus, and argues that such statements are probably not derived from Ion of Chios but from doxographies developed in the Peripatetic school.

855 Woodbury, Leonard. "Socrates and the Daughter of Aristides." *Phoenix*, 27 (1973), pp. 7-25.

Discusses the reported second marriage of Socrates with Myrto, the granddaughter of Aristides, and examines the sources which are responsible to this story. Argues that Diogenes Laetius (ii,26) is more reliable than Athenaeus (xiii,555d) and Plutarch (*Aristides*, xxvii), with respect to the information concerning Socrates' second marriage. Views the Aristotelian report found in Diogenes as an illustrative anecdote which lacks historical or biographical substance. Concludes that the story of Myrto is based on doubtful evidence, and points out its absence from the Platonic and Xenophontean testimonies.

856 Yankow, Robert Joseph. *Socratic 'episteme' in Two Plays of*

*Euripides: The Medea and the Hippolytus.* Doctoral dissertation. Fordham University, 1978.

Attempts to clarify the issue of whether Euripides' *Medea* and *Hippolytus* echo the Socratic conviction that knowledge is virtue. Notes that Euripides, no less than Aeschylus and Sophocles, was affected by contemporary ideological influences, and that in his plays there are clear instances of Socratic influence. Examines the Socratic notions of *episteme* and *arete*, and the Socratic doctrine of the identity between knowledge and virtue. Observes that the *Medea* and the *Hippolytus* have been interpreted as dramatic challenges to Socrates' conviction that knowledge results in virtuous action, but suggests that Euripides does support in the end this conviction: wrong action is explainable in terms of an absence of true *episteme*.

857 Yannoulidou, K. M. "Ποῦ ἔκειτο τὸ Σωκρατεῖον." *Platon*, 31 (1979), pp. 123-127.

Discusses the possible sites of Socrates' prison, and notes that the Hill of the Muses was so called in honor of Socrates, for his prison was probably located on the northern slope of that hill.

858 Yannoulidou, K. M. "Ποῦ ἔκειτο τὸ Σωκρατεῖον." *Platon*, 34-35 (1982-1983), pp. 72-76.

Comments on the reports concerning the fate of Socrates' remains, in particular on the alleged transfer of his body from Athens to Thessaly.

859 Zuccante, Giuseppe. "La donna nella dottrina di Socrate." *Rivista Filosofica*, 5, No. 6 (1903), pp. 13-55.

Examines Socrates' various utterances and opinions about women. Reviews the place and character of women in ancient Athens, and notes that in that context, women were expected to sacrifice themselves for the sake of their families and their country ("*la donna era sacrificata alla famiglia e alla razza*"). Observes that just as Socrates introduced revolutionary ideas in philosophy and politics, he was also able to advance new radical concepts with respect to womanhood.

## SPECIAL STUDIES

The annotations in this section include entries which refer to special or specific themes in Socratic philosophy. They focus on, but are not exclusive to, the following topics: Socratic ignorance, the *elenchus*, irony, dialectic, the Socratic spiritual voice or sign, and the problem of *akrasia*.

860 Albert, Ethel M. *et al.* "Knowledge and Virtue." *Great Traditions in Ethics*. New York: D. Van Nostrand, 1979, pp. 9-35.

Identifies the early Platonic dialogues as Socratic, and emphasizes the dialectical method as the procedure which helps deliver individuals of their latent ideas. Emphasizes the character of Socrates as a philosophical midwife.

861 Allen, Reginald E. "A Note on the Elenchus of Agathon. *Symposium* 199C-201C." *The Monist*, 50 (1966), pp. 460-463.

Argues that the inconsistencies between the account of beauty in the *Phaedrus* and in the *Symposium* are not inconsistencies of doctrine, but of language and context.

862 Allen, Reginald E. "Plato's Earlier Theory of Forms." *The Philosophy of Socrates: A Collection of Critical Essays*. Edited by Gregory Vlastos. Notre Dame, Ind.: University of Notre Dame Press, 1980, pp. 319-334.

Examines the emergence of Plato's theory of Forms as this appears in the early dialogues in general and in the *Euthyphro* in particular. Argues that in Socrates' quest for the definition of virtues (such as holiness), we can clearly detect an incipient movement towards the postulation of the theory of Ideal Forms, and that even in the early dialogues this theory involves a metaphysical claim. Concludes that the theory of Forms of the middle dialogues is neither identical to nor yet altogether different from the theory of the early dialogues: the former is directed towards issues not raised in the early dialogues, although it does incorporate elements found in its earlier formulation. Paper presented at Princeton University, March 14, 1967. Ref. 1477.

863 Allen, Reginald E. "The Socratic Paradox." *The Journal of the History of Ideas*, 21 (1960), pp. 256-265.

Argues that the Socratic paradox of the identity between knowledge and virtue has never been clearly explained. Maintains that for Socrates this apparent paradox was resolved within his own experience, and that through a direct intuition he was able to understand clearly that in his own life knowledge had to lead necessarily to virtue.

864 Amory, F. "εἴρων and εἰρωνεία." *Classica and Mediaevalia*, 33 (1981-1982), pp. 49-80.

Interprets the concept of irony, as this is manifested among the Greeks and the Romans, as a mediating principle between extremes, both in the context of problems of the individual and of the culture. Sees Socratic irony as a mediating agency between the new ideology of the Sophists and the traditional allegiance to civic and political responsibilities.

865 Arendt, Hannah. *The Life of the Mind: Thinking*. New York: Harcourt Brace Jovanovich, 1971, pp. 166-193.

Seeks an answer to the question, "What makes us think?" and suggests that the person of Socrates as a thinker whose very being represented apparently contradictory passions, thinking and acting, offers an opportunity for the full understanding of the question. Discusses the Socratic metaphor (Xenophon, *Memorabilia*, IV, iii, 14) which is used to express thinking ability, *i.e.*, that while the winds themselves are invisible, we feel their approach and they make themselves known. Concludes that the meaning of what Socrates did lies in his actual philosophical activities.

866 Ballard, Edward G. *Socratic Ignorance: An Essay on Platonic Self-Knowledge*. The Hague: Martinus Nijhoff, 1965.

Argues that Socratic ignorance is an integral and fundamental part of Platonic thought and bears crucially upon the problem of self-knowledge. Studies the problem of self-knowledge and self-ignorance in the light of Socrates' effort to maintain his integrity while remaining loyal to the Athenian state. Presents a four-part plan for exploring the complexities of the self: (1) the moral dimension of Socrates and his contribution to the understanding of the *psyche*; (2) character, both exhibited and developed by activity is examined through the complex role of the arts in society and the ends towards which they are to be directed; (3) an understanding of self-knowledge/ Socratic ignorance emerging as a factor in knowledge; and (4) a review of self-knowledge and self-ignorance. Interprets Socrates' irony as a consequence of his realization of the impossibility of obeying fully the Delphic command to know oneself. Ref. 1049.

867 Bambrough, R. "Socratic Paradox." *The Philosophical Quarterly*, 10 (1960), pp. 289-300.

Examines the Socratic contentions that virtue and knowledge are identical, and that evil is always the consequence of ignorance. Bases its analysis on a variety of passages from the Platonic dialogues and from Aristotles's *Nicomachean Ethics*.

868 Banu, I. "Appréciation critique du moment socratique dans l'histoire de la philosophie grecque." *Studii Clasice*, 2 (1960), pp. 99-125.

In Rumanian with abstracts in French and in Russian. Emphasizes the role played by Socrates in the controversy between materialism and idealism during his time. Observes that in spite of his subjectivism and conservative leanings, that controversy gave rise to important ethical developments which ultimately found their way into a dialectical materialistic concept of reality.

869 Barabas, Marina. "The Strangeness of Socrates." *Philosophical Investigations*, 9 (1986), pp. 89-110.

Discusses the issue of the gap that separates the ideal of philosophy, as manifested in Socrates, and the concerns and ideals of ordinary human life. Notes that although the gap is quite real, this circumstance does not justify the charge of arrogance and impiety which can be levelled against Socrates. Focuses on the Platonic representation of Socrates in the *Symposium*.

870 Beckman, James. *The Religious Dimension of Socrates' Thought*. Waterloo, Ontario: Wilfred Laurier University Press, 1979.

Stresses the importance of the religious dimension of Socrates' philosophical activities, and the significance of the mystical aspect of his quest for self-knowledge. Calls for a reassessment of current views concerning Socrates' religiosity. Contains an introductory chapter on the Socratic problem. Ref. 942.

871 Belfiore, E. "Elenchus, Epode and Magic. Socrates as Silenus." *Phoenix*, 34 (1980), pp. 128-137.

Observes that on the surface Socrates' discourse gives the impression of being magical, resembling the mystical music with which Silenus was able to seduce and enchant those around him. Insists, however, that as soon as his discourse and arguments are grasped through *elenchus* and *epode*, he proves to be something quite different from a magician or a seducer.

872 Berti, Enrico. "Ancient Greek Dialectic as Expression of Freedom of Thought and Speech." *The Journal of the History of Ideas*, 39 (1978), pp. 347-370.

Examines the relationship between Athenian democracy and free speech in the fifth century B.C., and the dialectical philosophy developed by the Sophists, Socrates and the Socratics (including both Plato and Aristotle). Argues that it was Socrates who succeeded in merging the two requirements of dialectic: (1) the value of opinions and (2) the principle of non-contradiction.

873 Bertondini, A. "Intorno al Socrate di Labriola e Spaventa." *Studi Urbinati di Storia, Filosofia e Letteratura*, 35 (1961), pp. 236-248.

Reviews and compares A. Labriola's *Socrate* and B. Spaventa's *Da Socrate ad Hegel* (Bari: Laterza, 1906). Ref. 261.

874 Blasucci, Savino. *L'ironia in Socrate e in Platone.* Trani: Vecchi, 1969.

Distinguishes sharply between the irony of Socrates and the irony of Plato, but admits that the latter is a direct off-spring of the former.

875 Blasucci, Savino. *Socrate, saggio sugli aspetti construttivi dell' ironia.* Milan: Marzorati Editore, 1972.

Discusses the concept of irony as this surfaces in Plato's early dialogues, and approaches the subject by examining the following themes: irony and science, irony and ethics, irony and education, irony and politics, and irony and religion. Discusses in the introductory chapter the relationship between Socrates and the Sophists. Regards the adequate understanding of irony as the key for the correct interpretation of Socrates' thought. Contains an extensive bibliography (pp. 209-247).

876 Boder, Werner. *Die sokratische Ironie in den platonischen Frühdialogen.* Amsterdam: Verlag B. R. Grüner, 1973.

Studies, in the first part, the problem of Socratic irony as this becomes manifested in the form of Socrates' con-fession of ignorance in the early dialogues. Comments on the relationship between modern concepts of irony and ancient ideas before Plato and in the dialogues. Observes that it is possible to distinguish Socratic irony from Platonic irony. Examines, in part two, the manifestation of irony in the *Apology*, and constructs in the last part a synthesis of its interpretation of the meaning of Socratic irony. Adds comments concerning the relationship between irony and *anamnesis*.

877 Brandis, C. A. "Uber die vorgeblich Subjektevität des Sokratischen Lehre." *Rheinisches Museum für Philologie*, 2 (1828), pp. 85-102.

Discusses the principle of subjectivity in Socrates' philosophy, and defines this principle in terms of the reorientation of the search of knowledge towards the person's inner self. Regards subjectivity as the basis of Socrates' ethical ideas. Disputes claims made concerning Socrates' subjective standpoint, and concerning the accuracy of Xenophon's reports.

878 Brickhouse, Thomas C. and Smith, Nicholas D. "Vlastos on the Elenchus." *Oxford Studies in Ancient Philosophy*. Edited by Julia Annas. Oxford: The Clarendon Press, 1984 (4 vols.), Vol. 2, pp. 185-195.

Agrees with Vlastos' position that there is no reason to doubt Socrates' remarks about his elenchical method, but suggests difficulties with Vlastos's 'constructivist' approach to the *elenchus*, this approach being problematic both on logical and textual grounds. Concludes that the *elenchus* was intended for others who would sincerely employ it, not for the master alone. Ref. 1023.

879 Brumbaugh, Robert S. "Doctrine and Dramatic Dates of Plato's Dialogues." *Essays in Ancient Greek Philosophy*. Albany: State University of New York Press, 1983 (2 vols.), Vol. 2, pp. 174-185.

Raises the question as to the doctrinal significance of several internal cross-references in the Platonic dialogues. Examines the issue through an analysis of many of the dialogues, including the *Phaedo, Lysis, Laches, and Charmides*.

880 Büchner, W. "Uber den Begriff der Eironeia." *Hermes*, 76 (1941), pp. 339-358.

Studies the meaning and use of irony in Socratic thought.

881 Burge, E. L. "The Irony of Socrates." *Antichthon*, 3 (1969), pp. 5-17.

Argues that those who interpret Socrates' profession of ignorance as irony or pretence are in error. Concludes that this profession represents a sincere and deeply held philosophical conviction, demonstrated by Plato in the *Apology*. Notes that Plato sought to transcend the agnosticism of Socrates, and that he used Socratic irony as an educational tool.

882 Burnet, John. "The Socratic Doctrine of the Soul."

*Proceedings of the British Academy*, 8 (1915/1916), pp. 235-260.

Examines the meaning and significance of the Socratic concept of the soul as this is developed throughout the Platonic dialogues. Maintains that Socrates was the real creator of the concept of soul that has exercised so great an influence on the development of Western culture. Emphasizes the metaphysical and ethical significance of that concept as it was understood by the Platonic Socrates.

883 Calogero, Guido. "Gorgias and the Socratic Principle *Nemo sua sponte peccat*." *The Journal of Hellenic Studies*, 77 (1957), pp. 12-17.

Reprinted in *Essays in Ancient Philosophy*. Edited by John P. Anton and George L. Kustas. Albany: State University of N.Y. Press, 1971, pp. 170-186. Attempts to establish parallels between the Platonic *Apology* and Gorgias' *Palamedes*. Argues for the essential identity of Socrates' statements defending himself (*Apology* 25c-e) and the sophistical argument developed by Gorgias (*Palamedes* 26), and suggests that in this instance Socrates made use of Gorgias' line of reasoning.

884 Camarero, Antonio. *Sócrates y las creéncias demoníacas griegas*. Bahía Blanca, Argentina: Instituto de Humanidades, Universidad del Sur, 1968.

Studies the general context within which the Greek notion of the demonic developed before and during Socrates' time. Reviews the various references to Socrates' spiritual voice given in the sources, and attempts to clarify Socrates' stance vis-à-vis the demonic against the background of popular ideas about the matter. Argues that an adequate interpretation of the *Apology* should convince us that the Platonic Socrates did not view the spiritual voice as a personal being.

885 Carlill, H. F. *Socrates or the Emancipation of Mankind*. London: Kegan Paul, Trench, Trubner & Co., 1927.

Discusses the trial of Socrates and his significance in the history of ideas against the background of early twentieth century developments in psychology. Speaks of Socrates as "humanity's first essay in self-consciousness."

886 Ciholas, P. "Socrates, Maker of New Gods." *The Classical Bulletin*, 57 (1981), pp. 17-20.

Finds it unfortunate that Meletus and the Athenians fell into the easy temptation of interpreting Socrates' divine voice or sign as the manifestation of a new private religion which was dangerous to the Athenian polity.

887 Cioran, E. M. "A Bouquet of Heads." *Hudson Review*, 15 (1962-1963), pp. 491-503.

Asks how Socrates, the promoter of rationalism, acted on the authority of inner voices, and asks whether this spiritual sign was either a purely psychological phenomenon or a profound spiritual reality.

888 Colbert James G. "El intectualismo ético de Sócrates." *Anuario Filosófico*, 6 (1973), pp. 11-28.

Discusses the Socratic contention that knowledge and virtue are inexorably related, and clarifies the import of this contention by an eclectic appeal to the testimonies of Plato and Xenophon, and by reference to Aristotle's critique of the Socratic view.

889 Concil, A. "El conócete a ti mismo del Edipo Rey a la Apología." *Revista de Estudios Clásicos*, 16 (1982), pp. 117-129.

Examines the import and significance of the maxim "Know Thyself" and sees in it the fundamental idea of Sophocles' *Oedipus*. Notes that the call for self-knowledge is that which forces Oedipus to undertake the quest for his identity. Observes that it is this same call for self-knowledge that activates Socrates' thought and activity.

890 Connors, Robert J. "Greek Rhetoric and the Transition from Orality." *Philosophy and Rhetoric*, 19 (1986), pp. 38-65.

Examines the relationship between poetry and rhetoric, and the power of rhetoric in an oral culture. Discusses

Plato's and Socrates' realization that rhetorical discourse is extremely powerful, almost like magic or drugs in its ability to influence those who listen. Compares it to the analytic and rational power of the dialectic, so brilliantly displayed by Socrates, and designed to question and break the spell of rhetorical discourse.

891 Cremona, A. "Filosofia del diritto e filosofia morale in Socrate." *Rivista Internazionale di Filosofia del Diritto*, 35 (1958), pp. 101-104.

Regards as Socrates' most important philosophical achievement, especially with respect to ethics and legal philosophy, the successful way in which he combined a desire to introduce moral reforms and a firm grasp of the social reality of his time.

892 Cumming, J. "The 'Daemon' of Socrates." *The Dublin University Magazine*, 82 (1873), pp. 97-108.

Studies the references to Socrates' spiritual or divine voice or sign in Plato's testimony, and offers a religiously oriented interpretation of the phenomenon.

893 Cybichowski, B. *Quae Socrates de diis et daemonio fuerint opiniones.* Bratislava, 1870.

Pamphlet (29 pp.) which collects various Socratic statements about the gods and about Socrates' spiritual sign.

894 Dampasis, I. N. "Αἱ ἰατρικαι ἀπόφεις τοῦ Σωκράτους." *Platon*, 24 (1972), pp. 230-243.

Examines various medical statements and allusions made by Socrates in Plato's dialogues, and concludes that they reflect certain Orphic and Pythagorean tendencies; notes the concept of the self (body and soul) as a unity, and the conviction that the knowledge of the soul is inseparable from the knowledge of the universe. Points out the sound anatomical knowledge imputed to Socrates by Plato.

895 Dénes, T. "Socrate et la valeur de la pédagogie." *Bulletin de l'Association Guillaume Budé*, 17 (1969), pp. 201-207.

Comments on Socrates' educational mission and commitment, and notes that for him, his function as an educator is fundamental. Discusses the influence and presence of Socrates as an extraordinary human being and teacher.

896 Dewhurst, David. "How Can I Know Myself?" *Philosophy*, 59 (1984), pp. 205-218.

Queries into the meaning of the Socratic injunction "Know Thyself" and attempts to develop an answer: Does Socrates mean for us to do something we inevitably do, or does he mean that we should acquire knowledge of our own minds? Approaches the issue by examining certain ideas of Freud, Hamlet, Kant, Beckett, Ryle, and T. S. Eliot, as well as the concept of self-deception.

897 Djuric, M. N. "Les sceptiques grecs." *Ziva Antika*, 8 (1958), pp. 3-20.

In Serbian with an abstract in French. Argues that clearly skeptical tendencies already existed in the Greek intellectual world among the Sophists, but that these tendencies were maintained under control among them by the philosophical activities of Socrates. Notes, however, that his most significant contribution is related to the critical analysis to which he subjected rationalistic and dogmatic ideas.

898 Dodds, E. R. "Plato and the Irrational." *The Journal of Hellenic Studies*, 65 (1945), pp. 16-25.

Raises the question as to whether Plato was able and willing to recognize the importance of irrational factors in determining human behavior. Argues that the intellectualist approach was invented neither by Socrates or Plato, and that Socrates was quite removed from being an 'unqualified rationalist'.

899 Drengson, Alan. R. "The Virtue of Socratic Ignorance." *The American Philosophical Quarterly*, 18 (1981), pp. 237-242.

Examines the Socratic claim that wisdom is to be found in the realization of our ignorance and in the pursuit of practical self-knowledge. Discusses the relationship between knowledge (wisdom) and ignorance, and attempts to shed light on the precise meaning of ignorance. Examines the Socratic contention that knowledge is a virtue, and ignorance is a vice, and concludes by interpreting Socrates' philosophy as a way of inquiry through which it is possible for us to live full human lives.

900 Dubarle, D. "Recherche socratique, recherche cartésienne et pensée chrétienne." *Revue des Sciences Philosophiques et Théologiques*, 27 (1938), pp. 369-385.

Devotes the first section to an examination of the basic ideas which appear to constitute the foundations of Socrates' ethical thought, namely a total commitment to the search for the truth and an effort to distinguish true knowledge from confused knowledge or opinion.

901 Du Prel, Carl. "Der Dämon des Sokrates." *Die Mystik der alten Griechen*. Leipzig: Ernst Günthers Verlag, 1888, pp. 121-170.

Reviews the testimonies concerning Socrates' divine voice or sign, and discusses the various interpretations of the phenomenon.

902 Ebert, Theodor. *Meinung und Wissen in der Philosophie Platons. Untersuchungen zum Charmides, Menon, und Staat.* Berlin: Gruyter, 1974.

Focuses on the relationship between *doxa* and *episteme*, and argues that Plato does not consider them distinct faculties with different proper objects.

903 Eldridge, Michael. *Philosophy as Religion: A Study in Critical Devotion*. Doctoral dissertation. The University of Florida, 1985.

Argues that if religion is defined as "the acknowledgement of a pervasive authoritative reality through a self-constituting practice," Socrates (as well as Spinoza and Dewey) can be viewed as religious in the practice of philosophy. Maintains that Socrates conceived of himself as serving God through the practice of dialectic, and that he assisted his gods in their effort to maintain the structure and vitality of the Athenian polity.

904 Elias, J. A. "'Socratic' vs. 'Platonic' Dialectic." *The Journal of the History of Philosophy*, 6 (1968), pp. 205-216.

Concludes, after examining the concept of dialectic in the early and middle dialogues, that there is a distinction between Socratic and Platonic dialectic, the former being characterized by a negative approach, the latter by a rationalistic and affirmative tone. Suggests that Plato eventually recognized the limitations of dialectic.

905 Elliott, R. K. "Socrates and Plato's Cave." *Kant-Studien*, 58 (1967), pp. 137-157.

Provides an examination and critique of the principles, goals, and characteristics of Socratic education.

906 Faggi, A. "Una sentenza socratica." *Atti della reale Accademia di Torino*, 64 (1929-1930),pp. 197-203.

Discusses the meaning and justification of Socrates' assertion that it is better to commit injustice with knowledge of one's actions than to act without any knowledge.

907 Ferejohn, Michael T. "Socratic Thought-Experiments and the Unity of Virtue Paradox." *Phronesis*, 29 (1984), pp. 105-122.

Argues against the thesis of T. Irwin in *Plato's Moral Theory* that a single argument for the unity of virtue can be found in *Euthydemus* 279-281, and in *Meno* 87-89. Explains the distinction between 'value indifferent' goods and wisdom as a good in itself, as this distinction is advanced in the *Euthydemus*, and clarifies it by reference to a distinctively Socratic thought experiment found in *Charmides* 173-174. Maintains that the *Euthydemus* reflects an unresolved perplexity because of the difficulty of fitting the virtues of courage, temperance, justice and piety within the above-mentioned distinction. Ref. 628.

908 Ferejohn, Michael T. "The Unity of Virtue and the Objects of Socratic Inquiry." *The Journal of the History of Philosophy*,

20 (1982), pp. 1-21.

Argues against G. Vlastos' reasons for denying that in the *Protagoras* Socrates defends a strict identity among the virtues. Also argues against an attempt to replace the 'meaning-view' of Socratic inquiry, and views such an attempt as the result of a misunderstanding and a false dichotomy. Defends the view according to which Socrates' understanding of the virtues would make them co-referential but not synonymous. Ref. 1543.

909 Ferrier, James Frederick. *Philosophical Works of the Late James Frederick Ferrier.* Edinburgh: William Blackwood & Sons, 1888 (3 vols.), Vol. 2, pp. 210-266.

Compares the Sophists and Socrates. Concludes that the Socratic quest leads to the recognition that thought is distinct from sensation and that it is a primary and indigenous product of the mind in virtue of its freedom and self-organization.

910 Festugière, A. J. *Les Trois 'Protreptiques' de Platon: Euthydème, Phédon, Epinomis.* Paris: Librairie Philosophique J. Vrin, 1973.

Contains seven lectures given at Oxford, May, 1947. Examines what the ancients called *le thème protreptique*, that is *l'exhortation à la sagesse* in the Platonic dialogues.

911 François, Claude. *Dissertation sur l'ironie de Socrate, sur son prétendu Démon familier et sur ses mouers.* Paris: Mémoires de Literature de l'Académie Royale des Inscriptions et Belles-Lettres, 1723, Vol. 4, pp. 360 ff.

Recounts the circumstances of Socrates' life in which countless examples of his virtuous customs are found. Discusses Socratic irony and the spiritual sign (*le démon*) which guided Socrates.

912 Fremling, M. *De genio Socrates.* London, 1793.

Offers a brief expository essay on Socrates' divine sign. Reviews the Platonic and Xenophontean passages pertinent to the subject.

913 Frieden, Ken. "Greek Gods, δαίμων, and Socrates' δαιμόνιον." *Genius and Monologue*. Ithaca, N.Y.: Cornell University Press, 1985, pp. 27-47.

Examines the meaning and significance of Socrates' δαιμόνιον, and the issue of whether in Socrates and Plato it is possible to detect a clear movement away from the ordinary polytheism of their time, towards the formulation of some form of monotheism. Notes the importance of approaching the problem by examining the meanings of terms such as δαίμων, θεός, and δαιμόνιον as these functioned in ancient Greece. Comments on Hegel's interpretation of the Socratic experience, and on Homer's and Hesiod's concept of δαίμων. Concludes that the Socratic δαιμόνιον represents a turn away from the popular δαίμονες, and that it 'subverts' popular polytheistic theological systems, and moves in the direction of an abstract conception of a monotheistic divinity.

914 Gauss, John. "Evaluation of Socrates." *Phi Beta Kappa* (1962), outside back cover.

A satirical evaluation of Socrates as a teacher. Gives low ratings for his personal appearance, his self-confidence, his preparation, and his knowledge of the subject. Finds him prone to suicide by poison when under duress, and notes his tendency to place students in embarrassing situations by asking questions. Recommends his dismissal as a teacher, and concludes that he has no place in education.

915 Geffcken, Johannes. "Zwei Sokratesworte." *Rheinisches Museum für Philologie*, 84 (1935), pp. 241-249.

Argues that the two phrases θεία μοῖρα and τόλμαι ἀμαθιάς express fundamentally Socratic ideas that reflect two different aspects of Socrates' philosophy.

916 Gigon, Olof. "Zum antiken Begriff der Harmonie." *Studium Generale*, 19 (1966), pp. 539-547.

Reviews the concept of harmony as it was conceived by the Greeks, and notes its three main manifestations: music, mathematics and physics. Comments on Socrates' understanding of harmony as this is manifested generally in philosophy, and more particulary in the notion of philosophical perfection.

917 Gnizo, F. P. "Il demone di Socrate e il suo messaggio." *Annali del Liceo classico G. Garibaldi di Palermo*, 14-16 (1977-1979), pp. 291-313.

Interprets the Socratic spiritual voice or sign as an audio-verbal hallucination and as a psychical condition. Notes that through the agency of his divine voice or sign, Socrates was able to transmit a concept of justice based on absolute principles by which, as if emanating from a divine source, philosophy stood on a level which transcended the human condition.

918 Gooch, Paul W. *Socratic Paradox in Plato: A Study in Virtue, Knowledge, and Related Concepts in Plato's Dialogues.* Doctoral dissertation. University of Toronto, 1970.

Develops an analysis of the relationship between virtue and knowledge in the Platonic dialogues. Examines this relationship in the context of Socrates' contention that knowledge is a sufficient condition of right action. Concludes that the intellectualist interpretation of the Socratic paradoxes is groundless and is not supported by an analysis of the texts. Notes that the two aphorisms "Virtue is knowledge" and "Vice is ignorance" should not be called Socratic paradoxes. Argues that what the Socratic-Platonic thesis means is simply that wrongdoing is irrational behavior.

919 Gordon, Robert M. "Socratic Definitions and 'Moral Neutrality'." *The Journal of Philosophy*, 61 (1964), pp. 433-450.

Identifies the 'Law of Moral Neutrality' according to which "no definition of moral terms or analysis of moral reasoning shall favor one set of moral principles over another, nor one answer to a moral question over another," as one of the laws Socrates appears to have violated. Presents a linguistic and etymological discussion, and concludes that the 'Law of Moral Neutrality' is either arbitrary or vacuous, and never of use in resolving disputes between conflicting analyses.

920 Gould, John. *The Development of Plato's Ethics.* Cambridge:

Cambridge University Press, 1954.

Proposes to disprove the "widely held" view that Socrates believed that the knowledge of moral facts entails by necessity morally correct behavior. Argues that the words ἐπιστήμη and ἐπίστασθαι mean 'knowing how' to accomplish a task, and confidence or subjective certainty, and claims that these meanings must be borne in mind in order to gain an adequate understanding of Socrates' identification of knowledge with virtue. Maintains that the sort of knowledge which Socrates has in mind in the *Gorgias* is not simply speculative but practical, that is, an ability to act. Concludes that Socrates' concept of knowledge involves "the ability to react instinctively" in the presence of various moral situations, and that the paradox often recognized in the Socratic position is more apparent than real. Ref. 1030, 1541.

921 Gourinat, Michel. "Socrate était-il un ironiste?" *Revue de Métaphysique et de Morale*, 91 (1986), pp. 339-353.

Observes that the primary and original meaning of 'irony' is 'dissimulation' or 'imposture', often in the sense of someone who hides his ignorance or pretends to know what he does not know. Notes that in the context of Socrates, irony refers to his feigned ignorance. Concludes that the transformation of the meaning of irony involves a misunderstanding of the Socratic maieutic.

922 Graf, Gerhard. *Die sokratische Aporie in Denken Platons*. Winterthur: Verlag P. G. Keller, 1963.

Examines the origins, significance, and implications of Socrates' ignorance or perplexity as this is reported in Plato's early dialogues, and notes that the Socratic stance can be detected not only in these dialogues but in the later dialogues as well. Reviews the value of Socrates' and Plato's myth-creating activities as ways to transcend the original Socratic impasse. Concludes with an examination of the Platonic Idea of the Good.

923 Gray, J. Glenn. "The Moral Responsibilites of Teachers of Philosophy." *Philosophy and the Civilizing Arts: Essays Presented to Herbert W. Scheider*. Athens, Ohio: Ohio University Press, 1974, pp. 370-377.

Maintains that the moral responsibility of philosophy teachers entails their being persons first and teachers afterwards, and that their function should not lead to indoctrination but to critial thought. Views Socrates as the "spiritual father of our discipline", and as the ideal teacher of philosophy. Stresses Socrates' commmitment to the clarification of ideas and beliefs: his desire to avoid "the original sin of philosophy" -- to think that we know what we do not know: his insistence on maintaining a private station in life, and his respect for language as a way of maintaining the purity of the soul.

924 Grimaldi, N. "Le shamanisme socratique. Réflexion sur le language dans la philosophie de Platon." *Revue de Metaphysique et de Morale*, 73 (1968), pp. 401-429.

Compares the method employed by Socrates in order to deliver the soul from ignorance and confusion, with that employed by the oriental shamans.

925 Grossman, Morris. "Drama and Dialectic: Ways of Philosophizing." *The Southern Journal of Philosophy*, 10 (1972), pp. 137-148.

Attempts to give expression to the belief that contemporary philosophy, marked by warring factions, avoids what could be a healthy synthesis. Appeals to Santayana's ideas on Plato and Socrates to develop the argument that dialectic and drama are best thought of as polarities and tensions between which philosophy properly moves.

926 Grote, George. *Mythology of the Greeks*. New York: William L. Allison, 1888.

Relates myth to religion and philosophy. Emphasizes the Socratic distinction between the religious and scientific points of view, which suggests that they are to be looked at and approached from radically different perspectives. Compares the position of Socrates with that of Hippocrates and Anaxagoras, and employs them to illustrate the Greek philosophical mind of the fifth century B. C.

927 Gulley, Norman. "The Interpretation of 'No one does wrong willingly' in Plato's Dialogues." *Phronesis*, 10 (1965), pp.

82-96.

Argues that the most accurate statement of Socrates' rejection of moral weakness is found in the *Protagoras*. Notes that the statements of Socrates on the subject in the *Gorgias* are limited and incomplete.

928 Gundert, Hermann. "Platon und das Daimonion des Sokrates." *Gymnasium*, 61 (1954), pp. 513-531.

Discusses the Socratic experience of the spiritual voice as this is reported by Plato. Comments on the distinction between Socrates' voice or sign and his *logos*, and interprets both as expressions of his soul. Stresses, however, the ironic overtones with which Socrates speaks of his experience.

929 Guthrie, W. K. C. "Plato's Views on the Nature of the Soul." *Plato (II): Ethics, Politics, and Philosophy: A Collection of Critical Essays*. Edited by Gregory Vlastos. Garden City, N.Y.: Doubleday, 1971, pp. 230-243.

Addresses itself to the following questions: What were Plato's beliefs about the nature of the human soul, and in what sense did he predicate immortality to it? Asks whether the dialogues speak with internal consistency about the soul. Maintains that the seeds of Plato's concept of the soul can be traced back to Socrates, and that even when the former went beyond the latter, no state of contradiction can be found between them: Plato held firmly the Socratic thesis that the chief purpose of human life is the care of the soul, and that the ultimate purpose of philosophy is the looking after the well-being of the soul (θεραπεύα ψυχῆς). Agrees with E. Ehnmark ("Socrates and the Immortality of the Soul." *Eranus*, 1946, pp. 105-122, published originally in *Recherches sur la tradition platonicienne, Entretiens*, tome III, Fondation Hardt, *Pour l'Etude de l'Antiquê Classique*, Vandoeuvres-Genève, 1957, pp. 2-19) on the idea that for Socrates the soul is immortal and is destined to an everlasting blessed existence. Concedes, that the specific doctrines of the *Phaedo* go far beyond the stance adopted by Socrates. Concedes also that it may be impossible to state with precision Socrates' views on the nature of the soul. For further comments, see p. 178 (Ref. 619). Ref. 1192.

930 Hackforth, Reginald. "Great Thinkers (1) Socrates." *Philosophy*, 8 (1933), pp. 259-272.

Acknowledges the 'Socratic problem', and argues that it is the dialectical method which characterizes Socrates' greatness.

931 Haden, James. "Socratic Ignorance." *New Essays on Socrates*. Edited by Eugene Kelly. Lanham, Md.: University Press of America, 1984, pp. 17-28.

Discusses the possible meanings that can be attached to Socrates' confession of ignorance. Views the interpretation of this ignorance in terms of Socrates' midwifery as an attractive but ultimately unproductive approach to the problem. Suggests that Socrates' confession of ignorance can be best elucidated by shedding light on the general intellectual and political history of Greece down to his time, and by understanding his commitment to the unity of excellence and knowledge; the complete unification of mind and feeling became the fundamental goal of the philosophical life. Ref. 1009.

932 Hathaway, Ronald F. "Explaining the Unity of the Platonic Dialogue." *Philosophy and Literature*, 8 (1984), pp. 195-208.

Refutes the position that the Platonic dialogues represent the 'Socratic' task alone. Questions the comparison between Plato's artfulness to other arts (*e.g.*, tragedy, satire, mime, music and architecture), and argues that if it is an art form, it is one unto itself. Also examines the arguments in favor of a linguistic analysis of the dialogues in terms of flavor and style. Concludes that the dialogues instantiate two things at once, namely, a symbolic token and a type of inquiry. Suggests that the dialogues are essentially united as art and as philosophy.

933 Hawtrey, R. S. W. "Socrates and the Acquisition of Knowledge." *Antichthon*, 6 (1972), pp. 1-9.

Argues that Socrates was not a skeptic -- that is a person who rejects the possibility of knowledge. Interprets Socrates' stance as being one that entails that true knowledge is attainable, but notes that the limitations of his language did not allow him to realize that the elenchical method could only yield technical, not moral knowledge.

934 Henry, M. D. "Socratic Piety and the Power of Reason." *New Essays on Socrates*. Edited by Eugene Kelly. Lanham, Md.: University Press of America, 1984, pp. 95-105.

Examines the Xenophontean and the Platonic accounts of Socrates' piety, and finds them to be markedly divergent: whereas the former described it in traditionalistic, ritualistic, and conventional terms, the latter emphasized its rational and critical nature. Argues that Plato's account of Socrates' piety portrays this as being in direct opposition to the ordinary piety promoted by the state. Concludes that Socrates' conception of the gods was radically different from the conventional conception, and that in this respect at least the accusation of Meletus was technically justified. Argues that Socratic piety is true piety because it is based on reason, not on superstitious faith. Ref. 960.

935 Herrmann, R. D. "Il logos socratico e il linguaggio." *Rivista di Filosofia*, 52 (1961), pp. 279-284.

Examines the significance and use of language in Plato's Socratic discourses (early and middle dialogues), and discovers its development in three interrelated dimensions: aesthetics, metaphysics, and logic. Observes that the common ground on which these dimensions rest for Socrates is his preoccupation with the use of language as an effective philosophical tool.

936 Hughen, Richard E. "Some Arguments in Support of the Socratic Thesis That There is No Such Thing as Weakness of the Will." *The Journal of Thought*, 17 (1982), pp. 85-93.

Supports the Socratic rejection of an ἀκρατής and claims that actions normally described as incontinent are caused by an absence of sufficient knowledge.

937 Högli, F. F. *Das Dämonium des Sokrates*. Bern, 1864.

Reviews various statements in Plato and Xenophon concerning Socrates' τὸ δαιμόνιον, and discusses some interpretations given of the phenomenon. Pamphlet (51 pp.).

938 Hyslop, James H. *The Ethics of Greek Philosophers: Socrates, Plato, and Aristotle.* New York: C. M. Higgins, 1903.

Lecture given before the Brooklyn Ethical Association (season 1896-1897).

939 Jackson, H. "The *Daimonion* of Socrates." *The Journal of Philology*, 5, (1874), pp. 232-247.

Proposes to clarify the problem of Socrates' divine sign or voice by examining the specific functions attributed to it by Xenophon and by Plato, and then to compile the views expressed by various scholars concerning those functions, in order to assess to what extent they are in accord with the reported facts. Insists that there is a gap between eccentricity and insanity, and that only the former is applicable to Socrates. Suggests that the Socratic voice could have been a sort of auditory hallucination which should not be confused with delusions of the mind.

940 Jannone, Antonio. "Sur les notions ἐκούσιον et ἀκούσιον dans la morale platoniciene." *Diotima*, 2 (1974), pp. 57-71.

Examines the content and implications of the Socratic paradoxes that virtue is wisdom and vice is ignorance, and that no one chooses wrong voluntarily. Concludes that Plato's formulation of such paradoxes reflects Socrates' conviction that evil is an involuntary course of behavior. Argues that Plato's view does not preclude freedom of the will on a metaphysical plane. Views Aristotle's treatment of the Socratic paradoxes as a way to resolve and develop them more completely.

941 Justi, B. J. C. *Uber den Genius des Sokrates.* Leipzig, 1779.

Discusses the Platonic and Xenophontean testimonies concerning Socrates' τὸ δαιμόνιον, and offers its own interpretation. Views it as essentially a religious phenomenon.

942 Kachi, Yukio. "Gods, Forms, and Socratic Piety." *Ancient*

*Philosophy*, 3 (1983), pp. 82-88.

Discusses J. Beckman's *The Religious Dimension of Socrates' Thought*. Argues that the contemplation of separate Forms is not Socratic, and that Socrates' conduct was basically guided by his view of the gods as perfect exemplifications of wisdom and the virtues, and that human existence is guided by Divine Providence. Ref. 870.

943 Kalinka, E. "Das Nichtwissen des Socrates." *Wiener Studien*, 50 (1932), pp. 36-46.

Comments on the apparent similarities between Socrates and the Sophists, but stresses the fact that his confession of ignorance differs substantially from their skeptical position. Argues that in spite of Socrates' ignorance, he held firmly to certain convictions such as his faith in his divine voice.

944 King, James. "Nonteaching and Its Significance for Education." *Educational Theory*, 26 (1976), pp. 223-230.

Explores the significance of Socrates' claim in the *Apology* that he was never anybody's teacher. Distinguishes the Socratic educative process (as exemplified in the *Gorgias*) from ordinary teaching and from rhetoric. Argues that the main feature of Socrates' approach to education is the conviction that before some things can be learned, others must be unlearned.

945 Klosko, George. "Criteria of Fallacy and Sophistry for Use in the Analysis of Platonic Dialogues." *The Classical Quarterly*, 33 (1983), pp. 363-374.

Maintains that some of the arguments or proofs used by Socrates contain a mixture of valid and invalid lines of reasoning, a circumstance that is exemplified by his appeal to sophistical methods of argumentation.

946 Klosko, George. "The Technical Conception of Virtue." *The Journal of the History of Philosophy*, 19 (1981), pp. 95-102.

Ref. 1425.

947 Kraut, Richard. "Comments on Gregory Vlastos' 'The Socratic Elenchus'." *Oxford Studies in Ancient Philosophy*. Edited by Julia Annas. Oxford: The Clarendon Press, 1983 (4 vols.), Vol. 1, pp. 59-70.

Raises questions about what Vlastos calls the problem of the *elenchus*, specifically Vlastos' contention that the *elenchus* is too weak to provide proof unless supported by two principles of methodology (A and B) which are to be found in the *Gorgias*: Principle A is "Everyone's moral beliefs always include a subset of true beliefs which entail the negation of each of their false moral beliefs," while Principle B is "the set of moral beliefs held by Socrates at any given time is consistent with A and B." Examines Vlastos' conclusion that A and B entail C, C being that "the set of moral beliefs held by Socrates at any given time is true." Ref. 1029.

948 Landmann, Michael. *Der Sokratismus als Wertethik*. Dornach: Dissertationen Verlag Knobel, 1943.

Doctoral dissertation at the University of Basel (1939). Discusses the Socratic thesis concerning the identity of knowledge and virtue, and devotes the last chapter to an examination of the Socratic concept of the idea of the Good.

949 Lélut, Louis F. *Du démon de Socrate: Specimen d'une application de la science psychologique à celle de l'histoire*. Paris: Trinquart, 1856.

Originally published in 1836. Examines the Socratic experience of the divine sign or voice, which is seen as a strictly psychological phenomenon. Compares it with other historical occurrences allegedly similar to that of Socrates, and concludes that what is involved in it is a case of mental alienation of a psychopathological origin. Assumes that Socrates not only heard voices but saw visions, and examines marginally the testimonies of Xenophon and Plato. Speaks of Socrates as a deranged individual (*Socrate était un fou*), and diagnoses his condition as madness (*folie*). Concludes that Socrates was a theosophist, a visionary, and simply a madman, and that this is the only true interpretation of him. Ref. 950.

950 Littré, E. "Du Démon de Socrate." *Médicine et médecins.* Paris, 1872.

Approaches the Socratic experience of the divine sign or voice from an allegedly scientific and medical point of view, and follows in general the approach taken by L. F. Lélut. Reaches the conclusion that in Socrates we come upon *une intelligence derangée*; that is, a disturbed and unbalanced individual. Ref. 949.

951 Lombardi, F. "Il discorso socratico." *Rivista di Filosofia*, 45 (1954), pp. 271-290.

Develops an analysis of the Socratic method as this is given expression in the Platonic dialogue form, and establishes a contrast between Plato's 'essentialism' and Socrates' unwillingness to move easily from the examination of particulars to general concepts.

952 Luckhardt, C. G. "Remorse, Regret and the Socratic Paradox." *Analysis*, 35 (1975), pp. 159-166.

Maintains that the reality of remorse and regret does not constitute evidence against the Socratic claim that no one can fail to do what he truly thinks he ought to do. Concludes that the embarrassment often felt by defenders of the Socratic claim is unjustified even in the presence of remorse and regret on the part of someone who thinks he has acted wrongly in spite of his better judgment.

953 MacNaghten, R. E. "Socrates and the Daimonion." *The Classical Review*, 28 (1914). pp. 185-189.

Reviews the characteristics and functions assigned by Plato and Xenophon to Socrates' divine sign. Discusses in detail Xenophon's use of the word δαιμόνιον.

954 Manning, H. E. *The Daemon of Socrates.* London: Longman & Green, 1872.

Discusses the manifestations of Socrates' demon or spiritual sign. Reviews various interpretations offered to account for it, and emphasizes the significance attached to it by Socrates.

955 Maritain, Jacques. "Socrate et la philosophie morale." *Mèlanges offerts à Etienne Gilson.* Toronto: Pontifical Institute of Mediaeval Studies, 1959, pp. 389-402.

Comments on various themes associated with Socrates' thought: the merging of the Good in a metaphysical sense and the Good in an ethical sense, the importance of teleological ethical considerations, and the identity between virtue and knowledge. Comments also on Socrates' opposition to the ethical relativism of the Sophists.

956 Mazzantini, Carlo. "La metafisica di Socrate." *Giornale di Metafisica*, 1 (1946), pp. 32-42.

Studies various aspects of the metaphysical dimension of Socrates' life and thought: his mysticism, the divine sign, and others. Concludes that Socrates' life was altogether guided by the voice of God (*"la voce divina"*) which led him to look for the true life beyond this physical life.

957 Méron, Evelyne. *Les idées morales: Des interlocuteurs de Socrate dans les dialogues platoniciens de jeunesse.* Paris: Librairie Philosophique J. Vrin, 1979.

Explores the relationship between Socratic morality and classical Greek morality. Suggests that modern European morality is derived from classical Greek morality and, quoting from *Ecclesiastes*, observes that there is nothing new under the sun.

958 Meyer, Michel. "Dialectic and Questioning: Socrates and Plato." *The American Philosophical Quarterly*, 17 (1980), pp. 281-289.

Examines the role of questioning in Socrates' philosophical practice, and comments on the emergence of dialectics in Plato's dialogues.

959 Miller, J. F. "The Socratic Meaning of Virtue." *The Southern Journal of Philosophy*, 9 (1971), pp. 141-150.

Understands Socrates' concept of virtue not only as knowledge that something is true, but as knowledge of how to act as the situation demands based on certain knowledge of what is truly good.

960 Mooney, Christopher P. "The Mystical Dimension of Socratic Piety." *New Essays on Socrates*. Edited by Eugene Kelly. Lanham, Md.: University Press of America, 1984.

Offers a commentary on M. Henry's "Socratic Piety and the Power of Reason." Suggests that his analysis overstresses the element of rationalism in Socrates, and overlooks the decidedly mystical or spiritual aspects of his vision and method. Agrees with the contention that the seeds of philosophical monotheism can be found in Socrates' religiosity. Reviews the etymology of the words 'piety' (εὐσέβεια) and 'holiness' (τὸ ὅσιον), and the connection between religiosity and patriotism among the Athenians. Quotes in full the *New York Daily News* editorial on Socrates (Dec. 12, 1971). Ref. 934, 1085.

961 More, Paul E. "The Socratic Revolution." *The Sceptical Approach to Religion*. Princeton, N.J.: Princeton University Press, 1934, pp. 27-49.

Emphasizes the role played by Socrates in the conceptual revolution in which the Greek mind moved from the mechanistic conceptions of the pre-Socratics to a teleological view of reality. Reviews the major ideas of the 'Socratic Revolution' by adducing the testimony of Socrates' autobiographical remarks in the *Phaedo*. Comments on the ideological differences between Socrates on the one hand and, on the other, Polus and Callicles.

962 Morichère, B. "Sur la méconnaissance de Socrate." *Revue de Metaphysique et de Morale*, 76 (1971), pp. 441-447.

Interprets Socrates' confession of ignorance as a manifestation of a subconscious sublimation of personality, and as a mechanism through which he sought to cover up his imperfections and his emotions. Argues that Socrates was compelled by a need to be admired and recognized, and that his aggressive character revealed itself under the innocent garb of ignorance.

963 Mulhern, J. J. "Aristotle and the Socratic Paradoxes." *The Journal of the History of Ideas*, 35 (1974), pp. 293-299.

Discusses Aristotle's treatment of the Socratic identification of knowledge and virtue, and the contention that no one does wrong knowingly. Outlines the Aristotelian view as advanced in Books 1-6 of the *Nicomachean Ethics* where the first Socratic paradox is ultimately judged too simplistic to be true. Reviews Aristotles's treatment of the second paradox (*Nicomachean Ethics*, Book VII), and concludes that this treatment resolves the paradox by isolating disposition as a quality of character that falls short of being habit.

964 Mulhern, J. J. "A Note on Stating the 'Socratic Paradox'." *The Journal of the History of Ideas*, 29 (1968), pp. 601-622.

Quotes Xenophon's *Memorabilia* specifically including two statements usually discussed in Socratic ethics: first that those who know what is noble and true will never choose otherwise, and secondly, that all virtues are wisdom as a starting position. Raises the question as to whether there are one or two paradoxes inferred. Demonstrates the relevant ambiguity by quoting the translations of various scholars, *e.g.*, Burnet, "no one intentionally is voluntarily bad"; Cornford, "no one does wrong wittingly"; Shorey, "no one intentionally does wrong"; Taylor, "all wrongdoing is involuntary." Divides these interpretations into those which include a reference to 'will' and those which do not. Suggests that those which refer to 'will' are methodologically incorrect because there was no such concept in ethics at the time.

965 Myers, Frederic W. H. "The Daemon of Socrates." *Proceedings of the Society for Psychical Research*, 5 (1888-1889), pp. 544ff.

Reviews the evidence concerning Socrates' spiritual voice or sign. Rejects those interpretations that see in this phenomenon any kind of madness or mental instability, and maintains that far from being madness, Socrates' experience is "wiser than our sanity itself." Establishes a comparison between this experience and that of Joan of Arc, and concludes that "we have no right to class Joan's monitions, any more than those of Socrates, as incipient madness," and that ultimately "it is Socrates and Joan who should be our types of sanity."

966 Nakhnikian, George. "Elentic Definitions." *The Philosophy of Socrates: A Collection of Critical Essays.* Edited by Gregory Vlastos. Notre Dame, Ind.: University of Notre Dame Press, 1980, pp. 125-157.

Examines the nature of definitions and the criteria for good definitions in what the author regards as Plato's Socratic dialogues. Compares the inconclusive character of Socrates' elenchical search for adequate definitions with Plato's own attempt to construct the definitions of moral states.

967 Nakhnikian, George. "The First Socratic Paradox." *The Journal of the History of Philosophy*, 11 (1973), pp. 1-17.

Defines the first Socratic paradox as the contention that no person wills evil, and that all desire is of what is good. Examines the relationship between this contention and psychological egoism, and Socrates' identification of knowledge and virtue. Concludes that Socrates' arguments in favor of the first paradox are not sound.

968 Nares, Robert. *An Essay on the Demon or Divination of Socrates.* London: T. Payne, 1782.

Pamphlet (53 pages) which explores the religious significance of Socrates' spiritual sign. Stresses the prophetic gift of Socrates, and opposes the interpretation of the Socratic sign as a manifestation of his internal consciousness; sees in it a form of divination.

969 Nelson, Leonard. *Socratic Method and Critical Philosophy.* Translated by Thomas K. Brown. New Haven: Yale University Press, 1949.

Collects in one volume a series of essays by Nelson. Argues that at the root of all intellectual reasoning there is an immediate knowledge which is not derived from anything else. Considers the Socratic method the ideal tool for self-examination. Concludes that the goal of philosophy, which is the clarification of concepts like 'good', 'right', 'I', and 'true', finds its greatest expression in this technique.

970 Ogilvy, James A. "Socratic Method, Platonic Method, and Authority." *Educational Theory*, 21 (1971), pp. 3-16.

Discusses the adaptation by Plato of Socrates' method of verbal questioning to the medium of writing. Observes that legitimate educational authority consists in the ability to practice the Socratic-Platonic method.

971 Olivieri, F. J. "Lo demónico en Sócrates." *Anales de Historia antigua* y *medieval*, 21-22 (1980-1981), pp. 242-257.

Discusses fourteen passages in the dialogues in which references are made to Socrates' spiritual sign or voice. Concludes that it is a mistake to interpret the Socratic experience in terms of a demon (*demonio*), and that it should be understood as a spiritual experience which allows the philosopher to transcend the sensible world.

972 Paisse, J. M. "La critique, source de sagesse." *Bulletin de l'Association Guillaume Budé*, 21 (1973), pp. 519-528.

Comments on the critical attitude developed by Socrates, and notes that this attitude is ultimately based on a commitment to undertake a reformation of oneself under the most strict dialectical discipline.

973 Paisse, J. M. "De la sagesse socratique." *Bulletin de l'Association Guillaume Budé*, 19 (1971), pp. 353-367.

Notes that the main objective of Socrates' wisdom was to stimulate his interlocutors and to compel them to develop their own ideas and examine their moral values.

974 Patocka, Jan. "Remarques sur le problème de Socrate." *Revue Philosophique de France et de l'Etranger*, 4-6 (1949), pp. 186-213.

Examines in detail the nature and implications of Socrates' confession of ignorance, and explores the issue by analyzing various possible responses to the Socratism of Socrates (*les réactions au Socratisme de Socrate*).

975 Penner, Terry. "The Unity of Virtue." Philosophical Review,

82 (1973), pp. 35-68.

Argues against those who see in Socrates' contention that 'virtue is one' a mere statement concerning the equivalence of virtues. Supports the view that Socrates' contention is that all virtues are really identical. Ref. 908.

976 Perez Ruiz, Franciso. "El justo es feliz y el injusto desgraciado: Justicia y felicidad en la *República* de Platón." *Pensamiento*, 40 (1948), pp. 257-296.

Examines Socrates' (Plato's) understanding of the relationship between the just life and the happy life, and discusses the general philosophical significance of that understanding. Reviews the reasons which led Socrates (Plato) to conceive of happiness as residing primarily in the individual soul.

977 Polansky, Ronald M. "Professor Vlastos' Analysis of Socratic Elenchus." *Oxford Studies in Ancient Philosophy*. Edited by Julia Annas. Oxford: The Clarendon Press, 1985 (4 vols.), Vol. 3, pp. 247-259.

Examines Vlastos' analysis of the Socratic *elenchus* and concludes that there are two problems: (1) that he assumes that all the premises used by Socrates in his elenchical arguments are moral beliefs, and would be considered true if Socrates' moral beliefs were true, and (2) that there is no need for Socrates to go through the elenchical argument, for the way in which he confirms the premises he can also confirm the conclusion. Suggests that this demonstrates that the *elenchus* is not a method of research for Socrates, but merely a means used to convey the results of his research to his interlocutors. Ref. 1023.

978 Potter, John P. *The Religion of Socrates*. London, 1831.

Outlines the religious beliefs and attitudes attributed by Plato and Xenophon to Socrates. Stresses his compliance with the externalities of Athenian religion, but points out his critical attitude towards the conceptual elements of that religion.

979 Pourrat, Henri. *Le Sage et son Démon, précédé de 'Le Démon*

*de Socrate' de Plutarque*. Paris, 1950.

Examines the function and significance of Socrates' spiritual sign according to the testimonies of Plato and Xenophon. Includes a French translation (by Ed. Des Places) of Plutarch's *On the Sign of Socrates*. Ref. 168.

980 Préaux, J. G. "Deus Socratis (De Varron et Cicéron à Tertullien)." *Revue Belge de Philologie et d'Histoire*, 35 (1957), pp. 333-355.

Comments on Tertullian's *De anima* (xii, 1-2), where Socrates' God is interpreted as a universal prime mover and as the soul of the world. Notes the agreement of this interpretation with Varro's Platonic concept of God.

981 Pusch, L. *Katechismus der Religion des Sokrates*. Leipzig, 1893.

Pamphlet (47 pages) which outlines the religious beliefs of Socrates.

982 Reilly, R. "Socrates' Moral Paradox." *The Southwestern Journal of Philosophy*, 8 (1977), pp. 101-107.

Argues that the Socratic contention that the unjust person is always involuntarily unjust does not preclude the possibility of moral weakness. Maintains that Socrates' commitment to ethical egoism renders that contention a logical truth. Concludes that the explanation of weakness is possible by denying the existence of only one primary criterion for determining better or worse courses of action. Argues against G. Santas' interpretation of the Socratic paradox concerning the impossibility of moral weakness. Ref. 995.

983 Ribbing, S. *Uber Sokrates Daimonion*. Upsala, 1870.

Examines the Socratic experience of the divine voice or sign, and concludes that the most appropriate avenue of interpretation is neither mystical or religious nor psychological, but ethical and philosophical. Views Socrates' experience as a symbolic manifestion of his moral or practical tact. Maintains that the essential aspect of

Socrates' philosophy is his emphasis on the primacy of ethical practice.

984 Robinson, Richard. "Elenchus." *A Collection of Critical Essays*. Edited by Gregory Vlastos. Notre Dame, Ind.: University of Notre Dame Press, 1980, pp. 78-93.

Examines the emergence and the development of the Socratic *elenchus* in Plato's early dialogues. Calls the *elenchus* "the outstanding method in Plato's early dialogues" which is clarified by extended references to the *Apology* and the *Meno*, as well as to the *Sophist*, emphasizing its personal character. Concludes with a critical appraisal of the *elenchus* and with comments on its transformation in the middle and late dialogues where "the elenchus changes into dialectic, the negative into the positive, pedagogy into discovery, morality into science." Ref. 1493.

985 Robinson, Richard. "Elenchus: Direct and Indirect." *A Collection of Critical Essays*. Edited by Gregory Vlastos. Notre Dame, Ind.: University of Notre Dame Press, 1980, pp. 94-109.

Presents a detailed analysis of the reasoning processes involved in the Socratic *elenchus*. Introduces a distinction between direct *elenchus* and indirect *elenchus*, the latter kind being characterized by its attempt to deduce a falsehood from the contradictory of that thesis. Maintains that the distinction is not always clear, and that in the Platonic texts it does not formally appear, but notes that it remains possible to detect in them its genesis.

986 Robinson, Richard. "Socratic Definition." *A Collection of Critical Essays*. Edited by Gregory Vlastos. Notre Dame, Ind.: University of Notre Dame Press, 1980, pp. 110-124.

Discusses the nature and scope of Socrates' preoccupation with definitions, and examines the grounds of his common dissatisfaction with answers to his recurrent question 'What is X?' Explores the issue of the justification for the Socratic contention (particulary present in the early dialogues) that the clarification of the essence must take precedence over any other questions about a given X. Undertakes a critique of the Socratic concern about precise definitions. Ref. 1018.

987 Röck, Hubert. *Der unverfälschte Sokrates.* Innsbruck, 1903.

Portrays Socrates as an atheist for whom religious rituals had only an external significance. Views as historically justified the charge of atheism which Aristophanes levelled against him. Studies in detail the nature and implications of the skepticism that may be attributed to Socrates.

988 Rodriguez Adrados, F. "Tradition et raison dans la pensée de Socrate." *Bulletin de l'Association Guillaume Budé*, 4 (1956), pp. 27-40.

Interprets the thrust of Socrates' mission as an effort to establish on a firm foundation certain ethical principles which had been reduced to individualistic and relativistic maxims by the Sophists. Observes that the Socratic mission was in agreement with ancient Athenian tradition, but that its endeavors called also for a critical appraisal of that tradition.

989 Rogers, Arthur Kenyon. "The Ethics of Socrates." *The Philosophical Review*, 34 (1925), pp. 117-144.

Discusses Socrates' view concerning the relationship between knowledge and virtue, and between ignorance and vice. Argues that the Platonic Socrates is presented as a moral reformer with mystical tendencies, while the Xenophontean Socrates lacks these traits.

990 Roochnik, David L. "Socrates' Use of the Techne-Analogy." *The Journal of the History of Philosophy*, 24 (1986), pp. 295-310.

Makes reference to T. Irwin's understanding of Socrates' use of *techne* in terms of craft, and that on this basis Socratic virtue simply means craft-knowledge. Observes, however, that in Plato's dialogues *techne* can refer to other than productive knowledge or craft, as in the case of mathematical knowledge.

991 Rossetti, Livio. "Socrate e il ruolo della dissimulazione nel processo educativo." *Pedagogia e Vita*, 1 (1974-1975), pp. 41-59.

Discusses Socrates' contention that he was not a teacher, and interprets this Socratic characteristic as a means through which he sought to influence and guide his associates. Argues that his method of 'dissimulation' was particulary effective in his endeavor to unsettle their convictions.

992 Roth, Robert J. "The Unknown Socrates' Unknown God." *God Knowable and Unknowable*. Edited by Robert J. Roth. New York: Fordham University Press, 1973, pp. 1-22.

Suggests that in the process of revealing to us the mind and person of Socrates, Plato attempted to unfold for us a glimpse of the 'person' who stands behind Socrates himself, that is, "the god" who ultimately guided him. Characterizes Plato's major concern as a desire "to elaborate reflectively a world in which Socrates' life, death, and the faith which grounded his unshakeable fidelity would make sense," that is, a moral cosmos. Examines the relationship between Plato's Forms and the popular notions about the gods.

993 Rudberg, G. "Wissen und Tugend. Eine Sokrates-Frage." *Symbolae Osloenses*, 25 (1947), pp. 20-25.

Comments on Socrates' conviction that knowledge is the necessary and sufficient condition for virtue, and concludes that the knowledge of which Socrates spoke is a sort of vision which embraces the road to follow and the goal to achieve.

994 Santas, Gerasimos X. "The Socratic Fallacy." *The Journal of the History of Philosophy*, 10 (1972), pp. 127-141.

Argues against the view that Socrates presupposes that the knowledge of the definition of a given virtue is a necessary condition in order to know that some specific action is virtuous.

995 Santas, Gerasimos X. "The Socratic Paradoxes." *The Philosophical Review*, 73 (1964), pp. 147-164.

Argues that a source of a common misunderstanding of Plato's ethics is a mistaken reading of the Socratic paradoxes (*i.e.*, that no one desires what is bad for himself, and that evil is the result of ignorance). Maintains that the Platonic Socrates does not actually deny the reality of moral weakness. Ref. 982.

996 Sarri, Franceso. *Socrate e la genesi storica dell' idea occidentale di anima*. Rome: Edizioni Abete, 1975, (2 vols.).

Examines the genesis and development of the concept of soul in four different yet interrelated dimensions: biological, personalist, metaphysical, and eschatological, and traces the genesis and development of that concept throughout the early writings of Plato and Xenophon in order to shed light on Socrates' own concept of soul.

997 Scharff, Robert C. "Socrates' Successful Inquiries." *Man and World*, 19 (1986), pp. 311-307.

Argues against the characterization of the early dialogues as paradoxical, and notes that their apparently truncated results reveal more about ourselves than about Socrates. Comments on the real meaning of a genuine Socratic inquiry -- one that promotes a continuous re-examination of human life. Emphasizes the Platonic representation of Socrates in the *Apology*.

998 Schmid, W. Thomas. "The Socratic Conception of Courage." *The History of Philosophy Quarterly*, 2 (1985), pp. 113-129.

Discusses two main traditions of Greek thought regarding courage, prior to the emergence of Socrates: the military tradition (which contributed to a change in the tactics of warfare), and the tradition which involved the concept of endurance (as exemplified by Odysseus). Suggests that the rationalism which developed in Athens in the fifth century B. C. produced a new conception of courage -- a skill conception -- which emphasizes competent individuals who, because they are informed about the true danger of situations, are better able to control fear. Discusses the role of the intellect in regard to courage in the *Laches*.

999 Schmid, W. Thomas. "Socratic Moderation and Self-Knowledge." *The Journal of the History of Philosophy*, 21 (1983), pp. 339-348.

Examines the historical background and the nature of the Socratic concept of moderation, and reviews the relationship of this concept with the ideal of self-knowledge. Discusses the justification for the assertion that the Socratic *elenchus* cleanses and liberates the person who subjects himself to it. Analyses the relationship between σωφροσύνη and moral wisdom.

1000 Schuhl, Pierre Maxime. *Etudes Platoniciennes*. Paris: Presses Universitaires de France, 1960.

Contains a collection of essays which have appeared elsewhere. Includes the following: "Remarques sur la technique de la répétition dans le *Phédon*," (pp. 118-126); "Platonisme et Socratisme après Platon," (pp. 129-174); "Montaigne et Socrate," (pp. 152-166); and "Le Médecin de soi-même: De Socrate à la Reine Christine," (pp. 167-171).

1001 Scolnicov, Samuel. "Reason and Passion in the Platonic Soul." *Dionysius*, 2 (1978), pp. 35-49.

Interprets Plato's conception of the soul as an attempt to resolve the paradox posed by Socrates that virtue is knowledge and that evil is always some form of ignorance. Stresses the nature of the Platonic soul as a complex unity whose parts are not heterogeneous, and emphasizes the fact that its differentiation stems from its temporary union with the body.

1002 Seeskin, Kenneth R. "Courage and Knowledge: A Perspective on the Socratic Paradox." *The Southern Journal of Philosophy*, 14 (1976), pp. 511-521.

Offers a new interpretation of the Socratic paradox that identifies the virtues (*e.g.*, courage) with knowledge.

1003 Seeskin, Kenneth R. "Socratic Philosophy and the Dialogue Form." *Philosophy and Literature*, 8 (1984), pp. 181-194.

Argues that not all philosophy is literature because it is written in the dialogue form, but that in the case of Socratic philosophy, the dialogue is the perfect form for the development of the Socratic *elenchus*. Highlighting the Socratic view of language that the written word is an image of the spoken word (*Phaedrus* 275d-e; Seventh Letter, 341-344), suggests that Plato's dialogues represent the closest approximation to the rigor of an actual refutation. Emphasizes the constructive rather than the destructive nature of the *elenchus*.

1004 Semerari, G. "Il principio del dialogo in Socrate." *Giornale Critico della Filosofia Italiana*, 3 (1953), pp. 437-456.

Studies the use and significance of the dialogue form as the instrument for the expression of Socrates' philosophical orientation. Views the dialogue form as the manifestation of the essence of Socratism, and comments on its relationship to Sophistical ideas and to Plato's philosophy.

1005 Sesonske, Alexander. "To Make the Weaker Argument Defeat the Stronger." *The Journal of the History of Philosophy*, 6 (1968), pp. 217-231.

Discusses the accusation against Socrates that he makes the weaker argument defeat the stronger, and argues that in defending himself he does not respond to that accusation but commits instead the same wrong of which he is being accused.

1006 Sichel, Betty A. "Is Socrates a Sophist?" *Paideia* (Special Plato Issue), 1976, pp. 141-152.

Examines the dilemma which arises from Socrates' criticism of Sophistical techniques and arguments, and his apparent use of them. Concludes that the dilemma must be resolved by reference to Socrates' purpose in using Sophistical techniques: he may have used Sophistical arguments, but his goals were vastly different from those of the Sophists, and on account of this, he cannot be viewed as a Sophist.

1007 Söderblom, Nathan. "Socrates: The Religion of Good Conscience." *The Living God: Basal Forms of Personal Religion*. London: Oxford University Press, 1933, pp. 234-263.

Discusses the place of Socrates in the development of ethics and religion, and comments briefly on the sources of information about him. Argues that the main element of his philosophy is not the examination and criticism of concepts (*i.e.*, his method), but his firm and unswerving faith. Comments on the significance of his spiritual voice, and notes that it simply acted as a source of guidance for him, not as the basis of his spiritual mission. Maintains that the basis of his 'religion' was his faith in the moral order of the universe and in the unconditional authority of the divine. Establishes a sharp distinction between Plato's mysticism and Socrates' religiousness.

1008 Sorel, Georges. *Le procès de Socrate*. Paris: Ancienne Librairie Germer Ballière et Cie., 1889.

Ref. 1105.

1009 Soupios, Michael. "Reason and Feeling in Socrates." *New Essays on Socrates*. Edited by Eugene Kelly. Lanham, Md.: University Press of America, 1884.

Offers a commentary on Haden's "Socratic Ignorance." Takes issue with Haden's interpretation of Socrates' confession of ignorance as an effort to establish a union between the cognitive and emotive dimensions of human existence, and challenges the tendency of superimposing on Socrates a modern existentialist outlook. Emphasizes the Socratic faith in reason which permeated the Greek world at large, although it recognizes Socrates' sensitivity to the extra-rational aspects of human life. Ref. 931.

1010 Spranger, E. "Sokrates." *Antike*, 7 (1931), pp. 271-278.

Argues that Socrates' philosophy contains two aspects which at first may appear to be mutually exclusive: a bent towards a skepticism which aimed at unsettling principles and convictions generally accepted, and a clear and firm conviction with respect to the most important ethical ideas.

1011 Stannard, J. "Socratic Eros and Platonic Dialectic." *Phronesis*, 4 (1959), pp. 120-134.

Interprets the significance of Plato's dialectical method as the unfolding of his understanding of the function of Socrates' concept of *eros* in the search for wisdom.

1012 Stenzel, Julius. "Zur Logik des Sokrates." *Studien zur Entwicklung der platonischen Dialektik von Sokrates zu Aristoteles.* Breslau, 1917; Leipzig, 1931.

Emphasizes the organic continuity between Socrates and Plato: "Every one of Plato's dialogues remains a debate between Plato and Socrates himself." Notes that the objective discussion and clarification of the problems raised by Socrates was more urgent for Plato than the mere literary controversy created by such problems.

1013 Strycker, Emile de. "The Unity of Knowledge and Love in Socrates' Conception of Virtue." *The International Philosophical Quarterly*, 6 (1966), pp. 428-444.

Maintains that the Platonic Socrates' identification of virtue and knowledge involves knowledge about human life as a whole, and about the ultimate end of all human striving (as distinguished from knowledge about a special and limited field, as the knowledge of an architect). Conceives of Socrates' concept of virtue as an indissoluble unity of love and knowledge of the Good.

1014 Suttle, Bruce Boehmer. *Moral Education and Incontinence: An Attempted Defense of the Socratic Dictum That One Cannot Knowingly Do That Which is Wrong.* Doctoral dissertation. University of Illinois, Urbana, 1980.

Studies the Socratic denial of *akrasia*, and notes that John Dewey has captured well the implications of the Socratic stance when he asserts that the most important problem of moral education concerns the relationship between knowledge and conduct. Maintains that the belief in and acceptance of *akrasia* rests upon a conceptual model which separates the intellect, the will, and the appetite, and criticizes this model as basically untenable. Concludes that in the light of analysis of moral conduct, the Socratic dictum is vindicated.

1015 Tarrant, Dorothy. "The Pseudo-Platonic Socrates." *The Classical Quarterly*, 32 (1938), pp. 167-173.

Examines all those dialogues which are not considered genuine or have doubt associated with their authorship, and asks whether they contribute anything to the Socratic tradition. Concludes that these dialogues are compatible and consistent with Socratic rather than Platonic themes and character, suggesting that they give expression to the older tradition.

1016 Tate, J. "Plato, Socrates and the Myths." *The Classical Quarterly*, 30 (1936), pp. 142-145.

Notes that the critical yet respectful attitude of Socrates towards the gods and the myths about the gods is in accord with what Plato says in *Laws* 10.887d-e with respect to mythical stories about the gods: to criticize such myths does not entail a rejection of the existence of the gods.

1017 Tejera, V. "The Use of Rhetoric and the Good of Politics." *Plato's Dialogues One By One: A Structural Interpretation*. New York: Irvington Press, 1984, pp. 61-74.

Describes how Socrates does not wish to meet with Gorgias in order to witness one of his famous rhetorical displays, but rather to engage Gorgias in dialectic -- a question and answer exchange. Focuses on Socratic irony and satire. Concludes that neither Gorgias nor Callicles nor Polus has succeeded in convincing Socrates that anything other than a just life of human excellence is at all worthwhile.

1018 Thomas, John E. "On the Duality of Socrates' 'What-is-X?' Question." *Laval Théologique et Philosophique*, 30 (1974), pp. 21-27.

Discusses the meaning of the typical Socratic question "What is X?" and examines the disagreement between R. Allen and R. Robinson over the interpretation of such a question. Shows how the question (according to Robinson) can be construed as a request either for an identifying mark of X, or for the specification of the essence of X. Attempts to provide an alternative interpretation of the question which would allow us to conceive of it as a request for both an identifying mark and an essential definition, and maintains that Socrates was tolerant about various interpretations. Reviews the *Euthyphro* (especially 6e) in order to clarify and exemplify the general issue. Ref. 986.

1019 Titus, Harold et al. *Living Issues in Philosophy*. New York: D. Van Nostrand, 1978, pp.13-15.

Emphasizes the Socratic dialectic as a deceptively simple technique in which, through a disciplined conversation, the interplay of ideas leads to the development of thought. Discusses other scattered references to Socrates and his attitude towards disobedience and skepticism.

1020 Toulmin, Stephen. *Reason in Ethics*. Cambridge: Cambridge University Press, 1968, p. 158.

Defines two types of moral reasoning which are distinct and which provide their own logical criteria: the 'reasons' for individual action and the 'reasons' for social practice. Examines Socrates as an example of the latter.

1021 Verdenius, W. J. "De Socratische methode." *Hermeneus*, 25 (1953), pp. 3-8.

Stresses the positive and constructive elements of the Socratic *elenchus*. Comments in particular on the meaning of the maxim "An unexamined life is not worth living" (*Apology* 28a).

1022 Villani, A. "Microsociologie et philosophie. Socrate, conducteur de réunions." *Revue de l'Enseignement Philosophique*, 26 (1976), pp. 1-19.

Reviews Socrates' pedagogical approach in his practice of dialogue or conversation, and concludes that he was neither a moralist nor a philosopher, but more properly speaking a 'group-discussion leader' who sought to redefine self-consciousness in terms of group-consciousness.

1023 Vlastos, Gregory. "Afterthoughts on the Socratic Elenchus." *Oxford Studies in Ancient Philosophy*. Edited by Julia Annas. Oxford: The Clarendon Press, 1983 (4 vols.), Vol. 1, 1983, pp. 71-74.

Presents a response to Kraut's comments on Vlastos' paper. Reconsiders and amends the author's earlier position that in the early dialogues Socrates believed that the truth was already within his adversaries despite their resistance to it, and that by the *elenchus* they are made to 'witness' the truth, this position emerging in the *Gorgias* as prior evidence. Ref. 878, 977.

1024 Vlastos, Gregory. "Happiness and Virtue in Socrates' Moral Theory." *Proceedings of the Cambridge Philological Society*, 210 (1984), pp. 181-213.

Comments on Socrates' thesis of the identity between happiness and virtue, and suggests that this thesis constitutes an approximation of a more sophisticated view, according to which, virtue would be supreme, but which would allow for happiness to retain some value in itself.

1025 Vlastos, Gregory. "The Paradox of Socrates." *University: A Princeton Magazine*, 21 (1964), pp. 19-24.

Examines the Platonic Socrates, and notes the paradoxical nature of the Socratic claim that the human soul is the only thing worth saving, and that it is only through knowledge that its salvation is possible. Argues that the paradox emerges as one considers Socrates' confession of ignorance. Emphasizes the importance of dialectics as the only method used in the Socratic quest for knowledge.

1026 Vlastos, Gregory. "Socrates' Contribution to the Greek Sense of Justice." *Archaiognosia*, 1 (1980), pp. 301-324.

Emphasizes those aspects of Athenian justice which were not beyond the application of primitive ideas of retribution, and notes that it was Socrates who attempted to bring the Athenian's sense of justice to a more sophisticated and philosophical level, a level in which virtue is not seen as a mere constituent of happiness but as its very essence.

1027 Vlastos, Gregory. "Socrates' Disavowal of Knowledge." *The Philosophical Quarterly*, 35 (1985), pp. 1-31.

Raises the question as to whether in the early dialogues, when Socrates claims to have no knowledge, he actually means it. Argues that both Gulley, who claims that Socrates does not believe this, and Irwin who does believe it, are wrong. Explains they can be wrong if Socrates uses variable words for 'knowing'. Contends that for Socrates it is elenchical reasoning which is highest in us.

1028 Vlastos, Gregory. "The Socratic *Elenchus*." *The Journal of Philosophy*, 79 (1982), pp. 711-714.

Shows how Socrates sought universally sound and true conclusions through the application of the *elenchus*. Notes, however, that he must have been aware of the fallible character of his method, since this method can be successful only in showing inconsistencies and contradictions in the interlocutor's arguments, without demonstrating the validity of one's own conclusions.

1029 Vlastos, Gregory. "The Socratic Elenchus." *Oxford Studies in Ancient Philosophy*. Edited by Julia Annas. Oxford: The Clarendon Press, 1983 (4 vols.), Vol. I, pp. 27-59.

Examines the various ways in which Socrates employs the *elenchus*, and notes that in all the early dialogues (except in the *Lysis*, the *Euthydemus*, and the *Hippias Major*) he does not investigate the rationale of the pattern of investigation which he uses, in contrast to the Socrates of the middle dialogues. Suggests that the *elenchus* has a double purpose: (1) to find out how every person 'ought' to live, and (2) to discover whether the particular person is living as he ought to live. Ref. 947.

1030 Vlastos, Gregory. "Socratic Knowledge and Platonic 'Pessimism'." *The Philosophical Review*, 66 (1957), pp. 226-238.

Argues that the Socratic identification of knowledge with virtue entails that knowing how to be a moral agent depends on the correct understanding of what actions are moral and what actions are immoral. Maintains that the Socratic *episteme*, even if understood (as Gould does) in the sense of moral confidence, can make a person totally invulnerable to emotions like rage, pleasure, love, and terror under conditions of stress. Ref. 920.

1031 Vogel, Cornelia J. de. "Two Major Problems Concerning Socrates." *Theta-Pi*, 2 (1973), pp. 18-39.

Discusses two major issues that arise in the context of W.

K. C. Guthrie's *Socrates*, namely, the alleged utilitarian tendencies of Socrates' ethical ideas, and the reported contempt for the body which Plato attributes to Socrates (*Phaedo* 61c-69c). Ref. 236.

1032 Vogel, Cornelia J. de. "What Philosophy Meant to the Greeks." *International Philosophical Quarterly*, 1 (1961), pp. 35-57.

Examines the close link between *theoria* and *praxis* (philosophy and moral life) which was one of the most distinctive traits of the Greek philosophers. Discusses the Socratic position as it is presented in the *Apology* as an example. Questions the Aristotelian interpretation of Socrates and suggests that Aristotle was mistaken when he concluded that for Socrates intellectual clearness and moral improvement were inseparable.

1033 Volguardsen, C. R. *Das 'Dämonium' des Sokrates und seine Interpreten*. Kiel, 1862.

Pamphlet (72 pp.) which recounts the details of Socrates' divine voice or sign (according to the testimonies of Plato and Xenophon). Discusses several ancient and modern interpretations of its sources and meaning.

1034 Waldenfels, Bernhard. *Das Sokratische Fragen. Aporie, Elenchos, Anamnesis*. Meisenheim: Verlag Anton Hain, 1961.

Suggests that there are three fundamental moments of Socrates' philosophical enterprise, and sees them as three distinct levels of thought in which the first level leads necessarily to the second, and the second level to the last. Identifies these moments as: (1) a state of perplexity in which the Socratic confession of ignorance appears as a conclusion; (2) the Socratic *elenchus* which emerges as a negative phase; and (3) the state of recollection which overcomes the two previous stages as a positive solution.

1035 Walsh, James J. "The Socratic Denial of *akrasia*." *The Philosophy of Socrates: A Collection of Critical Essays*. Edited by Gregory Vlastos. Notre Dame, Ind.: University of Notre Dame Press, 1980, pp. 235-263.

Examines Socrates' rejection of the possibility of *akrasia* in the light of Xenophon's and Plato's testimonies, and compares the problem raised by the Socratic position with the issues that arise from Euripides' *Medea* and *Hippolytus*. Views Socrates' assertion of the motivational supremacy of reason in the form of knowledge (*Protagoras* 352b-c) as a possible response to Euripides' dramatization of the moral conflict, and as a sophisticated philosophical rendition of the Socratic rejection of *akrasia* as this is reported by Xenophon. Comments on Aristotle's position vis-à-vis the Socratic thesis.

1036 Warbeke, John M. "Socrates." *The Searching Mind of Greece*. New York: F. S. Crofts, 1934, pp. 131-144.

Emphasizes the Socratic dialectic and the unity of theory and practice. Suggests that the Platonic theory of Forms is already evident in Socratic teaching, referring to Aristotle's observation that Socrates sought the universal in ethical matters.

1037 Warman, M. S. "Plato and Persuasion." *Greece and Rome*, 30 (1983), pp. 48-54.

Argues that the *Gorgias* represents fairly well the methods and views of Socrates, despite the Platonic overtones. Identifies as Socratic the belief in the primacy of the spoken word as a means to the truth; the belief that persuasion is more effective when addressed to individuals rather than to crowds; the commitment to a question and answer method; the scorn of rhetoric as it was practiced in Athenian courts; and the belief that the most important function of persuasion is to induce reflection on how to live a good life.

1038 Waterfall, Donald Ernest. *Plato and Aristotle on 'akrasia'*. Doctoral dissertation. Princeton University, 1969.

Attempts to clarify Plato's and Aristotle's treatment of *akrasia* and some of the psychological principles they appealed to in order to account for it. Observes the developmental changes in Plato's own view from the *Protagoras* (where through cognitive psychology he asserts the impossibility of *akrasia*), to the *Meno* and *Republic* III, to *Republic* IV (where he abandons his previous approach), and to the *Laws* (where he allows for the possibility of *akrasia*). Notes that Aristotle displays less willingness to abandon Socrates' original position than Plato. Analyzes the sections of the *Nicomachean Ethics* in which Aristotle endeavors to reconcile Socrates' view with the contentions of those who see in *akrasia* a conflict in the soul. Concludes by noting the difference between Plato and Aristotle: the former exhibits development and change, whereas the latter shows a desire to harmonize divergent views.

1039 Watson, Gary. "Skepticism About Weakness of Will." *The Philosophical Review*, 86 (1977), pp. 316-339.

Develops an interpretation of weakness of will on a non-Socratic basis. Argues that the Socratic interpretation is basically incorrect, and notes that, contrary to Socrates' view, it is possible for a person to act against his better judgment. Concludes that Socrates' position ignores the "morally and psychologically important complexity of human motivation."

1039a Wiggins, David. "Teleology and the Good in Plato's *Phaedo*." *Oxford Studies in Ancient Philosophy. A Festschrift for J. L. Ackril.* Edited by Michael Woods. Oxford: The Clarendon Press, 1986 (4 vols.), Vol. 4.

Examines *Phaedo* 99c2-d1 where Socrates speaks of his initial excitement and later disappointment at the works of Anaxagoras. Argues that the is teleological in intention, not formal in content.

1040 Wildauer, F. *Sokrates' Lehre vom Willen*. Innsbruck, 1877.

Interprets Socrates' philosophy as a fundamental contribution to the genesis of psychology, and views his concept of *psyche* as a basically psychological idea.

1041 Willing, August. *De Socratis daemonis quae antiquis temporibus fuerint opiniones*. Doctoral dissertation, University of Jena. Leipzig: B. G. Teubner, 1909.

Examines textually the passages in Xenophon and in Plato concerning the Socratic divine sign or voice. Reviews the opinions held by the Peripatetics, the Academicians, the Stoics, and the early Fathers of the Church, with respect to the meaning of Socrates' experience.

1042 Windelband, Wilhelm. "Uber Sokrates." *Präludien. Aufsätze und Rede zur Philosophie und ihrer Geschichte.* Tübingen, 1921, pp. 55-87.

Explores in particular Socrates' concept of soul, and concludes that with him, and through that concept, reason assumes the role of the true source of legislation for the conduct of life.

1043 Winsatt, William K. and Brooks, Cleanth. "Socrates and the Rhapsode." *Literary Criticism: A Short History.* New York: Alfred A. Knopf, 1965, pp. 3-20.

Discusses the beginnings of literary criticism among the early Greek poets, with emphasis on Aristophanes' the *Frogs*. Devotes considerable attention to the *Ion* and to the character of Socrates drawn therein. Views Socrates as "representing a spirit of criticism which was increasing with the sad experiences of the city state." Comments on the presence of literary criticism as this appears in other Platonic dialogues, as in the *Phaedrus*, the *Meno*, the *Republic*, and the *Symposium*.

1044 Wohlgemuth, L. "Die Lehre des historischen Sokrates." *Opuscula Philologica.* Vienna: Akademie Philologenverein, 1927, pp. 1-42.

Argues that the thesis of the identity of knowledge and virtue can be associated with the historical Socrates, and that this is supported by the testimonies of the *Memorabilia* and the early dialogues of Plato.

1045 Woodhead, W. D. "The *Daimonion* of Socrates." *Classical Philology*, 35 (1940), pp. 425-426.

Brief note which compares the Socratic experience of a spiritual sign or voice with an experience reported by William Hale White [Mark Rutherford] in his autobiography. Observes that all the references in the genuine Platonic dialogues to Socrates' experience are perfectly consistent with one another.

1046 Woodruff, Paul. "Socrates on the Parts of Virtue." *The Canadian Journal of Philosophy*, Supplement 2 (1976), pp. 101-116.

Explains the apparent paradox of Socrates' view of the virtues as one unity, by introducing various senses of 'essence' and 'accident'. Concludes that the Socratic position makes sense if we maintain that in essence all the virtues are one, but that in their accidental manifestations they are varied and different.

1047 Woodruff, Paul. "The Socratic Approach to Semantic Incompleteness." *Philosophy and Phenomenological Research*, 38 (1978), pp. 453-468.

Reviews Socrates' rule for adjectives by which he insists that everything to which an adjective is correctly applied displays a certain character (even when the same adjective has different meanings in different contexts). Examines how Plato inherited the Socratic rule, and what consequences this rule has for Plato's metaphysics.

1048 Zeyl, Donald J. "Socratic Virtue and Happiness." *Archiv für Geschichte der Philosophie*, 64 (1982), pp. 205-238.

Rejects the interpretation of Socrates as a moral solipsist, and notes that for him virtue is both a cause and an ingredient of happiness.

1049 Zimmerman, Michael E. "Socratic Ignorance and Authenticity." *Tulane Studies in Philosophy*, 29 (1980), pp. 133-150.

Examines the significance of Socrates' confession of ignorance against the background furnished by E. Ballard's *Socratic Ignorance*. Explains Ballard's interpretation of Socratic (Platonic) ignorance as 'existential loyalty', and discusses the relationship between such an interpretation and Heidegger's notion of authenticity. Ref. 866.

1050 Zuccante, Giuseppe. "Sul concetto del bene in Socrate a proposito del suo asserito utilitarismo." *Rivista di Filoso-*

*fia e Scienze*, 7 (1904), pp. 453ff.

Studies the concept of the good as this is conceived by Socrates, and concludes that it is ultimately supported by a commitment to utilitarian considerations.

1051 Zych, Paulette Marie. "Plato's Aphrodite Pandemos and Aphrodite Urania." *Sociologia Internationalis*, 16 (1978), pp. 1-2 and pp. 105-112.

Discusses the concept of various types of love in selected Platonic dialogues (the *Symposium*, the *Phaedrus*, and the *Lysis*). Pays particular attention to Socrates' discourses on art, virtue, and the nature of love.

# SOCRATES' TRIAL - GENERAL WORKS

The entries of this section contain information concerning general works on Socrates' trial. Entries related to the literature which discusses Plato's account of the trial are included in another section. References are given to works which are annotated elsewhere and which shed some light on Socrates' trial.

1052 Alsberg, Max. *Der Prozess des Sokrates im Lichte moderner Jurisprudenz und Psychologie.* Mannheim: J. Bensheimer, 1933.

Pamphlet (29 pp.) which gives a general account of Socrates' trial, and which explores a number of issues concerning its legality and background, as these can be assessed from a contemporary point of view.

1053 Aly, W. "Anytos, der Ankläger des Sokrates." *Neue Jahrbücher für klassische Altertum*, 31 (1913), pp. 169-193.

Examines the historical and literary information which is available concerning Anytus, and reviews his role as the chief prosecutor in Socrates' trial.

1054 Atkinson, Brooks. "Visit to Reconstructed Stoa of Attalos Recalls Trial and Death of Socrates." *The New York Times*, March 9, 1965, p. 32.

Commentary in the "Critic at Large" column of *The New York Times.* Establishes a comparison between the jury which sentenced Socrates and the House Committee on Un-American Activities, and describes the sentenced philosopher as an imposing historical figure whose trial and death are among the most fundamental events in the history of civilization, and an integral part of the intellectual foundation of the free world. Establishes a comparison of the agora of Socrates' time with the present archeological site. Describes the various remains kept today in the museum of the reconstructed Stoa of Attalos in Athens. Concludes with comments about hemlock and its effects, and notes that, as Plato says, it attacks the heart before it attacks the brain: in Socrates, "the heart always comes before the head."

1055 Beyschlag, F. *Die Anklage des Sokrates.* Neustadt, 1900.

Pamphlet (58 pp.) which outlines the indictment against Socrates. Studies the possible political implications tacitly contained in the accusations.

1056 Blumenthal, H. "Meletus the Accuser of Andocides and Meletus the Accuser of Socrates." *Philologus*, 117 (1973), pp. 167-178.

Argues for the view that the Meletus of Andocides' trial is the same person who prosecuted Socrates.

1057 Bourgeois, H. *Le tribunal des Heliastes et le procès de Socrate.* Paris, 1891.

Reviews the historical information concerning the Athenian jury system, and discusses the background and the actual conduct of Socrates' trial.

1058 Breitenbach, L. "Wer ist der κατήγορος in Xenophons Commentarien?" *Neue Jahrbücher für Philologie und Paedagogik*, 39 (1869), pp. 801-815.

Ref. 509.

1059 Brumbaugh, Robert S. "The Trial of Socrates." *Six Trials.* New York: Thomas Y. Crowell Company, 1969, pp. 9-23.

Chapter 1 of a volume (edited by Brumbaugh) which contains chapters on the trials of Socrates, Galileo, John Brown, Alfred Dreyfus, Sacco and Vanzetti, and John T. Scopes -- each chapter written by a different author. Views Socrates' trial as a dramatic confrontation between a new idea of human dignity and an ancient desire and need for social stability and tranquility. Discusses the political and ideological context of the trial, and summarizes the legal process by adducing the testimonies of Plato and Xenophon; regards the latter as providing only an incomplete account of the matter.

1060 Bury, J. B. "The Trial of Socrates." *Selected Essays of J. B. Bury.* Edited by H. Temperly. Cambridge: Cambridge

University Press, 1930. pp. 75-90.

Discusses the background, details, outcome, and sources of information of Socrates' trial. Comments on other similar trials and indictments in Athens (those involving Anaxagoras, Diogoras of Melos, Euripides, and Protagoras), and on the laws against irreligiosity (specifically the decree of Diopeithes). Argues that the real basis of the indictment against Socrates was more political than religious, and that the trial cannot be interpreted as a simple manifestation of hatred towards rationalism. Speaks of Meletus as the only real accuser of Socrates, Anytus and Lycon being only associated in the prosecution. Considers Plato's account of the trial an embellished and rhetorical rendition of Socrates' reply to Meletus, and notes that his *Apology* omits certain crucial elements which can be gathered from the account of Xenophon and from Polycrates' pamphlet. Notes that the speech delivered by Socrates after his sentence is an element in the Platonic testimony which appears to have been invented for dramatic and philosophical purposes. Concludes with comments on the allegation (made by Xenophon) that Socrates actually wanted to die at the time of the trial, and rejects this allegation as unfounded. Maintains that if Socrates "bore witness to any cause, it was to the cause of freedom of speech." Ref. 1082.

1061 Carlill, H. F. *Socrates or the Emancipation of Mankind.* London: Kegan Paul, Trench, Trubner & Co., 1927.

Begins with a brief examination of the intellectual process which led to the trial and execution of Socrates, and notes that the Socratic doctrine was truly the cultural suicide of the Greek national genius -- supporting thus Nietzsche's interpretation of Socrates' presence and influence. Develops various themes on the basis of its understanding of the meaning of Socrates' doctrine and trial (*e.g.*, the role of the unconscious in society).

1062 Casini, N. "Il processo di Socrate." *Iura*, 8 (1957), pp. 101-120.

Examines the evidence concerning Socrates' trial and the specific law under which he was tried and sentenced, and concludes that the jury had only two possible courses of action, once Socrates was found guilty: either a sentence of death or an insignificant fine. Ref. 1098.

1063 Chroust, Anton-Hermann. *Socrates: Man and Myth. The Two Socratic Apologies of Xenophon.* Notre Dame, Ind.: University of Notre Dame Press, 1957.

Ref. 511.

1064 Chroust, Anton-Hermann. "Xenophon, Polycrates, and the Indictment of Socrates." *Classica et Mediaevalia*, 16 (1955), pp. 1-17.

Ref. 512.

1065 Dover, Kenneth J. "The Freedom of the Intellectual in Greek Society." *Talanta*, 7 (1975), pp. 24-54.

Reviews historical and literary testimonies concerning cases of ideological persecution and prosecution of intellectuals during Socrates' time. Comments on the ways in which the examination of intellectual freedom (or lack of freedom) in Athens can shed light on the prosecution and condemnation of Socrates.

1066 Dresig, Siegmund F. *De Socrate iuste damnato.* Leipzig: Langenheim, 1738.

Reprinted in M. Montuori's *De Socrate iuste damnato* (pp. 101-114). Written in the form of a letter. Examines in detail the various charges contained in the indictment against Socrates, and concludes that each one of them was amply justified by reference to his attitude towards the gods and the Athenian polity. Portrays Socrates as a persistent and dangerous opponent of the Athenian democracy, and as a supporter of an aristocracy based on intelligence and ability. Concludes that the accusations and the sentence were fully justified within the political and social context of Athenian life. Ref. 398.

1067 Düring, I. "Socrates' Valedictory Words to His Judges." *Eranos Rudbergianus*, 44 (1946), pp. 90-104.

Contrasts the submissiveness of Socrates to the laws of the

Athenian polity (*e.g.*, as evidenced in the *Crito*) with his defiant and critical stance as a defendant (as this is made manifest in Plato's *Apology*).

1068 Duruy, Victor. "Lutte entre la religion et la philosophie au temps de Socrate." *Revue des Deux Mondes*, 1887, pp. 44-77.

Ref. 752.

1069 Edman, Irwin. "Socrates on Trial." *Atlantic Monthly*, 191 (1953), pp. 47-52.

Presents a biographical essay which deals mostly with "the turning point" in the life of Socrates, namely, his trial, which is described as a crucial moment in the history of humanity. Considers his refusal to escape and his serenity up to the moment of his death "a high moment in the history of civilization." Argues that Socrates was tried and sentenced for his way of life and for his commitment to reason. Suggests that to live the Socratic life is to follow his mission -- to follow reason wherever it leads.

1070 Erasmus, S. "Richterzahl und Stimmenverhältnisse im Sokratesprozess." *Gymnasium*, 71 (1964), pp. 40-42.

Reviews the conflicting testimonies of Plato (*Apology* 36a) and Diogenes Laertius (ii,41) concerning the number of votes cast against Socrates at the trial. Concludes that he must have been found guilty by 280 jurors (220 or 221 voting to acquit him), and sentenced to death by 360 (140 or 141 voting for him).

1071 Ferguson, A. S. "The Impiety of Socrates." *The Classical Journal*, 7 (1913), pp. 157-175.

Examines the concept of ἀσέβεια as this is relevant to the accusation against Socrates and to this trial. Notes that from the point of view of the prosecutors, especially Anytus, Socrates' divine sign must have been particularly disturbing and therefore something worthy of condemnation. Emphasizes Socrates' conviction that the 'new' accusers based their accusations on those of the old accusers (*i.e.*, Aristophanes), and notes that on that basis, Socrates' defense is justifiable, both legally and logically. Takes issue with Taylor's interpretation of Socrates' impiety in terms of Orphism and Pythagoreanism, and observes that if Socrates had been a Pythagorean or Orphic initiate, he would have surely defended *those* religious convictions before the jury. Ref. 496.

1072 Finley, M. I. "Censorship in Classical Antiquity." *The Times Literary Supplement*, 76 (1977), pp. 923-925.

Text of a lecture given at the Anglo-American Conference of Historians, London, July 6, 1977. Notes that in ancient societies the overwhelming importance of oral communication made it necessary for censorship to opt for the banishment (or for the execution) of offending persons. Uses the cases of Socrates and Carneades as illustrations. Observes that in these instances, the character of the audience affected allows us to understand the specific form of censorship which was applied to them.

1073 Fréret, N. *Observations sur les causes et sur quelques circonstances de la condemnation de Socrate.* Paris: *Mémoires de Literature de l'Académie Royal des Inscriptions et Belles Lettres*, 1723, Vol. 67, pp. 209-276.

Reprinted in M. Montuori's *De Socrate iuste damnato* (pp. 31-99). Endeavors to clarify the causes (both remote and immediate) of Socrates' trial, and to elucidate its juridical process. Observes that the Socratic trial is the sort of affair about which everybody talks a great deal, without there being a real effort to understand its actual circumstances. Concludes that the ultimate reason for the trial was Socrates' open opposition to the Athenian democracy, an opposition clearly manifested in the words and deeds of his disciples (*e.g.*, Critias, Charmides, Alcibiades, and Xenophon). Adds that a contributing factor for the trial must have been Socrates' fanatical conviction concerning the divine origin of his inspiration and mission. Ref. 398.

1074 Gebhardt, Ernst. *Polykrates' Anklage gegen Sokrates und Xenophons Erwiderung.* Doctoral dissertation. Johann Wolfgang Goethe Universität, Frankfurt, 1957.

Ref. 525.

1075 Gomperz, Heinrich. "Die Anklage gegen Sokrates in ihrer Bedeutung für die Sokratesforschung." *Neue Jahrbücher für das klassische Altertum*, 53 (1924), pp. 377-423.

Examines the content, signficance, and sources of the indictment against Socrates. Argues that Xenophon was probably better able to recognize and give an accurate account of the actual charges against Socrates than Plato, and that the latter was inclined to obscure them in his desire to create a philosophical idealization of his master.

1076 Gomperz, Heinrich. "Sokrates Haltung vor seinem Richtern." *Wiener Studien*, 54 (1936), pp. 32-42.

Reviews the evidence concerning Socrates' trial and in particular the historical value of Plato's testimony in that regard. Concludes that it is not altogether unreasonable to assume that Socrates made no formal defense at all, as is reported by Maximus of Tyre. Suggests that Plato's account of the trial is more a poetical construction than a historical report.

1077 Hart, Richard E. "Socrates on Trial." *New Essays on Socrates*. Edited by Eugene Kelly. Lanham, Md.: University Press of America, 1984, pp. 143-150.

Serves as a response to Brickhouse's and Smith's "Irony, Arrogance, and Sincerity in Plato's *Apology*." Argues that from the point of view of his accusers and jurors, Socrates did not seriously pursue his acquittal, and that his intention was not so much to defend himself against specific charges, but to vindicate philosophy at large and carry out the god's ethical directive. Agrees that it is an error to interpret Socrates' behavior in court as an instance of deliberate arrogance or sarcastic irony. Ref. 1124.

1078 Havelock, Eric A. "Why Was Socrates Tried?" *Studies in Honour of Gilbert Norwood*. Edited by Mary E. White. Toronto: University of Toronto Press, 1952, pp. 95-109.

Maintains that the chief accusation against Socrates was that he unsettled and challenged the ordinary and customary educational practices of the aristocratic Athenian class.

Argues that it was Plato's intention to conceal the main issues involved in Socrates' trial, and that he transformed Socrates' confession of ignorance into a rejection of his true educational mission.

1079 Hirzel, R. "Polykrates' Anklage und Lysias' Verteidigung des Sokrates." *Rheinisches Museum für Philologie*, 42 (1887), pp. 239ff.

Argues that Libanius and Xenophon must have relied for their apologetic writings on Lysias' *Apologia Socratis* (which is assumed to have been a direct reply to Polycrates' pamphlet against Socrates). Assigns to Plato's *Gorgias* a date prior to that of Polycrates' work, and rejects thereby the suggestion that the former was a rebuttal to the latter. Interprets Polycrates' work as a fictitious and posthumous indictment allegedly delivered by Anytus. Comments on the appearance of Anytus in the *Meno*, and on the alleged defense speech written by Lysias on behalf of Socrates.

1080 Kendall, Willmoore. "The People Versus Socrates Revisited." *Willmoore Kendall Contra Mundum*. New Rochelle, N.Y.: Arlington House, 1971, pp. 149-176.

Argues on behalf of a conservative assessment of the case of Socrates, and concludes that he was indeed guilty as charged. Disputes the attempts of 'intellectuals' to construct an image of Socrates as a champion of freedom of thought and speech.

1081 Limburg Brouwer, P. *Apologia Socratis contra Meliti redivivi calumniam*. Groningen (Holland), 1838.

Discusses the substance of Meletus' accusations against Socrates, as these are recounted by Plato. Emphasizes the gap that separated Socrates from the Sophists, and portrays him as a paradigm of moral life, in whom ideas and existence were fundamentally one. Criticizes the Hegelian interpretation of Socratic philosophy.

1082 Lofberg, J. O. "The Trial of Socrates." *The Classical Journal*, 23 (1928), pp. 601-609.

Criticizes Bury's interpretation of Socrates' trial, and maintains that he is mistaken in regarding Plato's *Apology* more as a dramatic and artistic creation than as a historical account, and as a testimony from which important components of the actual defense have been omitted. Argues against Bury's view which sees in Socrates' speech a reply only to the speech of Meletus. Ref. 1060.

1083 Marasco, G. "Il processi d'empietà nella democrazia ateniese." *Atene e Roma*, 21 (1976), pp. 113-131.

Reviews the history and nature of the Athenian law against irreligiosity. Observes that, although this law was essentially a means to preserve intact certain traditional religious beliefs and practices, it was in reality often used as a juridical mechanism for the service of personal or political purposes. Comments in particular on the trials of Anaxagoras, Phidias, Aspasia, Alcibiades, Andocides, and Socrates. Argues that in the instance of Socrates' trial, the charge of irreligiosity had undeniable hidden political roots. Notes that in the fourth century B.C. the law against irreligiosity was occasionally used as a weapon against Macedonian sympathizers.

1084 Markowski, H. "De Libanio Socratis defensore." *Breslauer Philologische Abhandlungen*, 40 (1910), pp. 1-196.

Reviews the content and purpose of Libanius' *Apologia Socratis*, and endeavors to reconstruct the specific charges of Polycrates against Socrates, as these emerge from Libanius' defense. Argues that these charges are basically nine: the undermining of democracy, the teaching of neglect towards religion, the corruption of the youth, the contempt for the most respected poets, the inducement of crime among his followers, the practice of secret vices, the endeavor to promote idleness, the tutorship of bad characters like Critias and Alcibiades, and the practice of Sophistical arts. Studies in detail the sources available to Libanius, and argues that his work was partly composed as a disguised attempt to vindicate the character and career of Emperor Julian.

1085 [Maury, Reuben.] "The Voice of the People." *The New York Daily News*, December 12, 1971, editorial page.

Editorial article (unsigned) presumably written by Maury. Speaks of Socrates' trial for corrupting the Athenian youth, and of his death by "a cup of poisonous liquid called hemlock." Notes that Socrates was in the habit of asking "embarrasing, meddlesome, impudent, or otherwise annoying questions," and suggests that ordinary "American folk" should easily understand how the Athenians felt about Socrates, and why "the old gentleman knock[ed] himself off."

1086 Meiser, K. "Zu den Deklamationen des Libanios über Sokrates." *Sitzungsberichte der Königlich Bayerischen Akademie der Wissenschaften*. Munich, 1910, pp. 1-26.

Reviews in detail the structure and content of Libanius' *Apologia Socratis*, and attempts to reconstruct on that basis Polycrates' indictment. Gives a comprehensive list of the specific accusations against Socrates, as these may have originally appeared in Polycrates' work.

1087 Menzel, A. "Untersuchungen zum Sokrates-Prozess." *Sitzungsberichte der Wiener Akademie*, No. 146 (1903), pp. 7ff.

Analyzes in detail the juridical issues relevant to Socrates' trial, in particular the historical transmission of the official indictment.

1088 Mesk, J. "Die Anklagerede des Polykrates gegen Sokrates." *Wiener Studien*, 32 (1911), pp. 56-84.

Ref. 539.

1089 Montgomery, John D. "The Unfinished Trial." *The State Versus Socrates: A Case Study in Civic Freedom*. Edited by John D. Montgomery. Boston: The Beacon Press, 1954, pp. 3-15.

Serves as the introduction to Montgomery's anthology. Maintains that the case of Socrates' trial demonstrates dramatically the inevitable contradiction between civic freedom and social order. Observes that his conviction and execution reveal the irrationalism and moral weakness of the Athenian political world. Ref. 293.

1090 Montuori, Mario. *Socrate. Dal mito alla storia*. Athens,

1967.

Endeavors to construct an interpretation of the philosophy of Socrates against the background of the causes and circumstances which brought about his indictment, trial, and execution. Attempts to counterbalance the sort of skepticism towards a possible solution of the Socratic problem which emerges from scholars like Gigon.

1091 Neumann, Harry. "Plato's *Defense of Socrates*: An Interpretation of Ancient and Modern Sophistry." *Liberal Education*, 56 (1970), pp. 458-475.

Interprets the allegation that Socrates was innocent as an example of modern sophistry, and as a manifestation of the tendency to transform philosophy into doctrine and ideology. Maintains that genuine philosophy does not hesitate to challenge and question even one's dearest convictions.

1092 Oldfather, W. A. "Socrates in Court." *The Classical Weekly*, 31 (1938), pp. 203-211.

Examines the evidence concerning Socrates' trial. Concludes that it is quite possible that Socrates did not make a formal defense before the jury. Calls attention to "the astonishing multiplicity of speeches ascribed to Socrates, or designed for Socrates, at the time of his trial, or composed in behalf of Socrates at some later date." Notes that Plato would have been amazed, had he learned that his *Apology* would often be taken to be an accurate account of Socrates' trial.

1093 Phillipson, Coleman. "The Target of Power Politics." *The State Versus Socrates: A Case Study in Civic Freedom*. Edited by John D. Montgomery. Boston: The Beacon Press, 1954, pp. 167-183.

Excerpted from Phillipson's *The Trial of Socrates*. Discusses the issue of whether the sentence passed on Socrates was justified. Concludes that while Socrates' death was a great triumph for philosophy and the Socratic spirit, it was also a 'triumph' for the politicians, for the votaries of tradition, for the enemies of innovation, and for the obscurantist segments of the population at large. Views in any attempt to justify the execution of Socrates "an arbitrary and arrogant assertion indicating moral obliquity and juridical anarchy." Ref. 1094.

1094 Phillipson, Coleman. *The Trial of Socrates.* London: Stevens & Sons, 1928.

Deals in a comprehensive way with practically all the major aspects and themes related to Socrates. Introduces the subject with a chapter on the historical and cultural context in which Socrates lived, and with a chapter on the sources of Socratic information (Plato, Xenophon, Aristophanes, Aristotle, Antisthenes, Aeschines, and Diogenes Laertius). Supports an eclectic and integrational approach to the Socratic problem, and claims that *all* the sources must be taken into account. Regards the following Platonic dialogues as most important for the reconstruction of the historical Socrates: the *Euthyphro*, the *Apology*, the *Crito*, the *Phaedo*, the *Symposium*, and the *Gorgias.* Devotes several individual chapters to the main events in Socrates' life, to his personal characteristics, to his fundamental ideas and doctrines, to the Socratic method, to the public hostility and prejudices against him, and to the meaning and impact of Aristophanes' *Clouds.* Deals with the trial and execution of Socrates in several chapters, and discusses subjects such as the immediate cause and political circumstances of the indictment, the law relating to impiety, the Athenian juridical system, the procedure before the trial, the trial itself, and the accusations, verdict, and sentence. Concludes with a chapter on Socrates' position and influence in history. Contains abundant comments and information on the legal and juridical aspects of the trial. Provides an extensive bibliography of ancient sources and modern writings on Socrates. Ref. 1093.

1095 Plumb, Robert K. "Socrates Linked to Find in Athens." *The New York Times*, December 29, 1953, p. 25.

Ref. 810.

1096 Ramello, P. "Due testimoni del processo contra Socrate. Platone e Senofonte." *Appunti di Filologia greco-latina*, 1 (1980), pp. 35-40.

Reviews the Platonic and Xenophontean testimonies concerning Socrates' trial, and concludes that while Xenophon reduces him to the level of an ordinary human being, Plato raises him to an idealized level of humanity.

1097 Raoss, M. "Ai margine del processo di Socrate." In *Seconda Miscellanea graeca e romana*. Rome: Studi pubbl. dall' Istituto Italiano per la storia antica, XX, 1968, pp. 47-291.

Examines the indictment, trial, and sentence of Socrates, against the background provided by our understanding of Isocrates' relevant testimony, the testimonies of Plato and Xenophon, Libanius' *Apologia Socratis*, and Polycrates' pamphlet.

1098 Reinach, J. "A proposito di 'Il processo di Socrate' di N. Casini." *Iura*, 9 (1958), pp. 121-122.

Comments on Casini's article, and discusses in particular Socrates' suggestion to the jury concerning the penalty which he deemed appropriate for himself. [There is a reply by Casini to Reinach's comments, in *Iura*, 10 (1959), pp. 114-117.]. Ref. 1062.

1099 Rexroth, Kenneth. "Plato: The Trial and Death of Socrates." *Classics Revisited*. New York: New Directions Publishing, 1986, pp. 48-52.

Originally published in 1969 (Avon Books). Gives a general account of the trial and death of Socrates, basing its comments on Plato's testimony (*Euthyphro*, *Apology*, *Crito*, and *Phaedo*). Regards the accusations against Socrates justified, inasmuch as he did in fact establish a new 'religion' -- a religion of civic piety based on the recognition of one's ignorance and on the constant nurturing of the soul. Sees Socrates as the founder of a special tradition of martyrdom -- "the just man just unto death."

1100 Roberts, Steven V. "Athens Ruin May Be Jail of Socrates." *The New York Times*, March 21, 1976, pp. 17.

Ref. 818.

1101 Robertson, John Charles. "The Athenians and Socrates." *Mixed Company*. Freeport, N.Y.: Books for Libraries Press, 1939, pp. 12-39.

Examines the religious, political, and social climate that made possible Socrates' trial. Maintains that, given the nature and practice of religion in Athens, the trial was not induced by real religious motivations. Argues that the trial was the result of the reaction of conservative citizens who sought to couterbalance the ideological decadence of the city, and who saw in Socrates a man who challenged its traditions and conventions in the name of individuality and critical thinking. Concludes that Socrates was indeed guilty of the charge of corrupting the youth, if by corruption we mean the teaching of rational and free inquiry.

1102 Scheid, Lucienne. "Le procès de Socrate et la justice." *Trois procès scandaleux*. Givors: A. Martel, 1955.

Discusses in Chapter 3 the process of Socrates' trial, conviction, and execution. Emphasizes its character as a travesty of justice. Deals in Chapters 1 and 2 with the trials and executions of Marie Antoinette and Jesus.

1103 "Site of Trial of Socrates Is Unearthed." *The New York Times*, June 22, 1970, p. 2.

Ref. 832.

1104 "Socrates' Death Sentence Is Appealed." *The New York Times*, April 1, 1927, p. 25.

Unsigned news report. Describes the appeal brought before the Greek Supreme Court on March 30, 1927, by M. Paradopoulos on behalf of Socrates. Notes that according to Paradopoulos' brief, the death sentence imposed on Socrates was a patent miscarriage of justice, and that, in his view, the honor of Greece requires a formal revision of the original verdict and a declaration of Socrates' complete innocence, in spite of the fact that 2325 years have passed since his sentence.

1105 Sorel, Georges. *Le procès de Socrate*. Paris: Ancienne

Librairie Germer Belière, 1889.

Regards Socrates as a great source of political and social decadence in the Greek world, and (along with the Sophists) as an influence which undermined the ancient morality of the Greeks. Supports the accusations raised by Aristophanes, as well as his ridicule of Socrates. Maintains that Socrates confused ethics, politics, law, and science, thereby leading his disciples into a condition of utter perplexity. Argues that he was unable to answer and solve the questions and problems he raised, and that his accusers were ultimately justified in viewing him as a threat to the social order. Disassociates the historical Socrates from dialogues such as the *Republic* and the *Symposium* (which are called "disgraceful"), but does not exonerate him from his guilt in having planted the seeds of Plato's philosophy. Regards Socrates' ethical doctrine as a specimen of legalistic utilitarianism.

1106 Stone, I. F. "I. F. Stone Breaks the Socrates Story." *The New York Times*, April 8, 1979, Section 6, pp. 22ff.

An interview with himself by journalist I. F. Stone. Attempts to shed new and decisive light on the trial of Socrates by appealing to primary source material allegedly ignored by historians. Regards our understanding of the trial as essential for an adequate appreciation of Socrates' position within the Athenian democracy. Maintains that both Plato and Xenophon, as avowed apologists for Socrates, deleted or minimized the political nature of the trial and the fundamental root of the indictment. Views Socrates' involvement with Critias and the Thirty, his remaining in Athens during the reign of terror, and his anti-democratic leanings, as the principal causes for the indictment, verdict, and sentence. Stresses the value of the testimony of Aeschines (the orator). Calls for a reassessment of Socrates' political views, and emphasizes his contempt for the principles and practices of democracy; notes that this contempt was shared by Plato and Xenophon. Ref. 1112.

1106a Stone, I. F. *The Trial of Socrates*. New York: Little, Brown, 1987.

Examines the background, circumstances, details, outcome, and sources of information of Socrates' trial, in an effort to resolve what it considers a most perplexing and crucial question, namely, how it was possible for a democratic and cultured society, which treasured and practiced freedom of speech, to have condemned to death a man as excellent and worthy of admiration as Socrates. Notes that "no other trial, except that of Jesus, has left so vivid an impression on the imagination of Western man as that of Socrates." Develops a portrait of Socrates as an enemy of democracy in general and of the Athenian democracy in particular. Argues that Socrates' speech in court served precisely the purpose he had in mind -- that is, to infuriate the jurors and assure his death sentence. Concludes that in theory and in practice, Socrates rejected throughout his life the very essence of the political principles on which the Athenian polity was based. Reviewed by Christopher Lehmann-Haupt (*The New York Times*, January 18, 1988, Section C, p. 20). Ref. 1106.

1107 Tate, J. "Greek for 'Atheism'." *The Classical Review*, 51 (1937), pp. 3-5.

Argues that the indictment against Socrates involved a clear charge of atheism -- not believing in the gods, and that the phrase οὐ νομίζειν θεούς does not merely mean 'not worshipping the gods', but 'not believing in the gods'.

1108 Taylor, Alfred E. "The Impiety of Socrates." *Varia Socratica. First Series*. Oxford: James Parker & Co., 1911, pp. 1-39.

Argues that the charge of impiety levelled against Socrates cannot be interpreted as one involving either atheism (either in the form of disbelief or in the form of a rejection of religious practices or rituals), or the possession of a private oracle (as exemplified in his divine sign). Rejects Xenophon's interpretation of the indictment, and charges him with both confusion and deceptiveness. Affirms that in the eyes of the prosecutors, Socrates' impiety was related to the suspicion of his being the central figure in an anti-democratic Pythagorean club which practised a 'foreign' cult. Suggests that such a suspicion is well established in undeniable facts about Socrates. Ref. 1144.

1109 Taylor, Alfred E. "The Security Risk: The Issue of Foreign

Allegiance." *The State Versus Socrates: A Case Study in Civic Freedom*. Edited by John D. Montgomery. Boston: The Beacon Press, 1954, pp. 55-61.

Excerpted from Taylor's *Varia Socratica*. Attempts to clarify the precise import of the accusations against Socrates, specifically the charge of irreligiosity. Maintains that before the actual prosecution, Socrates had not been the object of widespread popular resentment, and that Aristophanes' attack represented only the reaction of a small literary group. Concludes that the chief reason for the prosecution was the suspicion that Socrates was the central figure of an anti-democratic association, and that he was responsible for the importation of a foreign cult into Athens, namely, the Pythagorean cult. Finds Socrates guilty as charged in accordance with the existing laws. Ref. 689.

1110 Thomas, Will. *Die drei grossen Prozesse. Sokrates, Jesus, Galilei*. Krefeld: Scherpe Verlag, 1966.

Discusses in the first part the causes, circumstances, and outcome of Socrates' trial, and gives extended quotations from the Platonic *Apology*.

1111 Turlington, Bayly. "Socrates' Courtroom Ethics." *The American Bar Association Journal*, 59 (1973), pp. 505-509.

Examines the ethical implications of Socrates' defense as reported by Plato.

1112 Vlastos, Gregory. "On 'The Socrates Story'." *Political Theory*, 7 (1979), pp. 533-536.

Comments on the article by I. F. Stone in *The New York Times* (April 8, 1979). Points out that some of his statements are misleading, for instance, his allusion to the fact that Socrates did not leave Athens when the Thirty came to power. Observes that several thousand Athenians also stayed in Athens during the reign of the Thirty. Suggests that the entire Athenian jury system was on trial as Socrates was tried. Emphasizes the travesty of Socrates' ideas perpetrated by Aristophanes, and argues that Socrates' conviction was more the result of the animosity of his opponents towards the tenor and direction of his philosophical inquiries, than the consequence of personal hatred. Ref. 1106, 1301.

1113 "Who Killed Socrates?" *The New York Times*, March 17, 1940, Section 4, p. 8.

Unsigned article in the "Topics of the Times." Recalls the trial and death of Socrates in the context of Bertrand Russell's difficulties over his appointment at the City College in New York. Quotes Professor Morris R. Cohen who, in defending Russell, said: "The fair name of our city [New York] will suffer as did Athens for condemning Socrates as a corruptor of its youth." Notes that Socrates' trial was primarily a political reaction on the part of the newly re-established democracy, and observes that repression can come as easily from a democratic establishment as from reactionary and conservative regimes: "All majorities incline to lose patience with dissidents, democratic majorities or anti-democratic, capitalist majorities or proletarian."

1114 Zeller, Eduard. "The Arrogant Defendant: The Issue of Contempt of Court." *The State Versus Socrates: A Case Study in Civic Freedom*. Edited by John D. Montgomery. Boston: The Beacon Press, 1954, pp. 92-97.

Excerpted from Zeller's *Socrates and the Socratic Schools*. Reviews Socrates' language at his trial, and notes that it was his apparent incorrigible obstinacy that led many of the jurors to vote against him. Emphasizes Socrates' critical attitude towards the Athenian democracy, and his constant questioning of the laws and their moral foundation: to Socrates, "true virtue and right action are only possible when they spring from personal conviction." Observes that Athens was ignorant of that freedom of conviction which Socrates required. Ref. 360.

## STUDIES ON PLATO'S *APOLOGY*

The entries in this section focus on Plato's *Apology* and on those aspects of the trial of Socrates which are presented in the Platonic testimony.

1115 Allen, Reginald E. *Socrates and Legal Obligation*. Minneapolis: University of Minnesota Press, 1980.

Ref. 1234.

1116 Anastaplo, George. "Human Being and Citizen: A Beginning to the Study of the Apology of Socrates." *Human Being and Citizen: Essays on Virtue, Freedom, and the Common Good*. Chicago: Swallow Press, 1975, pp. 8-29.

Reviews the significance of Plato's *Apology*, specifically with respect to what it can teach about the meaningful relationship between the individual and the State. Constitutes an introductory study to the dialogue.

1117 Armleder, P. J. "Death in Plato's *Apologia*." *The Classical Bulletin*, 42 (1966), p. 46.

Argues that Socrates' statement that death is either an endless sleep or a change from this world to another should not be taken in a literal sense.

1118 Bassett, Samuel E. "Note on αἰνίττομαι, Plato *Apology* 27a, 21b." *The Classical Review*, 42 (1928), p. 58.

Comments on the riddle to which Socrates compares the wording of Meletus' accusations. Observes that the Platonic account of Socrates' trial appears to be "shot through and through with a light and gentle humour."

1119 Bonafante, L. and Raditsa, L. "Socrates' Defense and His Audience." *Bulletin of the American Society of Papyrologists*, 15 (1978), pp. 17-23.

Argues that in his defense Socrates made it clear that his trial was related to the restoration of the democracy. Notes that his unwillingness to side with any given political party or faction could have been construed by his enemies as political opportunism or as an attitude of contempt towards the state.

1120 Bonner, R. J. "The Legal Setting of Plato's *Apology*." *Classical Philology*, 3 (1908), pp. 177ff.

Examines the content and structure of Plato's *Apology* against the background of our knowledge of Athenian juridical and forensic practices.

1121 Bostock, David. *Plato's Phaedo.* Oxford: The Clarendon Press, 1986.

Ref. 1177.

1122 Brann, Eva. "The Offense of Socrates: A Re-reading of Plato's *Apology*." *Interpretation*, 7 (1978), pp. 1-21.

Interprets the *Apology* as an embodiment of Plato's recognition of the political dangers of philosophy. Argues that Socrates did not offer the jury an effective defense against the indictment, and that in fact his speech was deliberately offensive to civic sensibility. Emphasizes the recalcitrant attitude of Socrates vis-à-vis the jury. Recognizes Socrates' guilt within the context of the Athenian political institutions.

1123 Brickhouse, Thomas C. and Smith, Nicholas D. "The Formal Charges Against Socrates." *The Journal of the History of Philosophy*, 23 (1985), pp. 457-482.

Examines the early and later charges described in the *Apology*, focusing on Socrates' examination of Meletus, and argues that Socrates' interrogation of Meletus should not be construed merely as an attempt to show Meletus' ignorance, but as an endeavor to convince the jury of the worthlessness of the accusations. Concludes that Socrates' consummate philosophical skill demonstrates that his fanatical enemy cannot coherently believe that Socrates is guilty of the charges.

1124 Brickhouse, Thomas C. and Smith, Nicholas D. "Irony, Arrogance, and Sincerity in Plato's *Apology*." *New Essays on Socrates*. Edited by Eugene Kelly. Lanham, Md.: University Press of America, 1984, pp. 29-41.

Argues that the passages often quoted to exemplify Socrates' irony are misunderstood, since in them there is ample evidence of earnest moral conviction or commitment. Maintains that Socrates would have never used irony in a way which could have put in jeopardy the judicial process under which he was tried, for this would have violated a number of his most cherished moral principles. Ref. 1077.

1125 Brickhouse, Thomas C. and Smith, Nicholas D. "The Paradox of Socratic Ignorance in Plato's *Apology*." *The Journal of the History of Philosophy* 1, (1984), pp. 125-132.

Examines the apparent paradox entailed by Socrates' confession of ignorance and his absolute confidence in the value of his mission. Argues that his confidence is based on various spiritual 'signs', such as dreams, and that such confidence is ultimately consistent with his confession of ignorance. Finds a relationship between Socrates' confidence in his mission and his moral conviction that knowledge inexorably leads to virtue.

1126 Brickhouse, Thomas C. and Smith, Nicholas D. "Socrates' Proposed Penalty in Plato's *Apology*." *Archiv für Geschichte der Philosophie*, 64 (1982), pp. 1-22.

Argues that the penalty suggested by Socrates in the *Apology* is a sizable amount of money, and is in accord with his ethical sensitivity. Maintains that the testimony of Plato concerning the change in the number of jurors who rejected Socrates' offer and voted for his execution is probably not historically valid.

1127 Clay, Diskin. "Socrates' Mulishness and Heroism." *Phronesis*, 17 (1972), pp. 53-60.

Attempts to clarify, in a witty style, some of the apparent peculiarities found in Socrates' defense (Plato's *Apology*). Comments on Socrates' references to his divine sign and on his posture as a hero.

1128 Coulter, C. C. "The Tragic Structure of Plato's *Apology*." *The Philological Quarterly*, 1933, pp. 137-143.

Sees in Plato's *Apology*, not simply an account of Socrates' trial, but a masterful work of tragic art which reflects clearly the Aristotelian theory of art.

1129 Coulter, James A. "The Relation of the *Apology of Socrates* to Gorgias' *Defense of Palamedes* and Plato's Critique of Gorgianic Rhetoric." *Harvard Studies in Classical Philology*, 68 (1964), pp. 269-303.

Attempts to demonstrate that Plato's *Apology* is an example of the rhetorical counter-position to Gorgias' *Defense of Palamedes*. Shows that Plato's *Apology* is an intricate and extensive reworking of the actual trial.

1130 Daniel, J. and Polansky, Ronald M. "The Tale of the Delphic Oracle in Plato's *Apology*." *Ancient World*, 2 (1979), pp. 83-85.

Argues that the story of the Delphic pronouncement introduced by Plato in the *Apology* is specifically designed to vindicate the value of philosophy, and is not intended to serve the purpose of defending Socrates against the accusations.

1131 Delatte, Armand. "La figure de Socrate dans *l'Apologie* de Platon." *Bulletin des Lettres de l'Académie Belgique*, 36 (1950), pp. 213-226.

Examines the origin and meaning of Socrates' vocation as this is described in the *Apology*, and suggests the possibility of finding an earlier model for his vocation among the Pythagoreans. Emphasizes his conviction concerning the divine origin of his philosophical mission.

1132 Dihle, A. "Die Bedeutung der Gestalt des Sokrates für die Entstehung der Biographie." *Studien zur griechischen Biographie*. Göttingen, 1956, pp. 13-34.

Studies the biographical sketch of Socrates developed in Plato's *Apology*, and comments on its significance and value against the background of older forms of biographical writing. Compares the Platonic sketch with that developed by Xenophon.

1133 Dresig, Siegmund F. *De Socrate iuste damnato.* Leipzig: Langenheim, 1738.

Ref. 1066.

1134 Drexler, H. "Gedanken über den Sokrates der platonischen *Apologie*." *Emerita*, 29 (1961), pp. 177-201.

Studies the various conceptions of Socrates' personality, philosophical mission, ethical concepts, and trial, to which Plato's *Apology* has given rise, both among ancient interpreters and among modern ones.

1135 Feaver, Douglas and Hare, John. "The *Apology* as an Inverted Parody of Rhetoric." *Arethusa*, 14 (1981), pp. 205-216.

Regards the *Apology* as a paradigm example of forensic rhetorical irony, and insists that irony ultimately constitutes the permeating theme of all of Socrates' statements to the jury. Argues that "every section of Socrates' main speech is in fact a parody." Presents an examination of the 'idioms of rhetoric' used by Socrates in the *Apology*. Compares the *Apology* with the *Palamedes* of Gorgias in order to support the claim that the Platonic Socrates endeavors to imitate the orators.

1136 Ferguson, John. "An Athenian Remainder Sale." *The Journal of Classical Philology*, 65 (1970), p. 173.

Suggests that in *Apology* 26a, Plato is referring to a secondhand book store located near the agora.

1137 Fox, Marvin. "The Trials of Socrates: An Interpretation of the First Tetralogy." *Archiv für Philosophie*, 6 (1956), pp. 226-261.

Ref. 1365.

1138 Fraine, J. de. "Rhetorische gemeenplaatsen in de voorrede van de *Apologia Socrates.*" *Philologische Studien*, 1942, pp. 87-94.

Collects and examines examples of rhetorical *exordia* found in various Attic orators, and shows how they reappear in Plato's *Apology*, particularly in its introductory sections.

1139 Fréret, N. *Observations sur les causes et sur quelques circonstances de la condamnation de Socrate.* Paris: *Mémoires de Literature de l'Académie Royal des Inscriptions et Belles Lettres*, 1723, Vol. 67, pp. 209-76.

Ref. 1073.

1140 Galli, Gallo. "L'Apologia di Socrate." *Paideia*, 1947, pp. 273-292.

Concludes that even though the *Apology* contains the specific rhetorical and artistic import and form given to it by Plato, its substance is a faithful reflection of the Socratic spirit.

1141 Geissler, A. "Der Strafantrag in der platonischen *Apologie.*" *Blätter für das Gymnasial Schulwesen*, 42 (1906), pp. 381-391.

Claims that many elements found in the *Apology* are inventions on Plato's part, as is the case with the 'counter-penalty' proposed by Socrates.

1142 Gontar, David P. "The Problem of the Formal Charges in Plato's *Apology.*" *Tulane Studies in Philosophy*, 27 (1978), pp. 89-101.

Regards the *Apology* as an unsuccessful reply to Aristophanes' *Clouds*, and examines Socrates' arguments in his trial. Concludes that the representation of Socrates as a Sophist is perhaps not as farfetched or inaccurate as has been maintained by those who insist on 'canonizing' the Platonic Socrates. Argues that Socrates' rhetoric before the jury fails to rebut the charges against him, and shows his devious methods.

1143 Hackforth, Reginald. *The Composition of Plato's Apology.*

London: Cambridge University Press, 1933.

Presents a comprehensive study of the composition, structure, and contents of Plato's *Apology*. Compares and analyzes the relationship between Xenophon's *Apology* and Plato's work, and endeavors to clarify the motive (or motives) behind the writing of the latter. Examines separately the three major parts or speeches of Socrates' defense, and concludes with a statement which seeks to give us a 'total picture' of him. Endeavors to shed light on the relationship between Plato's *Apology* and the actual speech made by Socrates at his trial. Accepts as historically factual many of the details reported by Plato (*e.g.*, his own presence at the trial), but supports the view that the principal aim of the *Apology* is not to give us a journalistic account, but a composite philosophical representation of Socrates. Assigns the year 394 B. C. as a *terminus post quem* for the writing of the *Apology*. Denies any political implications of Socrates' trial. Maintains that Xenophon's *Apology* is independent of Plato's. Ref. 1168.

1144 Hathaway, Ronald F. "Law and the Moral Paradox in Plato's *Apology*." *The Journal of the History of Philosophy*, 8 (1970), pp. 127-142.

Discusses the apparently paradoxical position assumed by Socrates during his trial, and comments in detail on his cross-examination of Meletus. Notes that the Socratic interrogation of Meletus constitutes an effort to demonstrate the thesis that no person chooses evil knowingly.

1145 Hoerber, Robert G. "A Note on Plato, *Apology* XLII." *The Classical Bulletin*, 42 (1966), p. 92.

Maintains that the views expressed by Socrates about death (*Apology* 42) are not in contradiction with one another.

1146 Keaney, J. J. "Plato, *Apology* 32c8-d3." *The Classical Quarterly*, 30 (1980), pp. 296-298.

Attempts to demonstrate that Meletus, Socrates' accuser, is the same Meletus who brought charges against Andocides.

1147 Keseling, P. "Sophocles' *Antigone* in Platons *Apologie des Sokrates*." *Philologische Wochenschrift*, 1936, pp. 141-143.

Comments on the relationship and similarity between the concepts of death entertained by Antigone and by Socrates (*Apology* 40d-e). Detects the same similarity between Socrates' last words to the Athenians (*Apology* 42a) and Antigone's words at 559ff.

1148 Laguna, Théodore. de. "Interpretations of the *Apology*." *Philosophical Review*, 18 (1909), pp. 23-27.

Examines the accusations against Socrates, and notes in particular that his argument to defend himself from the charge of having led astray Critias, Charmides, and Alcibiades, while not rigidly conclusive, remains a strong *a priori* argument which is amply supplemented by *a posteriori* evidence.

1149 Limburg Brower, P. *Apologia Socratis contra Meliti redivivi calumniam*. Groningen, Holland, 1838.

Ref. 1081.

1150 Maas, Paul. "How Socrates Addressed the Jury." *The Classical Review*, 53 (1939), pp. 58-59.

Presents a brief notice on the specific words used by Socrates in the *Apology* in order to address the jurors. Observes that when speaking to the entire jury, Socrates refuses to give the jurors the honorable title of 'judges', and simply calls them 'men of Athens'.

1151 Masaracchia, A. "Senso e problemi dell' *Apologia* platonica." *Helikon*, 4 (1964), pp. 111-152.

Maintains that the main theme of the *Apology* is the conflict between the individual and the State, and the urgency of reforming the political context through the moral regeneration of the individual. Regards the *Apology* as a philosophical document, not as a historical or biographical statement about Socrates.

1152 Mulgan, R. G. "Socrates and Authority." *Greece and Rome*, 19 (1972), pp. 208-212.

Ref. 1275.

1153 Nadler, Steven. "Probability and Truth in the *Apology*." *Philosophy and Rhetoric*, 9 (1985), pp. 198-202.

Replies to K. Seeskin. Argues that Socrates' defense is even more of a parody than Seeskin would allow. Maintains that Socrates uses rhetoric in order to convince his jurors, and that his rhetoric is one based on probabilities. Ref. 1164.

1154 Nussbaum, G. "Some Problems in Plato's *Apology*." *Orpheus*, 8 (1961), pp. 53-64.

Notes that the basic principles of Socrates' philosophy, which Plato unfolds in his *Apology*, are the same ones which are attributed to Socrates in the other Socratic dialogues.

1155 Overman, Caroline A. *Plato's Apology: A Literary Approach*. Doctoral dissertation. Brown University, 1976.

Subjects the *Apology* to a critical analysis in which this work is treated as a self-contained entity, and in which several distinct but interrelated themes are explored. These themes include Socrates' "accustomed way of speaking," "the philosopher as hero," and "the philosopher as dialectician." Stresses the value of the literary approach to the *Apology*. Includes an annotated bibliography.

1156 Piérart, M. "Le second discours de Socrate à ses juges. Platon, *Apologie*." *Les Etudes Classiques*, 40 (1972), pp. 288-293.

Suggests that Socrates' speech to his judges is an expression of his philosophic ideal rather than a statement of well-defined arguments.

1157 Plass, P. "Socrates' Method of Hypothesis in the *Phaedo*." *Phronesis*, 5 (1960), pp. 103-115.

Examines the method employed by Socrates in *Phaedo* 100a-101f, and notes that the main difficulty to which his approach gives rise stems from the tension between the attempt at a rigorous systematization on Plato's part, and Socrates' apparent negligence in applying it.

1158 Pucci, P. "*Sofia* nell' *Apologia* platonica." *Maia*, 13 (1961), pp. 317-329.

Comments on the meaning of 'human wisdom' which is identified by Socrates in the *Apology* with false wisdom, and which is related to the wisdom of the Sophists. Adds that the conviction that God alone is truly wise is a Platonic idea more than a Socratic belief.

1159 Re, M. C. de. "Il processo di Socrate e la sua problematica nella critica moderna." *Atene e Rome*, 6 (1961), pp. 83-94.

Discusses the apparent paradox created by the passages of the *Apology* in which Socrates suggests as a penalty to be maintained at the Prytaneum, and his offer to pay a fine of thirty minae.

1160 Redfield, James. "A Lecture on Plato's *Apology*." *The Journal of General Education*, 15 (1963), pp. 93-108.

Gives a general presentation of the contents and structure of the *Apology*.

1161 Roochnik, David L. "*Apology* 40c4-41e7: Is Death Really a Gain?" *The Classical Journal*, 80 (1985), pp. 212-220.

Contends that Socrates' argument to the 220 ordinary citizens who voted for his acquittal was deliberately fallacious, presented by Socrates in order to give hope and comfort to these supporters of free speech. Notes, however, that Socrates' speech provides stimulation of thought for the attentive reader. Considers the possibility that this represents a Socratic myth.

1162 Rudberg, G. "Sokrates' Reden." *Symbolae Osloenses*, 24 (1945), pp. 8-15.

Reviews the structure and content of Plato's *Apology*, and attempts to identify in it those aspects and components that may be viewed as distinctively Socratic.

1163 Schmid, W. Thomas. "Socratic Moderation and Self-Knowledge." *The Journal of the History of Philosophy*, 21 (1983), pp. 339-348.

Ref. 999.

1164 Seeskin, Kenneth. "Is the 'Apology of Socrates' a Parody?" *Philosophy and Literature*, 6 (1982), pp. 94-105.

Views Plato's *Apology* as a well constructed parody of rhetorical commonplaces and accustomed phrases, and interprets it in the light of a particular speech attributed to Gorgias (by reference to which Plato constructed his work). Claims that the *Apology* allows us to gain a better understanding of Plato's attack on rhetoric in the *Gorgias*. Ref. 1153.

1165 Shero, L. R. "*Apology* 26d-e and the Writings of Anaxagoras." *The Classical Weekly*, 35 (1941-1942), pp. 219-220.

Ref. 830.

1166 Shero, L. R. "Plato's *Apology* and Xenophon's *Apology*." *The Classical Weekly*, 20 (1926), pp. 107-111.

Compares the two works, and concludes that Xenophon's is more historical than Plato's, but that the Platonic account, while more idealized and rhetorical, corresponds more adequately to the philosophical portrait of Socrates.

1167 Shorey, Paul. "Plato *Apology* 27E." *Selected Papers*. New York: Garland Publishing Company, 1980, pp. 452-454.

Originally published in *Classical Philology*, 23 (1928), pp. 68-70. Examines the phrase which centers on the Socratic interpretation that the individual who believes in gods also believes in demons. Emphasizes that contrary to many interpretations and translations (*e.g.*, Burnet), it cannot mean that the same person who believes in both believes in neither. Presents examples of several erroneous translations which highlight the grammatical oversights and ommissions which lead to this conclusion.

1168 Stocks, J. L. "Review of *The Composition of Plato's Apology* by R. Hackforth." *Philosophy*, 8 (1933), pp. 372-373.

Considers this work a middle ground between the extremes of total acceptance and total rejection in regard to whether the *Apology* represents or does not represent the actual speech at his trial. Ref. 1143.

1169 Strycker, Emile de. "Socrate et l'au-delà d'après l'*Apologie* platonicienne." *Les Etudes Classiques*, 18 (1950), pp. 269-284.

Defends the view that the Platonic *Apology* does not reveal so much the substance of Socrates' view of immortality, as the value and significance of the problem of immortality in general, and the traditional beliefs concerning immortality in particular. Argues that Socrates' apparent agnosticism is explainable as the result of his desire to convince his jurors that even if death were final, it would not be something evil for him.

1170 Tejera, V. "Plato's Tragic Humor. The *Apology* and the *Phaedo*." *Plato's Dialogues One by One: A Structural Interpretation*. New York: Irvington Publishers, 1984, pp. 9-30.

Ref. 1529.

1171 Winspear, Alban D. and Silverberg, Thomas. "The Enemy of the Poor: The Issue of Class Conflict." *The State vs. Socrates: A Case Study in Civic Freedom*. Edited by John D. Montgomery. Boston: The Beacon Press, 1954, pp. 80-91.

Extracted from *Who Was Socrates?* (pp. 76-85). Examines the *Apology*, and concludes that the real accusation against Socrates was related to his ideological views and activities, and that these were all directed towards the enhancement of the oligarchical party in Athens which oppressed and despised the working class. Ref. 356.

1172 Wolff, Erwin. *Platons Apologie*. Berlin, 1929.

Examines the text of Plato's *Apology*, and comments on the issue of the historicity of the reported speech of Socrates. Rejects the historical character of Plato's *Apology*. Establishes a parallelism between the ἀπορία into which the Delphic oracle plunged Socrates and the ἀπορία into which he himself plunged his interlocutors. Stresses the idea of the philosophical life which emerges from the *Apology*.

1173 Woodruff, Paul. "Review of *Socrates and Legal Obligation* by R. E. Allen." *The Journal of the History of Philosophy*, 21 (1983), pp. 93-94.

Ref. 1234, 1302.

## THE *PHAEDO*, DEATH, AND IMMORTALITY

This section includes annotations of works which discuss the themes of death, suicide, and immortality, as they appear in the context of Plato's *Phaedo*.

1174 Anderson, Albert. "Was Socrates Unwise to take the Hemlock?" *Harvard Theological Review*, 65 (1972), pp. 437-452.

Argues that Socrates drank the hemlock either because he believed that the sentence was indeed justified, or because he believed in the existence of a moral order in another world, not for the reasons presented in either the *Apology* or the *Crito*.

1175 Anton, John P. "The Ultimate Theme of the *Phaedo*." *Arethusa*, 1 (1968), pp. 94-102.

Argues that the ultimate thesis of the *Phaedo* is neither a discussion on the immortality of the soul nor an examination of the Ideal Theory of Forms, but "an existential demonstration of the attainability of the Platonic ideal of the good life."

1176 Battin, Margaret Pabst. *Ethical Issues in Suicide*. Englewood Cliffs, N.J.: Prentice-Hall, 1982.

Presents a comprehensive examination of various issues related to the ethical aspects of suicide. Discusses current views on suicide, and the traditional arguments for and against the morality of suicide. Mentions Socrates in a variety of places (pp. 34, 64-65, 84, 95, 103, 148, 178, 184, 188-189). Comments on the Socratic-Platonic idea of death as a release from the physical prison of the body -- an idea based on Pythagorean and Orphic teachings. Discusses the solution given in the *Phaedo* to the problem of suicide: "If one's goal [release] can be attained only in death, the question arises -- and it is an acute one for Socrates -- Why not hasten that death by suicide?" (p. 65).

1177 Bostock, David. *Plato's Phaedo*. Translated by D. Gallop. Oxford: The Clarendon Press, 1986.

Concentrates on the philosophical value of the *Phaedo* rather than on its literary and dramatic merits. Examines the arguments of the text in detail. Discusses the difference between the Socratic attitudes towards the immortality of the soul in the *Apology* and in the *Phaedo*.

1178 Brémond, André. "Un argument de Socrate contre la thèse de l'âme-harmonie." *Archives de Philosophie*, 9 (1932), pp. 63-74.

Comments on Burnet's appeal to the testimony of Olympiodorus in his explication of *Phaedo* 93b, and notes that such testimony supports another, more ordinary interpretation of the passage. Ref. 117.

1179 Campbell, M. "The Meaning of Immortality in the *Phaedo*." *Kinesis: A Graduate Journal of Philosophy*, 1 (1968), pp. 29-36.

Discusses the concept of immortality as it is presented in the *Phaedo*, and concludes that it describes the soul as imperishable, with an existence before birth and after death, and with a personal destiny exemplified by a purifying way of life.

1180 Capuder, A. "Note complémentaire au dernier mot de Socrate." *Ziva Antika*, 19 (1969), pp. 21-23.

Examines the passage of the *Phaedo* (118a) in which Plato describes the effect of the poison from the initial feelings in Socrates' legs to the final outcome.

1181 Carafides, J. L. "The Last Words of Socrates." *Platon*, 23 (1971), pp. 229-232.

Interprets the last words of Socrates as an expression of Pythagorean traditions, emphasizing the immortality and purification of the soul. Suggests that the cock is offered to Asclepius to show Socrates' belief that he was being healed from the sickness of life.

1182 Carbonara, Naddei M. "Il ricordo di Anassagora nel Fedone platonico." *Sophia*, 40 (1972), pp. 82-87.

Argues that the critique of Anaxagoras presented in the *Phaedo* is not a Socratic critique but one that belongs to the mature Plato.

1183 Castañeda, H. N. "Plato's *Phaedo* Theory of Relations." *The Journal of Philosophy*, 68 (1971), pp. 617-618.

Examines *Phaedo* 102b7-c4, and argues that no distinction is made between qualities and relations, relational propositions being reducible to qualitative facts.

1184 Cobb, William S. "Plato's Treatment of Immortality in the *Phaedo*." *The Southern Journal of Philosophy*, 15 (1977), pp. 173-188.

Suggests that the arguments for the immortality of the soul advanced in the *Phaedo* do not constitute a sound philosophical doctrine but a 'magic charm' whose purpose is to dispel the natural fear of death. Maintains that the structure of the final argument demonstrates the fallacy of begging the question, and that Plato himself was aware of this fallacy. Sees in Socrates' ultimate trial an element dramatically used by Plato.

1185 Cohen, Maurice. "Dying as Supreme Opportunity: A Comparison of Plato's *Phaedo* and *The Tibetan Book of the Dead*." *Philosophy East and West*, 26 (1976), pp. 317-327.

Compares these two theories of dying, each of which views dying as the culmination of life: something to be prepared for thoughtfully and rigorously. Suggests that the Socrates of the *Phaedo* acts as a moral and spiritual guide, that is, as a guru.

1186 Cressell, M. J. "Plato's Theory of Causality: *Phaedo* 95-106." *Australian Journal of Philosophy*, 49 (1971), pp. 244-249.

Examines this section where Socrates expresses dissatisfaction with several causal explanations and then provides a theory of causality which introduces the Forms. Concludes that the theory of causality presented in the

*Phaedo* does involve teleology.

1187 Cumont, Franz. "A propos des dernières paroles de Socrate." *Institut de France. Académie des Inscriptions et Belles-Lettres*, 1943, pp. 112-126.

Discusses two comments attributed by Plato to Socrates in the *Phaedo*: (1) that it is better for a person to die in silence, and (2) that the cock he owes to Aesklepius must be paid. Discovers in the first comment traces of Pythagorean beliefs and practices, but maintains that no definitive assertion can be made concerning the import of the second comment.

1188 Diaz Delgado, Ramón. *La muerte de Sócrates.* Barcelona: R. Dalman, 1960.

Studies Socrates' stance vis-à-vis the problem of death in general, and in particular his attitude towards his own death. Reviews the Platonic account of Socrates' last moments.

1189 Dorter, Kenneth. "Socrates on Life, Death and Suicide." *Laval Théologique et Philosophique*, 32 (1976), pp. 23-41.

Reviews in detail *Phaedo* 62a-69e. Argues that the paradox of death and suicide advanced in 62a is dialectically expressed and is ultimately resolved by an appeal to the concept of virtue. Examines also certain other exegetical issues related to the passage of the *Phaedo* under analysis.

1190 Duff, R. A. "Socrates Suicide?" *Proceedings of the Aristotelian Society*, 83 (1982-1983), pp. 35-48.

Compares and contrasts Socrates with persons who commit suicide in order to avoid execution, or who participate in their own executions. Examines Socrates' behavior, and shows the relationship between the definition of suicide and various conceptions of its ethical character. Argues that the concept of suicide does not necessarily apply to all those cases in which the agent has sought his own death.

1191 Eckstein, Jerome. *The Deathday of Socrates: Living, Dying and Immortality - The Theater of Ideas in Plato's Phaedo.* Frenchtown, N.J.: Columbia Publishing Co., 1981.

Analyzes the dialogue from a literary rather than from a philosophical perspective, and concludes that what have been hitherto considered literary devices, merely chit-chat, (*e.g.*, the recurring dream, and Phaedo's reference to Plato's absence at Socrates' death), suggest an uncertainty associated with Socrates' decision to die. The Socratic argument against suicide is viewed not as a *fait accompli*, but as the perfect culmination of the dialogue's beginning. Contains the complete translation of the *Phaedo*.

1192 Ehnmark, E. "Socrates and the Immortality of the Soul." *Eranos Rudbergianus*, 44 (1946), pp. 105-122.

Maintains that we can attribute to Socrates a belief in the immortality of the soul, and that in this respect there is no gap that separates Socrates from Plato. Ref. 619, 929.

1193 Ferguson, John. "Plato and *Phaedo*." *Museum Africum. West African Journal of Classical and Related Studies*, 1 (1972), pp. 9-17.

Argues that the *Phaedo* has the most developed dramatic structure of all the dialogues. Suggests that it was Plato's journey to Magna Graecia in 387 B.C., where he met Pythagorean communities, which helped Plato to develop the theme of immortality of the soul.

1194 Frede, Dorothea. "The Final Proof of the Immortality of the Soul in Plato's *Phaedo* 102a-107a." *Phronesis*, 23 (1978), pp. 27-41.

Examines the atypical final argument for the immortality of the soul, whereby Socrates confidently asserts the imperishability of the soul. Argues that Plato leaves the nature of the soul undefined, thus violating a Socratic 'rule' not to state that something possesses a particular quality if one has not grasped the nature of the thing itself. Suggests a Kantian formulation: this knowledge itself transcends experience.

1195 Frey, R. G. "Did Socrates Commit Suicide?" Reprinted in *Suicide: The Philosophical Issues*. Edited by M. Pabst Battin and David J. Mayo. New York: St. Martin's Press, 1980, pp. 35-38.

Adapted from Frey's article in *Philosophy*, 53 (1978), pp. 106-108. Maintains that in drinking the hemlock at the order of the government, Socrates did in fact commit suicide. Bases its conclusion on an analysis of what it is to commit suicide: suicide is killing oneself intentionally. Examines and rejects various interpretations that see in Socrates' action an involuntary self-killing, for instance, that Socrates did not want to die, that he was forced to drink the poison, that he was under duress, and that he drank it in order to comply with the law.

1196 Gavin, William. "Death: Acceptance or Denial: The Case of Socrates Re-examined." *Religious Humanism*, 11 (1977), pp. 134-139.

Argues that Socrates' stance towards death does not entail an attitude of acceptance or resignation. Insists that his stance is one of irony which implies defiance in the presence of an ambiguous situation. Views the portrayal of Socrates as a prescriptive idealization, not as a representational description.

1197 Gill, Christopher. "The Death of Socrates." *The Classical Quarterly*, 23 (1973), pp. 25-29.

Examines the discrepancy between Plato's description of Socrates' death by hemlock poisoning and modern medical accounts of such a process. Concludes that Plato selects and embellishes those aspects which he wishes to emphasize, and that he does not provide a literal description of what occurred. Suggests that Plato may have done the same in other parts of other dialogues.

1198 Gulley, Norman. "Review of *Platonic Love* by Thomas Gould." *The Classical Review*, 14 (1964), pp. 262-264.

Ref. 1390.

1199 Hicken, W. F. "*Phaedo* 93A11-94B3." *The Classical Quarterly*,

48 (1954), pp. 16-22.

Discusses Socrates' refutation of Simmias' argument according to which the soul is conceived as a sort of harmony.

1200 Kerényi, K. "Unsterblichkeit und Apollonreligion. Zum Verständnis von Platons *Phaidon*." *Antike*, 10 (1934), pp. 46-58.

Argues that there is in the *Phaedo* an unbreakable bond between the belief in the immortality of the soul and the cult of Apollo, and that Socrates' insistence in the necessity to purify one's soul is linked to an Apollonian notion.

1201 Lamartine, Alphonse de. *Homère et Socrate*. Paris: Michel Levy Frères, 1863.

Deals in the second part (pp. 119-213) with Socrates, primarily with his death. Recounts the details of Socrates' trial and execution. Reprints (pp. 172-207) the author's poem "La mort de Socrate." Concludes with an appraisal of Socrates as the most spiritual and the most honest among the Athenians, but as someone in whom charity or neighborly love had not been born as yet.

1202 Lange, S. "Emotion in Plato's *Phaedo*." *The Classical Journal*, 33 (1938), pp. 296-298.

Comments on the attitude of Socrates towards death, as he speaks in the *Phaedo*. Notes that this attitude is dominated by a peaceful emotion which resembles the mood associated with great mystics such as Saint Paul, Plotinus, and others.

1203 Leitz, A. "Gerechtigkeit und Gesetz bei Plato und Xenophon." *Der altsprachliche Unterricht*, 12 (1969), pp. 104-121.

Examines the attitude of Socrates towards the laws in the testimonies of Plato and Xenophon. Concludes that the Socratic position as outlined by Xenophon (specifically with respect to Socrates' condemnation) is severe and uncompromising, and is in accord with Antisthenes' attitude. Adds that in Plato's report we witness an effort on Socrates' part to discover a divine foundation for human laws.

1204 Loraux, N. "Donc Socrate est immortel." *Le Temps de la Réflexion*, 3 (1983), pp. 19-116.

Develops a general interpretation of the *Phaedo*, in which emphasis is made on the way in which Plato made use of Socrates and his death in order to construct an idealization of the philosopher. Notes that this idealization necessitates the separation of the soul from its physical abode, and that the idea of immortality which it entails is removed from the concept of civic immortality which was common in ancient times.

1205 Loriaux, R. "L'introduction du Phédon." *Les Etudes Classiques*, 34 (1966), pp. 209-230.

Contains a translation of and a commentary on the *Phaedo*. Attempts to show that all the themes developed in the dialogue reveal Socrates as a man whose entire life and thought are in perfect harmony through the agency of reason. Speaks of Socrates as a paradigmatic example of the true philosopher.

1206 Lukic, Miodrag. "Socrates and Indifference Towards Death." *The Southern Journal of Philosophy*, 9 (1971), pp. 393-398.

Suggests that Socrates endeavored to find a compromise position between the moral absoluteness of one who believes in eternal life on the one hand, and, on the other, the full participation in this world. Argues that Socrates failed in this endeavor.

1207 Mendelson, Alan. "Plato's *Phaedo* and the Frailty of Human Nature." *Dionysius*, 5 (1981), pp. 29-39.

Maintains that in the *Phaedo* there is a progression from rational argument and myth to action. Discusses the portrayal of Socrates as a believer in immortality, and explains the difficulties which skeptics like Simmias encounter in accepting views such as those of Socrates. Views Socrates' death as an event which finally demonstrated his belief in immortality.

1208 Mitsche, Charles. "La mort de Socrate." *Etudes*, 145 (1915), pp. 236-244.

Accepts the general veracity of Plato's account of Socrates' death in the *Phaedo*. Contains lengthy quotations from Alcibiades' speech in the *Symposium*, and reviews Socrates' attitude towards death. Concludes that from our knowledge of such an attitude, we can be certain that if Socrates were alive today, his sympathies would not be on the side of materialism or positivism, but on the side of a definitely religious orientation towards life and death.

1209 Morris, Michael. "Socrates' Last Argument." *Phronesis*, 30 (1985), pp. 223-248.

Examines the concluding Socratic argument in the *Phaedo* for the immortality of the soul, and concludes that although it is basically valid, it remains unsound. Argues that its major point does not involve a distinction of universals from particulars, and maintains that what Socrates really attempts to do is to clarify a semantical issue concerning the truth of certain seemingly uncomplicated propositions.

1210 Mueller, Gustav E. "The Unity of the *Phaidon*." *The Classical Journal*, 48 (1952-1953), pp. 129-139.

Reviews parts of the *Phaedo*, and reaches the conclusion that the dialogue is structured by reference to a strict principle of unity, as in a musical composition.

1211 O'Brien, D. "A Metaphor in Plato: 'Running Away' and 'Staying Behind' in the *Phaedo* and the *Timaeus*." *The Classical Quarterly*, 27 (1977), pp. 297-299.

Examines the metaphor of withdrawal from the last argument for the immortality of the soul in the *Phaedo*, and suggests that there is a paradox in that for Plato something stays as it is by 'running away', *e.g.*, fire continues to be fire by running away, escaping the cold. Examines similar metaphors in the *Timaeus*.

1212 O'Brien, D. "The Last Argument of Plato's *Phaedo*. I." *The Classical Quarterly*, 17 (1967), pp. 198-231.

Offers a new analysis of the last argument of the *Phaedo* for the immortality of the soul, with the purpose of discovering how Plato thought that he had arrived at the conclusion, rather than by evaluating its validity.

1213 O'Brien, D. "The Last Argument of Plato's *Phaedo*. II." *The Classical Quarterly*, 18 (1968), pp. 95-106.

Considers the arguments which make the soul imperishable, and suggests that the analysis of opposites presented by Plato hints that the soul resembles a being which exists necessarily and exists by itself, *e.g.*, the God of Anselm and Descartes. Argues that this is not what Plato intended, but that the last argument for the indestructibility of souls differs from the arguments for the indestructibility of the Forms.

1214 Peterman, John E. "The Socratic Suicide." *New Essays on Socrates*. Edited by Eugene Kelly. New York: University Press of America, pp. 3-15.

Attemps to examine the problem of Socrates' 'suicide' as this is recounted in Plato's *Phaedo*. Argues that it is essential to distinguish between the historical Socrates and the Platonic Socrates: the former did not choose death as a way to reinforce his philosophical contributions, and his death was not a privileged or special moment in his life, but a continuation of his activities. The Platonic Socrates, on the other hand, chooses death, but this choice must be understood against the background of Plato's dramatic creation. Ref. 1231a.

1215 Ritchie, D. G. "On Plato's *Phaedo*." *Mind*, 11 (1886), pp. 353-376.

Examines the arguments for the immortality of the soul, and concludes that Plato did not hold that the soul was immortal in itself, but that it is because it partakes in the divine nature and has the divine nature manifested in it. Suggests that immortality was for Plato a hope rather than a dogma.

1216 Roberts, W. R. "The End and the Beginning of Plato's *Phaedo*." *The Classical Weekly*, 21 (1927), pp. 10-17.

Comments on the absence of Plato, Xenophon, and Aristippus from Socrates' death scene.

1217 Scarrow, David S. "*Phaedo*, 106A-106E." *The Philosophical Review*, 70 (1961), pp. 245-253.

Acknowledges the difficulty many scholars have had in trying to interpret the final argument for the immortality of the soul. Disagrees with those who argue that to be deathless is to be indestructible. Examines the arguments which suggest that Plato made a blatant logical error. Argues that the Forms should not be considered as universals. Emphasizes the 'thing-like' character which Plato ascribes to the Ideal Forms, *e.g.*, justice is just.

1218 Smith, Morton. "Did Socrates Kill Himself Intentionally?" *Philosophy*, 55 (1980), pp. 253-254.

Argues that the fact that Socrates caused his own death knowingly does not entail that he killed himself intentionally.

1219 Smith, Nicholas D. "The Various Equals at Plato's *Phaedo* 74B-C." *The Journal of the History of Philosophy*, 18 (1980), pp. 1-7.

Ref. 1505.

1220 Strachan, J. C. G. "Who Did Forbid Suicide at *Phaedo* 62b?" *The Classical Quarterly*, 20 (1970), pp. 216-220.

Concludes that Plato adopted from the Orphic-Pythagorean school not only the body-prison doctrine, but perhaps the prohibition against suicide as well.

1221 Strycker, Emile de. "Socrate et l'au-delà d'après l'*Apologie* platonicienne." *Les Etudes Classiques*, 18 (1950), pp. 269-284.

Ref. 1169.

1222 Sweeney, Leo. "Safe and Cleverer. Answers in Plato's

Discussion of Participation and Immortality." *The Southern Journal of Philosophy*, 15 (1977), p. 239-252.

Examines *Phaedo* 100b, and comments on the reasons given by Socrates with respect to his 'safe' answer, specifically regarding the meaning of *aitia*.

1223 Taylor, C. C. W. "The Arguments in the *Phaedo* Concerning the Thesis that the Soul is a Harmonia." *Essays in Ancient Greek Philosophy*. Albany: The State University of N.Y. Press, 1971, pp. 217-231.

Examines the meaning of the thesis that the soul is a *harmonia*, and comments on the arguments Socrates uses in his response to Simmias's statement. Includes an appendix for the analysis of the arguments discussed.

1224 Tejera, Victorino. "Plato's Tragic Humor. The *Apology* and the *Phaedo*." *Plato's Dialogues One by One: A Structural Interpretation*. New York: Irvington Publishers, 1984, pp. 9-30.

Ref. 1529.

1225 Trainor, Paul. "Immortality, Transcendence, and the Autobiography of Socrates in the *Phaedo*. *The Southern Journal of Philosophy*, 21 (1983), pp. 595-610.

Ref. 848.

1226 Trotignon, P. "Sur la mort de Socrate." *Revue de Metaphysique et de Morale*, 81 (1976), pp. 1-10.

Argues that a careful reading of the *Phaedo* reveals that each one of the dramatic actions it portrays (Socrates' gestures, words, prayers, and agony) is a symbol which has some religious or metaphysical import. Claims that a mystic and symbolic interpretation of Socrates' death scene is supported by the testimony of Plato (in dialogues other than the *Phaedo*), and by passages from Porphyry, Plutarch and other writers.

1227 Tumarchin, A. "Der Unsterblichkeitsgedanke in Platons

Phädon." *Rheinsiches Museum*, 81 (1926), pp. 58-84.

Argues that the views attributed by Plato to Socrates in the *Phaedo* should be interpreted as supporting the spiritual value of a life devoted to philosophy rather than as attempting to demonstrate the idea of individual immortality.

1228 Verdenius, W. J. "Notes on Plato's *Phaedo*." *Mnemosyne*, 4 (1958), pp. 193-243.

Provides textual, grammatical, and interpretational comments on more than three hundred passages of the *Phaedo*. Furnishes critical notes on various English translations of the dialogue.

1229 Vlastos, Gregory. "Reasons and Causes in the *Phaedo*." *Platonic Studies*. Princeton, N.J.: Princeton University Press, 1981, pp. 76-110.

Examines the methodological and metaphysical preamble (95e-105c) to the final argument for the immortality of the soul made by Socrates, in an attempt to understand the teleological significance of the Forms.

1230 Walton, Richard E. "Socrates' Alleged Suicide." *The Journal of Value Inquiry*, 14 (1980), pp. 287-300.

Examines the issue of Socrates' alleged or apparent suicide in the light of Xenophon's claim that Socrates sought death by taking advantage of the indictment drawn against him. Claims that while Plato's testimony does not openly contradict that of Xenophon, the Platonic dialogues dealing with Socrates' trial and execution should not be read as involving an allegation of suicide: such dialogues are portions of a tragedy whose dramatic theme is the relationship between the individual and the State. Argues that even though the allegation of suicide cannot be conclusively settled, Socrates does appear to have approved self-destruction.

1231 Wedin, Michael V. " αὐτὰ τὰ ἴσα and the Argument at *Phaedo* 74B7-C5." *Phronesis*, 22 (1977), pp. 191-205.

Ref. 1549.

1231a West, Elinor Jane Maddock. "Plato and Socrates: The Men and Their Methods." *New Essays on Socrates*. Edited by Eugene Kelly. New York: University Press of America, 1984, pp. 131-136.

Comments on J. Peterman's discussion of Socrates' "killing off" of Simmias' argument. Ref. 1214.

1232 Wiggins, David. "Teleology and the Good in Plato's *Phaedo*." *Oxford Studies in Ancient Philosophy. A Festschrift for J. L. Ackrill*. Edited by Julia Annas and Michael Woods. Oxford: The Clarendon Press (4 vols.), Vol. 4.

Ref. 1039a.

## THE *CRITO* AND POLITICAL THEORY

The annotations in this section deal with Socrates' political ideas. The emphasis is on, but not exclusive to, Plato's *Crito*.

1233 Allen, Reginald E. "Law and Justice in Plato's *Crito*." *The Journal of Philosophy*, 69 (1972), pp. 562-566.

Argues that Socrates' arguments do not require absolute obedience to all laws: "to disobey a law or decree that enjoins the doing of injustice is not to injure the law." Maintains that Socrates' choice to comply with an unjust sentence is based on his view of judicial authority: to reject the authority of any specific sentence is to reject the authority of any judicially rendered sentence, which would imply a denial of all laws and of the legal foundation of society.

1234 Allen, Reginald E. *Socrates and Legal Obligation*. Minneapolis: University of Minnesota Press, 1980.

Deals with various issues related to Plato's *Apology* and *Crito*, and reproduces the full text of these two dialogues. Attempts to clarify certain elements in them which the author claims have remained obscure. Discusses, with respect to the *Apology*, the use of irony and rhetoric by Plato with the historical background of the accusations against Socrates, and with the issues of the legality and the historicity of the trial. Considers the issue of legal obligation in the *Crito*, and conludes that, while not establishing the right of revolution where citizenship is the result of voluntary agreement, it still does not condone passive obedience to the state. Views the Socratic argument in the *Crito* as an ancestor of the medieval writ of *assumpsit*, which in turn is the ancestor of our own contract laws. Rejects the idea that the Socrates of the *Apology* and the Socrates of the *Crito* stand in opposition to each other. Ref. 1172, 1302.

1235 Bambrough, R., editor. *Plato, Popper, and Politics*. New York: Barnes & Noble, 1968.

Contains fifteen short pieces dealing with Popper's *The Open Society and Its Enemies*, and with its assessment of Plato's political philosophy.

1236 Barker, Andrew. "Why Did Socrates Refuse to Escape?" *Phronesis*, 22 (1977), pp. 13-19.

Analyzes and criticizes the views on the *Crito* advanced by A. D. Woozley. Notes that Socrates' refusal to escape was the result of his unwillingness to commit an unjust act, since the commission of such an act would not only affect him, but would also affect his friends and his children. Ref. 1303.

1237 Beccari, A. "Socrate politico." *Convivium*, 2 (1930), pp. 430-450.

Sees as the kernel of Socrates' political philosophy his conviction that moral ideas must be injected into all political decisions and activities. Stresses the stance of Socrates as a revolutionary who fought for the freedom of thought, but who chose to die in order to remain faithful to the Athenian laws.

1238 Bendixen, Jakob F. *Über den tieferen Schriftsinn des revolutiönaren Sokrates und der gesetzlichen Athener*. Husum: 1839.

Examines the philosophical and political opposition between Socrates and his contemporaries.

1239 Bertman, M. A. "Socrates' Defence of Civil Obedience." *Studium Generale*, 24 (1971), pp. 576-582.

Also published in German as "Die Argumentation des Sokrates zugunsten des bürgerlichen Gehorsams," in *Conceptus*, 5 (1971), pp. 39-45. Examines the following concepts presented in the *Crito*: the responsibilities of the individual citizen toward the state, law and order, and the comparison of the State to a parent.

1240 Bethe, E. "Platons *Kriton*." *Philologische Wochenschrift*, 1932, pp. 957-960.

Regards the *Crito* as a masterpiece of dramatic art in which one should not expect to find decisive philosophical contributions.

1241 Birt, T. *Sokrates der Athener*. Leipzig, 1918.

Studies the political position of Socrates in the Athenian world, and outlines his views concerning the political ideas and practices of his world.

1242 Bleckly, H. *Socrates and the Athenians*. London: Kegan Paul, Trench & Co., 1884.

Pamphlet (70 pp.) which discusses the political and social context of Socrates, the Athenians' reaction to his questioning habit, and the basis and significance of the indictment against him.

1243 Börtzler, F. "Das wahre Gesicht des Sokrates." *Neue Jahrbücher für Wissenschaft und Jugendbildung.*

Comments on Socrates' repeated assertions concerning his ignorance. Interprets them as an attack against the ideal of democracy of his time.

1244 Brémond, André. "La politique de Socrate." *Archives de Philosophie*, 9 (1932), pp. 23-59.

Reviews the relationship between Socrates and the Athenian political establishment, and rejects the notion (developed by Taylor) that Socrates constituted himself as the master of an aristocratic conspiracy of foreign and secret leanings against the popular and democratic Athenian regime. Ref. 1108.

1245 Caprariis, V. de. "Umanesimo e politica di Socrate." *La Parole del Passato*, 8 (1953), pp. 264-302.

Views as the central theme of Socrates' political thought the identification between δίκαιον and νόμιμον. Argues that the basis of Socrates' view can be interpreted as an attempt to rework the myth of Protagoras. Insists that for Socrates the freedom to question and criticize the laws was fundamental.

1246 Congleton, Ann. "Two Kinds of Lawlessness: Plato's *Crito*." *Political Theory*, 2 (1974), pp. 432-446.

Argues that the question of whether there is a justice higher than the positive laws is not the central theme of the *Crito*. Maintains that an adequate understanding of the speech of the Laws is possible by reflecting carefully on the nature of the Socratic dialogue in general, and by appreciating the character of Crito, as he is portrayed in the first part of the *Crito*.

1247 Döring, A. *Die Lehre des Sokrates als soziales Reformsystem. Neuer Versuch zur Lösung des Problems der sokratischen Philosophie*. Munich: Beck, 1895.

Examines the import and implications of the Socratic doctrine specifically from a political and social point of view. Maintains that the testimony of Xenophon furnishes us with a historically reliable representation of Socrates, a testimony which is deemed to be uniform and systematic, and that Aristotle's testimony provides a summary statement of the Old Academy on Socrates. Views Plato's testimony as a means to use Socrates as the mouthpiece of his ideas. Notes that the end result of Socrates' message is the presentation of a system of *sozial-eudämonie* or a *sozial-eudämonistische Ideal*.

1248 Düring, I. "Socrates' Valedictory Words to His Judges." *Eranos Rudbergianus*, 44 (1946), pp. 90-104.

Ref. 1067.

1249 Dybikowski, J. "Socrates, Obedience, and the Law: Plato's *Crito*". *Dialogue*, 13 (1974), pp. 519-535.

Shows the way in which Socrates compels Crito to assess his proposal to escape from prison. Argues that a *prima facie* notion (or even a conditional concept) of obligation to obey the laws cannot be found in the *Crito*. Claims that Socrates' careless expression of respect for authority puts in question Popper's representation of a democratically oriented Socrates who was eventually betrayed by Plato.

Ref. 1283.

1250 Euben, J. Peter. "Philosophy and Politics in Plato's *Crito*." *Political Theory*, 6 (1978), pp. 149-172.

Investigates the apparent inconsistency between the rebellious Socrates of the *Apology* and the submissive Socrates of the *Crito*, not through the prism of civil disobedience, but through the relations between philosophy and politics. Concludes that the inconsistency was real and existential. Highlights the importance of citizenship for Socrates and of politics for the Greeks, these qualities being forcefully combined in Socratic philosophy.

1251 Farrell, Daniel M. "Illegal Actions, Universal Maxims and the Duty to Obey the Law." *Political Theory*, 6 (1978), pp. 173-189.

Argues that Socrates' arguments in the *Crito* are more compelling than usually acknowledged, and that they were meant to be taken at face value. Suggests that they provide at least a sketch of what ought to be the moral basis of political obligation.

1252 Forschhammer, Peter. *Die Athener und Sokrates. Die Gesetzlichen und der Revolutionär*. Berlin: Nicolarische Buchhandlung, 1837.

Examines the character of Socrates' philosophy from the point of view of his political relationship with the Athenian world. Emphasizes the inevitable tension which arises between the solidity of the socio-political establishment and the fluidity of the philosopher's mind. Endeavors to explain the specific import of Socrates' thought as an effort to resolve such tension. Regards Socrates as a great intellectual revolutionary both in theory and in practice, and emphasizes the destructive role played by Socrates in the context of the Athenian polity.

1253 Foulk, Gary F. "Socrates' Argument for not Escaping in the *Crito*." *The Personalist*, 55 (1974), pp. 356-359.

Attempts to clarify what Socrates regards as the central issue in his conversation with Crito. Concludes that

Socrates' argument is valid, even though one of its premises is clearly false, namely the premise about the nature of the agreement between an educated and mature person, and the State.

1254 Gabbert, Mont Robertson. *A Series of Six Radio Talks or Conversations with a Philosopher.* University of Pittsburgh, Radio Publication No. 15, 1925.

Broadcast from the University of Pittsburgh Studio of KDKA. Poses six questions to Socrates in the six talks which compose the series: (1) From Protagoras: Does the state have a divine origin? (2) From Callicles: Are might and right identical? (3) From Thrasymachus: Does might constitute right? (4) From Glaucon: Why are men moral? (5) Can a selfish man be a successful citizen? (6) From Crito: Would Socrates obey the eighteenth amendment?

1255 Gavin, William. "A Note on Socrates and 'the Law' in the *Crito.*" *Aitia*, 7 (1979), pp. 26-28.

Examines the apparent contradiction between Socrates' refusal to obey the law (when asked by the Thirty to arrest Leon of Salamis), and his announcement that on the one hand, should any legal body forbid philosophy, he would disobey it, and on the other, his argument against disobeying the laws (*Crito*). Resolves the issue by arguing that whereas Socrates does accept the existence of an unjust law (which ought to be disobeyed), he claims that there is no justification in opposing the nature of law in general: the spirit of the law should never be disobeyed.

1256 Giannantoni, Gabriele. "La pritania di Socrate nel 406 a. C." *Rivista Critica di Storia della Filosofia*, 17 (1962), pp. 3-25.

Ref. 765.

1257 Giannaras, A. "Platon und K. Popper: Zur Kritik der politischen Philosophie Platons." *Philosophia*, 3 (1973), pp. 208-255.

Examines Popper's interpretation of Plato's political philosophy as a paradigm of the totalitarianism of the 'closed society', and reviews Popper's allegation that Plato was guilty of unfaithfulness towards Socrates. Draws analogies with respect to Hegel's interpretation of Socrates, and argues that the Hegelian Socrates is indeed the critical perspective of that level of morality which corresponds to the open society. Comments on various reactions to the thesis advanced by K. Popper. Ref. 1283.

1258 Gomme, A. W. "The Structure of Plato's *Crito*." *Greece and Rome*, 5 (1958), pp. 45-51.

Interprets the structure and content of the *Crito* in terms of Aristotle's doctrine of μίνησις in the *Politics*. Attempts to show on this basis that Socrates as a tragic hero exhibits a great deal of virtue, while remaining thoroughly on a human level.

1259 Greenberg, N. A. "Socrates' Choice in the *Crito*." *Harvard Studies in Classical Philology*, 70 (1965), pp. 45-82.

Examines the opposition between Socrates' choice to remain loyal to the laws in the *Crito*, and his conviction in the *Apology* that one must always choose right over wrong. Resolves the apparent contradiction between these views by arguing that, in the end, Socrates chose to remain loyal to a heroic image of himself.

1260 Grote, George. "The Persistent Meddler: The Thirty Years of Athenian Tolerance." *The State versus Socrates: A Case Study in Civic Freedom*. Edited by John D. Montgomery. Boston: The Beacon Press, 1954, pp. 98-102.

Excerpted from *Plato and Other Companions of Socrates* (London: John Murray, 1867), Vol.I, pp. 256-265. Discusses Socrates' opposition to the 'King Nomos' whose prescriptive creed and unconscious sentiments are said to be *ratio ex fide, casu, and puerilibus notionibus*. Views Socrates as the great adversary of the irrationality and indolence of the Athenian world, and accounts for the circumstance that the polity did not eliminate the threat emanating from Socrates by reference to the "comparative tolerance of Athenian practice." Ref. 614.

1261 Harlap, Samuel. "Thrasymachus's Justice." *Political Theory*,

7 (1979), pp. 347-370.

Discusses and investigates the distinction between Thrasymachus' 'essentialist' view of justice and that of Socrates, maintaining that while Thrasymachus and Socrates may agree on the meaning of *justice*, they disagree on is its essence. Examines the meanings assigned to Thrasymachus' 'essentialism' by various scholars.

1262 Howe, Marvin. "A Greek Square in Queens Starts a Classic Debate." *The New York Times*, January 30, 1986, p. B1.

Argues in support of erecting statues of Socrates, Plato and Aristotle in a park in a Greek section of Queens, New York, because of their support of Athenian democracy. Refers to them as "the fathers of Athenian democracy." Ref. 1265.

1263 Jaeger, Werner. "The Defender of the State." *The State Versus Socrates: A Case Study in Civic Freedom*. Edited by John D. Montgomery. Boston: The Beacon Press, 1954, pp. 184-193

Excerpted from *Paideia: The Ideals of Greek Culture*, translated by Gilbert Highet (Oxford University Press, 1939), pp. 70-75. Describes Socrates' political and educational mission as one that called forth a re-establishment of the inward moral authority of the State, an accomplishment that could only begin by the regeneration of each person's individual soul. Maintains that unlike Plato, Socrates did not view his country as being beyond repair, or become engaged in the ideal construction of a utopic republic, but chose to live and die within the geographic and political confines of the Athenian polity.

1264 James, Gene G. "Socrates on Civil Disobedience and Rebellion." *The Southern Journal of Philosophy*, 11 (1973), pp. 119-127.

Examines three questions: (1) Is there consistency between the *Apology* and the *Crito* concerning the issue of civil disobedience? (2) Are Socrates' arguments in the *Crito* a sufficient answer to Crito? (3) Is civil disobedience or rebellion ever justified according to Socrates? Concludes that there is no consistency between Socrates' opinions in the *Apology* and those expressed in the *Crito*, and that even though his reply to Crito is adequate, we cannot infer from it that civil disobedience or rebellion must always be unjustified.

1265 Katz, Ellen. "No Supporters of Athenian Democracy." *New York Times*, Letter to the Editor, February 13, 1986, Section 1, p. 30.

Argues against a *New York Times* article in which it is claimed that Socrates, Plato and Aristotle were "the fathers of Athenian democracy." Ref. 1262.

1266 Korfmacher, William C. "Socrates on the 1960 Elections." *America*, 104 (1960), pp. 18-19.

Notes the great need to have a critical mind of the caliber of Socrates in order to subject the present political system and context (1960) to a severe examination: "Athens needed his vigorous leadership in the fifth century before Christ. America needs the same leadership in the campaign of 1960."

1267 Kraut, Richard. *Socrates and the State*. Princeton, N.J.: Princeton University Press, 1984.

Examines the nature and scope of Socrates' political position as this surfaces in the *Apology* and especially in the *Crito*, and reviews the question concerning the possibility of an ideological inconsistency between these two dialogues. Argues that it is a mistake to detect in the *Crito* a political philosophy that is offensively authoritarian: the *Crito* is not an open plea for unrestricted authority, civil stability, or the supremacy of the State over the individual. Interprets the speech of the 'Laws' in the *Crito* as an attempt to resolve the conflicts between the needs of the individual and the needs of the State, arguing that the Laws do not demand blind obedience. Sees no contradiction between the Socrates of the *Apology* and the Socrates of the *Crito*.

1268 MacLaughlin, Robert J. "Socrates and Political Disobedience." *Phronesis*, 21 (1976), pp. 185-197.

Argues, against the view expressed by G. Young, that the speech of the 'Laws' in the *Crito* can be reconciled with Socrates' position in the *Apology*. Comments on the *Euthyphro* and Book I of the *Republic*, and concludes that Socrates' philosophy of law allows the possibility and even the necessity of disobeying the laws in many cases, not only when the philosopher is forbidden to practice philosophy. Ref. 1305.

1269 Martin, Rex. "Socrates on Disobeying the Law." *The Review of Metaphysics*, 24 (1970), pp. 21-36.

Examines the arguments presented by Socrates on behalf of the 'Laws' in the *Crito*, and concludes that his position entails a complete commitment to obey all laws. Criticizes the Socratic position as unreasonable and too inclusive.

1270 Martin, Victor. "L'art royal ou la politique selon Socrate." *Alma Mater*, 1944, pp. 121-133.

Comments on Socrates' understanding of politics in terms of a technique or art which occupies the highest place among all techniques. Notes that, according to Socrates, the exclusive goal of all political knowledge and activity is the good of the person and the community.

1271 Martineau, Alain. "Socrate et Marcuse nous prèviennent-ils contre les tyrans?" *Revue de l'Université d'Ottawa*, 56 (196), pp.173-181.

Discusses Marcuse's appeal to Socrates as an example of a political subversive. Raises questions about the possibility of preventing tyranny if those who (like Marcuse) are expected to oppose it do not hesitate to justify the use of selective violence and subversion.

1272 McKeon, Richard. "The Choice of Socrates." *Great Moral Dilemmas in Literature, Past and Present*. Edited by R. M. MacIver. New York: Cooper Square Publishers, 1964, pp. 113-133.

Discusses various interpretations to which Socrates' paradoxical philosophy and life have given rise, and reviews several solutions proposed towards the resolution of the

Socratic problem. Devotes particular attention to the paradox of Socrates' death: a just man who is sentenced to die by a justly constituted jury. Comments at length on Socrates' refusal to escape and on various issues related to the *Crito*, and argues that "the final choice of Socrates, which brought his life to its close, was the consequence, logical as well as historical, of the choices and decisions which made up his life."

1273 McKeon, Richard. "The Interpretation of Political Theory and Practice in Ancient Athens." *The Journal of the History of Ideas*, 42 (1981), pp. 3-12.

Calls for the a reversal of the usual order of examining the relationship between philosophical speculation and the performance and interpretation of practical actions. Proceeds by an analysis of the Socratic dialectic.

1274 Momeyer, Richard W. "Socrates on Obedience and Disobedience to the Law." *Philosophical Research Archives*, 8 (1982).

Notes that the many attempts to resolve the apparent contradiction between Socrates' pledge to disobey the law if it asked him to abandon philosophy (*Apology* 29c-30c), and his assertion that legal authority must be obeyed in all circumstances (*Crito* 51b-c), have not been successful. Claims that this contradiction is real and unresolvable. Examines and rejects various attempts to resolve the contradiction, and remains unconvinced of the justification of saying either that one of Socrates' views really does not belong to him, or that one of the dialogues can be construed as motivated by mere rhetorical purposes.

1275 Mulgan, R. G. "Socrates and Authority." *Greece and Rome*, 19 (1972), pp. 208-212.

Examines the *Apology* and the *Crito* in an attempt to answer the question as to whether Socrates believed in freedom of conscience as a general right or duty of the individual to resist the state when it interferes with freedom, and concludes that Socrates does not believe that the individual has the right to disobey when his own values appear compromised by the legal authorities.

1276 Murphy, Jeffrie G. "The Socratic Theory of Legal Fidelity." *Violence and Aggression in the History of Ideas.* Edited by P. Wiener and John Fisher. New Brunswick, N.J.: Rutgers University Press, 1974, pp. 15-33.

Examines in detail the arguments of the *Crito* in order to shed light on the authentic Socratic position vis-à-vis the problem of legal obligation. Points out that Socrates' argument concerning his reputation implies the conviction that even if his reputation were to suffer (if he were to escape), he would not suffer an evil. Claims with respect to Socrates' 'threat' to the jurors (*Apology* 29d) that, rightly understood, it is not a threat to disobey the laws. Notes, however, that according to Socrates' words in the *Apology*, a command by God supersedes the commands of the laws, and that these must be disobeyed if God so orders.

1277 Nichols, Mary P. *Socrates and the Political Community: An Ancient Debate.* Albany: State University of New York Press, 1967.

Discusses the general philosophical significance of Socrates and the impact of his political stance by exploring the way in which Aristophanes, Plato, and Aristotle reacted to him. Attempts to demonstrate that the city portrayed by Socrates in the *Republic* resembles the thinking establishment described by Aristophanes in the *Clouds.* Discusses the relationship between Aristotle's establishment of politics as a science and the partial solutions of the political problem given by Plato.

1278 Organ, Troy Wilson. "Crito Apologizes." *The Personalist*, 38 (1957), pp. 366-371.

Develops a defense of the lifestyle of Crito as it appears in Plato's testimony. Presents Crito as if he, not Socrates, were on trial before an Athenian jury.

1279 Pangle, Thomas L. "Socrates on the Problem of Political Science Education." *Political Theory*, 13 (1985), pp. 112-137.

Identifies the malaise centering upon educational goals faced by contemporary political science as a new version of an ancient conundrum -- the conflict between education in citizenship, and education in political science, theory and philosophy. Focuses on the *Theages*, acknowledging but disagreeing with the contention of modern times, that this dialogue is not a true Platonic dialogue. Concludes that the wisdom of Socratic philosophy consists in the way in which it conforms to the demand to be a contribution to society.

1280 Payne, Thomas. "The Crito as a Mythological Mime." *Interpretation*, 11 (1983), pp. 1-23.

Relates the scene and arguments of the Crito to those of the *Iliad* (Book 9), where Odysseus seeks to persuade Achilles to remain in the Greek forces. Concludes that the *Crito* is basically a rehearsal of Homer's scene.

1281 Piovani, P. *Per una interpretazione unitaria del Critone*. Rome, 1947.

Examines in detail the grounds on which Socrates refuses to accept the opportunity to escape from jail, and chooses to obey the laws even if these are unjust. Argues that his stance in the *Crito* is in no way in opposition to his general philosophical principles.

1282 Popper, Karl R. "The Advocate of Democratic Criticism." *The State Versus Socrates: A Case in Civic Freedom*. Edited by John D. Montgomery. Boston: The Beacon Press, 54, pp. 160-166.

Excerpted from the *Open Society and Its Enemies* (Princeton, N.J.: Princeton University Press, 1950), Vol. 1, pp. 184-189. Distinguishes between the democratic and the totalitarian critics of the democratic form of government, and classifies Socrates among the former. Esteems the sort of criticism associated with Socrates as the very essence of democracy. Lists the following as features of Socrates' teaching: his intellectualism, his egalitarian theory of human reason, his stress on intellectual honesty and self-criticism, his equalitarian theory of justice, and his doctrine that it is better to be a victim of injustice than to inflict it upon others. Maintains that such ideas were ultimately the cause of his death. Ref. 1283.

1283 Popper, Karl R. *The Open Society and Its Enemies*. New York:

Harper Torchbooks, 1963 (2 vols).

Gives a historical account of the development of totalitarianism and authoritarianism in the Western world from Plato to the twentieth century. Views the course of civilization as a constant struggle between the advocates of an open society, in which humanness and reasonableness, equality and freedom, are prominent, and the proponents of a closed society who are committed to totalitarian and repressive ideals. Regards Plato as a paradigm of political totalitarianism, and accuses him of having used and misused the name and ideas of Socrates for the dissemination of his own political ideology. Makes abundant references to Socrates (especially Vol. 1, Chap. 10), and stresses his commitment to an egalitarian theory of human reason and justice. Discusses at length (Notes to Chapter 10, Vol. 1, pp. 293-318) the relationship between Socrates and Plato, and the issues related to the Socratic problem. Concludes that the Platonic Socrates can be regarded as a politically motivated fabrication, and that Plato's use of Socrates entails a patent case of ideological betrayal. Ref. 1249, 1257.

1284 Quandt, Kenneth. "Socratic Consolation: Rhetoric and Philosophy in Plato's *Crito*." *Philosophy and Rhetoric*, 15 (1982), pp. 238-256.

Maintains that the speech of the 'Laws' (with which the *Crito* concludes) develops an argument that fails to satisfy the requirements of valid reasoning stipulated by Socrates himself in the middle of the dialogue. Regards this speech as a rhetorical piece whose aim is more to offer Socrates a source of consolation than to convince him.

1285 Ray, A. Chadwick. "The Tacit Agreement in the *Crito*." *International Studies in Philosophy*, 12 (1980), pp. 47-54.

Argues that Socrates does not construe tacit agreements as establishing the duty to obey, and that the duty of promise-keeping is subordinate to the prohibition to do injury.

1286 Rosen, Frederick. "Obligation and Friendship in Plato's *Crito*." *Political Theory*, 1 (1973), pp. 307-316.

Explores the relationship between the dramatic details of the *Crito* and the philosophical lines of argumentation it advances.

1287 Rosivach, Vincent J. " οἱ πολλοί in the *Crito* (44b5-d10)." *The Classical Journal*, 76 (1981), pp. 289-297.

Suggests that Crito, as a dramatic character, represents at least to some extent *rhetoric*, whose purpose is not to obtain rational consent but rather to persuade. Argues that the dialogue should be read with Plato's upper class social values and language in mind, and that the language suggests that the upper class should be οἱ φρόνιμοι and see things as Socrates does, not as the members of the lower class, the οἱ πολλοί.

1288 Saxonhouse, Arlene W. "Eros and the Female in Greek Political Thought." *Political Theory*, 12 (1984), pp. 5-27.

Approaches the issue of how women are represented in ancient Greek political thought through an analysis of the *Symposium*. Calls attention to how flute music is repeatedly associated with the female and how Alciabiades recognizes that Socrates' words have the same power as the flute to control men's souls. Concludes that if we use the hermaphroditic Socrates as our model, we become complete individually because we have acknowledged both the female and male within us.

1289 Seuter, Nell W. "Socrates, Rhetoric and Civil Disobedience." *Southwestern Philosophical Studies*, 1 (1976), pp. 50-56.

Introduces two kinds of categories of civil disobedience: moral disobedience and political disobedience, and alleges that only the latter is characterized by public protest. Contends that Socrates' disobedience of government and judicial authority does not fit the model of civil disobedience as public protest. Compares Socrates' moral disobedience with that associated with Henry Thoreau.

1290 Shorey, Paul. "Note on Plato *Crito* 49E-50A." *Selected Papers*. Garland Publishing Co., 1980, pp. 456-457.

Originally published in *The Classical Journal*, 2 (1906-1907), pp. 80-81. Considers inaccurate those interpretations which suggest that this reference in the *Crito* means, "Do we abide by what we acknowledge to be just?" Argues that no good parallel can be found for such a construction. Suggests that Socrates is arguing from the principle of Attic law which states that all agreements which are not the result of fraud or duress must be honored.

1291 Skousgaard, Stephen. "Genuine Speech vs. Chatter: A Socratic Problematic." *Kinesis* 6, (1974), pp. 87-94.

Explores the social and political consequences of speech. Takes the Socratic dialogue as a paradigm of speech which is conducive to a sound political existence, and views the rhetoric associated with the Sophists as a model which promotes corrupt and chaotic political life.

1292 Spitz, David. "Socrates versus Hobbes on the Nature of Power." *Essays in the Liberal Idea of Freedom*. Tucson: The University of Arizona Press, 1964, pp. 23-27.

Examines Hobbes' definition of power as "the present means to obtain some future apparent Good." Analyzes the implications of this definition against the background provided by Socrates' comments on the vacuity of the power allegedly possessed by tyrants. Maintains that Hobbes' concept of power introduces an element missing in Socrates' concept, namely, an empirical dimension.

1293 Stephens, James. "Socrates on the Rule of Law." *The History of Philosophy Quarterly*, 2 (1985), pp. 3-10.

Argues that the apparent inconsistency between the Socratic position of the *Apology*, where Socrates is willing to disobey a court order forbidding him to practice philosophy in Athens, and the *Crito*, where he is willing to die rather than disobey the State, are true inconsistences in detail and in principle, and cannot be argued away on the basis of existing evidence.

1294 Uchiyama, K. "Nomos and Logos in Plato's *Crito*." *The Journal of Classical Studies*, 29 (1981), pp. 41-52.

In Japanese with an English summary. Argues that the only way to understand meaningfully Socrates' refusal to accept Crito's offer, is to see in his decision a resolution to comply with the *logos*, not merely a desire to obey the *nomos* of the State.

1295 Veyne, Paul. "Did the Greeks Invent Democracy." *Diogenes*, 124 (1983), pp. 1-32.

Suggests that if we were to return to ancient Athens, we would not find "the democratic semi-ideal of Western countries, but the mental climate of activist political parties" charged with many responsibilities. Suggests that the 'law' a good citizen respects (Xenophon, *Memorabilia*, I,ii,41) is much more than the laws as we understand them today, as it includes "all the laws, unwritten customs, political decisions, orders from authorities and more generally, the collective will which had a legitimacy beyond temporary legalities." Argues that this is the law to which Socrates' patriotism is tied in the *Crito*.

1296 Wade, Francis C. "In Defense of Socrates." *The Review of Metaphysics*, 25 (1971), pp. 311-325.

Maintains that the Socratic argument of obedience to the laws (as this is developed in the second half of the *Crito*) must be modified by two premises integral to Socrates' philosophy: (1) that under no circumstances should one do harm to another person, and (2) that one's obligation to obey the laws is contingent on their being just. Argues that Socrates' defiance of the jury in the *Apology* clearly supports this interpretation of the *Crito*. Argues that while the threat to disobey the jury (*Apology* 29d) may be justified (for an order to stop philosophizing would compel Socrates to commit injustice), his acceptance of the death penalty is also justified, even if the sentence was unjust: in the latter case Socrates would be compelled to *suffer* an injustice, not to commit injustice.

1297 Watson, Walter. "The Voice of the God." *New Essays on Socrates*. Edited by Eugene Kelly. Lanham, Md.: University Press of America, 1984. pp. 173-179.

Presents a commentary on Kostman. Argues against the view that the Socrates of the *Crito* abandoned the philosophical mission given to him by Apollo, by refusing to escape and by obeying the laws. Maintains that Socrates' mission required him not to act unjustly by escaping, and that it would have been impossible for him to continue his mission, had he chosen to escape. Ref. 1427.

1298 West, Thomas G. "Defending Socrates and Defending Politics." *Natural Right and Political Right: Essays in Honor of Harry V. Jaffa*. Edited by Thomas B. Silver and Peter W. Schramm. Durham: Carolina Academic Press, 1984, pp. 235-249.

Originally published in *Interpretation*, 9 (1983), pp. 383-397. Maintains that Socrates' political philosophy offers an alternative to the two prominent currents of political thought, liberalism and Marxism. Rejects the interpretation of Socrates as a liberal who stood in opposition to the State.

1299 Whelan, F. G. "Socrates and the 'Meddlesomeness' of the Athenians." *History of Political Thought*, 4 (1983), pp. 1-29.

Maintains that Socrates' definition and understanding of the concepts of justice and injustice in the *Republic* can only entail a rejection and a severe condemnation of Athenian political institutions and practices.

1300 Wood, Ellen Meiksins and Wood, Neal. *Class Ideology and Ancient Political Theory: Socrates, Plato and Aristotle in Social Context*. Oxford: Basil Blackwell, 1978, pp. 275ff.

Presents the premise that the classics of political theory are predominantly ideological and that to be understood they must be related to their social context. Presents Socrates as "the saint of the counter-revolution" and as the founder of a philosophical school in which Greek aristocratic ideas achieved their apotheosis. Views him not as a seeker of truth, but as the expounder of a pro-aristocratic ideology.

1301 Wood, Ellen Meiksins and Wood, Neal. "Socrates and Democracy." *Political Theory*, 14 (1986), pp. 55-82.

Disagrees with the position of Vlastos that Socrates preferred democracy to all other constitutions and that

Socrates was a democrat or, at the very least, a demophile. Focuses on the textual and historical account developed by Vlastos. Ref. 1112.

1302 Woodruff, Paul. "Review of Socrates and Legal Obligation by Reginald E. Allen." *The Journal of the History of Philosophy*, 21 (1983), pp. 93-95.

Considers Allen's work to be an essay on the history and philosophy of law rather than an explication of Platonic thought, and in this regard finds it fresh and filled with wit and humanness. Finds Allen's analysis of the core of the *Crito*, the relationship between Socrates and the Laws, an elegantly designed argument and a considerable achievement. Suggests that Allen's approach to the *Apology*, through the clever use of paradox, provides an interesting understanding of Socratic irony and rhetoric. Ref. 1234.

1303 Woozley, A. D. *Law and Obedience: The Arguments of Plato's Crito*. Chapel Hill: The University of North Carolina Press, 1979.

Analyzes Socrates' arguments in the *Crito* for not accepting the offer to escape. Views the Socrates of the *Crito* as an essentially historical character, and regards this dialogue as a substantially faithful representation of the actual Socrates. Examines the concept of duty in a three-fold manner: duty to avoid injustice, duty to obey the laws, and duty to obey the laws as parents. Discusses the notion of contractual duty, and the issue of disobedience as destructive of law. Regards Socrates' arguments as being "interestingly bad rather than uninterestingly good." Contains a new translation of the *Crito*. Ref. 1236.

1303a Woozley, A. D. "Socrates on Disobeying the Law." *The Philosophy of Socrates: A Collection of Critical Essays*. Edited by G. Vlastos. Notre Dame, Ind.: University of Notre Dame Press, 1971, pp. 299-318.

Examines the *Crito* and the *Apology* in an effort to understand the apparent inconsistency in the position of Socrates regarding a person's responsibility to obey the laws.

1304 Yaffe, Martin D. "Civil Disobedience and the Opinions of the Many: Plato's *Crito*." *The Modern Schoolman*, 54 (1977), pp. 123-136.

Explores the assumptions and implications of Socrates' comments on the opinions of the many, and the relationship of such comments to Socrates' plea on behalf of obeying the laws.

1305 Young, Gary. "Socrates and Obedience." *Phronesis*, 19 (1974), pp. 1-29.

Reviews the paradox entailed by Socrates' statement in the *Apology* that he will not abandon philosophy even if the law so commands him, and his contention in the *Crito* that every citizen ought to obey the laws in all circumstances. Argues that Socrates does not really uphold either position, and interprets Socrates' statements in the *Crito* as arguments to persuade Crito that life without philosophy is not worth living, and that philosophy outside Athens is impossible for him. Concludes that according to Socrates the standard of justice must be found through philosophy, not shown by a simple appeal to the laws. Ref. 1268.

1306 Younger, Irving. "Socrates and Us." *Commentary*, 70 (1980), pp. 46-49.

Recounts various details of Socrates' life, and develops a critical appraisal of the American democratic system against the background provided by Socrates' ideas and political context.

1307 Zeppi, S. "Βίος θεωρητικὸς ἢ βίος πολιτικός come ideali di vita nella filosofia preplatonica." *Logos* (1972), pp. 219-248.

Discusses the ideals of contemplative life and political life as these were harmoniously conceived by the pre-Socratics before the advent of the Sophists. Notes that among the Sophists (Protagoras, Gorgias, and Callicles) these two ideals became separated, and comments on Socrates' effort to create out of them a new synthesis in which theoretical endeavors and political involvement could be integrated.

# STUDIES ON THE PLATONIC DIALOGUES

Included in this section are those entries which are on selected works specifically related to studies of particular Platonic dialogues. There is a primary emphasis on the early dialogues, later dialogues being occasionally included if they reflect a specific Socratic theme, *e.g.*, dialectic. Entries for the *Apology* (where the emphasis is on the trial), the *Crito* (along with other works which focus on general political themes), and the *Phaedo* (where attention is given to the themes of death, dying, and immortality) are included in separate sections.

1308 Adams, E. W. "The Death of Socrates: A Point of Contact Between Two Worlds." *Hibbert Journal*, 22 (1924), pp. 515-526.

Suggests the abandonment of the tetralogical arrangement of the Platonic dialogues attributed to Thrasyllus in favor of a group of six dialogues which, it is claimed, complete a tragedy by a first-rate dramatist: (1) the *Meno* (characterized by the sudden entrance of Anytus); (2) the *Theaetetus* (an abrupt ending which presages evil); (3) the *Euthyphro* (Socrates frequenting the court of the King Archon, and the appearance of Meletus); (4) the *Apology*; (5) the *Crito*; and (6) the *Phaedo*. Concludes with the observation that Socrates' death proved that indeed man may deserve to be immortal.

1309 Adkins, A. W. H. "Arete, Techne, Democracy and Sophists: Protagoras 316B-328D." *The Journal of Hellenic Studies*, 93 (1973), pp. 3-12.

Reviews the ambiguities of the term *arete* in *Protagoras* 316b-328d, and notes that Protagoras confuses justice with political skill. Argues that Protagoras' speech is specifically designed to appeal to a wide variety of Athenian groups.

1310 Alderman, Harold. "Dialectic as Philosophical Care." *Man and World: An International Philosophical Review*, 6 (1973), pp. 206-219.

Argues that dialectic is "the philosopher's destructively

philosophical mode of caring." Examines passages from the *Euthyphro*, the *Ion*, the *Euthydemus*, and the *Apology*. Defines Socratic dialectic as the mode of caring "which insures that we remain open to the dual possibility of knowledge and ignorance, and to the proper role of man as the caretaker of speech."

1311 Anderson, Albert. "Socratic Reasoning in the *Euthyphro*." *The Review of Metaphysics*, 22 (1969), pp. 461-481.

Examines Socrates' arguments in the *Euthyphro*, particularly in 10a-c, and concludes that they are neither faulty nor immature, as it is sometimes alleged. Shows that Socrates' efforts move towards a lesson on good definition.

1312 Anderson, D. E. "Socrates' Concept of Piety." *The Journal of the History of Philosophy*, 5 (1967), pp. 1-3.

Examines the *Euthyphro*, *Apology* and *Crito*, and concludes that absolutes (*e.g.*, Eternal Forms) are denied, the only constant element being the dialectic, and that Socrates' death was a symbolic vindication of the dialectical process.

1313 Anton, John P. "Dialectic and Health in Plato's *Gorgias*: Presuppositions and Implications." *Ancient Philosophy*, 1 (1980), pp. 549-60.

Shows how in the *Gorgias* Plato develops conceptual means of distinguishing bodily health from mental health, and that he does so by going beyond the medical terminology of his context. Explains how the *Gorgias* accomplishes this by combining the art of medicine and dialectics, and by bringing mental health in line with coherent action as rational harmony. Interprets the Socrates of the *Gorgias* as a paradigm of rational harmony, and Callicles as the champion of discord or irrationality.

1314 Anton, John P. "The Secret of Plato's *Symposium*." *Diotima*, 2 (1974), pp. 27-47.

Maintains that the sense which emerges from Alcibiades' speech is that the failure of his relationship with Socrates was not the result of his own bad character alone, but also the consequence of Socrates' inability to communicate to him the teaching on love which had been given by Diotima to the philosopher.

1315 Ballard, Eduard G. "Plato's Movement from an Ethics of the Individual to a Science of Particulars." *Tulane Studies in Philosophy*, 6 (1957), pp.5-41.

Maintains that various ethical and political issues that are left unresolved in the *Republic* eventually led Plato to the formulation of a comprehensive theory of knowledge. Notes that the unresolved issues of the *Republic* (inherited from Socrates' ethical questions) are mainly concerned with the ethical domain as this pertains to the individual.

1316 Ballew, Lynne. "Review of *Plato: Hippias Major*, translated by Paul Woodruff." *The Journal of the History of Philosophy*, 22 (1984), pp.229-231.

Considers this a fine translation on the whole, but raises several points of discontent, *e.g.*, the translation of the two instances of ψυχή (296d8, 300c10) as 'mind' rather than 'soul' which confuses the functions of νοῦς and ψυχή, and waters down the earnestness of Socrates' search. Concludes that the work is of value to general readers as well as specialists.

1317 Barnes, Jonathan. "Socrates and the Jury, Part II." *Proceedings of the Aristotelian Society*, Supplement 54 (1980), pp. 193-206.

Discusses two of the paradoxes detected by Burnyeat in *Theaetetus* 201b. Introduces the notion of an 'epistemic category', and argues that by its application, the paradoxes appear less puzzling. Ref. 1336.

1318 Beatty, Joseph. "Review of *Socrates: Philosophy in Plato's Early Dialogues* by Gerasimos Santas." *The Journal of the History of Philosophy*, 20 (1982), pp. 303-306.

Considers this work as enriching an understanding of Socratic claims and arguments, yet expresses serious reservations about Santas' focus on only logical and discursive elements. Ref. 327.

1319 Bedu-Addo, J. T. "On the Alleged Abandonment of the Good in the *Phaedo*." *Apeiron*, 13 (1979), pp. 104-114.

Argues that it is unreasonable to conclude that in the *Phaedo* Socrates abandoned the search for the Good, and that this erroneous conclusion could be the result of not distinguishing the two biographical stages of Socrates represented in the dialogue (*i.e.*, the young Socrates and the old Socrates).

1320 Bedu-Addo, J. T. "The Role of the Hypothetical Method in the *Phaedo*." *Phronesis*, 24 (1979), pp. 111-132.

Explains that the hypothetical method is introduced right before the final proof of the immortality of the soul (102a-107a), and that it is a description of the philosopher's practice of death. Argues that it is a general statement of method, as well as the description of his 'second voyage' in search of the cause of generation, existence and destruction -- the *Good*.

1321 Ben, N. van der. *The Charmides* of Plato. Amsterdam: B. R. Grüner, 1985.

Contains notes to help facilitate an understanding of the text. Concludes that the wide range of topics mentioned are presented in a deliberately perplexing manner, especially the subject of knowledge. Includes a discussion of various passages which are presented in Greek.

1322 Benjamin, W. "Socrates." *The Philosophical Forum*, 15 (1983), pp. 52-54.

Reviews Socrates' idea of love in the *Symposium*, and concludes that he reveals himself to us as an almost in-human person who has little or no understanding of human love.

1323 Blits, Jan H. "The Holy and the Human: An Interpretation of Plato's *Euthyphro*." *Apeiron*, 14 (1980), pp. 19-40.

Reviews the contents and structure of the *Euthyphro*, and emphasizes Socrates' endeavor to reduce the concept of piety to strictly human terms (as distinguished from theological terms). Regards the 'failure' of the *Euthyphro* as more apparent than real, and notes that the concept of piety is well defined by the dialogue's dramatic structure and what Socrates says and does in it.

1324 Bluck, R. S. "Plato, *Gorgias* 493 C 1-3." *The Classical Review,* 13 (1963), pp. 263-264.

Suggests that what is presented is something approaching the bipartite division of the soul (as advanced in the *Meno* as the rational and the irrational) rather than an anticipation of the tripartite division of the soul.

1325 Brickhouse, Thomas C. and Smith, Nicholas D. "Justice and Dishonesty in Plato's *Republic*." *The Southern Journal of Philosophy*, 21 (1983), pp. 79-95.

Examines Book 2 of the *Republic*, focusing on whether a ruler should lie to the citizens. Concludes that the debate has been misdirected by critics and supporters alike, and should be addressed from the perspective of whether or not the moral justification Plato presents is defensible.

1326 Brickhouse, Thomas C. and Smith, Nicholas D. "The Formal Charges Against Socrates." *The Journal of the History of Philosophy*, 23 (1985), pp. 457-482.

Ref. 1123.

1327 Brickhouse, Thomas C. "Zeigler on Plato's *Gorgias* and Psychological Egoism." *The Personalist*, 60 (1979), pp. 451-454.

Examines Zeigler's view that the Socrates of the *Gorgias* does not endorse psychological egoism on the ground that virtue and happiness are one and the same state of the soul. Concludes that a version of psychological egoism is assumed in the *Gorgias* because of the fact that the identification of virtue and happiness is merely contingent: the enlightened person pursues virtue only because it is happiness.

1328 Brochard, Victor. "Sur le *Banquet* de Platon." *L'Année Philo-*

*sophique*, 18, (1907), pp. 1-12.

Reviews the significance of the concept of love as this is developed in Plato's *Symposium*, and comments on its relationship to the concepts of knowledge and virtue. Maintains that the views expressed by Socrates belong mostly to Plato.

1329 Brown, John H. "The Logic of the *Euthyphro* 10A-11B." *The Philosophical Quarterly*, 14 (1964), pp. 1-14.

Maintains that the argument employed by Socrates in *Euthyphro* 10a-11b is not a formally valid argument with unambiguous and plausible premises.

1330 Bruell, Christopher. "Socratic Politics and Self-Knowledge: An Interpretation of Plato's *Charmides*." *Interpretation*, 6 (1977), pp. 141-203.

Subjects to analysis Socrates' exhortation to Charmides to devote himself to the practice of moderation, and compares it to the one made to Alcibiades focusing on justice. Views such exhortations as intimately related to Socrates' own ongoing endeavor to attain to self-knowledge.

1331 Buford, Thomas O. "Plato on the Educational Consultant: An Interpretation of the *Laches*." *Idealistic Studies*, 7 (1977), pp. 151-171.

Argues that the central theme of the *Laches* is not (as is generally believed) the concept of courage as a virtue, but the nature of the educational consultant. Views the *Laches* as an incomplete investigation of certain issues related to the skill of giving educational advice.

1332 Burger, Ronna. *The Phaedo: A Platonic Labyrinth*. New Haven, Conn.: Yale University Press, 1984.

Emphasizes the significance of the dialogical form, and suggests that it more often than not displays the intellectual limitations of its characters. Argues that identifying a particular position as Platonic is not possible, because Plato nowhere identifies an idea as his own. Suggests that there is nothing which appears in the dialogue that is without philosophical significance. Notes that the *Phaedo* is generally viewed as the greatest source of Platonic thought since it gives expression to Plato's two most significant ideas, mainly, the theory of Ideal Forms and the belief in immortality. Examines the dialogue in terms of its structural division in two parts, and comments on the transformation of ideas from the first part to the second.

1333 Burger, Ronna. "Socratic Irony and the Platonic Art of Writing: The Self-Condemnation of the Written Word in Plato's *Phaedrus*." *The Southwestern Journal of Philosophy*, 9 (1978), pp. 113-126.

Examines Socrates' ironic depreciation of the written word in the *Phaedrus*, and the circumstance that in the Platonic dialogues there is no acknowledgment of their author as a writer. Makes use of the 'Egyptian story' in the *Phaedrus* to show that the written dialogue overcomes the dangers inherent in the written word to which Socrates makes specific reference.

1334 Burns, Steven. "Doing Business with the Gods." *The Canadian Journal of Philosophy*, 15 (1985), pp. 311-326.

Argues that Socrates' position in the *Euthyphro* results in a positive and substantive teaching about the nature of piety. Concludes that the Socratic concept of piety in terms of self-denying reverence towards the gods is in full accord with Socrates' own living example.

1335 Burnyeat, M. F. "Examples in Epistemology: Socrates, Theaetetus and G. E. Moore." *Philosophy*, 52 (1977), PP. 381-398.

States that the *Theaetatus* represents the most elaborate example of Socrates' dialectical method at work, this method being a procedure for working towards an analytic understanding of philosophically difficult concepts.

1336 Burnyeat, M. F. and Barnes, J. "Socrates and the Jury." *Proceedings of the Aristotelian Society*, Supplement 54 (1980), pp. 173-206.

Discovers three paradoxes in Plato's argument in *Theaetetus* 200d-201c, where it is claimed that knowledge is not true belief. Suggests a contrast between knowledge as justified true belief, and knowledge as the systematic understanding that comes from ourselves. Includes remarks on the *Meno*. Ref. 1317.

1337 Burnyeat, M. F. "Virtues in Action." *Socrates: A Collection of Critical Essays*. Edited by Gregory Vlastos. Notre Dame, Ind.: University of Notre Dame Press, 1980, pp. 209-234.

Discusses the treatment of virtue in *Laches* 190d-191e and 192a-193d, *Charmides* 159b-160d, *Euthyphro* 10a-11a, *Protagoras* 332a- 333b, and *Republic* 352d-354a. Emphasizes the Socratic position that virtue is knowledge, and examines the priority of *being* over *doing*, which the author associates with Socrates. Devotes considerable attention to the understanding of the concept character as this is significant in a moral sense.

1338 Calogero, Guido. "Gorgias and the Socratic Principle *Nemo sua sponte peccat*." *The Journal of Hellenic Studies*, 77 (1957), pp. 12-17.

Ref. 883.

1339 Candlish, S. "*Euthyphro* 6D-9B and its Misinterpretations." *Apeiron*, 17 (1983), pp. 28-32.

Comments on the *ad hominem* character of Socrates' argumentation against Euthyphro.

1340 Cappelletti, Angel J. "Eutifrón: La superación de la religión popular y el germen de la teología platónica." *Revista Latinoamerica de Filosofía*, 12 (1986), pp. 87-94.

Maintains that although the *Euthyphro* takes its point of departure from a strictly Socratic problem, namely, the definition of the idea of piety, it moves into a region of a distinctive Platonic texture, in which the idea of God (or the Divine) is related to the Ideal Forms.

1341 Cappelletti, Angel J. "Sobre la estructura dramática del

*Gorgias* de Platón." *Revista Venezolana de Filosofía*, 11 (1979), pp. 137-142.

Reviews the *Gorgias*, especially from the point of view of the confrontation between philosophy and political power, and between wisdom and oppression. Concludes that the dialogue exhibits the dramatic structure associated with tragedy, and that even the tragic chorus is not absent from it. Regards Socrates as a figure generally equivalent to the heroes of the tragedies.

1342 Carabba, C. "I molti *non sequitur* dell' *Eutifrone* platonico." *Sandalion*, 9 (1982), pp. 91-95.

Discovers many instances of faulty logical reasoning in the *Euthyphro*, and alleges that Socrates appealed to unsound arguments in order to refute the basic ideas of Euthyphro.

1343 Claus, David B. *Toward the Soul: An Inquiry into the Meaning of Psyche Before Plato*. New Haven: Yale University Press, 1981.

Presents an analysis of the semantic changes which the term ψυχή underwent during the archaic and classical periods: in Homer it was used to represent the 'life' lost at death as well as 'shade', as in the description of death in battle, whereas in the classical period it developed into the Platonic personal 'soul', which was characterized as the immortal and divine part of an individual, being the rational seat of moral choice. Concludes that Democritus stands apart in the pre-Socratic tradition in that although his interpretation is materialistic, it is Socratic in tone for it suggests an ethical program, happiness being dependent on the ψυχή. Provides a brief summary of the Socratic uses of 'soul' in Aristophanes and Xenophon, and an examination of the concept in the *Euthyphro, Apology, Crito, Ion, Laches, Lysis, Hippias Major, Hippias Minor, Alcibiades I, Charmides, Protagoras, Euthydemus, Menexenus and Gorgias*.

1344 Cobb, William S. "The Argument of the *Protagoras*." *Dialogue*, 21 (1982), pp. 713-731.

Notes that no major logical errors can be imputed to Socrates, when, in the *Protagoras*, he endeavors to examine the nature and essential unity of virtue.

1345 Cobb, William S. "Plato's Treatment of Immortality in the *Phaedo*." *The Southern Journal of Philosophy*, 15 (1977), pp. 173-188.

Ref. 1184.

1346 Coby, Patrick. "The Education of a Sophist: Aspects of Plato's *Protagoras*." *Interpretation*, 10 (1982), pp. 139-158.

Examines the characterization of the Sophist given in the *Protagoras*, and discusses the limitations of Sophistical education. Reviews Protagoras' contention of being the first Sophist who is able to combine personal safety with a reputation for wisdom. Explains the Socratic proposal for reforming Sophistical education: a science which permits the Sophist to retain his fame but which does not bring harm to others.

1347 Coby, Patrick. "Politics and the Poetic Ideal in Shakespeare's the *Tempest*." *Political Theory*, 11 (1983), pp. 215-243.

Analyzes and discusses the *Tempest* through the lens of the *Republic* where Socrates calls for the banning of poets. Examines Socrates' position that poetry should be rejected because it is twice removed from the truth, and that by exaggerating the comic and the tragic, it breeds an exaggerated attachment to human affairs. Argues that Shakespeare in the *Tempest* likewise elevates philosophy over poetry, but that for him both philosophy and poetry belong in the 'cave of politics'.

1348 Cohen, S. Marc. "Socrates on the Definition of Piety: *Euthyphro* 10A-11B." *Socrates: A Collection of Critical Essays*. Edited by Gregory Vlastos. Notre Dame, Ind.: University of Notre Dame Press, 1980, pp. 158-176.

Reprinted from *The Journal of the History of Philosophy*, 9 (1971). Analyzes the central argument in the *Euthyphro* (10a-11b) in which piety is defined as "what all the gods love," and stresses the idea that the Socratic critique of Euthyphro's definition does not show that piety cannot be defined in terms of what the gods love, but proves that such a definition is unjustified, if we assume that the gods love what is pious *because* it is pious.

1349 Cohen, Maurice. "Dying as Supreme Opportunity: A Comparison of Plato's *Phaedo* and the *Tibetan Book of the Dead*." *Philosophy East and West*, 26 (1976), pp. 317-327.

Ref. 1185.

1350 Cooper, John. "The *Gorgias* and Irwin's Socrates." *The Review of Metaphysics*, 35 (1982), p. 577-587.

Discusses how T. Irwin treats the *Gorgias* as transitional between Socratic moral theory and the Platonic theory of the *Republic* and other middle dialogues, and argues that this approach leads Socrates to contradict himself over central points expressed in earlier dialogues. Ref. 628.

1351 Delcourt, M. "Socrate, Ion et la poésie." *Bulletin de l'Association Guillaume Budé*, 1937, pp.4-14.

Notes that Ion's simplicity has often been exaggerated by the commentators, and maintains that as he reveals himself to us, Ion is a man who is not acquainted with the dialectical games in which Socrates forces him to participate. Emphasizes the Sophistical nature of Socrates' attitude towards him.

1352 Devereux, Daniel T. "Courage and Wisdom in Plato's *Laches*." *The Journal of the History of Philosophy*, 15 (1977), pp. 129-141.

Interprets the *Laches* as a sustained critique of the Socratic definition of courage as a form of knowledge. Examines the various conceptions of courage given in the *Laches*, and concludes that Plato's aim is to show that courage cannot be conceived of as a simple kind of knowledge. Argues (against the view advanced by Vlastos) that Socrates' critique of Nicias' definition of courage should be taken at face value. Concludes that the early dialogues (like the *Laches*) should not be interpreted as mere expository or apologetic accounts of Socrates' views and activities. Ref. 1540.

1353 Devereux, Daniel T. "Nature and Teaching in Plato's *Meno*." *Phronesis*, 23 (1978), pp. 118-126.

Examines the passage in the *Meno* where Socrates argues that virtue cannot be taught, and deals with the issue of whether such a passage stands in contradiction with the Socratic conviction that virtue and knowledge are identical. Concludes that even though the passage in the *Meno* is to be taken seriously, it does not conflict with Socrates' view of virtue and knowledge. Argues that Socrates' statement that virtue cannot be taught is relevant only within the context of Sophistical teaching.

1354 Devereux, Daniel T. "Socrates' First City in the *Republic*." *Apeiron*, 11 (1979), pp. 36-40.

Examines the philosophical purpose of the First City in the *Republic*, the so-called 'pig-state'. Argues that standard interpretations fail to clarify certain puzzling features of the First City. Compares it with Glaucon's statements concerning the origin of justice. Regards Socrates' conception of the First City as an answer to Glaucon's views, and as a representation of the genesis of the Ideal State.

1355 Dorter, Kenneth. *Plato's Phaedo: An Interpretation.* Toronto: University of Toronto Press, 1982.

Develops a reinterpretation of the *Phaedo* and of Platonic philosophy in general. Suggests that two attitudes which are usually considered antithetical, the analytical and the dramatic, are really complementary. Ref. 1383.

1356 Dorter, Kenneth. "The Significance of the Speeches in Plato's *Symposium*." *Philosophy and Rhetoric*, 2 (1969), pp. 215-234.

Examines the various speeches on love presented in the *Symposium*, and notes that they are so structured that each one functions as a corrective of the previous one, and that in Socrates' speech all the preceding ones are incorporated and corrected.

1357 Dorter, Kenneth. "Socrates' Refutation of Thrasymachus and Treatment of Virtue." *Philosophy and Rhetoric*, 7 (1974), pp. 25-46.

Examines Book 1 of the *Republic*, and inquires into the reason why there are the three views of justice represented by Cephalus, Polemarchus and Thrasymachus, which Socrates refutes. Assumes Book 1 to be an integral and organic part of the *Republic*, and analyzes it, as well as Books 2 and 3, in an attempt to understand Socrates' account of justice given in Book 4. Concludes that if one were to understand adequately any one of the highest virtues (wisdom, justice and temperance), one would comprehend the others as well. Notes that by understanding their inner essences as perspectives of the *Good*, we can appreciate their underlying unity.

1358 Duncan, Roger. "Courage in Plato's *Protagoras*." *Phronesis*, 23 (1978), pp. 216-228.

Argues from a Platonic perspective that the question of the nature of courage is, from a Protagorean point of view, in serious trouble, appearing more like folly. Suggests that there is a subtle web that connects the dialogues, threads being drawn between the *Protagoras*, the *Symposium*, and the *Theaetetus*.

1359 Dunshirn, A. *Der Humor des Sokrates*. Doctoral dissertation. University of Vienna, 1982.

Ref. 750.

1360 Dyson, M. "Knowledge and Hedonism in Plato's *Protagoras*." *The Journal of Hellenic Studies*, 96 (1976), pp. 32-45.

Examines the details of *Protagoras* 355-358 and Plato's position with respect to hedonism. Contrasts Socrates' view of the weakness of will as ignorance with Socratic accounts of the issue given by Xenophon and Aristotle. Concludes that the Socratic critique of hedonism is based on the absence of appropriate objects of knowledge provided by a hedonistic ethics.

1361 Dyson, M. "Some Problems Concerning Knowledge in Plato's *Charmides*." *Phronesis*, (1974), pp. 102-111.

Focuses mainly on four passages in the *Charmides* and their interpretations: first, the formulation of the definition of temperance as knowledge of knowledge, and then three other passages which are concerned with the utility of this understanding of knowledge of knowledge.

1362 Eckstein, Jerome. *The Deathday of Socrates: Living, Dying and Immortality -- The Theater of Ideas in Plato's Phaedo.* Frenchtown, N. J.: Columbia Publishing Co., 1981.

Ref. 1191.

1363 Ferejohn, Michael T. "Socratic Virtue as the Parts of Itself." *Philosophy and Phenomenological Research*, 44 (1984), pp. 377-388.

Examines the Socratic question concerning the relationship between knowledge and virtue through the arguments of the *Protagoras* and the *Laches*.

1364 Fineberg, S. "Plato's *Euthyphro* and the Myth of Proteus." *Transactions and Proceedings of the American Philological Association*, 112 (1982), pp. 65-70.

Argues that Socrates' understanding of χάρις (as the basis of piety) should be taken in the sense of a gift of beauty which commands respect and admiration for itself, not for what it confers or accepts. Compares Socrates' 'battle' with Euthyphro with the contest between Menelaus and Proteus.

1365 Fox, Marvin. "The Trials of Socrates: An Interpretation of the First Tetralogy." *Archiv für Philosophie*, 6 (1956), pp. 226-261.

Argues that, regardless of their dates of composition, the *Euthyphro*, the *Apology*, the *Crito*, and the *Phaedo*, are meant to be read in that sequence. Observes that the *Apology*, the *Crito*, and the *Phaedo* furnish us with three 'levels' of Socrates' trial. Views the *Euthyphro* as a 'foil' for the other three dialogues, and notes that what Plato intended to show through the character of Euthyphro was the very opposite of Socrates' character.

1366 Frede, Dorothea. "The Impossibility of Perfection: Socrates'

Criticism of Simonides' Poem in the *Protagoras*." *The Review of Metaphysics*, 39 (1986), pp. 729-753.

Argues that the *Proto-Protagoras* was designed to be a problematic dialogue exploring the exact nature of virtue and its teachability, and that the serious interpretation of Simonides' poem was a later addition designed to emphasize the aporetic nature of the dialogue.

1367 Friedländer, Paul. *Die Platonischen Schriften, Erste Periode*. Berlin: W. de Gruyter & Co., 1957.

Examines and analyzes the Platonic dialogues, devoting individual chapters to each dialogue. Deals with the dialogues under four categories: (1) *Protagoras* and the main body of aporetic dialogues in search of a definition (*Laches*, *Thrasymachus* [*Republic*], *Charmides*, *Euthyphro*, *Lysis*, and *Hippias Major*); (2) smaller early dialogues (*Hipparchus*, *Ion*, *Hippias Minor*, *Theages*); (3) self-portrait and disguises of the philosopher (*Apology*, *Crito*, *Euthydemus*, *Cratylus*, and *Menexenus*); and (4) "the Logos takes a stand" (*Alcibiades I*, *Gorgias*, and *Meno*).

1368 Friedländer, Paul. *Plato: The Dialogues, First Period*. Translated by Hans Meyerhoff. New York: Pantheon Books, 1964.

English translation of *Die Platonischen Schriften, Erste Periode*.

1369 Friedman, Joel I. "Plato's *Euthyphro* and Leibniz' Law." *Philosophia*, 12 (1982), pp. 1-20.

Attempts to formalize Socrates' argument that the pious is not the same as what is loved by the gods. Interprets this argument as being expressed in object-language, and as using higher-order Leibnizian law. Concludes that the Socratic argument is fatally flawed, and that there is no way of reconstructing faithfully and validly that argument either in the object-language or in meta-language.

1370 Furley, William D. "The Figure of Euthyphro in Plato's Dialogue." *Phronesis*, 30 (1985), pp. 201-208.

Presents the character of Euthyphro as a hard-line and

conservative representative of traditional religiosity in Athens. Rejects the interpretation that sees him as a theological innovator. Emphasizes two contrasting aspects revealed by his encounter with Socrates: (1) Socrates' stand against Euthyphro at the time when the former is accused of having broken traditional religious customs, and (2) Socrates' superiority on religious thought as contrasted with Euthyphro's simplistic traditionalism.

1371 Gagarin, M. "The Purpose of Plato's *Protagoras*." *Transactions and Proceedings of the American Philological Association*, 100 (1969), pp. 133-164.

Presents a detailed analysis of the *Protagoras*, and concludes that Plato handles Protagoras with respect. Suggests that Protagoras and Socrates use different means to reach the same conclusions about the teachability of virtue. Discusses Socrates' progress beyond the Sophists.

1372 Gagarin, Michael. "Socrates' Hybris and Alcibiades' Failure." *Phoenix*, 31 (1977), pp. 22-37.

Argues that Plato portrays Socrates in certain respects as a failure in the *Symposium*, most directly as a failure of love. Focuses on Alcibiades' statement, usually ignored in favor of his praise of Socrates, that he has mixed criticism of Socrates -- admitting to Socrates' personal achievement, Alcibiades makes us understand that his personal success has set him apart from others, thus making him hybristic.

1373 Galli, Gallo. "Saggio sull' *Eutifrone* i Platone." *Estudios de la Filosofía en homenaje al Prof. R. Mondolfo*, Fasc. 1, Tucumán, 1957, pp. 169-189.

Discusses the general structure of the *Euthyphro*, and concludes that Plato's treatment of piety reveals an oscillation between the Socratic approach to the problem and his own philosophical convictions.

1374 Galli, Gallo. *Socrate ed alcuni dialoghi Platonici*. Turin: G. Giappiachelli, 1958.

Contains an introductory essay on the life and philosophy

of Socrates, with special emphasis on the complexity of the Socratic problem. Devotes individual chapters to an examination and analysis of the following dialogues: *Apology*, *Symposium*, *Laches*, *Euthyphro*, *Lysis*, and *Ion*.

1375 Gallop, David. "Justice and Holiness in *Protagoras* 330-331." *Phronesis*, 6 (1961), pp. 86-93.

Argues that a careful reading of *Protagoras* 330-331 leads to the conclusion that Socrates' argument does not upset in any significant way the initial thesis of Protagoras.

1376 Gallop, David. "The Socratic Paradox in the *Protagoras*." *Phronesis*, 9 (1964), pp. 117-129.

Argues that the Socratic contention that behavior which is recognized as the most pleasant is always preferable, involves the fallacy of begging the question, as soon as the predicate 'preferable' is changed into 'preferred'. Maintains that the Socratic change would be justified only if we assume that people actually act rationally. Claims that this latter thesis is never demonstrated by Socrates. Discusses in detail the logic of Socrates' demonstration with respect to the issue of whether the pleasant and the good are one and the same thing.

1377 Garland, William J. "Notes on Two Socratic Arguments in *Republic* 1." *Apeiron*, 10 (1976), pp. 11-13.

Examines two arguments developed by Socrates against Thrasymachus (*Republic* 2, 336b-347e): (1) in which it is argued that every art or skill has an interest which is distinguishable from the interests of those who practice that art; and (2) in which Socrates maintains that a craftsman (*e.g.*, a shepherd) exercises two distinct skills: he takes care of his flock as a shepherd, and he gets paid as a wage earner. Concludes that both arguments are misleading and unsound because (1) there is little sense in talking abstractly about the interest of an art, and (2) wage earning cannot be classified as a skill.

1378 Garrett, Roland. "The Structure of Plato's *Euthyphro*." *The Southern Journal of Philosophy*, 12 (1974), pp. 165-183.

Explores the relationship between motion and rest in the unfolding structure of the *Euthyphro*. Shows how Socrates attempts to move Euthyphro from a position of restlessness and mobility to one of rest and stability, that is, from a condition of wavering ideas to one of solidly established knowledge.

1379 Geach, P. "Plato's *Euthyphro*: Analysis and Commentary." *The Monist*, 50 (1966), pp. 369-382.

Examines the *Euthyphro* in general and maintains that as one analyzes Socrates' struggle to reach the correct definition of virtue (specifically piety), one assumes that the proper understanding of the definition is a necessary condition for the precise determination of what actions are virtuous (pious). Pays close attention to the issue of the validity of the arguments advanced by Euthyphro and Socrates, and observes that they are generally not well developed.

1380 Geffcken, Johannes. "Studien zu Platons *Gorgias*." *Hermes*, 65 (1930), pp. 14ff.

Examines the content and structure of the *Gorgias* against the background of the anti-Socratic literature exemplified by Polycrates' pamphlet. Accepts the authenticity of Polycrates' work (as this can be reconstructed from Libanius' *Apologia Socratis*), and observes that Polycrates' charge that Socrates' private vices must have been worse than his public ones should be read in the context provided by *Apology* 31c. Notes that Polycrates' accusations against the Socratics might have led to their banishment, had such accusations not been answered. Interprets Plato's *Gorgias* as an attempt to counterbalance Polycrates' pamphlet.

1381 Gobry, I. "La recontre de Phédon et Echécrate." *Diotima*, 11 (1983), pp. 67-75.

Discusses the meeting between Phaedo and Echecrates at the beginning of the *Phaedo*, and argues that the introduction of this meeting on Plato's part gives a clear indication of the real meaning of the *Phaedo*. Views this meaning as the replacement of Socratic philosophy by a Pythagorean ideology. Notes that from Plato's point of view, Socrates' thought appeared to be truncated and useless, its depth and intensity notwithstanding, and that through the agency of

Archytas of Tarentum (who was Echecrates' teacher), Plato learned to transcend the parameters of Socratism by the acceptance of Pythagorean ideas.

1382 Goldberg, Larry. *A Commentary on Plato's Protagoras.* New York: Peter Lang, 1984.

Taking its clue from the *Phaedrus* (275d-278e) and the Seventh Letter (7.344c-d), views the *Protagoras* as a union of the playful and the serious. States, as its prime concern, the relationship between word and deed -- what the characters say and how they act. Approaches its analysis through the apparent pitting of Protagoras and Socrates against each other, and examines their respective positions. Suggests that an implicit subject of the dialogue is how Sophistical ideas bear on legislation, and that the underlying discussion between Plato and Socrates is about what kind of discourse should be utilized.

1383 Gooch, Paul W. "Review of *Plato's Phaedo: An Interpretation* by Kenneth Dorter." *The Journal of the History of Philosophy*, 23 (1985), pp. 99-100.

Considers this a useful and interesting study and interpretation which offers much to think about and tests other interpretations. Finds Dorter's arguments for the non-immortality of the soul in the traditional Platonic sense provocative and challenging. Ref. 1355.

1384 Gottlieb, E. "Zum Problem des *Euthyphron*." *Archiv für Geschichte der Philosophie*, 37 (1925), pp. 270-279.

Notes that for Socrates and for Plato the basis of ethical values does not derive its substance from religious ideas, as is the case in Euthyphro's understanding of the relationship between ethics and religious belief.

1385 Grube, G. M. A. "On the Authenticity of the *Hippias Major*." *The Classical Quarterly*, 20 (1926), pp. 134-148.

Argues that in this dialogue we have the same Socrates as in the other dialogues, but because of Hippias' conceit, Socrates appears more rude than usual. Concludes that spuriousness need not be assumed because some arguments may appear sophistical. Provides extensive Greek quotations from the *Hippias Major*, as well as from other dialogues.

1386 Guardini, Romano. *Der Tod des Sokrates. Eine Interpretation der Platonischen Schriften et Euthyphron, Apologie, Kriton, und Phaidon.* Berlin: H. Küpper, 1943.

Ref. 88.

1387 Guardini, Romano. *La mort de Socrate. Interprétation des dialogues philosophiques, Euthyphron, Apologie, Criton, Phédon.* Translated by Paul Ricoeur. Paris: Edition du Seuil, 1956.

French translation of Guardini's *Der Tod des Sokrates.* Ref. 88.

1388 Guardini, Romano. *The Death of Socrates: An Interpretation of the Platonic Dialogues Euthyphro, Apology, Crito, and Phaedo.* Translated by Basil Wrignton. New York: Sheed and Ward, 1948.

English translation of Guardini's *Der Tod des Sokrates.* Dialogues translated by F. Church. Ref. 88.

1389 Gulley, Norman. "Socrates' Thesis at *Protagoras* 358B-C." *Phoenix*, 25 (1971), pp. 118-123.

Interprets Socrates' contention that no one does wrong willingly and knowingly as maintaining that when someone does wrong voluntarily, the agent believes (falsely) that he is doing what is right.

1390 Gulley, Norman. "Review of *Platonic Love* by Thomas Gould." *The Classical Review* 14 (1964), pp. 262-264.

Discusses Gould's presentation of the *Phaedo*. States that through the 'clear implication of the theory of Forms' we learn that *reality* is entirely good and thereby provides deeper meaning to the Socratic notion of 'desire for the good'. Examines Christian, Romantic and Freudian interpretations of love.

1391 Hackforth, Reginald. "The ἀνεξέταστος βίος." *The Classical Review*, 59 (1945), pp. 1-4.

Advances the view that in the *Republic*, as well as in the later dialogues, Plato did not move away from his attachment and commitment to the Socratic method, and to the principle (stated clearly in the *Apology*), that the unexamined life is not worth living.

1392 Hackforth, Reginald. "Hedonism in Plato's *Protagoras*." *The Classical Quarterly*, 22 (1928), pp. 39-42.

Argues that the doctrine of hedonism advanced by Socrates in the *Protagoras* should be understood as having been meant in earnest and not ironically. Defends this interpretation by calling attention to the way in which Socrates compels Protagoras to agree with him, and to the manner in which Socrates forces his idea on the many who do not accept it initially. Suggests that the hedonistic position attributed by Plato to Socrates is a philosophical device through which Plato sought to resolve adequately the issues raised by Socrates in other contexts.

1393 Haden, James. "Friendship in Plato's *Lysis*." *The Review of Metaphysics*, 37 (1983), pp. 327-356.

Outlines a method of interpreting the earlier (Socratic) Platonic dialogues, and illustrates that method by an analysis of the *Lysis*. Explains the method in terms of Plato's choice of certain images which facilitate the adequate grasp of the concepts under examination. Claims that on this basis many of the confusions and disputes over the earlier dialogues can be resolved.

1394 Haden, James. "On Plato's Inconclusiveness." *The Classical Journal*, 44 (1969), pp. 219-224.

Suggests that although at the end of the *Euthyphro* we are back where we started from, Socrates has demonstrated that the path to truth should be pursued along the lines continuously rejected by Euthyphro.

1395 Hall, John C. "Plato: *Euthyphro* 10A1-11A10." *The Philosophical Quarterly*, 18 (1968), pp. 1-15.

Considers this passage the central argument of one of the 'weightiest' of the early Platonic dialogues, vital for an understanding of the relationship between religion and ethical knowledge as Plato understood it to be, and vital because it introduces the important terms πάθος and οὐσία.

1396 Hall, Robert W. "Techne and Morality in the *Gorgias*." *Essays in Ancient Greek Philosophy*. Albany: State University of New York Press, 1971, pp. 202-218.

Analyzes the *Gorgias* and concludes that it goes beyond the ethical doctrines of the earlier dialogues in which a *techne*-influenced ethic, based upon a standard of utilitarianism, is pursued. Argues that the *Gorgias* suggests a concept of inherent value by introducing a cosmic ordering principle which is the sustaining cause and source of all values, foreshadowing the Form of the Good, and presents Socrates as espousing a philosophical way of life apart from politics.

1397 Hammond, A. L. "*Euthyphro*, Mill and Mr. Lewis." *The Journal of Philosophy*, 49 (1952), pp. 377-392.

Examines the logical structure of the *Euthyphro*, with emphasis on its implications for ethics. Uses its conclusions as a basis for developing a critique of the ethical ideas of Mill, Dewey, and Lewis.

1398 Harrison, E. L. "Was Gorgias a Sophist?" *Phoenix*, 18 (1964), pp. 183-192.

Examines the *Apology*, the *Hippias Minor*, the *Protagoras*, and the *Gorgias* for Socrates' references and responses to Gorgias and Sophistry. Concludes that Gorgias was not a Sophist, but a person skilled in the art of rhetoric who could impart it to others or exercise it in the law courts of Athens.

1399 Henderson, T. Y. "In Defense of Thrasymachus." *The American Philosophical Quarterly*, 7 (1970), pp. 218-228.

Offers an interpretation of Thrasymachus' definition of justice in Book 1 of the *Republic*, and shows that his definition is internally consistent. Argues that Socrates' arguments to refute Thrasymachus are inadequate.

1400 Hiestand, Max. *Das sokratische Nichtwissen in Platons ersten Dialogen*. Zurich: Verlag Seldwyla. 1923.

Examines the sources, meaning, and implications of Socrates' confession of ignorance and of his refusal to come to any substantial conclusions about the meaning of ethical terms. Examines the following dialogues: *Ion*, *Hippias Minor*, *Laches*, *Charmides*, *Euthyphro*, and *Apology*.

1401 Hinrichs, G. "The *Euthydemus* as the Locus of the Socratic Elenchus." *The New Scholasticism*, 25 (1951), pp. 178-183.

Develops a negative critique of R. Robinson's *Plato's Earlier Dialectic*. Ref. 663.

1402 Hoerber, Robert G. "Plato's *Euthyphro*." Phronesis, 3 (1958), pp. 95-107.

Gives a general analysis of the dialogue. Views Socrates' argument as a 'straw-man' argument, which incorporates il-logical reasoning. Discusses the relationship between Euthyphro's idea of religion and the ideas of his contem-poraries, and comments on the historical basis for the sort of juridical basis discussed in the dialogue. Stresses the intimate relationship between the *Apology* and the *Euthy-phro*.

1403 Hoerber, Robert G. "Plato's *Laches*." *Classical Philology*, 63 (1968), pp. 95-105.

Examines how dramatic techniques are intertwined with the philosophical development of the meaning of 'courage', and offers clues to Plato's general philosophic perspective.

1404 Hogan, Richard. "Review of *Plato's Moral Theory: The Early and Middle Dialogues* by Terence Irwin." *The Journal of the History of Philosophy*, 19 (1981), pp. 103-105.

Considers Irwin's work an important contribution to the literature, presenting provocative interpretations which challenge the traditional explanations. Ref. 628.

1405 Hoopes, J. P. "Euthyphro's Case." *The Classical Bulletin*, 47 (1970), pp. 1-6.

Examines Euthyphro's arguments against his father, and concludes that it is Euthyphro who is impious, not Socrates. Concludes that Socrates represents the true paradigm of piety.

1406 Hornsby, R. "Significant Action in the *Symposium*." *The Classical Journal*, 52 (1956), pp. 37-40.

Comments on the dramatic structure of the *Symposium*, and explores the significance of Socrates' speech concerning his debt to Diotima.

1407 Hubbard, B. A. F. and Karnofsky, E. S. *Plato's Protagoras: A Socratic Commentary*. Chicago: The University of Chicago Press, 1982.

Examines the *Protagoras* and the use of the Socratic *elenchus* as this is directed to the concepts of virtue and wisdom.

1408 Huby, Pamela. *Plato and Modern Morality*. London: Macmillan, 1972.

Presents the position that those dialogues written shortly after the death of Socrates probably reflect his opinions fairly faithfully, and that as time went on Plato put more and more of his ideas into the mouth of Socrates.

1409 Humbert, J. "Le pamphlet de Polycrates et le *Gorgias* de Platon." *Revue de Philologie*, 5 (1931), pp. 20-77.

Argues that the *Gorgias* was written *after* Polycrates' Κατηγορία, and allows for the possibility of the former having been intended as a rebuttal of the latter. Detects the influence of Gorgias on Polycrates. Concludes that Polycrates' denunciation of Socrates is based on five interrelated allegations: (1) that Socrates taught young men to despise their parents and elders; (2) that Socrates chose to quote the most perverse and immoral lines from the poets; (3) that Socrates despised and taught others to despise the laws and institutions of the polity; (4) that he was given to idleness and political apathy, and taught others to imitate him; and (5) that he misled Alcibiades and Critias.

1410 Humbert, J. *Polycrates, l'Accusation de Socrate et le Gorgias.* Paris: 1930.

Examines the content of Polycrates' indictment of Socrates as this can be reconstructed from the testimony of Libanius. Argues that the *Gorgias* could be construed as a rebuttal to Polycrates' indictment. Ref. 158.

1411 Hyland, Drew A. *The Virtue of Philosophy: An Interpretation of Plato's Charmides.* Athens, Ohio: Ohio University Press, 1981.

Discusses the significance of the *Charmides'* treatment of σωφροσύνη, with special emphasis on its implications for the problem of self-knowledge.

1412 Ikushima, K. "An Analysis of the Dispute Between Thrasymachus and Socrates in Book A of Plato's *Republic.*" *The Journal of Classical Studies*, 13 (1965), pp. 87-97.

In Japanese with an English abstract. Reviews the discussion between Thrasymachus and Socrates against the background of Polemarchus' definition of justice. Notes that whereas Thrasymachus views human life as a war of all against all, Socrates extends the concept of justice advanced by Polemarchus, in order to erase the line which separates friends from enemies.

1413 Irwin, Terence. "Coercion and Objectivity in Plato's Dialectic." *Revue Internationale de Philosophie*," 40 (1986), pp. 49-74.

Examines the use of argument in the *Gorgias*, and notes that Plato was able to effect a meaningful transition from conversational argument to compelling argument, without falling into the temptation of creating a coercive argument. Notes that Plato's success stems from the fact that the rational compulsion of his arguments is derived from the qualities of his opponents. Ref. 1469.

1414 Jeffrey, Andrew. "Polemarchus and Socrates on Justice and Harm." *Phronesis*, 24 (1979), pp. 54-69.

Examines various interpretations of βλάπτειν in regard to Polemarchus' defense of the position that the just person is one who helps his friends and harms his enemies.

1415 Kahn, Charles H. "The Beautiful and the Genuine." *Oxford Studies in Ancient Philosophy*. Edited by Julia Annas. Oxford: The Clarendon Press, 1985 (4 vols.), Vol. 3, pp. 261-287.

Presents a discussion of *Plato, Hippias Major* by Paul Woodruff. Considers this a lively translation with a commentary which goes beyond the question of authenticity, (Kahn disagreeing with Woodruff's position that the *Hippias Major* is an authentic dialogue), and which makes important contributions to our understanding of Socrates' quest for definition. Ref. 1556.

1416 Kahn, Charles H. "Drama and Dialectic in Plato's *Gorgias*." *Oxford Studies in Ancient Philosophy*. Edited by Julia Annas. Oxford: The Clarendon Press, 1983 (4 vols.), Vol. 1, pp. 75-121.

Argues that the three arguments with Gorgias, Callicles and Polus are in a 'deep sense' *ad hominem*, being directed not only against the statements of the three, but against them as men, critically examining their lives.

1417 Kahn, Charles H. "Plato's Methodology in the *Laches*." *Revue Internationale de Philosophie*, 40 (1986), pp. 7-21.

Argues that the *Laches* functions as an introduction for a series of dialogues which deal with the concept of virtue. Views the *Laches* as a transition point between Plato's use of the dialogue form as a device and its use as a literary genre.

1418 Kauffman, Charles. "Enactment as Argument in the *Gorgias*." *Philosophy and Rhetoric*, 12 (1979), pp. 114-129.

Argues that although it is usually inferred that Socrates and Plato have nothing but disdain for rhetoric, there are references in the *Gorgias* which seem to suggest the possibility of an ideal and legitimate rhetoric. Reinterprets the *Gorgias* as an effort to resolve the apparent riddle which centers on the nature, scope, and function of rhetoric in the πόλις. Concludes that Socrates emerges not as the victorious protagonist, but as a tragic figure unable to recognize his own shortcomings. Notes that the Socrates of the *Gorgias* is merely a literary character invented by Plato to serve his own purposes.

1419 Kerferd, G. B. "The Doctrine of Thrasymachus in Plato's *Republic.*" *The Durham University Journal*, 40 (1947-1948), pp. 19-27.

Reviews the dialogue between Socrates and Thrasymachus in the *Republic*, and regards as unlikely the idea that it (along with the conversations with Cephalus and Polemarchus) could have been an initially independent dialogue from the rest of the *Republic*. Assumes a degree of historicity concerning Thrasymachus' views as reported by Plato, and argues for a certain continuity between his initial position and the eventual set of ideas which Socrates compels him to state.

1420 Kerferd, G. B. "Protagoras' Doctrine of Justice and Virtue in the *Protagoras* of Plato." *The Journal of Hellenic Studies*, 73 (1953), pp. 42-45.

Argues that because Protagoras has not made clear what he means by virtue, and that the common understanding holds that for Socrates it is impossible to determine whether virtue is teachable or not until an understanding of its nature is achieved, a vagueness remains, which points to confusion in the mind of Protagoras. Notes, however, that Protagoras' reply to Socrates is generally consistent.

1421 Kirwan, C. "Glaucon's Challenge." *Phronesis*, 10 (1965), pp. 102-173.

Maintains that Socrates succeeds in satisfying the demand imposed on him by Glaucon and Adeimantus in the early sections of the *Republic*, that demand being to demonstrate that justice is pleasant in itself and that its results are always pleasant.

1422 Klonoski, Richard J. "Setting and Characterization in Plato's *Euthyphro*." *Diálogos*, 19 (1984), pp. 123-140.

Argues that a close examination of the dramatic setting of the *Euthyphro*, and an adequate understanding of Euthyphro, allow us to appreciate Plato's purpose in writing the dialogue, its purpose being to develop a critique of the atmosphere of religious decay that occurred in Athens in and around the time of Socrates' trial.

1423 Klosko, George. "On the Analysis of *Protagoras* 351B-360E." *Phoenix*, 34 (1980), pp. 307-322.

Notes that the basis of Socrates' view of *akrasia* in the *Protagoras* is an egoistical interpretation of human behavior.

1424 Klosko, George. "The Refutation of Callicles in Plato's *Gorgias*." *Greece and Rome*, 31 (1984), pp. 126-139.

Explores Callicles' speech on immoralism (482c-484c) and the arguments employed by Socrates in order to refute him. Argues that Callicles is made to defend a position of extreme hedonism in order to allow Socrates to deal with hedonism in an effective manner.

1425 Klosko, George. "The Technical Conception of Virtue." *The Journal of the History of Philosophy*, 19 (1981), pp. 95-102.

Examines T. Irwin's *Plato's Moral Theory: The Early and Middle Dialogues*, focusing on his position that Socrates holds a technical conception of virtue ("Happiness is a determinate end to which virtue prescribes instrumental means"). Argues that the evidence does not support this interpretation. Concludes that Irwin fails to address serious issues, such as Plato's relationship to Socrates, and that although the book is ingenious, its arguments are not convincing. Ref. 628.

1426 Kosman, L. A. "*Charmides'* First Definition: Sophrosyne as Quietness." *Essays in Ancient Greek Philosophy*. Albany: State University of New York Press, 1983 (2 vols.), Vol. 2, pp. 174-185.

Examines the arguments and structure of the *Charmides*, and compares it with the *Laches*, focusing on the dialectic. Suggests an understanding of *sophrosyne* as "a virtue of self without self ... the wisdom of self-mastery in which wisdom, self, and mastery vanish, and what remains is the quiet, orderly effortless grace of skilled living," a perspective similar to Zen Buddhism.

1427 Kostman, James. "Socrates' Self-Betrayal and the 'Contradiction' Between the *Apology* and the *Crito*. *New Essays on Socrates*. Edited by Eugene Kelly. Lanham, Md.: University Press of America, 1984, pp. 107-130.

Examines the various reasons given by Socrates in the *Crito* for not escaping, and assesses the value and import of such reasons in the light of Socrates' announcement in his trial that he would be prepared to disobey the laws if he were ordered to desist from pursuing philosophy (*Apology* 29b-30c). Argues that the *Crito* proves to be a piece of philosophical fiction, and that the actual reasons for Socrates' acceptance of the death penalty can be found in Xenophon's *Apology* rather than in the *Crito*. Criticizes Woozley for his contention that Socrates would have obeyed an order to stop philosophizing. Criticizes Santas' and Vlastos' interpretations of the *Crito*. Ref. 1297, 1303, 1303a.

1428 LaDrière, Craig. "The Problem of Plato's *Ion*." *The Journal of Aesthetics and Art Criticism*, 10 (1951), pp. 26-37.

Argues that the fundamental Socratic stance throughout the *Ion* should not be construed as an attack against poetry, but as a severe critique of the art of literary criticism.

1429 Laguna, Théodore de. "The Problem of the *Laches*." *Mind*, 43 (1934), pp. 170-180.

Maintains that the *Laches* contains a polemic directed by Plato against Antisthenes and other Socratics who did not quite understand (from Plato's point of view) the Socratic thesis of the identity between knowledge and virtue. Sees an indication of this polemic in the fact that it is Nicias who argues Socrates' idea badly.

1430 Lesses, Glenn. *Desire and Motivation in Plato: Issues in the Psychology of the Early Dialogues and the Republic.* Doctoral dissertation. Indiana University, 1980.

Examines the accounts of desire to which Socrates and Plato appeal, and emphasizes the idea of moral behavior as a rational activity which underlies their moral psychology. Studies the chronology of Plato's dialogues. Develops its major themes on the thesis that for Socrates and Plato virtue is a craft which is both cognitive and affective. Observes that for Socrates all desire is belief about what is good. Argues against the idea that Plato rejected the Socratic interpretation of desire and its role in motivation.

1431 Levi, Adolfo. "La teoria della *philia* nel *Liside*." *Giornale di Metafisica*, 5 (1950), pp. 285-296.

Views the *Lysis* as standing between the *Symposium* and the *Republic*. Attempts to distinguish certain Platonic elements in the *Lysis* from those that are clearly attributable to Socrates.

1432 Levin, Donald Norman. "Some Observations Concerning Plato's *Lysis*." *Essays in Ancient Greek Philosophy.* Albany: State University of New York Press, 1971, pp. 236-258.

Attempts to demonstrate that the *Lysis* does not deal with questions concerning the nature of friendship in general, but with the essence of 'being a friend'. Concludes that the argument yields more than negative results, although the theory of reciprocity, as this is related to the issue of friendship, is abandoned.

1433 Lledó, Iñigo E. "La estructura dialéctica del Eutifrón platónico." Revista de Filosofía, 17 (1958), pp. 363-393.

Notes that even though the *Euthyphro* does not resolve any one of the various problems and issues it raises, it contains references and allusions to some of the most important ideas developed by Plato in later dialogues.

1434 Luce, J. V. "Plato, *Phaedo* 67C5." *The Classical Review*, 1 (1951), pp. 66-67.

Disagrees with Burnet's interpretation and translation, and concludes that his conjecture that Platonic thought is indebted to an Orphic prototype is unjustified. Ref. 117.

1435 Lycos, Kimon. *Plato on Justice and Power: Reading Book I of Plato's Republic*. Albany, N.Y.: State University of New York Press, 1987.

Develops as its main initial theme the idea that the function of the first book of the *Republic* is to show that justice, far from being an external possession to the soul, is an internal condition which requires discrimination and virtue. Views the introductory arguments of the *Republic* as essential to the entire work. Contains two parts: the dramatic characterization of the *Republic* (with emphasis on the presence of Thrasymachus), and a detailed analysis of the arguments. Concludes with a chapter, "The Socratic Vision," which reviews Socrates' concept of justice.

1436 Magalhães-Vilhena, V. de. "Le Socrate de *Gorgias* et l'action politique." *L'Information Littéraire*, 6 (1954), pp. 109-113.

Maintains that the evidence of the *Gorgias* leads us to conclude that Plato was not willing to abandon politics, and that he envisioned the necessity of becoming engaged in political activity by means other than direct political undertakings.

1437 Maguire, Joseph P. "Protagoras or Plato: II, the *Protagoras*." *Phronesis*, 22 (1977), pp. 103-122.

Examines the concepts of self-restraint and justice as these are employed in the first third of the *Protagoras* (to 328d). Reviews Socrates' ability to manipulate a moral formula advanced by Protagoras into a concept of moral virtue. Claims that the dramatic Protagoras is basically unrelated to the historical Protagoras.

1438 Maguire, Joseph P. "Thrasymachus -- or Plato?" *Phronesis*, 16 (1971), pp. 142-163.

Reviews the exchange between Socrates and Thrasymachus, and raises the question of whether Plato may have manipulated Thrasymachus' initial position in order to suit his own purposes.

1439 Manasse, E. M. "A Thematic Interpretation of Plato's *Apology* and *Crito*." *Philosophy and Phenomenological Research*, 40 (1980), pp. 393-400.

Reviews Luis Noussan-Lettry's *Spekulative Denken in Platons Fruhschriften: Apologie und Kriton*, in which the *Apology* and the *Crito* are understood not as historical documents but as philosophical pieces which are centered around a single thought: the πρᾶγμα of Socrates. Concludes that in spite of certain deficiences, Noussan-Lettry's analysis constitutes an original and enlightening approach.

1440 Mann, Oscar. *Quid censuerit Socrates de amicitia*. Rostochii: C. Boldt, 1873.

Offers an inaugural dissertation on Socrates' idea of friendship, basing itself mostly on Plato's *Lysis*.

1441 Martens, Ekkehard. *Das selbstbezügliche Wissen in Platons Charmides*. Munich: Carl Hanser Verlag, 1973.

Presents a detailed analysis of the arguments of the *Charmides* as they relate to the other dialogues of the Platonic corpus. Contains extensive notes and a detailed index of name references.

1442 Masaracchia, A. "Il *Carmide* di Platone." *Maia*, 3 (1959), pp. 161-180.

Views the *Charmides* as the bridge that links Socrates' concept of philosophy to Plato's own philosophy of life.

1443 McPherran, Mark L. "Socratic Piety in the *Euthyphro*." *The Journal of the History of Philosophy*, 23 (1985), pp. 283-309.

Compares two traditions, the constructivist, which considers the *Euthyphro* a positive Socratic doctrine on the nature of piety, and the anticonstructivist, which considers it merely a peirastic inquiry. Argues for a 'cautiously constructive' view which is consistent with the historical Socrates. Concludes that Socrates' methodological skepticism emerges as an expression of piety, more sincere than traditional Greek god-related piety.

1444 McTighe, Kevin. "Socrates on Desire for the Good and the Involuntariness of Wrongdoing: *Gorgias* 466A-468E." *Phronesis*, 29 (1984), pp. 193-236.

Examines the Socratic paradox that no one is voluntarily unjust. Argues that the paradox does not depend on the notion of desire as it emerges from this section of the *Gorgias* (*i.e.*, that no agent can desire or will to perform *X* if *X* is unjust or harmful), but that it depends upon the notion that all persons desire the apparent good -- what they conceive to be good for themselves.

1445 Mercant, Sebastián T. "Platón y una gramática del poder." *Pensamiento*, 37 (1981), pp. 287-312.

Discusses the issue raised in the *Gorgias*, namely, whether those who possess the command of language can also possess absolute political power. Reviews Socrates' answer to this question, and outlines what it calls 'the politics of language'. Concludes with comments on Socrates' 'language of philosophy', whose function is not the manipulation of the masses as in the case of the language of politics, but the clarification of the truth.

1446 Michaelides-Nouaros, Georges. "Une nouvelle évaluation du dialogue entre Thrasymaque et Socrate." Πρακτικὰ τῆς Ἀκαδημίας Ἀθηνῶν, 53 (1978), pp. 117-137.

In modern Greek, with a French summary. Discusses the dialogue between Socrates and Thrasymachus (*Republic* 1), and concludes that while Thrasymachus views political reality from the standpoint of a sociologist whose pessimism is justified by the actualities of the political world, Socrates approaches the issue from the vantage point of an optimistic philosopher who believes in the moral function of the State. Argues that the chief flaw of Thrasymachus' position is found in its exclusive attention to the elements of political power, and in its neglect of an element which would involve the ideological legitimation of political authority.

1447 Mignosi, P. "L'ascetismo di Eutifrone." *Rivista d'Italia*, 28 (1925), pp. 1122-1133.

Argues that Greek culture was moved by two fundamentally opposed forces, namely, rationalism and religious faith, and that these forces are personified in Socrates and Euthyphro. Emphasizes the impossibility of building a meaningful bridge between them, something that explains Plato's inability to bring the *Euthyphro* to a satisfactory conclusion.

1448 Miller, Clyde Lee. "The Prometheus Story in Plato's *Protagoras*." *Interpretation*, 7 (1978), pp. 22-32.

Analyzes the story of Prometheus, Epimetheus, and Zeus which Socrates hears from Protagoras (*Protagoras* 320c-322d). Comments on the dramatic roles played by Socrates and Protagoras, and appeals to the story in order to make better sense of such roles. Recognizes the significance of the story in the endeavor to understand the issue of political and moral virtue which is the controversy that engages Socrates and Protagoras.

1449 Miller, Clyde Lee. "Two Midpoints in Plato's *Protagoras*." *The Modern Schoolman*, 55 (1977), pp. 71-79.

Examines the dramatic interaction of the participants of the *Protagoras*, principally Socrates and Protagoras. Distinguishes as the first midpoint (335c) the moment when Socrates is about to leave the scene (after having revealed to Hippocrates the norms which measure Protagoras' activity as a teacher). Argues that the second midpoint (338c) resolves the impasse between Socrates and Protagoras, and allows the conversation to proceed on the terms proposed by Socrates.

1450 Moreau, J. "La Paradoxe Socratique." *Revue de Théologie et Philosophie*, 110 (1978), pp. 269-279.

Explains Socrates' contention in the *Protagoras* that no one does wrong willingly as an entailment from utilitarian considerations. Discusses the Socratic position from the point of view of a distinction between 'formal will' (the will that aims at the supreme good) and the will that chooses particular goods. Relates Socrates' view to those defended by Malebranche and Maurice Blondel.

1451 Morgan, Michael L. "The Continuity Theory of Reality in Plato's *Hippias Major*." *The Journal of the History of Philosophy*, 21 (1983), pp. 133-158.

Attempts to test the scope of Socrates' and Plato's metaphysical convictions as they emerge in the dialogue. Concludes that the theory of properties, parts and wholes is one which Socrates holds and which will be developed further by Plato in succeeding dialogues. Focuses on the Socratic *elenchus* and how it is used to explore the question, "What is beautiful?"

1452 Moulinier, L. "Socrate devant Protagoras." *Annales de la Faculté des Lettres et Sciences Humaines d'Aix*, 39 (1965), pp. 101-125.

Examines the confrontation between Socrates and Protagoras in the *Protagoras*, and views the Socratic contention concerning the impossibility of teaching virtue as the central issue of the debate. Includes a brief sketch of Protagoras' philosophical position.

1453 Moutafakis, Nicholas J. "Plato's Emergence in the *Euthyphro*." *The Journal of Critical Analysis*, 2 (1970), pp. 35-42.

Argues that the *Euthyphro* reflects an early manifestation of Plato's later thought. Questions the ordinarily accepted sequence, *Euthyphro-Apology-Crito*. Shows that the Greek text of the *Euthyphro* contains a mode of locution which suggests that the theory of Ideas is beginning to be expressed.

1454 Mulhern, J. J. "τρόπος and πολυτροπία in Plato's *Hippias Minor*." *Phoenix*, 22 (1968), pp. 283-288.

Discusses the subtle and paradoxical use of these terms in the complex arguments of the dialogue.

1455 Murphy, N. R. "The δεύτερος πλοῦς in the *Phaedo*." *The Classical Quarterly*, 30 (1936), pp. 40-47.

Presents an analysis of the meaning of *Phaedo* 99-107 including a paraphrase of the Greek text. Gives a linguistic analysis of the text in the first section, and deals in the second section with the general doctrine.

1456 Nehamas, Alexander. "Meno's Paradox and Socrates as a Teacher." *Oxford Studies in Ancient Philosophy*. Edited by Julia Annas. Oxford: Clarendon Press, 1985 (4 vols.), Vol. 3, pp. 1-30.

Argues that Plato took very seriously the paradox of *Meno* 80d, where Meno argues that all learning is impossible, as is evidenced from the development of Plato's own arguments.

1457 Neumann, Harry. "Diotima's Concept of Love." *The American Journal of Philology*, 86 (1965), pp. 33-59.

Maintains that there is a wide gap between Diotima's speech in the *Symposium* and Socrates' own concept of human immortality. Notes that it is not possible to ascertain whether the actual ideas of Plato agree with those of Socrates or those attributed to Diotima.

1458 Neumann, Harry. "On the Comedy of Plato's Aristophanes." *The American Journal of Philology*, 87 (1966), pp. 420-429.

Examines various components of Aristophanes' speech in the *Symposium*, and notes that from Diotima's perspective, such elements would have only been regarded as examples of comic rhetoric.

1459 Neumann, Harry. "The Problem of Piety in Plato's *Euthyphro*." *The Modern Schoolman*, 43 (1966), pp. 265-272.

Establishes a relationship between Euthyphro's personality and his belief in personal gods, and between this belief and his self-oriented concept of piety. Compares Euthyphro's notion of piety with Socrates' rational and impersonal way of dealing with this notion.

1460 Nichols, Mary P. "The *Republic's* Two Alternatives: Philosopher-Kings and Socrates." *Political Theory*, 12 (1984), pp. 252-274.

Comments that although Plato clearly believes that philosophy is the best way of life, he never tells us directly what is the meaning of philosophy. Regards the education of Plato's philosopher-kings as mathematical training which prepares them to rule over a communistic society in which ordinary citizens are treated as numbers, as if these were equal persons possessing no distinctive characteristics or needs. Argues that Plato implicitly contrasts the philosopher-kings with Socrates, for whom the complexity of each human life, rather than its simplicity, was the object of his inquiries. Concludes that Socratic philosophy is nurtured by the passions and attitudes of individuals; it is erotic and encourages questions, not control. Represents Socratic political philosophy as an alternative to the sort of intellectual tyranny entailed by the *Republic*.

1461 O'Brien, D. "A Metaphor in Plato: 'Running Away' and 'Staying Behind' in the *Phaedo* and the *Timaeus*." *The Classical Quarterly*, 27 (1977), pp. 297-299.

Ref. 1211.

1462 O'Brien, D. "The Last Argument of Plato's *Phaedo*. I." *The Classical Quarterly*, 17 (1967), pp. 198-231.

Ref. 1212.

1463 O'Brien, D. "The Last Argument of Plato's *Phaedo*. II." *The Classical Quarterly*, 18 (1968), pp. 95-106.

Ref. 1213.

1464 O'Brien, Michael J. "The 'Fallacy' in *Protagoras* 349-350C." *Transactions and Proceedings of the American Philological Association*, 92 (1961), pp. 408-417.

Argues that in the passage of the *Protagoras* under discussion, it is unreasonable to accuse Socrates of using unsound reasoning.

1465 O'Brien, Michael J. "The Unity of the *Laches*. *Essays in Ancient Greek Philosophy*. Albany: State University of New

York Press, 1971, pp. 303-315.

Presents an analysis of the *Laches*, and concludes that it is a balanced work of art, the cornerstone of its construction being the interplay between the Greek opposition of word and deed, or claim versus fact, an ingrained feature of Greek literary style before Plato.

1466 Perelman, Chaim. *The Realm of Rhetoric*. Translated by William Kluback. Notre Dame, Ind.: University of Notre Dame Press, 1982, pp. 185.

Emphasizes the distinguishing characteristics of Socratic irony by reference to the *Gorgias*. Suggests that Socrates, by verifying the explicit agreement of his interlocutor, can move on in the dialogue and lead his opponent into a contradiction. Concludes that the dialectic enables Socrates to reveal the internal inconsistencies of his opponents' opinions.

1467 Plochmann, G. K. "Socrates, the Stranger from Elea, and Some Others." *Classical Philology*, 49 (1954), pp. 223-231.

Comments on the roles and functions of Socrates (as a character in Plato's dialogues), and of other Platonic characters as vehicles through which Plato gave expression to the development of dialectical ideas.

1468 Preiswerk, R. *Neue philologische Untersuchungen zum 1. Buch des platonischen Staates*. Freiburg, Switzerland, 1939.

Ref. 658.

1469 Principe, Michael A. "Restraint of Desire in the *Gorgias*." *The Southern Journal of Philosophy*, 20 (1982)

Challenges T. Irwin's claim that the Socrates of the *Gorgias* is guilty of a serious inconsistency because he represents the position that knowledge is sufficient for virtue (the craft analogy), and that Socrates later presents arguments to the contrary. Ref. 1413.

1470 Rabinowitz, W. Gerson. "Platonic Piety: An Essay Towards the

Solution of an Enigma." *Phronesis*, 3 (1958), pp. 108-120.

Examines Socrates' treatment of the concept of piety in the *Euthyphro*, and concludes that the Socratic search is directed towards a notion of piety in which the gods are ultimately identified with mind (the apprehension of the Ideal Forms). Calls attention to the 'monstrousness' of the Athenians' condemnation of Socrates in view of the fact that he was a man who practiced true piety all his life.

1471 Race, William H. "Shame in Plato's *Gorgias*." *The Classical Journal*, 74 (1979), pp. 197-202.

Analyzes the various references to shame in the dialogue, and concludes that it does not consist in ignominious treatment by the powerful, for they are not powerful: it consists in ignorance in thinking that one knows when one does not know. Notes that Callicles typifies the shamelessness of the ignorant person.

1472 Reeve, M. D. "Socrates' Reply to Cebes in Plato's *Phaedo*." *Phronesis*, 20 (1975), pp. 199-208.

Maintains that Plato's argument in *Phaedo* 103c contains two fallacies correctly identified by D. Keyt, and that the objections raised by J. Schiller and H. Erbse are not well founded. Adds that Schiller and Erbse are mistaken in their acceptance of G. M. A. Grube's interpretation of *Phaedo* 104d.

1473 Rembert, Ronald B. *The Socratic Method in the Lysis, Meno and Gorgias: A Pedagogical Interpretation and Its Implications.* Doctoral dissertation. Emory University, 1950.

Argues that the typical portrayal of the Socratic *elenchus* as a single method accounts only for the interaction on the philosophical level where Socrates cross-examines his interlocutors for refutational purposes. Adds that that is not the only level upon which Socrates interacts: he engages people on the personal and pedagogical levels. Examines the interpretations of the Socratic method offered by R. Robinson, G. Vlastos, and J. Stenzel. Highlights major features of the Socratic method: the notion of philosophy as practice, friendship, truth and understanding, and the perfection of the soul. Examines the

*Lysis*, the *Meno*, and the *Gorgias* as dramatic contexts where the *elenchus* is developed. Ref. 984, 1012, 1028, 1029.

1474 Rendall, Steven. "Dialogue, Philosophy, and Rhetoric: The Example of Plato's *Gorgias*." *Philosophy and Rhetoric*, 10 (1977), pp. 165-179.

Regards the dialogue form as the ideal vehicle for Plato's concept of the philosophical activity as situational and rhetorical. Reviews the *Gorgias*, and discusses its conditions and aims, and its usefulness in resolving the Socratic-Platonic uneasiness with the written word. Examines the relationship between Plato's use of the dialogue form and the later history of the employment of this form.

1475 Ricci, Marcello. *Socrate, padre del nichilismo. Struttura logica e significato teoretico del discorsa socratico.* L'Aquila, Italy: L. U. Japadre Editore, 1971.

Discusses two groups of Socratic dialogues: (1) *Euthyphro*, *Charmides*, *Lysis*, *Republic I*, *Hippias Major*, and *Laches*; and (2) *Protagoras*, *Hippias Minor*, *Alcibiades I*, and *Apology*. Contains an appendix which gives a brief summary statement of the present state of the Socratic problem, and which reviews the ideas of some contemporary Socratic scholars.

1476 Rist, John M. "Knowledge and Value in Plato." *Phoenix*, 21 (1967), pp. 283-295.

Examines sections from the *Republic*, *Phaedo*, *Euthyphro* and other dialogues, and concludes that the Forms are both eternal objects of knowledge and standards of value. Argues that in the *Euthyphro* there is no theory of Transcendent Forms, and that, therefore, the 'holy' and 'unholy', although universals, are not Forms, since they can only be identified in the world of time and space.

1477 Rist, John M. "Plato's Earlier Theory of Forms." *Phoenix*, 29 (1975), pp. 336-357.

Questions R. Allen's view that in the so-called early dialogues there is a theory which is substantially different from the two-world theory presented in the *Phaedo* and represents an 'earlier' theory of Forms. Examines the *Euthyphro*, *Hippias Major*, *Hippias Minor*, *Euthydemus*, *Protagoras*, *Meno*, *Cratylus*, *Symposium* and *Phaedo*. Ref. 862.

1478 Ritchie, D. G. "On Plato's *Phaedo*." *Mind*, 11 (1886), pp. 353-376.

Ref. 1215.

1479 Robert F. "Sur trois dialogues de Platon (*Protagoras*, *Gorgias*, *Phèdre*)." *L'Information Littéraire*, 4 (1952), pp. 15-18.

Argues that the protagonist of the *Protagoras*, the *Gorgias*, and the *Phaedrus* is indeed the historical Socrates, and that in these three dialogues the kernel of Socrates' thought appears clearly as the basis on which all of Plato's subsequent thoughts would develop. Suggests that in the context of the *Gorgias* the character of Callicles is a literary device employed by Plato, through which he left for us an autobiographical detail: 'Callicles' is a mask which depicts Plato's own initial confrontation with the ethical stance of Socrates. Notes the similarity between this use of 'Callicles' and the role asigned to Hippocrates in the *Protagoras*.

1480 Rohatin, Dennis A. "The *Euthyphro* as Tragedy: A Brief Sketch." *Diálogos*, 9 (1973), pp. 147-151.

Argues that the tragic nature of the *Euthyphro* is the same as in nearly all other Platonic dialogues, a failure to produce a suitable intellectual partner for Socrates. Observes the inability of Euthyphro to understand basic moral distinctions (*e.g.*, between murder and mere negligence).

1481 Roochnik, David L. "*Apology* 40c4-41e7: Is Death Really a Gain?" *The Classical Journal*, 80 (1985), pp. 212-220.

Ref. 1161.

1482 Rose, L. E. "The δεύτερος πλοῦς in Plato's *Phaedo*." *The Monist*, 50 (1966), pp. 464-473.

Concludes that the δεύτερος πλοῦς is an explanation of things according to the ideas which are their formal causes, and is second best when compared with explanations by final causes.

1483 Rosen, Frederick. "Piety and Justice: Plato's *Euthyphro*." *Philosophy*, 42 (1968), pp. 105-115.

Maintains that in Socrates' view the concept of justice is more fundamental than that of piety as a bridge between the human and the divine realms.

1484 Rudberg, G. "Zum platonischen *Thrasymachos*." *Symbolae Osloenses*, 23 (1944), pp. 1-6.

Defends the thesis that the first book of the *Republic*, specifically 327a-354c, was originally an independent dialogue which was left by Plato in an unfinished and sketchy form, and which was later incorporated by him into his *Republic*.

1485 Rudebusch, George. "Plato on Sense and Reference." *Mind*, 44 (1985), pp. 526-537.

Examines the Socratic position that when one makes a judgement one must make that judgment about either a thing one knows or does not know. Argues that Plato was aware of Frege's solution, the possibility of partial knowledge, and rejected it.

1486 Salmsen, Friedrich. "Plato and the Concept of Soul (Psyche)." *Journal of the History of Ideas*, 44 (1983), pp. 355-368.

Examines the development of the concept of ψυχή through the ancient tragedies and several Platonic dialogues, including the *Apology*, *Phaedo*, Book 2 of the *Republic*, and the *Gorgias*. Reviews Burnet's thesis that it was Socrates who brought about the synthesis between the two older distinct religious and secular traditions which resulted in supreme value being attached to the soul. Suggests that we keep in mind that the basic Homeric meaning of ψυχή is that its presence means life and its absence means death.

1487 Santas, Gerasimos X. "Plato's *Protagoras* and Explanations of Weakness." *Socrates: A Collection of Critical Essays*. Edited by Gregory Vlastos. Notre Dame, Ind.: University of Notre Dame Press, 1980, pp. 264-298.

Reprinted from *The Philosophical Review*, 5 (1966), pp. 3-33. Discusses the philosophical problem of ἀκρασία by endeavoring to understand the various kinds of explanations offered in cases of moral weakness, and examines in detail Socrates' contention that such explanations are untenable or absurd (*Protagoras* 352-356c). Analyzes in detail what the author construes as limitations inherent in Socrates' rejection of ἀκρασία, principally his premise combining ethical and psychological hedonism.

1488 Santas, Gerasimos X. "Socrates at Work on Virtue and Knowledge in Plato's *Laches*." *Socrates: A Collection of Critical Essays*. Edited by Gregory Vlastos. Notre Dame, Ind.: University of Notre Dame Press, 1980, pp. 177-208.

Reprinted from *The Review of Metaphysics*, 22 (1969), pp. 433-460. Examines textually the sections of the *Laches* which deal with the nature of courage and its relationship to knowledge. Emphasizes the importance of two premises for the construction of Socrates' argument: (1) the analogy of virtue to knowledge in the arts and science, and (2) knowledge as the necessary and sufficient condition for the good. Concludes that within its very narrow conception of courage, the *Laches*, while failing to answer any questions in a definitive way, succeeds in addressing itself to practically all significant issues concerning courage.

1489 Saunders, T. J. "The Socratic Paradoxes in Plato's *Laws*. A Commentary on 859C-864B." *Hermes*, 96 (1968), pp. 421-434.

Identifies two Socratic paradoxes: (1) that an individual does not commit injustice knowingly, and (2) that virtue is knowledge. Concludes that the second paradox is modified since an individual may be dominated by passion: knowledge is necessary, but not sufficient for virtue.

1490 Saxonhouse, Arlene W. "An Unspoken Theme in Plato's *Gorgias*:

War." *Interpretation*, 11 (1983), pp. 139-170.

Discovers in the background of the *Gorgias* Thucydides' account of the Peloponnesian War, and sees Callicles as a symbolic figure who represents Athenian imperialism with all its confusions and inconsistencies. Discusses the role assigned to ἔρως in philosophy, rhetoric, and politics, and examines its function as it intermingles the Socratic discourse with the historical account of Thucydides.

1491 Sayre, Kenneth M. "The Method of Hypothesis: *Phaedo* 100A-101D." *Plato's Analytic Method*. Chicago: University of Chicago Press, 1969, pp. 3-56.

Constitutes primarily a commentary on the *Theaetetus* and the *Sophist*, including certain methodological passages in the *Phaedo*, *Meno*, *Republic*, and *Parmenides*. Suggests that the dialogues are teaching instruments through their structure as well as their content. Argues that the method of hypothesis adumbrated in the *Phaedo*, as to the way in which the Forms can be considered 'causes', is later tested and rejected in the *Theaetetus*.

1492 Scarrow, David S. "*Phaedo*, 106A.106E." *The Philosophical Review*, 70 (1961), pp. 245-253.

Ref. 1217.

1493 Schmid, W. Thomas. "Socrates' Practice of *Elenchus* in the *Charmides*." *Ancient Philosophy*, 1 (1981), pp. 141-147.

Argues that the *elenchus* (as exemplified in the *Charmides*) demands that the interlocutor commit himself to the practice and values entailed by a philosophical inquiry in which virtue is the ultimate goal. Opposes the view expressed by Richard Robinson (among others) which regards the Socratic *elenchus* merely as a critical and destructive undertaking, and which ignores Socrates' sensitivity towards the idiosyncratic requirements of the interlocutor. Emphasizes the genuine educational concern that seems to underlie the refutational (elenchical) approach taken by Socrates in the *Charmides*. Ref. 984.

1494 Schmid, W. Thomas. "Socratic Moderation and Self-Knowledge."

*The Journal of the History of Philosophy*, 21 (1983), pp. 339-348.

Examines the concept of moderation as it is explored in the *Charmides* and the *Apology*. Suggests the concept originally developed from Dorian culture which was characterized by a shared code of appropriate behavior and an ethic dependent upon external sanctions. Argues that in the *Apology* Socrates introduces a new application of the concept which until then had two main fields of application, (1) sexual conduct, and (2) interpersonal relations; the new concept being the intellectual life, the unique aspect of Socratic moderation. Stresses the idea conveyed by Socrates in his questioning of Charmides, namely, that self-questioning inevitably leads to moderation and self-knowledge.

1495 Schofield, M. "Socrates on Conversing with Doctors." *The Classical Quarterly*, 23 (1973), pp. 121-123.

Presents a fragment from the *Charmides* 170e3-171a7 (Burnet's text), where Socrates argues that the most one could claim for second order knowledge is that oneself or some other has knowledge, and that from this alone it is impossible to distinguish the charlatan from the true physician. Suggests that only if certain emendations are made to the text, can the text be worked out beyond the way it stands.

1496 Schuhl, Pierre Maxime. "Remarques sur la technique de la Répétition dans le *Phédon*." *Etudes Platoniciennes*. Paris: Presses Universitaires de France, 1960, pp. 118-126.

Published originally in *Revue des Etudes Grecques*, 41 (1948), pp. 373-380. Presents various Greek passages from the *Phaedo* which highlight Plato's repetition of terms. Suggests that these repetitions demonstrate that he did not think of the rhetoricians in a completely negative way.

1497 Sciacca, G. M. "Il *'Carmide'* e la ricerca d'un oggetto per la filosofia." *Rivista Critica di Storia della Filosofia*, 5 (1950), pp. 103-123.

Examines the arguments and structure of the *Charmides*, and concludes that the essence of Plato's dialectic is clearly presented in it. Comments on what it views as the general goal of Plato's philosophical system.

1498 Sciacca, M. F. "Il problema della giustizia nel libro Primo della *Repubblica* di Platone." *Studi sulla Filosofia antica*, 1935, pp. 95-130.

Recognizes in the first book of the *Republic* a separate dialogue, written as a complete and independent piece. Argues that in this dialogue the basic tenets of Socrates' philosophy can be found.

1499 Sharny, Richard. "*Euthyphro* 9D-11B: Analysis and Definition in Plato and Others." *Nous*, 6 (1972), pp. 119-137.

Argues, on the basis of an analysis of the concept of piety, that property identity is not involved in Socrates' definition. Insists that when Socrates talks about defining a concept he is not talking about what the concept is identical to, but about what it means after analysis. Notes that Socratic definition involves a species of formal cause. Concludes that Socratic definitions are not by synonym and do not involve identity of properties: a Socratic definition gives (or attempts to give) an analysis of the *definiendum*.

1500 Shiner, Roger A. and King-Farlow, John. *New Essays on Plato and the Pre-Socratics*. Ontario: Canadian Association for Publishing in Philosophy, 1976.

Issued as Supplementary Volume 2 for the *The Canadian Journal in Philosophy*. Includes four relevant essays: "Socrates on the Parts of Virtue," by Paul Woodruff (pp. 101-116); "Particulars in *Phaedo* 95e-107a," by F. C. White (pp. 129-148); "Relations in the *Phaedo*," by David Gallop (pp. 149-164); and "The *Phaedo's* Final Argument," by Kenneth Dorter (pp. 165-180).

1501 Shipton, K. M. W. "A Good Second Best: *Phaedo* 99Bff." *Phronesis*, 24 (1979), pp. 33-53.

Analyzes the implications of the δεύτερος πλοῦς passage in the *Phaedo*, and argues that it is neither a mechanistic nor a teleological account of causation, but is used to refer to the acquisition of knowledge; this knowledge being either divinely revealed truth or the discovery of truth by one's own efforts. Interprets this expression as the acquisition of a cognitive state; not indubitable truth but the closest approach human beings may attain.

1502 Sider, David. "Plato's Early Aesthetics: The *Hippias Major.*" *The Journal of Aesthetics and Art Criticism*, 35 (1977), pp. 465-470.

Views the *Hippias Major* as an authentic and early Platonic dialogue. Examines various themes associated with the concept of beauty as this emerges from the dialogue, particularly the absolute and permanent nature of beauty.

1503 Sider, David. "Plato's *Symposium* as Dionysian Festival." *Quaderni Urbinati di Cultura classica*, 33 (1980), pp. 41-56.

Interprets Plato's *Symposium* as a literary rendition of a Dionysian festival in which Socrates, as a Dionysian satyr, emerges as the sole victor. Emphasizes the relevance of the fact that the dialogue's literary time coincides with the Athenian celebration of the Dionysian festival.

1504 Smith, John Leigh. *Plato and the Paradox of False Statements: A Study of the Euthydemus and the Sophist.* Doctoral dissertation. University of Virginia, 1975.

Argues that there is a close relationship between the *Euthydemus* and the *Sophist*. Notes that the two Sophists of the *Euthydemus* fit the definition given in the *Sophist*. Notes that the refutation of the impossibility of making false statements is a doctrine maintained in both dialogues, and that the semantic relation between "other than" statements and negative statements is likewise developed in both dialogues. Observes that the deprecation of the study of language (as advanced in the *Euthydemus*) is a denial that the knowledge of words alone suffices for the acquisition of knowledge.

1505 Smith, Nicholas D. "The Various Equals at Plato's *Phaedo* 74B-C." *The Journal of the History of Philosophy*, 18 (1980), pp. 1-7.

Examines what sorts of objects Plato is referring to in

this argument which purports to suggest the existence of nonsensible entities in the reference "αὐτὰ τὰ ἴσα." Contrasts the standard view that the use of synonymous expressions refers to but one abstract entity, the Form of Equality, and M. V. Wedin's criticism of this view. Concludes that a modified form of the standard view is preferable. Ref. 1549.

1506 Sparshott, F. E. "Socrates and Thrasymachus." *The Monist*, 50 (1966), pp. 421-459.

Rejects the idea that Book 1 of the *Republic* can be conceived of as a separate and independent dialogue from the rest of the *Republic*, and argues that the arguments advanced by Socrates against Thrasymachus make sense only against the background of arguments developed in later books of the *Republic*, and in other dialogues such as the *Gorgias*.

1507 Spitzer, Adele. "Self-Reference of the *Gorgias*." *Philosophy and Rhetoric*, 8 (1975), pp. 1-22.

Argues that the *Gorgias* demonstrates the nature and defects of rhetoric through the words and actions of its characters, as well as by argument. Contends that the three protagonists, Gorgias, Polus and Callicles, represent the three facets of rhetoric as they emerged in fifth century Athens: (1) rhetoric as a technique and art form not attached to particular ends; (2) rhetoric consciously used to gain wealth and position; (3) rhetoric as politics, the actual practice of gaining these political ends. Concludes that although never specifically mentioned in the discourse, philosophy is the true art of justice, and that Socrates is its representative, and that by triumphing over the others, Socrates' art is shown to be the true statesmanship.

1508 Steidle, W. "Der Dialog *Laches* und Platons Verhältnis zu Athen in den Frühdialogen." *Museum Helveticum*, 7 (1950), pp. 129-146.

Argues that the *Laches* was the first dialogue written by Plato. Maintains that in the *Laches*, as well as in the *Apology* and the *Crito*, it is possible to discern some degree of optimism on Plato's part concerning the possibility of reforming through education the Athenian polity. Observes that Socrates' execution was not initially sufficient to destroy Plato's optimism. Comments on the relationship between the Socratic λόγος, and certain political and social aspects of Athenian life.

1509 Stokes, Michael C. *Plato's Socratic Conversations*. Baltimore: The John Hopkins University Press, 1986.

Intended to be a contribution to the study of Greek literature as well as Greek philosophy. Presents a method for reading the dialogues which is more characteristic of French and German scholars than the interpretative approach of English speaking scholars. Analyzes three dialogues (*Laches*, *Symposium*, and *Protagoras*) by paying close attention to the specific information as provided by Plato, and to their historical and political meanings.

1510 Stoops, John A. "The Rise of Formal Idealism." *Philosophy and Education in Western Civilization: Summaries and Interpretations for Schoolmen and Churchmen*. Danville, Ill.: The Interstate Printers and Publishers, 1971, pp. 43-81.

Suggests that the Sophists gave 'intellectual birth' to their critics, thus turning the midwifery metaphor away from Socrates.

1511 Stough, Charlotte L. "Forms and Explanation in the *Phaedo*." *Phronesis*, 20 (1975), pp. 1-30.

Proposes to examine the function of the Platonic Forms as set forth in *Phaedo* 95e-10be, and to determine the force of the claim that εἶδος is αἰτία. Concludes that although Plato's language was strikingly different than that of his predecessors, his discussion of the Forms as causes was reminiscent of their beliefs, *e.g.*, that air or fire were the causes of various physical phenomena.

1512 Strauss, Leo. "On Plato's *Apology of Socrates* and *Crito*." *Essays in Honor of Jacob Klein*. Annapolis, Md.: St. John's College Press, 1976, pp. 155-170.

Provides a brief account of the two dialogues.

1513 Sullivan, John P. "The Hedonism in Plato's *Protagoras*." *Phronesis*, 6 (1961), pp. 10-28.

Examines the Socratic contention that what is pleasant is what is good. Concludes that the Socratic argument is ultimately an *ad hominem* argument, and that as such it may allow for the use of false premises, the employment of which may help in the clarification of the argument. Insists that there are sufficient hints in the *Protagoras* which point to the fact that in his apparent acceptance of hedonism, Socrates was being ironical, and that this should be quite evident by reflecting on the emphasis made on the concept of τέλος. Argues that the sort of hedonism presented in the *Protagoras* is both psychological and ethical.

1514 Sweeney, Leo. "'Safe' and 'Cleverer' Answers in Plato's Discussion of Participation and Immortality." *The Southern Journal of Philosophy*, 15 (1977), pp. 239-252.

Ref.1222.

1515 Taft, Tracy Marie. *Socrates' Argument Against Tyranny in the Gorgias and in the Republic I-V*. Doctoral dissertation. State University of New York at Buffalo, 1976.

Analyzes in Chapter 1 Callicles' argument in the *Gorgias* that tyranny is naturally just, and Thrasymachus' claim in the *Republic* that tyranny is unjust but good. Concludes that Socrates' rejoinders are incomplete because he assumes an undefended premise in both cases, namely, that there is a valid analogy between the individual's good and the good of the community. Discusses in Chapter 2 the position taken by Glaucon and Adeimantus in *Republic* 2-4, and notes that Socrates' response is also incomplete. Notes in Chapter 3 that the missing Socratic argument is finally furnished in *Republic* 5, this argument being based in part on Socrates' distinction between knowledge and opinion. Suggests that the final Socratic argument entails a concept of the soul as a naturally social entity.

1516 Tarrant, Dorothy. "Plato, *Phaedo* 74A-B." *The Journal of Hellenic Studies*, 77 (1957), pp. 124-126.

Examines this passage in which the Forms are not yet

regarded as causes, but are introduced in each case as the perfect type of which so-named particulars imperfectly resemble. Gives careful attention to an analysis of the Greek terms and examines the interpretations of various scholars.

1517 Tarrant, Dorothy. "The Touch of Socrates." *The Classical Quarterly*, 52 (1938), pp. 167-173.

Ref. 841.

1518 Tate, J. "Plato, Socrates and the Myths." *The Classical Quarterly*, 30 (1936), pp. 142-145.

Examines the *Laws* and the *Euthyphro*, and concludes that although Socrates may have adversely criticized myths of the Uranus-Kronos-Zeus type, this need not imply his disbelief in the existence of the gods.

1519 Taylor, C. C. W. "The Arguments in the *Phaedo* Concerning the Thesis that the Soul is a Harmonia." *Essays in Ancient Greek Philosophy*. Albany: State University of New York Press, 1971, pp. 217-231.

Ref. 1223.

1520 Taylor, C. C. W. "Forms as Causes in the *Phaedo*." *Mind*, 82 (1969), pp. 45-59.

Concludes that although the dialogue provides no such statement about the Forms being causes, the explanations provided in terms of the theory of Forms suggest a teleological scheme.

1521 Taylor, C. C. W. "The End of the *Euthyphro*." *Phronesis*, 27 (1982), pp. 109-118.

Renews the discussion of the concluding sections of the *Euthyphro*. Argues that the *Euthyphro* along with the *Laches* and *Charmides* seeks to give an account of a single virtue, and that it fails to find it, although it imparts the message that the virtue in question is itself *goodness*, understood as knowledge of the good. Implicit is the corollary that each virtue is the same as each of the others.

1522 Tejera, Victorino. "The *Charmides*: Self-Knowledge and Knowledge of Knowledge." *Plato's Dialogues One by One: A Structural Interpretation.* New York: Irvington Publishers, 1984, pp. 155-170.

Calls attention to the definition of irony as 'covered up speech', and reminds us that the Platonic Socrates never feels obliged to give the short, straight answers he demands of his questioners. Suggests that Plato satirized many of his favorite doctrines, arguments and institutions.

1523 Tejera, Victorino. "Disputation, Education and Dialectic: The *Euthydemus* and the *Euthyphro.*" *Plato's Dialogues One by One: A Structural Interpretation.* New York: Irvington Publishers, 1984, pp. 257-272.

Considers the *Euthydemus* and the *Euthyphro* as complementary to each other. Suggests that the *Euthyphro* is "a dramatized object lesson in the logic of definition."

1524 Tejera, Victorino. "The Equivocity of Beauty: Or, Plato's Socrates and Hippias the Sophist." *Plato's Dialogues One by One: A Structural Interpretation.* New York: Irvington Publishers, 1984, pp. 297-312.

Raises the question as to what Plato does in this dialogue. Suggests that it points to yet more difficulties in the idealist theory of definition, when he tries to define an idea with many accepted meanings, and at the same time is unable to make it more manageable.

1525 Tejera, Victorino. "The Intellectual Pleasures and the Unity of the Moral Excellences: The *Philebus* and the *Laches.*" *Plato's Dialogues One by One: A Structural Interpretation.* New York: Irvington Publishers, 1984, pp. 325-338.

Argues that the *Philebus* shows that it is the conception and nature of intellectual courage, not dialectic or cosmology, which is of primary concern. Suggests that the *Philebus* and the *Laches* (as well as the *Charmides, Hippias Minor* and *Hippias Major*) supply the reader with parameters by which to judge the nature and limits of Socratic intellectualism. Highlights the *Laches* as emphasizing the unity of *all* specific human excellences through the Socratic moderation of definitions of courage.

1526 Tejera, Victorino. "Interdialogical Interlude I: On the Use of the Term 'Irony' in the Dialogues." *Plato's Dialogues One By One: A Structural Interpretation.* New York: Irvington Publishers, 1984, pp.75-84.

Examines Plato as the master of irony, and attempts to bring some clarity to the understanding of the nature of irony in order to appreciate how Plato's mastery of prose contributed to his being the great philosopher that he is.

1527 Tejera, Victorino. "Interdialogical Interlude II: Dialogue and Dialectic: The *Protagoras* and the *Parmenides.*" *Plato's Dialogues One by One: A Structural Interpretation.* New York: Irvington Publishers, 1984, pp. 85-92.

Draws attention to Aristotle's distinction between syllogistic reasoning, which is apodeictic, proceeding from true and primary premises, and dialectical reasoning, which proceeds from only generally accepted premises (*Topics*, Book 1), suggesting the "iffy" nature of this reasoning, which is not knowledge itself but the instrumentation of the search for knowledge. Characterizes Zeno's dialectic as elenchical, and sees the Platonic dialogues as a synthesis of the Zenonian refutative and the Aristotelian rhetorical methods.

1528 Tejera, Victorino. "Irony and Allegory in the *Phaedrus.*" *Philosophy and Rhetoric*, 8 (1975), pp. 71-87.

Discusses the relationship between Plato and Plato's Socrates, and how they viewed dialectic, rhetoric, philosophy, and writing.

1529 Tejera, Victorino. "Plato's Tragic Humor. The *Apology* and the *Phaedo.*" *Plato's Dialogues One by One: A Structural Interpretation.* New York: Irvington Publishers, 1984, pp. 9-30.

Begins by highlighting the humor often evidenced by Socrates, even in the most serious of circumstances. Argues that the *Apology* is not a judicial defense. Presents evidence of much Socratic irony in the *Phaedo*. States that because Plato teaches an art of philosophic interrogation, he may rightly be called a Socratic, but that there is a critical difference in that Plato practices his art in writing, and Socrates through personal contact and conversation, thus emphasizing the distinction between dialectic and dialogic.

1530 Tejera, Victorino. "Problems of Morality, Inspiration and Practice: The *Hippias Minor* and the *Ion*." *Plato's Dialogues One by One: A Structural Interpretation.* New York: Irvington Publishers, 1984, pp. 9-30.

Quotes extensively from both dialogues to demonstrate that in the *Hippias Minor* Socrates expounds the position that it is better to do wrong voluntarily than involuntarity (providing examples from medicine, wrestling and flute playing). Suggests that Ion is not a Sophist like Hippias, and that he is neither a rational nor a thoughtful critic.

1531 Tejera, Victorino. "The *Symposium*: Socrates, Eros and Aristophanes." *Plato's Dialogues One by One: A Structural Interpretation.* New York: Irvington Publishers, 1984, pp. 339-358.

Ref. 497.

1532 Teloh, Henry. *Socratic Education in Plato's Early Dialogues.* Notre Dame, Ind.: University of Notre Dame Press, 1986.

Examines Socrates' activity of διαλέγεθαι in the early dialogues, and notes that this activity is far more complex than many scholars are willing to recognize. Shows how the Socratic discussion covers a wide range of educational approaches, from the ἔλεγχος to the φυχαγωγία. Argues that the Socratic activity is not really a search for 'universally valid truth' but an attempt to investigate the belief structure of the person.

1533 Thom, Paul. "*Euthyphro* 9D-11B." *Philosophical Inquiry*, 1 (1978), pp. 5-10.

Analyzes Socrates' argument about piety, specifically his question to Euthyphro as to whether what is holy is holy because the gods approve of it, or whether they approve of it because it is holy in itself. Finds the Socratic argument either to be guilty of an equivocation on the term 'because', or simply to be redundant. Concludes that Euthyphro's apparent inconsistency stems from a mixture of his uncritical reverence towards the gods and a somewhat cynical interpretation of holiness.

1534 Trainor, Paul. "Immortality, Transcendence, and the Autobiography of Socrates in the *Phaedo*." *The Southern Journal of Philosophy*, 21 (1983), pp. 595-610.

Ref. 848.

1535 Versényi, Laszlo. *Holiness and Justice: An Interpretation of Plato's Euthyphro*. New York: University Press of America, 1982.

Develops a new interpretation of the *Euthyphro*, and argues that appearance notwithstanding, this early Platonic work offers a positive and constructive definition of holiness or piety. Explains the virtual absence of any discussion on piety in other dialogues on the basis of the fact that this virtue is dealt with in the *Euthyphro* in a definitive way. Views the *Euthyphro* as one of Plato's most important writings.

1536 Versényi, Lazlo. "Plato's *Lysis*." *Phronesis*, 20 (1975), pp. 185-198.

Attempts to show that contrary to common opinion, the *Lysis* does not lack substantive content. Emphasizes the harmony in form and in content between the *Lysis* and the other early Socratic dialogues. Argues that form and content are complementary aspects of the dialogue.

1537 Vlastos, Gregory. "Is the *Lysis* a Vehicle of Platonic Doctrine?" *Platonic Studies*. Princeton, N.J.: Princeton University Press, 1981, pp. 35-37.

Argues that there is no evidence of Plato's theory of Forms in the *Lysis*.

1538 Vlastos, Gregory. "Reasons and Causes in the *Phaedo*." *Platonic Studies*. Princeton, N.J.: Princeton University Press, 1981, pp. 76-110.

Ref. 1229.

1539 Vlastos, Gregory. "Socrates on Acrasia." *Phoenix*, 23 (1969), pp. 71-88.

Presents a detailed analysis of the *Protagoras* 352a-358d, specifically the passage where Socrates states that knowledge of good and evil constitutes a necessary and sufficient condition for virtue, and is a certain guarantee against the commission of evil deeds.

1540 Vlastos, Gregory. "Socrates on 'The Parts of Virtue'." *Platonic Studies*. Princeton, N.J.: Princeton University Press, 1981, pp. 418-423.

Argues for citing the texts of the *Laches, Euthyphro, Meno, Gorgias, Hippias Major* and *Protagoras* as evidence that Socrates believed courage to be a part of virtue. Ref. 1352.

1541 Vlastos, Gregory. "Socratic Knowledge and Platonic 'Pessimism'." *Platonic Studies*. Princeton, N.J.: Princeton University Press, 1981, pp. 204-217.

Presents a discussion of J. Gould's *The Development of Plato's Ethics*, focusing on Part 1, which deals with the early Socratic dialogues and Socrates' understanding of knowledge, and on Part 3 which examines the interval between the Socratic dialogues and the *Laws*. Ref. 920.

1542 Vlastos, Gregory. "The Individual as Object of Love in Plato." *Platonic Studies*. Princeton, N.J.: Princeton University Press, 1981, pp. 3-34.

Examines the Socratic concept of love as it is developed in the *Lysis*, and then analyses the Platonic understanding of love as it is unfolded in the *Republic*, the *Symposium* and the *Phaedrus*.

1543 Vlastos, Gregory. "The Unity of the Virtues in the *Protagoras*." *Platonic Studies*. Princeton, N.J.: University Press, 1981, pp. 221-269.

Examines the problem posed in the *Protagoras* by Socrates' use of formulas which appear to contradict both common sense and the procedural assumptions of his dialectic in his defense of the doctrine of the unity of virtues. Ref. 908.

1544 Vlastos, Gregory. "Was Polus Refuted?" *The American Journal of Philology*, 88 (1967), pp. 454-460.

Provides an analysis of the argument in the *Gorgias* in which Socrates contends that it is worse to do evil than to suffer evil, and in which a definition of the concept of καλόν is developed (*Gorgias* 474d-475e). Notes that the Socratic argument involves a conclusion that is incorrectly or elliptically stated, and states that the Socratic argument does not succeed in refuting Polus' position, unless its conclusion is restated.

1545 Vlastos, Gregory. "What Did Socrates Understand by His 'What is F?' Question." *Platonic Studies*. Princeton, N.J.: Princeton University Press, 1981, pp. 410-417.

Argues that in the *Laches*, when Socrates inquires into the essence of courage, what he is truly seeking is a semantical or 'constitutive' answer, not a psychological account of the conditions that render a person courageous.

1546 Vries, C. J., de. *A Commentary on the Phaedrus of Plato*. Amsterdam: Adolph M. Hakkert, 1969.

Designed for students, providing a sort of *ancilla*, enabling them to study the Greek text themselves. Offers no text of the dialogue, but includes an introduction, a synopsis of the dialogue, detailed annotations, and an *index graecitatis*.

1547 Walman, Theodore. "A Key to Plato's Early Dialogues." *Philosophy and the Civilizing Arts: Essays Presented to Herbert W. Schneider*. Edited by Craig Walton and John P. Anton. Athens, Ohio: Ohio University Press, 1974, pp. 60-88.

Argues that the early dialogues of Plato should not be interpreted merely as a testimony of Socrates' method and ideas, or solely as a dramatic monument constructed by Plato in honor of his beloved teacher, but as progressive steps along Plato's dialectical and mystic-mythical philosophical edifice. Maintains that the early dialogues express dramatically the initial stages in the allegories of the line and the cave developed in the *Republic*.

1548 Warner, M. "Love, Self, and Plato's *Symposium*." *The Philosophical Quarterly*, 29 (1979), pp. 329-339.

Maintains that Socrates' speech in the *Symposium* becomes truly significant if one assumes that the sort of love he has in mind is directed to the special qualitites of the person who is loved, not to some metaphysical self.

1549 Wedin, Michael V. "αὐτὰ τὰ ἴσα and the Argument at *Phaedo* 74B7-C5." *Phronesis*, 22 (1977), pp. 191-205.

Examines what he considers "a crisp but tricky argument" for the distinction between forms and sensible particulars, which appears as a small part of the larger argument for the doctrine that knowledge is recollection. Emphasizes Plato's interest in why knowledge of the Forms cannot be derived from sensible particulars. Ref. 1505.

1550 Weiss, Roslyn Esther. *The 'Socratic' Paradoxes in Plato's Hippias Major and Protagoras*. Doctoral dissertation. Columbia University, 1982.

Examines two 'immoral' doctrines found respectively in the *Hippias Major* and the *Protagoras*; (1) that the true man and the false man are one and the same, and that the good man may do wrong willingly, and (2) that pleasure is the good. Reviews the import and context of these doctrines against the background of the so-called Socratic paradoxes, and concludes that such doctrines are genuine views held by the Sophists. Notes that if this is the case, (1) Socrates is exonerated of the charge levelled against him on account of his paradoxical views, and (2) the Sophists should be the prime targets of such charges.

1551 Welch, C. "The *Euthyphro* and the Forms." *Giornale di*

*Metafisica*, 22 (1967), pp. 228-244.

Suggests that the main interest of the dialogue resides in the analysis presented of knowledge and comprehension.

1552 Weston, A. H. "The Question of Plato's *Euthyphro*." *The Classical Bulletin*, 27 (1951), pp. 57-58.

Argues that the *Euthyphro* should not be regarded as a mere exercise in logical reasoning. Maintains that in this dialogue Socrates advances constructive and positive ideas concerning the ideas of holiness and piety.

1553 White, F. C. "The Compresence of Opposites in *Phaedo* 102." *The Classical Quarterly*, 27 (1977), pp. 303-311.

Agrees with Cornford that the theory of Forms put forth in the *Phaedo* is identical with the theory as it is presented in the *Parmenides*.

1554 Wolz, Henry G. "The Paradox of Piety in Plato's *Euthyphro* in the Light of Heidegger's Conception of Authenticity." *The Southern Journal of Philosophy*, 12 (1974), pp. 493-511.

Discusses in detail the central argument of the *Euthyphro* (10a-11b). Argues that the common understanding of the *Euthyphro* ignores the import of the central argument, no less than the paradox which arises from a concept of piety both as the fulfillment of God's will *and* as moral excellence. Appeals to Heidegger's concept of authenticity in order to develop a concept of piety as moral excellence which is not altogether divorced from God's will.

1555 Wolz, Henry G. "The Republic in the Light of the Socratic Method." *The Modern Schoolman*, 32 (1954-1955), pp. 115-142.

Argues that the Socratic *elenchus* remains intact throughout the *Republic*, and that the development of this dialogue can be interpreted as an 'illustration' of the Socratic *elenchus*. Maintains also that the Socratism of the early dialogues is evident in the *Statesman* and the *Laws*.

1556 Woodruff, Paul. "Socrates and Ontology: The Evidence of the

*Hippias Major*." *Phronesis*, 23 (1978), pp. 101-117.

Examines the significance and role of the Ideal Forms in the *Hippias Major*, and concludes that they are not ontologically prior to their instances. Argues that Socrates views the Ideal Forms as not separable from objects, and that he shows no real interest in their ontological status. Classifies the *Hippias Major* as a Socratic or early dialogue. Ref. 1415.

1557 Zaslarsky, Robert. "The Platonic Godfather: A Note on the *Protagoras* Myth." *The Journal of Value Inquiry*, 16 (1982), pp. 79-82.

Discusses the question of whether virtue is teachable, as this question is raised and answered in the *Protagoras*. Interprets Protagoras' answer as equating the teaching of virtue with punishment, and Socrates' view as identifying virtue with knowledge. Understands Socrates' solution as implying that virtue is not teachable, and that of Protagoras as affirming the teachability of virtue. Raises the issue as to whether or not it may be necessary to introduce a third possibility.

1558 Zeyl, Donald J. "Socrates and Hedonism: *Protagoras* 351B-358D." *Phronesis*, 25 (1980), pp. 250-269.

Argues that the hedonistic arguments developed by Socrates in the *Protagoras* against *akrasia* should not be ascribed to him. Examines closely various key passages, and concludes that the *Protagoras* does not necessitate the presence of a hedonistic Socrates.

# SOCRATES, JESUS, AND CHRISTIANITY

This section includes annotations of works in which a comparison is established between Socrates and Jesus, or between the Socratic literature and the Christian Gospels, or in which the influence of Socrates' life and philosophy on Christianity is explored. Several references are given to works annotated elsewhere which contain the opinions expressed by the Fathers of the Church on Socrates and Socratic philosophy.

1559 Alarco, Luis Felipe. *Sócrates y Jesús ante la muerte*. Lima: Universidad Major de San Marcos, 1972.

Reviews the circumstances and background of the trials and executions of Socrates and Jesus, and comments on their similarities and differences. Analyzes the attitudes of Socrates and Jesus with respect to death.

1560 Barr, David Lawrence. *Toward a Definition of the Gospel Genre: A Generic Analysis and Comparison of the Synoptic Gospels and the Socratic Dialogues by Means of Aristotle's Theory of Tragedy*. Doctoral dissertation. The Florida State University, 1974.

Considers the issue of whether the Gospels, as a literary genre, can be descriptively related to other literary ancient works, specifically to the Socratic dialogues. Argues that a direct comparison between them cannot be established, but that an indirect comparison can be developed by appealing to Aristotle's concept of tragedy. Notes that on this basis there are many similarities and dissimilarities between the Gospels and the dialogues: they are different, for instance, in the kind of *katharsis* which they achieve, but they are remarkably similar in what concerns their respective objects, manners of expression, means, and purpose.

1561 Baur, F. C. "Das Christliche des Platonismus, oder Sokrates und Christus." *Drei Abhandlungen zur Geschichte der Alten Philosophie und ihres Verhältnisses zum Christentum*. Edited by Eduard Zeller. Leipzig, 1876, pp. 228ff.

Originally published in *Tübinger Zeitschrift für Theologie*, 3 (1837), pp. 1-154. Compares the relationship between the testimony of Xenophon and the testimony of Plato, with the relationship between the Synoptic Gospels and the Gospel according to Saint John: just as the Synoptic Gospels describe the external and human presence of Jesus, so the writings of Xenophon unveil for us only the surface and public aspects of Socrates; and just as Saint John recognizes the divinity of Jesus, so the Platonic Socrates reveals himself to us as an ideal and more than human person. Classifies (in agreement with Diogenes Laertius) the Platonic dialogues into narrative and dramatic dialogues, and assigns to the first group a more historical value with respect to Socrates. Views the dramatic dialogues as expressions of Plato's free creativeness. Devotes much of its attention to the task of establishing parallels between Socrates and Jesus, and concludes that in many respects they stood on the same ethical ground, although recognizes the immense gap that separates them: while Jesus is divine, Socrates only approaches the divine.

1562 Belmont, Paul. *Le testament de Socrate*. Paris: Hermann et Cie, 1938.

Ref. 187.

1563 Benz, E. "Christus und Sokrates in der alten Kirche. Ein Beitrag zum altkirchlichen Verständnis des Märtyrers und des Martyriums." *Zeitschrift für die Neutestamentliche Wissenschaft*, 43 (1950-1951), pp. 195-224.

Studies and comments on the common practice among some of the early Fathers of the Church to appeal to the example of the condemnation and death of Socrates as an instance of the persecution and sufferings endured by the just and the good. Notes that for the Fathers, Socrates often stood as a paradigm of commitment to the search for the truth even in the presence of danger and death. Stresses the significance of *Republic* 2.361 in this regard.

1564 Bowman, F. P. "La *confirmatio christianorum per Socratica* dans le romantisme français." *Revue des Sciences Humaines*, 1966, pp. 217-226.

Notes the frequent comparisons established between Jesus

and Socrates during the nineteenth century in the midst of the romantic movement in France. Comments on the superiority generally accorded to Jesus, and explains this circumstance as a consequence of the distrust towards reason and logic on the part of the representatives of the romantic movement.

1565 Brun, Jean. "La mort de Socrate et la mort de Jésus." *Etudes Théologiques et Religieuses*, 35 (1960), pp. 197-204.

Studies the various ways in which the deaths of Socrates and Jesus display similarities, but notes that their dissimilarities are more evident and pronounced.

1566 Campbell, Gabriel. "Socrates, the Predecessor of Christ." *Bibliotheca Sacra*, 74 (1917), pp. 194-222.

Recounts various details of Socrates' life, and comments on his basic philosophical ideas. Emphasizes the virtuous character of his life and his firm faith in the providence of the gods and the efficacy of prayer. Concludes with comments on Socrates' martyrdom, and notes that he, like Jesus, died for the sake of the truth: "Socrates had to give his life for the truth. Jesus of Nazareth was nailed to the cross. Nevertheless, the sun is brightening the sky. God's truth is marching on."

1567 Capizzi, Antonio. *Socrate. Antologia di teste.* Florence: La Nuova Italia, 1974.

Ref. 140.

1568 Carus, Paul. "Socrates, a Forerunner of Christianity." *The Open Court*, 21 (1907), pp. 523-527.

Regards Socrates as a moral teacher whose ideas were part of the Christ spirit that was destined to come in the person of Jesus. Stresses the Socratic doctrine of returning love and forgiveness for hatred and persecution, and notes that at least in this aspect Socrates can be considered a true forerunner of Christianity. Includes a photograph of Socrates' prison in Athens.

1569 Courtney, W. L. "Socrates, Buddha, and Christ." *The North American Review*, 77 (1885), pp. 63-77.

Compares and discusses the similarities in the ethical teachings of Socrates, Buddha, and Jesus. Notes that in spite of the cultural and historical differences, their ethical contributions are remakably in agreement with one another.

1570 Davar, Firoze C. *Socrates and Christ*. Ahmedabad, India: Gujarat University Press, 1972.

Maintains that the reconciliation between philosophy and religion, each recognizing and acknowledging the strengths of the other, leads to the elevation of the individual. Notes that Socrates and Jesus represent respectively the personification of philosophy and religion.

1571 Déman, Thomas. *Socrate et Jésus*. Paris: L'Artisan du Livre, 1944.

Compares the messages of Socrates and Jesus, and draws parallels between their missions. Considers the question of whether it is possible to see in Socrates the first pre-Christian martyr. Discusses the possibility of discovering in Socrates' critical attitude towards anthropomorphic polytheism an effort to advance towards transcendent monotheism. Concludes that although there are clear and unquestionable parallels between Socrates and Jesus, it is not justifiable to place them on the same plane: "*On retrouve Socrate dans le passé; Jésus -- il est celui qui nous attendons.*"

1572 Dunne, Mary Rachel. *Kierkegaard and Socratic Ignorance: A Study of the Task of a Philosopher in Relationship to Christianity*. Doctoral dissertation. University of Notre Dame, 1970.

Ref. 1650.

1573 Eberhard, Johann A. *Examen de la doctrine touchant le salut de payens, ou Nouvelle apologie pour Socrate*. Translated by C. M. F. Dumas. Amsterdam: E. van Harrevelt, 1778.

French translation of Eberhard's *Neue Apologie des Sokrates*. Ref. 1574.

1574 Eberhard, Johann A. *Neue Apologie des Sokrates; oder, Untersuchung des Lehre von der Seeligkeit der Heiden*. Berlin: F. Nikolai, 1776-1778.

Examines the traditional theological issue concerning the spiritual salvation of non-Christians. Approaches this issue by constructing an apologetic eulogy of Socrates who is viewed as a man who, although outside of the Christian faith, deserved eternal bliss in the presence of God.

1575 Erasmus of Rotterdam, Desiderius. *Convivium religiosum. Colloquia familiaria*. Basel: John Fobren, 1522.

Ref. 1656.

1576 Fascher, E. "Sokrates und Christus. Eine Studie zur aktuellen Aufgabe der Religionsphänomenologie." *Zeitschrift für die Neutestamentliche Wissenschaft*, 45 (1954), pp. 1-41.

Establishes a detailed comparison and juxtaposition between the lives, personalities, and ethical teachings of Jesus and Socrates.

1577 Ferguson, John. *Socrates: A Source Book*. London: Macmillan, 1970.

Ref. 144.

1578 Fichter, J. H. "A Christian Attitude on Socrates." *The Catholic World*, 157 (1943), pp. 488-490.

Attempts to demonstrate, by an appeal to the *Crito*, that the philosophy of Socrates is essentially in agreement with Christian ethical principles, inasmuch as it maintains that evil may not be done either to requite evil or to obtain a worthy end. Calls attention to the Christian character of Socrates' statement in the *Crito*, namely, that "we ought neither to requite wrong with wrong nor to do evil to anyone, no matter what he may have done to us." Compares this statement with Jesus' command: "Love your enemies; do good to them who persecute you."

1579 Geffcken, Johannes. *Sokrates und das alte Christentum.* Heidelberg: Carl Winter, 1908.

Pamphlet (45 pp.) which examines the influence of and the reactions to Socrates among the early Fathers of the Church. Comments on the parallelisms established between Socrates and Jesus, and between the message of the Christian faith and the essence of what the Fathers of the Church understood by Platonism.

1580 Giannatoni, Gabriele. *Socrate. Tutte le testimonianze da Aristofane e Senofonte ai padri cristiani.* Bari: Editori Laterza, 1971.

Ref. 143.

1581 Gilson, Etienne. "La connaissance de soi-même et le socratisme chrétien." *L'Esprit de la philosophie médiévale.* Paris, 1944, pp. 1-22.

Discusses the meaning and significance of the Delphic "Know thyself" which played so crucial a role in the formation of Socrates' mission, and explores its implications in the context of a Christian interpretation of the meaning of human existence. Notes that for Socrates, the Delphic command was a recommendation to seek a virtuous life. Traces the history of the call for self-knowledge among Christian philosophers and writers, and among the Biblical Jews. Concludes with comments on Pascal's understanding of the meaning of the Christian *nosce teipsum*, which is seen in part as a development of the Socratic call for self-knowledge, and which is regarded as central to the problem of Christian philosophy.

1582 Gilson, Etienne. "Self-knoweldge and Christian Socratism." *The Spirit of Mediaeval Philosophy.* Translated by A. H. C. Downes. New York: Charles Scribner's Sons, 1936, pp. 209-228.

English translation of Gilson's "La connaissance de soi-même et le socratisme chrétien." Ref. 1581.

1583 Hamann, Johann Georg. *Socratic Memorabilia: A Translation and Commentary*. Edited and translated by James C. O'Flaherty. Baltimore: The Johns Hopkins Press, 1967.

Contains a reprint of the German text of Hamann's *Sokratische Denkwürdigkeiten* (Amsterdam, 1759), and an accompanying annotated English translation. Includes O'Flaherty's "Concept of Form in the *Socratic Memorabilia*," as well as an extensive bibliography. Ref. 1727.

1584 Hamann, Johann Georg. *Sokratische Memorabilia*. Stuttgart: Reclam, 1968.

Originally published in Amsterdam in 1759, and in Hamann's *Sämtliche Werke* (edited by Josef Nadler, Vienna, 1950, 6 vols., Vol. 2, pp. 57-82). Reconstructs the image of Socrates as a man of faith and as a forerunner of Jesus. Recounts the major moments and aspects of Socrates' life, and makes abundant references to primary and secondary sources. Contends that the philosophers of the Enlightenment misrepresented and misunderstood the Socratic message by seeing in it an endorsement of absolute rationalism. Attempts to establish the primacy of faith and feeling in the philosophy of Socrates, and interprets his divine voice or sign as a manifestation of the presence of the Holy Ghost in him. Constructs a parallelism between Socrates' doctrine of true ignorance and knowledge, and some of the doctrines of Saint Paul.

1585 Hamilton, Edith. "Socrates." *Witness to the Truth*. New York: W. W. Norton & Co., 1957, pp. 23-40.

Establishes a comparison between Jesus and Socrates, and finds a number of important similarities between them. Reviews the social and political vicissitudes of Socrates, and emphasizes the pedagogical impact of his presence. Regards his lack of dogmatism as a most essential component of his philosophical stance. Speaks of his divinely appointed search for truth, and of his clearly defined purpose and rigorous method.

1586 Harnack, A. *Sokrates und die alte Kirche*. Gissen: J. Richer, 1900.

Studies the diverse reactions of the early Fathers of the

Church to Socrates. Reviews the various attempts in the first centuries of the Christian era to establish a juxtaposition between Socrates and Jesus.

1587 Hommel, H. "Herrenworte im Lichte sokratischer Uberlieferung." *Zeitschrift für die Neutestamentliche Wissenschaft*, 57 (1966), pp. 1-23.

Comments on the extraordinary number of similarities between the sayings attributed to Jesus in the Gospels and the ethical ideas imputed to Socrates in various Socratic discourses.

1588 Horne, T. H. *The Deaths of Socrates and Jesus Contrasted.* London, 1852.

Printed version of a sermon delivered by the author. Compares the attitudes of Socrates and Jesus towards their deaths, and stresses the profound spirituality with which both (in different degrees and for different reasons) went through the final human physical experience. Emphasizes the Socratic human response and the divine compliance of Jesus at the moment of death.

1589 Jackson, D. "Socrates and Christianity." *Classical Folia*, 31 (1977), pp. 189-206.

Reviews the interpretations and influence of Socrates among the early Fathers of the Church. Maintains that in the view of some of them, Socrates was either a precursor of Christianity or someone who approached the ideas of the Christian faith. Notes the influence of his asceticism on the development of Christian ascetic ideals. Comments on the role of Christian Socratism during medieval times.

1590 Kaufmann, George. "Socrates and Christ." *Harvard Studies in Classical Philology*. Cambridge, Mass.: Harvard University Press, 1951.

Contains information about the iconographic traditions of late classical times and the Byzantine period concerning the representations of Jesus and Socrates.

1591 Kranz, W. "Die Frömmigkeit des Sokrates." *Theologische Studien und Kritiken*, 108 (1937-1938), pp. 265-281.

Studies the concept of piety or religious devotion which can be found in the life and ideas of Socrates, and compares it with its manifestations in the life and doctrine of Jesus. Argues that there are in that respect profound differences between Socrates and Jesus, but that, those differences notwithstanding, there is a common ground which can be identified as their profound and overwhelming relationship with God or the divine.

1592 Lamartine, Alphonse de. *La mort de Socrate.* Paris: L'Advocat, Libraire, 1823.

Ref. 1810.

1593 Leist, Fritz. *Moses - Sokrates - Jesus. Um die Begegnung mit der biblischen und Antiken Welt.* Frankfurt am Main: Verlag Josef Knecht, 1959.

Devotes its third chapter to Socrates, and begins with an examination of the historical, philosophical, and religious relationship between Socrates and Jesus. Provides a general sketch of the biography and doctrine of Socrates.

1594 Less, D. Gottfried. "Parallel des Genius Sokrates' mit den Wundern Christi." *Deutsches Museum*, 1777, pp. 302-310.

Establishes a comparison between the divine voice which guided Socrates and the divine inspiration of the Holy Spirit which acted on Jesus.

1595 Lindenbaur, Erich. *Der Tod des Socrates und das Sterben Jesu.* Stuttgart: Calwer Verlag, 1971.

Discusses the deaths of Socrates and Jesus, and notes that in them we have the highest expressions of humanism and Christianity.

1596 Linn, John Blair. *A Letter to Joseph Priestley in Answer to his Performance Entitled Socrates and Jesus Compared.* Philadelphia: J. Conrad & Co, 1803.

Reviews and criticizes Priestley's *Socrates and Christ Compared*. Ref. 1604.

1597 Lloyd, Alfred H. "The Death of Socrates." *Citizenship and Salvation; or, Greek and Jew: A Study in the Philosophy of History*. Boston: Little, Brown & Company, 1897, pp. 1-62.

Views the death of Socrates as the symbolic moment which signaled the collapse of the Greek world, and as an anticipation of the death of Jesus which constitutes the birth of the new world of temporal and spiritual freedom.

1598 Mendonça, Eduardo Prado de. *O socratismo cristão e os origens da metafisica moderna*. São Paulo: Editora Convivio, 1975.

Develops the theme of Christian Socratism, which is compared and contrasted with Christian Aristotelianism and Christian Platonism. Concludes with a statement on the meaning of Christian Socratism, to which it attributes two essential elements: (1) the thesis that Christian revelation is ultimately self-knowledge, and (2) that self-knowledge is basically the knowledge of God.

1599 Mill, John Stuart. "The Search for Truth: The Unending Trial of Freedom." *The State Versus Socrates: A Case Study in Civic Freedom*. Edited by John D. Montgomery. Boston: The Beacon Press, 1954, pp. 222-226.

Excerpted from Mill's *On Liberty* (New York: Holt, 1874). Compares the trial and execution of Socrates with those of Jesus, and finds them extraordinary examples of judicial iniquity: in both, the accusers sought to make of their victims exactly the opposite of what they were in reality. Maintains that experience refutes as a plain falsehood the commomplace dictum that truth always triumphs over persecution. Notes that the progress in freedom and tolerance since ancient times has been more apparent than real.

1600 Miller, D. L. "Rhythmus of Silenus in a Poetics of Christ: Images of the Great Teacher." *Eranos-Jahrbuch*, 47 (1978), pp. 67-121.

Notes that the image of Socrates can be vaguely recognized

behind the image of Jesus, and that beneath the outline of the Socratic image we can discern the features of Silenus. Relates this recognition to the consideration of mystical intoxication or divine enthusiasm. Comments on the passage in *Mark* 1:5 where reference is made to the total sensual satisfaction which is brought about by intoxication.

1601 Moss, A. E. *Socrates, Buddha, and Jesus.* London: Watts & Co., 1885.

Pamphlet (15 pp.) in which the ethical principles of Socrates, Buddha, and Jesus are compared. Observes the great similarities between them.

1602 Muñoz Valle, I. "Las figuras modélicas del mundo clásico y los mártires cristianos." *Orpheus*, 21 (1974), pp. 25-43.

Studies the problem of paradigmatic continuity between the ideals of perfect humanity among the pagans (*e.g.*, Socrates and Seneca) and their counterpart among the early Christians (*i.e.*, the Christian martyrs). Concludes that the Christian ideology succeeded in developing more fully the sketches of human perfection (such as Socrates) created in the pagan classical world.

1603 Natali, G. *Socrate nel giudizio dei padri apologisti.* Ascoli, Italy, 1912.

Reviews and discusses the views and interpretations about Socrates and Socratic philosophy held by the early fathers of the Church, principally Saint Justin, Saint Augustine, Eusebius, and Tertullian.

1604 Priestley, Joseph. *Socrates and Jesus Compared.* Philadelphia: P. Byrne, 1803.

Pamphlet (60 pp.) which discusses the similarities between the ethical teachings of Socrates and those of Jesus. Emphasizes the unmistakable common denominator which underlies their moral views, but recognizes that their ultimate sources are fundamentally different. Ref. 1596.

1605 Romero, Francisco. "La cuestión socrática." *Nosotros*, No.

227 (1928), pp. 111ff.

Ref. 409.

1606 Santayana, George. *Dialogues in Limbo*. New York: Charles Scribner's Sons, 1926.

Ref. 1839.

1607 Scott, John Adams. *Socrates and Christ: A Lecture Given at Northwestern University*. Evanston, Ill.: The Northwestern University Press, 1928.

Stresses the common elements between the moral doctrines of Jesus and those of Socrates.

1608 "Socrates and the Revelation of God." *The Spectator*, 102 (1909), pp. 85-86.

Unsigned article. Maintains that the soul of Socrates led him as far along the way of Truth as was at all possible four hundred years before the revelation of God made possible through the advent of Jesus.

1609 Spiegelberg, Herbert. *The Socratic Enigma*. New York: The Library of Liberal Arts, 1964.

Ref. 149.

1610 Tapscott, F. T. "Socratic Anticipation of Christianity." *Bibliotheca Sacra*, 92 (1935), pp. 58-76.

Comments on the relationship between the ethical ideals entailed by the philosophical message of Socrates and the moral values preached by Christianity, and observes that the former are clearly a prelude to the latter.

1611 Toynbee, Arnold J. "The Search for a Prophet: Socrates and Jesus." *The State Versus Socrates: A Case Study in Civic Freedom*. Edited by John D. Montgomery. Boston: The Beacon Press, 1954, pp. 203-214.

Reprinted from Toynbee's *A Study of History* (New York: Oxford University Press, Vol. 6, pp. 486-495). Attempts to test the theory that the correspondence between divine and pagan heroes may be the result of the transference of legends and myths from one culture to another. Develops eighteen sets of parallels between Socrates and Jesus in which similar characteristics, activities, and ideas are attributed to both.

1612 Vircillo, Domenico. "Etica socratica e etica evangelica." *Sapienza*, 27 (1974), pp. 50-69.

Reviews the significance of F. Bartolone's understanding of Socrates, an understanding which interprets Socrates' philosophy as the kernel of human thought and essentially a moral revelation. Examines this idea against the background provided by the revelation of the Christian Gospels, and concludes that there is an insoluble contradiction in Bartolone's position.

1613 Wenley, Robert. M. "The Search for a Prophet: The Uniqueness of Jesus." *The State Versus Socrates: A Case Study in Civic Freedom*. Edited by John D. Montgomery. Boston: The Beacon Press, 1954, pp. 215-221.

Excerpted from Wenley's *Socrates and Christ: A Study in the Philosophy of Religion*. Ref. 1614.

1614 Wenley, Robert M. *Socrates and Christ: A Study in the Philosophy of Religion*. Edinburgh: William Blackwood, 1889.

Examines the many parallels that can be readily found between the life and character of Socrates and those of Jesus, and concludes that, in what concerns the externalities, those parallels are remarkable and point to a common denominator between the Greek philosopher and the founder of Christianity: they lived simply and with no concern for wealth, since their kingdoms were not of this world; they taught by parable and in simple dialogue, and were moved by a spiritual force through which they sought to move people to virtue and purity; they claimed to be willing to obey God alone, and they both suffered and were tried and executed; and they left no writings, and yet their influence has been overwhelming. Maintains, however, that the similarities do not extend beyond the mere externalities of their lives, for even though Socrates can be viewed as an ethical herald for the coming of Christianity, the gap that separates him from Jesus is immense: Socrates simply pointed the way to the truth and the light, but Jesus is the truth and the light.

1615 Zinzendorf, Nikolaus Ludwig. *Der teutsche Sokrates, das ist: Aufrichtige Anzeige verschiedener nicht so wohl unbekannter als vielmehr in Abfall gerathener Haupt-Wahrheiten.* Leipzig, 1732.

Examines the principal doctrines of Socrates, and concludes that the only appropriate way to understand and interpret his message is by recognizing in him a man who anticipated, both in word and in deed, the advent of Jesus. Assesses Socrates' thought from a pietistic point of view.

# THE INFLUENCE OF SOCRATES

The entries included in this section contain information about works which discuss the influence of Socrates on various philosophical and literary movements or figures of ancient and modern times, as well as about works of influential modern writers who have advanced distinct views on Socrates and his philosophy.

1616 Abma, Erik. *Sokrates in der deutschen Literatur. Deutsche Quellen und Studien.* Nymwegen, 1949.

Examines the presence and influence of Socrates in various major German philosophical and literary writings of modern times. Pays particular attention to the many interpretations given of Socrates' divine voice or sign on the part of German writers. Notes the adequacy of Hamann's summary statement concerning those interpretations (p. 130). Ref. 1583.

1617 Anastaplo, George. "Citizen and Human Being: Thoreau, Socrates, and Civil Disobedience." *Human Being and Citizen: Essays on Virtue, Freedom, and the Common Good.* Chicago: The Swallow Press, 1975, pp. 203-213 and 313-316.

Explores the political ideas of Henry Thoreau, and establishes a comparison between them and those attributed to Socrates. Deals in particular with the issue of civil disobedience as this was conceived by Thoreau, and contrasts his ideas with those which emerge from the Platonic Socrates in the *Crito*.

1618 Armaingaud, A. "Montaigne, Socrate et Epicure." *La Nouvelle Revue*, 42 (1919), pp. 97-107 and 215-224.

Reviews the many references to Socrates and to Epicurus in Montaigne's *Essais*, and attempts to delineate the multiplicity of their images created by Montaigne.

1619 Atkins, Elizabeth. "Points of Contact Between Byron and Socrates." *Publications of the Modern Language Association of America.* Edited by Carleton Brown. New York: Kraus Reprint

Corporation, 1966, Vol. 41, pp. 402-423.

Discusses the influence of Socrates (the Socrates of Plato's writings) on Byron. Notes that the poet's attachment is greater to Socrates than to Plato. Explores the impact of two Socratic themes on Byron's mind: the confession of ignorance, and the Socratic irony. Observes the presence of the Socratic influence on Byron's melancholy temperament and on his attitude of peaceful resignation.

1620 Beatty, Joseph. "Thinking and Moral Considerations: Socrates and Arendt's Eichmann." *The Journal of Value Inquiry*, 10 (1976), pp. 266-278.

Examines Hannah Arendt's contention that Socratic and Kantian thinking is inexorably related to a moral sense. Analyzes her arguments for explaining a peculiarly modern phenomenon, namely, the commission of evil deeds on a massive scale by an agent who cannot either know or feel the wrongness of his deed. Argues that Arendt's arguments involve some sort of question-begging, and concludes that those arguments actually undermine her assessment of Eichmann's guilt, and her condoning his actual punishment.

1621 Bergmann, J. "Sokrates in der judischen Literatur." *Monatschrift für die Geschichte und Wissenschaft des Judentums*, 80 (1936), pp. 1-13.

Discusses the ideological portraits and the various interpretations of Socrates among Jewish scholars of the eighteenth and nineteenth centuries.

1622 Berland, K. J. H. "Bringing Philosophy Down From the Heavens: Socrates and the New Science." *The Journal of the History of Ideas*, 47 (1986), pp. 299-308.

Observes that the legendary authority of Socrates has often been used on both sides of a number of important controversies. Examines the role played by his ideas in the debate concerning the opposition between the New Science and morality. Reviews the interpretation given to the idea that Socrates called philosophy down from the heavens, and explores its implications: Does it constitute a caution against scientific investigation, or is it an endorsement of it? Documents seventeenth and eighteenth century English polemics in this respect, and comments in particular on Amyas Bushe's figure of a Newtonian Socrates.

1623 Betz, Joseph. "Dewey and Socrates." *Transactions of the Peirce Society*, 16 (1980), pp. 329-356.

Explains the apparent ambiguity of John Dewey's appraisal of Socrates, and interprets this appraisal in two senses: (1) a conception of Socrates as the first true philosopher and as someone who defined and practiced philosophy in the style typical of Dewey, and (2) an understanding of Socrates as someone who was an accomplice in the development of a classical tradition (which Dewey calls 'harmful'). Investigates the ramifications of the tension created by this possibly inconsistent attitude on Dewey's part.

1624 Bickel, E. "Seneca und Seneca-Mythus." *Altertum*, 5 (1959), pp. 90-100.

Discusses various themes and factors related to the formation of legends and myths around the person and ideas of Seneca. Examines in particular the legendary relationship between Seneca and Socrates, specifically with respect to the circumstances of their violent deaths. Comments on the artistic way in which this relationship was conceived in late classical times.

1625 Bignone, Ettore. *Studi sul pensiero antico.* Naples, 1938, pp. 44-51.

Reviews the influence of Socrates on the Cynics and the Cyrenaics, and discusses the question of whether there is a common Socratic element among the diverse Socratic schools.

1626 Blasucci, Savino. *Nietzsche e Socrate. Significato di una polemica.* Bari: Levante, 1983.

Regards Socrates and Nietzsche as the most significant thinkers of antiquity and modern times respectively. Discusses at length the ambivalent attitude of Nietzsche towards Socrates, an attitude which combines elements of great attraction and great repulsion. Comments on the ideological extremes to which the two philosophers were committed: Socrates gravitated towards the ideal of perfect rationalism, while Nietzsche functioned in a spiritual-intuitive (*psico-intuitiva*) atmosphere. Ref. 1723.

1627 Bock, Friedrich. *Untersuchungen zu Plutarchs Schrift* Περὶ τοῦ Σωκράτους δαιμόνιου. Munich: Wolf & Sohn, 1910.

Constitutes a detailed analysis of Plutarch's *De genio Socratis*. Contains a section on the history of the scholarship related to this work, as well as a section on the sources available to Plutarch, and a study of the demonology associated with Plutarch. Concludes with comments on Xenophon's references to Socrates' divine voice or sign, which are contrasted with those found in Plutarch. Ref. 169.

1628 Böhm, Benno. *Sokrates im achtzehnten Jahrhundert: Studien zum Werdegange des modernen Persönlichkeitsbewusstseins.* Neumünster: Karl Wachholtz, 1966.

Originally published in Leipzig in 1929. Studies the transformations of the image of Socrates through the eyes of his rationalistic and romantic admirers in the eighteenth century, especially in the context of the German *Aufklärung*. Shows how Socrates became the symbol of rationalism for writers such as Mendelssohn, Hamann, Tennemann, and Voltaire. Speaks of Socrates as the 'touchstone' through which those writers often sought to reach an understanding of their own ideas, and refers to him as the prototype of the modern man. Notes that the Socratic problem, properly so-called, arose in the nineteenth century mostly as a result of the investigations of Schleiermacher.

1629 Bonser, Robert Dale. *The Role of Socrates in the Thought of Søren Kierkegaard.* Doctoral dissertation. University of California at Santa Barbara, 1985.

Examines Socrates' role in the formation of Kierkegaard's thought. Notes that the two most critical questions for Kierkegaard were: (1) What does it mean to be a human being, and (2) What is the meaning of Christianity for each person. Argues that Kierkegaard approached Socrates for an answer to the first question, and that he found in him various hints in order to answer the second. Stresses the importance of Socrates for Kierkegaard as an ideal teacher, and emphasizes the non-political character of Kierkegaard's philosophy -- an element which he inherited from Socrates. Ref. 1692.

1630 Brenning, E. "Die Gestalt des Sokrates in der Literatur des vorigen Jahrhunderts." *Bremer Festschrift zur 45. Versammlung deutscher Philologen und Schulmänner*. Bremen, 1899, pp. 421-481.

Reviews the influence of Socrates' life and ideas among the major figures of German literature in the eighteenth century.

1631 Broecker, W. "Plotin, un platonisme sans Socrate." *Annales de la Faculté des Lettres et Sciences Humaines d'Aix*, 43 (1967), pp. 107-126.

Maintains that even though Plotinus remained firmly grounded on the principles of Plato's philosophy, he was never a spiritual disciple of Socrates. Emphasizes the total absence of Socratic doubt and open-ended inquiry in the philosophy of Plotinus.

1632 Buehner, Thomas Lee. *"The Birth of Tragedy": The Re-Birth of Tragic Thought in the Music-Practising Socrates*. Doctoral dissertation. Duquesne University, 1978.

Develops an interpretation of Nietzsche's *The Birth of Tragedy*, and concentrates its attention on the phenomena of Socrates and the development of rational or dialectical thought. Maintains that Socrates and Euripides sounded "the death-knell of tragedy," and that through logical thought they subsumed art and tragedy under rationality. Discusses the possibility of a rebirth of tragedy after the age of Socratism, and finds that possibility in the "music-practising Socrates." Observes that Socratism feels within itself a sense of the inexplicable and the unintelligible, and that this need is manifested in Socrates' decision to set poetry to music shortly before his death. Views the "music-practising" Socrates as the tragic thinker who understands the limitations of ethics and morality, and who envisions the rebirth of tragedy. Ref. 1723.

1633 Calesi, Vasile. *The 'Death of Socrates' in Diderot and the Eighteenth Century Philosophers.* Doctoral dissertation. The Ohio State University, 1963.

Stresses the similarities between the repression of free thought and expression in France during the eighteenth century and the Athenian religious intolerance at the end of the fifth century B.C., especially in the context of Socrates' trial. Notes the role played by Palissot and other comic French playwrights in the attack against the philosophers -- something reminiscent of Aristophanes and the Athenian comic poets who also attacked philosophers and men of ideas. Observes how the Encyclopaedists (Diderot, Voltaire, and others) appealed to Socrates, and how his image underwent several changes in their hands: Socrates as the father of philosophy, as the martyr for freedom, and as a symbol for the immortality of ideas. Maintains that the symbol of Socrates' death was often used by the *philosophes* as a defensive weapon against their attackers. Comments on the ways in which Voltaire, Diderot, and Rousseau were identified with Socrates.

1634 Calogero, Guido. *Erasmo, Socrate e il Nuovo Testamento.* Rome: Accademia Nazionale del Lincei, 1972.

Pamphlet (20 pp.) which contains a speech delivered on the occasion of the 500th anniversary of the birth of Erasmus. Examines the influence of Socrates on Erasmus, and quotes abundantly from the latter's letters. Ref. 1656.

1635 Carter, R. E. "Saint John Chrysostom's Rhetorical Use of the Socratic Distinction Between Kingship and Tyranny." *Traditio,* 14 (1958), pp. 367-371.

Comments on Saint John Chrysostom's appeal to the Socratic distinction between a king and a tyrant, and explores the various ways in which such a distinction allowed him to defend the Christian point of view in the context of several controversies.

1636 Christodolou, K. "Socrate chez Montaigne et Pascal." *Diotima,* 7 (1979), pp. 39-50.

Reviews Montaigne's description and interpretation of Socrates as a soul of diverse levels of depth. Examines

Pascal's reaction to the Socrates of Montaigne, and analyses his ambivalence towards the pagan ideal of virtue which Montaigne recognized in the Greek philosopher.

1637 Cohen, Cynthia B. "The Trials of Socrates and Joseph K." *Philosophy and Literature*, 4 (1980), pp. 212-228.

Compares and contrasts Socrates and Joseph K (Kafka's character). Argues that Socrates' confession of ignorance rests on only one of three possible meanings of ignorance, one that overlooks the nature and function of particulars, while relying too heavily on a deductively derived awareness of universal principles. Explains how Joseph K, on the other hand, restricts himself to the realm of conflicting particulars, and refuses to liberate himself by an appeal to generalization.

1638 Cohen, Maurice. "Confucius and Socrates." *The Journal of Chinese Philosophy*, 3 (1976), pp. 159-168.

Examines the similarities and differences between the philosophical activities of Socrates and Confucius, and stresses their common unwillingness to define the chief concepts with which they were concerned. Attributes such unwillingness to their commitment to a practical and reformist moral mission. Draws attention to the influence of their traditions and to the ways in which they have influenced each other.

1639 Craft, Jimmy Lee. *Some Remarks on Socrates and Wittgenstein*. Doctoral dissertation. University of Texas at Austin, 1977.

Establishes a comparison between Socrates' doctrine of recollection (as developed in the *Meno*) and Wittgenstein's doctrine of grammatical reminders (with special emphasis on *Philosophical Investigations*, Sections 1-24). Endeavors to shed light (1) on the difficulty of distinguishing a description of the uses of language from a description of the form of words used, and (2) on the conception of the working of language created by the failure to recognize that distinction.

1640 Criscuolo, U. "Sull' epistola di Giulano imperatore al filosofo Temistio," *Koinonia*, 7 (1983), pp. 89-111.

Reviews and analyzes the major ideas and principles enunciated by Julian in his letter to Themistius. Notes the importance attached by Julian to the example set by Socrates, with its accompanying implications: a commitment to the spirit of philosophy and to the quest for self-knowledge, and the urgency of injecting rational principles into political affairs.

1641 Dannhauser, Werner J. *Nietzsche's View of Socrates.* Ithaca, N.Y.: Cornell University Press, 1974.

Attempts to elucidate several critical aspects of Nietzsche's philosophy by the light provided by an appreciation of his understanding of Socrates. Relies on certain insights of Lukács' *Der Zerstörung der Vernunft.* Observes that Kaufmann's interpretation does not shed enough light on the ambiguities of Nietzsche's thought. Traces and documents practically all of Nietzsche's references to Socrates, and notes his superb understanding of the critical spirit of Socratic philosophy. Emphasizes the persistent contest which Nietzsche sustained against the Socratic spirit, especially with respect to ethical ideas. Calls attention to the positive and negative stances of Nietzsche towards Socrates: positive towards the man, but negative towards him as the advocate of Socratism. Notes that Nietzsche's insistence that his writings should always be questioned reflects the influence of Socrates' dialectical method. Ref. 1723.

1641a De Grazia, Sebastian. "Crossings to Another World: Machiavelli and Others." *The Journal of the History of Ideas*, 45 (1984), pp. 145-151.

Establishes a comparison between Socrates' anticipation of death as a journey to another world (*Apology* 40e-41c) and Machiavelli's comments to Francesco Vettori in 1513 concerning his nightly conversations with great spirits of antiquity. Discusses also how others (*e.g.*, Lucian and Petrach) understood or visualized the passage from this world to the world of the dead.

1642 Déman, Thomas. "Socrate dans l'oeuvre de Saint Thomas d'Aquin." *Revue des Sciences Philosophiques et Théologiques*, 29 (1940), pp. 177-205.

Examines the references to Socrates in the writings of Saint Thomas Aquinas, and comments on his understanding and appreciation of Socrates as the embodiment of the philosophical life. Notes that he was not quite able to comprehend fully the import and extent of the moral revolution brought about by Socrates.

1643 Derrida, Jacques. *La carte postale de Socrate à Freud et au-delà.* Paris: Flammarion, 1980.

Develops a mock-epistolary discussion concerning the controversy surrounding the authenticity and import of the Platonic letters. Uses this discussion as a point of departure for a wider treatment of the problem of human relationship. Deals with *Beyond the Pleasure Principle* and with Lacan's psychoanalytic interpretation of "The Purloined Letter." Aims at clarifying the problem of the relationship between written messages and actual human situation.

1644 Derrida, Jacques. *The Post Card: From Socrates to Freud and Beyond.* Translated by Alan Bass. Chicago: The University of Chicago Press, 1987.

English translation of Derrida's *La carte postale de Socrate à Freud et au-delà.* Ref. 1643.

1645 Dilman, Ilham. "Socrates and Dostoyevsky on Punishment." *Philosophy and Literature*, 1 (1976), pp. 66-78.

Examines Socrates' view that punishment reintegrates the wrong-doer with the good, and regards this idea of punishment as neither retributive nor therapeutic. Understands the Socratic concept of punishment as one in which the pain inflicted is a source of moral awakening. Relates the Socratic position to that advanced by Dostoyevsky in *Crime and Punishment.*

1646 Di Lorenzo, Raymond. "The Critique of Socrates in Cicero's *De oratore: Ornatus* and the Nature of Wisdom." *Philosophy and Rhetoric*, 11 (1978), pp. 247-261.

Attempts to show how Cicero's notion of *ornatus* functions as the underlying principle of his critique of Socrates as a philosopher. Examines the role played by Licinus Crassus as the ideal orator, and compares his representation in Cicero's works with the portrait of Socrates created by Plato.

1647 Dimundo, R. "Da Socrate a Eumolpo. Degradazione dei personaggi e delle funzioni nella novella del fanciullo di Pergamo." *Materiali e Discussioni per l'analisi dei testi classici*, 10-11 (1983), pp. 255-265.

Analyzes the parallelism that can be constructed between the relationship of Socrates and Alcibiades on the one hand, and, on the other, the relationship of Eumolpus and the boy from Pergamum in the novel of Petronius. Relies on Plato's *Symposium* for its description of the relationship between Socrates and Alcibiades.

1648 Döring, Klaus. *Exemplum Socratis. Studien zur Sokratesnachwirkung in der Kynisch-stoischen Popularphilosophie der frühen Kaiserzeit und im frühen Christentum.* Wiesbaden: Franz Steiner Verlag, 1979.

Contains a general introduction which discusses the reception and impact of Socrates in the ancient Greek and Roman world. Devotes one chapter to the influence of Socrates on Seneca, and one chapter to Epictetus' debt to Socrates' philosophy and example. Reviews the impact of Socrates on Dio Chrysostomus and on the early Christian martyrs. Includes one chapter on the spurious Socratic and Xenophontean epistles. Provides an extended bibliography.

1649 Dudley, Donald R. *A History of Cynicism: From Diogenes to the 6th Century A.D.* Chicago: Ares Publishers, 1980.

Originally published by Cambridge University Press in 1937. Discusses the development of Cynicism from the middle of the fourth century B.C. to the end of Roman times. Deals with the relationship between Diogenes of Sinope and Antisthenes, and between Antisthenes and Socrates. Maintains that true Cynicism can only be traced back to Diogenes of Sinope, and argues that the representation of Antisthenes as the founder of the Cynic movement is a late fabrication of Hellenistic time. Rejects as unhistorical the succession Socrates-Antisthenes-Diogenes, and thus argues against the interpretation of Socrates as the real source of Cynicism.

1650 Dunne, Mary Rachel. *Kierkegaard and Socratic Ignorance: A Study of the Task of a Philosopher in Relationship to Christianity*. Doctoral dissertation. University of Notre Dame, 1970.

Takes as its point of departure Harold Durfee's "The Second Stage of Kierkegaard's Scholarship in America" (*International Philosophical Quarterly*, 3, 1963, pp. 121-139), where it is argued that Kierkegaard's philosophy of religion virtually eliminated the philosophical need to come to grips with the problem of ultimate reality. Develops an analysis of the relationship (and 'dis-relationship') between philosophy and Christianity, and finds that Socrates (who for Kierkegaard represents philosophy at its best) is the key to the solution of the problem. Explores the negative and positive significance of Socrates' confession of ignorance in terms of the religious questions, "What is God, and what is the self?" Works out a Socratic analysis of the answers developed by Hegel and Feuerbach, exposing what it views as its failures. Notes that the Socratic position allows us to move from the 'known' to the 'unknown' and to paradox. Concludes that the Socratic inwardness entailed by Socrates' ignorance is "the correct posture" of someone who wishes to be related to Christianity: "The task of the philosopher in relation to Christianity is to discover his own ignorance and in so doing to become able to provide the same therapeutic service to others" -- an exercise reminiscent of the repentance preached by John the Baptist. Ref. 1692.

1651 Dunshirn, A. *Der Humor des Sokrates*. Doctoral dissertation. University of Vienna, 1982.

Ref. 750.

1652 Eichthal, Gustave. *Socrate et notre temps. Théologie de Socrate. Dogme et providence*. Paris, 1881.

Examines Socrates' thought against the background of religious issues and problems of the nineteenth century. Views Socrates as the true precursor of classical theology and as the real source of theodicy. Maintains that he was able to give to his ideas the true structure of a theological system.

1653 Ellerman, Carl Paul. *Nietzsche: The Mask of Truth and the Death of the Socratic Man.* Doctoral dissertation. Syracuse University, 1976.

Begins with the exploration of the question of whether the human species is to be guided in its present predicament by a Socratic will to truth, or by an antithetical will to fiction, illusion, and myth. Focuses its analysis of Nietzsche on his paradoxical relationship both to truth in a Socratic sense and to a Dionysian will to fiction and illusion. Examines his atheism with reference to his archetypal Socratic quest to abolish fiction, illusion, and myth. Discusses his "vituperative condemnation" of Christianity and his attack on radical meaninglessness or nihilism. Regards him as an author who "used-up his life in the Socratic service of truth." Concludes with comments on the post-Nietzschean man: he is a character in search of himself, who "must lose his authors in order to become an authentic creator of himself." Ref. 1723.

1654 Ellis, Madeleine B. *Rousseau's Socratic Aemilian Myths: A Literary Collation of Emile and The Social Contract.* Columbus: Ohio State University Press, 1977.

Examines the structure and content of Rousseau's *Emile* and *The Social Contract*, stressing the organic continuity between them. Deals extensively and in great detail with Rousseau's two major sources of inspiration, namely, Jesus and Socrates. Studies all the explicit references to Socrates in the two works under consideration, and discusses the influence of the Platonic Socrates in the formation of Rousseau's thought. Notes that Socrates was his acknowledged master, and that countless Socratic themes appear repeatedly and clearly throughout his writings, specifically with respect to his ideas on happiness, friendship, gymnastics and training, wealth and poverty, wisdom, family life, and politics. Emphasizes the genuinely Socratic character of Rousseau's philosophical mission. Comments on certain similarities between Socrates and Rousseau, in particular in what concerns their spirit of independence and the political vicissitudes that beset them.

1655 Erasmus of Rotterdam, Desiderius. *The Godly Feast. The Colloquies of Erasmus.* Translated by Craig R. Thompson. Chicago: The University of Chicago Press, 1965, pp. 46-78.

Annotated English translation of Erasmus' *Colloquia familiaria*, including his *Convivium religiosum*. Ref. 1656.

1656 Erasmus of Rotterdam, Desiderius. *Convivium religiosum. Colloquia familiaria.* Basel: John Froben, 1522.

[There are no works by Erasmus specifically dealing with Socrates. And yet, the name of Socrates appears repeatedly throughout his voluminous writings. Of particular interest, for instance, are the references to Socrates in the *Colloquia familiaria*: Socrates is said to have brought down philosophy from Heaven (*De utilitate colloquium*); Socrates' glory is said to be the result of his virtuous life (*Philodoxus*); the uncouth behavior of Xanthippe is described (*Convivium poeticum*); Socrates' patience and forebearance are extolled (*Nephalion symposion*). But the most celebrated, important, and lengthiest statement about Socrates is found in the *Convivium religiosum.*]

Compares Socrates' ideas about life and death with those of Cicero and those of Saint Paul. Notes that for Socrates "the human soul is placed in this body as if in a garrison which it must not abandon except by the commander's order, or remain in it longer than suits him who stationed it here." Recalls that Saint Paul speaks of the body as a tabernacle: "For we who are in this tabernacle do groan, being burdened") -- words reminiscent of Socrates. Praises Socrates' words to Crito just before the execution: "Whether God will approve of my works, I do not know; certainly I have tried hard to please him. Yet I have good hope that he will accept my efforts." Concludes with the following words about Socrates: "An admirable spirit, surely, in one who did not know Christ and the Sacred Scriptures. And so, when I read such things about him, I cannot avoid exclaiming: Holy Socrates, pray for us!" (*Sancte Socrates, ora pro nobis*). Ref. 1634, 1710.

1657 Erde, Edmund L. "Founding Morality: Hume v. Plato, or Hume and Plato." *The Southwestern Journal of Philosophy*, 9 (1978), pp. 19-25.

Attempts to correct Hume's commentary on the *Crito*, and

seeks to clarify the grounds of morality and community. Argues that Hume is mistaken in believing that the *Crito* is incompatible with his idea that the moral force of a social contract depends on an antecedent moral context in which promises have a moral meaning. Relates the notion of such a context to the idea of governmental paternalism.

1658 Field, Guy C. "Socrates and Plato in Post-Aristotelian Tradition." *The Classical Quarterly*, 18 (1924), pp. 127-136; 19 (1925), pp. 1-14.

Ref. 604.

1659 Fiore, Benjamin. *The Function of Personal Example in the Socratic and Pastoral Epistles*. Doctoral dissertation. Yale University, 1982.

Ref. 759.

1660 Franceschini, E. "Il liber philosophorum moralium antiquorum. Testo critico." *Atti del Reale Istituto Veneto di Scienze, Lettere ed Arti*, 41 (1931-1932), pp. 393-597.

Critical annotated edition of the Latin version of a chapter on Socrates of an ancient work of the middle of the eleventh century, and which goes back to Arabic sources. Contains a list of ancient books on Socrates and a compilation of apoththegms attributed to him.

1661 Friedländer, Paul. "Socrates Enters Rome." *The American Journal of Philology*, 66 (1945), pp. 337ff.

Reprinted in Friedländer's *Plato: An Introduction* (Part 2, Chapter 18). Establishes a textual and ideological comparison between Polybius' statements on the education and character of Scipio Africanus Minor (*On Virtues and Vices, Histories*, xxxi, 23-30) and Plato's *Alcibiades I*. Argues that Polybius must have been acquainted with Plato's dialogue. Sees in Polybius' reported relationship with Scipio a distinct echo of the relationship between Socrates and the young Alcibiades, and concludes that the educational force of the Socratic spirit must have been powerfully at work in the Roman world of Polybius, who can be regarded as one of the principal agencies in the transference of the Socratic influence from Greece to Rome. Adds a concluding section on a comparison between the *Alcibiades I* and Aristotle's *Eroticus* (*Fragmenta*, 96). Ref. 608.

1662 Friedman, John A. "The Nature of the Dialogue: Freud and Socrates." *Human Studies*, 2 (1959), pp. 229-246.

Studies the significant commonality of reflection that determines the Socratic dialogue and the psychoanalytical technique associated with Freud. Explores the role played by the confession of ignorance as an initial stage in both, and stresses the importance of affectively determined guidance and the ideal identification with the interlocutor which characterize both the Socratic dialogue and psychoanalytic therapy.

1663 Friedrich, R. "Euripidaristophanizein and Nietzschesokratizein: Aristophanes, Nietzsche, and the Death of Tragedy." *Dionysius*, 4 (1980), pp. 5-36.

Notes the striking similarity between Aristophanes' paradoxical stance towards Euripides and Nietzsche's apparently ambivalent attitude towards Socrates. Maintains that just as Aristophanes attacked Euripides while being himself influenced by the spirit of tragedy, Nietzsche incorrectly blamed the rationalism of Socrates without providing a meaningful substitute for it. Ref. 1723.

1664 Fries, Carl. *Das philosophische Gespräch von Hiob bis Platon*. Tübingen, 1904.

Maintains that the most adequate approach to Socrates is one that allows us to see him as a philosopher endowed with a host of oriental ornaments. Claims that in him we can discern the presence of themes derived from the Upanishads and from Buddhism. Endeavors to establish a correlation between the heroic Socrates created by Plato on the one hand, and on the other the oriental sage Yajnavalkya and the traditional saints of Buddhism.

1665 Galluci, Gerald M. *Freud: A Socratic Man*. Doctoral dissertation. University of Pittsburgh, 1978.

Notes that through the impact of Freudian psychoanalysis, contemporary political philosophers have discovered that man is a much more complex phenomenon than was thought to be in previous times. Argues that by his discovery of the unconscious, Freud was able to bring about a corrected view of human nature, and that thereby he became relevant as a political philosopher for whom the mind is explainable in terms of a conflict between internal authority and the individual. Maintains that Freud was a political philosopher of the internal *polis* -- the *polis* which engaged so intensely the imagination of Socrates. Points out that Freud, just like Socrates, practiced the art of the "care of the soul" as a genuine Socratic statesman.

1666 Geffcken, Johannes. "Antiplatonika." *Hermes*, 64 (1929), pp. 87-110.

Reviews various anti-Socratic and anti-Platonic literary currents in antiquity, from Socrates' death to the second century B.C. Discusses specifically the significance of Aristoxenus as a representative of those currents.

1667 Giannaras, A. "Platon und K. Popper: Zur Kritik der politischen Philosophie Platons." *Philosophia*, 3 (1973), pp. 208-255.

Ref. 1257.

1668 Groarke, Leo. "The Socratic Dictum and the Importance of Philosophy." *Teaching Philosophy*, 8 (1985), pp. 193-196.

Examines the significance of Socrates' ideas as the foundation of education, and argues that philosophy and the teaching of philosophy have an important part to play in all modern democratic societies.

1669 Guilhamet, Leon. "Socrates and Post-Socratic Satire." *The Journal of the History of Ideas*, 46 (1985), pp. 3-12.

Examines the relationship between Socrates and satire, as this genre was developed in the ancient world after Aristophanes and Plato. Begins with an analysis of the work of Lucilius (180-102 B.C.) and Lucian. Includes a discussion of satirical literature in the Renaissance and the eighteenth century (Erasmus, Rabelais, and Diderot). Calls attention to the fact that it was not until the nineteenth century that scholars began to recognize a clear distinction between Socrates and Plato.

1670 Guy, Alain. "Le socratisme d' Amedée Ponceau." *Revue de Metaphysique et de Morale*, 73 (1968), pp. 361-363.

Gives a brief analysis of the Socratic method as it is employed in Ponceau's chief work, *Initiation philosophique.*

1671 Hamann, Johann Georg. *Sokratische Denkwürdigkeiten.* Stuttgart: Reclam, 1968.

Ref. 1583.

1672 Hammond, A. L. "*Euthyphro*, Mill, and Mr. Lewis." *The Journal of Philosophy*, 49 (1952), pp. 377-392.

Ref. 1397.

1673 Harrison, Derek. "Keeping It Alive." *Teaching Philosophy*, 8 (1985), pp. 201-206.

Deals with the significance and the effectiveness of presentation of Socrates' image and method among students in introductory philosophy courses. Stresses the importance of Socrates' cleverness, youthfulness, idealism, and non-conformity for the educational experience.

1674 Hasse, H. *Das Problem des Sokrates bei Friedrich Nietzsche.* Leipzig, 1918.

Examines Nietzsche's assessment of Socrates as the great originator of European cultural decadence. Attempts to resolve the apparent contradiction between Nietzsche's great admiration for Socrates and his contempt of the ethical ideals for which Socratic philosophy stands. Ref. 1723.

1675 Hathaway, Ronald F. "Cicero, *De republica* II, and His Socratic View of History." *The Journal of the History of*

*Ideas*, 29 (1968), pp. 3-12.

Argues that the ambiguity which derives from Cicero's *De republic* is the result of the influence of Socrates' political philosophy, and not the consequence of the concept of natural law associated with Stoicism. Suggests that Scipio's defense of the Roman polity is Socratic, in so far as it recognizes that despite the tension between nature and the laws, there exists "a natural articulation" of justice.

1676 Hathaway, Ronald F. "The Neoplatonist Interpretation of Plato: Remarks on Its Decisive Characteristics." *The Journal of the History of Philosophy*, 7 (1969), pp. 19-26.

Notes that the neo-Platonic interpretations of Plato's philosophy tend to ignore the Socratic elements of the dialogues and pay little attention to the genuine character of Socrates' perplexity and confession of ignorance.

1677 Hegel, Georg F. W. *Lectures on the History of Philosophy*. Translated by E. S. Haldane. London: Routledge & Kegan Paul, 1963 (3 vols.), Vol. 1, pp. 384-448.

Lectures delivered between 1805 and 1830 which cover the entire history of philosophy. Part 1, Chapter 2, deals with Socrates. Views him as the great embodiment of subjective consciousness, and as the focal point for the emergence of the universal Self. Attributes to Socrates the true origin of moral philosophy. Deals in great detail with the development of the Socratic method, with Socrates' intellectual midwifery, and with his confession of ignorance. Interprets the Socratic divine voice or sign as a manifestation of pure subjective consciousness (*i.e.*, conscience). Examines the testimonies of Aristophanes, Xenophon, and Plato, and concludes that it is chiefly in Xenophon that we can find the final point reached by Socrates in the development of his philosophy. Attempts to understand the Athenians' decision to destroy Socrates: the objective (tribal) consciousness could not tolerate the existence of pure subjectivity in its midst. Ref. 1700.

1678 Hertel, Wolf. *Sokrates in der deutschen Dichtung der Aufklärung. Ein Beitrag zur Geistesgeschichte des 18. Jahrhunderts*. Doctoral dissertation. University of Munich, 1921.

Examines the interpretation of Socrates among major poets and writers of the German Enlightenment. Stresses the reverence with which some of them (for instance, Wieland) treated Socrates.

1679 Hess, M. Whitecomb. "Kierkegaard and Socrates." *The Christian Century*, 82 (1965), pp. 736-738.

Takes issue with existentialists (like Sartre) who have allegedly derived their irrational and atheistic philosophy from Socrates and Kierkegaard. Argues that Socrates' call for self-knowledge moved Kierkegaard to a recognition of the self's awareness of its relationship to God in Christ. Maintains that what Socrates had seen as the beginning of wisdom, Kierkegaard regarded as the beginning of life, that is, the life of the spirit in the presence of God. Ref. 1692.

1680 Hildebrandt, Kurt. *Nietzsches Wettkampf mit Sokrates und Plato.* Dresden: Sybillen, 1922.

Offers a chronological analysis of Nietzsche's writings. Explains his paradoxical attitude towards Socrates by introducing a sharp distinction between 'Socratism' and the personality of Socrates. Claims that Nietzsche's opposition and contempt were directed at the former, inasmuch as it represented for him a decadent tendency which stood for plebeian values, and a rationalistic and intellectualistic stance towards human existence. Maintains that Nietzsche's admiration and affection were for Socrates as a man. Ref. 1723.

1681 Hock, R. F. "Simon the Shoemaker as an Ideal Cynic." *Greek, Roman and Byzantine Studies*, 17 (1976), pp. 41-53.

Discusses the significance of Simon and his reported association with Socrates. Observes that the legends and traditions about Simon have often been built around the question of whether the philosopher, as a true Cynic, should associate himself only with ordinary people, not with kings and oligarchs.

1682 Holt, Edwin B. *The Freudian Wish and Its Place in Ethics.* New York: H. Holt & Co., 1915, pp. 141, 145, 148.

Defends the basic principles of Socratic ethics from the standpoint of psychoanalysis, and sees Freudian ethics as a literal and concrete justification of the Socratic doctrines.

1683 "Hopes to See Socrates." *The New York Times*, June 28, 1932, p. 10.

Unsigned news report which comments on Harry A. Ironside's remarks about Socrates, in his speech at the meeting of the New York Summer School of Theology. Quotes Ironside's statement: "I hope to see Socrates in heaven. I only hope God spoke to the old man and got him into heaven."

1684 Hu Shih. "The Scientific Spirit and Method of Chinese Philosophy." *The Chinese Mind*. Edited by Charles A. Moore. Honolulu: University of Hawaii Press, 1967, pp. 104-131.

Establishes a comparison between Socrates and Confucius, and notes that in both instances we come upon individuals who did not profess to be wise men but merely men who loved wisdom. Discusses the Confucian tradition, and observes that it always encouraged independent thinking. Comments on the 'Socratic tradition' of Confucius which led Chu Hsi to formulate a set of principles on the spirit, method, and procedure of scientific research and investigation.

1685 Jagu, Amand. *Epictète et Platon. Essai sur les relations du stoïcisme et du platonisme à propos de la morale des "Entretiens."* Paris, 1946.

Discusses the influence of Socrates on Epictetus, and in particular the portrait of the ideal wise man drawn by Epictetus in his *Discourses* on the basis of his understanding of the philosophy and personality of Socrates.

1686 Jöel, Karl. "Die Auffassung der Kynischen Sokratik." *Archiv für Geschichte der Philosophie*, 20 (1907), pp. 1-24 and 147-170.

Discusses the influence of Socrates' ideas on the development of Cynicism. Expresses reservations concerning the idea that the Cynic movement can be traced back directly to Socrates.

1687 Jordan, James N. "Socrates' Wisdom and Kant's Virtue." *The Southwestern Journal of Philosophy*, 4 (1973), pp. 7-23.

Establishes a comparison between the Kantian account of the Good Will and Socrates' arguments concerning wisdom in the *Euthydemus* and the *Meno*. Concludes that there is a remarkable similarity between them, and that both anticipate to some extent G. E. Moore's principle of organic wholes. Discusses various allegedly inaccurate interpretations of the Kantian position (such as those advanced by Paton, Ross, and Broad).

1688 Katz, Ellen L. *Niels Bohr: Philosopher-Physicist*. Doctoral dissertation. New York University, 1986.

Discusses in the concluding section of Chapter 5 (pp. 161-172) the influence of Socrates in the development of Bohr's thought. Notes that of all the ancient philosophers, it was Socrates who had the greatest influence on Bohr, and that this influence probably came to him through the agency of Kierkegaard. Finds many similarities between the personalities and approaches to the problems of philosophy of Socrates and Bohr: their commitment to the unity of theory and practice, their pursuit of knowledge in an atmosphere of openness and questioning, and their overwhelming commitment to the search for truth. Comments also on the paradoxical character of their methods and conclusions.

1689 Kaufmann, Walter. "Nietzsche's Admiration for Socrates." *Nietzsche: Philosopher, Psychologist, Antichrist*. New York: Vintage Books, 1968, pp. 319-411.

Views Nietzsche's admiration for Socrates as the focal point of all his philosophy, especially of his ideas concerning reason and morality. Argues that Nietzsche's conception of his task was modelled in part after Socrates' own understanding of his mission. Discusses the interpretation of Socrates in *The Birth of Tragedy*, where he appears as a semi-god in whom Apollo and Dionysus are mysteriously fused. Draws attention to the influence of the Platonic *Symposium* in Nietzsche's understanding of the Socratic presence, and emphasizes the distinction between 'Socratism' (which Nietzsche despised) and Socrates himself (whom Nietzsche loved and admired). Expands on the representation of Socrates as a decisive turning point in history, and on Nietzsche's concept on him as the highest human ideal: the passionate man who is able to master fully all his emotions. Relates the paradoxical and contradictory texture of Nietzsche's thought and personality to the similar texture that can be discerned in Socrates. Makes abundant allusions to several works of Nietzsche. Ref. 1722, 1723.

1690 Kellerman, Frederick. *Montaigne's Socrates*. Doctoral dissertation. Indiana University, 1954.

Traces the development of Montaigne's interpretation of Socrates, and notes that an understanding of the Socratic influence on Montaigne is essential for an adequate appreciation of the *Essais*. Recounts the various allusions to Socrates in the editions of the *Essais*: fifteen in 1580, twenty-eight in 1588, and seventy-two 1592. Observes that Montaigne's image of Socrates is mostly un-Platonic, and that he rejected many features of Plato's Socrates, while accepting the veracity of Xenophon's testimony. Recognizes several important Socratic elements as having played a crucial role in Montaigne: the skeptical tendency, Socrates' wise ignorance, the call to self-knowledge and self-abasement, and the pedagogical method and goal. Maintains that Socrates acted as a moral guide for the development of Montaigne's ethical ideas.

1691 Kierkegaard, Søren. *The Concept of Irony, with Constant Reference to Socrates*. Translated by Lee M. Capel. New York: Harper & Row Publishers, 1965.

English translation of Kierkegaard's *Om Begrebet Ironi med stadigt Hensyn til Socrates*. Ref. 1692.

1692 Kierkegaard, Søren. *Om Begrebet Ironi med stadigt Hensyn til Socrates*. Copenhagen, 1841.

Develops the concept of irony as an existential stance of suspension which transcends ordinary humor and intellectual skepticism, and which expresses in a fundamental way the individual's confrontation with the duality of finitude and infinity. Views irony as the 'mastered moment' in which the self is successful in realizing fully its actuality. Takes as its point of departure Socrates' memorable irony, and retains it as the underlying theme of all its reflections. Interprets the genesis of Socrates' irony as a manifestation of the duality of his personality: in him, the external and the internal selves did not form a harmonious unity. Argues that the Socratic presence can only be apprehended by means of an 'internal calculation.' Develops this method by eliciting a phenomenological account of Socrates from Xenophon, Plato, and Aristophanes. Finds the idea of irony absent from Xenophon's account, and deems this account to be superficial and prosaic, although faithful to the externalities of Socrates. Discovers a real ironical opposition in the seeminigly contradictory accounts of Plato and Xenophon. Devotes considerable attention to Plato's *Symposium*, *Protagoras*, *Phaedo*, *Apology*, and *Republic* (Book 1) -- that is, those dialogues in which the Socratic irony emerges most clearly to the foreground. Examines the phenomenon of Socrates' divine voice or sign, as well as the accusations levelled against him at the trial, and finds in them confirming hints concerning its interpretation of Socrates' irony. Reviews and criticizes Hegel's understanding of the Socratic philosophy, and delves into the question of whether we can view Socrates as the real founder of morality. Contains sections which deal with the development of the concept of irony in Fichte, Schlegel, and other German philosophers. Ref. 1629, 1650, 1677, 1679, 1700, 1702, 1715, 1717, 1742, 1745, 1755, 1770.

1693 Kivy, Peter. "Socrates' Discovery: Some Historical Reflections." *The Journal of Aesthetics and Art Criticism*, 39 (1981), pp. 303-314.

Discusses the "problem of taste" as this was viewed in England in the eighteenth century, and traces its roots to various sources, including Socrates' critique of the poets, and his contention that poetical inspiration entails some sort of divine possession.

1694 Kleve, K. "Naso magister erat. Sed quis Nasonis magister?" *Symbolae Osloenses*, 58 (1983), pp. 89-109.

Argues that an examination of the literary context of Ovid's *ars amatoria* leads us to conclude that the Latin poet was not the originator of didactic-erotic poetry, but that he belongs to a literary tradition that can be traced back to Epicurus, and to Socrates and the Sophists.

1695 Knös, B. "Les citations grecques de Montaigne." *Eranos*, 44 (1946), pp. 460-483.

Collects and comments on the numerous quotations of and references to Greek philosophers throughout Montaigne's *Essais*, with emphasis on those which reveal his appreciation and understanding of Socrates, who is referred to as "the master of masters."

1696 Landmann, Michael. "Socrates as a Precursor of Phenomenology." *Philosophy and Phenomenological Research*, 2 (1941-1942), pp. 15ff.

Regards Socrates as the precursor of Husserl's phenomenology, and discovers in him the seeds of the conceptual substantialism of phenomenologists. Maintains that traces of Husserl's concept of *Wesenschau* can be readily found in Socrates.

1697 Langan, J. "Socrates and Cicero: Two Approaches to the Role of Philosophy." *The Classical Bulletin*, 37 (1960), pp. 17-19 and 25.

Compares and contrasts the attitudes of Socrates and Cicero towards the issues of old age and death. Stresses the idealistic texture of the Socratic stance and the pragmatic tendencies of that of Cicero.

1698 Lanza, D. "La massima epicurea Nulla è per noi la morte." *Siculorum Gymnasium*, 33 (1980), pp. 357-365.

Reviews Epicurus' concept of death as a total privation of sensation and as a state of nothingness which can no longer affect the dead. Observes that in Socrates and in Aristotle we come upon a similar contemptuous concept of death.

1699 Larock, V. "Le Socrate 'oriental' de Bergson." *Réseau*, 18-19 (1972), pp. 47-57.

Discusses Bergson's interpretation and portrayal of Socrates in his *Les deux sources de la morale et de la religion*. Observes that the mystical and 'oriental' features of that portrayal may be the result of the influence of Plato's *Apology* on Bergson's understanding of Socrates.

1700 Larouche-Tanguay, Camillia. "Hegel et Kierkegaard: L'ironie comme thème philosophique." *Laval Théologique et Philosophique*, 39 (1983), pp. 269-282.

Argues that the fundamental differences between Hegel and Kierkegaard emerge to the foreground as one examines their interpretations of the meaning of Socrates' irony. Ref. 1677, 1692.

1701 Lévêque, C. "La vie socratique et la vie cynique." *Séances et Travaux de l'Académie des Sciences Morales et Politiques*, 127 (1887), pp. 199-201.

Discusses the sources of the Cynics' concept of the ideal life, and draws a comparison between the Socratic ideal (for instance, as developed by Antisthenes) and the Cynic ideal.

1702 Levi, Albert W. "A Hundred Years After Kierkegaard." *The Kenyon Review*, 18 (1956), pp. 169-182.

Explores the way in which Kierkegaard gave expression to the three critical stages in a person's life: (1) the aesthetic stage, which is characterized by hedonism, and is illustrated by Mozart's *Don Juan*; (2) the ethical stage, which is animated by personal commitment from earnest choice, and is exemplified by Socrates; and (3) the religious stage, where through faith in God the postulates of human morality are transcended. Notes that Kierkegaard views the Socrates of the *Crito* as a man fulfilling an obligation -- a decision carefully chosen after travelling ethical crossroads. Ref. 1703.

1703 Levi, Albert W. "The Idea of Socrates: The Philosophic Hero in the Nineteenth Century." *The Journal of the History of Ideas*, 17 (1956), pp. 89-108.

Reviews the philosophical portrayals of Socrates created by nineteenth century philosophers, and discusses the significance of Socratic thought in the writings of Hegel, Kierkegaard, J. S. Mill, and Nietzsche. Notes that although it may remain always impossible to delineate with precision the features of the historical Socrates, the quest for the significance and meaning of his philosophical message is an important process. Ref. 1702.

1704 Llamzon, Benjamin S. "Philosophy in the University: Athena or Socrates." *The Thomist*, 40 (1976), pp. 635-664.

Examines the clash between philosophy and tradition, as this develops in the context of university education in general and of catholic university education in particular. Contends that wisdom can emerge in two ways: either from society and tradition, or from self-examination and self-questioning. Speaks of the former way as "Athena's wisdom," and of the latter as Socratic. Attempts to resolve the conflict that arises between these two approaches in education, and suggests the possibility of transcending that conflict in order to arrive at an integrational solution.

1705 Lombardo, Joseph. "Husserl's Method in Phenomenology and the Socratic Method of Teaching." *Aitia*, 8 (1980), pp. 10-16.

Discusses the method involved in Husserl's genetic phenomenology, and explores the ways in which it can be applied to the teaching of philosophy. Discovers in Husserl's approach an application of the Socratic teaching. Emphasizes the importance and relevance of developing classroom teaching models that lead the learner from the concrete to the abstract, and from the particular to the general, and notes that such models can be readily found in Socrates' own pedagogical activities.

1706 Lundgren, Lars O. *Sokratesbilden. Fran Aristofanes till Nietzsche*. Stockholm: Almquist & Wiksell International, 1978.

Ref. 390.

1707 Mahood, G. H. "Socrates and Confucius: Moral Agents or Moral Philosophers." *Philosophy East and West*, 21 (1971), pp. 177-188.

Deals with the issue of whether it is relevant to an understanding of Socrates and Confucius as moral agents to examine their roles as practical moral philosophers. Rejects the contrast between Socrates the theoretician and Confucius the moralist, and the idea that their activities in the realm of moral experience belonged to two different dimensions.

1708 Mainberger, G. K. "Typologie der Nihilisme." *Annuaire de la Societé Suisse de Philosophie*, 42 (1983), pp. 125-146.

Discusses the meaning and development of nihilism, and argues that its history begins among the Greeks with Empedocles, Socrates, and Pyrrho, while among the Romans with Quintilian and among the Christians with Saint Augustine.

1709 Maranhão, Tulio. *Therapeutic Discourse and Socratic Dialogue: A Cultural Critique*. Madison: The University of Wisconsin Press, 1986.

Constructs an analysis of therapeutic discourse and Socratic dialogue, around the critical question, "What is it that really cures?" Applies its findings to psychoanalytic and family therapy situations, and adduces examples in which a typical Socratic dialogue is employed in such situations.

1710 Marcel, R. "Saint Socrate, patron de l'humanisme." *Revue Internationale de Philosophie*, 5 (1951), pp. 135-143.

Reviews the significance accorded to Socrates by the great humanists of the Renaissance. Comments on the process by which he was transformed into an ideal of human holiness by writers such as Erasmus. Ref. 1656.

1711 Martineau, Alain. "Socrate et Marcuse nous préviennent-ils contre les tyrans?" *Revue de l'Université d'Ottawa*, 56 (1986), pp. 173-181.

Discusses Marcuse's reference to Socrates' political subversiveness. Raises questions about the possibility of preventing tyranny, if those who are expected to oppose it do not hesitate to justify the use of selective violence and subversion.

1712 Matross, Ronald Philip. *Socratic Methods in Counseling and Psychotherapy.* Doctoral dissertation. University of Minnesota, 1975.

Attempts to determine the extent to which Socratic questioning can effect changes beyond those anticipated by an interviewer's overt conclusions. Suggests in its conclusion that Socratic questioning about specific modes of behavior can bring about changes in self-perception which are not attributable to the interviewer's statement of opinion.

1713 McAuley, Allyn David. *Western Rationalism and the Problem of Socrates.* Doctoral dissertation. University of California at Santa Cruz, 1980.

Maintains the following theses: (1) that major contemporary schools of moral and political philosophy view the Western tradition as a declining one; (2) that such an attitude is the result of a mistaken interpretation of the 'rationalistic' origins of that tradition; (3) that a study of the origins of Western rationalism shows that such an interpretation is misguided; and (4) that the assumption that the Western tradition is in decline is mistaken. Examines Nietzsche's critique of Western values and his assessment of Socrates' role in the history of those values. Ref. 1723.

1714 Metropoulos, Nicholas Demetrius. *The Relevance of the Socratic Method to Contemporary Adult Education.* Doctoral dissertation. Arizona State University, 1974.

Investigates the scope and effectiveness of the Socratic method as a tool for helping adult students achieve an increased awareness of value meanings, as these apply to the person and to others. Traces the influence of the Socratic method throughout Western educational theory, and examines its present-day use. Analyses the potential value of the Socratic method for adult education, and concludes with a proposal which shows a theoretical adult education program which incorporates the Socratic method.

1715 Morris, T. F. "Kierkegaard's Understanding of Socrates." *The International Journal for Philosophy of Religion*, 19 (1986), pp. 105-112.

Approaches Kierkegaard's understanding of Socrates through his description of the person who is related to God with infinite passion. Concludes that for Kierkegaard there are two types of Socratic religiousness: one in which the eternal is desired as a response to doubts about the relationship to God, and the other in which there is an abstaining from temporal things because they are less than eternal. Ref. 1692.

1716 Naddei Carbonara, M. "Socrate e i socratici minori in Diogene Laerzio e nello Zibaldone." *Atti dell' Accademia Pontaniana*, 30 (1981), pp. 247-268.

Develops an analysis of Leopardi's understanding and appreciation of Socrates and the minor Socratics. Stresses Leopardi's critical and respectful attitude towards Socrates, and points out the influence of Diogenes Laertius in Leopardi's acquaintance with Socrates and his circle.

1717 Nagley, Winfield E. "Kierkegaard's Early and Later View of Socratic Irony." *Thought*, 55 (1980), pp. 271-282.

Discusses Kierkegaard's confession in the *Concluding Unscientific Postscript*, namely, that his early assessment of Socrates in his *The Concept of Irony* was onesided and incomplete. Explains how in Kierkegaard's later view, Socrates appears as a true existential philosopher, as an ethicist, and as a deeply religious man. Argues that Kierkegaard's humorous 'confession' is really an admission of guilt for having misrepresented the Socratic presence. Ref. 1692.

1718 Naumann, H. "Die Gestalt des Sokrates und ihre Wirkungen auf die Weltliteratur." *Der altsprachliche Unterricht*, 12 (1969), 2, pp. 64-103.

Ref. 476.

1719 Nebel, Gerhard. *Sokrates*. Stuttgart: Ernst Klett Verlag, 1969.

Ref. 305.

1720 Neumann, Harry. "Is Philosophy Still Possible?" *The Thomist*, 36 (1972), pp. 545-565.

Argues that the perplexitity of philosophers as how to live best has often compelled them to question and challenge the morality of their specific contexts: thus, Socrates opposed civic piety in the name of a global morality, and, in later times, Rousseau stood against a global morality in the name of local and patriotic values. Questions whether in contemporary regimes, Socrates' accusers would not have been more philosophical than he, and whether under such regimes, philosophy (in Socrates' sense) would have been possible.

1721 Nietszche, Friedrich W. *The Birth of Tragedy from the Spirit of Music*. Translated by Clifton P. Fadiman. *The Philosophy of Nietzsche*. New York: The Modern Library, 1954, pp. 947-1088.

English translation of Nietzsche's *Die Geburt der Tragödie, oder Griechentum und Pessimismus*. Ref. 1723.

1722 Nietzsche, Friedrich W. *Der Wille zur Machte. Versuch einer Umwertung aller Werte*. Stuttgart: Alfred Kröner, 1964.

Originally published in 1901. Discusses or mentions Socrates and Socratic philosophy (Socratism) in a variety of places, for instance, in Sections 274, 427, 429-433, 435, 437, 441-443, and 578. Regards the appearance of Socrates as the advent of decadence among the Greeks and as the prelude of the decadence of the Western world. Views Socrates as the advocate *par excellence* of plebeian or non-aristocratic mob morality, and condemns the Socratic equation 'reason=virtue=happiness' as an absurd piece of morbid sophistry. Recognizes in Socrates the triumph of dialectics and slave morality over the true spirit of vitality and strength which had animated the Greek world before him.

1723 Nietzsche, Friedrich W. *Die Geburt der Tragödie, oder Griechentum und Pessimismus. Nietzsches Werke*. Salzburg: Verlag Das Bergland-Buch, n.d. (2 vols.), Vol. 1, pp. 589-661.

Originally published in 1872. Advances an interpretation of the ancient Greek tragic art in terms of two fundamental human modes of existence and expression: the Apollonian and the Dionysian. Conceives the former as the spirit of rationality and harmony, and the latter as the spirit of irrationality and passion. Discusses the presence and influence of Socrates and Socratism, and views him as the antithesis of the Dionysian spirit. Maintains that it was under the influence of Socratism that Euripides was successful in combating and vanquishing Aeschylean tragedy. Speaks of Socrates as "the most puzzling phenomenon of antiquity," whose death became an ideal of noble Greek youths. Interprets him as the archetype of the 'theoretical' man, who in the name of pure rationality was able to defeat permanently the Dionysian spirit that had permeated the earlier Greek world. Contrasts the somber pessimism of the ancient tragedians with the theoretical optimism of the Apollonian Socrates, for whom the nature of things is ultimately explainable in the light of reason. Argues that in the transformation of the Greek mind from a Dionysian mode to an Apollonian texture, Socrates was responsible for the advent of decadence in the Greek world. The main sections which deal specifically with Socrates are 12, 13, 14, and 15. Ref. 1626, 1632, 1653, 1663, 1674, 1680, 1689, 1713, 1739, 1744, 1765, 1772.

1724 Nietzsche, Friedrich W. "The Futile Intellectual: Vulgarity Versus Art." *The State Versus Socrates: A Case Study in Civic Freedom*. Edited by John D. Montgomery. Boston: The Beacon Press, 1954, pp. 103-110.

Excerpted from Nietzsche's *Beyond Good and Evil* and *The Birth of Tragedy* (*The Philosophy of Nietzsche*, New York: The Modern Library, 1927, pp. 100-101 and 263-270). Defines Socratism as the conviction that "no one desires to injure himself, hence all evil is done unwittingly." Regards this idea as a manifestation of a plebeian mentality ("This mode of reasoning savours of the populace"). Blames Socrates for having taken the side of reason against natural human instincts, and the side of knowledge against that of faith. Declares him to be the prototype of the theoretical optimist who views knowledge as a universal panacea. Ref. 1723.

1725 Nietzsche, Friedrich W. *The Will to Power*. Translated by Walter Kaufmann and R. J. Hollingdale. New York: Random House, 1967.

English translation of Nietzsche's *Der Wille zur Macht*.

Edited with commentary and facsimiles of pages of the original Ms. Ref. 1722.

1726 O'Brien, Charles H. "Jacob Burckhardt: The Historian as Socratic Humanist." *The Journal of Thought*, 16 (1981), pp. 51-73.

Discusses the affinity between the humanism of Burckhardt and that of Socrates, and concludes that they have in common certain personalist political and educational principles, as well as a commitment to promote enlightenment in the community. Argues that the 'realism' inherent in Burckhardt did not hinder his humanistic orientation, but served as a controlling factor in order to render it effective in the service of society.

1727 O'Flaherty, James C. "The Concept of Form in the *Socratic Memorabilia*." *Hamann's Socratic Memorabilia*. Edited and translated by James C. O'Flaherty. Baltimore: The Johns Hopkins Press, 1967, pp. 3-131.

Serves as the introduction to O'Flaherty's translation of Hamann's *Socratic Memorabilia*. Discusses the influence of Hellenism and Christianity on the development of Hamann's thought, and notes that these two ideological currents were seen by him as parts of a cultural and spiritual continuum. Comments on the influence of Socrates on Hamann. Emphasizes the role played by Socrates as a source of challenge to the rationalism of many of the philosophers of the Enlightenment. Develops a detailed analysis of Hamann's Socratic work, with particular attention to the relationship between its outward form (the style) and its inward form (the essential and dramatic unity of the work). Devotes one chapter to Hamann's biography and literary work, and one chapter to the issue of the genesis of the *Socratic Memorabilia*. Ref. 1583.

1728 Pecorino, Philip A. "The Midwife's Trickery or Teaching Philosophy: A Provocation." *Aitia*, 3 (1975), pp. 13-17.

Argues that the Socratic approach to teaching philosophy entails that the teacher should provoke, guide, and seduce the students, and, at times, go as far as to deceive them for methodological purposes.

1729 Perkinson, Henry J. *Since Socrates: Studies in the History of Western Education*. New York: Longman, 1980.

Contains original interpretative essays on the educational philosophy and influence of Socrates, Plato, Saint Augustine, Descartes, Locke, Rousseau, J. S. Mill, Dewey, and K. Popper. Examines each philosopher's educational ideas as integral components of his general philosophical outlook, and as elements of his intellectual development. Maintains that educational theory has been authoritarian since the time of Socrates, and that Popper's idea of education promises to lead us towards a non-authoritarian point of view.

1730 Pincherle, Mario. *La cicuta e la croce*. Ancona: Filelfo, 1977.

Develops the thesis that the real roots of Socrates (and even of the entire Hellenic civilization) are to be found in the Eastern world. Discovers a hidden symbolism in the hemlock cup drunk by Socrates, and establishes a parallelism between that symbol and the symbol of the Cross. Written mostly in the form of a dialogue.

1731 Pitkin, Walter B. "Then Came Socrates." *On My Own*. New York, 1944, pp. 235ff.

Recounts autobiographically Pitkin's first encounter with Socrates through the agency of Alfred H. Lloyd at the University of Michigan. Speaks of Socrates as "the only influence of the first magnitude between Thales and Dewey on Pitkin's own thought." Views Socrates as "the world's most magnificent Social Misfit," through whose questioning the tiny souls and midget minds of the two eternal racketeers of culture -- the priests and the politicians -- were effectively exposed.

1732 Popper, Karl R. *The Open Society and Its Enemies*. New York: Harper Torchbooks, 1963 (2 vols.).

Ref. 1283.

1733 Powell, Clifford John. *Didactic and Socratic Supervision with Novice Counselors: Effects on Anxiety and Ratings of the*

*Supervisory Experience*. Doctoral dissertation. University of Denver, 1983.

Contrasts the use of an information giving approach (didactic) with an approach which stresses self-discovery learning (Socratic) for novice counselors. Examines the differential effects on supervisees with respect to levels of anxiety, and observes that anxiety levels decrease significantly in the case of didactic subjects, but that they increase for Socratic subjects. Draws conclusions concerning the relative advantages and usefulness of both approaches.

1734 Raschini, Maria. *Interpretazioni socratische*. Milan: Marzorati Editore, 1970 (2 vols.).

Contains an introductory essay which discusses the Socratic problem and the reliability of the sources. Deals in Part 1 with various interpretations of Socrates from 1400 to 1700 (Cristoforo Landino, Gianozzo Manetti, Marsilio Ficino, Erasmus, Galileo, Campanella, Francis Bacon, and Vico), and in Part 2 with the different interpretations of Socrates developed during the Enlightenment (Bayle, Voltaire, Diderot and the Encyclopaedists, Rousseau, Mendelssohn, and Lessing). Ref. 1759.

1735 Richmond, William Kenneth. *Socrates and the Modern World: An Essay in the Philosophy of Education*. London: Alvin Redman, 1954.

Attempts to develop a new interpretation of Socrates in order to show the vitality of his message for the twentieth century. Emphasizes the influence of Socrates on education. Examines various conversations between Socrates and his interlocutors (in Plato's dialogues), and endeavors to clarify the sort of relationship between teacher and student which emerges from the Socratic paradigms. Maintains that only by an appeal to Socrates' call for self-examination, will modern education and contemporary civilization stand on a firm foundation. Compares Socrates with K. Jung (Chapter 3) and with Jesus (Chapter 4).

1736 Riley, Mark T. "The Epicurean Criticism of Socrates." *Phoenix*, 34 (1980), pp. 55-68.

Discusses the Epicureans' criticism of Socrates, and explains how and why they interpreted Socratic irony as an unwillingness to assist people genuinely and sincerely, and Socrates' confession of ignorance as a manifestation of hypocrisy. Argues that the Epicureans raised objections against Socrates' behavior rather than against his particular ideas, and that they viewed him as a man who did not say what he meant or thought, and who did not practice what he taught. Bases its comments on the texts of Philodemus of Gadara.

1737 Rist, John M. "Plotinus and the Daimonion of Socrates." *Phoenix*, 17 (1963), pp. 13-24.

Comments on various themes related to Plotinus' biography by Porphyry, specifically the transformation undergone by the interpretation of Socrates' divine voice or sign. Notes that this transformation, as manifested in Plotinus, reveals a trend towards the popularization or vulgarization of the phenomenon.

1738 Rosen, S. "Socrates' Dream." *Theoria*, 42 (1976), pp. 161-188.

Studies the import, limits, and goals of contempoary analytical thought, and sees in it an attempt to bring into reality Socrates' dream. Interprets this dream as a vision in which a synthetic understanding of reality is made possible.

1739 Sandvoss, E. *Sokrates und Nietzsche*. Leiden: E. J. Brill, 1966.

Reviews Nietzsche's conception of Socrates as the originator of cultural decadence among the Greeks, and discusses Nietzsche's paradoxical stance towards the Socratic phenomenon, that is, his immense admiration for Socrates, and his profound contempt towards the moral principles of Socratic philosophy. Ref. 1723.

1740 "Santayana and Socrates." *The New York Times*, August 1, 1926, Section 2, p. 4.

Unsigned literary commentary. Reviews Santayana's dialogue

on self-government (in *Dialogues in Limbo*), in which a stranger and Socrates are depicted in a conversation about the relationship between good government and the government that rests on the will of the governed. Notes that Santayana plays well the part of Glaucon-Polemarchus-Adeimantus, and approaches the issues in the style of the best of modern newspaper interviewers. Ref. 1839.

1741 Santayana, George. *Dialogues in Limbo*. New York: Charles Scribner's Sons, 1926.

Ref. 1839.

1742 Sarf, Harold. "Reflections on Kierkegaard's Socrates." *The Journal of the History of Ideas*, 44 (1983), pp. 255-276.

Attempts to clarify the precise nature of Kierkegaard's personal and intellectual relationship to Socrates, and comments on the way in which his understanding of Christianity affected that relationship. Stresses the significance of Socrates' irony in the formation of Kierkegaard's philosophy. Examines the distinction introduced by Kierkegaard between Socrates and Plato. Notes that "the image of Socrates as noble and simple, as honest and thoughtful, as a penetrating conversationalist, and as a philosopher who humbly admitted his ignorance among the cultured," appears to be based on Kierkegaard's reading and appreciation of Plato's *Symposium*. Observes that for Kierkegaard Socrates was "the highest embodiment of humanity that had hitherto been attained." Ref. 1692.

1743 Scheda, G. "Die Todesstunde Kaiser Julians." *Historia*, 15 (1966), pp. 380-383.

Comments on the descriptions of Julian's death given by Libanius and Ammianus Marcellinus, and notes the similarities between them and the descriptions of Socrates' death. Argues that in creating such similarities, those writers were attempting to vindicate the memory of the pagan emperor, who, after his death, was being attacked by the Christians.

1744 Schmidt, Hermann Josef. *Nietzsche und Sokrates; philosophische Untersuchungen zu Nietzsches Sokratesbild*. Meisenheim: Anton Hain, 1969.

Provides an exhaustive examination of Nietzsche's interpretation of Socrates as a person and as a philosopher. Reviews in detail the import of Nietzsche's seemingly ambivalent conclusions concerning the significance of the Socratic phenomenon. Endeavors to shed light on Nietzsche's motives for having undertaken a critique of Socrates, and distinguishes the motive that may be deemed subtantial from those of a personal nature. Comments on Nietzsche's 'ambition' to influence his culture as powerfully as Socrates influenced his own. Ref. 1723.

1745 Schottländer, Rudolf. "Søren Kierkegaards Sokratesauffassung." *Philosophischer Anzeiger*. Tübingen, 1927, pp. 27ff.

Discusses Kierkegaard's interpretation of Socrates. Explores the significance of his understanding of Socratic irony, especially against the background of Hegel's philosophy. 1692.

1746 Schuetz, P. "Oedipus wider Sokrates." *Antaios*, 2 (1960), pp. 259-265.

Develops an interpretation of the Oedipus myth in the light provided by Socrates' philosophy.

1747 Schuhl, Pierre Maxime. "Le médecin de soi-même. De Socrate à la reine Christine." *Etudes platoniciennes*. Paris: Presses Universitaires de France, 1960, pp. 167-174.

Discusses the distinction between the knowledge conveyed by a physician concerning the state of health of a patient and the knowledge that the patient might have about his own health. Makes reference to the violent disagreement between philosophical knowledge and medical knowledge during the time of Queen Christine of Sweden. Comments on the Xenophontean Socrates who argues that it would be difficult to find a physician who can know us better than we know ourselves. Stresses Socrates' distrust for scientific knowledge in general.

1748 Schuhl, Pierre Maxime. "Montaigne et Socrate." *Etudes platoniciennes*. Paris: Presses Universitaires de France, 1960, pp. 152-166.

Establishes a comparison between the thought of Montaigne and that of Socrates by quoting extensively from Montaigne's references to Socrates. Concludes that in spite of their profound differences, Montaigne was a genuine disciple of Socrates.

1749 Schweingruber, F. "Sokrates und Epiktek." *Hermes*, 78 (1943), pp. 52-79.

Deals with the extent and depth of Socrates' influence in the formation of the Stoicism associated with Epictetus, and comments in particular on the role of the Aristotelian model of 'the man of great soul' (which appears to have been inspired in part by Socrates' character and life) in the Stoic notion of the ideal wise man.

1750 Shannon, Mark Edward. *Socrates as Ethical Model in the "Essais" of Montaigne*. Doctoral dissertation. Stanford University, 1977.

Develops a comprehensive examination of the portrayal of Socrates in Montaigne's *Essais*. Begins by outlining the great Socratic revival of the fifteenth and sixteenth centuries, and shows how that revival culminated with Montaigne's work. Notes that his Socrates -- as much as the Socrates of Petrarch, Bruni, Ficino, and Erasmus -- is a syncretistic image, that is, the product of a double loyalty -- to classical ideals and to the Christian faith. Observes, however, that Montaigne did not wish to fuse Socrates and Jesus, but that he sought to make each one of them supreme in his own realm. Studies the gradual development of Socrates in Montaigne's work, from an illustrious name at first, to the foremost ethical ideal in the end. Comments on Montaigne's admiration for Cato the Younger, and establishes a juxtaposition between Montaigne's portrait of Cato and his portrait of Socrates; argues that the latter emerges in triumph over the former.

1751 Shubart, Robert Franz. *From Socrates to Thomas: An Emblemic Epoch, as Seen Through Its Philosophy and Its Visual Aesthetics*. Doctoral dissertation. New York University, 1980.

Deals with Socrates only marginally. Views his death as the beginning of an epoch which would last until the year 1323 -- the date of the canonization of Saint Thomas Aquinas. Argues that this epoch "deserves salutory recognition and continuing investigative analysis as a special entity," for it was a period during which the West lost and finally recovered its classical heritage. Speaks of Socrates' execution as an event which was precipitated by the Peloponnesian tragedy of 431-404 B.C.

1752 Sigad, Ran. "Fichte, Sartre, Socrates." *Iyuun*, 29 (1980), pp. 37-43.

Examines Fichte's *Vocation of Man*, which is interpreted as an existentialist expression of an attitude towards life. Compares Fichte's philosophical outlook with that of Sartre. Relates Fichte's analysis and understanding of consciousness to Socrates' quest for self-knowledge, and emphasizes that in both instances, the analysis of consciousness is followed by a profession of faith.

1753 Slings, S. R. "Epictetus en Socrates. Kennis, deugd en vrijheid." *Lampas*, 16 (1983), pp. 65-85.

Considers the major ethical principles and teachings of Epictetus to be specific and practical responses and solutions to the problems inherent in the Socratic paradoxes. Text in Dutch with an English abstract.

1754 Somariva, G. "Eumolpo, un Socrate epicureo nel *Satyricon.*" *Annali della Scuola Normale Superiori di Pisa* , 14 (1984), pp. 25-58.

Observes that the *Satyricon* as a *Bildungroman* or psychological novel belongs to a tradition that goes from the writings of Varro to the genre of the picaresque novel. Compares Eumolpus (Petronius' character) to Socrates, and speaks of him as a new Epicurean Socrates.

1755 Stack, George J. *Kierkegaard's Existential Ethics.* Alabama: University of Alabama Press, 1977, pp. 1-17, 25ff, 118ff, 175, 181, and 182.

Focuses on the phenomenological analysis and interpretation

of Socrates developed by Kierkegaard in his *The Concept of Irony*. Stresses Kierkegaard's representation of Socrates as the paradigm of the ethical individual, and notes that Kierkegaard, like Socrates, solved his philosophical perplexities by turning his doubts inwards. Ref. 1692.

1756 Steinkraus, Warren E. "Socrates, Confucius, and the Rectification of Names." *Philosophy East and West*, 30 (1980), pp. 261-264.

Recalls Fénelon's imaginary dialogue between Socrates and Confucius, and notes the striking parallels between the Greek and the Chinese philosophers -- parallels recognized, for instance, by Guthrie and Fung Yu Lan. Argues that on the issue of the rectification of names, however, it is not clear that Socrates and Confucius stood on the same ground, or had the same aim in mind. Insists that Socrates' statement in *Phaedo* 115e (namely, that inaccurate language brings evil to the soul) would have been given a different interpretation by Confucius, for whom language had a social significance.

1757 Sugiyana, Yoshimu. "J. G. Hamanns *Sokratische Denkwürdigkeiten*. Eine geistesgeschichtliche Betrachtung." *Doitsu Bangaku*, 12 (1954), pp. 12-25.

Gives an analysis of Hamann's work on Socrates, and attempts to examine its significance within its specific historical context. Ref. 1583.

1758 Sutton, Anne. "Socrates, Paranhi and Quinces." *Catholic World*, 128 (1929), pp. 571-574.

Relates how since her childhood, Socrates had attracted the author, and how she had later compared him with the Javanese philosopher and poet Pangiri Paranhi. Explains how she once left her husband with a bushel of quinces, as she went to hear Paranhi speak, and how she was disappointed and sickened by his heinous rhetoric. Concludes with the comment that there are very few things that can truly stand the test of time, and among them one can surely include Socrates and quinces.

1759 Sweeney, Leo. "Foreign Books on Greek Philosophers: Socrates and Plato." *The Modern Schoolman*, 50 (1972), pp. 76-86.

Discusses among other books, M. A. Raschini's *Interpretazioni Socratische*, and raises the issue (mainly in the context of Raschini's work) of whether Socrates can be understood as nothing but a 'given' that can be structured by other philosophers into various types of Socratism. Ref. 1734.

1760 Sypher, Wylie. "Nietzsche and Socrates in Messina." *The Partisan Review*, 16 (1949), pp. 702-713.

Examines Shakespeare's *Much Ado About Nothing*, and suggests that the clown in the drama may be interpreted as occupying two extreme positions which might be designated as Nietzschean and Socratic. Maintains that Socrates was a εἴρων, that is, a mocker and a follower of Apollo and dialectic, while Nietzsche was "the votary of Dionysus the ecstatic, the exuberant, the possessed."

1761 Szarmach, M. "Ἐρωτικοὶ λόγοι von Maximus Tyrios." *Eos*, 70 (1982), pp. 61-69.

Reviews four lectures on love by Maximus of Tyre (c. 125-185), and calls attention to his debt to earlier treatments of the subject, including, for instance, the Platonic rendition of Socrates' idea of love. Notes the influence of this Socratic idea on the formation of Maximus' understanding of homosexual love.

1762 Tarcov, Susan Fleckman. *Swift and Socrates: A Study of the Ancients-Moderns Theme in "A Tale of a Tub."* Doctoral dissertation. Brandeis University, 1977.

Studies the 'Ancients-Moderns' distinction in Swift, and claims that a precise understanding of this idea is crucial for an appreciation of his *The Battle of Books*, *A Tale of a Tub*, and *Gulliver's Travels*. Notes that the distinction is based on a political theme, namely, the Ancients' concept of liberty and public spirit, and the Moderns' search for personal security. Maintains that for Swift, the highest virtue was not public virtue, but the moral virtues of friendship and benevolence found in Socrates and in Jesus. Observes that, like Thomas More, Swift sought to reconcile antiquity with Christianity, and that Socrates played an important role in this reconciliation.

1763 Thullier, Pierre. *Socrate fonctionnaire. Essai sur (et contre) la philosophie universitaire.* Paris: Editions Robert Laffont, 1970.

Develops a polemic against university philosophy and against the professors of philosophy who, on the one hand, claim to represent Socrates and his spirit of free inquiry, but who, on the other, are merely state functionaries who have lost touch with the social and political reality of their time, and who act as the representatives of the educational establishment.

1763a Tillich, Paul. "Socrates (A Speech Delivered by Paulus)." *From Place to Place: Travels With Paul Tillich, Travels Without Paul Tillich* by Hannah Tillich. New York: Stein and Day, 1976, pp. 86-91.

Speaks of Socrates as the very embodiment of the spirit of philosophy or as philosophy "incarnated in a personal existence." Emphasizes the importance of Socrates as the greatest of the creative educators, and as the philosopher who understood perfectly well the task of education as growth in intellectual and spiritual autonomy. Notes the significance of the use of dialogue for the search of objective truth in the realm of the mind -- a search initiated by Socrates in his effort to transcend the subjectivism of the Sophists and the bare objectivism of the natural philosophers. Stresses the value of the Socratic contention that virtue is teachable, a contention which ultimately implies that knowledge (understood as "a matter of the total man" and not merely in the sense of information) can guide human existence. Views Socrates as a paradigm example of the reality of an existential transformation.

1764 Tod, Marcus N. "Sidelights on Greek Philosophers." *The Journal of Hellenic Studies*, 77 (1957), pp. 132-141.

Examines the way in which epigraphical discoveries may have contributed to our understanding of Greek philosophy. Views Socrates as the first among Athenian philosophers who initiated a new chapter in Greek thought. Discusses the Parian chronicle (an anonymous compilation of chronological tables of outstanding personalities and events in Greek history, where philosophy appears in the persons of Socrates, Anaxagoras, and Aristotle). Mentions the mosaic at Syrian Apamea (dated between A.D. 350 and 400), in which Socrates is shown presiding over six unnamed philosophers, and notes that this detail should give us an idea of Socrates' popularity among Syrian pagans of that time. Observes that the main philosophical schools of antiquity invariably traced their ancestry to Socrates.

1765 Troncoso, Alfredo. "Nietzsche y el intento de ir más allá de Sócrates." *Logos*, 12 (1984), pp. 63-86.

Studies Nietzsche's conviction that the 'true' philosophical spirit can be found more clearly in the pre-Socratics than in Socrates himself, and interprets the Nietzschean attempt to transcend Socrates as an endeavor to go beyond the metaphysical stance created by the Socratic presence. Analyzes the scope and magnitude of Nietzsche's effort, and draws attention to its shortcomings. Concludes with comments on the significance of our understanding of Nietzsche's stance vis-à-vis Socrates as an important element for the appreciation of the history of Western thought. Ref. 1723.

1766 Trousson, Raymond. *Socrate devant Voltaire, Diderot et Rousseau. La conscience en face du mythe.* Paris: Lettres Modernes, 1967.

Contains an introductory chapter which outlines the transformations of Socrates in late classical, Christian, and medieval times, and during the Renaissance. Deals in separate chapters with the portrayals of Socrates created by Voltaire, Diderot, and Rousseau. Shows how each one of them draws different conclusions from the same facts available to them: the Socrates of Voltaire is a realistic (and almost cynical) deist; the Socrates of Diderot is a man caught in self-contradiction and a man of great sincerity; and the Socrates of Rousseau is a man of passion and faith. Observes that, as the legendary and symbolic Socrates grows and develops in the minds of his three great interpreters, the historical Socrates recedes more and more into the background.

1767 Waddington, Raymond B. "Socrates in Montaigne's *Traicté de la* physionomie." *Modern Language Quarterly*, 41 (1980), pp. 328-345.

Discusses the characterization of Socrates in Montaigne's essay on physiognomy, with emphasis on the issue of Socrates' alleged physical ugliness. Notes that this essay constitutes Montaigne's most direct and extended treatment of Socrates.

1768 Walker, James Henry. *The Perception Contrast of the Socratic Theory of Recollection with the Ideas of Husserl's Phenomenology: A Historical Interpretation.* Doctoral dissertation. Boston College, 1981.

Reviews and traces the possible grounds for regarding Socrates' notion of 'recollection' as a theory of human perception, in which the idea of imagination-perception plays a decisive role. Reviews the concepts of perception which functioned among the pre-Socratics, and discusses Aristotle's distinction between 'reminiscence' and 'memory.' Examines the concept of recollection in the philosophies of Descartes, Kant, Sartre, and Husserl.

1769 Walton, Craig. "Ramus and Socrates." *Proceedings of the American Philosophical Society*, 114 (1970), pp. 119-139.

Examines the influence of Socrates on the development of the dialectics of Petrus Ramus (Pièrre de la Ramée, 1515-1572). Acknowledges the marked differences between the French humanist and the Greek philosopher, but stresses the fact that the former's philosophical inspiration was in part the result of his acquaintance with Socratic thought.

1770 Weiss, Raymond L. "Kierkegaard's 'Return' to Socrates." *The New Scholastism*, 45 (1971), pp. 573-583.

Examines Kierkegaard's endeavor to revive Socratic dialectics in the form of an existential dialectic (that is, subjective thinking). Concludes that Kierkegaard's view of existence and his adherence to nineteenth century scholarship did not allow him to develop a genuine restoration of Socratic dialectics. Ref. 1692.

1771 Zinzendorf, Nikolaus Ludwig. *Der teutsche Sokrates, das ist:*

*Aufrichtige Anzeige verschiedener nicht so wohl unbekannter als vielmehr in Abfall gerathener Haupt-Wahrheiten.* Leipzig, 1732.

Ref. 1615.

1772 Zuckert, Catherine. "Nietzsche's Rereading of Plato." *Political Theory*, 13 (1985), pp. 213-238.

Stresses the Nietzschean concept of Socrates as the philosopher who detroyed the spirit of tragedy in the name of a relentless search for absolute intelligibility. Notes that the Nietzschean Socrates appears as the source of meaning for the human herd, and that it is through his death that his influence has been truly felt. Ref. 1723.

# FICTION, POETRY, DRAMA

The following entries reflect the Socratic influence in various forms of art and literature. Included in this section are plays, poems, novels, musical compositions, fictional essays, films, cassette-tapes, phonodiscs, television programs, and modern paintings.

1773 Alastos, Donos. *Socrates Tried: Drama Reconstruction.* London: Zeno Publishers, 1966.

Recreates in a dramatic setting the trial of Socrates, and adds to the information supplied by Plato's *Apology* a number of imaginative elements.

1774 Allen, Steve. "Meeting of Minds. Show #11." *Meeting of Minds* (Second Series). New York: Crown Publishers, 1979.

Offers a television script which creates a discussion between Francis Bacon, Socrates, Emiliano Zapata, and Susan B. Anthony, on topics related to philosophy and social reform.

1775 Allen, Woody. "My Apology." *Side Effects.* New York: Random House, 1975, pp. 33-40.

Presents a short dialogue between Allen (who has been sentenced to death and is about to drink hemlock poison) and Agathon and Simmias. Written as a witty parody of the last scene of the *Phaedo.* Notes in the introductory remarks that "of all famous men who ever lived, the one [Allen] would most like to have been was Socrates." Observes, too, that by his death, "Socrates gave his life authentic meaning, something [Allen's] existence lacks totally."

1776 Almeida, Franciso Antonio de. *La pazienza di Socrate.* Lisbon, 1733.

Opera in three acts. Libretto is based on Minato's text (which was already used by Draghi in 1680, and by Caldara and Reutter in 1731). Represents the oldest Italian opera by a Portuguese composer which is partly extant (third act only).

1777 Anderson, Maxwell. *Barefoot in Athens.* New York: William Sloane Associates, 1951.

Presents a two-act dramatization of three episodes of Socrates' last days. Recreates conversations between Socrates and various historical characters such as Crito, Xanthippe, Lamprocles, Critias, Pausanias, Meletus, and others. Depicts Socrates in his home, at the trial, and in prison. Develops its dramatic settings around the theme of the danger of silencing criticism in a democracy. Departs substantially from the information supplied by the primary sources (*e.g.*, as when it describes how the Spartan king Pausanias visits Socrates in prison). Ref. 181, 1778.

1778 *Barefoot in Athens.* Motion Picture. Princeton, N.J.: Films for the Humanities (FFH775D). 76 min., color, videotape.

Based on Maxwell Anderson's *Barefoot in Athens.* Centers on Socrates' trial, specifically on the charges of introducing new divinities and corrupting young men. Draws special attention to Socrates' opportunities to escape and to his refusal to abandon his philosophical principles. Peter Ustinov plays the part of Socrates. Ref. 1777.

1779 Baring, Maurice. *Xant[h]ippe and Socrates. Diminutive Dramas.* Boston: Houghton Mifflin Co., 1911, pp. 216-24.

Short play based on a conversation between Socrates and Xanthippe, in which she is portrayed as a naggy woman arguing with him about the supper she has cooked for him.

1780 Beals, Michael. *The Tragedy of Socrates.* Philadelphia: Dorrance & Co., 1971.

Play in five parts. Concludes with the scene of Socrates' death.

1781 Becket, Andrew. *Socrates: A Dramatic Poem.* London: G. Wilkie, 1806.

Offers a lengthy poetical composition (70 pp.) which portrays Socrates in the context of his trial and death. Written on the model of ancient Greek tragic writing.

1782 Bloch-Michel, Jean. *Ctepsippe.* Paris: Gallimard, 1964.

Drama in four acts which includes the following characters: Xanthippe, Socrates, Ctepsippe, Crito, Phaedo, Simmias, and Cebes.

1783 Bovio, Giovanni. *Socrate (dall' Eutifrone).* Turin: Casa Editrice Nazionale, 1904.

Presents a play which calls for the following characters: Socrates, Xanthippe, Lamprocles, Meletus, Lycon, Chaerephon, Euthyphro, and four others. Places the scene in an Athenian public square, and the conversation deals with the accusations which Meletus and Lycon are about to bring against Socrates.

1784 Brayne, F. L. *Socrates in an Indian Village.* London: Oxford University Press, 1929.

Pictures Socrates in an Indian village, asking questions about subjects like plumbing, cattle, and everyday life. Emphasizes those aspects of Socratic questioning which are directed to materialistic concerns, and seeks to place Socrates in the context of rural India.

1785 Brayne, F. L. *Socrates Persists in India.* London: Oxford University Press, 1932.

Depicts Socrates in conversation in India. Creates thirty-three dialogues, in most of which the inquisitive Socrates attempts to raise the consciousness of his interlocutors about social issues. Provides seven cartoons intended to illustrate graphically some of the Socratic messages.

1786 Brecht, Bertolt. "Der verwundete Sokrates." *Bertolt Brecht. Gesammelte Werke.* Frankfurt am Main: Suhrkamp Verlag, 1967 (20 vols.), Vol. 11, pp. 286-303.

Short story written in 1939. Describes how Socrates took

part in a battle against the Persians, and how he wounded himself accidentally by stepping on a thorn, as he was in the process of running away from the enemy. Describes how he was mistakenly declared to be the hero of the battle. Includes scenes with Xanthippe, Antisthenes, and Alcibiades. Concludes with Socrates' revelation of the embarrassing truth: he was not a hero but merely a wounded man who scared away the enemy with his shouts of pain.

1787 Brecht, Bertolt. "Socrates Wounded." *Bertolt Brecht. Short Stories 1921-1946.* Edited by John Willet and Ralph Manheim. Translated by Ivonne Kapp, Hugh Rorrison, and Antony Tatlow. London: Methuen, 1983, pp. 139-153.

English translation of Brecht's "Der verwundete Sokrates." Ref. 1786.

1788 Brémond, André. "Socrate et le poète." *Le charme et la raison.* Le Puy: X. Mappus Editeur, 1943.

Develops an imaginary conversation between Hippias the rhapsodist and Socrates concerning the latter's suggestion that poets ought to be exiled as dangerous and useless persons. Makes Hippias alert Socrates to the fact that he himself might be exiled, should his suggestion be taken seriously, to which Socrates is made to reply that his critique of poets is based on his love and admiration for them, and that he himself would like to possess the magic charm of poetry, if this charm could be joined to a complete control of all emotions. Has Socrates delineate his ideal poet: a human being more universal than Homer, whose knowledge would penetrate all mysteries, and whose control over his passions would be complete.

1789 Caldara, Antonio and Reutter, Hermann S. *La pazienza di Socrate con due moglie.* Vienna, 1731.

Opera in three acts. Text by Nicolo Minato. First performed in Vienna on January 17, 1731. The beginning of the first act and the entire third act were written by Caldara, and the rest of the opera by Reutter.

1790 Clarín [Alas, Leopoldo]. "The Cock of Socrates." Translated by M. M. Lasley. *Spanish Stories and Tales.* Edited by

Harriet de Onío. New York: Alfred A. Knopf, 1954, pp. 44-48.

Describes how, after Socrates died, Crito went about looking for a cock to sacrifice to Asklepius, and how providentially he found a magnificent cock which belonged to Gorgias. Creates a dialogue between the cock (who despises Sophists and philosophers, and who pleads for his life, alleging that Socrates' last words were ironic), and Crito (who, as a religious fanatic, is intent on complying with his Master's wish). Concludes with the killing of the cock by Crito, as the cock had sought refuge by a statue of Athena.

1791 Collot d'Herbois, J. M. *Le Procès de Socrate, ou le régime des anciens temps.* Paris: Chez la Veuve Duchesne, 1791.

Comedy in three acts. Written in prose.

1792 David, Jacques Louis. *The Death of Socrates.* 1787. Painting. 59"x78". The Metropolitan Museum of Art. New York. (Wolfe Fund, 1931).

Depicts, in a neoclassic style, David's interpretation of the death of Socrates. Represents Socrates as the founder of a religion of reason, Christ-like in appearance, surrounded by twelve disciples. Places Plato in Socrates' prison cell as Socrates drinks the hemlock.

1793 *The Death of Socrates.* Motion Picture. BBC-TV, London, 1968. 45 min., black & white, 16 mm. Directed by Jonathan Miller.

Offers a modern reconstruction of Plato's *Crito* and *Phaedo.* Stresses the fact that political persecution has persisted for the 2500 years since Socrates' execution. Presents Socrates' arguments for the immortality of the soul. Leo McKern plays the role of Socrates. Reviewed in *The New York Times*, June 10, 1971, p. 87, by John J. O'Connor.

1794 Deutsch, Babette. *Mask of Silenus: A Novel About Socrates.* New York: Simon & Schuster, 1933.

Recreates in a semi-fictional fashion the last days of Socrates. Bases its narrative and dialogues on the testimonies of Plato, Xenophon, and other ancient sources, and remains generally within the parameters established by them. Portrays various aspects of Socrates' domestic life: his relationships with Xanthippe, Myrto, and Lamprocles. Describes the immediate antecedents of the trial and the proceedings of the trial itself, and concludes with an account of Socrates' execution. Builds its image of Socrates around three themes which the author regards as the basic components of the Socratic message: the spirit of free inquiry, the inviolability of the individual, and the honesty and courage that underlie the concept of human dignity.

1795 Donnelly, Eleanor C. "Socrates". *The Catholic World*, 78 (1904), p. 508.

Short poem in which Socrates' spiritual voice is equated with the voice of God, and in which his almost Christian truth and selflessness are praised.

1796 Draghi, Antonio. *La patienza di Socrate con due moglie.* Prague, 1680.

Opera in three acts. Text by Nicolo Minato. Ballet music composed by J. H. Schmelzer. Performed first in Prague on January 6, 1680, the first opera ever produced at Prague.

1797 *The Drinking Party.* Motion Picture. BBC-TV, London, 1968. 40 min., black & white, 16mm.

Presents Plato's *Symposium* in a contemporary setting as an after-dinner discussion among four men attending a college reunion.

1798 Epstein, Lee. "Dialogues of Polemarchus." *The Open Court*, 42 (1928), pp. 488-491.

Creates a short dialogue between Thrasymachus and Socrates in which the fictitious author (Polemarchus) proposes to correct the Platonic account of the conversation of the middle of Book 5 of the *Republic*.

1799 Faucett, Lawrence. *The Thinking Shop of Socrates: A Realistic Reconstruction of the Life of Socrates, Stressing his*

*Ideas of Education, Democracy, and God.* Tokyo: Shinozaki Shorin, 1957.

Dramatic reconstruction. Takes more than ninety percent of its lines from the writings of Plato, Aristophanes, Xenophon, Diogenes Laertius, and other classical authors.

1800 Frischer, B. "On Reconstructing the Portrait of Epicurus and Identifying the Socrates of the Lysippus." *California Studies in Classical Antiquity*, 12 (1979), pp. 121-154.

Argues that seventeenth and eighteenth century reconstructions and identifications of portraits of philosophers are often unreliable. Attempts to show that the Ludovisi Socrates is probably not Socrates, and that if it somehow turns out to be Socrates, this is merely the result of a chance identification in the seventeenth century.

1801 Giannini, Humberto. *Sócrates o el Oráculo de Delfos.* Santiago de Chile: Editorial Universitaria, 1970.

Dialogue in which over eighteen characters participate, the most significant role being assigned to Socrates. Euthyphro, Xanthippe, Callicles, Anytus, Meletus, Crito, Phaedo and other acquaintances and relations of Socrates are engaged in a discussion (divided into two acts) in which the hidden presence of the Delphic oracle in Socrates' life is brought to the foreground. Concludes with a description of Socrates death.

1802 Godel, Roger. *Socrate et le sage indien: Cheminements vers la sagesse.* Paris: Société d'edition Les Belles Lettres, 1976.

Poses the rhetorical question about what a conversation would have been like between Socrates and a visiting Indian sage. Permits an entrance into the thoughts and beliefs of each. Identifies the Socratic quest for true knowledge of oneself as a parallel to the Hindu quest for knowing one's true nature.

1803 Grazebrook, Owen F. *Socrates Among His Peers.* London: Paul Kegan, Trench, Trubner & Co., 1927.

Describes in three imaginary conversations what an Athenian

company might have said concerning death and the hereafter, and justice and the Kingdom of Heaven. Presents three conversations which are entitled, "Night and the Dream," "The Verdict," and "The City of God," with Socrates as a participant only in the first conversation, but with Socratic themes (both biographical and ideological) as the basis of all of the conversations.

1804 Highet, Gilbert. "A Socrates Dialogue." *The Classical Papers of Gilbert Highet.* Edited by Robert J. Ball. New York: Columbia University Press, 1983, pp. 332-335. *New York Herald Tribune*, October 28, 1951, Section 4, pp. 1-2.

Recreates a conversation between Socrates and Maxwell Anderson (the author of *Barefoot in Athens*) in which the author is asked about his motives for writing a play about Socrates. Makes Anderson explain how his play deals with the freedom of the human mind. Develops various themes such as the differences between Socrates and his disciples, principally Plato, and the fabrications which they built around his teachings. Ref. 1777.

1805 Housman, Lawrence. *The Death of Socrates.* London: Sidgwick and Jackson, 1925.

Recreates scenes from the *Crito* and the *Phaedo* in a dramatic setting, suitable for a stage performance. Adopts and transforms the original Platonic account to suit its dramatic requirements.

1806 Janson, H. W. "The Death of Socrates." *History of Art*. Englewood Cliffs, N.J.: Prentice-Hall, 1962. pp. 472-473 (plate #709).

Discusses the technical qualities of Jacques Louis David's painting of Socrates' death scene, in which the lighting is sharply focused, casting direct shadows, and is inspired by Caravaggio, as is the firm detail. Suggests that the composition seems to unfold like a relief, while the figures appear as solid as statues. Concludes that the idealism of the neo-classical style is tempered by these details, and that a quality of life emerges from the painting.

1807 Kaiser, Georg. *Alkibiades Saved.* Translated by Bayard Quincy Morgan. *Anthology of German Expressionist Drama: A Prelude to the Absurd.* Edited by Walter H. Sokel. Garden City, N.Y.: Doubleday, 1963, pp. 204-264.

Drama in three acts.

1808 Kerr, H. T. "Rossellini's 'Socrates' -- A Colloquy." *Theology Today*, 31 (1974), pp. 199-204.

Reviews Rossellini's film *Socrates*, by way of a dialogue among several Platonists. Includes as participants Diogenes Allen, George Thomas, George Hendry, Mary Mulder, and Daniel Migliore. Emphasizes the parallels established by Rossellini between Socrates and Jesus. Ref. 1835.

1809 Kreft, Peter. *The Unaborted Socrates: A Dramatic Debate on the Issues Surrounding Abortion.* Downers Grove, Ill.: Intervarsity Press, 1983.

Contains three dialogues in which Socrates is the chief participant: Socrates in an abortion clinic, Socrates at a philosophy convention, and Socrates in a psychiatric ward. Included in the dialogues is a character named Dr. Rex Herrod (an abortionist), who deals with various ethical issues related to abortion.

1810 Lamartine, Alphonse de. *La mort de Socrate.* Paris: L'Advocat, Libraire, 1823.

Reconstructs poetically the last moments of Socrates, basing its creation on the testimony of Plato's *Phaedo.* Compares the death of Socrates with the death of Jesus, and has Socrates foretell the advent of true religion and the worship of the one true God. Depicts the soul of the departed Socrates in a place where the Platonic world of Ideas and the Christian heaven are one and the same. Puts in Socrates' mouth these words which reflect the spirit of the entire poem: *"La vie est le combat, la mort est la victoire, et la terre est pour nous l'autel expiatoire."*

1811 *The Legacy of Socrates: The Oratory of Philosophy's Patron Saint Dramatically Recreated.* Hollywood, Ca.: The Center for Cassette Studies. 25 min.

Recreates on this audio-cassette tape, in a dramatized style, Socrates' trial and last hours in prison. Uses brief excerpts from Plato's testimony and adapts them freely for literary effectiveness. Contains a brief fictional dialogue between Socrates and Xenophon, and two quotations from Locke and Goethe in support of the ideas for which Socrates is supposed to have stood.

1812 Levinson, Alfred. *Socrates Wounded. New American Plays.* Edited by Robert W. Corrigan. New York: Hill and Wang, 1965 (2 vols.), Vol. 1, pp. 45-82.

Written in 1959. Two act comedy which shows how Socrates was mistakenly credited with singly halting the enemy line in battle, when in fact he was simply attempting to escape from the enemy. Based (according to the author) on a tale by Bertolt Brecht. Ref. 1786.

1813 Linguet, S. H. *Socrate.* Amsterdam: M. Rey, 1764.

Presents a tragedy in five acts. Describes Socrates in prison, punished for having taught that true religion is unrelated to the rituals and dogmas invented by priests. Portrays the priests as the true enemies and accusers of Socrates, and Anytus as a spokesman for the clergy.

1814 Linklater, Eric. *The Raft and Socrates Asks Why.* London: MacMillan, 1942.

Presents the second conversation ("Socrates Asks Why," pp. 54-121) which takes place in the loggia of a country club in Elysium. Participating are the following characters: Socrates, Abraham Lincoln, Voltaire, Dr. Johnson, and Beethoven, who discuss contemporary themes related to the American participation in World War II.

1815 Llovet, Enrique. *Sócrates.* Madrid: Escelicer, 1972.

Recreates in a dramatic setting Socrates' execution. Cast calls for ten actors.

1816 Lorenz, Friedrich. *Sokrates.* Vienna: F. Speidelsche Verlagsbuchhandlung, 1938.

Novel based on the life of Socrates. Devotes the first part to the fictional treatment of the relationship between Socrates and Pericles, and the second part to the elaboration of the relationship between Socrates and Xanthippe.

1817 Mauthner, Fritz. *Mrs. Socrates.* Translated by Jacob W. Hartmann. New York: International Publishers, 1926.

Reconstructs in this novel the character and biography of Xanthippe. Describes her relationship with Socrates as his wife and companion, and her activites among a number of Socrates' associates (Alcibiades, Aspasia, and others). Recounts various aspects of Athenian society, as well as many particulars about Socrates' life: his military campaigns, his depiction in Aristophanes' *Clouds*, his trial and refusal to escape, and his execution. Concludes with a chapter on Xanthippe's old age and death. Uses various historical and philosophical sources to create a romantic tale about Xanthippe.

1818 Mercier, Louis-Sebastien. *La maison de Socrate le Sage.* Paris: Duminil-Lesueur, 1809.

Presents in this five act comedy aspects of Socrates' domestic life. Describes his relationship with Xanthippe and Myrto (who is in love with Alcibiades). Portrays Euclides of Megara's secret visits to Socrates. Recounts the patience and jealousy of Xanthippe.

1819 *The Minds of Men*. Motion Picture. Princeton, N.J.: Films for the Humanities (FFH706D). 52 min., color, videotape.

Presents an overview of the lives and philosophical outlooks of Socrates and Plato, stressing their keen curiosity concerning the issue of human nature and the place of man in the context of the universe at large. Contains sections on Herodotus and Thucydides.

1820 Mohnnau, Ralph Günther. *Sokrates oder das Ärgernis der Philosophie.* Frankfurt: Alpha Literatur Verlag, 1974.

Includes the following characters in this drama in twelve scenes: Socrates, Antiphon, Charmides, Phaedo, Chaerephon,

Plato, Hippias, Alcibiades, Critias, Charicles, Aristophanes, Xanthippe, Meletus, Lycon, Anytus, and Callias. Covers the years between 411 and 399 B.C.

1820a Mori, Tuyosi. *Socrates and the Three Little Pigs.* Illustrated by Mitsumasa Anno. New York: Putnam, 1986.

Appropriate for children seven years and older. Introduces combinatorial analysis with a tale about a wolf named Socrates, and his attempt to determine in which of five houses three little pigs are hiding so that he can eat them. Presents two additional characters who assist Socrates: his wife Xanthippe and his friend Pythagoras the frog.

1821 Murdoch, Iris. *Above the Gods: A Dialogue About Religion. Acastos: Two Platonic Dialogues.* New York: Viking, 1987, pp. 67-121.

Includes in its cast seven characters: Socrates, Plato, Alcibiades, Acastos, Timonax, Antagoras, and a servant. Presents a conversation held in Athens in the late fifth century B. C. Develops a discussion about religion, that is, about the belief in the gods and the human practices that honor them. Allows Socrates to sum up his views in these words: "Religion and virtue are not always allies, religion is many things and must be subject to justice and truth. We can't always learn virtue from loving [the] good, we often have to live by external rules.... Man is not the measure of all things, we don't just invent our values, we live by a higher law, yet we can't fully explain how this is so."

1822 Murdoch, Iris. *Art and Eros: A Dialogue About Art. Acastos: Two Platonic Dialogues.* New York: Viking, 1987, pp. 9-66.

First performed in 1980. Includes in the cast Socrates, Plato, Callistos, Acastos, Mantias, and Deximenes. Presents a conversation among the characters in Athens in the late fifth century B. C., and focuses its discussions on the nature and function of art, specifically theatrical art. At the end, shows how Plato, disenchanted with all artistic endeavors, promises to destroy all his poetic creations, while Socrates sums up his views on art in these terms: "It may even be that ... good art tells us more truth about our lives and our world than any other kind of thinking or speculation ... and perhaps the language of art is the most universal and enduring kind of human thought."

1823 Myers, Irvin H. "Socrates Up to Date: A Dialogue Regarding Time." *Atlantic Monthly*, 143 (1929), pp. 78-83.

Presents a dialogue with the dramatic characters of Socrates and Crito, who discourse on the nature of time. Concludes with Socrates asserting that time is purely subjective or relative, "Therefore, O Crito, there is no such thing as time. We live in the eternal *now*."

1824 Ner, Henri. *Les veritables entretiens de Socrate.* Paris: Editions Athéna, 1922.

Arranged in four books, the author creates a series of recollections as if from the pen of Antisthenes. Written in a style reminiscent of Xenophon's *Memorabilia*, Antisthenes' recollections appear to be intended as corrections of the Platonic account of Socrates' character, ideas, trial and death. Describes Plato as the worst enemy of Socrates.

1825 Neumann, Frederick. *Uber das Lachen, und studien Über den Platonischen Sokrates.* The Hague: Martinus Nijhoff, 1971.

Contains a Socratic sonnet, an essay on the nature of laughter, and an examination of two early Platonic dialogues (the *Hippias Minor* and the *Protagoras*). Concludes with a section on the relationship between virtue and art in Plato's early dialogues.

1826 Palissot de Montenoy, C. "Socrate et Erasme." *Dialogues historiques et critiques. Oeuvres Complètes de M. Palissot.* London: Jean François Bastien, 1779, Vol. 16, pp. 169-181.

Reprinted in Montuori' *De Socrate iuste damnato* (Amsterdam: J. C. Gieben, 1981), pp. 139-146. Creates a conversation between Socrates and Erasmus in which the former attempts to cleanse from the latter's mind some of the features associated with the exalted portrait of Socrates painted by Plato. Amused by the process of canonization to which he has been subjected (including by Erasmus himself), Socrates speaks freely of the questionable morality of his youth.

Observes the senselessness of accusing Aristophanes of calumny, and suggests that the sentence passed on him was ultimately justified. Regards his trial as the inevitable outcome of the imprudence of his youth and of the political views and activities of his mature years. Ref. 398.

1827 Pastoret de Calian. *Socrate.* Montauban: Vincent Teulières, 1789.

Portrays in this tragedy in five acts Socrates as the enemy of superstitious and idolatrous religion, and as the advocate of the religion of reason and nature. Represents Socrates in love with Myrto who actually loves Meletus: Myrto marries Socrates only to save him, but Meletus, in a fit of jealousy, accuses Socrates of irreligiosity.

1828 Pick, Robert. *The Escape of Socrates.* New York: Alfred A. Knopf, 1954.

Bases this historical novel on the life and times of Socrates. Makes use of the testimonies of the primary sources, and adds a number of purely fictional components. Emphasizes the Socratic irony. Translates the language of the sources into a sort of vernacular street-English with the intention of injecting a good dosage of realism into the scenes and characters.

1829 Pierard, M. Charles. *La mort de Socrate.* Paris: Bibliothèque Nationale de France, 9282, c.1763, pp. 270-306.

Unpublished tragedy in five acts. Describes the scene of Socrates' last hours in prison. Recreates characters and details in a highly imaginative manner: Alcibiades and Xenophon are ready to rescue Socrates with a force of ten thousand soldiers, while Aristophanes, Plato, and Pericles endeavor to convince Socrates to recant. Introduces a certain Ismina who is allegedly Socrates' daughter and Alcibiades' fiancée.

1830 Ratti, Federico Valerio. *Socrate: Tragedia.* Florence: Vallecchi, 1927.

Presented in this drama in four acts are various scenes which depict Xanthippe in conversation with her children, the machinations of Anytus and Lycon against Socrates, and the death scene. Crito, Phaedo, Plato, Critobulus, Simmias, Cebes, and Antisthenes are portrayed in conversation with Socrates.

1831 Reid, Charles Sloan. "Socrates". *The Open Court*, 45 (1931), p. 640.

Short poem which extols Socrates' victory over dogma and death.

1832 Renault, Mary. *The Last of the Wine.* New York: Pantheon Books, 1956.

Novel in which Socrates is the central figure.

1833 Richards, I. A. *Why So, Socrates? A Dramatic Version of Plato's Dialogues Euthyphro, Apology, Crito, Phaedo.* Cambridge: Cambridge University Press, 1964.

Recreates in four acts the scenes and sequences portrayed and developed by Plato in the *Euthyphro*, the *Apology,* the *Crito,* and the *Phaedo.* Assigns the dramatic conversations to the following characters: Socrates, Euthyphro, Crito, Critobulus, Phaedo, Apollodorus, Cebes, Simmias, Xanthippe, and the prison keeper. Generally follows the plan and development of the Platonic texts.

1834 Richet, Charles R. *Sokrato. Kvarakta tragedio.* Translated by Jean Couteaux. Paris: Acetebla ce al Tradukinto, 1914.

In Esperanto. Drama in four acts which concludes with the death scene of Socrates.

1835 Rossellini, Roberto. *Socrate. La TV di Rossellini, Socrate, Pascal, Agostino d'Ippona.* Rome: Coines Edizioni, 1972, pp. 21-107.

Presents the script by Rossellini of his television film *Socrates* (produced by RAI Radiotelevisione Italiana). Based on the testimonies of Plato, Xenophon, Diogenes Laertius, and Aristotle, with dramatic accommodations. Ref. 1808.

1836 Rothschild, Richard. *Jefferson, Lenin, Socrates. Three Gods Give an Evening to Politics.* New York: Random House, 1936.

Portrays Jefferson (the individualist), Lenin (the collectivist), and Socrates (the Greek) engaged in an after-dinner discussion in which the great divergences among their ideologies are emphasized. Discussed are the following salient topics: political freedom and social restraints, experimentation in social affairs, the destiny of people and states, and the future of humanity.

1837 Saint-Pierre, Bernardin de. *La Mort de Socrate. Oeuvres Complètes.* Brussels: A. Wahlen, 1820 (12 vols.), Vol. 1, pp. 646-666.

Bases this dialogue on the testimonies of Plato, Xenophon, and Plutarch. Portrays Socrates as the advocate of natural and rational religion, and as a believer in one universal God who is manifest to all rational and good human beings. Speaks of Socrates' rejection of materialism and atheism. Describes his sentence as the unjust reward for his wisdom.

1838 Saix, Guillot de. *Socrate et les fables.* Paris: Editions de la Revue Moderne, 1963.

Contains a collection of forty short poems (56 pp.) about Socrates' life, character, and death. Addresses subjects as varied as Socrates' parents, Xanthippe, the Socratic cosmopolitanism, the drinking of the hemlock poison, and others.

1839 Santayana, George. *Dialogues in Limbo.* New York: Charles Scribner's Sons, 1926.

Constructs a fictional conversation between a stranger who visits Hades and the ghosts of Democritus, Alcibiades, Aristippus, Dionysius the Younger, Socrates, and Avicenna. Depicts Socrates in conversation with the stranger in three dialogues: two of them on the idea of self-government, and one on philanthropy; in the former, Socrates hears from the stranger about the mode of self-government which is known in the twentieth century as democracy, and in that context expresses his bafflement at that form of government. Defines philanthropy, in the latter dialogue, as the love of that beauty and goodness in people which, if realized, would make them happy. Discusses several meaningful points on philanthropy concerning the relationship between Jesus' idea of charity and Socrates' definition of philanthropy.

1840 Santayana, George. "The Hidden Soul." *Atlantic Monthly*, 181 (1948), pp. 54-57.

Presents the second dialogue of the trilogy published by the *Atlantic Monthly*, with three characters, Socrates and Alcibiades who are shades, and a stranger who is alive and able to communicate with them through incantations, and who speaks with each separately. Offers an interpretation of Socrates by Alcibiades who argues that although there are Sophistical aspects to Socrates' manner, these are only skin-deep, providing a forum for his satirical humor which hides a sensitive and tender goodness. Considers Socrates worthy of the admiration of all.

1841 Santayana, George. "The Libertine." *Atlantic Monthly*, 181 (1948), pp. 28-31.

Represents the first of three dialogues published in successive issues of the *Atlantic Monthly* in the Spring of 1948. Presents a dialogue between Alcibiades, who is in the realm of shades, and a stranger, who is alive and can summon 'ghosts' and force them to speak to him against their will. Discusses the relationship between Socrates and Alcibiades both before and after their deaths.

1842 Santayana, George. "The Vortex of Dialectic." *Atlantic Monthly*, 181 (1948), pp. 51-58.

Presents the third dialogue of the *Atlantic Monthly* series, which includes a three-way discussion between Socrates, Alcibiades, and a stranger. Considers the comment made by the stranger to Alcibiades, that it was a misfortune for Alcibiades to be so handsome, and exemplifies the *elenchus* by having Socrates question the stranger (who is nervous at the questioning) about his reasons for reaching that conclusion about Alcibiades.

1843 Satie, Erik. *Socrate*. Prague, 1925.

Symphonic drama in three parts for orchestra and voices.

Originally published in 1919, and first performed in Paris on February 14, 1920, by the Societé Nationale de Musique. Makes use of passages from V. Cousins's French translation of Plato's dialogues which are specifically related to various moments of Socrates' life.

1844 Sauvigny, E. Billardon de. *La mort de Socrate.* Paris: Prault le Jeune, 1763.

Depicts Socrates, in this tragedy in three acts, as the victim of the bigotry and fanaticism of his contemporaries. Describes Anytus as the hateful high priest who convinces the Areopagus to sentence Socrates, and portrays the Athenians as they revolted against and punished him for his wickedness. Portrays Socrates as the archenemy of the priests and of superstitious religious credulity.

1845 Schiller, F. C. S. "F. C. S. Schiller's Supercelestial Politics." *The Personalist*, 50 (1969), pp. 5-32.

Constructs a dialogue among Socrates, Plato, and Aristotle, as they contemplate from heaven the struggles of human beings. Depicts Plato and Aristotle as happy in the ideal realm, but not Socrates who announces his conversion to Christianity. Concludes with a debate on the relationship between the individual and the state.

1846 Schütz, Wilhelm Wolfgang. *Der Fall des Sokrates. Eine Auklage.* Zurich: Verlag der Arche, 1970, 94 pp.

Includes the following characters in this drama in six scenes: Socrates, Meletus, Crito, Diotima, the accuser, a general, and others.

1847 Schwartz, Delmore. "Socrates' Ghost Must Haunt Me Now." *A Comprehensive Anthology of American Poetry.* Edited by Conrad Aiken. New York: The Modern Library, 1929, p. 462.

Short poem (19 lines). Describes how the ghost of Socrates comes to the poet in order to remind him of his ignorance and give him hope.

1848 Sears, Willis G. *Socrates. A Play to Develop a Thought on*

*Truth.* Omaha: Festner Printing Co., 1918.

Takes place in Socrates' prison on the day of his execution. Calls for three characters: Socrates, Criticles, and a prison guard.

1849 Seiler, Conrad. *The Husband of Xanthippe, and Other Plays.* Boston: Walter H. Baker Company, 1929.

Dramatically set in Athens, c. 399 B.C., this play about Socrates includes the following characters: Xanthippe, Socrates, Phaedo, Apollodorus, and Critobulus. Suggests that Xanthippe's intolerable 'shrewishness' can be regarded as the major reason for Socrates' ultimate choice of death over life.

1850 Simpkins, J. M. [Sawyer, J. M.]. *A Little Confab with Socrates.* Boston: Meador Publishing Co., 1946.

Creates an imaginary conversation between a farmer from Maine and Socrates, who has come all the way (in space and time) to spend a day with an American of the mid-twentieth century.

1851 Sinclair, Lister. *Socrates: A Drama in Three Acts.* Agincourt: Book Society of Canada, 1957.

Set in the Athenian agora, in the houses of Philip and Agathon, in the court of the King-Archon, and in the prison, this drama in three acts calls for thirty actors. Compresses and alters the various events in order to suit its dramatic interests.

1852 Stockmyer, John G. *The Death of Socrates.* Phonodisc, 42 min. Gladstone, Missouri: Stockmyer Educational Materials, n.d.

Recounts Socrates' execution as if it were being reported by a newscaster. Provides a study-guide and a bibliography.

1853 Strassberg, Sara. *Sócrates.* Buenos Aires: Ismael Colombo, 1971.

Includes, in this drama in three acts, a cast of Socrates, Anytus, Critias, Crito, Alcibiades, Chaerephon, Antiphon, Myrto, and Phaedo. Recounts in the last act the death of Socrates.

1854 Strindberg, August. "Hemicycle of Athens." *Historical Miniatures*. Translated by Claud Field. Freeport, N.Y.: Books for Libraries Press, 1972, pp. 28-64.

English translation of Strindberg's short story included in his *Historiska mimiatyrer*. Originally published in 1913. Creates a series of conversations dramatically set in Athens during the plague of 429 B. C. Assigns the main role to Socrates, and includes, among the participants, Alcibiades, Pericles, Euripides, Antisthenes, Plato, Protagoras, Cleon, a visiting Jew, Anytus, and others. Portrays Anytus as a man in search of an opportunity to destroy Socrates and his friends.

1855 Strindberg, August. *Historical Miniatures*. Translated by Claud Field. Freeport, N.Y.: Books for Libraries Press, 1972, pp. 82-88.

English translation of Strindberg's short story included in his *Historiska miniatyrer*. Originally published in 1913. Contains three dialogues: (1) Socrates and Euripides, shortly after the defeat of Athens in 404 B.C.; (2) Socrates and Aspasia, about the same time; and (3) Socrates in prison where he dies accompanied by Plato and other friends.

1856 Strozier, Robert M. "Under the Agnus Castus Tree, By the Banks of the Old Ilissus." *Atlantic Monthly*, 239 (1977), pp. 86-87.

Dialogue between Socrates and various friends (Hermogenes, Lysimachus, Charmides, Plato, and others).

1857 Telemann, Georg Phillipp. *Der geduldige Socrates*. Hamburg, 1721.

Opera in three acts. Based on Nicolo Minato's text *La patienza di Socrate con duo moglie*. Text by J. V. König. First performed in Hamburg, on January 28, 1721.

1858 Tollinton, R. B. "Socrates in Zion." *The Hibbert Journal*, 30 (1932), pp. 545-560.

Written as a dialogue representing the work of a young man named Sophron, an Athenian by birth, who had spent time with Socrates and who, after a business trip to Jerusalem, wondered what Socrates would say about this city since the customs of the Jews and the Greeks were so different. Offers Socrates free passage to Jerusalem, and is pleased to learn that Socrates will go, because his inner voice tells him to do so. Introduces Socrates to Rabbi Ben-Azrah in Jerusalem, who then spend the evening discoursing, Socrates raising many questions regarding the nature of the God of the Jews.

1859 Valéry, Paul. *L'Ame et la danse. Eupalinos ou l'architecte, précédé de L'Ame et la danse*. Paris: La Nouvelle Revue Francaise, 1923.

Develops a fictional dialogue in Hades among Socrates, Phaedrus, and Eryximachus the physician. Contemplating the spectacle of a dancing girl, the characters discourse on truth and falsehood, and reality and appearance; they discover that there is something 'Socratic' in dancing ("this monumental walk with no object but itself"). Replying to Socrates' request for a cure for the tedium of living (itself the inexorable result of seeing the world as it really is), the answer is given that such cure can only be "the intoxication due to action," and this, in its turn, is clearly recognized in the precise, rhythmical and liberating dancing of the girl: "Is not great dancing the liberation of our bodies, which are wholly possessed by the spirit of falsehood"?

1860 Valéry, Paul. *The Dance and the Soul. Selected Writings*. Translated by Dorothy Bussy. New York: New Directions Publishing Corporation, 1950, pp. 184-198.

English translation of Valéry's *L'Ame et la danse. Eupalinos ou l'architecte, précédé de L'Ame et la danse*. Ref. 1859.

1861 Valéry, Paul. *Eupalinos ou l'architecte, précédé de L'Ame et la danse*. Paris: La Nouvelle Revue Francaise, 1923.

Creates a fictional dialogue in Hades between Socrates and Phaedrus, which leads eventually to a narration of a conversation between Phaedrus and Eupalinos of Megara, the architect. Deals with the relationship between thinking and the creative process in art, and makes Socrates confess that if he were to commence his life anew, he would not seek the god in the realm of thought alone, but in the realm of artistic construction.

1862 Valéry, Paul. *Eupalinos, or the Architect. Selected Writings.* Translated by William McCausland Stewart. New York: New Directions Publishing Corporation, 1950 (originally 1923), pp. 162-183.

English translation of Valéry's *Eupalinos ou l'architecte, précédé de L'Ame et la danse.* Ref. 1861.

1863 Valéry, Paul. *Orgueil pour orgueil. Mélange.* Paris: Gallimard, 1941.

Offers a short prose poem which presents a brief exchange between Anaxagoras and Socrates: Anaxagoras speaks of his desire to find a way to overcome his intellectual defeat at Socrates' hands, while Socrates discovers, in Anaxagoras, a manifestation of pride.

1864 Valéry, Paul. *Pride for Pride. Dialogues.* Translated by William McCausland Stewart. *The Collected Works of Paul Valéry.* New York: Pantheon Press, 1956 (16 vols.), Vol. 4, p. 13.

English translation of Valéry's *Orgueil pour orgueil.* Ref. 1863.

1865 Valéry, Paul. *Socrates and His Physician. Dialogues.* Translated by William McCausland Stewart. *The Collected Works of Paul Valéry.* New York: Pantheon Books, 1956 (16 vols.), Vol. 4, pp. 1-10.

English translation of Valéry's *Socrate et son médecin.* Ref. 1866.

1866 Valéry, Paul. *Socrate et son médecin.* Paris: Editions de la

N. R. F., 1931.

Published in the same volume as Valery's *L'Idée fixe.* Creates a fictional dialogue between Socrates and Eryximachus, the physician. Includes a conversation in which the physician's art of dealing with innumerable ills is compared with Socrates' unending search for answers in the realm of ideas.

1867 Vernet, Jacob. *Dialogues socratiques.* Halle, 1753.

Originally published in 1746. Creates imaginary conversations in which Socrates appears to be an instrument for the expression and advancement of educational ideas. Conveys the notion that if knowledge is to be meaningful, it must be morally and practically useful.

1868 Voltaire. [Arouet, François Marie]. *Socrate: Ouvrage dramatique en trois actes. Oeuvres Complètes de Voltaire.* Paris: Garnier Frères, 1877-1885 (52 vols.), pp. 361-396.

Published in 1759 as if translated from the English by M. Fatema, from a drama by M. Thomson. Presents the following *dramatis personae*: Socrates, Crito, Anytus, Meletus, Xanthippe, Aglae (a young Athenian lady brought up by Socrates), Sophronimus (a young Athenian brought up by Socrates), Drixa, Terpander, and Acros (friends of Anytus). Describes Socrates' fate as being the result of the machinations of priests and political fanatics. Spoken by Crito, the last words of the play are indicative of Voltaire's theme: "At least may his wisdom teach mankind that temples should be raised to God alone!"

1868a Voltaire. [Arouet, François Marie]. *Socrates: A Drama in Three Acts. The Works of Voltaire.* Translated by William F. Flenung. Paris: E. R. DuMont, 1901 (52 vols.), Vol. 16, pp. 270-315.

English translation of Voltaire's *Socrates.* Ref. 1868.

1869 Woodruff, Douglas. "Socrates in London." *With a Merry Heart: A Treasury of Humor by Catholic Writers.* Edited by Paul J. Phelan. London: Longmans, Green & Co., 1943, pp. 341-349.

Short story, originally published in Woodruff's *Plato's Brittania* (New York: G. P. Putnam). Describes a visit by Socrates to London, as he accompanied a certain young man named Mylon who wished to study among the English. Recounts Socrates' adventures in the city, and his visit to the Athenaeum Club, where he sought in vain to find sophisticated persons. Notes that the Londoners whom Socrates found were quite unable to engage in serious talk, and that the most refined activity was doing cross-word puzzles.

# DICTIONARIES, ENCYCLOPAEDIAS, HISTORIES

The annotations of this section include references to Socrates found in philosophy dictionaries and encyclopaedia articles, and as they appear in more general histories of philosophy which highlight his relationship to the various philosophical traditions.

1871 Asmus, Valentin F. "Socrates." *The Great Soviet Encyclopaedia.* Moscow, 1947, Vol. 52, pp. 26-27.

Stresses Socrates' political ideas, which are interpreted as oligarchical and aristocratic, and as pieces of propaganda against democratic ideas and institutions. Views Socrates as the basic source of idealistic philosophy.

1872 Avery, Catherine B., editor. "Socrates." *The New Century Classical Handbook.* New York: Appleton-Century-Crofts, 1962, pp. 1018-1019.

Provides a brief biographical notice on Socrates. Summarizes the major moments and developments of his life.

1873 Belfort Bax, Ernest. *A Handbook of the History of Philosophy*. London: George Bell & Sons, 1888, pp. 44-50.

Deals with Socrates and the minor Socratics under Greek Philosophy, Epoch 2 (pp. 44-50). Regards Socrates' conviction concerning the identity of knowledge and virtue as the main, if not the only, thesis of his philosophy. Recognizes two major contributions associated with him: the development of the introspective method and the ethical and individualistic tendency of all his work.

1874 Benn, Alfred William. "Socrates." *Early Greek Philosophy*. London: Constable & Co., 1914, pp. 100-123.

Comments on the testimonies of Aristophanes, Xenophon, Plato, and Aristotle. Explains the major differences between Socrates and the Sophists, and comments on the meaning of Socratic irony. Considers Xenophon a more trustworthy source than Plato in as much as Xenophon states that Socrates claimed ignorance only about natural philosophy. Notes that Plato, however, seems more reliable when he emphasizes how the Socratic method is employed and how it demonstrates that the logician does not need to know specific facts, but is able to expose the flaws in reasoning.

1875 Benn, Alfred William. "The Place of Socrates in Greek Philosophy." *The Greek Philosophers.* London: Kegan, Paul, Trench & Co., 1882 (2 vols.), Vol. 1, pp. 108-170.

Offers a detailed listing of the topics explored in the chapter, which is broken into seven sections. Covers a number of aspects of Socrates' philosophy and emphasizes his moral character.

1876 Bowder, Diana, editor. "Socrates." *Who Was Who in the Greek World.* Ithaca: Cornell University Press, 1982, pp. 190-191.

Presents a standard portrait of the historic Socrates from a Platonic perspective.

1877 Bréhier, Emile. *The History of Philosophy: The Hellenic Age.* Translated by Joseph Thomas. Chicago: The University of Chicago Press, 1965, pp. 80-87.

General history of philosophy from the pre-Socratics to Aristotle. Chapter 11 (pp. 80-87) deals with Socrates. Reviews the major biographical details and the different views entertained by scholars (E. Wolff, O. Gigon and others) concerning the accuracy of the sources. Discusses briefly Socrates' political views and posture, and summarizes various elements of the Socratic teaching. Views Socrates as a political conservative whose criticism was directed not at the laws and the religious practices, but at men and their human qualities.

1878 Brumbaugh, Robert S. "Socrates: The Search for the Self." *The Philosophers of Greece.* Albany: State University of New York Press, 1981, pp. 123-132.

Gives a brief account of the major biographical and ideological aspects of Socrates. Notes that "the very example of Socrates' own life and death reminds us of the importance of human intelligence, and of the freedom to use that intelligence." Places Socrates within the general context of Greek philosophy at the crucial moment when attention was directed to the human being and to ethical problems.

1879 Burnet, John. *Greek Philosophy: Thales to Plato*. London: Macmillan, 1964, pp. 102-156.

Provides a general history of Greek philosophy from the pre-Socratics to Plato. Chapters 8, 9, and 10 deal with Socrates -- his life, his philosophy, and his trial and death. Maintains that it is in Plato, not in Xenophon, that we can find a trustworthy portrait of Socrates. Attributes to Socrates doctrines generally associated with Plato: the immortality of the soul and the idea of reincarnation. Regards the Aristophanic and Xenophontean images of Socrates as distorted images of the Platonic Socrates. Views the doctrine of Ideal Forms as rightfully belonging to Socrates, and rejects as unsound the procedure of distinguishing Socratic from Platonic dialogues by reference to the absence or presence of that doctrine. Concludes that there is no justification for seeing in the Platonic Socrates a fiction, and still less a falsification of the historical Socrates. Closes the discussion with comments on the trial and death of Socrates.

1880 Burnet, John. "Socrates." *Encyclopaedia of Religion and Ethics.* New York: Charles Scribner's Sons, n.d., Vol. 11, pp. 665-672.

Discusses Socrates under the following headings: chronology, early references, the comic poets, Antisthenes and Aeschines, Plato, early reputation of Socrates, the mission of Socrates, his concept of soul, his trial and death, and the idea that virtue and knowledge are identical. Maintains that we are bound to regard all the Platonic dialogues in which Socrates is the main speaker as primarily intended to expound his teaching. Views the application of Pythagorean principles to questions of morals as the chief occupation of Socrates.

1881 Bury, J. B. "The Age of Illumination." *The Cambridge Ancient History.* Cambridge: Cambridge University Press, 1978, Vol.5, pp. 376-397.

Examines the intellectual character of Socrates' time, and discusses his reaction against Ionian philosophy. Outlines the characteristics of the Sophistical movement, and explains the contributions of Gorgias, Protagoras, Prodicus and Hippias. Reviews the historical information concerning the blasphemy trials at Athens. Examines the main biographical information about Socrates, and comments briefly on the nature of the principal primary sources. Minimizes the value of Xenophon's testimony, and refers to the worth of the *Memorabilia* as 'negligible'. Expresses his agreement with A. E. Taylor's assessment of Xenophon.

1882 Copleston, Frederick. *A History of Philosophy*. Garden City, N. Y.: Image Books, 1962 (9 vols.), Vol. 1, Part 1, pp. 117-136.

General history of philosophy from the Milesian Rationalists to the 20th century. Vol. 1, Part 1, Chapter 14, deals with Socrates (pp. 117-136). Reviews the major biographical details, and discusses the nature and scope of the Socratic problem. Supports Hackforth's insistence on attaching great weight to the Aristotelian contention that the theory of Ideal Forms belongs to Plato, not to Socrates. Summarizes the principal themes associated with Socrates' philosophical activity, and maintains that Socrates' polytheism notwithstanding, it is possible to detect in him a tendency towards a purer conception of the Deity. Comments briefly on Socrates' trial and execution. Chapter 15 addresses itself to the development of the minor Socratic schools (pp. 137-144).

1883 Cornford, Francis MacDonald. "The Athenian Philosophical Schools." *The Cambridge Ancient History.* Cambridge: Cambridge University Press, 1978, Vol. 6, pp. 302-310.

Examines the major sources of our information concerning Socrates' philosophy, and concludes that the only Aristophanic element of historical value may be the characterization of Socrates as an ascetic. Views Xenophon's testimony as valuable only in so far as it provides a means for determining where Plato's testimony went beyond the historical Socrates. Reviews succintly three aspects of Socrates: his doctrine, his religion and his character.

1884 Cushman, Herbert Ernest. "Socrates." *A Beginner's History of Philosophy*. Boston: Houghton Mifflin, 1910 (2 vols.). Vol. 1, pp. 74-97.

Considers Socrates and Aristophanes as two responses to the Sophistical movement. Suggests that Socrates is the central figure in this age of critical inquiry. Examines the personality and life of Socrates, the relationship between Socrates and Aristophanes, the relationship between Socrates and the Sophists, the unsystematic character of Socratic philosophy, the Socratic ideal and what it involves, the Socratic method, Socrates and Athens, the logical expedients of Socrates, Socrates and the minor Socratics, and the Cynic and Cyrenaic schools.

1885 Cushman, Robert E. "Socrates." *The Encyclopaedia of Religion*. Edited by Mincea Eliade. New York: Macmillan, 1987 (15 vols.), Vol. 13, pp. 401-403.

Recounts various details of Socrates' life, and gives a brief account of his philosophical views. Argues that "by general consent Plato's dialogues are the incomparable thesaurus for the quest of the historical Socrates." Views Socrates as "the funnel and solvent through which the ancient Hellenic *ethos* embracing both the religious and scientific questing of the human spirit" found its way into our culture.

1886 Diderot, Denis. "Socratique, ou histoire de la philosophie de Socrate." *Oeuvres Complètes de Diderot*. Paris: Garnier Frères, 1876 (20 vols.), Vol. 17, pp. 151-166.

Originally published in 1751. Summarizes the major events of Socrates' life and the chief tenets of his thought. Speaks of him as the philosopher *par excellence* of all times, and as a man of consummate prudence and experience through whom others learned to love truth and virtue. Praises Socrates for his insistence that moral values and virtue must be pursued before knowledge of the world. Recounts an incident (not found in the primary sources) in which Socrates claims not to know how to write in order to avoid signing an accusation against an innocent man during the reign of the Thirty. Emphasizes Socrates' contempt for the polytheism of his contemporaries, and suggests that by the use of his powerful reasoning abilities he was able to raise himself to the conception of one universal God.

1887 Durant, Will. "Socrates." *The Life of Greece.* New York: Simon & Schuster, 1939, pp. 364-373.

Treats Socrates under three subsections: The Mask of Silenus, Portrait of a Gadfly, and the Philosophy of Socrates. Discusses the content and relative historical value of the testimonies of Plato, Xenophon and Aristophanes. Emphasizes the constructive skepticism of the Socratic position, and concludes with remarks on the accusations and trial of Socrates. Regards him as a martyr and saint in Greek history. Gives abundant references to primary and secondary sources.

1888 Durant, Will. *The Story of Philosophy.* New York: Garden City Publishing Co., 1943, pp. 7-13.

Presents only the Platonic Socrates and emphasizes the *Crito.* Gives a straightforward presentation of Plato's dialogues, highlighting the Socratic quest as an undermining of contemporary Athenian values.

1889 Escohotado, Antonio. *De physis a polis. La evolución del pensamiento filosófico griego desde Tales a Sócrates.* Barcelona: Editorial Anagrama, 1957.

Traces the development of Greek thought from the earliest pre-Socratics to Socrates. Discusses the place of Socrates in this development (pp. 178ff), and emphasizes the importance of two elements in his philosophy: the search for true knowledge within the self and the identity of knowledge and virtue.

1890 Fénelon, François de Salignac. "Socrate." *Abregé de la vie des plus illustres philosophes de l'Antiquité.* Paris: A. Payen, 1830.

Offers a brief biographical notice which recounts various generally accepted historical facts of Socrates.

1891 Fénelon, François de Salignac. "Socrates". *Great Men and Famous Women.* New York: Selmar Hess, 1894, Vol. 2, pp. 38-43.

English translation of Fénelon's "Socrate." Ref. 1890.

1892 Field, Guy C. "Socrates." *The Oxford Classical Dictionary.* Oxford: The Clarendon Press, 1953, pp. 845-846.

Gives a summary statement of Socrates' life and principal doctrines. Emphasizes the disagreement that prevails among scholars concerning the interpretation of these doctrines. Argues that, contrary to the testimony of certain ancient authorities, it is unreasonable to view Socrates as the *sole* agency responsible for the shift from objectivism to subjectivism (*e.g.,* from cosmology to ethics), which affected Greek thought in the late fifth century B.C.

1893 Flew Anthony. Editorial consultant. "Socrates, Socratic Fallacy and Socratic Method." *A Dictionary of Philosophy.* New York: St. Martin's Press, 1979, p. 306.

Provides a preface by A. Flew in which he explains that this is essentially a dictionary rather than an encyclopaedia, the majority of items being key words and phrases. Gives only a very short entry, acknowledging that whether in the work of Plato, Xenophon or Aristophanes, it is impossible to distinguish facts from embellishment. Mentions the scenario of the *Phaedo* without interpretation. Suggests the Socratic method was successful because Plato could *script* the answers as well as the questions. Presents a table of symbols and abbreviations as well as extensive cross-references.

1894 Fuller, B. A. G. *A History of Philosophy.* Revised by Sterling M. McMurrin. New York: Holt, Rinehart & Winston, 1955, pp. 108-114.

General history of philosophy from the pre-Socratics to the 20th century. Part 1, Chapter 9 (pp. 108-114), deals with Socrates. Reviews the principal aspects of his biography and discusses the following themes: the Socratic method, Socrates' growing unpopularity and his trial, his denial of Sophistic relativism, and his conception of virtue as a natural endowment. Recognizes the difficulty of determining the precise nature of Socrates' metaphysical convictions, and emphasizes the moralistic or ethical orientation of his philosophy. Acknowledges the complexity of deciding with finality the issue of Socrates' definition of the ultimate good.

1895 Fuller, B. A. G. "Socrates." *History of Greek Philosophy*. New York: Henry Holt & Co., 1931, pp. 43-87.

Provides a thorough historical review and philosophical perspective from which to assess the contributions of Socrates. Discourses on various interpretations which have been offered in an attempt to shed light on the Socratic philosophy. Explores the various Socratic paradoxes and the significance of dialectics.

1896 Fung Yu Lan. *A Short History of Chinese Philosophy*. New York: The Free Press, 1948, 10ff, 45-46.

Discusses the idea that Chinese philosophers were all different grades of Socrates. Draws parallels between Confucius and Socrates, who both lived during turbulent times and were constantly engaged in dialogues with their contemporaries.

1897 Gilmore, D. Percy. "Socrates". *The New Schaff-Herzog Encyclopedia of Religious Knowledge*. Edited by Samuel Macauley Jackson. Grand Rapids, Mich.: Baker Book House, 1959, Vol. 10, pp. 494-495.

Presents a brief biographical notice on Socrates. Places his birth at Palania (on the east of Mt. Hymettus, near modern Liopesi, 8 miles from Athens). Stresses his belief in "the existence of one supreme Divinity, the creator and disposer of the universe, all-powerful, omniscient and omnipresent, perfectly wise and just and good." Compares Socrates' argument for the existence of God with that of Paley in his *Natural Theology*.

1898 Ginzburg, Benjamin. "Socrates". *Encyclopedia of the Social Sciences*. New York: Macmillan, 1959 (15 vols.), Vol. 13, pp. 247-248.

Brief biographical sketch. Views Socrates as "the real founder of Greek philosophical ethics, bringing into moral inquiry a spirit of intellectual criticism and personal sincerity which it had lacked and without which it would have been futile and even mischievous."

1899 Gomperz, Theodor. *Greek Thinkers: A History of Ancient*

*Philosophy*. Translated by G. G. Berry, London: John Murray, 1964 (4 vols.).

Originally published in 1905. Covers the years 600 to 400 B.C. Books 4 and 5 (Vol. 11, pp. 3-118) deal with the background, biography and philosophy of Socrates. Introduces the subject with two chapters on the cultural and ideological context of the 5th century Athenian world. Reviews Socrates' life, teaching, and trial, and examines in detail the various theories associated with his philosophy. Seeks an integration of the Platonic and Xenophontean testimonies, and pays close attention to the Aristotelian references to Socrates. Stresses the impossibility of making dogmatic statements concerning Socrates' convictions and emphasizes the possibility of finding in him a reconciliation between simple religious beliefs and a critical philosophical stance. Abundantly annotated with references to primary and secondary sources. Ref. 1925.

1900 Hammond, Lewis M. "Socrates." *The World Book Encyclopedia*, 17 (1969), p. 463.

Presents the Platonic Socrates, emphasizing the *Apology* and the *Crito*. Discusses Socratic ethical philosophy which is characterized by the distinction between knowledge and opinion, and is pursued by his relentless questioning. Discusses the stereotype of Xanthippe as a shrew.

1901 Hegel, Georg F. W. Lectures on the History of Philosophy. Translated by E. S. Haldane. London: Routledge and Kegan Paul, 1963 (3 vols.), Vol. 1, pp. 384-448.

Ref. 1677.

1902 Huby, Pamela M. "Socrates and Plato." *A Critical History of Western Philosophy*. Edited by D. J. O'Connor. New York: The Free Press, 1964, pp. 14-35.

Reviews the major biographical and ideological aspects of Socrates and Plato. Discusses in detail the Socratic method in its application to the search for definitions. Finds the Socratic search generally misguided, although not entirely useless. Maintains that it is impossible to distinguish sharply between the contributions of Socrates and those of Plato, but concedes that the study of Plato's early dialogues may give us some hints towards the reconstruction of the historical Socrates.

1903 Jackson, Henry. "Socrates." *The Encyclopaedia Britannica* (11th edition). Cambridge: Cambridge University Press, 1911, Vol. 25, pp. 331-338.

Gives a general biographical and ideological description of Socrates, and includes a brief description of the Socratics. Stresses the following topics and themes: Socrates' mode of life, the assessment of his contemporaries about him, Plato's Socratic panegyric, the development of the dialectical method, the function of maieutic in the testimonies of Plato and Xenophon, Socrates' work in induction and definition, the thesis concerning the identity of virtue and knowledge, and the Socratic vision of the Good.

1904 Kidd, I. G. "Socrates." *The Encyclopedia of Philosophy*. Edited by Paul Edwards. New York: Macmillan, 1967, Vols. 7-8, pp. 480-486.

Identifies the Socratic problem and two extreme responses to it: Burnet and Taylor, who conclude that it is the Platonic Socrates who is the only historical Socrates, and the agnostics, who argue that we know hardly anything about the historical Socrates. Argues that contradiction should be an opportunity for a cultural examination of all sources and their historical background. Discusses the relationship between Socrates and the Sophists, focusing on Socrates' interest on words and arguments, and on the political and social influence of Socrates as a representative of a serious challenge to the Athenian system of education which rested upon the acceptance of received assumptions. Also discusses Socrates' relationship to religion and the force of his philosophical personality, highlighted by his questioning and dialectic. Distinguishes between the difference in form (as well as content) between Xenophon and Plato, suggesting that Xenophon's anectodal account was only of local interest, while Plato's dialogues stimulated the development of Western philosophy.

1905 Lamprecht, Sterling P. *Our Philosophical Traditions: A Brief History of Philosophy in Western Civilization*. New York: Appleton-Century-Crofts, 1955, pp. 27-31.

Deals with Socrates in Chapter 11 (pp. 27-31). Reviews the major biographical details. Maintains that it remains impossible to establish a precise line of demarcation between Socrates and Plato, and argues that Burnet's and Taylor's ideas concerning the presence of the historical Socrates in Plato's dialogues are not convincing. Relies on the Aristotelian testimony in order to determine the content and scope of Socrates' philosophy. Emphasizes the openness and curiosity of the Socratic enterprise.

1906 Lewes, George Henry. *The Biographical History of Philosophy.* New York: D. Appleton and Co., 1883 (2 vols.).

Presents a general history of philosophy, from the early Greeks to the middle of the nineteenth century. Directs its attention more to the characters and lives of the philosophers than to their philosophical contributions. Discusses Socrates under "The Fourth Epoque" (Vol. 1, pp. 122-168). Deals with the philosophy of Socrates (pp. 148-168), and emphaszies the Socratic method, which is compared with Bacon's induction.

1907 Losev, A. F. "Socrates." *Great Soviet Encyclopedia.* New York: Macmillan, 1980, Vol. 24, p. 270.

Offers a short biographical statement about Socrates. Refers to him as one of the founders of political dialectics, and mentions Marx's references to Socrates as "the embodiment of philosophy" and as "philosophy personified."

1908 Moreri, L. "Socrate." *Le Grand Dictionnaire historique ou mélange curieux de l'histoire sacrée et profane.* Paris: D. Thierry, 1683 (2 vols.).

Gives a brief biographical notice of Socrates. Refers to him as the one who succeeded in purifying the spirit of pagan philosophy.

1909 Müller, K. O. "The New Beginning of Attic Training: Foundation of the Socratic Schools." *A History of the Literature of Ancient Greece.* Translated by George C. Lewis and John W. Donaldson. London: Loughaus, Green & Co., 1884 (3 vols.), Vol. 2, pp. 161-182.

Reviews the philosophical contributions of Socrates, and concludes that his presence (even in the absence of any written works from him) constituted a decisive influence on the development of literature among the Greeks. Sees Socrates as a superb representative of the intellectual middle class in Athens, and as a representative of the literary party. Recognizes as Socrates' major contributions the development of the dialectical method and the reorientation of philosophy towards moral and political issues.

1910 O'Neill, W. H. "Socrates." *New Catholic Encyclopedia.* New York: McGraw-Hill Book Co., 1967, Vol. 13, pp. 407-408.

Summarizes the major aspects of Socrates' life and philosophy. Views him as a religious man who recognized the limits of human reason and the need to consult the gods.

1911 Parker, G. F. "Socrates." *A Short Account of Greek Philosophy from Thales to Epicurus.* New York: Barnes & Noble, 1967, pp. 85-89.

Presents a general description of Socrates' biography and philosophy, and attempts to explain the sense in which it is justifiable to affirm that "Socrates was the pivot on which the course of European thought swung around." Emphasizes the two main philosophical ideas associated with him, namely, that virtue is knowledge, and that an unexamined life is not worth living.

1912 Reese, William L. "Socrates." *Dictionary of Philosophy and Religion: Eastern and Western Thought.* New Jersey: Humanities Press, 1980, pp. 537-538.

Presents several encyclopaedic features, including an analysis of the thought of major philosophers, as well as an attempt at an explication of terms which are based on the conceptual systems from which they were developed. Offers a standard Platonic biography of Socrates, making mention of the Aristotelian testimony. Ignores the testimonies of Xenophon and Aristophanes. Contains extensive cross-references.

1913 Robinson, John Mansley. "Review of *A History of Greek*

*Philosophy*, Vol. 3 by W. K. C. Guthrie." *The Journal of the History of Philosophy*, 11 (1971), pp. 376-383.

Presents a detailed review of the volume, *The Fifth Century Enlightenment*, which is divided by Guthrie into two sections: the first dealing with the Sophists and the second with Socrates. Analyzes Guthrie's interpretation of the Sophists which focuses not simply on rhetoric and persuasion, but on the important ideas introduced and explored by them -- ideas which have fostered an intellectual movement with long-standing permanent results. Disagrees with Guthrie's interpretation which gives high standing to Aristotle's remarks on Socrates, and argues that there is nothing unique to the Aristotelian perspective, all of it being available in the Platonic dialogues. Considers Guthrie's full paraphrase of Aristophanes' *Clouds*, which was his attempt to develop his own answer to the question of the relationship between Socrates and Aristophanes, as inadequate and unsuccessful. Concludes that there are serious questions about how far a historian can go when trying to assess the philosophical significance of a thinker. Ref. 236.

1914 Robinson, John M. *An Introduction to Early Greek Philosophy.* New York: Houghton Mifflin Co., 1968, pp. 239-284.

Deals, in Chapter 12, with the emergence of the Sophists (Protagoras, Antiphon, Callicles), and devotes Chapter 13 to the ideological reaction against the Sophistical movement, a reaction embodied principally in Socrates. Contains extended quotations from Aristophanes' *Clouds*, Plato's *Apology*, and fragments from the Sophists (Gorgias, Protagoras and Critias). Views the Sophists as responsible for the "unseating of Zeus," that is, for the undermining of the traditional ethical and religious ideas and ideals of the pre-Socratic Greek world. Comments on the reactions of Aristophanes and Plato to the breakdown of values.

1915 Robinson, Richard. "Socrates." *The Concise Encyclopedia of Western Philosophy and Philosophers.* Edited by J. O. Urmson. New York: Hawthorne Books, 1960, pp. 347-350.

Comments on the extent, nature, and value of the testimonies of Aristophanes, Xenophon, Aristotle, and Plato. Notes that the testimony of Plato, especially in the *Phaedo*, should be viewed as more dramatically significant than historically accurate. Emphasizes Socrates' "superb championship of the ideal of reason, and his high and clear conception of what reason demands."

1916 Rodier, G. "Socrate." *La Grande Encyclopédie.* Paris: Societé Anonyme de la Grande Encyclopédie, n.d., Vol. 30, pp. 177-184.

Provides a general reference about Socrates' life and philosophy. Observes that in Socrates there was a perfect harmony of thought and character, and of doctrine and action. Contains an extensive bibliography.

1917 Ross, Donald A. "Socrates." *The McGraw-Hill Encyclopedia of World Biography.* New York: The McGraw-Hill Book Co., 1973, Vol. 10, pp. 115-118.

Provides a brief biographical sketch and a summary statement of Socrates' ideas.

1918 Ruggiero, Guido de. "Socrate." *Storia della Filosofia. La Filosofia greca.* Bari: Editori Laterza, 1963 (10 vols.), Vol. 1, pp. 233-285.

Originally published in 1918. Deals with Socrates in four sections: (1) the Socratic problem, in which it discusses the emergence of Socrates in the world of Sophistical thought, and his relationship with the natural philosophers; (2) Socrates' life, in which the early Socratic dialogues are seen as historically important; (3) the development of Socrates' ethical science (*la scienza morale*), in which emphasis is made on Socrates' determination to establish moral principles on a rational basis; and (4) the death of Socrates.

1919 Russell, Bertrand. *A History of Western Philosophy.* New York: Simon & Schuster, 1945.

Deals with the history of philosophy in the West, from the rise of Greek civilization to the philosophy of logical analysis in the twentieth century. Book 1, Chapter 11 (pp. 82-93) discusses Socrates. Speaks of the testimony of Xenophon as superficial and composed of dull and commonplace reports, and as philosophically inconsequential.

Uses the *Apology* as the point of reference for most of its comments on Socrates. Detects in this testimony a number of elements which are designated as 'religious,' and compares the Socrates depicted in it by Plato as 'a Christian martyr or a Puritan.' Recognizes, in the Platonic Socrates an anticipation of the Cynics and the Stoics. Regards the early dialogues as the most reliable source of information concerning Socrates' philosophy.

1920 Russell, Bertrand. *Wisdom of the West: A Historical Survey of Western Philosophy in Its Social and Political Setting.* London: Crescent Books, 1959.

Contrasts Socrates with the Sophists. Focuses on Plato's *Apology* as a piece of historical writing. States that by acknowledging the distinction between Plato and Socrates, it is reasonable to assert that it is the doctrines of the Platonic Socrates which have so greatly influenced the development of philosophy.

1921 Schopenhauer, Arthur. "Socrates." *Fragments of the History of Philosophy. Selected Essays of Arthur Schopenhauer.* Translated by Ernest Belfort Box. London: George Bell & Sons, 1909, pp. 45-52.

English translation of Schopenhauer's "Sokrates." Ref. 1922.

1922 Schopenhauer, Arthur. "Sokrates." *Fragments zur Geschichte der Philosophie. Schopenhauers Sämtliche Werke.* Edited by Max Frischeiser-Hohler. Berlin: A. Weichert, Verlag, n.d. (8 vols.), Vol. 6, pp. 45-48.

Comments on Socrates' physiognomy, and observes that "a fat belly does not belong to the signs of genius." States that Socrates' choice to leave no writings indicates an absence of "high mental powers." Compares Socrates' philosophy with that of Kant, and finds a number of parallels between them; in particular, their skepticism with respect to metaphysical claims.

1923 Schwegler, Albert. *Handbook of the History of Philosophy.* Translated by James Hutchison Sterling. Edinburgh: Oliver and Boyd, 1868.

Represents a general history of philosophy, from the pre-Socratics to Hegel. Chapter 12 (pp. 39-52) deals with Socrates, and its headings include Socrates' personality, Socrates and Aristophanes, the condemnation of Socrates, the general character of Socratic philosophizing, the sources of the Socratic philosophy, and the Socratic doctrine of virtue. Rejects the suggestion that we can distinguish an exoteric (Xenophontean) Socrates from an esoteric (Platonic) Socrates, and insists that we have no right to view Plato as the true source. Regards the Socrates of Xenophon (particularly in the *Memorabilia*) as perhaps the closest historical portrait of Socrates and his doctrines (inasmuch as we can truly assume the reality of such doctrines).

1924 Shestov, Lev. *Athens and Jerusalem.* Translated by Bernard Martin. New York: Simon & Schuster, 1966.

Scattered throughout are numerous references which discuss the Socratic philosophical practice from an existentialist perspective. Suggests that we are not justified in assuming that reason will find in the world more good than evil. Considers Socrates to have laid the foundations of scientific knowledge as well as of autonomous ethics.

1925 Shorey Paul. "Review of *Greek Thinkers: A History of Ancient Philosophy* by Theodor Gomperz." *Selected Papers.* New York: Garland Publishing Co., 1980, pp. 446-450

Considers the translation excellent and readable, a skillful blend of history with discussion of ideas, demonstrating a modern and rational scientific point of view. Suggests that in Gomperz's discussion of the Socratic problem the distinction between the positive and negative use of induction is exaggerated. Appeared originally in *Classical Philology,* 23 (1928), pp. 68-70. Ref. 1899.

1926 Stace, W. T. *A Critical History of Greek Philosophy.* New York: St. Martin's Press, 1967.

Offers a general survey of Greek philosophy, from its origins among the Ionians to Neo-Platonism. Chapter 10 (pp. 127-154) deals with Socrates. Reviews the major moments of his life and the principle aspects of his educational activities. Quotes the concluding paragraphs of the *Phaedo*. Emphasizes the ethical orientation of Socratic philosophy, and its commitment to rationalism particularly the idea that virtue is ultimately knowledge. Chapter 11 (pp. 155-163) gives a brief account of the minor Socratics who are referred to (in contradistinction to Plato) as 'the semi-Socratics'.

1927 Stumpf, Samuel Enoch. *Socrates to Sartre: A History of Philosophy.* New York: McGraw-Hill Book Company, 1966.

Deals with Socrates in Part 1, Chapter 2 (pp. 31-47). Examines Socrates' philosophy against the cultural and ideological climate of the Sophistical movement. Reviews the details of Socrates' life, and emphasizes the common character which the testimonies of Aristophanes, Xenophon and Plato disclose. Views Socrates' intellectual midwifery and his concern with arriving at adequate definitions of moral states as the principal contributions associated with him.

1928 Taylor, Alfred E. "Socrates." *Encyclopaedia Britannica*, 1957, Vol. 20, pp. 915-920.

Offers a standard encyclopaedia article. Summarizes major biographical details. Presents, in the subsections, brief discussions of Socrates' personal characteristics, religion, mode of life, the nature and causes of his legal indictment, the Socratic method and the principal doctrines associated with him, and his political views. Gives a succinct account of the development of the Socratics. Lists standard reference works on Socrates.

1929 Tennemann, W. G. *A Manual of the History of Philosophy.* Revised by J. R. Morell. Translated by Arthur Johnson. London: George Bell & Sons, 1878.

Represents a general handbook of the history of philosophy from the ancient oriental philosophers to modern European thinkers. Part 1, Chapter 2 (section 1, pp. 86-42) deals with Socrates. Gives an extended list of sources and ancient biobibliographical references, and summarizes the major details of Socrates' life. Speaks of Socrates' desire to develop correct ideas concerning moral and religious obligation, and concerning the purpose of human life and its perfection as the exclusive object of his philosophy. Emphasizes the spiritual aspects of Socratic thought and Socrates' complete acceptance of divine providence.

1930 Thilly, Frank. "Socrates." *A History of Philosophy.* New York: Henry Holt & Co., 1914, pp. 50-57.

Identifies the chief concern of Socrates as one that meets the challenge of Sophistry which, by undermining knowledge, also undermined morality and the State. Emphasizes the *elenchus* as a means of achieving definition of terms.

1931 Ueberweg, Friedrich. "Socrates of Athens." *A History of Ancient Philosophy*. Translated by G. S. Morris. London: Hodder & Stoughton, 1874 (2 vols.), Vol. 1, pp. 80-88.

English translation of Ueberweg's "Sokrates von Athen." Ref. 1932.

1932 Ueberweg, Friedrich. "Sokrates von Athen." *Grundriss der Geschichte der Philosophie des Alterthums.* Berlin: Ernst Siegfried Mittler und Sohn, 1874 (4 vols.), Vol. 1, pp. 110-121.

Originally published in 1862. Gives a detailed biographical account of Socrates and a sketch of his philosophical contributions, with abundant references to primary and secondary sources, and to modern works. Observes that Plato and Xenophon agree in most respects in their testimonies, but notes that the Platonic portrait is more delicately drawn. Regards the Socratic identification of virtue with knowledge as the main source of problems for Socrates' successors.

1933 Voltaire [Arouet, François Marie]. "Socrate." *Dictionnaire philosophique. Oeuvres Complètes de Voltaire.* Paris: Garnier Frères, 1879 (52 vols.), Vol. 20, pp. 428-430.

Written in 1756. Depicts Socrates in conversation with two Athenians whom he attempts to convince of the reasonableness of monotheism (expressed in rationalistic language). Maintains that Socrates was condemned to death for his belief in the unity of God.

1934 Voltaire [Arouet, François Marie]. "Socrates." *A Philosophical Dictionary. The Works of Voltaire.* Paris: E. R. DuMont, 1901 (52 vols.), Vol. 13, pp. 233ff.

English translation of Voltaire's "Socrate." Ref. 1933.

1935 Weber, Alfred and Perry, Ralph Barton. *History of Philosophy* by A. Weber. Translated by Frank Thilly. *Philosophy Since 1860* by Ralph B. Perry. New York: Charles Scribner's Sons, 1896, pp. 44ff and throughout text.

Suggests that the fundamental Socratic principle, the very 'soul' of his philosophy, relates to the relationship between knowledge and will: the more a person thinks and knows, the better he will act. Believes that Socrates' heroic death has led to an exaggeration of his importance at the expense of his predecessors.

1936 Windelband, Wilhelm. *A History of Philosophy.* Translated by James H. Tufts. New York: Macmillan, 1906, pp. 76-82.

English translation of Windelband's *Lehrbuch der Geschichte der Philosophie.* Ref. 1937.

1937 Windelband, Wilhelm. *Lehrbuch der Geschichte der Philosophie.* Tübingen: J. C. B. Mohr, 1903, pp. 74-78.

Deals with Socrates in Part 1, Chapter 7 (pp. 76-82). Views the development of Socrates' philosophy as a direct reaction to the Sophistical movement, and as an attempt to transcend the relativism and subjectivism of the Sophists. Regards as Socrates' most important contributions his insistence on the necessity of objective standards in the moral estimation of human beings and their actions, and his conviction that knowledge and virtue are fundamentally one reality. Classifies this latter view as an example of psychological intellectualism.

1938 Zeller, Eduard. *Outlines of the History of Greek Philosophy.* Revised by Wilhelm Nestle. Translated by L. R. Palmer. London: Routledge and Kegan Paul, 1931.

Offers a general history of Greek philosophy, from the pre-Socratics to Neo-Platonism. Deals with Socrates under the Second Period, Chapter 1 (paragraphs 24-28, pp. 95-105). Reviews the main details of Socrates' biography, and maintains that the most trustworthy sources of information concerning Socrates' philosophy are the *Apology* and the *Symposium*, Xenophon's and Aristotle's testimonies being useful only in so far as they do not contradict that of Plato. Recognizes the difficulty of speaking of a Socratic system, and argues that Socrates did not give any precise formulations of doctrine. Views Socrates' ethics as a special instance of intellectual determinism and concludes with comments on Socrates' trial and execution. Speaks of his death as "the apotheosis of philosophy and the philosopher."

# INDEX OF AUTHORS